ORGB⁷

Organizational Behavior

Seventh Edition

Debra L. Nelson

Janaki Gooty

James Campbell Quick

Australia • Brazil • Canada • Mexico • Singapore • United Kingdom • United States

ORGB, **Seventh Edition**
Debra L. Nelson, Janaki Gooty, and James Campbell Quick

SVP, Product Management: Cheryl Costantini

VP, Product Management: Thais Alencar

Portfolio Product Director: Joe Sabatino

Portfolio Product Manager: Michael Worls

Learning Designer: Emma Train

Subject Matter Expert: Tahia Macias

Content Manager: Sibasis Pradhan, Lumina Datamatics Ltd., and Kathryn Begley

Digital Project Manager: Beth Ross

Marketing Director: Mary Reynolds

Marketing Manager: Danielle Dornbusch

Content Acquisition Analyst: Erin McCullough

Production Service: Lumina Datamatics Ltd.

Designer: Sara Greenwood

Cover Image Source: vs148/Shutterstock.com

For product information and technology assistance, contact us at
**Cengage Customer & Sales Support, 1-800-354-9706
or support.cengage.com.**

For permission to use material from this text or product, submit all requests online at **www.copyright.com.**

Library of Congress Control Number: 2024912788

ISBN: 978-0-357-89918-2

Cengage
5191 Natorp Boulevard
Mason, OH 45040
USA

Cengage is a leading provider of customized learning solutions. Our employees reside in nearly 40 different countries and serve digital learners in 165 countries around the world. Find your local representative at **www.cengage.com.**

To learn more about Cengage platforms and services, register or access your online learning solution, or purchase materials for your course, visit **www.cengage.com.**

Printed at CLDPC, USA, 01-25

Brief Contents

Contents

Chapter 5 Motivation and Work

Chapter 6 Learning and Performance Management

Chapter 7 Stress and Well-Being at Work

Part 3 Interpersonal Processes and Behavior

Chapter 8 Communication

Chapter 9 Work Teams and Groups

Chapter 16 Organizational Culture

Chapter 17 Career Management

Chapter 18 Managing Change

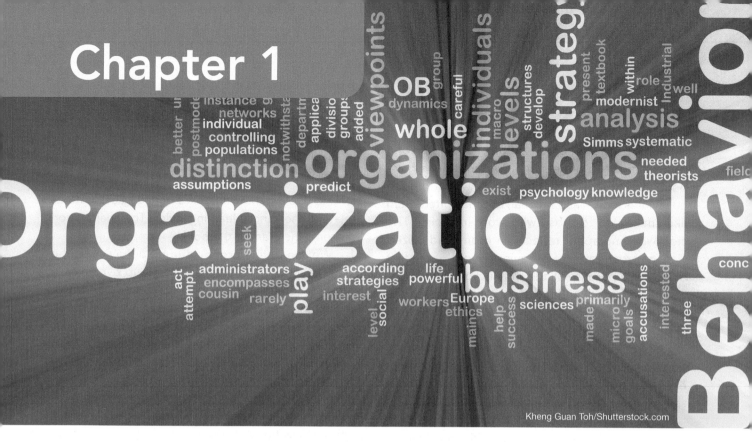

Chapter 1

Organizational Behavior and Opportunity

Learning Objectives

1-1 Define organizational behavior.

1-2 Identify four action steps for responding positively to change.

1-3 Identify the important internal and external system components of an organization.

1-4 Describe the formal and informal elements of an organization.

1-5 Identify factors that contribute to the diversity of organizations in the economy.

1-6 Describe the opportunities that change creates for organizational behavior.

1-7 Demonstrate the value of objective knowledge and skill development in the study of organizational behavior.

1-1 Human Behavior in Organizations

Human behavior in organizations is complex and often difficult to understand. Organizations have been described as clockworks in which human behavior is logical and rational, but they often seem like snake pits to those who work in them.[1] The clockwork metaphor reflects an orderly, idealized view of organizational behavior devoid of conflict or dilemma because all the working parts (the people) mesh smoothly. The snake pit metaphor, on the other hand, conveys the daily conflict, distress, and struggle in organizations. Each metaphor reflects reality from a different perspective—the organization's versus the individual's. The snake pit metaphor expresses the dark side of human behavior, which is seen at its extreme in cases of road rage and workplace violence. Workplace incivility has become commonplace in many organizations, with an estimated 50 percent of workers saying that they experience uncivil behavior weekly.[2] Incivility has negative affective (e.g., anger, sadness), cognitive, and behavioral consequences for instigators, targets, and witnesses of such negative behaviors. In contrast, the clockwork metaphor expresses the view of organizations as healthy and productive systems in which individuals have a clear sense of the shared vision and values, are personally invested in outcomes, feel that their contributions are significant, and receive support and respect from the organization's leadership.[3]

This chapter serves as an introduction to the complex subject of organizational behavior. The first section provides an overview of human behavior in organizations, its interdisciplinary origins, and its responses to change. The second section presents an organizational context within which behavior occurs. The third section highlights the **opportunities** that exist in times of **change** and **challenge** for people at work.[4] The fourth section addresses

> Organizations have been described as clockworks, but they often seem like snake pits.

the ways people learn about organizational behavior and explains how the text's pedagogical features relate to the various learning styles. The final section presents the plan for the book.

We can define **organizational behavior** as the study of individual behavior and group dynamics in organizations. The study of organizational behavior is primarily concerned with the psychosocial, interpersonal, and behavioral dynamics in organizations. However, organizational variables that affect human behavior at work are also relevant to the study of organizational behavior. These organizational variables include jobs, the design of work, communication, performance appraisal, organizational design, and organizational structure.

1-1a Understanding Human Behavior

The vast majority of theories and models of human behavior fall into two basic categories: that of an internal perspective and that of an external perspective. The internal perspective looks at workers' minds to understand their behavior. It is psychodynamically oriented, and its proponents understand human behavior in terms of the thoughts, feelings, past experiences, and needs of the individual. The internal perspective explains people's actions and behavior in terms of their histories and personal value systems. The idea of this perspective is that internal processes of thinking, feeling, perceiving, and judging lead people to act in specific ways; therefore, people are best understood from the inside, and their behavior is best interpreted alongside their thoughts and feelings. The internal perspective has given rise to a wide range of motivational and leadership theories.

The external perspective, on the other hand, focuses on factors outside the person to understand behavior, that is, external events, consequences, and environmental forces. This perspective excludes consideration of a person's history, feelings, thoughts, and personal value system in interpreting actions and behavior. Thus, it has given rise to an alternative set of motivational and leadership theories, which

opportunities Favorable times or chances for progress and advancement.

change The transformation or modification of an organization and/or its stakeholders.

challenge The call to competition, contest, or battle.

organizational behavior The study of individual behavior and group dynamics in organizations.

are covered in Chapters 5 and 12. The internal and external perspectives offer alternative explanations for human behavior. For example, the internal perspective might say Mary is an outstanding employee because she has a high need for achievement and thus performs well, whereas the external perspective might say it is because she is extremely well paid for her work. Kurt Lewin combined both perspectives with his claim that behavior is a function of both the person and the environment.[5]

1-1b Interdisciplinary Influences

Organizational behavior is a blended discipline that has grown out of contributions from numerous earlier fields of study. The sciences of psychology, sociology, engineering, anthropology, management, and medicine have all contributed to our understanding of human behavior in organizations.

Psychology, the science of human behavior, was developed during the closing decades of the nineteenth century. Psychology traces its origins to philosophy and the science of physiology. One of the most prominent early psychologists, William James, held a degree in medicine (MD). Since its beginnings, psychology has branched into a number of specialized fields, including clinical, experimental, military, organizational, and social psychology. Organizational psychology frequently overlaps with organizational behavior; for instance, both investigate work motivation.[6] Johnson & Johnson, Valero Energy, and Chaparral Steel all used long-standing psychological research to develop their sophisticated personnel selection methods.[7]

Sociology, the science of society, has contributed greatly to our knowledge of group and intergroup dynamics. Because sociology takes society rather than the individual as its point of departure, sociologists focus on the variety of roles within a society or culture, the norms and standards of behavior in groups, and the consequences of compliant and deviant behavior. Individuals have a role set that is determined by their social position, and roles affect how people interact within organizations. The Professional Role Behaviors Survey, for example, studied how the roles of various medical practitioners changed during hospital restructuring and how these changes influenced organizational behavior and culture.[8]

Engineering is the applied science of energy and matter. It enhances our understanding of the design

of work. Frederick Taylor took basic engineering ideas and applied them to human behavior at work, influencing the early study of organizational behavior.[9] With his engineering background, Taylor placed special emphasis on human productivity and efficiency in work behavior. Job preparation and performance shifted from a long apprenticeship and a creative, problem-solving approach to work to training in and automated performance of simplified tasks. A study published in 1990 showed that Taylor's notions of performance standards and differential piece-rate systems were still shaping organizational goal-setting programs at Black & Decker, IBM, and Weyerhaeuser at that time.[10]

Anthropology, the science of human learned behavior, is especially important to our understanding of *organizational culture*. In fact, anthropological research has been used to examine the effects of efficient organizational cultures on organizational performance[11] and the ways pathological personalities may lead to dysfunctional organizational cultures.[12] In one case study, Schwartz used a psychodynamic, anthropological mode of inquiry to explore corporate decay at General Motors and NASA.[13]

Management, originally called *administrative science*, is the study of overseeing activities and supervising people in organizations. It includes the design, implementation, and management of various administrative and organizational systems. March and Simon take the human organization as their point of departure to investigate administrative practices that enhance the effectiveness of the systems.[14] Management is the first discipline to take the modern corporation as the unit of analysis, a viewpoint that distinguishes its contribution to the study of organizational behavior.

Medicine, the applied science of treating diseases to enhance an individual's health and well-being, focuses on both physical and psychological health

---

psychology The science of human behavior.

sociology The science of society.

engineering The applied science of energy and matter.

anthropology The science of human learned behavior.

management The study of overseeing activities and supervising people in organizations.

medicine The applied science of healing or treating diseases to enhance an individual's health and well-being.

as well as industrial mental health.[15] As modern care defeats acute diseases, medical attention is shifting to more chronic diseases such as hypertension and to issues involved in occupational health and well-being.[16] These trends have contributed to the growth of corporate *wellness programs* such as Johnson & Johnson's "Live for Life Program." Moreover, *ergonomics* has gained increasing attention as a way to prevent medical problems resulting from poor design of workstations, resulting in the loss of billions of dollars from higher healthcare costs and lower worker productivity.[17] Such costs can be cut nearly in half by implementing the results of medical research into better workplace design.[18]

1-2 Behavior in Times of Change

Early research of individuals and organizations in the midst of environmental change found that people often experience change as a threat and respond by relying on well-learned and dominant forms of behavior.[19] That is, people often become rigid and reactive in the midst of change, rather than open and responsive. This behavior works well in the face of gradual, incremental change. However, rigid and well-learned behavior may be a counterproductive response to significant change, such as outsourcing. Prompted by dramatic advances in Internet and networking technology, outsourcing has been unavoidable in much of American industry.[20] Yet factors such as employee attrition and the potential for data loss have caused many companies to modify their outsourcing strategies to keep both talent and information within the organization.[21] Big changes disrupt people's habitual behavior and force them to learn new skills, often creating discomfort and discontent. To such employees Eric Brown, CEO of PlusFactor, recommends looking for the positive opportunities in change and viewing challenge as a good rather than bad experience. His action steps for adapting to change are to (1) have a positive attitude, (2) ask questions, (3) listen to the answers, and (4) be committed to success.[22]

Success is never guaranteed, however, and change sometimes results in failure. Some of the world's greatest leaders, such as Winston Churchill, experienced dramatic failures before they achieved lasting success. It was their capacity to learn from the failure and to

Hot Trend

How Do Leaders React to Crises?

Leaders, like all people, respond to changes in their environment. A crisis is a specific type of change that has the potential to negatively affect an organization and its stakeholders. In recent years, researchers have become interested in how leaders respond to organization-relevant crises. One group of researchers looked at both the 2008 financial crisis and the 2020 Covid-19 pandemic to explore this question. They predicted that, when faced with a crisis, leaders would engage in more narrow information processing and tighten their control over organizational processes. The authors called this "directive leadership."

In two separate papers, the authors tested their hypothesis. In the first, they used data from over 20,000 managers during the 2008 financial crisis and found that leaders increased their use of directive leadership from 2007 to 2009. In their second paper, the authors used data from over 27,000 managers during the Covid-19 pandemic and similarly found that leaders increased their use of directive leadership in the early months of the global pandemic. Further, they found that leaders in areas where the Covid-19 death rate was higher were even more likely to engage in directive leadership.

These studies provide evidence suggesting that leaders tend to respond to crises by narrowing their information processing and tightening their control over organizational processes. Crises, as a particular type of change, seem to predict a particular set of behaviors among organization leaders. More work will be needed to investigate the factors that might change this relationship or make it stronger. Further, a key question is how effective this behavioral tendency is; researchers are just beginning to explore these and other important questions in the literature on change and crisis management.

Sources: H. Garretsen, J. I. Stoker, D. Soudis, & H. Wendt. "The pandemic that shocked managers across the world: The impact of the COVID-19 crisis on leadership behavior." The Leadership Quarterly (2022).

J. I. Stoker, H. Garretsen, & D. Soudis. "Tightening the leash after a threat: A multilevel event study on leadership behavior following the financial crisis." The Leadership Quarterly, 30(2019), 199–214.

Climate change presents a major challenge for the ways businesses operate across the world.

respond positively to new opportunities that helped them overcome early setbacks. Knowing this, one venture capitalist with whom the authors have worked likes to ask an executive who is seeking to build a business to tell them about their greatest failure. They want to hear how the executive responded to the failure and what they learned from the experience.

So change carries both the risk of failure and the opportunity for success; our behavior often determines the outcome. Moreover, success can come through the accumulation of small wins and through the use of microprocesses, as has been found with middle managers engaged in institutional change. Finally, companies can improve their performance in the emerging China market during uncertain times and economic transitions by engendering trust between the business and state bureaucrats.[23,24]

1-3 The Organizational Context

A complete understanding of organizational behavior requires an understanding of both human behavior and of the organizational context—that is, the specific setting—within which behavior is acted out.

1-3a Organizations as Open Systems

Just as two different perspectives offer complementary explanations for human behavior, two views shape complementary explanations of organizations. Organizations are open systems of interacting components, including people, tasks, technology, and structure. These internal components also interact with components in the organization's task environment.

Today, the corporation is the dominant organizational form for much of the Western world, but other organizational forms have dominated other societies. Religious organizations, such as the temple corporations of ancient Mesopotamia and the churches in colonial America, can often dominate society.[25] So can military organizations, such as the clans of the Scottish Highlands and the regional armies of the People's Republic of China.[26] All of these societies are woven together by family organizations, which themselves may vary from nuclear and extended families to small, collective communities.[27] The purpose and structure of religious, military, and family organizational forms varies, but people within different organizations often behave alike. In fact, early discoveries about power and leadership in work organizations were remarkably similar to findings about power and leadership within families.[28]

Because organizations are so varied in function, manufacturing products such as aircraft components or delivering services such as money management, for example, we must first understand the open system components of an organization and its task environment in order to see how the organization performs.

Accordingly, Katz and Kahn in one study, and Leavitt in another, established open system frameworks for understanding organizations.[29] The four major internal components are task, people, technology, and structure. These four components, along with the organization's inputs, outputs, and key elements in the task environment, are depicted in Figure 1.1. The **task** of the organization is its mission, purpose, or goal for existing. The **people** are the human resources of the organization. The **technology** is the wide range of tools, knowledge,

and/or techniques used to transform inputs into outputs. The **structure** involves the systems of communication, authority and roles, and workflow.

In addition to these major internal components, the organization as a system also has an external task environment composed of different constituents such as suppliers, customers, and federal regulators. Thompson describes the task environment as that element of the environment related to the organization's degree of goal attainment, or its basic task.[30] A number of organizations are using or considering the use of Twitter as a way of networking into elements of their task environments.[31] For example, NASA uses Twitter to update followers on the status of upcoming shuttle flights.

The organization system works by taking inputs, converting them into throughputs, and delivering outputs to its task environment. *Inputs* are the human, informational, material, and financial resources used by the organization. *Throughputs* are the materials and resources as they are transformed by the organization's technology component. Once the transformation is complete, they become *outputs* for customers, consumers, and clients. The actions of suppliers, customers, regulators, and other elements of the task environment affect the organization and the behavior of people at work. The role of

task An organization's mission, purpose, or goal for existing.

people The human resources of an organization.

technology The tools, knowledge, and/or techniques used to transform inputs into outputs.

structure The systems of communication, authority and roles, and workflow.

Figure 1.1 An Open-Systems View of Organization

Source: Based on H. Leavitt, "Applied Organizational Change in Industry: Structural, Technological, and Humanistic Approaches," in J. G. March, ed., *Handbook of Organizations* (Chicago: Rand McNally, 1965), 1145.

modern corporations has expanded to include corporate social responsibility. Customers expect these organizations to be good corporate citizens, creating social value as well as financial wealth for their shareholders.[32] Organizational transparency contributes to trust in organization–stakeholder relationships, which is good for the health and well-being of the organization.[33]

1-4 The Formal and Informal Organization

The open systems view of organizations suggests that they are designed like clockwork (recall the clockwork metaphor described at the beginning of this chapter), with a neat, precise, interrelated functioning. The **formal organization** is the official, legitimate, and most visible part of the organization, and it enables people to think of organizations in logical and rational ways. The snake pit metaphor mentioned earlier originates from the study of the **informal organization**, which is unofficial and less visible. The **Hawthorne studies**, conducted during the 1920s and 1930s, first suggested the importance of the informal elements. During the so-called interview study, the third of the four Hawthorne studies, the researchers began to fully appreciate the informal elements of the Hawthorne Works as an organization.[34] The formal and informal elements of the organization are depicted in Figure 1.2.

Google tops reputation rankings for corporate social responsibility.

Because the formal and informal elements of an organization can sometimes conflict, we must understand both. Such conflicts erupted in many organizations during the early years of the twentieth century and were embodied in the union–management strife of that era. Sometimes these formal–informal conflicts escalated into violence. For example, supervisors at the Homestead Works of U.S. Steel during the 1920s were issued pistols "just in case" they felt it necessary to shoot unruly, dangerous steelworkers. However, during that same era, the progressive Eastman Kodak company provided financial backing for employees' neighborhood communities, such as Meadowbrook in Rochester, New York. Kodak's concern for employees and attention to informal issues made unions unnecessary at the company.

The informal elements of the organization are often points of diagnostic and intervention activities in organizational development, though the formal elements must always be considered because they provide the context for the informal.[35] It is the informal elements involving people's feelings, thoughts, and attitudes about their work that most affect their behavior and performance, but individual behavior plays out in the context of both the formal and informal elements of the system, becoming, in the process, organizational behavior. Employees' moods,

Figure 1.2 Formal and Informal Organization

Formal organization (overt)
Goals and objectives
Policies and procedures
Job descriptions
Financial resources
Authority structure
Communication channels
Products and services

Social surface

Informal organization (covert)
Beliefs and assumptions
Perceptions and attitudes
Values
Feelings (fear, joy, anger, trust, and hope)
Group norms
Informal leaders

formal organization The official, legitimate, and most visible part of the system.

informal organization The unofficial and less visible part of the system.

Hawthorne studies Studies conducted during the 1920s and 1930s that suggested the importance of the informal organization.

The open systems view of an organization suggests that it is designed and run like clockwork.

emotions, and dispositions all influence critical organizational outcomes such as job performance, decision making, creativity, turnover, teamwork, negotiation, and leadership.[36]

1-5 Diversity of Organizations

Most attempts to explain or predict organizational behavior rely heavily on factors within the organization and give less weight to external environmental considerations.[37] Yet organizational behavior always occurs in the context of a specific organizational setting, so students can benefit from being sensitive to that industrial context and from developing an appreciation for the diversity of various organizations.[38]

Large and small organizations operate in each sector of the economy: the private, manufacturing, service, government, and nonprofit sectors. In the private sector are a great variety of organizations that play an important role in the economy. The manufacturing sector includes the production of basic materials, such as steel, and the production

Inclusive Conversations

Does Remote Work Improve Diversity?

At the peak of the COVID-19 pandemic, many leaders struggled to determine the most effective work modality, whether in-office, remotely, or a combination of the two. When it comes to improving workforce diversity, Meta claimed that remote work enabled the organization to achieve its diversity goals two years ahead of schedule. According to Maxine Williams, Meta's chief diversity officer, individuals who accepted job offers for remote positions were "substantially more likely" to come from diverse communities, whether racial, ethnic, gender, veteran, or ability status. The numbers seemed to support Williams' statement. Though Meta did not have a specific goal to increase the number of disability hires, disabled workers rose from 4.7% to 6.2% with the advent of remote work. Meta has since updated its policy to require employees to work at least three days a week in the office. Even so, the company remains committed to distributed work as a means of fostering relationships and collaboration, all elements of an inclusive work culture where employees can be themselves. Some research has found that Black people and other underrepresented groups benefit from distributed work because they can spend less time code-switching—adjusting their speech, appearance, and behavior to fit into the dominant work culture. Indeed, employees who code-switch expend energy that is better spent performing actual work duties. By allowing hybrid modalities, organizations like Meta enable employees to be themselves, continuing to reap diversity benefits in the process.

1. How does improving workforce diversity present a challenge for leaders?
   Students will provide a variety of answers to this question, but they may focus on diversity as a challenge for leaders and the idea that different employees benefit from different work modalities.

2. Were you aware of code-switching prior to reading this feature? What do you think about this practice as a way for some employees to fit into workplace culture?
   Students from different racial and ethnic backgrounds may be more likely to describe experiences with code-switching. Encourage them to expand on their experiences, explaining why they felt they had to engage in this behavior.

Source: Tslpursky, G. (2022, October 23). How remote work can improve workforce diversity. Psychology Today, https://www. psychologytoday.com/us/blog/intentional-insights/202210/how-remote-work-can-improve-workforce-diversity; Vanian, J. (2023, June 1). Meta will require employees to return to the office three days a week starting in September. CNBC, https://www.cnbc.com/2023/06/01/ meta-will-require-employees-to-return-to-the-office-three-days-a-week-starting-in-september.html.

of finished products, such as automobiles and electronic equipment. The service sector includes transportation, financial services, insurance, and retail sales. The government sectors, which provide essential infrastructure, and nonprofit organizations are important to our collective well-being because they meet needs that other sectors do not address. For example, in France, the not-for-profit Action Tank has discovered a solution for poor consumers who find access to even low-cost products and services out of their reach.[39]

Hundreds of small, medium-sized, and large organizations contribute to the economic health and human welfare of the United States. Throughout this book, we provide examples from a variety of organizations to help you develop a greater appreciation for your own organization and for others in the diverse world of private business enterprises and nonprofit organizations.

1-6 Change Creates Opportunities

Global competition, which is a leading force driving change at work, has increased significantly during the past few decades, especially in industries such as banking, finance, and air transportation. As a result, change has accelerated and, with it, both opportunities and risks. Corporate competition creates performance and cost pressures, changes that have a ripple effect on people and their behavior at work. Although one such risk for employees is the marginalization of part-time professionals, good management practice can ensure their integration.[40] Furthermore, although competition may lead to downsizing and restructuring, it also provides the opportunity for revitalization.[41] And small companies don't necessarily lose in this competitive environment. Scientech, a small power and energy company, needed to enhance its managerial talent and service quality to meet the challenges of growth and big-company competitors, and it consequently improved its performance. Thus, competition spurred its increased success.

Product and service quality are the major ways that companies can win in a competitive environment. IBM, Control Data Services, Inc., Northwest Airlines (now Delta), and Southwest Airlines all used problem-solving skills to achieve high-quality products and services in their attempts to deal with

> Winning in a competitive industry can be a transient victory; staying ahead of the competition requires constant change.

competitive forces. Change in the coffee industry has been a key stimulus for both Caribou Coffee and Starbucks as they innovate and improve.

Too much change, however, leads to chaos, and too little change leads to stagnation. Also, winning in a competitive industry can be a transient victory; staying ahead of the competition requires constant change.

1-6a Global Competition in Business

Managers and executives in the United States face radical change in response to increased global competition. According to noted economist Lester Thurow, this competition is characterized by intense rivalry between the United States, Japan, and Europe in core industries.[42] As a result, all categories of employees face increased pressure to be productive and to add value to the firm. Moreover, corporate warfare and competition make employment uncertain for people in companies or industries that pursue cost-cutting strategies to achieve economic success. Five months after taking over as CEO of Microsoft, Satya Nadella notified employees of impending organizational changes, not limited to job cuts, required for the technology giant to return to its core business.[43] The global competition in the automotive industry among Japanese, U.S., and European car companies exemplifies the intensity that other industries can expect in the future.

In the midst of this international competition, managers must at the same time pay attention to changes and pressures within their own countries. This was exemplified in the in-depth study of a "whole-system" change program in the Scottish national healthcare system where the multilevel dynamics underlying organizational change and adaption were examined.[44] Managers must work across inter-organizational boundaries to ensure effective adaptation in bringing about successful organizational change. Global, economic, and organizational changes have dramatic effects on the study and management of organizational behavior.

Managers must work across national boundaries to ensure success in a global business environment.

1-6b Customer Focused for High Quality

Global competition has challenged organizations to become more customer focused, to meet changing product and service demands, and to exceed customers' expectations of high quality. Quality has the potential to give organizations in viable industries a competitive edge against international competition. By aiming to be number one in experience, for example, Caribou Coffee competes with a customer-focused, high-quality approach.

Quality has become a rubric for products and services of high status. *Total quality* is defined in many ways.[45] *Total quality management (TQM)* is the total dedication to continuous improvement and to

---

Organizational Example

Technology Change and the AI Domino Effect

Change in technology has the potential to create opportunities for businesses and entrepreneurs. A clear example of this can be found in the ongoing development of ChatGPT, an artificially intelligent chatbot created by the small group at OpenAI. ChatGPT has captured the attention of millions of people as well as large organizations like Microsoft who signed a multibillion-dollar deal with OpenAI.

While artificial intelligence technology had been developing for some time, the creators behind ChatGPT noted that previous versions of their chatbot were not as skilled at mimicking conversations. This seemingly small addition, combined with ChatGPT's release to the general public, led to a stunning amount of attention in a short period of time.

This attention created further opportunities for innovation. As ChatGPT became more popular, educators around the world realized that some students were using it to cheat on essays and other graded assignments. This change has led to a flurry of activity designed to provide a solution. Take GPTZero, an AI tool designed by Princeton computer science major Edward Tian. The tool is designed to detect the likelihood of a text having been generated by ChatGPT or other AI chatbots.

Others have developed similar anti-cheating tools and the race to develop the best is likely far from over. This situation exemplifies how change can create a domino effect: technology change leads to an innovation (e.g., ChatGPT), which leads to a change (e.g., AI-fueled cheating), which creates opportunity for more innovation (e.g., tools that detect AI-cheating). This tool, like all technology, does have its limitations too though.

Sources: E. Bowman. "A college student created an app that can tell whether AI wrote an essay." NPR, 2023; W. D. Heaven. "The inside story of how ChatGPT was built from the people who made it." MIT Technology Review, 2023.

customers so that the customers' needs are met and their expectations exceeded. This customer-oriented philosophy of management has important implications for virtually all aspects of organizational behavior. Quality cannot be optimized because customer needs and expectations are always changing, but it is embedded in highly successful organizations. Part of what has catapulted Toyota to the top of the auto industry is its attention to quality and detail throughout the organization. Even though TQM consulting has experienced a boom-to-bust cycle, the main concepts underlying its initial rise in popularity are here to stay.

Quality improvement enhances the probability of organizational success in increasingly competitive industries. One study of 193 general medical hospitals examined seven TQM practices and found them positively related to the financial performance of the hospital.[46] Indeed, quality improvement is an enduring feature of an organization's culture and of the economic competition we face today. It leads to competitive advantage through customer responsiveness, results acceleration, and resource effectiveness.[47] In evaluating quality improvement ideas for people at work, three key questions should be asked: (1) Does the idea improve customer response? (2) Does the idea accelerate results? and (3) Does the idea increase the effectiveness of resources? A "yes" answer means the idea should be implemented to improve quality.

Six Sigma is a philosophy for company-wide quality improvement developed by Motorola and popularized by General Electric. Characterized by its customer-driven approach, through its emphasis on using quantitative data to make decisions and its priority of saving money,[48] it has evolved into a high-performance system for executing business strategy. Part of its quality program is a twelve-step problem-solving method specifically designed to lead a Six Sigma "Black Belt" to significant improvement within a defined process. It tackles problems in four phases: (1) measure, (2) analyze, (3) improve, and (4) control. In addition, it forces executives to align the right objective and targets, and it forces quality improvement teams to mobilize for action in order to accelerate and monitor sustained improvement. Six Sigma is set up so that it can be applied to a range of situations, from manufacturing settings to service work environments.

Any quality control method has some success and some failure, and some methods may work better in a given organization than others due to differences in organizational culture. One study, with a strong emphasis on exploring statistical modeling techniques, compared Six Sigma to two other methods for quality improvement (specifically, Taguchi's methods and the Shainin system) and found it to be the most complete strategy of the three.[49] On the other hand, statistical data on the actual economic effect of Six Sigma is lacking, and the method has come under some critique.[50] It is important for managers to consider which of a variety of options is best for their organization.

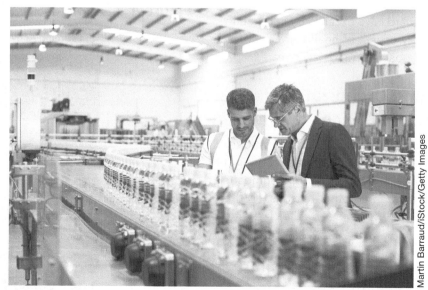

Martin Barraud/iStock/Getty Images

Quality is a customer-oriented philosophy of management with important implications for virtually all aspects of organizational behavior.

1-6c Behavior and Quality at Work

Whereas total quality may draw on reliability engineering or just-in-time management, total quality improvement can succeed only when employees have the skills and authority to respond to customer needs.[51] Total quality has important direct effects on the behavior of employees at all levels in the organization, not just on employees working directly with customers. Thus, chief executives can advance total quality by engaging in participative management, being willing to change things, focusing quality efforts on customer service (not cost cutting), including quality as a criterion in reward systems, improving the flow of information regarding quality-improvement successes or failures, and being actively and personally involved in quality efforts. While serving as chair of Motorola, George Fisher emphasized the behavioral attributes of leadership, cooperation, communication, and participation as important elements in the company's Six Sigma program.

Quality improvement is crucial to competitive success. The U.S. Department of Commerce sponsors an annual award in the name of Malcolm Baldrige, former secretary of commerce in the Reagan administration, to recognize companies excelling in quality improvement and management. The Malcolm Baldrige National Quality Award examination evaluates an organization in seven categories: leadership, information and analysis, strategic quality planning, human resource utilization, quality assurance of products and services, quality results, and customer satisfaction. Hospitals and health systems that have won the Malcolm Baldrige Award have excelled by integrating innovation into every aspect of healthcare delivery, from leadership and goal-setting to patient care.[52]

1-6d Managing Organizational Behavior in Changing Times

Over and above the challenge of quality improvement to meet international competition, managing organizational behavior during changing times is challenging for at least three other reasons: (1) the increasing globalization of organizations' operating territory, (2) the increasing diversity of organizational workforces, and (3) the continuing demand for higher levels of moral and ethical behavior at work.

Each of these three issues is explored in detail in Chapter 2 and highlighted throughout the text as they appear intertwined with contemporary organizational practices. For example, the issue of women in the workplace concerns workforce diversity and at the same time overlaps with the globalization issue.

1-7 Learning about Organizational Behavior

The study of organizational behavior is based on scientific knowledge and applied practice. It involves abstract ideas, such as valence and expectancy in motivation, as well as concrete matters, such as observable behaviors and medical symptoms of distress at work. Therefore, learning about organizational behavior includes at least three activities, as shown in Figure 1.3. First, the science of organizational behavior requires the mastery of a certain body of **objective knowledge**. Objective knowledge results from research, experimentation, and scientific observation. Second, the practice of organizational behavior requires **skill development** based on

objective knowledge Knowledge that results from research and scientific activities.

skill development The mastery of abilities essential to successful functioning in organizations.

Figure 1.3 Learning about Organizational Behavior

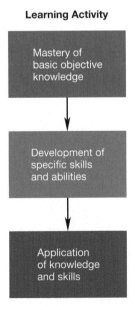

Learning Activity

Mastery of basic objective knowledge

↓

Development of specific skills and abilities

↓

Application of knowledge and skills

YOU

Learning style inventory

Directions: This 24-item survey is not timed. Answer each question as honestly as you can. Place a check on the appropriate line after each statement.

	OFTEN	SOMETIMES	SELDOM
1. Can remember more about a subject through the lecture method with information, explanations, and discussion.	—	—	—
2. Prefer information to be written on the chalkboard, with the use of visual aids and assigned readings.	—	—	—
3. Like to write things down or to take notes for visual review.	—	—	—
4. Prefer to use posters, models, or actual practice and some activities in class.	—	—	—
5. Require explanations of diagrams, graphs, or visual directions.	—	—	—
6. Enjoy working with my hands or making things.	—	—	—
7. Am skillful with and enjoy developing and making graphs and charts.	—	—	—
8. Can tell if sounds match when presented with pairs of sounds.	—	—	—
9. Remember best by writing things down several times.	—	—	—
10. Can understand and follow directions on maps.	—	—	—
11. Do better at academic subjects by listening to lectures and tapes.	—	—	—
12. Play with coins or keys in pockets.	—	—	—
13. Learn to spell better by repeating the word out loud than by writing the word on paper.	—	—	—
14. Can better understand a news development by reading about it in the paper than by listening to the radio.	—	—	—
15. Chew gum, smoke, or snack during studies.	—	—	—
16. Feel the best way to remember is to picture it in my head.	—	—	—
17. Learn spelling by "finger spelling" words.	—	—	—
18. Would rather listen to a good lecture or speech than read about the same material in a textbook.	—	—	—
19. Am good at working and solving jigsaw puzzles and mazes.	—	—	—
20. Grip objects in hands during learning period.	—	—	—
21. Prefer listening to the news on the radio rather than reading about it in the newspaper.	—	—	—
22. Obtain information on an interesting subject by reading relevant materials.	—	—	—
23. Feel comfortable touching others, hugging, hand-shaking, etc.	—	—	—
24. Follow oral directions better than written ones.	—	—	—

Scoring Procedures:

Score 5 points for each OFTEN, 3 points for each SOMETIMES, and 1 point for each SELDOM.

Visual Preference Score: 5 points each for questions 2 + 3 + 7 + 10 + 14 + 16 + 19 + 22 = _____

Auditory Preference Score: 5 points each for questions 1 + 5 + 8 + 11 + 13 + 18 + 21 + 24 = _____

Tactile Preference Score: 5 points each for questions 4 + 6 + 9 + 12 + 15 + 17 + 20 + 23 = _____

Source: Adapted from J. N. Gardner and A. J. Jewler, *Your college experience: Strategies for Success*, Third concise edition (Belmont, CA: Wadsworth/ITP, 1998), 62–63; E. Jensen, *Student Success Secrets*, 4th ed. (Hauppauge, NY: Barron's, 1996), 33–36.

knowledge and an understanding of oneself in order to master the abilities essential to success. Third, both objective knowledge and skill development must be applied in real-world settings.

Learning can be challenging and fun if student diversity is addressed in the learning process, when students have more options and can take greater responsibility as coproducers.[53] Teaching and learning styles should be aligned carefully, and educators should be aware that teaching is no longer merely verbal and visual but has now become virtual.[54] If you are a visual learner, use charts, maps, Power-Point slides, videos, the Internet, notes, or flash cards and write things out for visual review. If you are an auditory learner, then listen, take notes during lectures, consider taping them so that you can fill in gaps later, review your notes frequently, and recite key concepts aloud. If you are a tactile learner, trace words as you are saying them, write down facts several times, and make study sheets.

1-7a Objective Knowledge

In any field of study, objective knowledge is developed through basic and applied research. Since the early research on scientific management, research on organizational behavior has continued to provide objective knowledge involving theories, conceptual models, and various research findings. In this book, the objective knowledge in each chapter is reflected in the supporting notes. Mastering the concepts and ideas that come from these notes enables you to discuss intelligently topics such as motivation and work behavior[55] as well as stress and health.[56]

We encourage instructors and students of organizational behavior to think critically about the objective knowledge that has been gained in the study of organizational behavior. Only by engaging in critical thinking can one question or challenge the results of specific research or consider how such research should be applied in a particular work setting. Rote memorization does not prepare students to appreciate the complexity of specific theories or the intricacies of interrelated concepts, ideas, and topics. Critical thinking, by contrast, enables students to identify inconsistencies and limitations in the current body of objective knowledge.

Critical thinking, based on knowledge and understanding of basic ideas, leads to inquisitive exploration and is a key to accepting the responsibility of coproducer in the learning process. A questioning, probing attitude is at the core of critical thinking. The student of organizational behavior should evolve into a critical consumer of knowledge related to organizational behavior—one who is able to intelligently question the latest research results and distinguish plausible, sound, new approaches from fads that lack substance or adequate foundation. Ideally, the student of organizational behavior develops into a scientific, professional manager who is knowledgeable in the art and science of organizational behavior.

1-7b Skill Development

Learning about organizational behavior requires doing as well as knowing. Furthermore, the development of skills and abilities requires that students be challenged by the instructor and by themselves.

The U.S. Department of Labor tries to ensure that people acquire the necessary skills to be successful in the workplace.[57] The essential skills identified by the department are (1) resource management skills, such as time management; (2) information management skills, such as data interpretation; (3) personal interaction skills, such as teamwork; (4) systems behavior and performance skills, such as cause–effect relationships; and (5) technology utilization skills, such as troubleshooting. Many of these skills, such as decision making and information management, are directly related to the study of organizational behavior.[58] Employers increasingly demand that workers possess effective teamwork and collaboration skills. Eighty percent of employers surveyed cited the ability to work in groups as a highly desirable attribute of recruits.[59]

Developing skills is different from acquiring objective knowledge because it requires structured practice and feedback. A key function of experiential learning is engaging the student in individual or group activities that are systematically reviewed, leading to new skills and understandings. However, objective knowledge acquisition and skill development are interrelated, as shown in Figure 1.4. The student engages in an individual- or group-structured activity and then systematically reviews that activity, gaining new or modified knowledge and skills.

Figure 1.4 Learning from Structured Activity

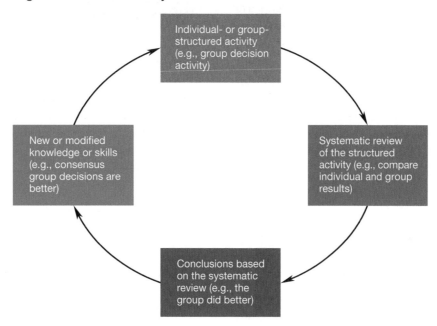

If skill development and structured learning occur in this way, there should be an inherently self-correcting element to learning because of the modification of the student's knowledge and skills over time.[60] To ensure that skill development does occur and that the learning is self-correcting as it occurs, three basic guidelines must be followed.

First, students must accept responsibility for their own behavior, actions, and learning. This is key to the coproducer role in the learning process. A group cannot learn for its members. Members must accept responsibility for what they each individually do and learn. Denial of responsibility helps no one, least of all the learner.

Second, each student must actively participate in the individual- or group-structured learning activity. Structured learning is not passive; it is active. In group activities, everyone suffers if just one person adopts a passive attitude. All must actively participate.

Third, each student must be open to new information, new skills, new ideas, and experimentation. This does not mean that students should be indiscriminately open. It does mean that students should have nondefensive, open attitudes so that they can learn and adjust to new ideas.

1-7c Application of Knowledge and Skills

Understanding organizational behavior includes an appreciation and understanding of working realities as well as of science and of oneself. One of the advantages of structured, experiential learning is that a person can explore new behaviors and skills in a comparatively safe environment. Fortunately, losing your temper in a classroom activity and learning about the potentially adverse impact on other people will have dramatically different consequences from losing your temper with an important customer in a tense work situation. Thus, learning spaces that offer the interface of student learning styles with institutional learning environments give learners safe spaces to engage their brains to form abstract hypotheses, to actively test these hypotheses through concrete experiences, and to reflectively observe the outcomes in behavior and experience.[61] The ultimate objective of skill application and experiential learning is that one transfers the process employed in learning from structured activities in the classroom and learning spaces to learning from unstructured opportunities in the workplace.

Although organizational behavior is an applied discipline, students are not "trained" in organizational behavior. Rather, they are "educated" in organizational behavior and are coproducers in learning. The distinction between these two modes of learning is found in the degree of direct and immediate applicability of either knowledge or skills. As an activity, training ties objective knowledge or skill development more directly to specific applications. By contrast, education enhances a person's residual pool of objective knowledge and skills that may then be selectively applied later—sometimes significantly

> Learning about organizational behavior requires doing as well as knowing.

later—when the opportunity presents itself. Hence, education is consistent with the concept of lifelong learning. Especially in a growing area of knowledge such as organizational behavior, the student can think of the first course as the outset of lifelong learning about the subject.

Experiential Exercise

What's Changing at Work?

This exercise provides an opportunity to discuss changes occurring in your workplace and university. These changes may be for the better or the worse. However, rather than evaluating whether they are good or bad changes, begin by simply identifying the changes that are occurring. Later, you can evaluate whether they are good or bad.

Step 1. The class forms into groups of approximately six members each. Each group elects a spokesperson and answers the following questions. The group should spend at least five minutes on each question. Make sure that each member of the group makes a contribution to each question. The spokesperson for each group should be ready to share the group's collective responses.

   a. *What are the changes occurring in your workplace and university?* Members should focus both on internal changes, such as reorganizations, and on external changes, such as new customers or competitors. Develop a list of the changes discussed in your group.
   b. *What are the forces that are driving the changes?* To answer this question, look for the causes of the changes that

members of the group are observing. For example, a reorganization may be caused by new business opportunities, by new technologies, or by a combination of factors.
   c. *What signs of resistance to change do you see occurring?* Change is not always easy for people or organizations. Do you see signs of resistance, such as frustration, anger, increased absences, or other forms of discomfort with the changes you observe?

Step 2. Once you have answered the three questions in Step 1, your group needs to spend some time evaluating whether these changes are good or bad. Decide whether each change on the list developed in Step 1a is good or bad. In addition, answer the question "Why?" That is, "why is this change good? Why is that change bad?"

Step 3. Each group shares the results of its answers to the questions in Step 1 and its evaluation of the changes completed in Step 2. Cross-team questions and discussion follow.

Step 4. Your instructor may allow a few minutes at the end of the class period to comment on his or her perceptions of changes occurring within the university or businesses with which he or she is familiar.

Learning Objectives

1-1 **Define organizational behavior.** Organizational behavior is individual behavior and group dynamics in organizations. The foundation of organizational behavior is human behavior, so the study of OB involves understanding workers' behavior in terms of their history and personal value systems and examining the external factors to which a person is subject. Organizational behavior has grown out of contributions from psychology, sociology, engineering, anthropology, management, and medicine.

1-2 **Identify four action steps for responding positively in times of change.** Change is an opportunity when one has a positive attitude, asks questions, listens, and is committed to succeed. People in change situations often become rigid and reactive, rather than open and responsive. This behavior works well in the face of gradual, incremental change. However, rigid and well-learned behavior may be counterproductive responses to significant change.

1-3 **Identify the important system components of an organization.**

1-4 **Describe the formal and informal elements of an organization.** Organizations have formal and informal elements within them. The formal organization is the official, legitimate, and most visible part that enables people to think of organizations in logical and rational ways. The informal organization is unofficial and less visible. The informal elements of the organization are often points of diagnostic and intervention activities in organization development.

1-5 **Identify factors that contribute to the diversity of organizations in the economy.** The United States has the largest economy in the world. It is composed of manufacturing organizations, service organizations, privately owned companies, and nonprofit organizations; all contribute to our national well-being. Understanding a variety of organizations will help you develop a greater appreciation for your own organization and for others in the world of private business enterprises and nonprofit organizations.

1-6 **Describe the opportunities that change creates for organizational behavior.** The changes and challenges that managers face are driven by international competition and customer demands. Managers in this environment must be aware of the risks associated with downsizing and the marginalization of part-time workers. Organizations also face regular challenges in the areas of globalization, workforce diversity, ethics and character, and technological innovation.

1-7 **Demonstrate the value of objective knowledge and skill development in the study of organizational behavior.** Although organizational behavior is an applied discipline, a student is not "trained" in organizational behavior. Rather, one is "educated" in organizational behavior and is a coproducer in learning. To enrich your study of organizational behavior, take the learning style inventory on this card.

Key Terms

anthropology The science of human learned behavior. (p. 3)

challenge The call to competition, contest, or battle. (p. 2)

change The transformation or modification of an organization and/or its stakeholders. (p. 2)

engineering The applied science of energy and matter. (p. 3)

formal organization The official, legitimate, and most visible part of the system. (p. 7)

Hawthorne studies Studies conducted during the 1920s and 1930s that suggested the importance of the informal organization. (p. 7)

informal organization The unofficial and less visible part of the system. (p. 7)

management The study of overseeing activities and supervising people in organizations. (p. 3)

medicine The applied science of healing or treating diseases to enhance an individual's health and well-being. (p. 3)

objective knowledge Knowledge that results from research and scientific activities. (p. 12)

opportunities Favorable times or chances for progress and advancement. (p. 2)

organizational behavior The study of individual behavior and group dynamics in organizations. (p. 2)

people The human resources of an organization. (p. 6)

psychology The science of human behavior. (p. 3)

skill development The mastery of abilities essential to successful functioning in organizations. (p. 12)

sociology The science of society. (p. 3)

structure The systems of communication, authority and roles, and workflow. (p. 6)

task An organization's mission, purpose, or goal for existing. (p. 6)

technology The tools, knowledge, and/or techniques used to transform inputs into outputs. (p. 6)

Ethical Dilemma

Kaya is a manager at Renew, Inc., an innovative car restoration company. Renew started as a small start up in southern California and has been expanding for the last 10 years. Their method of removing rust from cars and preventing its return has become very popular with lower income families who need to keep a car as long as possible.

With their growth and the proximity to Mexico, Kaya is considering proposing an international move to the owners of the company. She believes that expanding into Mexico will be very profitable. Her research has indicated that there is a large population in northern Mexico who could use Renew's services. The only issue is that her research also revealed that a normal and acceptable business practice in Mexico is to offer bribes to officials to get the necessary paperwork to incorporate in the country.

Kaya knows that Cyrus, the founder and president of Renew, has very strict ethical business practices and would never agree to do this. Kaya also knows that she could easily manage this process without Cyrus ever knowing. Cyrus would not be involved in setting up operations in Mexico. She could easily hide the bribes.

Kaya is really torn. She knows that this move would be great for the company. But she also knows that Cyrus would never want to be involved in something like this. But if she does it, is Cyrus really involved?

1. What are Kaya's options in this situation?

2. Of those options you considered, which one should Kaya choose? Why?

Chapter 2

PeachShutterStock/Shutterstock.com

Challenges for Managers

Learning Objectives

2-1 Describe the factors that affect organizations competing in the global economy.

2-2 Explain how cultural differences form the basis of work-related attitudes.

2-3 Describe the challenges and positive influences diversity brings to today's business environment.

2-4 Discuss the role of ethics, character, and personal integrity in the organization.

2-5 Explain five issues that pose ethical dilemmas for managers.

The challenges that managers face today stem from the fact that businesses exist within a complex and shifting global environment.[1] The COVID-19 pandemic, the continuing rise of China economically and militarily, and the Russian invasion of Ukraine have placed significant pressure on businesses and commerce around the world. The resulting challenges for managers can be viewed as both opportunities and threats.[2] Globalization may be in a difficult transition period but it is not dead.[3] Managers continue to have three sets of challenges in the new era emerging in the shadow of the COVID-19 business world. These challenges are: (1) competing in a global economy, with all of its complexity and complications;[4] (2) managing an increasingly diverse and complex workforce;[5] and (3) operating with ethics, character, and personal integrity.[6]

2-1 Competing in the Global Economy

Business conducted across national borders used to be referred to as *international* activity, a term implying that the individual's or the organization's nationality is held strongly in consciousness.[7] *Globalization,* by contrast, suggests that the world is free from national boundaries and is borderless.[8] U.S. workers now compete with workers in other countries. Organizations from other countries, such as the auto manufacturers Toyota, Nissan, Volkswagen, and Daimler Benz, have well established business interests in the United States.

Similarly, what were once called *multinational organizations* (organizations that did business in several countries) are now referred to as **transnational organizations,** indicating that the global viewpoint supersedes national issues.[9] Transnational organizations such as 3M, IBM, and Coca-Cola operate worldwide across long distances and employ a multicultural mix of workers.

2-1a Social and Political Changes

Social and political upheavals have led organizations to change the way they conduct business as a result of thinking globally. Toyota, for example, is one Japanese

---

transnational organization An organization in which the global viewpoint supersedes national issues.

guanxi The Chinese practice of building networks for social exchange.

What major challenges must managers overcome to remain competitive?

company thinking big, thinking globally, and thinking differently by learning to speak to the 60-million-strong Generation Y, or so-called millennials.[10]

Business ventures in China have become increasingly complex for U.S. companies given the rising international competition between the U.S. and Chinese economies. One challenge U.S. managers face is understanding Chinese ways of doing business, ways that have been shaped by the Communist Party, socialism, feudalistic values, and **guanxi** (building networks for social exchange). Once *guanxi* is established, individuals can ask favors of each other with the expectation that the favor will be returned. Thus, many Chinese use *guanxi,* or personal connections, to conduct business or obtain jobs.

The concept of *guanxi* is not unique to China. There are similar concepts in many other countries, including Russia and Haiti. It is a broad term that can mean anything from strongly loyal relationships to ceremonial gift giving, sometimes seen as bribery. *Guanxi* is more common in societies with underdeveloped legal support for private businesses.[11]

Americans can learn to build their own *guanxi* so as to interact effectively with Chinese managers. This would involve understanding the Chinese chain of command and negotiating slow, general agreements. Using the foreign government as a local franchisee may be effective in China. For example, KFC's operation in China is a joint venture between KFC (60 percent) and two Chinese government bodies (40 percent).[12]

The opening of trade barriers is a third issue that affects organizations competing in a global economy. In 1993, the European Union integrated fifteen nations into a single market by removing trade barriers. At that time, the member nations of the European Union were Austria, Belgium, Denmark, Finland, France, Germany, Greece, Ireland, Italy, Luxembourg, the Netherlands, Portugal, Spain, Sweden, and the United Kingdom. By 2007 Bulgaria, Cyprus, the Czech Republic, Estonia, Hungary, Latvia, Lithuania, Malta, Poland, Romania, Slovakia, and Slovenia had joined. Croatia joined the EU in 2014, and then the UK became the only sovereign nation to exit the EU in 2020 via BREXIT, leading to major commerce challenges.

Still, Europe's integration provides many opportunities for U.S. organizations to engage hundreds of millions of potential customers. Companies such as Ford Motor Company and IBM, which entered the market early with wholly owned subsidiaries, were able to capitalize on their much anticipated head start.[13] With BREXIT and deepening integration of the EU, global commerce has become more complex.

The United States, Canada, and Mexico replaced the North American Free Trade Agreement (NAFTA), which took effect in 1994, with the U.S.–Mexico–Canada Agreement (USMCA) that entered into force on July 1, 2020. With NAFTA, organizations found promising new markets for their products, and many companies located plants in Mexico to take advantage of low labor costs. However, this led to one of the limitations of NAFTA for the U.S., which was net job losses. The Trump Administration renegotiated the NAFTA trade agreement, resulting in the USMCA now in effect.

Managers must think globally and in the context of changing international trade agreements and alignments. Entering global markets requires long-term strategies accompanied by contingency plans for changing business realities. The Organizational Example below discusses how Walt and Roy Disney set their cartoon studio on a trajectory to become a major global enterprise.

2-1b Cultural Differences

Managers need to not only understand the climate and culture of their own organizations,[14] they must also understand cultural differences and diversity. Whether managing culturally diverse individuals within a single location or managing individuals at remote locations around the globe, organizations must appreciate the differences among cultures. Edgar Schein suggests that to understand an organization's culture or, more broadly, any culture, one should dig below the surface

Companies like IBM are transnational and are recognized around the world.

Peter Horree/Alamy Stock Photo

Organizational Example

100 Years of Wonder and Magic

Walt Disney and his brother Roy established the Disney Brothers Cartoon Studio in 1923, and Mickey Mouse was born five years later in 1928. From humble beginnings, Disneyland was later launched in Anaheim, California in 1955 as a $17 million revolutionary vacation destination. Since then, Disney has grown into a full-blown global enterprise. Celebrating 100 Years of Wonder in 2023, The Walt Disney Company is a diversified global entertainment business with operations in five major segments: Media Networks, Parks and Resorts, Studio Entertainment, Consumer Products, and Interactive. Disney is an innovator and a leader in its major market segments, with a market capitalization approaching $200 billion. When told that others were stealing his ideas, Walt Disney is reported to have said he could create new ideas faster than anyone else could steal them. Disney now operates in 59 markets across 29 countries, truly a global business born in a cartoon studio.

Source: J. Baxter, B. Steele, and Staff of the Walt Disney Archives, *The Story of Disney: 100 Years of Wonder* (Glendale, Calif.: Disney Publishing, 2023).

of visible artifacts and uncover the basic underlying assumptions at the core of the culture.[15]

Microcultural differences (i.e., differences within cultures) are key to our understanding of the global work environment.[16] One such difference is the gap between generations, which Toyota, as previously mentioned, is addressing by learning to speak to the 60-million-strong millennial Generation Y.[17]

When considering differences among cultures, symbols are extremely important because they can generate misunderstanding or inhibit communication if they are interpreted incorrectly. Consider the thumbs-up sign, which means approval in the United States but is an obscene gesture in Australia. Consider also the Windows icon representing a manila file folder, which is meaningless to Europeans who have never used such folders.[18]

Do cultural differences translate into differences in work-related attitudes? To answer this question, the pioneering Dutch researcher Geert Hofstede, with his colleagues, surveyed 160,000 managers and employees of IBM working in sixty different countries. Thus, the researchers were able to study individuals from the same company in the same jobs but living in different countries. They found that national culture explains more differences in work-related attitudes than does age, gender, profession, or position in the organization. The accompanying Inclusive Conversation on this page explores a CHIP manufacture's encounter with national culture differences. Five dimensions of cultural differences that formed the basis for work-related attitudes were identified (Figure 2.1).[19]

Management careers have taken on a global dimension in that working in transnational organizations may give managers the opportunity to work in other countries. **Expatriate managers,** those who work in a country other than their home country, benefit greatly from knowledge of cultural differences.

International executives are executives whose jobs have international scope, whether they have an expatriate assignment or deal with international issues. What kind of competencies should an individual develop to prepare for an international career? Some key competencies are integrity, insightfulness, risk taking, courage to take a stand, and ability to bring out the best in people. Learning-oriented attributes of international executives include cultural adventurousness, flexibility, openness to criticism, desire to seek learning opportunities, and sensitivity to cultural differences.[20] Further, strong human capital generally has a positive effect on internationalization.[21] Notice that all these qualities are based on core competencies and

expatriate manager A manager who works in a country other than her or his home country.

Inclusive Conversations

Chip Manufacturer Experiences National Culture Differences in Move to the U.S.

The CHIPS and Science Act of 2022 expanded domestic manufacturing, including microchip production, in the U.S., a move intended to prevent supply chain disruptions and microchip shortages due to a series of events, from trade wars to natural disasters in Asia-Pacific region, to COVID-19. Taiwan Semiconductor Manufacturing Company (TSMC), the world's largest producer of advanced computer chips, took advantage of this opportunity.

TSMC invested $40 billion dollars to build a semiconductor plant in Arizona, and with over 75% of its existing employees being of Taiwanese origin, a major challenge for the company will be to learn to blend two employee work cultures. While Taiwanese employees are willing work long hours and sacrifice their weekends to work at TSMC, American workers are less likely to make such sacrifices. A former TSMC engineer noted that the most difficult thing about chip wafer manufacturing wasn't the technology, but personnel management. While Taiwanese employees did what they were told, without question, American employees challenged managers and asked if there might be better methods and rejected new assignments, making standardization more difficult than what TSMC was accustomed to with Taiwanese employees. According to the engineer, "Americans are the most difficult to manage."

1. Do you agree with the Taiwanese engineer's assessment of the difficulty with managing American workers? Why or why not?

2. What aspects of national culture are most important for TSMC to understand as the company tries to blend its workers? Explain.

Source: Fusion Worldwide, "The Global Chip Shortage: A Timeline of Unfortunate Events" (October 11, 2021), https://info.fusionww.com/blog/the-global-chip-shortage-a-timeline-of-unfortunate-events; J. Liu and P. Mozur, "Inside Taiwanese Chip Giant, a U.S. Expansion Stokes Tensions," *The New York Times* (February 22, 2023), https://www.nytimes.com/2023/02/22/technology/tsmc-arizona-factory-tensions.html.

Figure 2.1 Hofstede's Dimensions of Cultural Differences

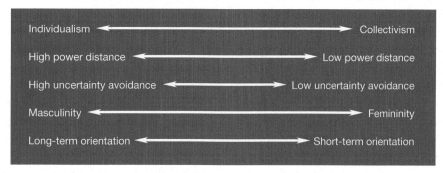

Individualism	⟷	Collectivism
High power distance	⟷	Low power distance
High uncertainty avoidance	⟷	Low uncertainty avoidance
Masculinity	⟷	Femininity
Long-term orientation	⟷	Short-term orientation

Source: Based on Academy of Management, P.O. Box 3020, Briarcliff Manor, NY 10510-8020. Cultural Constraints in Management Theories. G. Hofstede, Academy of Management Executive 7 (1993).

the ability to learn from experience. Sensitivity to the families of international executives is important too, especially children transitioning to university life.[22]

Because workplace customs vary widely, understanding cultural differences becomes especially important for companies that are considering opening foreign offices. It is wise to do the research in advance. Consulate offices and companies operating within the foreign country provide excellent information about national customs and legal requirements. Table 2.1

Table 2.1 Business Guide to Cultural Differences

Country	Appointments	Dress	Gifts	Negotiations
Japan	Punctuality is a necessity. It is considered rude to be late.	Conservative dress is the norm for men and women in large- to medium-sized companies, though pastel shirts are common. One may be expected to remove shoes in temples and homes, as well as in some ryokan (inn) style restaurants. In that case, slip-on shoes should be worn.	Important part of Japanese business protocol. Gifts are typically exchanged among colleagues on July 15 and January 1 to commemorate midyear and the year's end, respectively.	Business cards (*mishit*) are an important part of doing business and key for establishing credentials. One side of your card should be in English and the other in Japanese. It is an asset to include information such as membership in professional associations.
Mexico	Punctuality is not always as much of a priority. Nonetheless, Mexicans are accustomed to North Americans arriving on time, and most Mexicans in business, if not government, will try to return the favor.	Dark, conservative suits and ties are the norm for most men. Standard office attire for women includes dresses, skirted suits, or skirts and blouses. Femininity is strongly encouraged in women's dress.	Not usually a requirement in business dealings, though presenting a small gift is generally appreciated as a gesture of goodwill. If giving a gift, be aware that inquiring about what the receiver would like to receive may offend.	Mexicans avoid directly saying "no." A "no" is often disguised in responses such as "maybe" or "we'll see." You should also use this indirect approach in your dealings. Otherwise, your Mexican counterparts may perceive you as being rude and pushy.
Saudi Arabia	It is customary to make appointments for times of day rather than precise hours. The importance Saudis attach to courtesy and hospitality can cause delays that prevent keeping to a strict schedule.	The only absolute requirement of dress code is modesty. For men, this means covering everything from navel to knee. In public, women are required to cover everything except the face, hands, and feet by wearing an *abaya* (standard black cloak) and headscarf.	Should only be given to the most intimate of friends. For a Saudi to receive a present from a lesser acquaintance is so embarrassing that it is considered offensive.	Business cards are common but not essential. If used, R common practice is to have both English and Arabic printed on the same side so that neither language is perceived as less important by being on the reverse of the same card.

Source: Adapted from information obtained from business culture guides accessed online at http://www.Executiveplanet.Com.

presents a business guide to cultural differences in three countries: Japan, Mexico, and Saudi Arabia.

Another reality affecting global business practices is the cost of layoffs in other countries. As the economy has become more global, downsizing has presented challenges worldwide. For example, dismissing a forty-five-year-old middle manager with twenty years of service and a $50,000 annual salary varied in cost from a low of $13,000 in Ireland to a high of $130,000 in Italy.[23] Laying off this manager in the United States would have cost approximately $19,000. The wide variability in costs stems from the various legal protections that certain countries give workers. In Italy, laid-off employees must receive a so-called notice period payment (one year's pay if they have nine years or more of service) plus a severance payment (based on pay and years of service). U.S. companies operating overseas often adopt the European tradition of training and retraining workers to avoid overstaffing and potential layoffs. Appreciating the customs and rules for doing business in another country is essential to global success.

2-2 Cultural Differences and Work-Related Attitudes

Hofstede's work has implications for work-related attitudes. We'll now take a closer look at how his five dimensions of cultural differences are manifest in a variety of countries.

2-2a Individualism versus Collectivism

In cultures where individualism predominates, the social framework is loose and employees put loyalty to themselves and their families ahead of loyalty to their company and work group. Cultures

characterized by collectivism, on the other hand, are tightly knit social frameworks in which individual members depend strongly on others and group decisions are valued and accepted.

North American and European cultures are individualistic in orientation. Managers in Great Britain and the Netherlands, for example, emphasize and encourage individual achievement. In contrast, in collectivist cultures, such as Israeli *kibbutzim* and Japan, people view group loyalty and unity as paramount. Collectivistic managers seek to fit harmoniously within the group and encourage their employees to do the same. The world's regions are patterned with varying degrees of this cultural difference.

2-2b Power Distance

Power distance relates to the acceptance of the unequal distribution of power. In countries with a high power distance, bosses are afforded more authority, which is seldom bypassed, titles are used, and formality is the rule. Managers and employees in such countries see one another as fundamentally different kinds of people. India, Venezuela, and Mexico all demonstrate high power distance.

In societies with low power distance, people believe in minimizing inequality. People at various power levels in these countries are less threatened by and more willing to trust one another. Managers and employees judge each other on a basis of equality. Managers are given authority only if they have expertise. Employees frequently bypass the boss in order to get work done in countries with a low power distance, such as Denmark and Australia.

In feminine cultures, relationships and concern for others are emphasized. Nations with feminine cultures include Denmark, Sweden, the Netherlands, and Norway.

individualism A cultural orientation in which people belong to loose social frameworks and their primary concern is for themselves and their families.

collectivism A cultural orientation in which individuals belong to tightly knit social frameworks and depend strongly on extended families or clans.

power distance The degree to which a culture accepts unequal distribution of power.

2-2c Uncertainty Avoidance

Cultures with high uncertainty avoidance are concerned with security and tend to avoid conflict. People in such cultures tend to seek consensus in an effort to moderate the threat of life's inherent uncertainty. Cultures with low uncertainty avoidance tolerate ambiguity better. People are more willing to take risks and are more comfortable with individual differences. Conflict is seen as constructive, and people accept dissenting viewpoints. Accordingly, Norwegians and Australians value job mobility because they have low uncertainty avoidance; Japan and Italy are characterized by high uncertainty avoidance, and so, not surprisingly, their cultures emphasize career stability.

2-2d Masculinity versus Femininity

In cultures characterized by traditional masculinity, assertiveness and materialism are valued. Men, the idea goes, should be assertive, tough, and decisive, whereas women should be nurturing, modest, and tender.[24] Money and possessions are very important in this viewpoint, and performance is what counts. Achievement is admired. Cultures characterized by traditional femininity emphasize relationships and concern for others. Men and women are expected to assume both assertive and nurturing roles. Quality of life is very important, and people and the environment are emphasized.

Later in the chapter the emerging perspectives on sexual orientation and gender diversity beyond Hofstede's binary framework are discussed.

2-2e Time Orientation

Cultures also differ in time orientation. A culture's values may be oriented toward the future (long-term orientation) or toward the past and present (short-term orientation).[25] In China, which has a long-term orientation, values such as thrift and persistence, which look toward the future, are emphasized. Russians generally have a short-term orientation and particularly value respect for tradition (past) and meeting social obligations (present).

Hofstede found the United States to be the most individualistic country of any he studied. It ranked among the countries with weak power distance, and its level of uncertainty avoidance indicated a tolerance of uncertainty. The United States also ranked as a masculine culture with a short-term orientation.

> In cultures with low power distance, managers are more likely to consult employees and work with them to achieve harmonious results.

These values have shaped U.S. management theory, so Hofstede's work casts doubt on the universal applicability of U.S. management theories. Because these dimensions vary widely, management practices should be adjusted to account for cultural differences. Managers in transnational organizations must learn as much as they can about other cultures in order to lead their culturally diverse organizations effectively.

2-2f Developing Cross-Cultural Sensitivity

In today's multicultural environment, it is imperative that organizations help their employees recognize and appreciate cultural differences. One way companies do this is through cultural sensitivity training. IBM's cultural sensitivity program, Global Citizens Portfolio, consists of flexible spending accounts that employees can use to enhance their training and in turn benefit the company.[26] Another way to develop sensitivity is by using cross-cultural task forces or teams. The Milwaukee-based GE Medical Systems Group (GEMS), with 19,000 employees working worldwide, has developed a vehicle for bringing together managers from each of its three regions (the Americas, Europe, and Asia) to work on a variety of business projects. Their Global Leadership Program forms several work groups made up of managers from various regions and has them work together on important projects, such as worldwide employee integration, to increase employees' sense of belonging throughout the GEMS international organization.[27] Because cultural differences are constantly in flux, it is important for managers to foster up-to-date knowledge of relevant cultural trends.

uncertainty avoidance The degree to which a culture tolerates ambiguity and uncertainty.

masculinity A cultural orientation in which assertiveness and materialism are valued.

femininity A cultural orientation in which relationships and concern for others are valued.

time orientation Whether a culture's values are oriented toward the future (long-term orientation) or toward the past and present (short-term orientation).

The globalization of business affects all parts of the organization, but particularly human resource management. Human resource managers must adopt a global view of human resource planning, recruitment and selection, compensation, and training and development. This means that they must possess a working knowledge of the legal systems in various countries as well as of global economics, culture, and customs. Not only do HR managers prepare U.S. workers to live outside their native country, but they also help foreign employees interact with U.S. culture. Global human resource management is a complex field, one that is critical to organizations' success in the global marketplace.

2-3 The Richly Diverse Workforce

Cultural differences are just one dimension of workforce diversity. **Diversity** encompasses all individual differences, both surface-level differences such as gender, national origin, age, and race and deep-level differences such as personality, religion, social status, and sexual orientation. Bell and Leopold present a comprehensive and detailed examination of diversity in organizations, to include theoretical background, critical legislation, and consideration of a dozen or more specific, identifiable groups and categories.[28] Managers benefit from fully appreciating the breadth and depth of workforce diversity as a basis for understanding those with whom they work, for motivating those who work for them, and for communicating effectively with each employee.

The American Psychological Association (APA) is a richly diverse workforce of 150,000 professionals and staff. As the premier publisher of psychological and behavior science in the world for over a century, APA has honed a high set of ethical, legal, and professional standards for scholarly research and publication.[29] Adhering to these high standards is essential in selecting research that underpins sound knowledge and professional practice concerning organizational behavior. One of the distinguishing

diversity All forms of difference among individuals, including culture, gender, age, ability, religion, personality, social status, and sexual orientation.

features of APA is a strong emphasis on inclusiveness, bias-free language, and interpersonal respect. APA's two general bias-free language guidelines are equally applicable in the scientific community and the business community. These are: (1) describe individuals and groups in the appropriate level of specificity and (2) be sensitive to labels.[30] We ascribe to these bias-free guidelines throughout our writing, recognizing that historically these guidelines have not always been in place more broadly. In addition to these two general bias-free guidelines, APA has a set of seven specific guidelines, which focus on: racial and ethnic identity, gender, age, disability, sexual orientation, socioeconomic status, and intersectionality. Our emphasis is on ethnic diversity, gender diversity, age diversity, ability diversity, sexual orientation, and gender identity.

2-3a Ethnic Diversity

The globalization of business is not the only force promoting cultural and ethnic diversity in the workplace. Changing domestic demographics also affect organizations' cultural diversity. COVID-19 caused a broad-based downturn in the labor market during 2020, and the recovery of workers has been slow and uneven. Regardless of racial or ethnic group, education is a key asset for economic and career advancement. Higher levels of education are associated with higher earned incomes. As a group, college graduates earn 96 percent more than high school graduates while those with advanced and professional degrees earn 62 to 88 percent more respectively than college graduates.[31] There is strength in diversity and there is power in education. Education empowers the individual while diversity empowers the group. Johnson & Johnson's Global Diversity and Inclusion initiative for its 132,000+ employees is one example of an organization aiming to incorporate the strengths of a diverse workforce.

In sum, the globalization of business and changing demographic trends present organizations with a culturally diverse workforce, creating challenges, risks, and opportunities. The challenge is to harness the wealth of differences provided by cultural diversity. The risk is that prejudices and stereotypes may prevent managers and employees from developing synergies to benefit the organization. The opportunity is for businesses to reach new and

Barang/Shutterstock.com

Women are creating businesses at a faster rate than ever before.

untapped communities. Diversity of the workforce was a major factor in the innovation that drove the dot-com boom in Silicon Valley, illustrating that the benefits of a diverse workforce make good management of these challenges, risks, and opportunities, important.[32]

2-3b Gender Diversity

The number of women in the U.S. labor force reached its peak in 1999 with a rate of 60 percent. Since then, the participation rate for women (as for men) declined to 57.2 percent in 2013.[33]

Women are better prepared to contribute in organizations than ever before because they earn 51 percent of all doctorates, 60 percent of master's degrees, and 57 percent of all bachelor's degrees.[34] But their share of authority and compensation is not increasing commensurately with their education and participation in the workforce. Half of the males in the workforce occupy line positions, compared to only one-quarter of women in business.[35] In 2019, the National Association for Female Executives again named IBM and Aetna as top companies for executive women, the only two companies to appear on the NAFE top companies list for all 21 years of its existence.[36] When the Bureau of Labor Statistics began measuring in the 1960s, women's earnings were 62 percent of men's. Since 2004, that number has fluctuated between 80 percent and 83 percent.[37] Group comparisons never reveal the whole story, thus calling for further in-depth analysis and comparisons. In addition, the movement of women into the workforce over the past fifty-plus years has led to a

significant increase in household and national economic well-being.[38]

The **glass ceiling** is a transparent barrier that keeps women from rising above a certain organization level In the United States, it has been rare to find women in positions above middle management.[39] Although growth in opportunities for women to attain executive positions can be challenging, the situation is improving for women in the boardroom. Women hold 28.2 percent of board seats in S&P 500 companies, up from 15 percent in 2010.[40] Research has shown that companies that have gender-diverse board leadership performed better across dimensions of corporate social performance (CSP).[41] The ultimate glass ceiling may well be the professional partnership. Although women account for 34 percent of legal professionals, they account for only 21 percent of the partners.[42] Women are preserving their professional identities during pregnancy through strategies such as keeping up the same work pace and not asking for special accommodations.[43]

Globally, the leadership picture for women is improving. For example, the number of female political leaders has grown dramatically worldwide in recent decades. In the 1970s, there were only five such leaders. In the 1990s, twenty-one female leaders came into power, and today women around the world are leading major global companies. Indra Nooyi is a leading example of a global executive, honored in her native India while serving as CEO and Chairman of PepsiCo for twelve years, an unusually long tenure for any CEO.[44] In addition, Nooyi mentored at least nine future CEOs from within PepsiCo as she developed the next generation.

Removing obstacles to women's success is in the best interests of their organizations and all concerned. By helping female employees achieve their potential, they help maximize the talents of the entire U.S. workforce. Therefore, it is wise for organizations to develop policies that promote equity in pay and benefits, to encourage benefit programs for women's unique needs, and to provide equal starting salaries for jobs of equal value.

glass ceiling A transparent barrier that keeps women from rising above a certain level in organizations.

Corporations that shatter the glass ceiling share several practices:

1. Upper managers demonstrate support for the advancement of women.

2. Leaders incorporate practices into their diversity management programs to ensure that women perceive the organization as attractive.[45]

3. Women are represented on standing committees addressing key strategic business issues and are targeted for participation in executive education programs.

4. Systems are put in place to identify women with high potential for advancement.[46]

Companies such as IBM and Ernst & Young work for diversity not only by offering excellent programs for advancing and developing women executives, but also by judging supervisors based on their active support for such endeavors.[47]

2-3c Age Diversity

The graying of the U.S. workforce is another source of workplace diversity. Older Americans, aged 65 or older, number 58 million, or 17 percent of the U.S. population. That equates to more than one in every six individuals. Over 10.6 million (18.9 percent) Americans 65 and older were in the workforce in 2021. The 65 and over population is projected to increase to over 80 million by 2040.[48] The Fact Fact on page 29 is about the era of older employees.

This change in worker profile has profound implications for organizations. The job crunch among middle-aged workers will intensify as companies seek flatter organizational structures and eliminate middle-management jobs. Older workers are often higher paid, and companies that employ large numbers of aging baby boomers may find these pay scales a handicap to competitiveness.[49] Paid volunteerism, however, can be a draw to younger generations.[50] Conversely, a more experienced, stable, reliable, and healthier workforce can pay dividends to companies. One study showed that age diversity among employees in Western companies had a positive impact on profitability.[51] The baby boomers are well trained and educated, and their knowledge is a definite asset to organizations.

The aging workforce is increasing intergenerational tensions between the generations.[52] As organizations flatten, workers traditionally segregated by old corporate hierarchies find themselves working together. Four generations are cooperating: the *silent generation* (people born from 1930 through 1945), a small group that includes most organizations' top managers; the *baby boomers* (people born from 1946 through 1964), whose substantial numbers give them a strong influence; the *baby bust generation*, popularly known as *Generation X* (those born from 1965 through 1976); and the subsequent generation, tentatively called *Generation Y, millennial*, or the *baby boomlet* (those born after 1976).[53] The millennial often bring new challenges to the workplace because of their early access to technology and their continuing connection to parents.[54]

The differences in attitudes and values among these four generations can be substantial, and managers struggle to integrate their workers into a cohesive group. Most leadership positions are currently held by members of the silent generation. Baby boomers tend to (1) regard the silent generation as complacent, (2) strive for moral rights in the workplace, and (3) take a more activist position regarding employee rights. The baby busters, newer to the workplace, are often impatient, want short-term gratification, and value a greater balance between family and work. They scorn the achievement orientation and materialism of the baby boomers. Members of Generation Y, on the other hand, place high importance on independence and creativity, and they are less inclined to settle for work that is not in line with their values.

Younger workers may have false impressions of older workers, viewing them as resistant to change, unable to learn new work methods, less physically capable, and less creative than younger employees. Research indicates, however, that older employees are more satisfied with their jobs, more committed to the organization, and more internally motivated than their younger cohorts.[55] Research finds ageist stereotypes and perceptions about older workers, with implications for intended and actual behaviors directed at older workers.[56] Motivating aging workers and helping them maintain high levels of contribution to the organization is a key task for managers.

2-3d Ability Diversity

Employees with different abilities present yet another form of diversity. Individuals with disabilities are an underutilized human resource. An estimated 50 million individuals with disabilities live in the United States, and their unemployment rate is estimated

The Era of Older Employees

The share of Americans 55 and up who participate in the workforce is growing as the number of older Americans swell, especially in the 75 and older age groups. Despite the dents to long-term life expectancy growth caused by COVID-19, there has been a significant increase from life expectancies in the 60s in the 1940s to life expectancies in the 70s and 80s in 2023. Those in the prime working years (25 to 54) are expected to hold steady at 80 percent labor-force participation from 2001 to 2031 while the 16- to 24-year-old workers are expected to drop to about 50 percent participation in 2031 from over 60 percent in 2001. The participation rates for 55- to 64-year-old workers are climbing and expected to near 70 percent by 2031. The two groups of workers aged 65 to 74 and those 75 and older are increasing their participation rates too.

Source: C. Hymowitz, "Here Comes the 60-Year Career," *The Wall Street Journal* (February 13, 2023): R1, R12–R13.

to exceed 50 percent.[57] Nevertheless, they have entered the workforce in greater numbers since the Americans with Disabilities Act went into effect in the summer of 1992. The act defines a person with a disability as "anyone possessing a physical or mental impairment that substantially limits one or more major life activities."[58] Under this law, employers are required to make reasonable accommodations to permit workers with disabilities to perform jobs. The act's protection encompasses a broad range of illnesses that produce disabilities, including acquired immune deficiency syndrome (AIDS), cancer, hypertension, anxiety disorders, dyslexia, blindness, and cerebral palsy, to name only a few.

Source: McDonald's

McDonald's early McJOBS initiative for those with disabilities has given way to McHire Jobs that are competitive and flexible.

Some companies recognized the value of employing workers with disabilities long before the legislation. In 1981, McDonald's created McJOBS, a corporate plan to recruit, train, and retain individuals with disabilities, which has hired more than 9,000 mentally and physically challenged individuals.[59] Its participants include workers with visual, hearing, or orthopedic impairments; learning disabilities; and developmental disabilities. McJOBS held sensitivity training sessions with managers and crew members before workers go onsite to help workers without disabilities understand what it means to be a worker with a disabling condition. McJOBS paved the way for McDonald's McHire Jobs with competitive benefits and flexible working hours.

2-3e Sexual Orientation and Gender Diversity

APA's umbrella term "sexual and gender minorities" refers to multiple sexual and/or gender minority groups, terms used by the Office on Sexual Orientation and Gender Diversity at APA and the Sexual & Gender Minority Research Office at the National Institutes of Health.[60] Definitions in the domain of sexual orientation and gender diversity are evolving so the best practice is to allow employees and groups of employees to self-identify with their specific descriptive terms. In addition to the terminology, the scientific research is psychology and medicine are evolving around the issues of sexual orientation and gender identity.

To work toward an inclusive and respectful workplace calls for the avoidance of inaccurate and pejorative terms and for the use of specific and inclusive terms. There are a wide range of specific and inclusive terms for sexual orientation, such as LGBTQ+. The University of Washington School of Medicine (UW Medicine) is a top ranked medical school that has published an LGBTQ+ Inclusive Glossary of terms that are specific and well defined.[61] Managers benefit from listening to the medical and psychological communities as each call into question the previously accepted binary nature of sex, and gender. Where the binary paradigm has been used, or is used, in scientific research, that research cannot be retrofitted or revised in most cases.

The most inclusive language for individual differences includes terms "sex assigned at birth," "legal sex" (identifying sex listed on IDs and official documents, such as passports, driver's license, military

The workforce is increasingly diverse in many ways, reflecting the nation's diverse population.

identification card), "sexual orientation," "gender identity." This level of specificity and discernment in information is increasingly included along with "race" and "ethnicity" in employment records and research protocols. While this level of specificity and inclusiveness is not yet universal, the United States Supreme Court in a landmark civil rights case held that Title VII of the Civil Rights Act of 1964 protects employees against discrimination because they are gay or transgender.[62]

2-3f Valuing Diversity

Diversity involves more than culture, gender, age, ability, and personality. Diversity encompasses religion, social status, sexual orientation, social identities, and so much more. Diversity enriches the heterogeneity to the workforce.

Managers must combat prejudice and discrimination to manage diversity. *Prejudice* is an attitude, whereas *discrimination* describes behavior. Both diminish organizational productivity in that they present obstacles to promoting and compensating good workers fairly. Discrimination poses challenges to an organization's ability to attract and recruit prospective workers, retain good human talent, and maintain positive work environments that employees perceive as fair and inclusive.[63] The potential for unfair treatment increases as the workforce becomes

increasingly diverse. Combating stereotypes is essential. For example, a recent study revealed that male bosses sometimes hold certain stereotypes that negatively influence their interaction with female employees of color.[64] Open communication can help clarify misperceptions and clear the way for advancement.

Diversity helps organizations in many ways. Some organizations recognize the potential benefits of proactively working to increase the diversity of their workforces. Kentucky Fried Chicken (KFC) has a long track record of working to attract and retain female and minority-group executives, using diversity as the tie breaker between two equally qualified people.[65] Alcon Laboratories is another company with a long track record of appreciating diversity Alcon has two key ideas that drive their approach. First, people work best when they are valued and when diversity is considered. Second, when people feel valued, they build relationships and work together as a team.[66] Even majority-group managers may be more supportive of diversity training if they appreciate their own ethnic identity. One evaluation of diversity training found that participants preferred training with a traditional title and a broad focus.[67] Further, women were found to react more positively to diversity training than were men. A conclusion from the evaluation was that companies should measure the effects of training so that they can monitor its positive payoffs.

Managing diversity helps companies become more competitive, but effective diversity management involves more than simply being a good corporate citizen or complying with affirmative action.[68] Managing diversity requires a painful examination of employees' hidden assumptions. Having empathy, being able to see and understand the viewpoints of others, is an essential component of Emotional Intelligence (EI) and important for developing and maintaining relationships with others, whether minority or majority. Biases and prejudices about people's differences must be uncovered and dealt with so that differences can be celebrated and used to their full advantage.

2-3g Diversity's Benefits and Problems

Although diversity has the potential to enhance organizational performance, it may pose some problems as well. Table 2.2 summarizes the main benefits and problems with diversity at work. The first main benefit of diversity management is that it helps firms attract and retain the best available human talent. The companies topping the lists of the best places to work are usually excellent at managing diversity. A second benefit is that diversity aids marketing efforts. Just as workforces are diversifying, so are markets. A diverse workforce, therefore, can improve a company's marketing plans by drawing on insights from various employees' cultural backgrounds. Third, diversity promotes creativity and innovation. The most innovative companies, such as Hewlett-Packard, deliberately build diverse teams to foster creativity. Fourth, diversity improves problem-solving. Diverse groups bring

> The toughest problems for managers to resolve include employee theft, environmental issues, comparable worth of employees, conflicts of interest, and sexual harassment.

more expertise and experience to bear on problems and decisions, and they encourage higher levels of critical thinking. Fifth, diversity enhances organizational flexibility because it makes an organization challenge old assumptions and become more adaptable. These five benefits add up to competitive advantage for companies with well-managed diversity.

We must also recognize diversity's potential problems. Five problems are particularly notable: resistance to change, lack of cohesiveness, communication problems, interpersonal conflicts, and slower decision-making. People are attracted to and are more comfortable with others like themselves. Thus, it stands to reason that workers may resist diversity efforts when they are forced to interact with others unlike themselves. Managers should be prepared for this resistance rather than

Table 2.2 The Benefits and Problems of Diversity

Benefits	Problems
• Attracts and retains the best talent	• Resistance to change
• Improves marketing efforts	• Lack of cohesiveness
• Promotes creativity and innovation	• Communication problems
• Results in better problem solving	• Interpersonal conflicts
• Enhances organizational flexibility	• Slower decision making

Scottish moral philosopher Adam Smith presented a doctrine of natural liberty.

Heartland Arts/Shutterstock.com

naively assuming that everybody supports diversity. Another difficulty with diversity is the issue of cohesiveness, that invisible glue that holds a group together. Cohesive groups have higher morale and better communication, but diverse groups take longer to achieve cohesiveness, so they may also take longer to develop high morale.

Another obstacle to performance in diverse groups is communication. Culturally diverse groups may encounter special communication barriers. Misunderstandings can lower work group effectiveness by creating conflict and hampering decision-making.[69]

2-4 Ethics, Character, and Personal Integrity

Biographical research of business and world leaders over the past 150 years found character to be a cornerstone of health and well-being, instrumental to commercial and economic success.[70] Character is the foundation for ethical behavior and the avoidance of unethical conduct that harms the individual and others. Among the toughest ethical problems for managers are employee theft, environmental harms, comparable worth of employees, conflicts of interest, and sexual harassment.[71] Ethical leadership and good character can be a powerful antidote for these problems, contributing to group ethical voice and to positive ethical performance.[72]

Ethical theories help us understand, evaluate, and classify moral arguments; make decisions; and then defend conclusions about what is right and wrong. Ethical theories may focus on a person's intentions, on their actions and behavior, or on the consequences of their behavior. Character or virtue ethics is concerned with intentions. Rule-based ethics is concerned with our actions and behaviors. Consequential theories of ethics are focused on the consequences or results of one's actions and behavior.

character theory An ethical theory that emphasizes the character, personal virtues, and intent of the individual.

rule-based theory An ethical theory that emphasizes the character of the act itself rather than its effects.

2-4a Character Theories of Ethics

Virtue ethics, of which **character theories** of ethics are a type, offer an alternative to understanding behavior in terms of self-interest or rules. Character theories of ethics emphasize the character of the individual and the intent of the person instead of the character of the act itself or its consequences. These virtue-ethics theories are based on Aristotle's view of ethics, which focused on an individual's inner character and virtuousness rather than on outward behavior. Thus, the good person who acted out of virtuous and right intentions was one with integrity and ultimately good ethical standards. Robert Solomon is the best-known advocate of this Aristotelian approach to business ethics.[73] He advocates a business ethics theory centered on the individual within the corporation, emphasizing personal virtues as well as corporate roles. Solomon's six dimensions of virtue ethics are community, excellence, role identity, integrity, judgment (*phronesis* in Greek), and holism. Adam Smith identified three key virtues, which are noted below. At the heart of character and virtue ethics is emotional intelligence, a central component in leader and follower development. The *Goolsby Leadership Academy* at the University of Texas at Arlington emphasizes the development of emotional competencies, such as empathy, compassion, and self-control. For the emotionally competent person of good character, integrity comes first.[74] Organizational factors may negatively affect an otherwise virtuous individual. Workers who experience increased anxiety and feel threatened at work may engage in unethical behavior despite having good intentions.[75]

2-4b Rule-Based Theories of Ethics

Rule-based theories of ethics emphasize the character of the act itself, not its effects, in arriving at universal moral rights and wrongs.[76] Moral rights, the basis for legal rights, are associated with such theories. In a theological context, the Bible, the Talmud, and the Koran are rule-based guides to ethical behavior. Immanuel Kant worked toward the ultimate moral principle in formulating his *categorical imperative,* a universal standard of behavior.[77] Kant argued that individuals should be treated with respect and dignity and that they should not be used as a means to an end. He argued that we should put ourselves in the other

> People need ethical theories to guide them through complex, difficult, and often confusing moral choices and ethical decisions.

Figure 2.2 The Four-Way Test

The Four-Way Test
of What We Think, Say, or Do

1. Is it the TRUTH?

2. Is it FAIR to all concerned?

3. Will it build GOODWILL and better friendships?

4. Will it be BENEFICIAL to all concerned?

person's position and ask whether we would make the same decision if we were in that person's situation.

2-4c Consequential Theories of Ethics

Consequential theories of ethics emphasize the consequences or results of behavior. John Stuart Mill's *utilitarianism,* a well-known consequential theory, suggests that the consequences of an action determine whether it is right or wrong.[78] Good is the ultimate moral value, and we should maximize good effects for the greatest number of people. But do good ethics make for good business? Right actions do not always produce good consequences, and good consequences do not always follow right actions. And how do we determine the greatest good? The protection of what is good for minorities is critically important in a free, good society.

Corporations and business enterprises tend to subscribe to consequential ethics, partly due to the persuasive arguments of the Scottish moral philosopher Adam Smith.[79] He believed that the self-interest of human beings is God's providence, not the government's. Smith set forth a doctrine of *natural liberty,* presenting the classical argument for open-market competition and free trade. Within this framework, people should be allowed to pursue what is in their economic self-interest, and the natural efficiency of the marketplace will then serve the well-being of society. However, Smith was mindful of the interests of others and argued for three key virtues: prudence, which is good self-care; justice, which is doing no harm to others; and beneficence, which is doing good for others.[80]

2-4d Codes of Conduct and Ethics

Codes of conduct and ethics are designed to translate ethical theories into standards of ethical behavior as a basis for moral action. Business as a profession does not have a universal code of conduct or ethics. However, business leader and Rotary President Herbert J. Taylor developed The Four-Way Test of the things a

person thinks, says, and does, as shown in Figure 2.2. This test helped his company build a significant strategic advantage through good character and moral behavior, thus engineering one of the great business turnarounds of the 1930s.[81] Now used in more than 166 nations by 1.4 million Rotarians, this test focuses the questioner on key ethical and moral questions. Using The Four-Way Test and Rotary Minority-Owned Business Awards, the Rotary Club of Fort Worth, Texas grew their membership of color by four times in two years.[82] Rotarian John Barfield used The Four-Way Test as the cornerstone of his two billion-dollar enterprise.[83]

Beyond the individual and professional level, corporate culture is another excellent starting point for addressing ethics and morality. For example, the U.S. Department of Defense Standards of Conduct specify the range of ethics topics, such as conflicts of interest, and ethics resources available to ensure ethical behavior within all U.S. military personnel. In other cases, corporate ethics appear as a credo. Johnson & Johnson's credo, shown in Figure 2.3, helped hundreds of employees ethically address criminal tampering with Tylenol products. The J&J Credo has guided the company's decision-making since 1943.

Individual codes of ethics, professional oaths, and organizational credos must all be anchored in a moral, ethical framework because ethical theories are the only way to question and improve our current standards. However, even though a universal right and wrong may exist, it would be hard to agree on a single code of ethics to which all individuals, professions, and organizations can subscribe.

consequential theory An ethical theory that emphasizes the consequences or results of behavior.

Figure 2.3 The Johnson & Johnson Credo

We believe our first responsibility is to the doctors, nurses, and patients, to mothers and all others who use our products and services. In meeting their needs everything we do must be of high quality. We must constantly strive to reduce our costs in order to maintain reasonable prices. Customers' orders must be serviced promptly and accurately. Our suppliers and distributors must have an opportunity to make a fair profit.

We are responsible to our employees, the men and women who work with us throughout the world. Everyone must be considered as an individual. We must respect their dignity and recognize their merit. They must have a sense of security in their jobs. Compensation must be fair and adequate, and working conditions clean, orderly, and safe. Employees must feel free to make suggestions and complaints. There must be equal opportunity for employment, development, and advancement for those qualified. We must provide competent management, and their actions must be just and ethical.

We are responsible to the communities in which we live and work and to the world community as well. We must be good citizens—support good works and charities and bear our fair share of taxes. We must encourage civic improvements and better health and education. We must maintain in good order the property we are privileged to use, protecting the environment and natural resources.

Our final responsibility is to our stockholders. Business must make a sound profit. We must experiment with new ideas. Research must be carried on, innovative programs developed and mistakes paid for. New equipment must be purchased, new facilities provided, and new products launched. Reserves must be created to provide for adverse times. When we operate according to these principles, the stockholders should realize a fair return.

Source: "Our Credo," http://www.jnj.com/wps/wcm/connect/c7933f004f5563df9e22be1bb31559c7/jnj_ourcredo_english _us_8.5x11_cmyk .pdf?MOD=AJPERES.

2-5 Ethical Dilemmas Facing the Modern Organization

People need ethical theories to guide them through complex, difficult, and often confusing moral choices and ethical decisions. Contemporary organizations experience a wide variety of ethical and moral dilemmas. In this section, we address employee rights, sexual harassment, organizational justice, and whistle-blowing. We conclude with a discussion of social responsibility and codes of ethics.

2-5a Employee Rights

Managing the rights of employees at work creates many ethical dilemmas in organizations. Drug testing, free speech, downsizing and layoffs, and due process are but a few of the employee rights issues that managers face.

These dilemmas include privacy issues related to technology. Many feel that computerized monitoring constitutes an invasion of privacy. Using employee data from computerized information systems presents many ethical concerns. New software allows employers to tap into their employees' address books and e-mail contacts to obtain new potential clients and discern who in the company might be best suited to approach them.[84] Safeguarding the employee's right to privacy while preserving access to the data for those who need it forces managers to balance competing interests.

The reality of AIDS in the workplace also illustrates the difficulties managers face in balancing various interests. Managers may encounter a conflict between the rights of HIV-infected workers and the rights of their coworkers who feel threatened. But laws protect HIV-infected workers. The Americans with Disabilities Act (ADA) requires employees to treat HIV-infected workers as disabled individuals and to make reasonable accommodations for them. But ADA cannot encompass all of the ethical dilemmas involved.

Confidentiality may also present challenges. Employers are not required to make concessions to coworkers, but they are obligated to educate, reassure, and provide emotional support to them. Some employees with HIV or AIDS fear stigmatization or reprisals and do not want their condition known by their coworkers. Management should discuss the ramifications of trying to maintain confidentiality and should assure affected employees that every effort will be made to prevent negative consequences for them in the workplace.[85]

2-5b Sexual Harassment

According to the Equal Employment Opportunity Commission, sexual harassment is unwelcome verbal or physical sexual attention that affects an employee's job conditions or creates a hostile working environment.[86] Supreme Court rulings tend to blame companies when managers create a sexually hostile working environment. Sexual harassment is more likely to occur in some organizations than in others—for example, in male-dominated workplaces.[87] In some organizations, employees risk their jobs by complaining of sexual harassment or are not taken seriously, and perpetrators are rarely punished. While there has been progress since the 1990s in addressing sexual harassment, the problem continues. Emerging evidence suggests that bystander interventions can be effective in preventing and/or managing incidences of workplace sexual harassment.[88] Everyone in the workplace has responsibility for this endemic problem. Managers can defend themselves by demonstrating that they took action to eliminate workplace harassment and that the complaining employee did not take advantage of company procedures to deal with harassment. Even the best sexual harassment policy, however, will not absolve a company when harassment leads to firing, demotions, or undesirable working assignments.[89] How much do you know about sexual harassment? Complete the YOU exercise on page 36 to get an idea.

There are three types of sexual harassment. *Gender harassment* includes crude comments or behaviors that convey hostility toward a particular gender. *Unwanted sexual attention* involves unwanted touching or repeated pressures for dates. *Sexual coercion* consists of implicit or explicit demands for sexual favors by threatening negative job-related consequences or promising job-related rewards.[90] Recent theory has focused attention on the aggressive behavior of sexual harassers.[91]

Sexual harassment costs the typical *Fortune* 500 company $6.7 million per year in absenteeism, turnover, and lost productivity. Valeant Pharmaceuticals International paid out millions to settle four sexual harassment complaints against former CEO Milan Panic. Plaintiffs may now sue for compensatory and punitive damages in addition to back pay. And these costs do not take into account the negative publicity

that sexual harassment cases may attract. Moreover, victims of sexual harassment who do not report the problem are less satisfied with their work, supervisors, and coworkers, and they may psychologically withdraw at work. They may suffer poorer mental health and even exhibit symptoms of post-traumatic stress disorder in conjunction with the harassment experience. Some victims report alcohol abuse, depression, headaches, and nausea.[92]

Several companies have created comprehensive sexual harassment programs. Atlantic Richfield (ARCO), owned by British Petroleum and a player in the male-dominated energy industry, has a handbook on preventing sexual harassment that includes phone numbers of state agencies where employees can file complaints. The openness seems to work. Lawsuits rarely happen at ARCO. When employees make sexual harassment complaints, the company investigates thoroughly. ARCO fired the captain of an oil tanker for sexually harassing coworkers. Not all sexual behavior among employees is harmful or harassing in nature. Workplace interactions between organizational members that have sexual connotations but not perceived by any of the parties as being threatening or harassing are considered social sexual behavior. Examples of social sexual behavior include flirting, sharing sexual stories or jokes, complimenting physical appearance, or gentle touching. Social sexual behavior in the workplace can have numerous psychological, emotional, and relational benefits for those involved. Among the benefits are increased self-esteem, energy, vigor, and creativity. There is also evidence that social sexual behavior can enhance group cohesion and camaraderie.[93]

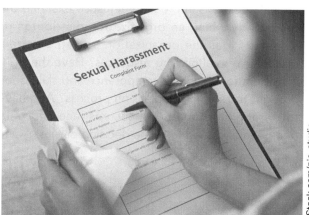

Sexual harassment costs the typical *Fortune 500* company $6.7 million per year in absenteeism, turnover, and lost productivity.

2-5c Organizational Justice

Organizational justice also generates moral and ethical dilemmas at work. **Distributive justice** concerns the fairness of outcomes individuals receive. For example, during former President George H. W. Bush's 1992 visit, Japanese CEOs questioned the distributive justice of keeping American CEOs' salaries so high while many companies were struggling and laying off workers.

Procedural justice concerns the fairness of the process by which outcomes are allocated. The ethical questions in procedural justice examine the process by which an organization distributes its resources. Has the organization used the correct procedures in allocating resources? Have the right considerations, such as competence and skill, been brought to bear in the decision process? And have the wrong considerations, such as race and gender, been excluded from the decision process? One

study of work scheduling found that advance notice and consistency, two dimensions of procedural justice, reduced voluntary turnover.[94] Some research suggests cultural differences in the effects of distributive and procedural justice.[95]

2-5d Whistle-Blowing

Whistle-blowers are employees who inform authorities of wrongdoings by their companies or coworkers. Depending on their situations, whistle-blowers may be perceived as either public heroes or vile wretches. Those seen as heroes generally report serious and high-magnitude ethical breaches widely perceived as abhorrent.[96] Others may see the whistle-blower as a wretch if they feel the act of whistle-blowing is more offensive than the situation reported. One of the most well-known whistle-blowers, Edward Snowden is hailed as a hero by some for revealing the extent of the U.S. government domestic surveillance program. However, others consider Snowden a disgruntled NSA contractor who participated in industrial espionage.[97]

Whistle-blowing is a powerful influence on corporate America because committed organizational members sometimes engage in unethical behavior in an intense desire to succeed. Organizations can manage

distributive justice The fairness of outcomes that individuals receive in an organization.

procedural justice The fairness of the process by which outcomes are allocated in an organization.

whistle-blower An employee who informs authorities of the wrongdoings of her or his company or coworkers.

whistle-blowing by explaining the conditions that are appropriate for disclosing wrongdoing. Clearly delineating wrongful behavior and the appropriate ways to respond are important organizational actions.

2-5e Corporate Social Responsibility

Corporate **social responsibility** is an organization's obligation to behave ethically in its social environment. Ethical conduct at the individual level can translate into social responsibility at the organizational level. Multiple stakeholders in society expect organizations to engage in socially responsible actions. Servant leaders play an important role in creating, implementing, and sustaining socially responsible behaviors.[98]

Current concerns include protecting the environment, promoting worker safety, supporting social issues, and investing in the community, among others. Some organizations, such as IBM, loan executives to inner-city schools to teach science and math. Some companies have even tried to build a Brand around social responsibility, such as the Just Coffee Cooperative, which sponsors trips to coffee-producing regions in order to build customer loyalty to the cause and their brand.[99] Firms that are seen as socially responsible have a competitive advantage in attracting applicants.[100] American Apparel, however, tried to build a brand around the fact that they produce garments locally rather than in foreign

Warren Price Photography/Shutterstock.com

J&J's rapid, transparent response to deaths from Tylenol that had been tampered with was viewed as highly socially responsible.

sweatshops but found that, as attractive as its ethics might have been to customers, sex appeal was more effective in actually selling its product.[101]

social responsibility The obligation of an organization to behave ethically in its social environment.

Experiential Exercise

International Orientations

1. **Preparation (preclass)**

   Read the background on the International Orientation Scale and the case study "Office Supplies International—Marketing Associate," complete the ratings and questions, and fill out the self-assessment inventory.

2. **Group discussions**

   Groups of four to six people discuss their answers to the case study questions and their own responses to the self-assessment.

3. **Class discussion**

   Instructor leads a discussion on the International Orientation Scale and the difficulties and challenges of adjusting to a new culture. Why do some people adjust more easily than others?

What can you do to adjust to a new culture? What can you regularly do that will help you adjust in the future to almost any new culture?

Office Supplies International—Marketing Associate

Jonathan Fraser is a marketing associate for a large multinational corporation, Office Supplies International (OSI), in Buffalo, New York. He is being considered for a transfer to the international division of OSI. This position will require that he spend between one and three years working abroad in one of OSI's three foreign subsidiaries: OSI-France, OSI-Japan, or OSI-Australia. This transfer is considered a fast-track career move at OSI, and Jonathan feels honored to be in the running for the position.

Jonathan has been working at OSI since he graduated with his bachelor's degree in marketing ten years ago. He is married and has lived and worked in Buffalo all his life. Jonathan's parents are first-generation German Americans. His grandparents, although deceased, spoke only German at home and upheld many of their ethnic traditions. His parents, although quite "Americanized," have retained some of their German traditions. To communicate better with his grandparents, Jonathan took German in high school but never used it because his grandparents had passed away.

In college, Jonathan joined the German Club and was a club officer for two years. His other collegiate extracurricular activity was playing for the varsity baseball team. Jonathan still enjoys playing in a summer softball league with his college friends. Given his athletic interests, he volunteered to be the athletic programming coordinator at OSI, where he organizes the company's softball and volleyball teams. Jonathan has been making steady progress at OSI. Last year, he was named marketing associate of the year.

His wife, Sue, is also a Buffalo native. She teaches English literature at the high school in one of the middle-class suburbs of Buffalo. Sue took five years off after she had a baby but returned to teaching this year when Janine, their five-year-old daughter, started kindergarten. She is happy to be resuming her career. One or two nights a week, Sue volunteers at the city mission where she works as a career counselor and a basic skills trainer. For fun, she takes pottery and ethnic cooking classes.

Both Sue and Jonathan are excited about the potential transfer and accompanying pay raise. They are, however, also feeling apprehensive and cautious. Neither Sue nor Jonathan has ever lived away from their families in Buffalo, and Sue is concerned about giving up her newly reestablished career. Their daughter Janine has just started school, and Jonathan and Sue are uncertain whether living abroad is the best thing for her at her age.

Using the following three-point scale, rate Jonathan and Sue as potential expatriates. Write a sentence or two on why you gave the ratings you did.

Rating Scale

1. Based on this dimension, this person would adjust well to living abroad.

2. Based on this dimension, this person may or may not adjust well to living abroad.

3. Based on this dimension, this person would not adjust well to living abroad.

Jonathan's International Orientation

Rating dimension	Rating and reason for rating
International attitudes	
Foreign experiences	
Comfort with differences	
Participation in cultural events	

Sue's International Orientation

Rating dimension	Rating and reason for rating
International attitudes	
Foreign experiences	
Comfort with differences	
Participation in cultural events	

Discussion Questions: Office Supplies International

1. Imagine that you are the international human resource manager for OSI. Your job is to interview Jonathan and Sue to determine whether they should be sent abroad. What are some of the questions you would ask? What critical information do you feel is missing? It might be helpful to role-play the three parts and evaluate your classmates' responses as Jonathan and Sue.

2. Suppose France is the country where they would be sent. To what extent would your ratings change? What else would you change about the way you are assessing the couple?

3. Answer the same questions, except this time they are being sent to Japan. Repeat the exercise for Australia.

4. For those dimensions that you rated Sue and Jonathan either 2 or 3 (indicating that they might have a potential adjustment problem), what would you suggest for training and development? What might be included in a training program?

5. Reflect on your own life for a moment and give yourself a rating on each of the following dimensions. Justify why you rated yourself as you did. Do you feel you would adjust well to living abroad? What might be difficult for you?

Rating dimension	Rating and reason for rating France, Japan, Australia (or other)
International attitudes	
Foreign experiences	
Comfort with differences	
Participation in cultural events	

6. Generally, what are some of the potential problems a dual-career couple might face? What are some of the solutions to those problems?

7. How would the ages of children affect the expatriate's assignment? At what age should the children's international orientations be assessed along with their parents?

International Orientation Scale

The following sample items are taken from the International Orientation Scale. Answer each question and give yourself a score for each dimension. The highest possible score for any dimension is 20 points.

Dimension 1: International Attitudes

Use the following scale to answer questions Q1 through Q4.

1. *Strongly agree*
2. *Agree somewhat*
3. *Maybe or unsure*
4. *Disagree somewhat*
5. *Strongly disagree*

Q1. Foreign language skills should be taught as early as elementary school._____

Q2. Traveling the world is a priority in my life._____

Q3. A yearlong overseas assignment (from my company) would be a fantastic opportunity for my family and me._____

Q4. Other countries fascinate me._____

Total Dimension 1_____

Dimension 2: Foreign Experiences

Q1. I have studied a foreign language.

1. Never
2. For less than a year
3. For a year
4. For a few years
5. For several years

Q2. I am fluent in another language.

1. I don't know another language.
2. I am limited to very short and simple phrases.
3. I know basic grammatical structure and speak with a limited vocabulary.
4. I understand conversation on most topics.
5. I am very fluent in another language.

Q3. I have spent time overseas (traveling, studying abroad, etc.).

1. Never
2. About a week
3. A few weeks
4. A few months
5. Several months or years

Q4. I was overseas before the age of 18.

1. Never
2. About a week
3. A few weeks
4. A few months
5. Several months or years

Total Dimension 2_____

Dimension 3: Comfort with Differences

Use the following scale for questions Q1 through Q4.

1. *Quite similar*
2. *Mostly similar*
3. *Somewhat different*
4. *Quite different*
5. *Extremely different*

Q1. My friends' career goals, interests, and education are_____

Q2. My friends' ethnic backgrounds are_____

Q3. My friends' religious affiliations are_____

Q4. My friends' first languages are_____

Total Dimension 3_____

Dimension 4: Participation in Cultural Events

Use the following scale to answer questions Q1 through Q4.

1. Never
2. Seldom
3. Sometimes
4. Frequently
5. As often as possible

Q1. I eat at a variety of ethnic restaurants, e.g., Greek, Polynesian, Thai, German._____

Q2. I watch the major networks' world news programs._____

Q3. I attend ethnic festivals._____
Q4. I visit art galleries and museums._____
Total Dimension 4_____

Self-Assessment Discussion Questions:

Do any of these scores surprise you?

Would you like to improve your international orientation? If so, what could you do to change various aspects of your life?

Source: "Office Supplies International—Marketing Associate" by Paula Caligiuri. Copyright © 1994 by Paula Caligiuri, Ph.D. Reprinted by permission of the author

Learning Objectives

2-1 **Describe the factors that affect organizations competing in the global economy.** Globalization suggests that the world is free from national boundaries. In transnational organizations, the global viewpoint supersedes national issues; organizations operate across long distances and employ a multicultural mix of workers. Social and political issues affect global operations and strategy development.

2-2 **Explain how cultural differences form the basis of work-related attitudes.** Individualistic cultures emphasize and encourage individual achievement, whereas collectivist cultures view group loyalty and unity as paramount. Other factors affecting work-related attitudes are power distance, uncertainty avoidance, masculinity versus femininity, and time orientation. Developing cross-cultural sensitivity training, cultural task forces, and global human resource management is critical to success.

2-3 **Describe the challenges and positive influences diversity brings to today's business environment.** Diversity encompasses all forms of differences among individuals, including culture, gender, age, ability, religion, personality, social status, and sexual orientation. The benefits of diversity are human talent, marketing, creativity and innovation, problem-solving, and flexibility. Potential problems are resistance to change, lack of cohesiveness, communication, conflicts, and decision-making.

2-4 **Discuss the role of ethics, character, and personal integrity in the organization.** Ethical theories help us understand, evaluate, and classify moral arguments; make decisions; and defend conclusions about what is right and wrong. Ethical theories can be classified as consequential, rule based, or character.

2-5 **Explain five issues that pose ethical dilemmas for managers.** Organizations experience a variety of ethical and moral dilemmas such as employee rights, sexual harassment, organizational justice, whistleblowing, and social responsibility. Managers can use ethical theories to guide them through moral choices and ethical decisions.

Key Terms

character theory An ethical theory that emphasizes the character, personal virtues, and intent of the individual. (p. 32)

collectivism A cultural orientation in which individuals belong to tightly knit social frameworks and depend strongly on extended families or clans. (p. 24)

consequential theory An ethical theory that emphasizes the consequences or results of behavior. (p. 33)

distributive justice The fairness of outcomes that individuals receive in an organization. (p. 36)

diversity All forms of difference among individuals, including culture, gender, age, ability, religion, personality, social status, and sexual orientation. (p. 26)

expatriate manager A manager who works in a country other than her or his home country. (p. 22)

femininity A cultural orientation in which relationships and concern for others are valued. (p. 25)

glass ceiling A transparent barrier that keeps women from rising above a certain level in organizations. (p. 27)

guanxi The Chinese practice of building networks for social exchange. (p. 20)

individualism A cultural orientation in which people belong to loose social frameworks and their primary concern is for themselves and their families. (p. 24)

masculinity A cultural orientation in which assertiveness and materialism are valued. (p. 25)

power distance The degree to which a culture accepts unequal distribution of power. (p. 24)

procedural justice The fairness of the process by which outcomes are allocated in an organization. (p. 36)

rule-based theory An ethical theory that emphasizes the character of the act itself rather than its effects. (p. 32)

social responsibility The obligation of an organization to behave ethically in its social environment. (p. 37)

time orientation Whether a culture's values are oriented toward the future (long-term orientation) or

toward the past and present (short-term orientation). (p. 25)

transnational organization An organization in which the global viewpoint supersedes national issues. (p. 20)

uncertainty avoidance The degree to which a culture tolerates ambiguity and uncertainty. (p. 25)

whistle-blower An employee who informs authorities of the wrongdoings of her or his company or coworkers. (p. 36)

What About You?

Planning for a Global Career

Think of a country you would like to work in, do business in, or visit. Find out about its culture, using Hofstede's dimensions as guidelines. You can use a variety of sources to accomplish this, particularly your school library, government offices, faculty members, or others who have global experience.

Answer the following questions:

1. Is the culture individualistic or collectivist?

2. Is the power distance high or low?

3. Is uncertainty avoidance high or low?

4. Is the country masculine or feminine in its orientation?

5. Is the time orientation short term or long term?

6. How did you arrive at your answers to the first five questions?

7. How will these characteristics affect business practices in the country you chose to investigate?

Ethical Dilemma

Roman works for Warehouse Partners, a large warehousing firm. He is the manager of a facility in a large metropolitan city. He is looking to hire a supervisor. In the process of hiring, he meets John, a candidate who has all the knowledge and experience needed to be successful in the job. Roman has been looking for a supervisor for a while and it looks like he has found the ideal person.

During the interview, Roman takes the time to try to get to know the candidates. In his conversations with John, he begins to get the sense that John is conservative. While his conservative views are not a problem, Roman has concerns about how well John would fit into the organization.

Warehouse Partners has very open hiring policies, especially for facilities operating in sanctuary cities. Many of the warehouse workers John would be supervising are legally hired undocumented immigrants. And because of the location and organization, the workers were very open about discussing this situation.

Roman has a strong feeling that John will not approve of undocumented workers. He also believes that the workers will quickly become aware of John's disapproval. Roman wants to be fair to everyone who is depending on him to manage the organization, but he feels conflicted. On one hand, he believes that John is the best candidate for the job. He deserves to be hired and from a legal and moral perspective his views should not even be considered. However, he also has a duty to his current employees to hire someone who will accept the company's hiring policies and who will not make their jobs unpleasant.

1. Using consequential, rule-based, and character theories, evaluate Roman's options.
2. What should Roman do? Why?

Chapter 3

Kasefoto/Shutterstock.com

Personality, Perception, and Attribution

Learning Objectives

3-1   Describe individual differences and why they are important in understanding organizational behavior.

3-2   Articulate key personality traits including how they influence behavior in organizations.

3-3   Discuss how personality theories may be applied in organizations.

3-4   Explain the factors that affect social perception.

3-5   Explain five common barriers to social perception and the difficulties they cause.

3-6   Explain the attribution process and how attributions affect managerial behavior.

3-1 Individual Differences and Organizational Behavior

Over the next two chapters, we'll explore the concept of **individual differences**. Individuals are unique in terms of their skills, abilities, personalities, perceptions, attitudes, emotions, and ethics. Hence, individual differences represent the essence of the challenge of management. Managers must often work with people who possess a multitude of varying characteristics, so the more managers understand individual differences, the better they can work with others.

The basis for understanding individual differences stems from Kurt Lewin's early contention that behavior is a function of the person and the environment.[1] He expressed this idea in an equation: $B = f(P, E)$, where B = behavior, P = person, and E = environment. Lewin's idea has been developed further by the **interactional psychology** approach.[2] Basically, this approach says that we must know something about the person and something about the situation in order to understand human behavior. There are four basic propositions of interactional psychology:

1. Behavior is a function of continuous, multidirectional interaction between the person and the situation.

2. The person is active in this process, both changing their situations and being changed by them.

3. People vary in many characteristics, including cognitive, affective, motivational, and ability factors.

4. Two aspects of a situation are important: the objective situation and the person's subjective view of the situation.[3]

The interactional psychology approach points out the need to study both persons and situations. The *person* consists of individual elements such as personality, perception, attribution, attitudes, emotions, and ethics. The *situation* consists of the environment the person operates in, including the organization, work group, personal life situation, job characteristics, and other environmental influences. The effect of personal and environmental differences on organizational behavior is shown visually in Figure 3.1. In this chapter, we'll address skills and abilities, personality, perception, and attribution. Chapter 4 will deal with attitudes, emotions, and ethics.

individual differences The way in which factors such as skills, abilities, personalities, perceptions, attitudes, values, and ethics differ from one individual to another.

interactional psychology The psychological approach to understanding human behavior that involves knowing something about the person and about the situation.

Figure 3.1 Variables Influencing Individual Behavior

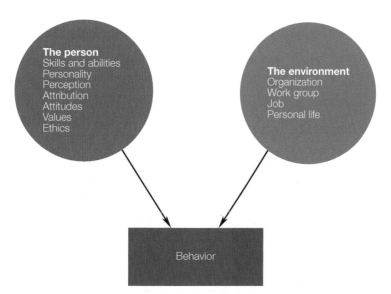

> Individuals are unique in terms of their skills, abilities, personalities, perceptions, attitudes, emotions, and ethics.

3-1a Skills and Abilities

Many skills and abilities influence work outcomes. Nearly 100 years ago, Charles Spearman introduced the concept of *general mental ability (GMA)* as a measure of an individual's innate cognitive intelligence.[4] GMA, which includes a person's skills and abilities, is the single best predictor of work performance across many occupations and across different cultures.[5]

3-2 Personality and Organizations

What makes an individual behave consistently in a variety of situations? **Personality** is the relatively stable set of characteristics that influences an individual's behavior and lends it consistency. Although researchers debate what determines personality, we conclude that it has several origins. One determinant is heredity. Researchers have found that identical twins who were separated at birth and raised in very different situations nevertheless shared personality traits and job preferences. In fact, about half

---

personality A relatively stable set of characteristics that influence an individual's behavior.

trait theory A personality theory that advocates breaking down behavior patterns into a series of observable traits in order to understand human behavior.

---

of the variations in traits such as extraversion, impulsiveness, and flexibility were shared by identical twins who grew up separately.[6] Thus, genes appear to influence personality.

Environment also determines personality, shaping it through family influences, cultural influences, educational influences, and other environmental factors. Two major theories of personality are the trait theory and the integrative approach. Each theory has influenced the study of personality in organizations.

3-2a Trait Theory

Some early personality researchers believed that we must break down behavior patterns into a series of observable traits in order to understand individuals. According to **trait theory**, the combination of these traits forms an individual's personality. Gordon Allport, a leading theorist, saw traits as broad, general guides that lend consistency to behavior.[7] Thousands of traits have been identified over the years. Raymond Cattell, another prominent theorist, identified sixteen traits that formed the basis for differences in individual behavior. He described traits in binary pairs such as self-assured/apprehensive, reserved/outgoing, and submissive/dominant.[8]

One popular personality classification involves the so-called Big Five. These traits (described in Table 3.1) include extraversion, agreeableness, conscientiousness, emotional stability, and openness to experience.[9] The Big Five are broad, global traits associated with behaviors at work. For example, from preliminary research, we know that introverted and conscientious employees are less likely to be absent from work.[10] Individuals with high agreeableness tend to rate others more leniently on peer evaluations, while those with high conscientiousness tend to be tougher raters.[11] In terms of work stress,

Table 3.1 The Big Five Personality Traits

Extraversion	The person is gregarious, assertive, and sociable (as opposed to reserved, timid, and quiet).
Agreeableness	The person is cooperative, warm, and agreeable (rather than cold, disagreeable, and antagonistic).
Conscientiousness	The person is hardworking, organized, and dependable (as opposed to lazy, disorganized, and unreliable).
Emotional stability	The person is calm, self-confident, and cool (as opposed to insecure, anxious, and depressed).
Openness to experience	The person is creative, curious, and cultured (rather than practical with narrow interests).

Sources: P. T. Costa and R. R. McCrae, *The NEO-PI Personality Inventory* (Odessa, Fla.: Psychological Assessment Resources, 1992); J. F. Salgado, "The Five Factor Model of Personality and Job Performance in the European Community," *Journal of Applied Psychology* 82 (1997): 30–43.

employees who are extraverted, conscientious, and open to experience fare better. They're less likely to let stress result in a negative mood.[12] Across many occupations, conscientious people are more motivated and perform better than others.[13]

But different patterns of the Big Five traits are related to high performance in different occupations and work situations. For customer service jobs, individuals high in emotional stability, agreeableness, and openness to experience perform best. Managers with emotional stability are top performers.[14] People who are emotionally stable (as opposed to neurotic) hold up better in decision-making under time and social pressure, and people who are more agreeable have a tougher time making decisions under pressure.[15] Studies have also shown that an extreme amount of any trait harms organizations. Interestingly, highly conscientious and emotionally stable individuals perform worse on the job than those with more moderate levels of both traits. The reasons could be that very conscientious individuals may be overly rigid, inflexible, and compulsive,

paying too much attention to small details at the expense of larger goals. Friends see the downsides to having high levels of the traits. Highly extraverted people may be seen as loud, and highly agreeable individuals may be labeled people pleasers.[16] It seems that any Big Five trait maximized or minimized can become a liability.

The Big Five framework is helpful for understanding cultural differences and has held up well when applied to Western cultures, particularly among Spanish and Mexican populations.[17] But it remains to be seen whether the Big Five traits will emerge in studies of non-Western cultures.[18] Personality traits are also relevant to *cultural intelligence*, which, in the workplace, means how we adapt to cultural differences.[19]

The Big Five continues to be a popular organizing framework and taxonomy of traits.[20] But the trait approach has many critics. Some theorists argue that simply identifying traits is not enough because personality is dynamic and never completely stable. In addition to traits, it is essential to also account for the influence of situations on behavior.[21]

Inclusive Conversations

When Using Personality Traits Lead to Bias

A study conducted by Textio designed to investigate language bias found that using personality traits for performance evaluations is not only unactionable but may also expose racial, ethnic, and gender bias.

The study analyzed two sets of data. One set of data came from employees on the quality of performance feedback they received during their performance evaluations; the other set, from language patterns on written performance feedback of 25,000 individuals across 250 different organizations. Researchers identified words in the written feedback documents that described employee personality, including 'brilliant,' 'opinionated,' 'nice,' and 'abrasive.'

Taken together, the study revealed that employees did indeed receive different kinds of feedback, and that feedback differed by both race and ethnicity and gender. For example, Asians were described as 'brilliant' more than twice as often as white people and more than four times as often as Black or Latinx employees. Women, Blacks, Latinx, and older workers reported receiving the lowest-quality feedback. The researchers suggested that while personality-laden terms imply innate characteristics about employees, they do not supply feedback that employees can use to change their behavior.

1. What are the implications of the study's finding that women, Blacks, Latinx, and older employees receiving the lowest-quality (vague and unactionable) performance feedback?

   The implications of receiving low-quality feedback are significant. Over time, employees who receive consistent vague and unactionable feedback will likely see reduced growth opportunities and increased intention to quit.

2. How would you describe employer expectations of workers they characterize as 'genius' and 'nice' compared with employees characterized as 'abrasive' and 'opinionated'?

   Though using personality characteristics is ineffective for motivating employee performance, using these words during employee reviews is indicative of how evaluators view the worth and value of employees, potentially setting up biases in employee experiences, opportunities, and outcomes.

Source: K. Snyder and A. Lee, "No More 'Abrasive,' 'Opinionated,' or 'Nice': Why Managers Need to Stop Giving Women and People Color Feedback on Their Personality," *Fortune*, June 15 (2022), https://fortune.com/2022/06/15/performance-reviews-bias-gender-race-language-textio-kieran-snyder-aileen-lee/.

3-2b Integrative Approach

In response to the criticisms of trait theory, researchers have taken a broader, more **integrative approach** to the study of personality.[22] This integrative approach focuses on both personal dispositions and situational variables as combined predictors of behavior. *Dispositions* are the tendencies of an individual to respond to situations in consistent ways. They include emotions, cognitions, attitudes, expectations, and fantasies.[23] Influenced by both genes and experiences, dispositions can be modified.

A recent study of how personality affects status offers a good example of how an integrative approach can be applied to better understand organizations. The study looked at a variety of personality variables that affected not only the actual status held by an individual, but also how that individual perceived their status as well as how the person's status was viewed by others. The most important variable was leadership identity, though the leader's self-perception was determined largely by emotional stability and agreeableness. Meanwhile, extraversion and conscientiousness most affected how the leader was perceived by others.[24]

3-2c Personality Characteristics in Organizations

Managers should learn as much as possible about personality in order to understand and better relate to their employees, which is why we devote much attention to the subject of personality in this text. Although researchers have identified hundreds of personality characteristics, we have selected a few with particularly strong influences on individual behavior in organizations. *Core self-evaluation (CSE)* involves a broad set of personality traits that articulates an individual's concept of themselves.[25] CSE is concerned with people's locus of control, self-esteem, generalized self-efficacy, and emotional stability. It predicts both goal-directed behavior and performance, even in non-U.S. cultures (e.g.,

Japan).[26] All these aspects of CSE will be examined shortly. In addition to the traits associated with CSE, we will consider the personality traits of self-monitoring and positive/negative affect.

Can managers predict the behavior of their employees from their personalities? Not completely. Recall that the interactional psychology model (Figure 3.1) requires both dispositional and situational variables to predict behavior. As we consider the following personality variables, then, keep in mind that they are only one piece of the personality puzzle.

When weighing the role of situation, it is important to understand that situations vary in strength. **Strong situations** overwhelm the effects of individual personalities. These situations are interpreted in the same way by different individuals, evoke agreement on the appropriate behavior in the situation, and provide cues to appropriate behavior. For example, at performance appraisal sessions, employees know to listen to their bosses and to contribute when asked to, so this is a strong situation.

Weak situations are open to many interpretations. They provide few cues to appropriate behavior and no obvious rewards for any particular behavior. Individual personalities thus have a greater influence in weak situations than in strong situations. An informal meeting without an agenda might be a weak situation. Because organizations present combinations of strong and weak situations, personality affects behavior more in some situations than in others.[27]

Following are explanations of the various aspects of personality involved in CSE plus the traits of self-monitoring and positive/negative affect. Locus

integrative approach The broad theory that describes personality as a composite of an individual's psychological processes.

strong situation A situation that overwhelms the effects of individual personalities by providing strong cues for appropriate behavior.

Rasulov/Shutterstock.com

of control, self-efficacy, self-esteem, and the effects of emotional stability together constitute the core self-evaluations. CSE is a strong predictor of both job satisfaction and job performance, next only to GMA. Employees with high CSE are more likely to offer suggestions and ideas for improving the organization in which they work, and this helps companies prevent crises, improve processes, and perform better overall.[28]

Locus of Control   An individual's generalized belief about internal (self) versus external (situation or others) control is called **locus of control**. People who believe they control what happens to them have an internal locus of control, whereas people who believe that circumstances or other people control their fate have an external locus of control.[29] In an organization, people with an internal locus of control (called *internals*) often report higher job satisfaction, exhibit superior job performance, are more likely to assume managerial positions, and tend to prefer participative management styles more than those with an external locus of control (*externals*).[30]

Internals and externals have similar positive reactions to being promoted, including high job satisfaction, job involvement, and organizational commitment. However, internals remain happy long after the promotion, whereas externals' joy over the promotion is short-lived. This might occur because externals do not believe their own performance led to the promotion.[31]

Knowing about locus of control can prove valuable to managers. Because internals believe they control what happens to them, they will want to exercise control in their work environments. Internals don't react well to close supervision, so managers should give them considerable voice in how work is performed. Externals, by contrast, may appreciate more structured work settings and prefer not to participate in decision-making.

Self-Efficacy   People's **general self-efficacy** is their overall view of themselves as being able to perform effectively in a wide variety of situations.[32] Employees with high general self-efficacy have more confidence in their job-related abilities and other personal resources (e.g., energy, influence over others) that help them function effectively on the job. People with low general self-efficacy often feel ineffective at work and may express doubts about performing new tasks well. Previous success or performance is one of the most important determinants of self-efficacy. People

who trust their own efficacy tend to attempt difficult tasks, persist in overcoming obstacles, and experience less anxiety when faced with adversity.[33] Because they are confident in their capability to provide meaningful input, they value the opportunity to participate in decision-making.[34] High self-efficacy has also been related to higher job satisfaction and performance.[35]

Another form of self-efficacy, called *task-specific self-efficacy*, describes a person's belief that they can perform a specific task. ("I believe I can do this sales presentation today.") In contrast, general self-efficacy is broader. ("I believe I can perform well in just about any part of the job.")

Self-Esteem   **Self-esteem** is an individual's general feeling of self-worth. Individuals with high self-esteem have positive feelings about themselves, perceive themselves to have strengths as well as weaknesses, and believe their strengths are more important than their weaknesses.[36] Individuals with low self-esteem view themselves negatively. They are more strongly affected by what other people think of them, and they compliment individuals who give them positive feedback while cutting down people who give them negative feedback.[37]

Evaluations from others affect our self-esteem. You might be liked for who you are, or you might be liked for your achievements. Being liked for who you are is more stable, and people with self-esteem stemming from this type of reaction from other people are usually able to be less defensive and more honest with themselves. Being liked for your achievements is more unstable; self-esteem resulting from this type of reaction waxes and wanes depending on the magnitude of achievements.[38]

Self-esteem affects attitudes and behavior in organizations. People with high self-esteem perform better and are more satisfied with their jobs.[39] They tend to seek out higher-status jobs.[40] A work team made up of individuals with high self-esteem is more likely to succeed than a team with low or average self-esteem.[41]

locus of control   An individual's generalized belief about internal control (self-control) versus external control (control by the situation or by others).

general self-efficacy   An individual's general belief that they are capable of meeting job demands in a wide variety of situations.

self-esteem   An individual's general feeling of self-worth.

High self-esteem, however, can be too much of a good thing. People with inflated self-esteem may brag inappropriately when they find themselves in stressful situations.[42] Very high self-esteem may also lead to overconfidence and relationship conflicts.[43] Such individuals may shift their social identities to protect themselves when they do not live up to some standard. For example, if Denise outperforms Teresa on a statistics exam, Teresa may convince herself that Denise is not really a good person to compare herself with because Denise is an engineering major and Teresa is a physical education major. Teresa's high self-esteem protects her from this unfavorable though, in truth, valid comparison, which might otherwise prompt her to improve her knowledge of statistics.[44]

Self-esteem may be strongly affected by situations. Success tends to raise self-esteem, whereas failure lowers it. Managers should thus encourage employees to raise their self-esteem by giving them appropriate challenges and opportunities for success.

Self-Monitoring Self-monitoring—the extent to which people base their behavior on cues from other people and situations—has a huge impact on behavior in organizations.[45] High self-monitors pay attention to what is appropriate in particular situations and to the behavior of other people, and they behave accordingly. Low self-monitors, by contrast, pay less attention to situational cues and act from internal states instead. As a result, low self-monitors behave consistently across situations. High self-monitors, because their behavior varies with the situation, appear more unpredictable and less consistent but in practice are actually more effective at work because they respond appropriately to changes in the organizational situation. For example, one study of managers at a recruitment firm found

> Individuals with positive affect are more likely to help others at work and engage in more organizational citizenship behaviors ... and have fewer absentee days.

that high self-monitors were more likely to offer emotional help to people dealing with work-related anxiety. Low self-monitors, on the other hand, were unlikely to offer such emotional support.[46]

According to our research, high self-monitors get promoted because they accomplish tasks by meeting the expectations of others and because they seek out central positions in social networks.[47] They are also more likely to use self-promotion to make others aware of their skills and accomplishments.[48] However, the high self-monitors' flexibility may not be suited for every job, and the tendency to move may not fit every organization.[49]

Because high self-monitors base their behavior on cues from others and from the situation, they demonstrate higher levels of managerial self-awareness. This means that, as managers, they assess their own workplace behavior accurately.[50] Managers who are high self-monitors are also good at reading their employees' needs and changing the way they interact with employees.[51]

We can further speculate that high self-monitors respond more readily to work group norms, organizational culture, and supervisory feedback than do low self-monitors, who adhere more to internal guidelines for behavior ("I am who I am"). In addition, high self-monitors may support the trend toward work teams because they can easily assume flexible roles.

3-2d The Dark Triad

Toxic traits also play a role in work life, and a constellation of three dangerous traits has been called the "**Dark Triad**." These traits include **Machiavellianism**, **narcissism**, and **psychopathy**. Each trait alone, or in combination, can create havoc in organizations. Machiavellianism is a tendency to manipulate others in pursuit of one's goals. "What's in it for me?" is a Machiavellian catch phrase. Individuals who are Machiavellian tend to lack empathy and believe that the ends justify the means in terms of getting what they want. (We will discuss Machiavellianism in more detail in Chapter 12 as it

---

self-monitoring The extent to which people base their behavior on cues from other people and situations.

Dark Triad A group of three toxic personality traits—Machiavellianism, narcissism, and psychopathology—that can cause harm in organizations.

Machiavellianism A willingness to manipulate others for personal benefit.

narcissism A preoccupation with self-focus and need for admiration.

psychopathy A lack of concern for others and inability to show conscience or regret.

YOU

Are You a High or Low Self-Monitor?

For the following items, circle T (true) if the statement is characteristic of your behavior. Circle F (false) if the statement does not reflect your behavior.

1.	I find it hard to imitate the behavior of other people.	T	F
2.	At parties and social gatherings, I do not attempt to do or say things that others will like.	T	F
3.	I can only argue for ideas that I already believe.	T	F
4.	I can make impromptu speeches even on topics about which I have almost no information.	T	F
5.	I guess I put on a show to impress or entertain others.	T	F
6.	I would probably make a good actor.	T	F
7.	In a group of people, I am rarely the center of attention.	T	F
8.	In different situations and with different people, I often act like very different persons.	T	F
9.	I am not particularly good at making other people like me.	T	F
10.	I am not always the person I appear to be.	T	F
11.	I would not change my opinions (or the way I do things) in order to please others or win their favor.	T	F
12.	I have considered being an entertainer.	T	F
13.	I have never been good at games like charades or at improvisational acting.	T	F
14.	I have trouble changing my behavior to suit different people and different situations.	T	F
15.	At a party, I let others keep the jokes and stories going.	T	F
16.	I feel a bit awkward in company and do not show up quite as well as I should.	T	F
17.	I can look anyone in the eye and tell a lie with a straight face (if it is for a good cause).	T	F
18.	I may deceive people by being friendly when I really dislike them.	T	F

Scoring:

To score this questionnaire, give yourself one point for each of the following items that you answered T (true): 4, 5, 6, 8, 10, 12, 17, and 18. Now give yourself one point for each of the following items you answered F (false): 1, 2, 3, 7, 9, 11, 13, 14, 15, and 16.

Add both subtotals to find your overall score. If you scored 11 or above, you are probably a high self-monitor. If you scored 10 or under, you are probably a low self-monitor.

Source: M. Snyder, *Public Appearances, Private Realities: The Psychology of Self-Monitoring* (New York: W. H. Freeman and Company, 1987)

relates to power.) Narcissism includes a grandiose view of self, arrogance, a substantial need to be admired, and an extreme sense of entitlement. Narcissists believe that ordinary rules don't apply to them, and like Machiavellians, lack empathy. Narcissists and Machiavellians are some of the most difficult people to be around at work.

Psychopathy, the third trait in the Dark Triad, is characterized by selfishness, a decided lack of concern for other people, and a lack of regret when they break rules or cause harm. Psychopaths know right from wrong, but they just don't care. The three Dark Triad traits share a focus on self-oriented behavior rather than other-directed or organization-directed behavior.

NotionPic/Shutterstock.com

Individually or collectively, these three traits produce toxic outcomes at work.[52] All three Dark Triad traits lead to dishonesty and faking in interviews, and to the use of hard (strong-arm) attempts at influencing others.[53] What if a leader has Dark Triad traits? No one enjoys working for a psychopathic leader, so job satisfaction plummets and employees leave the organization.[54] Machiavellian leaders leave employees emotionally exhausted unless the work climate prevents hostile behavior.[55] Narcissists fancy themselves as great leaders, but often derail from abusive supervision. All three traits may exemplify "kiss up, kick down" management style. Dark Triad leaders covet a favorable impression with their own bosses, while at the same time displaying their toxic behaviors to peers and subordinates.[56]

Leaders must be aware of the Dark Triad, and understand that these traits can lead to unethical behavior. And, it's important to recognize that reputation, what others see, is perhaps more important than the individual's self-perception.[57] It's easy to deceive yourself about negative characteristics, but coworkers will not be fooled. In addition, there is evidence that

projective test A personality test that elicits an individual's response to abstract stimuli.

behavioral measures Personality assessments that involve observing an individual's behavior in a controlled situation.

self-report questionnaire A common personality assessment that involves an individual's responses to a series of questions.

the "selfie generation" means that narcissism is on the rise. This is not an indictment of younger generations, but merely an observation that culture is changing over time. Popular songs and books are more focused on the self, children are given unique names, and social media perpetuates self-focus.[58] There is also evidence that some narcissists are driven by insecurity.[59]

3-3 Application of Personality Theory in Organizations

To apply personality theories in their organizations, managers first must measure the personalities of their organizations' members. Projective tests, behavioral measures, and self-report questionnaires can all be used to measure personality.

3-3a Common Personality Measurement Tools

During **projective tests**, individuals are shown a picture, abstract image, or photo and are asked to describe what they see or to tell a story about it. The rationale behind projective tests is that each individual responds to the stimulus in a way that reflects their unique personality. The Rorschach ink blot test is commonly used to assess personality.[60] Like other projective tests, however, it has low reliability. The individual being assessed may look at the same picture and see different things at different times. In addition, the assessor might apply their own biases in interpreting the information about the individual's personality.

Behavioral measures of personality examine an individual's behavior in a controlled situation. We might assess a person's sociability, for example, by counting the number of times they approach strangers at a party. The behavior is scored to produce an index of personality. Some potential problems with behavioral measures include the observer's ability to stay focused and the way the observer interprets the behavior. Additionally, some people behave differently when they know they are being observed.

The most common method of assessing personality is the **self-report questionnaire**. An individual responds to a series of questions, usually in an agree/disagree or true/false format. One of the more widely recognized questionnaires is the *Minnesota*

Multiphasic Personality Inventory (MMPI), a comprehensive test assessing a variety of traits that can help diagnose several neurotic or psychotic disorders. Another self-report questionnaire, the *NEO Personality Inventory*, measures the Big Five traits. Self-report questionnaires also suffer from potential biases. It is difficult to view your own personality objectively. People often answer the questionnaires in terms of how they want to be seen rather than as they really are.

3-3b Carl Jung and the Myers-Briggs Type Indicator® Instrument

Another approach to applying personality theory in organizations is the Jungian approach and its measurement tool, the *Myers-Briggs Type Indicator®* *(MBTI)*. This instrument was developed to measure ideas about individual differences advocated by the Swiss psychologist Carl Jung. Many organizations use the MBTI instrument, and we will focus on it as an example of how some organizations use personality concepts to help employees appreciate diversity.

Jung built his work on the notion that people are fundamentally different but also fundamentally alike. His classic treatise *Psychological Types* proposed that the population was made up of two basic types: Extraverted types and Introverted types.[61] He went on to identify two types of Perceiving (Sensing and Intuition) and two types of Judgment (Thinking and Feeling). Perceiving (how we gather information) and Judging (how we make decisions) represent the two universal basic mental functions.

Jung suggested that human similarities and differences could be understood by combining preferences. We prefer and choose one way of doing things over another. We are not exclusively one way or another; rather, we have a preference for Extraversion or Introversion, just as we have a preference for right-handedness or left-handedness. Jung's type theory argues that no preferences are better than others. Differences are to be understood, celebrated, and appreciated.

During the 1940s, the mother-daughter team of Katherine Briggs and Isabel Briggs Myers became fascinated with individual differences among people and with Jung's work. They developed the **Myers-Briggs Type Indicator® (MBTI) instrument** to put Jung's type theory into practical use. The MBTI instrument is used extensively in organizations as a basis

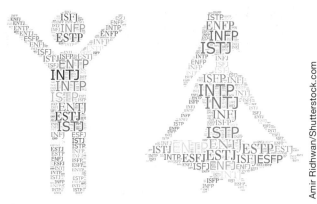

The Myers-Briggs Type Indicator is a common way to measure differences in individuals.

for understanding individual differences. More than 2 million people complete the instrument per year in the United States, and it is frequently used by *Fortune 500* companies.[62] The MBTI instrument has been used in career counseling, team building, conflict management, and understanding management styles.[63]

The Preferences There are four scale dichotomies in type theory: Extraversion/Introversion, Sensing/Intuition, Thinking/Feeling, and Judging/Perceiving. Table 3.2 shows these preferences. The combination of these preferences makes up an individual's psychological type.

Extraversion/Introversion The Extraversion/Introversion preference represents where you find energy. Jung's theory holds that the Extraversion/Introversion preference reflects the most important distinction among individuals. The Extraverted type (E) is energized by interaction with other people. The Introverted type (I) is energized by time alone. Extraverted types typically have a wide social network, whereas Introverted types have a more narrow range of relationships. As articulated by Jung, this preference has nothing to do with social skills. Many introverts have excellent social skills but prefer

Myers-Briggs Type Indicator® (MBTI) instrument
An instrument developed to measure Carl Jung's theory of individual differences.

Extraversion Being energized by interaction with other people.

Introversion Being energized by spending time alone.

Table 3.2 Type Theory Preferences and Descriptions

Extraversion	Introversion		Thinking	Feeling
Outgoing	Quiet		Analytical	Subjective
Publicly expressive	Reserved		Clarity	Harmony
Interacting	Concentrating		Head	Heart
Speaks, then thinks	Thinks, then speaks		Justice	Mercy
Gregarious	Reflective		Rules	Circumstance
Sensing	**Intuition**		**Judging**	**Perceiving**
Practical	General		Structured	Flexible
Specific	Abstract		Time oriented	Open ended
Feet on the ground	Head in the clouds		Decisive	Exploring
Details	Possibilities		Makes lists/uses them	Makes lists/loses them
Concrete	Theoretical		Organized	Spontaneous

Source: Adapted from *Introduction to Type®*, Sixth Edition by Isabel Briggs Myers. Copyright 1998, 2011 by CPP, Inc. All rights reserved.

Introverts Can Be Great Leaders

Do you have to be an extravert to be a leader? Some of the most influential leaders in business and politics would disagree—they're introverts!

- Former U.S. president Barack Obama
- Marissa Mayer, cofounder of Sunshine and former CEO of Yahoo!
- Wendy Kopp, founder of Teach for America
- Warren Buffett, famous investor and philanthropist, CEO of Berkshire Hathaway
- Tim Cook, CEO of Apple
- Deb Liu, CEO of Ancestry.com

Vasilis Ververidis/123RF

Rich Fury/Getty Images

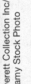
Everett Collection Inc/Alamy Stock Photo

Abaca Press/Alamy Stock Photo

Introverted leaders may succeed because of their natural capacity for introspection and thoughtful communication. They spend a lot of time listening and are more open to others' ideas, inviting diverse viewpoints. Rather than interacting with a great number of people, introverts form genuine, deep ties to a smaller network of people they can rely on.

It's important to remember that introversion means getting energy from time alone. It has nothing to do with social skills; in fact, many of the leaders mentioned above have great social skills.

Laura Hutton/Shutterstock.com

Shelby Knowles/Bloomberg/Getty Images

Source: D. P. Blevins. Shi, "3 Reasons Introverts Can Be Good Leaders," *Fast Company*, July 5 (2022), https://www.fastcompany.com/90761870/3-reasons-introverts-can-be-good-leaders?partner=rss&utm_source=rss&utm_medium=feed&utm_campaign=rss+fastcompany&utm_content=rss.

the internal world of ideas, thoughts, and concepts. Extraverts represent approximately 49 percent of the U.S. population, and introverts represent about 51 percent, indicating a fairly even split.[64] Our U.S. culture rewards and nurtures extraverts. In work settings, extraverts prefer variety and do not mind being interrupted by phone calls or visits. They communicate freely but, on the negative side, may say things that they regret later. Deb Liu, CEO of Ancestry.com, is a natural introvert for whom extraversion is a learned skill that she developed over time.

Introverts prefer to concentrate quietly and think things through privately. They are detail oriented and do not mind working on a project for a long time; but they dislike telephone interruptions and may have trouble recalling names and faces.

Sensing/Intuition The Sensing/Intuition preference represents perception or information gathering. The Sensing type (S) pays attention to information gathered through the five senses and to what actually exists. The Intuitive type (N) pays attention to a "sixth sense" and to what could be rather than to what actually exists. Approximately 70 percent of people in the United States are Sensing types.[65]

At work, Sensing types prefer specific answers to questions and can be frustrated by vague instructions. They like jobs yielding tangible results and would rather use established skills than learn new ones. Intuitive types like solving new problems and are impatient with routine details. They enjoy learning new skills more than actually using them. They tend to think about several things at once and may appear absent-minded. They like figuring out how things work just for the fun of it.

Thinking/Feeling The Thinking/Feeling preference describes the way we prefer to make decisions. The Thinking preference (T) makes decisions in a logical, objective fashion, whereas the Feeling preference (F) makes decisions in a personal, value-oriented way. The general U.S. population is divided 40/60 on the Thinking/Feeling type preference, respectively. But, interestingly, the majority of males are Thinking types, whereas the majority of females are Feeling types. It is the one preference in type theory that has a strong gender difference. Thinking types tend to analyze decisions, while Feeling types sympathize. Thinking types try to be impersonal, whereas Feeling types base their decisions on how the outcome will affect the people involved.

In work settings, Thinking types tend to show less emotion. They also tend to be less comfortable with others' emotional expressions and respond more readily to other people's thoughts. They tend to be firm minded and like putting things into a logical framework. Feeling types, by contrast, are comfortable with emotion in the workplace. They enjoy pleasing people and receiving frequent praise and encouragement.

Judging/Perceiving The Judging/Perceiving dichotomy reflects one's orientation to the outer world. The Judging preference (J) loves closure. They prefer to lead planned, organized lives and like making decisions. On the other hand, Perceivers (P) prefer flexible and spontaneous lives and like to keep options open. Imagine two people, one with a preference for Judging and the other for Perceiving, going out for dinner. J asks P to choose a restaurant, and P suggests ten alternatives. J just wants to decide and get on with it, whereas P wants to explore all the options.

Judging types love getting things accomplished and delight in checking off completed tasks on their calendars. Perceiving types generally adopt a wait-and-see attitude, collecting new information instead of drawing conclusions. Perceiving types are curious and welcome new information. They may start many projects without finishing them.

The Sixteen Types The preferences combine to form sixteen distinct types, as shown in Table 3.3. For example, the ESTJ type has Extraversion, Sensing, Thinking, and Judging preferences. ESTJs see the world as it is (S); make decisions objectively (T); and like structure, schedules, and order (J). Combining these qualities with their preference for interacting with others makes them ideal managers. ESTJs are dependable, practical, and able to get any job done. They are conscious of the chain of command and see

Sensing Gathering information through the five senses and focusing on what actually exists.

Intuition Gathering information through a "sixth sense" and focusing on what could be.

Thinking Making decisions in a logical, objective fashion.

Feeling Making decisions in a personal, value-oriented way.

Judging Preferring closure and completion in making decisions.

Perceiving Preferring to explore many alternatives with flexibility and spontaneity.

work as a series of goals to be reached by following rules and regulations. They may have little tolerance for disorganization and have a high need for control. Research results from the *MBTI Atlas* show that most of the 7,463 managers studied were ESTJs.[66]

The MBTI instrument has been found to have good reliability and validity as a measurement instrument for identifying type.[67] There are no good or bad types; each has its own strengths and weaknesses. Type influences learning style, teaching style, and choice of occupation. A study of the MBTI types of engineering students at Georgia Tech determined that STs and NTs were more attracted to engineering. Es and Fs were more likely to withdraw from engineering courses.[68] Type can also determine an individual's decision-making and management styles.

How Companies Use MBTI More than 88 percent of the Fortune 500 companies in 115 countries use the MBTI.[69] In organizations, effective MBTI training focuses on the gifts that each type brings to the workplace. Promoting the knowledge that both extraverts and introverts bring different positive behaviors to the leadership role is one example.[70] Companies such as AT&T, Amazon, ExxonMobil, and JetBlue use the MBTI instrument in their management development programs so that leaders can discover their own management style, and better understand their employees. The MBTI instrument can also be used for team building, and resources are available to help managers learn how to do so effectively. Consulting firms like McKinsey, Bain, and Deloitte use the MBTI instrument to show teams that diversity and differences lead to successful performance.

Managers value type theory for its simplicity and accuracy. But information from the MBTI instrument can be misused in organizational settings. Some inappropriate uses include labeling one's coworkers, claiming results as a convenient excuse that one simply can't work with a particular coworker, and avoiding responsibility for learning to work flexibly with others. Although personality type is not an excuse for inappropriate behavior, if used well, type theory helps managers develop self-awareness and interpersonal

skills. It also helps in building teams that capitalize on individuals' strengths and foster appreciation of individual team members' differences.

3-4 Social Perception

Perception is another psychological process that creates individual differences. As the primary vehicle through which we come to understand ourselves and our world, perception adds meaning to information gathered via the five senses of touch, smell, hearing, vision, and taste. Virtually all management activities rely on perception. Here, we focus specifically on **social perception**, or the process of interpreting information about another person.

The *selection interview* highlights the importance of perception. The consequences of a bad match between an individual and the organization are devastating for both parties, so accurate data must be gathered. First interviews are typically brief, and the candidate is usually one of many seen by an interviewer during a day. The interviewer often makes an accept or reject decision in the first four to five minutes based on her or his perception of the candidate.[71]

Social perception affects how people perceive each other when going through a life change such as pregnancy. Pregnant people are often viewed negatively in the workplace due to stereotypes, and women have historically worked hard to maintain their professional images by maintaining their work pace, going the extra mile, and not requesting accommodations.[72] They want to avoid being perceived as less capable, less career oriented, and less committed to the organization. Having to worry about how others see them can lead to burnout. Pregnant employees do not see themselves as different professionally during a pregnancy; it's the changing perceptions of others that make working during pregnancy a challenge.

Perception is often culturally determined. Based on our cultural backgrounds, we tend to perceive things in certain ways. Read the following sentence: *Finished files are the result of years of scientific study combined with the experience of years.* Now quickly count the number of *Fs* in the sentence. Individuals who speak English as a second language see all six *Fs*. Most native English speakers report that there are three *Fs* because they are culturally conditioned to ignore unimportant words like *of*.[73] Culture can affect

social perception The process of interpreting information about another person.

Table 3.3 Characteristics Frequently Associated with Each Type

Sensing Types		Intuitive Types	
ISTJ	**ISFJ**	**INFJ**	**INTJ**
Quiet, serious, earn success by thoroughness and dependability. Practical, matter-of-fact, realistic, and responsible. Decides logically what should be done and works toward it steadily, regardless of distractions. Takes pleasure in making everything orderly and organized—work, home, and life. Values traditions and loyalty.	Quiet, friendly, responsible, and conscientious. Committed and steady in meeting obligations. Thorough, painstaking, and accurate. Loyal, considerate, notices and remembers specifics about people who are important, concerned with how others feel. Strives to create an orderly and harmonious environment at work and at home.	Seeks meaning and connection in ideas, relationships, and material possessions. Wants to understand what motivates people and is insightful about others. Conscientious and committed to firm values. Develops a clear vision about how best to serve the common good. Organized and decisive in implementing their vision.	Has an original mind and great drive for implementing ideas and achieving goals. Quickly sees patterns in external events and develops long-range explanatory perspectives. When committed, organizes a job and carries it through. Skeptical and independent, has high standards of competence and performance for self and others.
ISTP	**ISFP**	**INFP**	**INTP**
Tolerant and flexible, quiet observer until a problem appears, then acts quickly to find workable solutions. Analyzes what makes things work and readily gets through large amounts of data to isolate the core of practical problems. Interested in cause and effect, organizes facts using logical principles, values efficiency.	Quiet, friendly, sensitive, and kind. Enjoys the present moment, and the immediate environment. Likes to have their own space and to work within a selected time frame. Loyal and committed to personal values and to people who are important to them. Dislikes disagreements and conflicts, does not force opinions or values on others.	Idealistic, loyal to values and to people who are important to them. Wants an external life that is congruent with values. Curious, quick to see possibilities, can be a catalyst for implementing ideas. Seeks to understand people and to help them fulfill their potential. Adaptable, flexible, and accepting unless a value is threatened.	Seeks to develop logical explanations for everything that interests them. Theoretical and abstract, interested more in ideas than in social interaction. Quiet, contained, flexible, and adaptable. Has unusual ability to focus in depth to solve problems in area of interest. Skeptical, sometimes critical, always analytical.
ESTP	**ESFP**	**ENFP**	**ENTP**
Flexible and tolerant, takes a pragmatic approach focused on immediate results. Finds theories and conceptual explanations boring. Wants to act energetically to solve the problem. Focuses on the here and now, spontaneous, enjoys each moment that they can be active with others. Enjoys material comforts and style. Learns best through doing.	Outgoing, friendly, and accepting. Exuberant lover of life, people, and material comforts. Enjoys working with others to make things happen. Brings common sense and a realistic approach to their work and makes work fun. Flexible and spontaneous, adapts readily to new people and environments. Learns best by trying a new skill with other people.	Warmly enthusiastic and imaginative. Sees life as full of possibilities. Makes connections between events and information very quickly, and confidently proceeds based on the patterns they see. Wants a lot of affirmation from others, and readily gives appreciation and support. Spontaneous and flexible, often relies on their ability to improvise and verbal fluency.	Quick, ingenious, stimulating, alert, and outspoken. Resourceful in solving new and challenging problems. Adept at generating conceptual possibilities and then analyzing them strategically. Good at reading other people. Bored by routine, will seldom do the same thing the same way, apt to turn to one new interest after another.
ESTJ	**ESFJ**	**ENFJ**	**ENTJ**
Practical, realistic, matter-of-fact. Decisive, quickly moves to implement decisions. Organizes projects and people to get things done, focuses on getting results in the most efficient way possible. Takes care of routine details. Has a clear set of logical standards, systematically follows them and wants others to do so also. Forceful in implementing plans.	Warmhearted, conscientious, and cooperative. Wants harmony in the environment, works with determination to establish it. Likes to work with others to complete tasks accurately and on time. Loyal, follows through even in small matters. Notices what others need in their day-to-day lives and tries to provide it. Wants to be appreciated for who they are and for their contribution.	Warm, empathetic, responsive, and responsible. Highly attuned to the emotions, needs, and motivations of others. Finds potential in everyone, wants to help others fulfill their potential. May act as a catalyst for individual and group growth. Loyal, responsive to praise and criticism. Sociable, facilitates others in a group, and provides inspiring leadership.	Frank, decisive, assumes leadership readily. Quickly sees logical and inefficient procedures and policies, develops and implements comprehensive systems to solve organizational problems. Enjoys long-term planning and goal setting. Usually well informed, well read, enjoys expanding knowledge and passing it on to others. Forceful in presenting ideas.

Note: I = Introversion; E = Extraversion; S = Sensing; N = Intuition; T = Thinking; F = Feeling; J = Judging; and P = Perceiving.

Although personality type is not an excuse for inappropriate behavior, if used well, type theory helps managers develop interpersonal skills.

our interpretation of the data we gather as well as the meaning we add to it. In other words, our culture can affect our social perception. Valuing diversity, including cultural diversity, has been recognized as a key to international competitiveness, so managers need good social perception skills.[74]

Three major categories of factors influence our perception of others: characteristics of ourselves as perceivers, characteristics of the target person we are perceiving, and characteristics of the situation in which the interaction takes place. Figure 3.2 models social perception.

3-4a Characteristics of the Perceiver

Several characteristics of the perceiver can affect social perception. The perceiver uses *perceptual lenses* to shape their view of the target, especially

if it is a new encounter. Perceptual lenses are filters used by the perceiver to make a quick initial assessment. The most often used lenses include the trust lens (are you friend or foe?), the power lens (are you useful to me?), and the ego lens (which of us is superior?). You can use knowledge of perceptual lenses to ensure that you're perceived accurately. For the trust lens, project warmth and competence through appropriate eye contact, smiling, and good posture. For the power lens, make yourself instrumental through assurances that you can help the perceiver reach mutual goals. For the ego lens, be modest and inclusive, and create a sense of "us."[75]

The perceiver's *attitudes* also affect social perception. Suppose you are interviewing candidates for a very important position in your organization—a position that requires negotiating contracts with suppliers, most of whom are male. You may feel that women are not capable of holding their own in tough negotiations. This attitude will doubtlessly affect your perceptions of the female candidates you interview.

Mood can have a strong influence on the way we perceive someone.[76] We think differently when we are happy than we do when we are depressed. We also remember information that matches our

Figure 3.2 A Model for Social Perception

Characteristics of the perceiver
• Perceptual lenses
• Attitudes
• Mood
• Self-concept
• Cognitive structure

Characteristics of the target
• Physical appearance
• Verbal communication
• Nonverbal cues
• Intentions

Barriers
Selective perception
Stereotyping
First-impression error
Projection
Self-fulfilling prophecies

Social perception

Characteristics of the situation
• Context of the interaction
• Strength of situational cues

mood state better than information that is inconsistent with it. When in a positive mood, we form more positive impressions of others. When in a negative mood, we tend to evaluate others unfavorably.

Another factor that can affect social perception is the perceiver's *self-concept*. An individual with a positive self-concept tends to notice positive attributes in another person. In contrast, a negative self-concept can lead a perceiver to pick out negative traits in another person. The better we understand ourselves, the more accurate our perceptions of others.

Cognitive structure, an individual's pattern of thinking, also affects social perception. Some people tend to perceive physical traits such as height, weight, and appearance more readily. Others focus on central traits, or personality dispositions. Cognitive complexity allows a person to perceive multiple characteristics of another person rather than attending to just a few traits.

theshots.co/Shutterstock.com

3-4b Characteristics of the Target

Characteristics of the target (the person being perceived) influence social perception in various ways. *Physical appearance* plays a big role in our perception of others. The perceiver will notice physical features such as height, weight, estimated age, race, and gender. Clothing says a great deal about a person. Blue pinstriped suits, for example, suggest banking or Wall Street. Perceivers tend to notice physical appearance characteristics that contrast with the norm, that are intense, or that are new or unusual.[77] A loud person, one who dresses outlandishly, a very tall person, or a hyperactive child will be noticed because they contrast with what is commonly encountered. Novel individuals such as newcomers or people of underrepresented racial or ethnic groups also attract attention.

The way you dress influences how people perceive you. Physical attractiveness often colors our entire impression of another person. Interviewers rate attractive candidates more favorably and award them higher starting salaries.[78] But people who are perceived as physically attractive face some nonbeneficial stereotypes as well.

Verbal communication from a target affects our perception of that person. We listen to the topics discussed and their tone of voice and accent, and we make judgments based on this input.

Nonverbal communication conveys a great deal of information about the target. Eye contact, facial expressions, body movements, and posture all are deciphered by the perceiver in an attempt to form an impression of the target. Awareness of cultural differences is particularly important when it comes to nonverbal communication because some nonverbal signals mean very different things in different cultures. The "okay" sign in the United States (forming a circle with the thumb and forefinger) is an insult in South America. Facial expressions, however, seem to have universal meanings. Individuals from different cultures can recognize and decipher expressions the same way.[79]

The *intentions* of the target are inferred by the perceiver who observes the target's behavior. We may see our boss appear in our office doorway and think, "Oh no! I'm about to get more work to do." Or we may perceive that the boss's intention is to congratulate us on a recent success. In any case, the perceiver's interpretation of the target's intentions affects the way the perceiver views the target.

3-4c Characteristics of the Situation

The situation in which the interaction between the perceiver and the target takes place, the *social context*, also influences perception. Meeting your professor in their office affects your impression differently than meeting your professor in a local restaurant would. Social context is very important in Japan. Business conversations after working hours or at lunch are taboo. If you try to talk business during these times, you may be perceived as rude.[80]

The *strength of situational cues* also affects social perception. As discussed earlier in the chapter, some situations provide strong cues about appropriate behavior. In these situations, we assume that the individual's behavior can be accounted for by the situation and may not reflect the individual's disposition. This is the **discounting principle** in social perception.[81] For example, you may encounter an automobile salesperson who has a warm and personable manner, asks about your work and hobbies, and seems genuinely interested in your taste in cars. Yet you probably cannot assume that this behavior reflects the salesperson's personality because of the influence of the situation. This person is trying to sell you a car and probably treats all customers in this manner.

3-5 Barriers to Social Perception

It would be wonderful if all of us had accurate social perception skills. Unfortunately, barriers often prevent us from perceiving others accurately. Five barriers to social perception are selective perception, stereotyping, first-impression error, projection, and self-fulfilling prophecies.

Selective perception is our tendency to prefer information that supports our viewpoints. Individuals often ignore information that threatens their viewpoints. Suppose, for example, that a sales manager is evaluating the performance of his employees. One employee does not get along well with colleagues and rarely completes sales reports on time. This employee, however, generates the most new sales contracts in the office. The sales manager may ignore the negative information, choosing to evaluate the salesperson only on contracts generated. The manager is exercising selective perception.

A **stereotype** is a generalization about a group of people. Stereotypes reduce information about other people to a workable level so that it can be compiled efficiently. Stereotypes become even stronger when they are shared with and validated by others.[82] Some stereotypes are accurate and serve as useful perceptual guidelines, but, of course, many are inaccurate and do much harm, generating false impressions that may never be tested or changed.

Stereotypes about different generations present challenges in the workplace. Older workers may see Millennials and Generation Z employees as entitled and unfocused, but stereotypes of older workers also exist. Ageism is prejudice or discrimination either for or against an age group. With four generations in the workforce, employees use stereotypes as shortcuts to categorize their coworkers, and these stereotypes can lead to misunderstandings and even obstacles to performance. Managers can create positive intergenerational climates by encouraging interactions between the coworkers of different generations, promoting cross-generational mentoring relationships, and creating a work environment that is inclusive and healthy for people of all ages.[83]

Attractiveness is a powerful stereotype. We assume that attractive individuals are also warm, kind, sensitive, poised, sociable, outgoing, independent, and strong. However, a study of romantic relationships showed that most attractive individuals do not fit the stereotype apart from possessing good social skills and being popular.[84] Some individuals may seem to us to fit the stereotype of attractiveness because our behavior elicits from them behavior that confirms the stereotype. Consider, for example, a situation in which you meet an attractive fellow student. Chances are that you respond positively to this person because you assume they are warm, sociable, and so on. Even though the person may not possess these traits, your positive response may bring out these behaviors in the person. Thus, your interaction may be channeled to confirm the stereotype.[85]

Stereotyping pervades work life. Neurodiverse individuals often face stereotypes, especially about leadership. These stereotypes arise from the ableist assumption that the full range of jobs is not suitable for neurodiverse people. As a result, 46 percent of autistic adults in the workforce are overeducated or overqualified for the roles they are in. Making the world of work more inclusive of neurodivergent employees will require examining ableist assumptions and debunking stereotypes.[86]

Gender stereotypes also create bias at work. Both men and women are likely to be viewed

discounting principle The assumption that an individual's behavior is accounted for by the situation.

selective perception The tendency to select information that supports our individual viewpoints while discounting information that threatens our viewpoints.

stereotype A generalization about a group of people.

badly at work when they violate traditional gender norms, and certainly people who align elsewhere on the gender continuum face stereotyping in the workplace. Men who cry at work (seen as gender atypical behavior) are rated lower in performance and leadership ability.[87] The "science is male" stereotype is also harmful and often prevents women from pursuing careers in STEM.[88] The way others perceive "bottom-line mentality," a focus on obtaining bottom-line results at work, differs along gender lines. Men are likely to be mistreated for not showing enough bottom-line mentality, whereas women are more likely to be mistreated for showing too much bottom-line mentality.[89] Also, female leaders' abusive supervision is viewed even more negatively than when male leaders are abusive, because it is seen as female-atypical behavior.[90] Transgender individuals are often stigmatized as "confused" or "mentally ill" for not conforming to traditional gender stereotypes.[91] As a result, 47 percent of transgender employees report daily experiences of discriminatory behaviors like transphobic remarks, being ignored, and pressure to act in traditionally gendered ways.[92] Awareness of, and debunking of, gender stereotypes and how they affect workplace behavior and outcomes is essential.

First impressions are lasting impressions, so the saying goes. We tend to remember what we perceive first about a person, and sometimes we are quite reluctant to change our initial impressions.[93] **First-impression** occurs when we observe a very brief bit of a person's behavior in our first encounter and infer that this behavior reflects what the person is really like. Such primacy effects can be particularly dangerous in interviews, given that we form first impressions quickly and that these impressions may be the basis for long-term employment relationships.

What factors do interviewers rely on when forming first impressions? Perceptions of the candidate, such as whether they like the person, whether they trust the person, and whether or not the person seems credible, all influence the interviewer's decision. Something as seemingly unimportant as the pitch of your voice can leave a lasting impression.

Speakers with lower vocal pitch are believed to be more competent, more dominant, and more assertive than those with higher voices. Men whose voices are high enough that they sound feminine are judged the least favorably of all by interviewers. This finding is ironic, given that research has found that students with higher vocal pitch tend to earn better grades.[94]

Projection, also known as the *false-consensus effect*, causes inaccurate perceptions of others. When we project, we assume that our own beliefs and values are commonly held and normative, and we overestimate the number of others who share them. People who are different are viewed as unusual and even deviant. Projection occurs most often when you surround yourself with others similar to you. You may overlook important information about others when you assume we are all alike and in agreement.[95]

Self-fulfilling prophecies, also called the *Pygmalion effect*, interfere with social perception in that our expectations affect the way we interact with others such that we provoke the very response we expect. Early studies of self-fulfilling prophecy were conducted in elementary school classrooms. Teachers were given bogus information that some of their pupils had high intellectual potential. These pupils were chosen randomly; there were really no differences among the students. Eight months later, the "gifted" pupils scored significantly higher on an IQ test. The teachers' expectations elicited growth from these students because they had given them tougher assignments and more feedback on their performance.[96]

A manager's expectations of an individual affect both the manager's behavior toward the individual and the individual's response. For example, suppose your initial impression is that an employee has the potential to move up in the organization. Chances are you will spend a great deal of time coaching and counseling the employee, providing challenging assignments, and grooming the individual for success. Managers can harness the power of the Pygmalion effect to improve productivity in the organization simply by expecting positive results from a group of employees.[97]

first-impression Forming lasting opinions about an individual based on initial perceptions.

projection Overestimating the number of people who share our own beliefs, values, and behaviors.

self-fulfilling prophecy Allowing expectations about people to affect our interaction with them in such a way that those expectations are fulfilled.

Is the Tattoo Taboo Fading?

There was a time in the recent past when impressions of tattooed employees in the workplace were not favorable, because hiring managers were fearful of damage to the company's image. New research shows, however, that although customers may hold either negative or positive views of tattoos, they do not show negative attitudes or behaviors toward tattooed employees. In jobs that require artistic skills, employees with tattoos are viewed more positively. When looking for a job, it's best to check the company's culture, and highlight your skills, knowledge, and experiences. Overall, it's good news that the stigma around tattoos may be shifting.

Dean Drobot/Shutterstock.com

Source: E. Ruggs and M. R. Hebl, "Do Employees' Tattoos Leave a Mark on Customers' Reactions to Products and Organizations," *Journal of Organizational Behavior*, February 24 (2022), https://onlinelibrary.wiley.com/doi/10.1002/job.2616.

3-5a Impression Management

Most people want to make favorable impressions on others. This is particularly true in organizations where individuals compete for jobs, favorable performance evaluations, and salary increases. The process by which individuals try to control the impressions others have of them is called **impression management**. Individuals use several techniques to control others' impressions of them.[98]

Some impression management techniques are *self-enhancing*. Name-dropping, or mentioning an association with important people in the hope of improving one's image, is often used. Controlling one's appearance is another self-enhancing technique for impression management. Individuals dress carefully for interviews because they want to "look the part" in order to get the job. Self-descriptions, or statements about one's characteristics, are used to manage impressions as well.

Another group of impression management techniques are *other-enhancing*. They focus on the individual on whom one is trying to make an impression rather than on oneself. People often use flattery and favors to win approval. Agreeing with someone's opinion can create a positive impression. People with disabilities, for example, often use other-enhancing techniques. They may feel that they must take it upon themselves to make others comfortable interacting with them. Impression management techniques help them prevent potential avoidance by others.[99]

Leaders, as the face of organizations, engage in impression management. If the company is in a highly publicized decline and their own compensation depends on company performance, leaders increase their impression management behaviors.[100] And firms often tailor their impression management techniques to different stakeholders such as local press, international press, and financial analysts, to manipulate each group's view of the company's performance.[101]

So impression management does seem to influence others' impressions. As long as the impressions conveyed are accurate, this process benefits organizations. If the impressions are found to be false, however, the result is a strongly negative overall impression. Furthermore, excessive impression management can lead to the perception that the user is manipulative or insincere.[102]

impression management The process by which individuals try to control the impressions others have of them.

3-6 Attribution in Organizations

Human beings are innately curious. We want to know *why* people behave the way they do. We also seek to understand and explain our own behavior. **Attribution theory** explains how we pinpoint the causes of our own behavior (and therefore our performance) and that of other people.[103]

3-6a Internal and External Attributions

We can attribute events to an internal source of responsibility (something within the individual's control) or an external source (something outside the individual's control). Suppose you perform well on an exam. You might say you aced the test because you are smart or because you studied hard; this internal attribution credits your ability or effort. Alternatively, you might make an external attribution for your performance by saying it was an easy test or that you had good luck.

Attribution patterns differ among individuals.[104] Achievement-oriented individuals attribute their success to ability and their failures to lack of effort—both internal causes. Failure-oriented individuals attribute their failures to lack of ability and may develop feelings of incompetence (or even depression) as a result.[105] Women managers are less likely to attribute their success to their own ability. This may be because they are adhering to social norms that compel women to be modest or because they believe that success has more do to with hard work than ability.[106]

Attribution theory has many applications in the workplace. The way you explain your own behavior affects your motivation. If you believe careful preparation and rehearsal led to your successful presentation, you're likely to take credit for the performance and to have a sense of self-efficacy about future presentations. If, however, you believe that you were just lucky, you may not be motivated to repeat the performance because you believe you had little influence on the outcome.

Lots of attributions are made during employment interviews when candidates are asked to explain the causes of previous performance. Candidates want to give interviewers reasons to hire them ("I work well with people, so I'm looking for a managerial job"). Research shows that successful candidates make different attributions for negative outcome than unsuccessful ones. Successful candidates are willing to make internal attributions for negative events. Unsuccessful candidates blame negative outcomes on things beyond their control, giving interviewers the impression that they failed to learn from the event and that they will likely blame others when something goes wrong in the workplace.[107]

3-6b Attributional Biases

The attribution process may be affected by two very common problems: The first is the tendency to make attributions to internal causes when focusing on someone else's behavior, known as the **fundamental attribution error**.[108] A manager may attribute an employee's poor performance to laziness (an internal cause), when in fact the employee may simply be suffering from work overload (an external cause). The other error, **self-serving bias**, occurs when focusing on one's own behavior. Individuals tend to make internal attributions for their own successes and external attributions for their own failures.[109] In other words, when we succeed, we take credit for it; when we fail, we blame the situation on other people.

Both biases were illustrated in a study of healthcare managers asked to cite the causes of their employees' poor performance.[110] The managers claimed that internal causes (their employees' lack of effort or lack of ability) explained their employees' poor performance. When the employees were asked to pinpoint the cause of their own performance problems, they blamed a lack of support from the managers (an external cause), which illustrates self-serving bias.

Stereotypes can affect attributions, and one particularly harmful stereotype is the "angry Black woman," which portrays Black women as aggressive

attribution theory A theory that explains how individuals pinpoint the causes of their own and others' behavior.

fundamental attribution error The tendency to make attributions to internal causes when focusing on someone else's behavior.

self-serving bias The tendency to attribute one's successes to internal causes and one's failures to external causes.

and hostile when interacting with others. When Black women display anger at work, observers are more likely to make internal attributions for their behavior (it's her fault, not the situation). This leads to negative performance evaluations, and negative assessments of leadership potential. Inaccurate internal attributions are damaging, and Black women are continually underrepresented in leadership positions. The first step toward eradicating the stereotype of the angry Black woman and the attribution error it produces is to make employees aware of the stereotype and the harm it creates in the workplace. It's also important to dispel the stereotype; research shows no evidence that Black women are angrier in the workplace. Displays of anger can be legitimate responses brought on by unfair treatment and lack of social justice at work.[111]

There are cultural differences in these two attribution errors. In fatalistic cultures, such as India, people tend to believe that fate is responsible for much that happens. People in such cultures tend to emphasize external causes of behavior.[112] In China, people are taught that hard work is the route to accomplishment. When faced with either a success or a failure, Chinese individuals first reflect on whether they tried hard enough or whether their attitude was correct. Thus, in analyzing a cause, they first look to their own effort.[113]

The way individuals interpret the events around them has a strong influence on their behavior.

Are successes from luck or skill?

People in general try to understand the causes of behavior so that they can predict and control future behavior, and managers certainly do this. Hence, they use attributions in all aspects of their jobs. Especially in evaluating performance and rewarding employees, managers must determine the causes of behavior and a perceived source of responsibility.

Attribution theory explains how performance evaluation judgments can lead to differential rewards. A supervisor attributing an employee's good performance to internal causes such as effort or ability may give a larger raise than a supervisor attributing the good performance to external causes like help from others or good training. Managers are often called on to explain their own actions as well, and in doing so they make attributions about the causes of their own behavior. We continue our discussion of attributions in Chapter 6.

Experiential Exercise

Management Styles*

Part I. This questionnaire will help you determine your preferences. For each item, circle either a or b. If you feel both a and b are true, decide which one is more like you even if it is only slightly more true.

1. I would rather
   a. solve a new and complicated problem.
   b. work on something I have done before.

2. I like to
   a. work alone in a quiet place.
   b. be where the action is.

3. I want a boss who
   a. establishes and applies criteria in decisions.
   b. considers individual needs and makes exceptions.

4. When I work on a project, I
   a. like to finish it and get some closure.
   b. often leave it open for possible changes.

5. When making a decision, the most important considerations are
   a. rational thoughts, ideas, and data.
   b. people's feelings and values.

6. On a project, I tend to
   a. think it over and over before deciding how to proceed.
   b. start working on it right away, thinking about it as I go along.

7. When working on a project, I prefer to
   a. maintain as much control as possible.
   b. explore various options.

8. In my work, I prefer to
   a. work on several projects at a time and learn as much as possible about each one.
   b. have one project that is challenging and that keeps me busy.

9. I often
   a. make lists and plans whenever I start something and may hate to seriously alter my plans.
   b. avoid plans and let things progress as I work on them.

10. When discussing a problem with colleagues, it is easy for me to
    a. see "the big picture."
    b. grasp the specifics of the situation.

11. When the phone rings in my office or at home, I usually
    a. consider it an interruption.
    b. do not mind answering it.

12. Which word describes you better?
    a. Analytical
    b. Empathetic

13. When I am working on an assignment, I tend to
    a. work steadily and consistently.
    b. work in bursts of energy with "downtime" in between.

14. When I listen to someone talk on a subject, I usually try to
    a. relate it to my own experience and see if it fits.
    b. assess and analyze the message.

15. When I come up with new ideas, I generally
    a. "go for it."
    b. like to contemplate the ideas some more.

16. When working on a project, I prefer to
    a. narrow the scope so it is clearly defined.
    b. broaden the scope to include related aspects.

17. When I read something, I usually
    a. confine my thoughts to what is written there.
    b. read between the lines and relate the words to other ideas.

18. When I have to make a decision in a hurry, I often
    a. feel uncomfortable and wish I had more information.
    b. am able to do so with available data.

19. In a meeting, I tend to
    a. continue formulating my ideas as I talk about them.
    b. only speak out after I have carefully thought the issue through.

20. In work, I prefer spending a great deal of time on issues of
    a. ideas.
    b. people.

21. In meetings, I am most often annoyed with people who
    a. come up with many sketchy ideas.
    b. lengthen meetings with many practical details.

22. I am a
    a. morning person.
    b. night owl.

23. What is your style in preparing for a meeting?
    a. I am willing to go in and be responsive.
    b. I like to be fully prepared and usually sketch an outline of the meeting.

24. In a meeting, I would prefer for people to
    a. display a fuller range of emotions.
    b. be more task oriented.

25. I would rather work for an organization where
    a. my job is intellectually stimulating.
    b. I am committed to its goals and mission.

26. On weekends, I tend to
    a. plan what I will do.
    b. just see what happens and decide as I go along.

27. I am more
    a. outgoing.
    b. contemplative.

28. I would rather work for a boss who is
    a. full of new ideas.
    b. practical.

In the following, choose the word in each pair that appeals to you more:

29. a. Social
    b. Theoretical

30. a. Ingenuity
    b. Practicality

31. a. Organized
    b. Adaptable

32. a. Active
    b. Concentrating

Scoring Key

Count one point for each item listed below that you have circled in the inventory.

Score for I	Score for E	Score for S	Score for N
2a	2b	1b	1a
6a	6b	10b	10a
11a	11b	13a	13b
15b	15a	16a	16b
19b	19a	17a	17b
22a	22b	21a	21b
27b	27a	28b	28a
32b	32a	30b	30a
Total ____	____	____	____

Circle the one with more points: I or E.		Circle the one with more points: S or N.	
Score for T	Score for F	Score for J	Score for P
3a	3b	4a	4b
5a	5b	7a	7b
12a	12b	8b	8a
14b	14a	9a	9b
20a	20b	18b	18a
24b	24a	23b	23a
25a	25b	26a	26b
29b	29a	31a	31b
Total ____	____	____	____

Circle the one with more points: T or F.	Circle the one with more points: J or P.
Your score is	
I or E ____	T or F ____
S or N ____	J or P ____

Part II. The purpose of this part of the exercise is to give you experience in understanding some of the individual differences Carl Jung proposed.

Step 1. Your instructor will assign you to a group.

Step 2. Your group is a team of individuals who want to start a business. You are to develop a mission statement and a name for your business.

Step 3. After you have completed the second step, analyze the decision process that occurred within the group. How did you decide on your company's name and mission?

Step 4. Your instructor will have each group report to the class the name and mission of the company, and then the decision process used. Your instructor will give you some additional information about the exercise and provide some interesting insights about your management style.

*Note: The "Personality Inventory" instrument is not associated with CPP, Inc., Isabel Myers Briggs, or the MBTI® or Myers–Briggs Type Indicator® trademarks.

Source: From D. Marcic and P. Nutt, "Personality Inventory," in D. Marcic, ed., *Organizational Behavior: Experiences and Cases* (St. Paul, MN: West, 1989), 9–16. Reprinted by permission.

Learning Objectives

3-1 **Describe individual differences and explain why they are important in understanding organizational behavior.** Individual differences are skills, abilities, personalities, perceptions, attitudes, emotions, and ethics. To understand human behavior, we must know something about the person and something about the organization, work group, personal life situation, job characteristics, and environmental influences.

3-2 **Articulate key personality traits and explain how they influence behavior in organizations.** Personality is an individual difference that lends consistency to a person's

behavior. Two major theories, integrative approach and trait theory, state that personality affects attitude, performance, attendance, motivation, satisfaction, commitment, and occupational success at work.

3-3 **Discuss how personality theories may be applied in organizations.** Managers assess the personalities of their organizations' members with projective tests, behavioral measures, and self-report questionnaires. These tests give practical insight into the personality and psychological traits of workers such as decision-making skills, management style, thought processes, diversity, and tolerance.

3-4 **Define social perception and explain the factors that affect it.** Social perception is the process of interpreting information about another person. Management perceptions are affected by perceptual lenses, attitude, mood, and cognitive structure. The target's physical appearance, communication skills, and perceived intentions as well as characteristics of the situation influence perception. In an organization, virtually all management activities rely on perception.

3-5 **Identify five common barriers to social perception and explain the difficulties they cause.** In organizations, expectations of an individual affect both the manager's behavior toward the individual and the individual's response. Five barriers to social perception are selective perception, stereotyping, first-impression error, projection, and self-fulfilling prophecies. Understanding social perception in organizations may lead to favorable performance evaluations, salary increases, and help individuals compete for jobs.

3-6 **Explain the attribution process and how attributions affect managerial behavior.** Attribution theory explains how we pinpoint the causes of our own behavior (and performance) and that of others. Attribution theory has many applications in the workplace. We can attribute events to an internal source of responsibility or an external source. In other words, when we succeed, we take credit for it (internal source); when we fail, we blame the situation on other people (external source).

Key Terms

attribution theory A theory that explains how individuals pinpoint the causes of their own and others' behavior. (p. 61)

behavioral measures Personality assessments that involve observing an individual's behavior in a controlled situation. (p. 50)

Dark Triad A group of three toxic personality traits—Machiavellianism, narcissism, and psychopathology—that can cause harm in organizations. (p. 48)

discounting principle The assumption that an individual's behavior is accounted for by the situation. (p. 58)

Extraversion Being energized by interaction with other people. (p. 51)

Feeling Making decisions in a personal, value-oriented way. (p. 53)

first-impression Forming lasting opinions about an individual based on initial perceptions. (p. 59)

fundamental attribution error The tendency to make attributions to internal causes when focusing on someone else's behavior. (p. 61)

general self-efficacy An individual's general belief that they are capable of meeting job demands in a wide variety of situations. (p. 47)

impression management The process by which individuals try to control the impressions others have of them. (p. 60)

individual differences The way in which factors such as skills, abilities, personalities, perceptions, attitudes, values, and ethics differ from one individual to another. (p. 43)

integrative approach The broad theory that describes personality as a composite of an individual's psychological processes. (p. 46)

interactional psychology The psychological approach to understanding human behavior that involves knowing something about the person and about the situation. (p. 43)

Introversion Being energized by spending time alone. (p. 51)

Intuition Gathering information through a "sixth sense" and focusing on what could be. (p. 53)

Judging Preferring closure and completion in making decisions. (p. 53)

locus of control An individual's generalized belief about internal control (self-control) versus external control (control by the situation or by others). (p. 47)

Machiavellianism A willingness to manipulate others for personal benefit. (p. 48)

Myers-Briggs Type Indicator® (MBTI) instrument An instrument developed to measure Carl Jung's theory of individual differences. (p. 51)

narcissism A preoccupation with self-focus and need for admiration. (p. 48)

Perceiving Preferring to explore many alternatives with flexibility and spontaneity. (p. 53)

personality A relatively stable set of characteristics that influence an individual's behavior. (p. 44)

projection Overestimating the number of people who share our own beliefs, values, and behaviors. (p. 59)

projective test A personality test that elicits an individual's response to abstract stimuli. (p. 50)

psychopathy A lack of concern for others and inability to show conscience or regret. (p. 48)

selective perception The tendency to select information that supports our individual viewpoints while discounting information that threatens our viewpoints. (p. 58)

self-esteem An individual's general feeling of self-worth. (p. 47)

self-fulfilling prophecy Allowing expectations about people to affect our interaction with them in such a way that those expectations are fulfilled. (p. 59)

self-monitoring The extent to which people base their behavior on cues from other people and situations. (p. 48)

self-report questionnaire A common personality assessment that involves an individual's responses to a series of questions. (p. 50)

self-serving bias The tendency to attribute one's successes to internal causes and one's failures to external causes. (p. 61)

Sensing Gathering information through the five senses and focusing on what actually exists. (p. 53)

social perception The process of interpreting information about another person. (p. 54)

stereotype A generalization about a group of people. (p. 58)

strong situation A situation that overwhelms the effects of individual personalities by providing strong cues for appropriate behavior. (p. 46)

Thinking Making decisions in a logical, objective fashion. (p. 53)

trait theory A personality theory that advocates breaking down behavior patterns into a series of observable traits in order to understand human behavior. (p. 44)

Ethical Dilemma

Renee is a manager at National Insurance Agency. Due to growth in the company, she is in the process of hiring a new actuary for her department. She has reviewed the resumes of all applicants and conducted six interviews. She has narrowed down the pool to three people. All are equally qualified, and she believes any one of them would be a great asset to the company. Now it is time to get input from others in the department and from the vice president to whom Renee reports.

Each candidate is set up with a day of interviews. The day includes interviews with individuals throughout the department and the vice president. After all three candidates have been interviewed, Renee collects feedback from all constituents and reviews the data. There is great consensus that Jack Donahue is the best candidate. He has the education and experience and was a great fit with the other members of the group. Everyone agreed except the vice president, Mike Terry. Renee calls Mike to discuss this issue and finds that Mike wants to choose Myra Chen. When asked why, Mike states that "Asians are always better at math and therefore she should be the natural choice."

Renee is very disappointed in Mike. She agrees that Myra is very talented and capable, but she was not a good fit with the other people. She wants to challenge Mike on his stereotyping but is concerned about his reaction.

1. Using consequential, rule-based, and character theories, evaluate Mike's actions.

2. What should Renee do? Why?

Chapter 4

iStock.com/Siphotography

Attitudes, Emotions, and Ethics

Learning Objectives

4-1 Explain the significance of job attitudes in the workplace.

4-2 Describe how job attitudes are formed.

4-3 Identify sources of job satisfaction and commitment.

4-4 Distinguish between organizational citizenship and counterproductive work behaviors.

4-5 Identify the characteristics of the source, target, and message that affect persuasion.

4-6 Discuss the importance of emotions at work.

4-7 Contrast the effects of individual and organizational influences on ethical behavior.

4-8 Identify the factors that affect ethical behavior.

4-1 Attitudes

An **attitude** is a psychological tendency expressed when we evaluate a particular entity with some degree of favor or disfavor.[1] Since we respond favorably or unfavorably toward many things such as coworkers, our own appearance, or politics, we have attitudes toward many things. Attitudes can drive and explain behavior in general, so they are an important factor in the workplace. Managers complain about workers with "bad attitudes" and conduct "attitude adjustment" talks. Poor performance attributed to bad attitude can often stem from lack of motivation, minimal feedback, lack of trust in management, or other problems. On the positive side, recognition and praise from colleagues and supervisors can positively impact an individual's attitudes and job performance.[2]

Thus, managers should understand the antecedents to attitudes as well as their consequences. They also need to understand the different components of attitudes, how attitudes are formed, the major attitudes that affect work behavior, and how to use persuasion to change attitudes.

4-1a The ABC Model

An individual does not have an attitude until they respond to an entity (person, object, situation, or issue) on an affective, behavioral, or cognitive basis. We can break attitudes down into three components, as depicted in Table 4.1. These three

> We may be supportive, passive, or hostile, depending on our attitude.

components compose what we call the *ABC model* of an attitude.[3,3a]

Affect is the emotional component of an attitude. It refers to an individual's feeling about something or someone. Statements such as "I like this" or "I prefer that" reflect the affective component of an attitude. Affect can be measured by self-report questionnaires as well as physiological indicators such as blood pressure, which show emotional changes by measuring physiological arousal.

The second component is *behavioral intent* toward an object or person. Here, it is important to note that a behavioral intent may not actually lead to a particular behavior, but it has the potential to affect behaviors. Our attitudes toward women in management, for example, may be inferred from observing the way we treat a female supervisor. We may be supportive, passive, or hostile, depending on our attitude. The behavioral component of an attitude is measured by observing actual behavior. A recent study found that we rarely study *actual* behavior in organizational behavior. Instead, a majority of research confuses actual behaviors with perceptions of observers or intentions to behave in a particular way.[4]

The third component of an attitude, *cognition* (thought), reflects a person's perceptions or beliefs. Cognitive elements are evaluative beliefs measured by attitude scales or by asking about thoughts. The statement "I think my boss is supportive" reflects the cognitive component of an attitude.

The ABC model shows that we must assess all three components to understand an attitude.

attitude A psychological tendency expressed by evaluating something with a degree of favor or disfavor.

affect The emotional component of an attitude.

Table 4.1 The ABC Model of an Attitude

	Component	Measured By	Example
A	Affect	Physiological indicators Verbal statements about feelings	I like my boss.
B	Behavioral intent	Observed behavior Verbal statements about intentions	I want to transfer to another department.
C	Cognition	Attitude scales Verbal statements about beliefs	I believe my boss plays favorites at work.

Source: Adapted from M. J. Rosenberg and C. I. Hovland, "Cognitive, Affective, and Behavioral Components of Attitude," in M. J. Rosenberg, C. I. Hovland, W. J. McGuire, R. P. Abelson, and J. H. Brehm, eds., *Attitude Organization and Change* (New Haven, Conn.: Yale University Press, 1960).

Suppose, for example, you want to evaluate your employees' attitudes toward *flextime* (flexible work scheduling). You would want to determine how they feel about the policy (affect), whether they would participate in it (behavioral intention), and what they think about it (cognition). The most common method of attitude measurement, however, is the attitude scale, which measures only the cognitive component.

4-1b Cognitive Dissonance

As rational beings, people prefer consistency (consonance) between their attitudes and behavior. Anything that disrupts this consistency causes tension (dissonance), which motivates individuals to change either their attitudes or their behavior to maintain consistency. The tension produced by a conflict between attitudes and behavior is **cognitive dissonance**.[5]

Suppose, for example, you are a vegetarian as a matter of choice. If you work in a fast food industry where you are required to serve or handle meat-based products, you will feel discomfort because of the conflict between your attitude towards meat and required behavior on the job. When we feel cognitive dissonance we are motivated to reduce it in a variety of ways. For example, you might try to change your attitude towards meat or you might try to switch to a role that does not involve coming into contact with it (e.g., the cashier). Alternatively, you might rationalize that the required behavior is not a problem. These attempts try to restore equilibrium between the attitude and required behavior, thereby eliminating the tension from cognitive dissonance.

Managers need to understand cognitive dissonance because employees often find themselves in situations in which their attitudes conflict with their behavior. Employees who display sudden shifts in behavior may be attempting to reduce such dissonance. Some employees find the conflicts between strongly held attitudes and required work behavior so uncomfortable that they leave the organization to escape the dissonance.

Employees can also experience ambivalence in organizations.[6] Ambivalence refers to a positive **and** negative orientation toward an object, a task, people, or the work environment. The difference between dissonance and ambivalence is that dissonance creates a conflict because there is an attitude to behavior disconnect, whereas ambivalence involves both favorable and unfavorable attitudes towards the same object. Consider Tesla, for example. An employee at Tesla might work there because they have a favorable attitude towards the company's commitment to electric vehicles and innovation. The same employee might have an unfavorable attitude towards the company when their CEO, Elon Musk, is in the news for disruptive behavior or there are widespread recalls of Teslas. The employee then experiences ambivalence towards their employer.

Interestingly, when people experience intense ambivalence, it is uncomfortable, just as in cognitive dissonance. They typically try to resolve the ambivalence in a variety of ways, but the science on this is rather scarce. Some authors suggest that being comfortable with ambivalence and accepting it is a mark of wisdom.

4-2 Attitude Formation

Attitudes are learned. Our responses to people and issues evolve over time. Two major influences on attitudes are direct experience and social learning.

Direct experience with something strongly influences attitudes toward it. How do you know that you like biology or dislike math? You have probably formed these attitudes from experience studying the subjects. Research has shown that attitudes derived from direct experience are stronger, held more confidently, and more resistant to change than attitudes formed through indirect experience.[7] These attitudes are powerful because of their availability; they are easily accessed and active in our cognitive processes.[8] When attitudes are available, we can call them quickly into consciousness.

cognitive dissonance A state of tension produced when an individual experiences conflict between attitudes and behavior.

In **social learning**, the family, peer groups, religious organizations, and culture shape an individual's attitudes indirectly.[9] Children adopt certain attitudes when their parents reinforce attitudes they approve. This is evident from the fact that very young children express political preferences similar to those held by their parents. Later, peer pressure molds attitudes through group acceptance of individuals who express popular attitudes and through sanctions, such as exclusion from the group, placed on individuals who espouse unpopular attitudes. Substantial social learning occurs through *modeling*, in which individuals acquire attitudes by observing others. After overhearing other individuals expressing opinions or watching them engage in behaviors that reflect an attitude, the observer adopts the attitude.

Culture also plays a definitive role in attitude development. Consider, for example, the contrast in the North American and European attitudes toward vacation and leisure. The typical vacation in the United States is two weeks. In Europe, longer vacations are the norm. In some countries, *holiday* means everyone taking a month off. The European attitude is that an investment in longer vacations is important to health and performance.

Intriguingly much of our social learning, especially among younger generations, is driven by social media influences such as Twitter, TikTok, and Instagram. Several studies have found that certain types of content and individuals can reliably change users' attitudes about a range of issues. Perhaps that is why being an "influencer" on social media has become big business.[10]

4-2a Attitudes and Behavior

The correspondence between attitude and behavior has concerned organizational behaviorists and social psychologists for quite some time. Can attitudes predict behaviors such as being absent from work or quitting your job? Some studies suggested that they can, because attitudes and behavior are closely linked, while others found no relationship

social learning The process of deriving attitudes from family, peer groups, religious organizations, and culture.

at all. Researchers also focused on when attitudes predict behavior and when they do not. Attitude–behavior correspondence depends on five things: attitude specificity, attitude relevance, timing of measurement, personality factors, and social constraints.

Individuals possess both general and specific attitudes. You may favor a woman's right to reproductive freedom (a general attitude) and prefer pro-choice political candidates (a specific attitude) without attending pro-choice rallies or donating to Planned Parenthood. That you don't perform these behaviors appears to weaken the link between your attitude and behaviors. However, given a choice between a pro-choice and an anti-abortion political candidate, you will probably vote for the pro-choice candidate. In this case, your attitude seems quite predictive of your behavior. The more specific the attitude, the stronger is its link to behavior.[11]

Another factor that affects the attitude–behavior link is relevance.[12] Attitudes that address an issue in which we have some self-interest are more relevant for us, and our subsequent behavior is consistent with our expressed attitude. Consider a proposal to raise income taxes for those earning $150,000 or more. If you are a student, you may not find the issue of great personal relevance. Individuals in that income bracket, however, might find it highly relevant. Their attitude toward the issue would be strongly predictive of whether they would vote for the tax increase.

The timing of the measurement is still another factor affecting attitude–behavior correspondence. The shorter the time is between the attitude measurement and the observed behavior, the stronger the relationship. For example, voter preference polls taken close to an election are more accurate than earlier polls.

Personality factors also influence the attitude–behavior link. One personality disposition that affects the consistency between attitudes and behavior is *self-monitoring*. Recall from the discussion of personality characteristics in Chapter 3 that low self-monitors rely on their internal states when making decisions about behavior, while high self-monitors are more responsive to situational cues. Low self-monitors therefore display greater correspondence between their attitudes and behaviors.[13]

High self-monitors may display little correspondence between their attitudes and behavior because they behave according to signals from others and from the environment.

Finally, *social constraints* affect the relationship between attitudes and behavior.[14] The social context provides information about acceptable attitudes and behaviors.[15] New employees in an organization are exposed to the attitudes of their work group.[16] For example, a new employee might be socialized to observe the attitudes in their work group regarding timeliness or recycling, and follow these norms regardless of their own attitudes on the matter.

4-2b Work Attitudes

Attitudes at work are important because, directly or indirectly, they affect work behavior. Chief among the things that negatively affect employees' work attitudes are demanding jobs over which employees have little control.[17] A study concerned with how to prevent turnover in nursing found that commitment to the profession was one factor, but nurses' attitudes were significantly affected by whether or not they had flexibility in their schedules, could get enough time off, and had opportunities to learn new

skills and advance. A major factor was the tension between patient care and hospital profits. The nurses in this study said that they felt called to make a difference in their patients' lives, but sometimes worried they could not offer patients adequate care and attention due to competing interests.[18] In contrast to the nursing situation in that study, another study found that a positive psychological climate was enough to generate positive attitudes and good performance in various jobs.[19]

4-3 Job Satisfaction

Job satisfaction is a pleasurable or positive emotional state resulting from the appraisal of one's job or job experiences.[20] It has been treated both as a general attitude and as satisfaction with five specific dimensions of the job: pay, the work itself, promotion opportunities, supervision, and coworkers.[21]

An individual may hold different attitudes toward various aspects of a job. For example, an employee may like their job responsibilities but be dissatisfied with the opportunities for promotion. Characteristics of individuals also affect job satisfaction.[22] Those with high negative affectivity are more likely to be

job satisfaction A pleasurable or positive emotional state resulting from the appraisal of one's job or job experiences.

Coworkers can be an important source of satisfaction on the job.

Inclusive Conversations

Work Accommodations and the Job Satisfaction of Workers with Disabilities

What is the impact of receiving a work accommodation on the job satisfaction of workers with disabilities? A recent study examined this question using 596 participants from a variety of national and state agencies that serve individuals with disabilities. According to the Americans with Disabilities Act (ADA), employers have a duty to provide reasonable accommodations for workers with disabilities who can perform the essential functions of the job. The study's researchers examined the effect that psychosocial factors, such as self-efficacy, positive and negative affect, ADA knowledge, workplace support, knowledge of accommodations, and work goals had on workers receiving an ADA accommodation and whether receiving that accommodation would result in increased job satisfaction and performance. Of the psychosocial factors the researchers examined, only worker support was found to affect whether disabled employees received accommodations and whether receipt of accommodations had an impact on job satisfaction and performance. The bottom line… It is important that disabled workers have an inclusive and supportive environment to receive the accommodations they require and for those accommodations to improve their satisfaction and job performance.

1. Workplace support was identified by this study as important for the job satisfaction of workers with disabilities. Can you identify other individual or organizational factors that might also have a positive effect on job satisfaction of disabled workers?

2. Why do you believe having knowledge of the ADA had no impact on employees with disabilities receiving an accommodation?

Source: Dong, S., Eto, O., Liu, L, & Villaquiran, A. (2023, January). *Work*. 1-13.

dissatisfied with their jobs. Challenging work, valued rewards, opportunities for advancement, competent supervision, and supportive coworkers are dimensions of the job that can lead to satisfaction. What may surprise you is that pay is only marginally related to job satisfaction. Well-paid individuals are only slightly more satisfied than relatively poorly paid individuals.[23]

There are several measures of job satisfaction. One of the most widely used measures comes from the *Job Descriptive Index (JDI)*. This index measures the specific facets of satisfaction by asking employees to respond "yes," "no," or "cannot decide" to a series of statements describing their jobs. Another popular measure is the *Minnesota Satisfaction Questionnaire (MSQ)*.[24] This survey also asks employees to respond to statements about their jobs using a five-point scale that ranges from very dissatisfied to very satisfied. Figure 4.1 presents some sample items from each questionnaire.

Managers and employees believe that happy or satisfied employees are more productive at work. Most of us feel more satisfied than usual when we believe that we are performing better than usual.[25]

But research on the relationship between job satisfaction and performance has shown it to be more complex than that. If job satisfaction always improved performance, then the manager's job would simply be to keep workers happy. Although this may be the case for certain individuals, research has shown that job satisfaction for most people is only one of several causes of good performance. Another view holds that good performance causes satisfaction, yet some high performers are not satisfied with their jobs. It is important to consider all of the potential variables when considering job satisfaction.[26]

The lack of a clear relationship between satisfaction and performance can be explained by the intervening role of rewards. Employees who receive valuable rewards are more satisfied. In addition, employees who receive rewards that are contingent on performance (the higher the performance, the larger the reward) tend to perform better. Rewards thus influence both satisfaction and performance. The key to influencing both satisfaction and performance through rewards is that the rewards are valued by employees and are tied directly to performance.

Figure 4.1 Sample Items from Satisfaction Questionnaires

Job Descriptive Index

Think of the work you do at present. How well does each of the following words or phrases describe your work? In the blank beside each word given below, write

_____Y_____ for "Yes" if it describes your work
_____N_____ for "No" if it does NOT describe it
_____?_____ if you cannot decide

WORK ON YOUR PRESENT JOB:

_____ Routine
_____ Satisfying
_____ Good

Think of the majority of the people who you work with now or the people you meet in connection with your work. How well does each of the following words or phrases describe these people? In the blank beside each word, write

_____Y_____ for "Yes" if it describes the people you work with
_____N_____ for "No" if it does NOT describe them
_____?_____ if you cannot decide

COWORKERS (PEOPLE):

_____ Boring
_____ Responsible
_____ Intelligent

Minnesota Satisfaction Questionnaire

1 = Very dissatisfied
2 = Dissatisfied
3 = I can't decide whether I am satisfied or not
4 = Satisfied
5 = Very satisfied

On my present job, this is how I feel about:

_____ The chance to work alone on the job (independence)
_____ My chances for advancement on this job (advancement)
_____ The chance to tell people what to do (authority)
_____ The praise I get for a good job (recognition)
_____ My pay and the amount of work I do (compensation)

Source: The Job Descriptive Index is copyrighted by Bowling Green State University. The complete forms, scoring key, instructions, and norms can be obtained from the JDI Office, Department of Psychology, Bowling Green State University, Bowling Green, OH 43403. Minnesota Satisfaction Questionnaire from D. J. Weiss, R. V. Davis, G. W. England, and L. H. Lofquist, *Manual for the Minnesota Satisfaction Questionnaire* (University of Minnesota Vocational Psychology Research, 1967).

4-4 Organizational Citizenship Versus Counterproductive Work Behavior

Job satisfaction encourages **organizational citizenship behavior (OCB)**—behavior that is above and beyond the call of duty. Satisfied employees are more likely to help their coworkers, make positive comments about the company, and refrain from complaining when things at work go poorly.[27] Going beyond the call of duty is especially important to organizations using teams, as employees in teams depend on extra help from each other to get things accomplished.

Satisfied workers are more likely to want to give something back to the organization—that is, to engage in OCBs because they want to reciprocate their positive experiences.[28] Often, employees may feel that their OCBs are not recognized because they

organizational citizenship behavior (OCB) Behavior that is above and beyond the call of duty.

YOU

Assess Your Job Satisfaction

Think of the job you have now or a job you've had in the past. Indicate how satisfied you are with each aspect of your job below, using the following scale:

1 = Extremely dissatisfied
2 = Dissatisfied
3 = Slightly dissatisfied
4 = Neutral
5 = Slightly satisfied
6 = Satisfied
7 = Extremely satisfied

1. The amount of job security I have.
2. The amount of pay and fringe benefits I receive.
3. The amount of personal growth and development I get in doing my job.
4. The people I talk to and work with on my job.
5. The degree of respect and fair treatment I receive from my boss.
6. The feeling of worthwhile accomplishment I get from doing my job.
7. The chance to get to know other people while on the job.
8. The amount of support and guidance I receive from my supervisor.
9. The degree to which I am fairly paid for what I contribute to this organization.
10. The amount of independent thought and action I can exercise in my job.
11. How secure things look for me in the future in this organization.
12. The chance to help other people while at work.
13. The amount of challenge in my job.

14. The overall quality of the supervision I receive on my work.

Now compute your scores for the facets of job satisfaction.

Pay satisfaction:

Q2 + Q9 = Divided by 2

Security satisfaction:

Q1 + Q1 = Divided by 2

Social satisfaction:

Q4 + Q7 + Q12 = Divided by 3

Supervisory satisfaction:

Q5 + Q8 + Q14 = Divided by 3

Growth satisfaction:

Q3 + Q6 + Q10 + Q13 = Divided by 4

Scores on the facets range from 1 to 7. (Scores lower than 4 suggest there is room for change.)

This questionnaire is an abbreviated version of the Job Diagnostic Survey, a widely used tool for assessing individuals' attitudes about their jobs. Compare your scores on each facet with the following norms for a large sample of managers.

Pay satisfaction:	4.6
Security satisfaction:	5.2
Social satisfaction:	5.6
Supervisory satisfaction:	5.2
Growth satisfaction:	5.3

How do your scores compare? Are there actions you can take to improve your job satisfaction?

Source: J. R. Hackman and G. R. Oldman, *Work Redesign* (Upper Saddle River, NJ: Pearson Education, Inc., 1980).

occur outside the confines of normal job responsibilities, but they do indeed influence performance evaluations. Employees who help others, suggest innovations, and develop their skills receive higher performance ratings.[29]

OCBs can be directed at different facets of an organization, determined according to individual attitudes. For example, affect tends to direct OCBs toward other people, while cognition directs OCBs toward the organization.

Performing OCBs at work has multiple benefits for employees. OCBs help individuals see their work as more meaningful and promote employee well-being. You might think that performing these extra behaviors depletes employees' energy. Research shows the opposite—that OCBs actually enhance employee energy and vigor.[30]

When OCBs are the norm within a team, members are more likely to engage in OCBs. The impact of one person's OCB can spread throughout an entire team and spill over into the organization.[31] It should be recognized, though, that employees who over-engage in OCBs can become exhausted because of the toll it takes on their personal energy resources.[32] Organizations can help individuals avoid fatigue and exhaustion from OCBs by providing a supportive environment, encouraging strong team-work, and by not pressuring employees for OCBs.[33] The impact of one worker's OCBs can thus spread throughout an entire department.

Researchers have found a strong link between job satisfaction and organizational performance, although, as mentioned earlier, the relationship between the two factors is more complex than one might think. Nevertheless, overall, companies with satisfied workers have better performance than companies with dissatisfied workers.[34] This may be due to the more intangible elements of performance, such as OCB, that contribute to organizational effectiveness but aren't necessarily captured by measuring individual job performance.

Job satisfaction connects to other important outcomes. Dissatisfied workers are more likely to skip work and quit their jobs, driving up the cost of turnover. Furthermore, dissatisfied workers report more psychological and medical problems than do satisfied employees.[35]

One factor that leads to dissatisfaction at work is a misfit between an individual's values and the organization's values, or a lack of *person–organization fit*. People who feel that their values don't mesh with the organization's values experience job dissatisfaction and eventually leave the organization.[36]

Like all attitudes, job satisfaction is influenced by culture. A recent study of job satisfaction rates in forty-nine countries found a close link between job characteristics and job satisfaction in countries with higher incomes, higher individualism, and lower power distance than in countries with lower incomes, lower individualism (higher collectivism), and higher power distance.[37] As employees from different cultures may have differing job expectations, there may be no single prescription for increasing the job satisfaction of a multicultural workforce. Researchers found in China's hotel and restaurant industry that high-performance human resource practices such as promotions from within, flexible job assignments, long-term results-oriented appraisals, and job security fostered service-oriented OCBs. Such OCBs were in turn linked to lower turnover and higher productivity at the organizational level.[38]

Nature Improves Work Attitudes

Managers who want to improve employees' job satisfaction and organizational commitment may want to redesign their workplaces. Research has shown that exposure to nature and being in sunlight while at work improved work attitudes, and even indirect sunlight boosted employees' moods at work. Natural elements in the workplace can be views out of windows, office plants, or simple things such as nature scenes as art or screen savers.

Amazon is bringing nature to downtown Seattle by constructing Spheres, which use natural elements to inspire employees. The spheres will be filled with botanical gardens and tree canopies three stories high, along with indoor creeks. Employees will be able to hold meetings, take breaks, and eat lunch in the spheres, and hopefully come up with more creative ideas.

David Ryder/Getty Images News/Getty Images

Source: M. An, S. M. Colarelli, K. O'Brien, and M. E. Boyajian, "Why We Need More Nature at Work: Effects of Natural Elements and Sunlight on Employee Mental Health and Work Attitudes," *PLOS One*, May 2016, http://journals.plos.org/plosone/article?id=10.1371/journal.pone.0155614; N. Wingfield, "Forget Beanbag Chairs. Amazon Is Giving Its Workers Treehouses," *New York Times*, July 10, 2016, https://www.nytimes.com/2016/07/11/technology/forget-beanbag-chairs-amazon-is-giving-its-workers-treehouses.html.

When employees are dissatisfied with their jobs, they are more likely to engage in **counterproductive work behavior (CWB)**, which is defined as any voluntary, attitude-driven behavior that violates organizational norms and causes some degree of harm to the organization, coworkers, or supervisors.[39] CWB can include calling in sick when you're not, coming in late, putting little effort into your work, taking property from work without permission, gossiping about others, and sabotaging others' projects. Negative events in the business world, such as downsizing and technological insecurities, are generally considered responsible for spikes in counterproductive work behavior. Layoffs, for example, may inspire employees to develop negative attitudes, to feel anger and hostility toward the organization, and to retaliate. Even when an employee keeps their job but believes the procedure used to determine the layoff is unfair, they may still take revenge against the manager. Perceived unfairness at work is a major cause of deviance, sabotage, and retaliation. Managers must prevent and manage CWB to keep it from damaging performance. One way to do that is to encourage positive attitudes among employees by providing a supportive organizational climate. Communicating to employees that their contributions are valued and that the company cares about their well-being can help prevent CWB.[40] While most of research examined CWB at the individual employee level, some research indicates that such CWB at the team or department level can have detrimental effects for team or department outcomes. Team CWB has moderate negative effects on team productivity, turnover, customer satisfaction, and profitability.[41]

counterproductive work behavior Behavior that violates organizational norms and causes harm to the organization and/or employees.

organizational commitment The strength of an individual's identification with an organization.

affective commitment Organizational commitment based on an individual's desire to remain in an organization.

continuance commitment Organizational commitment based on the fact that an individual cannot afford to leave.

normative commitment Organizational commitment based on an individual's perceived obligation to remain with an organization.

4-4a Organizational Commitment and Job Satisfaction

The strength of an individual's identification with an organization is known as **organizational commitment**. There are three kinds of organizational commitment: affective, continuance, and normative. **Affective commitment** is an employee's intention to remain in an organization because of a strong desire to do so. Affective commitment encompasses loyalty and a deep concern for the organization's welfare based on three factors: a belief in the goals and values of the organization, a willingness to put forth effort on behalf of the organization, and a desire to remain a member of the organization.[42]

Continuance commitment is an employee's tendency to remain in an organization because they cannot afford to leave.[43] Sometimes employees believe that they will lose a great deal of their investments in time, effort, and benefits if they leave. **Normative commitment** is a perceived obligation to remain with the organization. Individuals who experience normative commitment stay with the organization because they feel they should.[44]

Certain organizational conditions, such as participation in decision making and job security, encourage commitment. And so do job characteristics such as autonomy, responsibility, role clarity, and interesting work.[45] Affective and normative commitments are related to lower rates of absenteeism, higher quality of work, increased productivity, and overall performance.[46] Managers should encourage affective commitment in particular because committed individuals expend more task-related effort and are less likely to leave the organization.[47]

Managers can increase affective commitment by communicating their appreciation of employees' contributions and concern for employees' well-being.[48] Affective commitment also increases when the organization and employees share the same values and when the organization emphasizes values like moral integrity, fairness, creativity, and openness.[49] Negative experiences at work, such as perceived age discrimination, diminish affective commitment.[50]

Attitudes such as satisfaction and commitment are more important than ever. The COVID-19 global pandemic and a changing work environment has led to record high levels of burnout and disengagement. More and more employees are engaging in "quiet quitting,"

Affective and normative commitments are related to lower rates of absenteeism, higher quality of work, increased productivity, and overall performance. Still, job satisfaction shows the strongest link with performance and turnover. If a manager had to pick one attitude only to focus on, job satisfaction is the most important one!

a term used to describe low morale and lack of productivity. To minimize quiet quitting and improve commitment, managers should focus on recognizing employee differences and foster good work relationships.[51]

4-5 Persuasion and Attitude Change

The days of command-and-control management, in which executives simply told employees what to do, are over. Modern managers must instead aim to change employee attitudes and thus need to be skilled in the art of persuasion.[52] Through persuasion, one individual (the source) tries to change the attitude of another person (the target) in regard to a certain issue (the message). Certain characteristics of the source, target, and message affect the persuasion process.

4-5a Source Characteristics

Three major characteristics of the source affect persuasion: expertise, trustworthiness, and attractiveness.[53] A source who is perceived as an expert is particularly persuasive. Testimonials, for example, are the third most effective technique in advertising, after corporate responsibility and emotional appeal. Endorsers of a product are effective when they are perceived as trustworthy, attractive, or similar to the consumer, or when they represent an image the consumer would like to adopt.[54]

4-5b Target Characteristics

Individuals with low self-esteem are more likely to change their attitudes in response to persuasion than are individuals with high self-esteem. Individuals who hold very extreme attitudes are more resistant to persuasion, and people who are in a good mood are easier to persuade.[55] Undoubtedly, individuals

differ widely in their responsiveness to persuasion. Managers must recognize these differences and realize that their attempts to change attitudes may not be universally accepted.

4-5c Message Characteristics

Suppose you want to persuade your employees that an unpopular policy is a positive change. Should you present one side of the issue or both sides? Given that your employees are already negatively inclined toward the policy, you will have more success in changing their attitudes if you present both sides. This shows support for one side of the issue while acknowledging that another side does exist. Moreover, refuting the other side rather than ignoring it makes it harder for the targets to hang on to their negative attitudes.

Persuasion is a delicate skill. Undisguised deliberate attempts at changing attitudes may drive employees' attitudes in the opposite direction. This is most likely to occur when the target of the persuasive communication feels their freedom is threatened.[56] Less threatening approaches are less likely to elicit negative reactions. The emotional tone of the message is also important. Messages framed with the same emotion as that felt by the receiver are more persuasive.[57]

4-5d Cognitive Routes to Persuasion

The source, target, and message characteristics are weighed differently in the two cognitive routes to persuasion, the central route and the peripheral route, as shown in the *elaboration likelihood model* of persuasion in Figure 4.2.[58] The routes are differentiated by the amount of elaboration, or scrutiny, that the target is motivated to give to the message.

The *central route* to persuasion involves direct cognitive processing of the message's content. In this route, individuals think carefully about issues that are personally relevant. The listener may nod his head at strong arguments and shake his head at weak ones.[59] Logical and convincing arguments are needed to change attitudes by this route.

In the *peripheral route* to persuasion, the individual is not motivated to pay much attention to the message's content because they are distracted or perceive the message as personally irrelevant. Instead, they are persuaded by characteristics of the persuader such as expertise, trustworthiness, and

Figure 4.2 The Elaboration Likelihood Model of Persuasion

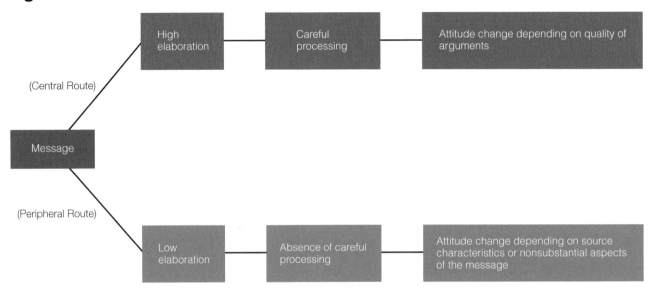

Source: Adapted from R. E. Petty and J. T. Cacioppo, "The Elaboration Likelihood Model of Persuasion," in L. Berkowitz, ed., *Advances in Experimental Social Psychology*, vol. 19 (New York: Academic Press, 1986), 123–205.

attractiveness. The individual may also be persuaded by statistics, the number of arguments presented, or the method of presentation—none of which relate to the actual content of the message.

The elaboration likelihood model shows that the target's level of involvement with the issue is important. That involvement also determines which route to persuasion will be more effective. In some cases, attitude change comes about through both the central and the peripheral routes. To cover all of the bases, managers should structure the content of their messages carefully, develop their own effective persuasive attributes, and choose a method of presentation that will appeal to the audience.[60]

4-6 Emotions and Moods at Work

Emotions are discrete and fairly short-lived feelings that have a specific, known cause. An emotion like anger, for example, may arise because a

emotion a short-lived response to an event or interaction that causes bodily changes and motivates one to act

colleague was rude to you. Or you may feel happy because you got a promotion. *Moods*, on the other hand, are typically classified as positive or negative and are made up of various emotions. Moods typically last longer than emotions and don't have a specific cause. Traditional management theories did not place a premium on studying the effects of employees' moods and emotions because they were thought to be bad for rational decision making at work. Ideas about management centered around the stereotypical ideal employee who kept their emotions in check and behaved in a totally rational, nonemotional manner. Research has proven that emotions and cognitions are intertwined and that both are normal parts of human functioning and decision making.[61]

4-6a Emotions

Emotions (e.g., anger, joy, pride, hostility) are short-lived, intense reactions to an event. Employees have to cope with both positive and negative events at work on a daily basis, and these events, in turn, lead to emotions. When events at work are positive and goals are being met, employees experience positive emotions. But when events at work are perceived as negative, the opposite can be true.[62] It is helpful to think of emotions as signals. When you experience positive outcomes, it is like a green light at a traffic stop, signaling "keep going." When obstacles arise, it is similar to a red light or negative emotions, which are signals to stop, carefully assess the environment, and then move forward. In most Western cultures, we are socialized to seek positive emotions and avoid negative emotions. In reality, this is almost impossible to do. Can you imagine driving through a busy intersection with no stop signs or traffic signals? It would be complete chaos and quite dangerous. Emotions, in turn, impact both work attitudes and work behaviors.

Positive emotions are related to better cognitive functioning, physical and psychological health, and coping mechanisms.[63] They are linked with organizational outcomes such as creativity, health, teamwork, leadership, and job performance.[64] Individuals differ in their capacity to experience both positive emotions (e.g., happiness, pride) and negative emotions (e.g., anger, fear, guilt).[65] This trait-like capacity, also known as positive affectivity, leads to repeated experiences of positive emotions whereas trait negative affectivity is related to the tendency to experience more negative emotions.[66] Overall, people who experience more positive emotions than negative emotions are more successful across a variety of life domains and report higher life satisfaction. An unbalanced occurrence of negative emotions, on the other hand, leads to unhealthy coping behaviors and lowered cardiovascular function and physical health.[67]

When one is satisfied with their job, it is possible that they experience more positive emotions such as gratitude for good coworkers, supervisors, or meaningful work. Work could spark feelings of curiosity or interest, and may relate to satisfaction with the work itself.[68]

4-6b Moods

Moods are feeling states that are more enduring than emotions and have no clear cause. Moods are one level above emotions since they are made up of a variety of emotions. Individuals experiencing a strongly positive mood at work feel excited, enthusiastic, and peppy, while individuals experiencing a less positive mood feel dull and sluggish. Individuals experiencing a negative mood at work feel distressed, hostile, or jittery, while those experiencing a less negative mood are calm and relaxed.[69]

Positive moods at work lead to better work performance and OCBs and decrease counterproductive work behavior. Positive moods at work lead to better work performance and more OCBs, whereas negative moods lead to absenteeism and turnover intentions.[70] Awareness of whether you are a morning person or an evening person in terms of your energy can allow you to better regulate your mood. Individuals are more energetic at their preferred times of day, and in better moods.

4-6c Emotional Contagion at Work

Intuitively, it is easy to see that emotions influence workplace behavior. They drive employee decision making, stock markets, and are even used as a manipulative tool to ensure desired outcomes from conflicts or negotiations.[71] The influence of emotion at work is extended by **emotional contagion**, which is the dynamic process through which emotions are transferred from one person to another, either consciously or unconsciously, through nonverbal channels. Emotions serve as social information. We infer information about an individual's intent, attitudes, and behaviors from their emotion expressions.[72]

Emotions need to be managed at work because they spread easily. Emotional contagion occurs primarily through nonverbal cues and the basic human tendency to mimic each other's facial expressions, body language, speech patterns, vocal tones, and even emotions. Contagion affects any job involving interpersonal or virtual interactions. Positive emotions that travel through a work group due to emotional contagion produce cooperation and task performance.[73]

When organizations and their employees experience change and/or huge losses, they may struggle to recover. Good leaders can help by using compassion to heal and rebuild employee morale.[74] Organizations need to give employees a comfortable place to share their mutual grief and trauma.

emotional contagion A dynamic process through which the emotions of one person are transferred to another, either consciously or unconsciously, through nonverbal channels.

These issues can be resolved by caring leaders who are willing to share their emotions with employees. Such emotional contagion can create emotional climate as well. The collective, shared emotions such as fear, anxiety, or sadness create toxic emotional climates, whereas collective shared emotions of compassion, elevation, awe, inspiration, and empathy can create positive, nurturing work climates. For example, in early 2020 when the COVID-19 pandemic first began and people were in lockdown, the usage of social media for garnering health information peaked. This usage of social media to gain medical information has been labeled an infodemic by some and caused heightened panic, fear, and anxiety for users.[75]

4-6d Emotional Intelligence

Emotional intelligence (EI) is the ability to recognize and manage emotion in oneself and in others. EI is made up of several types of abilities: perceiving, understanding, facilitating, and regulating emotion.[76] This type of intelligence is thought to be an important ability for many types of jobs and to be a fundamental aspect of leadership. EI seems to facilitate job performance in a sequential fashion. Having the ability to perceive emotions allows one to better understand emotions, which then increases emotion regulation. Being able to regulate your emotion, in turn, helps as you display appropriate emotions in the workplace, which allows you to perform better at work.

Although self-report measures are often used to measure EI, they are not always accurate, since individuals do not always have a good perspective as to their own abilities. Studies indicate that colleagues are quite accurate in rating an individual's emotional intelligence. Whereas others tend to rate us on our behavior, we tend to rate ourselves on our intentions.[77]

4-6e Emotional Labor

It is clear that moods and emotions impact employees and organizations a great deal. Positive moods and emotions bring about positive outcomes. This can be particularly true for highly interpersonal jobs like customer service representatives, flight attendants, and, oftentimes, professors, who are expected to express positive emotions and suppress any anger or hostility they may be feeling. *Emotional labor* is the work that employees do to control their feelings and expression of emotions in the workplace and is a type of emotion regulation.[78]

Often organizations have specific rules regarding emotional expression called *display rules*. There are two primary types of emotional labor used to meet these display rules: deep acting and surface acting. *Deep acting* involves attempting to feel the emotion one is displaying. Picturing a beautiful mountain vista or thinking about a pleasant memory are examples of deep acting. *Surface acting* is faking an emotion to meet the display rules. Surface acting causes *emotional dissonance*, or a discrepancy between one's felt emotion and one's expressed emotion. Surface acting can result in negative outcomes such as burnout, negative mood, and work withdrawal. Deep acting, in general, seems to have positive consequences and has been related to positive mood at work as well as high-quality customer service performance and reduced burnout.[79,79a]

4.6f Emotion Regulation

We now understand that emotions are a part of the work experience. Much like our thoughts about various aspects of the work environment (e.g., supervisor, coworkers, deadlines), we cannot ask employees to leave their feelings at the door. So, what can managers do with employee emotions and what can employees themselves do with it? Emotional intelligence, as discussed earlier, is an ability that helps us manage and regulate emotions. It is trait-like and thus a somewhat stable characteristic. Emotion regulation refers to specific strategies that can be used to manage emotions and is associated with a variety of positive outcomes at work and in life.[80]

We can each down-regulate (minimize) our negative emotion experiences through either an antecedent focus or a response focus—the former refers to attempts to alter the cause of the emotion while the latter focuses on how to change the emotion response itself. For example, you might feel angered by a coworker who insults you. By adopting an antecedent focus, you can try to reinterpret the insult as a growth opportunity (cognitive reappraisal), or you can choose to avoid interacting with this coworker (situation modification). If neither is practically feasible, you might choose to disengage from the anger by going on a walk or watching your favorite show on Netflix (disengagement), or you might choose to completely suppress the felt anger and not express it to anyone (suppression). The same strategies can be used by managers to regulate the negative emotions of their employees. When emotion regulation is used in this way to minimize another person's negative emotions, it is known as interpersonal emotional management strategies or IEMS.

In general, antecedent-focused emotion regulation is effective as IEMS but the response-focused strategies can backfire and lead to poorer quality interpersonal relationships.[81,81a]

4-7 Ethical Behavior

Ethics is the study of moral values and moral behavior. **Ethical behavior** involves acting in ways consistent with one's personal values and the commonly held values of the organization and society.[82] Paying attention to ethical issues pays off for companies. In the early 1990s, James Burke, then CEO of Johnson & Johnson, put together a list of companies committed to ethics. The group included Johnson & Johnson, Coca-Cola, Gerber, Kodak, 3M, and Pitney Bowes. A recent study showed that over a forty-year period, the market value of these organizations grew at an annual rate of 11.3 percent, as compared to 6.2 percent for the Dow Jones industrials as a whole.[83] Doing the right thing can have a positive effect on an organization's performance.[84]

Ethical behavior in firms can also lead to practical benefits, particularly by attracting new talent. Firms with better reputations attract more applicants, creating a larger hiring pool, and evidence suggests that respected firms can choose higher-quality applicants.[85] For example, Timberland's strong value system helps the company attract and recruit the best talent and maintain a solid reputation with investors.

Failure to handle situations ethically can hurt companies. Employees who are laid off or terminated are very concerned about the quality of treatment they receive. Honestly explaining the reasons for the dismissal and preserving the dignity of the employee will reduce the likelihood of employees

initiating a claim against the company. One study showed that less than 1 percent of employees who felt the company was being honest filed a claim. More than 17 percent of those who felt the company was being less than honest filed claims.[86] Conversely, ethical actions can be a boon to organizations. Australia's former prime minister, Kevin Rudd, apologized publicly for the ill treatment of Aborigines on the part of the national government. Even before the issue of financial compensation was addressed, this action built trust and hope among Australians of all races.[87]

Unethical behavior by employees can affect individuals, work teams, and even the organization. Organizations thus depend on individuals to act ethically. For this reason, more and more firms are starting to monitor their employees' Internet usage. Although some employees complain that this monitoring violates their privacy, the courts tend to disagree, arguing that companies have the right to monitor employees' use of company-owned hardware and software.

Michael Smyth was fired from his job with Pillsbury Company after employees read inflammatory comments he made in several e-mails to his supervisor. Smyth sued for wrongful termination, claiming that the firm had violated his right to privacy after telling employees their e-mail would remain confidential. Despite these promises, the court ruled that Smyth had no reasonable expectation of privacy while using the firm's equipment. Further, it said, Smyth's right to privacy was outweighed by the firm's need to conduct business in a professional manner. Only future court cases will clarify where a firm's effort to monitor potentially unethical behavior actually violates its own ethical code.[88] Nonetheless, today's high-intensity business environment only increases the need for strong ethics programs.

Managers often struggle to align the ideal of ethical behavior with the reality of everyday business practices. Violations of the public's trust are costly. When Mattel recalled 20.5 million toys that were manufactured in China because they contained

ethical behavior Acting in ways consistent with one's personal values and the commonly held values of the organization and society.

Table 4.2 Ethical Issues from One Week in the Life of *The Wall Street Journal*

1.	Stealing	Taking things that don't belong to you
2.	Lying	Saying things you know aren't true
3.	Fraud and deceit	Creating or perpetuating false impressions
4.	Conflict of interest and influence buying	Bribes, payoffs, and kickbacks
5.	Hiding or divulging information	Concealing information that another party has a right to know or failing to protect personal or proprietary information
6.	Cheating	Taking unfair advantage of a situation
7.	Personal decadence	Aiming below excellence in terms of work performance (e.g., careless or sloppy work)
8.	Interpersonal abuse	Behaviors that are abusive of others (e.g., sexism, racism, emotional abuse)
9.	Organizational abuse	Organizational practices that abuse members (e.g., inequitable compensation, misuses of power)
10.	Rule violations	Breaking organizational rules
11.	Accessory to unethical acts	Knowing about unethical behavior and failing to report it
12.	Ethical dilemmas	Choosing between two equally desirable or undesirable options

Source: Kluwer Academic Publishers and Journal of Business Ethics, 11, 1992, 255–265, A Menu of Moral Issues: One Week in the Life of The Wall Street Journal, J. O. Cherrington and D. J. Cherrington.

lead, its public image suffered greatly. The company attempted to undo the damages through a national advertising campaign.[89] Firms can experience lower accounting returns and slow sales growth for as long as five years after having been convicted of illegal corporate behavior.[90]

Individuals face complex ethical issues at work. A one-week review of *The Wall Street Journal* revealed more than sixty articles dealing with ethical issues in business.[91] As Table 4.2 suggests, few of these issues are clear-cut. They depend on the specifics of the situation, and their interpretation depends on the characteristics of the individuals examining them. Consider lying, for instance. Many business people tell white lies. Is this acceptable? The perception of what constitutes ethical versus unethical behavior in organizations varies among individuals.

4-8 Factors that Affect Ethical Behavior

Two sets of factors—individual characteristics and organizational factors—influence ethical behavior.[92] In this section, we'll look at the individual influences

on ethical behavior. Ethical decision making requires three qualities of individuals[93]:

1. The competence to identify ethical issues and evaluate the consequences of alternative courses of action.

2. The self-confidence to seek out different opinions about the issue and decide what is right in terms of a particular situation.

3. Tough-mindedness—the willingness to make decisions when all that needs to be known cannot be known and when the ethical issue has no established, unambiguous solution.

4. The capacity to experience moral emotions, such as guilt, anger, sympathy, elevation, shame, gratitude, disgust, or contempt, is fundamental to acting ethically. In fact, if a person cannot feel these emotions, they will be less likely to do the right thing.[94,94a]

Which individual characteristics lead to these qualities? According to our model, they are value systems, locus of control, Machiavellianism, and cognitive moral development. Figure 4.3 illustrates these, as well as the organizational

Hot Trend

Values Alignment Pays Off in Creativity and Innovation

We all know that when employees and their employers' values align, it is easier to encourage ethical behaviors and avoid unethical behaviors in organizations. But does such an alignment and subsequent ethical behaviors help or hurt creativity? For example, we often hear stories about how the most creative people are rule breakers. A recent study shows this does not always hold true.

Research shows that *value alignment* between employees and employers could create a psychologically safe workplace, which in turn can encourage them to think in morally imaginative ways. Patagonia's employees created emission free clothing from recycled plastic materials due to such values alignment. The study suggests that employers could encourage work moralization—that is incorporating moral or ethical considerations in one's work. Such work moralization stems from repeated experience of moral dilemmas, which encourage high level divergent thinking. This type of divergent thinking in turn can turn on the creative process. Work moralization can lead to innovations such as the three-pronged seat belt used by the Volvo company, or electric vehicle makers' concerns for the environment.

Source: Kundro, T. G. (2023). The benefits and burdens of work moralization on creativity. *Academy of Management Journal*, 66(4), 1183–1208.

influences, which we will examine throughout the remainder of the book.

4-8a Values

Different values generate different ethical behaviors. **Values** are enduring beliefs that a specific mode of conduct or end state of existence is personally or socially preferable to an opposite or converse mode of conduct or end state of existence.[95] This definition was proposed by Rokeach, an early scholar of human values. As individuals grow and mature, they learn values, although these may change as an individual develops a sense of self. Cultures, societies, and organizations shape values. Parents and other respected role models influence value development by providing guidance about what is right and

> **values** Enduring beliefs that a specific mode of conduct or end state of existence is personally or socially preferable to an opposite or converse mode of conduct or end state of existence.

Figure 4.3 Individual/Organizational Model of Ethical Behavior

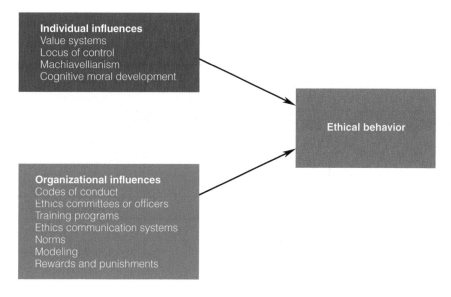

wrong. Like general beliefs about right and wrong, values form the basis for ethical behavior. Though values vary widely among individuals, we use them to evaluate our own behavior and that of others.

Instrumental and Terminal Values Rokeach distinguished between two types of values: instrumental and terminal. Instrumental values shape the acceptable behaviors that can be used to achieve some goal or end state. Instrumental values identified by Rokeach include ambition, honesty, self-sufficiency, and courage. Terminal values influence the goals to be achieved or the end states of existence. Rokeach identified happiness, love, pleasure, self-respect, and freedom among the terminal values. Table 4.3 gives a complete list of instrumental and terminal values. Terminal and instrumental values work in concert by providing individuals with goals to strive for and acceptable ways to achieve those goals.

Americans' rankings of instrumental and terminal values have been remarkably stable over time.[96] The highest ranked instrumental values were honesty, ambition, responsibility, forgiveness,

open-mindedness, and courage. The highest ranked terminal values were world peace, family security, freedom, happiness, self-respect, and wisdom.

Age also affects values. Baby Boomers' values contrast with those of Generation Z (those born after 1996), who are just entering the workforce. This generation is the most technologically savvy, most diverse racially and ethnically, and values societal change and family more so than previous generations did. They are also on track to be the most educated generation yet.[97]

This contrasts with the more driven, work-oriented value system of the boomers. The baby boomers place a huge emphasis on achievement values at work. Their successors in Generations X and Y are markedly different. Generation X values self-reliance, individualism, and balance between family and work life. Generation Y (popularly known as Millennials) values freedom in scheduling and embraces a work-to-live mind-set rather than the live-to-work approach of the baby boomers.[98]

Work Values Work values influence individuals' perceptions of right and wrong on the job.[99] Four work values are achievement, concern for others, honesty, and fairness.[100] *Achievement* is a concern for the advancement of one's career; it drives people to work hard and seek opportunities to develop new skills. *Concern for others* is shown in caring, compassionate behaviors such as encouraging others or helping

instrumental values Values that shape the acceptable behaviors that can be used to achieve some goal or end state.

terminal values Values that influence the goals to be achieved or the end states of existence.

Table 4.3 Instrumental and Terminal Values

Instrumental Values		
Honesty	Ambition	Responsibility
Forgiveness	Open-mindedness	Courage
Helpfulness	Cleanliness	Competence
Self-control	Affection/love	Cheerfulness
Independence	Politeness	Intelligence
Obedience	Rationality	Imagination
Terminal Values		
World peace	Family security	Freedom
Happiness	Self-respect	Wisdom
Equality	Salvation	Prosperity
Achievement	Friendship	National security
Inner peace	Mature love	Social respect
Beauty in art and nature	Pleasure	Exciting, active life

Source: Based on *The Nature of Human Values* by Milton Rokeach.

them with difficult tasks. These behaviors also constitute organizational citizenship. *Honesty* is providing accurate information and refusing to mislead others for personal gain. *Fairness* means remaining impartial while recognizing different points of view.

Individuals rank these values in terms of their relative importance in their work lives.[101] Employees who share their supervisor's values are more satisfied with their jobs and more committed to the organization.[102] Values also have profound effects on job choice. Although traditionally pay and advancement potential have had the strongest influences on job choice decisions, one study found that three other work values—achievement, concern for others, and fairness—had greater influence.[103] This means that organizations recruiting job candidates should pay careful attention to individuals' values and to the messages their organizations send about company values.

Cultural Differences in Values Organizations facing the challenges of an increasingly diverse workforce and a global marketplace must understand culture's influence on values. Doing business in a global marketplace often means encountering a clash of values among different cultures. Consider loyalty, for example. In Japan, loyalty means "compassionate overtime." Even when you have no work yourself, you should stay late to provide moral support for your peers who are working late.[104] In contrast, Koreans value loyalty to the person for whom one works.[105] In the United States, family and other personal loyalties are held above loyalty to the company or one's supervisor.

Cultures differ in the individual contributions they value at work. Collectivist cultures like China and Mexico value a person's contributions to relationships in the work team. By contrast, individualist cultures (the United States, the Netherlands) value a person's contribution to task accomplishment. Both collectivist and individualist cultures, however, value rewards based on individual performance.[106] Iran's collectivist managers demonstrate little tolerance for ambiguity, high need for structure, and willingness to sacrifice for the good of society—all values they derive from Islam, which promotes belonging, harmony, humility, and simplicity.[107]

Values also affect individuals' views of what constitutes authority. French managers value authority as a right of office and rank. Their behavior reflects this value, as they tend to exercise power based on their position in the organization. By contrast, managers from the Netherlands value group inputs to decisions and expect employees to challenge and discuss their decisions.[108]

We may be prone to judging the value systems of others, but we should resist this tendency. Tolerating

Organizational Example

A L'Oréal Chemist Creates Makeup for Women of Color

Diversity, Equity, and Inclusion (DEI) have become central work values in the world of business. One company that has created quite a buzz for its efforts to produce inclusive makeup products is L'Oréal Paris. The global cosmetics industry is valued at $197 billion and growing at a rate of 4% each year. Back in 2014, even before DEI efforts became front and center, the company's new market sales (anything outside the United States and Western Europe) totaled 39.6% of its overall sales. L'Oréal Paris realized then that the global market for makeup, particularly for women of color, needs to be addressed. They created a women of color makeup lab. Yet, many of the products being developed did not resonate in tests of these products with women customers.

Balanda Atis, a chemist in the company's mascara lab, took it upon herself to understand why, as it was a deeply personal issue for her. As a woman who grew up in a Haitian community, she felt most makeup lines made women of color look too red and too dull. She enlisted the help of two scientist friends, and they created a little side project to collect data on which materials work best for darker skin tones. Their research took them across the country and after much testing, the team had a breakthrough when they found a pigment rarely used until then in makeup: ultramarine blue. The newly developed makeup lines for Maybelline and Lancôme—both owned by L'Oréal Paris—included Atis' work and she now heads the women of color lab for the company. Atis' story represents how one's values can create new career paths as well as successful business ventures.

Source: E. Segran, "The Full Spectrum," *Fast Company* 199 (2015): 54–56.

diverse values can help us understand other cultures. The value systems of other nations are not necessarily right or wrong; they are merely different.

4-8b Locus of Control

Another individual influence on ethical behavior is locus of control. Recall from Chapter 3 that individuals with an internal locus of control believe that they control events in their lives and that they are responsible for their own experiences. Those with an external locus of control believe that outside forces such as fate, chance, or other people control what happens to them.[109]

Internals are more likely than externals to take personal responsibility for the consequences of their ethical or unethical behavior. Externals are more apt to believe that external forces caused their ethical or unethical behavior. Research has shown that internals make more ethical decisions than do externals.[110] Internals also are more resistant to social pressure and are less willing to hurt another person even if ordered to do so by an authority figure.[111]

4-8c Machiavellianism

Machiavellianism also influences ethical behavior. Niccolò Machiavelli was a sixteenth-century Italian statesman famous for writing *The Prince*, a guide for acquiring and using power.[112] He suggested that manipulating others was the best way to achieve power. **Machiavellianism**, then, is a personality characteristic involving one's willingness to do whatever it takes to get one's own way.

A high-Mach individual operates from the notion that it is better to be feared than loved. High-Machs tend to be deceitful, have a cynical view of human nature, and care little for conventional notions of right and wrong.[113] They are skilled manipulators, relying on their persuasive abilities. Low-Machs, in contrast, value loyalty and relationships. They are less willing to manipulate others for personal gain and are concerned with others' opinions.

Machiavellianism A personality characteristic involving one's willingness to do whatever it takes to get one's own way.

cognitive moral development The process of moving through stages of maturity with regard to making ethical decisions.

"The first method for estimating the intelligence of a ruler is to look at the men he has around him."
—Niccolo Machiavelli
(1469–1527)
The Prince

High-Machs believe that the desired ends justify any means, so they feel it's fine to manipulate others in order to achieve a goal.[114] They are emotionally detached from other people and focus on the objective aspects of situations. High-Machs are also more likely to engage in ethically questionable behavior.[115] Employees can counter Machiavellian individuals by focusing on teamwork instead of one-on-one relationships where high-Machs have the upper hand. Making interpersonal agreements public reduces their susceptibility to Machiavellian manipulation.

4-8d Cognitive Moral Development

An individual's level of **cognitive moral development** also affects ethical behavior. Psychologist Lawrence Kohlberg proposed that as individuals mature, they move through a series of six stages of moral development (Table 4.4).[116] With each successive stage, they become less dependent on other people's opinions of right and wrong and less self-centered

Table 4.4 Kohlberg's Stages of Cognitive Moral Development

Level I	Premoral	Reward, punishment, self-interest
Level II	Conventional	Expectations of other people and society
Level III	Principled	Universal values and personal ethical principles

(focusing less on their own interests). At higher levels of moral development, individuals are concerned with broad principles of justice and with their self-chosen ethical principles. Kohlberg's model focuses on the decision-making process and on how individuals justify ethical decisions. His cognitive developmental theory explains how people decide what is right and wrong and how the decision-making process changes through interaction with peers and the environment.

Cognitive moral development occurs at three levels, each consisting of two stages. At Level I, called the *premoral level*, a person's ethical decisions are based on rewards, punishments, and self-interest. In Stage 1, people obey rules to avoid punishment. In Stage 2, people obey rules only if it is in their immediate interest to do so.

At Level II, the *conventional level*, people focus on the expectations of others. In Stage 3, individuals try to live up to the expectations of people close to them. In Stage 4, they broaden their perspective to include the laws and norms of the larger society. They fulfill duties and obligations to contribute to society.

At Level III, the *principled level*, universal values determine what is right. The individual sees beyond laws, rules, and the expectations of other people. In Stage 5, individuals are aware that people have diverse value systems. They uphold their own values even if others disagree. Individuals in Stage 5 make decisions based on principles of justice and rights. For example, someone who decides to picket an abortion clinic just because their religion bans abortion is not a Stage 5 individual. A person who arrives at the same decision through a complex decision process based on justice and rights may be a Stage 5 individual. The key is the process rather than the decision itself. In Stage 6, the individual follows self-selected ethical principles. Stage 6 individuals act according to their own

self-selected ethical principles, even when these principles conflict with a law.

As individuals mature, their moral development passes through these stages in an irreversible sequence. Research suggests that most adults are in Stage 3 or 4. Most adults thus never reach the principled level of development (Stages 5 and 6).

Kohlberg's model of cognitive moral development has been supported by a great deal of research since it was proposed more than thirty years ago. Individuals at higher stages of development are less likely to cheat, more likely to engage in whistle-blowing, and more likely to make ethical business decisions.[117]

But Kohlberg's model has also been criticized. Carol Gilligan, for example, argues that the model does not take gender differences into account. Kohlberg's model was developed from a twenty-year study of eighty-four boys.[118] Gilligan contends that women's moral development follows a different pattern, one based not on individual rights and rules but on responsibility and relationships. Women and men face the same moral dilemmas but approach them from different perspectives—men from the perspective of equal respect and women from the perspective of compassion and care. But researchers who reviewed the research on these gender differences concluded that the differences may not be as strong as Gilligan originally suggested.[119]

In general, though, evidence supports the idea that men and women view ethics differently. A large-scale review of sixty-six studies found that women were more likely than men to perceive certain business practices as unethical. Young women were more likely than young men to see breaking the rules and acting on insider information as unethical. Both men and women agreed that collusion, conflicts of interest, and stealing are unethical. It takes about twenty-one years for this gender gap to disappear. Men seem to become more ethical with more work experience; the longer they are in the workforce, the more their attitudes resemble those held by women. That said, age and experience are related for both genders. Experienced workers of either gender are more likely to think that lying, bribing, stealing, and colluding are unethical.[120]

Individual differences in values, locus of control, Machiavellianism, and cognitive moral development all influence ethical behavior in organizations.

Organizations might use this knowledge to promote ethical behavior by hiring individuals who share the organization's values or hiring only internals, low-Machs, and individuals at higher stages of cognitive moral development. Such strategies, however, obviously present both practical and legal problems.

Training may be a safer way to use this knowledge. Evidence suggests that training can increase cognitive moral development. Organizations could help individuals move to higher stages of moral development by providing educational seminars. That said, values, locus of control, Machiavellianism, and cognitive moral development are fairly stable in adults.

The best way to use the knowledge of individual differences may be to recognize that they help explain why ethical behavior differs among individuals and to focus managerial efforts on creating a work situation supporting ethical behavior.

Most workers are responsive to external influences. They do not act as independent ethical agents but look to their organization for guidance. Managers can offer such guidance by exercising the organizational influences listed in Figure 4.3. They can encourage ethical behavior through codes of conduct, ethics committees, ethics communication systems, training, norms, modeling, and rewards and punishments, as shown in Figure 4.3. We discuss these areas further in Chapter 16.

Experiential Exercise

Chinese, Indian, and American Values

Purpose: To learn some differences among Chinese, Indian, and American value systems.

Group size: Any number of groups of five to eight people.

Time required: 50+ minutes

Exercise Schedule

1. **Complete rankings (preclass)**

   Students rank the fifteen values either for Chinese and American orientations or for Indian and American systems. If time permits, all three can be done.

	Unit time	Total time
2. **Small groups (optional)**	15 min	15 min

   Groups of five to eight members try to achieve consensus on the ranking values for Chinese and American cultures.

3. **Group presentations (optional)**	15 min	30 min

   Each group presents its rankings and discusses reasons for making those decisions.

4. **Discussion**	20 min	50 min

   Instructor leads a discussion on the differences between Chinese and American value systems and presents the correct rankings.

Value Rankings

Rank each of the fifteen values below according to what you think they are in the Chinese, Indian (from India), and American cultures. Use "1" as the most important value for the culture and "15" as the least important value for that culture.

Value	American	Chinese	**Indian**
Achievement			
Deference			
Order			
Exhibition			
Autonomy			
Affiliation			
Passion			
Supporting			
Dominance			
Humility			
Nurturing			
Change			
Achievement			
Deference			
Order			
Exhibition			
Endurance			
Heterosexuality			
Aggression			

Some Definitions

Intraception: The tendency to be governed by subjective factors, such as feelings, fantasies, speculations, and aspirations; the other side of extraception, where one is governed by concrete, clearly observable physical conditions.

Succorance: Willingness to help another or to offer relief.

Abasement: To lower oneself in rank, prestige, or esteem.

Internal/External Locus of Control

Consider American and Chinese groups. Which would tend to have more internal locus of control (tendency to feel in control of one's destiny, that rewards come as a result of hard work, perseverance, and responsibility)? Which would be more external (fate, luck, or other outside forces control destiny)?

Machiavellianism

This concept was defined by Christie and Geis as the belief that one can manipulate and deceive people for personal gain. Do you think Americans or Chinese would score higher on the Machiavellian scale?

Discussion Questions

1. What are some main differences among the cultures? Did any pattern emerge?
2. Were you surprised by the results?
3. What behaviors could you expect in business dealings with Chinese (or Indians) based on their value system?
4. How do American values dictate Americans' behaviors in business situations?

Source: "Chinese, Indian, and American Values" by Dorothy Marcic, copyright 1993. Adapted from Michael Harris Bond, ed., *The Psychology of the Chinese People*, Hong Kong: Oxford University Press, 200 Madison Ave., NY 10016, 1986. The selection used here is a portion of "Chinese Personality and Its Change," by Kuo-Shu Yang, pp. 106–170.

Learning Objectives

4-1 Explain the ABC model of an attitude. Attitudes are closely linked to behavior and are an integral part of the world of work. Attitudes are a response to an entity (person, object, situation, or issue) on an affective, cognitive, or behavioral basis. People prefer consistency between attitudes and behavior. Disruption causes tension, which motivates individuals to change attitudes or behavior to maintain consistency. The tension produced by a conflict between attitudes and behavior is *cognitive dissonance.*

4-2 Describe how attitudes are formed. Attitudes are learned. Influences on attitudes are direct experience and social learning. Culture also plays a definitive role in attitude development. Attitude–behavior correspondence depends on five things: attitude specificity, attitude relevance, timing of measurement, personality factors, and social constraints. Attitudes affect work behavior. Demanding jobs over which employees have little control negatively affect their work attitudes. A positive psychological climate can generate positive attitudes and good performance.

4-3 Identify sources of job satisfaction and commitment. *Job satisfaction* is a pleasurable or positive emotional state resulting from the appraisal of one's job or job experiences. It has been treated as a general attitude and as satisfaction with five specific dimensions of the job: pay, the work itself, promotion opportunities, supervision, and coworkers. Rewards are key to influencing both job satisfaction and work performance if valued by employees and tied directly to performance.

4-4 Distinguish between organizational citizenship and workplace deviance behaviors. Individuals who identify strongly with the organization are more likely to perform *organizational citizenship behavior*—behavior above and beyond the call of duty. A misfit between an individual's and the organization's values is called a lack of person–organization fit. Dissatisfied workers are likely to skip work and quit jobs. *Workplace deviance behavior* is a result of negative attitudes and consists of counterproductive behavior that violates organizational norms and harms others or the organization.

4-5 Identify the characteristics of the source, target, and message that affect persuasion. Through persuasion, one individual (the source) tries to change the attitude of another person (the target). Three major characteristics of the source affect persuasion: expertise, trustworthiness, and attractiveness. Targets with low self-esteem or in a good mood are easier to persuade. Individuals with extreme attitudes or high self-esteem are more resistant. The elaboration likelihood model proposes that persuasion occurs either through a central route or peripheral route, differentiated by the amount of elaboration, scrutiny, or motivation in the message.

4-6 **Discuss the definition and importance of emotions at work.** Emotions are mental states including feelings, physiological changes, and the inclination to act and are normal parts of human functioning and decision making. Positive emotions that travel through a work group produce cooperation and task performance. The opposite also occurs when negative emotions destroy morale and performance.

4-7 **Contrast the effects of individual and organizational influences on ethical behavior.** *Ethical behavior* is behavior that is consistent with one's personal values and the commonly held values of the organization and society. Firms with better reputations attract more applicants, creating a larger hiring pool, and evidence suggests that respected firms can choose higher-quality applicants. Unethical behavior by employees can affect individuals, work teams, and even the organization.

4-8 **Identify the factors that affect ethical behavior.** Factors that influence an individual's ethical behavior are values, locus of control, *Machiavellianism* (one's willingness to do whatever it takes to get one's own way), and an individual's level of *cognitive moral development*. Organizations can offer guidance by encouraging ethical behavior through codes of conduct, ethics committees, ethics communication systems, training, norms, modeling, and rewards and punishments.

Key Terms

affect The emotional component of an attitude. (p. 68)

affective commitment Organizational commitment based on an individual's desire to remain in an organization. (p. 76)

attitude A psychological tendency expressed by evaluating something with a degree of favor or disfavor. (p. 68)

cognitive dissonance A state of tension produced when an individual experiences conflict between attitudes and behavior. (p. 69)

cognitive moral development The process of moving through stages of maturity with regard to making ethical decisions. (p. 86)

continuance commitment Organizational commitment based on the fact that an individual cannot afford to leave. (p. 76)

counterproductive work behavior Behavior that violates organizational norms and causes harm to the organization and/or employees. (p. 76)

emotional contagion A dynamic process through which the emotions of one person are transferred to another, either consciously or unconsciously, through nonverbal channels. (p. 79)

emotions a short-lived response to an event or interaction that causes bodily changes and motivates one to act. (p. 78)

ethical behavior Acting in ways consistent with one's personal values and the commonly held values of the organization and society. (p. 81)

instrumental values Values that shape the acceptable behaviors that can be used to achieve some goal or end state. (p. 84)

job satisfaction A pleasurable or positive emotional state resulting from the appraisal of one's job or job experiences. (p. 71)

Machiavellianism A personality characteristic involving one's willingness to do whatever it takes to get one's own way. (p. 86)

normative commitment Organizational commitment based on an individual's perceived obligation to remain with an organization. (p. 76)

organizational citizenship behavior (OCB) Behavior that is above and beyond the call of duty. (p. 73)

organizational commitment The strength of an individual's identification with an organization. (p. 76)

social learning The process of deriving attitudes from family, peer groups, religious organizations, and culture. (p. 70)

terminal values Values that influence the goals to be achieved or the end states of existence. (p. 84)

values Enduring beliefs that a specific mode of conduct or end state of existence is personally or socially preferable to an opposite or converse mode of conduct or end state of existence. (p. 83)

Ethical Dilemma

Mina is the director of the customer service division of Advanced Manufacturing. Advanced produces computer components, and effectively servicing customers is crucial to its success. Recently, Mina implemented a new customer service protocol. Since the implementation, customer evaluations have been improving for all the center's employees except for Sally.

Mina is surprised as Sally has worked for Advanced for over five years and has been one of the best employees she has. Mina calls Sally into her office to discuss the problem. Sally is a natural leader of the group and Mina wants to fix this as soon as possible before it begins to affect the other employees.

During the meeting, Mina finds out that Sally really dislikes the new protocol. She thinks it is not client friendly. It seems that Sally's attitude about the protocol is coming across to clients as rudeness. Sally believes that the new system is intrusive and puts the client on the spot to answer questions that should not be asked. She tells Mina that she cannot continue asking what she feels are inappropriate questions of people and if she must, she will have to look for another job.

Mina ends the meeting feeling very conflicted. She feels the protocol is important and helps to get at the client's problem faster and more effectively. But Sally has a right to honor her own values. Mina does not want to lose Sally to another company. If she allows Sally to go back to the old system, what will the other employees think? Will they too want to return to the previous process?

1. Using consequential, rule-based, and character theories, evaluate Mina's options.

2. What should Mina's teammates do? Why?

Erin Clark/Boston Globe/Getty Images

Chapter 5

Motivation and Work

Learning Objectives

5-1 Define motivation and articulate different views of how individuals are motivated at work.

5-2 Explain Maslow's hierarchy of needs and its two main modifications.

5-3 Discuss how the needs for achievement, power, and affiliation influence an individual's behavior in the workplace.

5-4 Describe the two-factor theory of motivation.

5-5 Explain two new ideas in human motivation.

5-6 Describe the role of inequity in motivation.

5-7 Describe the expectancy theory of motivation.

5-8 Describe the cultural differences in motivation.

5-1 Motivation and Work Behavior

Motivation is the process of arousing and sustaining goal-directed behavior. Motivation theories attempt to explain and predict observable behavior. They may be broadly classified into internal, process, and external theories. *Internal theories* of motivation give primary consideration to variables within the individual that lead to motivation and behavior. Maslow's hierarchy of needs is a good example of an internal theory. *Process theories* of motivation, such as expectancy theory, emphasize the nature of the interaction between the individual and the environment. *External theories* of motivation focus on the elements in the environment, including the consequences of behavior, as the basis for understanding and explaining people's behavior at work. A review of motivation related to work over the past century categorized the theories, findings, and advances according to their primary focus on (a) motives and traits (content); (b) features of the job, work role, and work environment (context); and (c) the mechanisms and processes involved in choice and striving (processes).[1] This is the first of three chapters addressing the full set of motivation theories, research, and practice, the other two being Chapters 6 and 14.

5-1a Internal Needs

Philosophers and scholars have theorized for centuries about human needs and motives. During the past century, researchers have focused on motivation in a business context.[2] Max Weber, an early German sociologist, argued that the meaning of work lies not in the work itself but in its deeper potential for contributing to a person's ultimate salvation.[3] Weber, and later Milton Blood, understood this *Protestant ethic*, with its foundations in Calvinist thought, as the fuel for human industriousness. The Protestant ethic encouraged hard work on the grounds that prosperous workers were more likely to find a place in heaven.

Sigmund Freud proposed a more complex motivational theory, suggesting that a person's organizational life was founded on the compulsion to work and the power of love.[4] He emphasized the unconscious mind's influence on human motivation. **Psychoanalysis** is Freud's method for delving into the unconscious mind to better understand a person's motives and needs. Thus, the psychoanalytic approach can help explain irrational and self-destructive behaviors such as suicide or workplace violence.[5] Analyzing a person's unconscious needs and motives can help us understand such traumatic work events. The psychoanalytic approach also helps explain deviant behavior in the workplace.

Freud's thought served as the basis for subsequent *need theories* of motivation. Research suggests that people's deeper feelings transcend culture, with most people caring deeply about the same few things.[6] Factors that make employees motivated and loyal to the organization include fair compensation and the trust and respect of their supervisors. Intrinsic motivation varies by the individual and is positively correlated with some personality traits. For example, an employee who performs a work task for the pure satisfaction of doing so tends to be more conscientious, open to experience, and agreeable the following day.[7] Managers who are more supportive and less controlling appear to elicit more intrinsic motivation from their employees.

5-1b External Incentives

Most economic assumptions about human motivation emphasize financial incentives. The Scottish political economist and moral philosopher Adam Smith argued that a person's **self-interest** was determined by God, not the government.[8] Smith laid the cornerstone for the free enterprise system of economics when he formulated the so-called

> A comprehensive approach to understanding motivation, behavior, and performance must consider all three elements of the work situation and how they interact.

motivation The process of arousing and sustaining goal-directed behavior.

psychoanalysis Sigmund Freud's method for delving into the unconscious mind to better understand a person's motives and needs.

self-interest What is in the best interest of and benefit to an individual.

invisible hand and the free market to explain the motivation for individual behavior. The "invisible hand" refers to the unseen forces of a free market system that shape the most efficient use of people, money, and resources for productive ends. Smith assumed that people are motivated by self-interest for economic gain to provide the necessities and conveniences of life. Thus, employees are most productive when motivated by self-interest.

The more collective wealth an economy can produce, the better individuals can fulfill their self-interest. Technology and labor efficiency are two ways of promoting greater collective wealth. Technology is crucial to Smith's view because he believed that the productivity of a nation's labor force determines its wealth. Therefore, a more efficient and effective labor force yields greater abundance for the nation. Technology acts as a force multiplier for the productivity of labor.[9]

Frederick Taylor, the founder of *scientific management*, also examined labor efficiency and effectiveness.[10] His goal was to change the relationship between management and labor from one of conflict to one of cooperation.[11] Taylor believed the basis of the conflict was the division of the profits. Instead of continuing this conflict, labor and management should work together to enlarge total profits.

Early organizational scholars assumed that people were motivated by self-interest and economic gain. Consequently, they developed differential piece-rate systems of pay emphasizing external incentives. Modern management practices, such as employee recognition programs, flexible benefit packages, and stock ownership plans, stem from Smith's and Taylor's original theories. They emphasize external incentives, which may take either strictly economic form or more material form, such as outstanding employee plaques. Whataburger has developed the WhataGames in which the best employees compete for bragging rights and medals.[12] This training-and-loyalty exercise reduces turnover and builds commitment.

Some approaches, however, suggest that economic motives alone are not sufficient and need to be combined with other external motives. The Hawthorne studies, mentioned in Chapter 1 as the first to recognize informal aspects of an organization,

Hot Trend

Does Intrinsic Motivation Have a Downside?

Common knowledge would say that it's good to be intrinsically motivated; that is, to be motivated to do something not for the reward, but for the enjoyment of the task itself. Research in organizational behavior largely validates this common knowledge: when people are intrinsically motivated they are more likely to persist in a task and are more satisfied with the results and their work as a whole.

However, recent research has identified contexts where intrinsic motivation is not so positive. It seems that intrinsic motivation has at least two downsides. First, it can actually diminish people's motivation on subsequent tasks. Because people at work conduct a variety of tasks and not just one, some tasks are likely to be perceived as intrinsically motivating while others are not. Research shows that when an employee works on a task that is intrinsically motivating to them, they are subsequently *less* motivated when they turn to tasks that they do not find intrinsically motivating. The explanation here seems to be boredom: employees turning to a less intrinsically motivating task find themselves more bored with it after completing an intrinsically motivating one, thus reducing their persistence and effort.

A second downside to intrinsic motivation involves interpersonal relationships at work. Research has shown that employees who are more intrinsically motivated on average sometimes *moralize* the concept, meaning they see it as a moral virtue to be intrinsically motivated and a moral deficiency to not be. This influences how these employees will interact with others at work. Specifically, highly intrinsically motivated employees are more likely to selectively offer help, only providing it to those they see as similarly intrinsically motivated (e.g., morally virtuous). Those who are perceived as low in intrinsic motivation (and thus morally deficient) are then less likely to receive help on tasks.

Sources: A. Fishbach, & K. Woolley. "The Structure of Intrinsic Motivation." *Annual Review of Organizational Psychology and Organizational Behavior*, 9 (2022): 339–363.
M. Kwon, J. L. Cunningham, & J. M. Jachimowicz. "Discerning Saints: Moralization of Intrinsic Motivation and Selective Prosociality at Work." *Academy of Management Journal*, 66 (2023): 1625–1650.
J. Shin, & A. M. Grant. "Bored by Interest: How Intrinsic Motivation in One Task Can Reduce Performance on Other Tasks." *Academy of Management Journal*, 62 (2019): 415–436.

also studied what motivates people to be productive. They not only confirmed the positive effects of pay incentives on productivity but also demonstrated the importance of social and interpersonal motives.[13] Other people constitute yet another external motive. Executives have recently championed so-called enlightened self-interest. Self-interest is concern for one's own needs; enlightened self-interest recognizes others' interests as well.

In still other approaches, external and internal motivations are combined. Psychological ownership considers both psychological needs and external incentives to motivate workers. One study of 800 managers and employees in three different organizations found that "feelings of ownership" of an organization increased organizational citizenship behavior.[14]

Working from home may motivate employees to be more productive.

martin-dm/E+/Getty Images

5-2 Maslow's Need Hierarchy

Abraham Maslow, a psychologist, proposed a theory of motivation that went beyond just physical and economic needs to emphasize psychological and interpersonal needs as well. The core of Maslow's theory is a hierarchy of five categories of need.[15] Although he recognized that factors other than one's needs (e.g., culture) determine behavior, his theory focused on specifying people's internal needs. As shown in Figure 5.1, Maslow labeled the five levels of

his *need hierarchy* as physiological needs, safety and security needs, love (social) needs, esteem needs, and the need for self-actualization. He conceptually derived the five need categories from the early thoughts of William James and John Dewey, coupled with the psychodynamic thinking of Sigmund Freud and Alfred Adler.[16]

One distinguishing feature of Maslow's need hierarchy is the *progression hypothesis*, which suggests that as one level of need is met, a person progresses to the next higher level of need as a source of motivation. Hence, people progress up the hierarchy as they successively gratify each level of need. Maslow understood the lowest level of ungratified needs to motivate behavior.

Managers can make the most of Maslow's need hierarchy for success in their teams by recognizing

Figure 5.1 Human Needs, Theory X, and Theory Y

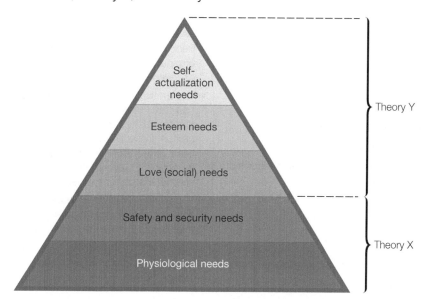

that each individual has a unique set of needs and therefore gearing incentives to meet various needs. The physiological need for sleep is instrumentally important for employee performance, safety, health, and even employee attitudes.[17] The need for security might be filled by a good retirement plan. Some employees have a high need for social interaction, and opportunities for after-work tennis or racquetball may fill those needs. Needs for status and self-actualization can be filled by opportunities to work with higher-ups or to work on projects that particularly suit the individual's skills and interests.[18]

5-2a Theory X and Theory Y

Maslow's need hierarchy has been applied to organizational behavior in two key ways. Douglas McGregor strove to explain motivation by grouping the physiological and safety needs as lower-order needs and the social, esteem, and self-actualization needs as upper-order needs. According to McGregor's theory, managers can

make one of two sets of assumptions about an individual depending on the factors that motivate their behavior. McGregor's **Theory X** assumptions are appropriate for employees motivated by lower-order needs, while **Theory Y** assumptions apply to employees motivated by higher-order needs. These assumptions are listed in Table 5.1 and have been mapped onto Maslow's hierarchy, from which they derive, in Figure 5.1.[19] McGregor understood the responsibility of management to be the same under both sets of assumptions. Specifically, "Management is responsible for organizing the elements of productive enterprise—money, materials, equipment, people—in the interest of economic ends."[20] Trust in top level leaders has been found to trickle-up from trust in direct supervisors, hence making these relationships a key to the benefits of having employees' trust.[21] Employees are more likely to identify with and motivated to achieve organizational outcomes when leaders formulate messages appropriately.[22] Whole Foods founder and CEO John Mackey relies on Maslow's hierarchy of needs in motivating employees.[23]

5-2b ERG Theory

Clayton Alderfer recognized Maslow's contribution to understanding motivation yet believed that the original need hierarchy didn't accurately identify and categorize human needs.[24] He proposed the **ERG theory** of motivation, which grouped human needs into only three basic categories: existence,

> **Theory X** A set of assumptions managers might apply to individuals who are motivated by lower-order needs.
>
> **Theory Y** A set of assumptions managers might apply to individuals who are motivated by higher-order needs.
>
> **ERG theory** A theory that organizes human needs into the categories of existence, relatedness, and growth.

Table 5.1 Mcgregor's Assumptions About People

Theory X	Theory Y
• People are by nature indolent. That is, they work as little as possible. • People lack ambition, dislike responsibility, and prefer to be led. • People are inherently self-centered and indifferent to organizational needs. • People are by nature resistant to change. • People are gullible and not very bright, the ready dupes of the charlatan and the demagogue.	• People are not by nature passive or resistant to organizational needs. They have become so as a result of experience in organizations. • The motivation, the potential for development, the capacity for assuming responsibility, and the readiness to direct behavior toward organizational goals are all present in people. Management does not put them there. It is a responsibility of management to make it possible for people to recognize and develop these human characteristics for themselves. • The essential task of management is to arrange conditions and methods of operation so that people can achieve their own goals best by directing their own efforts toward organizational objectives.

Source: Excerpted from "MacGregor's Assumptions about People" from Management Review, November 1957, American Management Association, New York, NY.

relatedness, and growth.[25] Alderfer classified Maslow's physiological and physical safety needs in an *existence need* category. The interpersonal safety, love, and interpersonal esteem needs were reclassified in a *relatedness need* category. Finally, a *growth need* category encompassed Maslow's self-actualization and self-esteem needs.

ERG theory also supplemented Maslow's original progression hypothesis with a *regression hypothesis*. Alderfer's regression hypothesis suggests that when people are frustrated by their inability to meet needs at the next higher level in the hierarchy, they regress to the next lower category of needs and intensify their desire to gratify those needs. Hence, ERG theory explains both progressive need gratification and regression when people face frustration.

5-3 McClelland's Need Theory

A second major need theory of motivation focuses on personality and learned needs. Henry Murray developed a long list of motives and manifest needs in his early studies of personality.[26] Inspired by Murray's work, David McClelland identified three learned, or acquired, needs, called **manifest needs** because they are easily perceived.[27] These are the needs for *achievement*, *power*, and *affiliation*. Some individuals have a high need for achievement, while others have a moderate or low need for achievement. The same is true for the other two needs. A manager may have a strong need for power, a moderate need for achievement, and a weak need for affiliation. Different needs are dominant in different people, and each need has different implications for people's behavior. Companies such as American Express recognize the importance of such diverse employee needs by creating and maintaining family-friendly policies.

5-3a Need for Achievement

The **need for achievement** encompasses excellence, competition, challenging goals, persistence, and overcoming difficulties.[28] People with a high need for achievement thus seek performance excellence, enjoy difficult and challenging goals, persevere, and are competitive. The *Murray Thematic Apperception Test (TAT)*, a projective test such as those discussed in Chapter 3,

was used as an early measure of the achievement motive. It was further developed by McClelland and his associates, although it has been criticized, and alternative instruments have been developed.[29]

McClelland found that people with a high need for achievement perform better than those lacking such a need. Such individuals share these three characteristics: First, they set goals that are moderately difficult yet achievable. Second, they like to receive feedback on their progress toward these goals. Third, they do not like having external events or other people interfere with their progress toward the goals.

In addition, high achievers (1) often hope and plan for success; (2) may be quite content to work alone or with other people, whichever is more appropriate to their task; and (3) like being very good at what they do so and, accordingly, tend to develop expertise and competence in their chosen endeavors. Groups consisting of high-achieving members may experience conflict over how to get work tasks accomplished as members attempt to demonstrate their individual task-related contributions.[30] The need for achievement is consistent across countries for adults who are employed full-time, but researchers have found international differences in the tendency for achievement.[31] Achievement tendencies are highest in the United States, an individualistic culture, and lowest in collectivist societies such as Japan and Hungary.[32]

5-3b Need for Power

The **need for power** includes the desire to influence others, the urge to change people or events, and the wish to make a difference in life. The need for power is interpersonal because it involves influence over other people. McClelland distinguishes between *socialized power*, which is used for the benefit of many, and *personalized power*, which is

---

manifest needs Learned or acquired needs that are easily perceived.

need for achievement A manifest need that concerns excellence, competition, challenging goals, persistence, and overcoming difficulties.

need for power A manifest need that concerns the desire to influence others, change people or events, and make a difference in life.

David McClelland

AP Images/Sean Kardon

used for individual gain. The former is a constructive force, while the latter may be a very disruptive or even destructive force.

According to McClelland's research, the best managers have a very high need for socialized power

as opposed to personalized power.[33] They are concerned for others; have an interest in organizational goals; and want to be useful to the larger group, organization, and society. For example, the CEO of Management Sciences for Health, Jonathan D. Quick, MD, displayed a high need for interactive, or socialized, power on the McClelland need profile while showing a very low need for imperial power, both of which are strong positive traits.

5-3c Need for Affiliation

The **need for affiliation** is an urge to establish and maintain warm, close, intimate relationships with others.[34] People with a high need for affiliation are motivated to express their emotions to others and expect them to do the same in return. They find conflicts disturbing and are strongly motivated to work through any such barriers to closeness. The need for relationships is important not only in McClelland's theory but also in each of the theories we have discussed so far.

Over and above these three needs for achievement, power, and affiliation, Murray's manifest needs theory also included the need for autonomy. This is the desire for independence and freedom from constraints. People with a high need for autonomy prefer to work alone and to control the pace of their work. They dislike bureaucratic rules, regulations, and procedures.

Figure 5.2 shows the parallel structures of Maslow's, McGregor's, Alderfer's, and McClelland's theories of motivation.

need for affiliation A manifest need to establish and maintain warm, close, intimate relationships with other people.

Figure 5.2 Need Theories of Motivation

	Maslow	McGregor	Alderfer	McClelland
	Self-actualization		Growth	Need for achievement
Higher order needs	Esteem — Self / Interpersonal	Theory Y		Need for power
	Belongingness (social and love)		Relatedness	Need for affiliation
Lower order needs	Safety and security — Interpersonal / Physical	Theory X		
	Physiological		Existence	

5-4 Herzberg's Two-Factor Theory

In developing his *two-factor theory of motivation*, Frederick Herzberg departed from need-based theories and examined the critical incident experiences of people at work.[35] Herzberg's original study included 200 engineers and accountants in western Pennsylvania during the 1950s. He asked them to describe two important incidents at their jobs: one that was very satisfying and made them feel exceptionally good at work and another that was very dissatisfying and made them feel exceptionally bad.

Herzberg and his colleagues believed that people had two sets of needs: one based on avoiding pain and one stemming from the desire for psychological growth. Conditions in the work environment would affect one or the other of these two needs. Work conditions related to satisfaction of the need for psychological growth were labeled **motivation factors**. Work conditions related to dissatisfaction caused by discomfort or pain were labeled **hygiene factors**. Motivation factors relate to job satisfaction, and hygiene factors relate to job dissatisfaction.[36] Table 5.2 lists the motivation factors and hygiene factors included in the following discussion.

5-4a Motivation Factors

Job enrichment involves building motivation factors into a job and, according to Herzberg, creates job satisfaction. In his original research, Herzberg identified motivation factors as responsibility, achievement, recognition, advancement, and the work itself. When these factors are present, they improve a worker's effort and performance. Table 5.2 lists salary as a motivational factor based on some studies.

iQoncept/Shutterstock.com

Acceptance of this idea has led many organizational reward systems to include financial benefits such as stock options as part of an employee's compensation package. Work team climate could be a motivation factor as well. One study found that teams that have a climate of trust, support, and transparency have higher intrinsic motivation which enhanced individual creativity.[37]

Motivation factors lead to positive mental health. They challenge people to grow, contribute to the work environment, and invest themselves in the organization. The absence of these factors does

motivation factor A work condition that satisfies the need for psychological growth.

hygiene factor A work condition that generates dissatisfaction due to discomfort or pain.

Table 5.2 The Motivation-Hygiene Theory of Motivation

Motivation factors that contribute to job satisfaction when they are present:	Hygiene factors that contribute to job dissatisfaction when they are absent:
• Achievement	• Company policy and administration
• Recognition of achievement	• Supervision
• Work itself	• Interpersonal relations
• Responsibility	• Working conditions
• Advancement	• Salary
• Growth	• Status
• Salary	• Security

What's Important to Employees?

There are many possible rewards that employees may receive. Listed below are ten possible job reward factors. Rank these factors three times. First, rank them as you think the average employee would rank them. Second, rank them as you think the average employee's supervisor would rank them for the employee. Finally, rank them according to what you consider important.

Your instructor has normative data for 1,000 employees and their supervisors that will help you interpret your results and put them in the context of Maslow's need hierarchy and Herzberg's two-factor theory of motivation.

Employee	Supervisor	You	
			1. Job security
			2. Full appreciation of work done
			3. Promotion and growth in the organization
			4. Good wages
			5. Interesting work
			6. Good working conditions
			7. Tactful discipline
			8. Sympathetic help with personal problems
			9. Personal loyalty to employees
			10. A feeling of being in on things

not lead to dissatisfaction, but rather to feelings of neutrality. Motivation factors are the more important of the two sets of factors because they directly affect a person's drive to do a good job. When they are absent, a person lacks the motivation to perform well and achieve excellence.

5-4b Hygiene Factors

Hygiene factors are completely distinct from the motivation factors and are unrelated to the drive to achieve and do excellent work. While motivation factors create job satisfaction if present or feelings of neutrality if absent, absent or insufficient hygiene factors result in job dissatisfaction. Herzberg's hygiene factors include company policy and administration, technical supervision, interpersonal relations with one's supervisor, working conditions, salary, and status. Good hygiene factors cannot stimulate psychological growth or human development, but they are necessary to prevent job dissatisfaction.

When these hygiene factors are poor or absent, the dissatisfied employee complains about poor supervision, poor medical benefits, or whatever hygiene factor is poor. One method that employees use to determine the quality of supervision they receive is by the level of fairness they perceive the supervisor uses when enacting company policies. However, the supervisor's motives may have a greater impact on employee perceptions of workplace fairness.[38] Even in unfair work environments, employees and managers can still enact fairness for the good of the workplace.[39] Even in the absence of good hygiene factors, employees may still be very motivated to perform their jobs well if the motivation factors are present.

Two conclusions can be drawn. First, hygiene factors are important to a certain level but unimportant beyond that threshold. Second, the presence of motivation factors is essential to enhancing employee motivation to excel at work.

5-4c Critique of the Two-Factor Theory

One critique of the theory surrounded the classification of the two factors. Some data have shown that a factor may not fit exclusively into either the hygiene or motivation categories. For example, employees generally classify pay as both a hygiene factor and a motivation factor. A second critique of the theory does not account for individual differences. Differences in age, sex, social status, education, or occupational level may influence the classification of factors. A third concern is that intrinsic job factors like the workflow process may be more important in determining satisfaction or dissatisfaction on the job. Finally, much of the supporting data for the theory is based on the *critical-incident technique*. Despite the critiques, Herzberg's was the first motivation theory developed specifically to predict motivation in work settings, thus having important implications for the design of work as we will discuss in Chapter 14.[40]

5-5 Two New Ideas in Motivation

Two new ideas in motivation have emerged in the past decade. One centers on eustress, strength, and hope. This idea comes from the new discipline of *positive organizational behavior*. A second new idea centers on positive energy and full engagement, translating what was learned from high-performance athletes for the use of *Fortune* 500 executives and managers. In addition, supporting a family (family motivation) provides a powerful source of motivation that can boost performance in the workplace, even when a person's intrinsic motivation is low, by providing energy.[41] However, family motivation does not reduce work stress.

5-5a Eustress, Strength, and Hope

Eustress (for "euphoria + stress") is healthy, normal stress. Stress is the energy we experience when confronted with a challenging or difficult situation. Such situations can produce *distress*, a negative response such as frustration or fear, which leads to

unhealthy and unproductive results, or eustress, a positive response to challenges that generates energy and motivates an individual to achieve. Eustress leads us to invest in strengths, find meaning in work, display courage and principled action, and draw on positive emotions at work.[42] This positive perspective on organizational life encourages optimism, hope, and health for people at work. Instead of focusing on the individual's needs or the rewards or punishment meted out in the work environment, the idea of encouraging eustress is to focus on the individual's interpretation of or response to events. An assumption underlying eustress is that although things happen that are out of our control, we can control our response to a situation. Thus, we can control distress by reframing our perspective on a situation. Eustress is a healthy and positive motivational force for individuals who harness its energy for productive work and organizational contributions.

5-5b Positive Energy and Full Engagement

The second new concept in motivation, Jim Loehr's *full engagement* idea, uses lessons learned from professional athletes.[43] The central tenets are that an individual should manage energy rather than time and should strategically disengage from certain activities to balance the power of full engagement.[44] This approach suggests that individuals do not need to be activated by unmet needs but are already activated by their own physical, emotional, mental, and spiritual energy. Managers should therefore help individuals learn to manage their energy so that they can build positive energy and capacity for work.

Loehr's concept stresses the role of energy recovery in overall performance. Some individuals work best by putting forth productive energy for short periods and then taking time to rest and reenergize. This mimics the human body's potential to build or enhance its capacity, enabling the individual to sustain a high level of performance in the face of increasing work demands. Organizations with high levels of employee engagement have strong financial performance, even in volatile economic conditions.[45]

eustress Healthy, normal stress.

5-6 Social Exchange and Equity Theory

Equity theory is a social exchange process approach to motivation that focuses on the interaction between an individual and the environment. In contrast to needs theories based on internal motivation, equity theory is concerned with the social processes that influence motivation and behavior. Power and exchange are important considerations in understanding human behavior.[46] Accounting for such external factors, Amitai Etzioni developed three categories of exchange relationships that people have with organizations: committed, calculated, and alienated involvements.[47] Committed relations have high positive intensity, calculated relationships have low positive or low negative intensity, and alienated relationships have high negative intensity. Committed relationships may characterize a person's involvement with a religious group, and alienated relationships may characterize a person's incarceration in a prison. These three categories will be discussed further in Chapter 11.

5-6a Demands and Contributions

Calculated involvements are based on the notion of social exchange in which each party in the relationship demands certain things of the other and contributes accordingly to the exchange. Business partnerships and commercial deals are both calculated involvements. When both parties to the exchange benefit, the relationship has a positive orientation. When losses occur or conflicts arise, the relationship has a negative orientation. Figure 5.3 offers a model for examining calculated exchange relationships.

Demands Each party to the exchange makes demands on the other. The organization expresses its demands on the individual in the form of goal or mission statements, job expectations, performance objectives, and performance feedback. The individual expresses demands, or needs, in the form of expectations of the organization. Employee need fulfillment and the feeling of belonging are both important to a healthy exchange and to organizational membership.[48] These needs may be viewed from the perspective of Maslow, Alderfer, Herzberg, or McClelland. When employees are well taken care of by the company, they take care of the business even in very difficult times.

Contributions Just as each party to the exchange makes demands on the other, each also contributes to the relationship. These contributions are the basis for satisfying the demands expressed by the other party. Employees satisfy organizational demands

Figure 5.3 The Individual–Organizational Exchange Relationship

Source: Adapted from McGraw-Hill, Inc, J. P. Campbell, M. D. Dunnette, E. E. Lawler, III, and K. E. Weick, Jr., *Managerial Behavior, Performance, and Effectiveness*.

sesame/DigitalVision Vectors/Getty Images

Individuals compare their outcome/input ratio to that of other people and determine equity or inequity.

through a range of contributions, including their skills, abilities, knowledge, energy, professional contacts, and native talents. As people grow and develop over time, they are able to increasingly satisfy the range of demands and expectations placed on them by the organization.

In a similar fashion, organizations contribute to the exchange relationship to meet individual needs. These contributions include salary, benefits, advancement opportunities, security, status, and social affiliation. Some organizations are richer in resources and better able to meet employee needs than other organizations. One of the concerns that both individuals and organizations have is whether the relationship is a fair deal or an equitable arrangement for both members of the relationship. Social exchange relationship perceptions are influenced by executive leadership style, organizational culture, and employment approach, which in turn have an effect on commitment and performance, though not organizational citizenship behavior (OCB), discussed in Chapter 4.[49]

5-6b Adams' Theory of Inequity

Ideas about social process and exchange advocated by Etzioni and others provide a context for understanding fairness, equity, and inequity in work relationships. Stacy Adams developed the idea that **inequity** in the social exchange process is a particularly important motivator. Adams' *theory of inequity* suggests that people are motivated when they find themselves in situations of inequity, or unfairness.[50] Inequity occurs when a person receives more or less than they believe they deserve based on their effort and/or contribution. Inequity creates tension, which in turn motivates a person to take action to resolve the inequity.

A perception of inequity arises when people consider their inputs (their contributions to the relationship) and their outcomes (the organization's contributions to the relationship) according to an input/outcome ratio, which they compare to that of a generalized "other," or *comparison other*. Figure 5.4 shows two inequity scenarios for a single situation, one negative and one positive. The negative inequity in (b) could occur, for example, if the comparison

> **inequity** A situation in which a person perceives that they are receiving less than they are giving or is giving less than they are receiving.

Organizational Example

Celebrating Employees at Bank of America

In the employee-organization exchange relationship, organizations provide contributions that go beyond the financial. Consider Bank of America: the financial institution signals a culture that rewards employees, and "appreciates and celebrates achievement year-round at all levels." The bank lists specific opportunities like teammate recognition, point-based rewards, and celebrations for anniversaries and long-term service to the company.

From this list, it is clear that status and social affiliation are contributions that Bank of America offers to its employees and signals to its potential applicants. Of course, financial compensation matters too: the organization also notes that they have offered $4 billion in extra compensation to their employees since 2017. These kinds of contributions make Bank of America more attractive to talented employees and helps them retain high-performers.

In sum, Bank of America, like other companies, rewards employees both by meeting financial needs and by meeting needs such as affiliation and belonging. Consistent evaluation and recognition of performance helps motivate employees and meet basic needs.

Source: Bank of America. "Recognizing and Rewarding Performance" (2023).

Figure 5.4 Equity and Inequity at Work

	Person	Comparison other
(a) Equity	$\dfrac{\text{Outcomes}}{\text{Inputs}}$	$=$ $\dfrac{\text{Outcomes}}{\text{Inputs}}$
(b) Negative Inequity	$\dfrac{\text{Outcomes}}{\text{Inputs}}$	$<$ $\dfrac{\text{Outcomes}}{\text{Inputs}}$
(c) Positive Inequity	$\dfrac{\text{Outcomes}}{\text{Inputs}}$	$>$ $\dfrac{\text{Outcomes}}{\text{Inputs}}$

> People believe there is a correlation between the effort they put forth, the performance they achieve, and the outcomes they receive.

other earned a higher salary, while inequity in (c) could occur if the person had more vacation time, all else being equal in both cases. Although not illustrated in the example, nontangible inputs such as emotional investment and nontangible outcomes such as job satisfaction may enter into a person's equity equation.

Pay inequity has been a thorny issue for women in some companies. Eastman Kodak and other companies have made real progress in addressing the issue of pay equity.[51] Globalization also presents a challenge for pay equity. As organizations grow internationally, they may have trouble determining pay and benefit equity/inequity across national borders.

Adams considers a situation in which there is inequity in only one variable to be a first level of inequity. A more severe, second level of inequity would occur, for example, in a situation where the inputs of a person experiencing negative inequity, as in Figure 5.4(b), are also greater than those of the comparison other. Inequalities in one (inputs or outcomes) coupled with equality in the other (inputs or outcomes) are experienced as a less severe inequity than inequalities in both inputs and outcomes. One drawback of Adams's theory is that it does not provide a way of determining whether some inputs or some outcomes are more important than others.

5-6c The Resolution of Inequity

Once a person establishes the existence of an inequity, they might use a number of strategies to restore equity. Adams's theory provides seven basic

equity sensitive An individual who prefers an equity ratio equal to that of their comparison other.

strategies for restoring equity: (1) alter the person's outcomes, (2) alter the person's inputs, (3) alter the comparison other's outcomes, (4) alter the comparison other's inputs, (5) change who is used as a comparison other, (6) rationalize the inequity, and (7) leave the organizational situation.

Each of the first four strategies could involve a wide variety of tactics. For example, if an employee has a strategy to increase their income by $11,000 per year to restore equity, the tactic might be a meeting between the employee and their manager concerning the issue of salary equity. Another tactic would be for the person to work with the company's compensation specialists.

The selection of a strategy and a set of tactics is a sensitive issue with possible long-term consequences. In this example, a strategy aimed at reducing the comparison other's outcomes may have the desired short-term effect of restoring equity but reduce morale and productivity in the long term. The equity theory does not include a hierarchy predicting which inequity-reduction strategy a person will or should choose, but it is nevertheless a reminder of the importance of fairness. Pay dispersion (the amount of allowable differences between employee pay) has the ability to enhance or diminish employee motivation. Employees will generally be motivated when pay dispersion strategies are based on performance.[52]

5-6d New Perspectives on Equity Theory

Equity theory has been revised in light of new theories and research. One important theoretical revision proposes three types of individuals based on preferences for equity.[53] **Equity sensitives** prefer equity based on the originally formed theory. In other words, they want the relationship between their own input and output to be equal to that of their comparison other. Equity sensitivity contributes to the extent to which employees feel obligated to help in the workplace. Equity sensitive

Inclusive Conversations

Why Are Gen Z Workers So Motivated by Pay?

With her bachelor's degree in hand, Marieta targeted only jobs that would pay her a six-figure salary. Family members expressed concern that her goals were unreasonable, that she should not be so obsessed with money. Marieta is not alone in her quest to earn high salaries early in her career. Seventy-four percent of U.S. Gen Z college graduates surveyed prioritized salary and stability over benefits, employer brand, and a fast-growing field. Are Gen Z workers obsessed with money? Not necessarily. Experts attribute Gen Zers' desire for high pay to two primary factors. First, most Gen Z workers grew up watching their mostly Generation X parents struggle with financial obligations during multiple global recessions and an economic downturn. Next, many Gen Zers graduated college during the Covid-19 pandemic amid increased costs, rising inflation, and mounting student loan debt. It is reasonable that this generation of workers would want to avoid the instability and uncertainty their parents faced by shoring up their own financial futures. Why is this generation so laser-focused on earning high salaries? The simple answer is these workers want to be able to cover their costs, and they view pay as the way to achieve that goal.

1. Do you consider some Gen Zers' quest for six-figure salaries out of college reasonable? Why or why not?

2. Earning high salaries is reasonable in job markets that support them. Speculate how job seekers might respond if they are unable to maintain their targeted salaries.

Source: Carnegie, M. (2023, May 31). Why Gen Z are So Motivated by Pay. *BBC*, https://www.bbc.com/worklife/article/20230530-why-gen-z-are-so-motivated-by-pay.

---

employees who monitor resources they receive from their supervisors may feel less obligated to engage in helping behaviors if they perceive they have been provided with fewer resources.[54] **Benevolents** are comfortable with an equity ratio less than that of their comparison other.[55] These people may be thought of as givers. **Entitleds** are comfortable only with an equity ratio greater than that of their comparison other.[56] These people may be thought of as takers.

Equity in pay is an important factor in motivation because pay is often thought to relate to a person's self-imposed performance expectations. But one study suggests that a person's organizational position also

> **benevolent** An individual who is comfortable with an equity ratio less than that of their comparison other.
>
> **entitled** An individual who is comfortable with an equity ratio greater than that of their comparison other.

As women age, their pay relative to the pay of men of the same age decreases

Median hourly earnings of women in the U.S. as a % of the median hourly earnings of men of the same age, starting at ages 25 to 34 in the years shown and ending at the ages reached in 2022

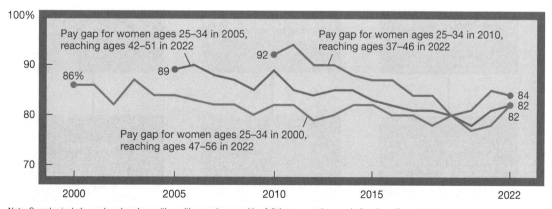

Note: Samples include employed workers with positive earnings, working full time or part time, excluding the self-employed.

Source: Pew Research Center analysis of the Current Population Survey outgoing rotation group files (IPUMS).

Source: Pew Research Center. Extracted from: https://www.pewresearch.org/social-trends/2023/03/01/the-enduring-grip-of-the-gender-pay-gap/

influences self-imposed performance expectations and may be a more important factor than pay.[57] Specifically, a two-level move up in an organization with no additional pay creates a higher self-imposed performance expectation than a one-level move up with modest additional pay. Similarly, a two-level move down in an organization with no reduction in pay creates a lower self-imposed performance expectation than a one-level move down with a modest decrease in pay.

Unfortunately, inequity and organizational injustice can also generate dysfunctional behavior.[58] More seriously, workplace injustice can trigger aggressive reactions that harm both individuals and the organization. Fortunately, only a small number of individuals respond to such unfairness through dysfunctional behavior.[59]

Increasing, decreasing, or constant experiences of inequity over time may have very different consequences for people.[60] Equity theory can help companies implement two-tiered wage structures such as the one used by American Airlines in the early 1990s. In a two-tiered system, one group of employees receives different pay and benefits than another group of employees. Such a system can, however, generate perceptions of inequity, especially where the value of equal pay for equal

work is strongly held. Research suggests that unions and management may want to consider work location and employment status (part-time versus full-time) prior to implementing a two-tiered system.[61]

5-7 Expectancy Theory of Motivation

In addition to individual needs and social exchange, motivation can also be explained in terms of an individual's perception of the performance process. Victor Vroom's *expectancy theory* of motivation is a cognitive process theory founded on two basic notions. First, Vroom assumes that people expect certain outcomes of behavior and performance, which may be thought of as rewards, or consequences of behavior. Second, people believe there is a correlation between the effort they put forth, the performance they achieve, and the outcomes they receive. Expectancy theory has been used in a wide variety of contexts, including test-taking motivation among students.[62]

The key constructs in the expectancy theory of motivation are the valence of an outcome, expectancy, and instrumentality.[63] **Valence** is the value, or importance, one places on a particular reward. **Expectancy** is the belief that effort leads to performance (e.g., "If I try harder, I can do better"). **Instrumentality** is the belief that performance is related to rewards (e.g., "If I perform better, I will get more pay"). Figure 5.5 models the expectancy theory notions of effort, performance, and rewards.

valence The value or importance one places on a particular reward.

expectancy The belief that effort leads to performance.

instrumentality The belief that performance is related to rewards.

Figure 5.5 An Expectancy Model for Motivation

Effort	Performance	Reward

Perceived effort–performance probability

Perceived performance–reward probability

Perceived value of rewards

"What are my chances of getting the job done if I put forth the necessary effort?"

"What are my chances of getting the rewards I value if I satisfactorily complete the job?"

"What rewards do I value?"

Valence, expectancy, and instrumentality all influence a person's motivation. The perceived relationship between effort and performance varies from person to person and from activity to activity. One person might believe that an increase in effort has a direct, positive effect on performance. Another person might have a very different set of beliefs about the link between effort and performance. In a similar fashion, people's beliefs about the link between performance and reward vary. From a motivation perspective, it is the person's belief about the relationships between these constructs that is important, not the actual nature of the relationship.

Managers can use expectancy theory to design *motivation programs*.[64] Sometimes called *performance planning* or *evaluation systems*, these motivation programs are meant to enhance a person's belief that effort will improve performance and therefore lead to better pay. Valence and expectancy are particularly important in establishing priorities for people pursuing multiple goals.[65]

Valence is the third key idea within the expectancy theory of motivation. Different people value different rewards. One person prefers salary to benefits, whereas another person prefers just the reverse. In fact, employees vary greatly with respect to the link between work and pay, as well as how much they value money.[66]

5-7a Motivational Problems

Expectancy theory attributes motivational problems to three basic causes: disbelief in a relationship between effort and performance, disbelief in a relationship between performance and rewards, and lack of desire for the rewards offered. If the motivational problem stems from the person's belief that effort will not improve performance, the solution lies in altering this belief. The person can be shown how an increase in effort or an alteration in the kind of effort put forth can be converted into improved performance.

If the motivational problem is related to the person's belief that performance will not result in rewards, the solution also lies in altering that belief. The person can be shown how an increase in performance or a somewhat altered form of performance will be converted into rewards. If, however, the motivational problem is related to the value placed on certain rewards, there are two possible solutions: to alter the value placed on the rewards or to alter the rewards themselves.

Research results on expectancy theory have been mixed.[67] The theory predicts job satisfaction accurately, but its complexity makes it difficult to test the full model, and the measures of instrumentality, valence, and expectancy have only weak validity.[68] In addition, measuring expectancy constructs is time-consuming, and the values for each construct change over time for an individual. Finally, the theory assumes that the individual is totally rational and acts as a minicomputer, calculating probabilities and values. In reality, the theory may be more complex than the way people typically function.

5-7b Motivation and Moral Maturity

Expectancy theory predicts that people will work to maximize their personal outcomes. This is consistent with Adam Smith's idea of working for one's own self-interest. Both suggest that people work to benefit themselves alone. Expectancy theory cannot explain altruistic behavior. Therefore, it may be necessary to consider an individual's **moral maturity** in order to understand altruistic, fair, and equitable behavior. Moral maturity is the measure of a person's cognitive moral development, as discussed in Chapter 4. Morally mature people behave based on universal ethical principles, while morally immature people behave based on egocentric motivations.[69]

5-8 Cultural Differences in Motivation

Most motivation theories in use today have been developed by and about Americans.[70] When researchers have examined the universality of these theories, they have found cultural differences, at least with regard to Maslow's, McClelland's, and Herzberg's theories. For example, while self-actualization is the pinnacle need for Americans in Maslow's need hierarchy, security may be the most important need for people in cultures with a high need to avoid uncertainty.[71] Although

moral maturity The measure of a person's cognitive moral development.

Andrew Flavin/Shutterstock.com

Motivation theories developed in Western contexts might or might not apply in other parts of the world.

achievement is an important need for Americans, research suggests that other cultures do not value achievement as much as Americans do. Similarly, in cultures that place a high value on individual achievement and autonomy, employees are more motivated when their firm engages in socially responsible practices.[72]

The two-factor theory has been tested in other countries as well. Results in New Zealand did not replicate the results found in the United States; supervision and interpersonal relationships were important motivators in New Zealand, as opposed to the importance of hygienic factors as in America.[73] Researchers examining equity theory in cross-cultural contexts have suggested reexamining equity preferences, selection of referent others, and reactions to inequity.[74] Finally, expectancy theory may hold up well in cultures that value individualism but break down in more collectivist cultures that value cooperative efforts. In collectivist cultures, rewards are more closely tied to group and team efforts, and expectancy theory is ill equipped to deal with such differences.[75]

Experiential Exercise

What Do You Need from Work?

This exercise provides an opportunity to discuss your basic needs and those of other students in your class. Refer back to You 5.2, and review your ranking of the ten possible job reward factors. Think about basic needs you may have that are possibly work-related and yet would not be satisfied by one or another of these ten job reward factors.

Step 1. The class will form into groups of approximately six members each. Each group will elect a spokesperson and answer the following questions. The group should spend at least five minutes on the first question and ensure that each group member contributes. The second question will probably take up to fifteen minutes for your group to answer. The spokesperson should be ready to share the group's answers.

a. *What important basic needs do you have that are not addressed by one or another of these ten job reward factors?* Members should focus on the whole range of needs discussed in the different need theories of motivation covered in Chapter 5. Develop a list of the basic needs overlooked by these ten factors.

b. *What is important to members of your group?* Rank all job reward factors (the original ten and any new ones your group came up with in Step 1) in terms of their importance for your group. If group members disagree about the rankings, take time to discuss the differences among group members. Work for consensus and note points of disagreement.

Step 2. Each group will share the results of its answers to the questions in Step 1. Cross-team questions and discussion follow.

Step 3. If your instructor has not already shared the normative data for 1,000 employees and their supervisors mentioned in You 5.2, the instructor may do that at this time.

Step 4 (Optional). Your instructor may ask you to discuss the similarities and differences in your group's rankings with the employee and supervisory normative rankings. If so, spend some time addressing two questions.

a. *What underlying reasons do you think may account for the differences that exist?*

b. *How have the needs of employees and supervisors changed over the past twenty years? Are they likely to change in the future?*

Learning Objectives

5-1 **Define motivation and articulate different views of how individuals are motivated at work.** *Motivation* is the process of arousing and sustaining goal-directed behavior. Motivation theories may be broadly classified into internal, process, and external theories. A comprehensive approach to understanding motivation, behavior, and performance must consider three elements of the work situation—the individual, the job, and the work environment—and how these elements interact.

5-2 **Explain Maslow's hierarchy of needs and its two main modifications.** Douglas McGregor used Maslow's need theory to explain motivation. McGregor's Theory X assumptions are appropriate for employees motivated by lower order needs—physiological and safety needs. Theory Y assumptions apply to employees motivated by higher order needs—social, esteem, and self-actualization. Clayton Alderfer's ERG theory of motivation grouped human needs into three basic categories: existence, relatedness, and growth. He explains both progressive need gratification and regression when people face frustration.

5-3 **Discuss how the needs for achievement, power, and affiliation influence an individual's behavior in the workplace.** David McClelland identified three learned or acquired needs, called manifest needs. The *need for achievement* encompasses excellence, competition, challenging goals, persistence, and overcoming difficulties. The *need for power* includes the desire to influence others, the urge to change people or events, and the wish to make a difference in life. The *need for affiliation* means an urge to establish and maintain warm, close, intimate relationships with others.

5-4 **Describe the two-factor theory of motivation.** Frederick Herzberg's two-factor theory examined experiences that satisfied or dissatisfied people at work. Motivation factors relate to job satisfaction; hygiene factors relate to job dissatisfaction. Motivation factors are responsibility, achievement, recognition, advancement, and the work itself. Hygiene factors are company policy and administration, technical supervision, salary, interpersonal relations with one's supervisor, working conditions, salary, and status. Excellent hygiene factors result in employees being *not dissatisfied*.

5-5 **Explain two new ideas in human motivation.** Positive organizational scholarship links eustress to investing in strengths, finding positive meaning in work, displaying courage and principled action, and drawing on positive emotions at work. A second idea, by Jim Loehr, centers on positive energy and full engagement. This approach suggests that individuals do not need to be activated by fulfilling unmet needs but are already activated by their own physical, emotional, mental, and spiritual energy.

5-6 **Describe the role of inequity in motivation.** Equity theory is a social exchange process theory of motivation that focuses on the individual-environment interaction. Individuals and organizations want an equitable arrangement for both members of the relationship. Inequity occurs when a person receives more, or less, than the person believes is deserved based on effort and/or contribution.

5-7 **Describe the expectancy theory of motivation.** Vroom's expectancy theory of motivation focuses on personal perceptions of the performance process. The key constructs in the expectancy theory of motivation are *valence, expectancy,* and *instrumentality*. Valence is the value or importance one places on a particular reward. Expectancy is the belief that effort leads to performance. Instrumentality is the belief that performance is related to rewards.

5-8 **Describe the cultural differences in motivation.** Most motivation theories in use today have been developed by and about Americans. When researchers have examined the universality of these theories, they have found that the studies did not replicate the results found in the United States due to cultural differences.

Key Terms

benevolent An individual who is comfortable with an equity ratio less than that of their comparison other. (p. 105)

entitled An individual who is comfortable with an equity ratio greater than that of their comparison other. (p. 105)

equity sensitive An individual who prefers an equity ratio equal to that of their comparison other. (p. 104)

ERG theory A theory that organizes human needs into the categories of existence, relatedness, and growth. (p. 96)

eustress Healthy, normal stress. (p. 101)

expectancy The belief that effort leads to performance. (p. 106)

hygiene factor A work condition that generates dissatisfaction due to discomfort or pain. (p. 99)

inequity A situation in which a person perceives that they are receiving less than they are giving or is giving less than they are receiving. (p. 103)

instrumentality The belief that performance is related to rewards. (p. 106)

manifest needs Learned or acquired needs that are easily perceived. (p. 97)

moral maturity The measure of a person's cognitive moral development. (p. 107)

motivation The process of arousing and sustaining goal-directed behavior. (p. 93)

motivation factor A work condition that satisfies the need for psychological growth. (p. 99)

need for achievement A manifest need that concerns excellence, competition, challenging goals, persistence, and overcoming difficulties. (p. 97)

need for affiliation A manifest need to establish and maintain warm, close, intimate relationships with other people. (p. 98)

need for power A manifest need that concerns the desire to influence others, change people or events, and make a difference in life. (p. 97)

psychoanalysis Sigmund Freud's method for delving into the unconscious mind to better understand a person's motives and needs. (p. 93)

self-interest What is in the best interest of and benefit to an individual. (p. 93)

Theory X A set of assumptions managers might apply to individuals who are motivated by lower-order needs. (p. 96)

Theory Y A set of assumptions managers might apply to individuals who are motivated by higher-order needs. (p. 96)

valence The value or importance one places on a particular reward. (p. 106)

Ethical Dilemma

Amir is a team leader for a production group at New Trends, a product design business. New Trends partners with clients to take their ideas and create prototypes of the new product the client wants to develop. Clients pay New Trends for the initial development work. If the product is adopted, a percentage of the projected revenue of the product is also paid to the company. Business has been very good lately.

The production group employees are paid a very good salary. And as team leader, Amir also receives a bonus for every one of the products that is adopted from his team. However, New Trends has been slow in paying bonuses and did not pay Amir the last bonus at all. This situation is frustrating Amir and making him reconsider his feelings about New Trends.

Amir's team got a new assignment. It is a very complex assignment with a very short delivery timeline. This project will take a lot of overtime to create a good prototype in time to meet the needs of the client. Amir is not very motivated to take on this new project. He wonders why he should put in the additional effort needed for this project. Recently his efforts have not given him the rewards he has been promised.

But this project is for a new big client that could lead to many new projects which, in the long run, could be very good for the company and ultimately the members of his team. He does not want to let everyone down, but he feels like he is not being rewarded for his efforts.

1. Using consequential, rule-based, and character theories, evaluate Amir's choices.

2. What should Amir do? Why?

vs148/Shutterstock.com

Chapter 6

Learning and Performance Management

Learning Objectives

6-1 Describe behavioral theories of learning.

6-2 Describe social and cognitive theories of learning.

6-3 Explain how goal setting can be used to direct learning and performance.

6-4 Define performance and identify the tools used to measure it.

6-5 Explain the importance of performance feedback, including how it can be delivered effectively.

6-6 Identify major ways managers can reward performance.

6-7 List two strategies for correcting poor performance.

6-1 Behavioral Models of Learning in Organizations

Learning is a change in behavior acquired through experience. It helps guide and direct motivated behavior. Learning may begin with the cognitive activity of developing knowledge about a subject, which then leads to a change in behavior. Alternatively, the behaviorist approach to learning assumes that observable behavior is a function of its consequences. Behaviorists argue that learning stems from classical and operant conditioning. Machine learning is a subfield of computer science that evolved from the study of pattern recognition and computational learning theory in artificial intelligence.[1] The concept of machine learning is extrapolated from human learning, the principal focus of the first section in this chapter.

6-1a Classical Conditioning

Classical conditioning is the process of modifying behavior by pairing a conditioned stimulus with an unconditioned stimulus to elicit an unconditioned response. Its discovery is largely the result of Russian physiologist Ivan Pavlov's research in the early 1900s. Pavlov's professional exchanges with Walter B. Cannon and other American researchers brought his ideas to prominence in the United States.[2]

Classical conditioning builds on the natural reaction of an unconditioned response to an unconditioned stimulus. In dogs, this might be the natural production of saliva (unconditioned response) in response to the presentation of meat (unconditioned stimulus). By presenting a conditioned stimulus (e.g., a ringing bell) simultaneously with the unconditioned stimulus (meat), the researcher trained the dog to develop a conditioned response (salivation).

---

learning A change in behavior acquired through experience.

classical conditioning Modifying behavior by pairing a conditioned stimulus with an unconditioned stimulus to elicit an unconditioned response.

operant conditioning Modifying behavior through the use of positive or negative consequences following specific behaviors.

> Reinforcement and punishment are used to manage good and bad behavior.

After enough trials, the dog salivated at the sound of a bell, even when no meat was presented.

As demonstrated by B. F. Skinner, classical conditioning may occur similarly in humans.[3] For example, people working at a computer terminal may get lower back tension (unconditioned response) from poor posture (unconditioned stimulus). If they become aware of that tension only when the manager appears (conditioned stimulus), then they may develop a conditioned response (lower back tension) to the appearance of the manager.

But classical conditioning has limited applicability to human behavior in organizations for three reasons. First, humans are more complex than dogs and less amenable to simple cause-and-effect conditioning. Second, the behavioral environments in organizations are complex and not very amenable to single stimulus–response manipulations. Third, the human capacity for decision making can override simple conditioning.

6-1b Operant Conditioning

Operant conditioning is the process of modifying behavior by following specific behaviors with positive or negative consequences.[4] These consequences influence behavior through three strategies: reinforcement, punishment, and extinction. Management pioneer Fred Luthans and his colleagues used *organizational behavior modification (OBM)* to shape behavior in a variety of organizations.[5] OBM employs three types of consequences: financial reinforcement, nonfinancial reinforcement, and social reinforcement. A major review of OBM's influence in organizations found that it had significant and positive influence on task performance in both manufacturing and service organizations but that the effects were most powerful in manufacturing organizations.[6] In a study of pay for performance, more productive employees chose performance-based compensation over fixed compensation when given a choice.[7] However, regardless of which pay scheme employees chose, all produced more under a pay-for-performance scheme. And while attitudes about pay for performance continue to vary according to cultural values, research suggests that its use may be rising cross-culturally.[8]

6-1c Reinforcement Theory

Reinforcement theory holds that reinforcement enhances desirable behavior, whereas punishment and extinction diminish undesirable behavior. This theory is central to the design and administration of organizational reward systems, which are a key factor in attracting and retaining top employees. Strategic rewards help motivate behavior, actions, and accomplishments, all of which advance the organization toward specific business goals.[9] In addition to cash rewards such as bonuses, strategic rewards include training and educational opportunities, stock options, and recognition awards such as travel.

Reinforcement and punishment represent the positive and negative consequences of behavior. **Positive consequences** are the results that the person finds attractive or pleasurable. They might include a pay increase, bonus, promotion, transfer to a more desirable geographic location, or praise from a supervisor. **Negative consequences** are the results that the person finds unattractive or aversive. They might include disciplinary action, an undesirable transfer, a demotion, or harsh criticism from a supervisor. The recipient of the consequences defines them as positive or negative. Therefore, individual personality differences as well as gender and cultural differences may be important in their classification.

Following a specific behavior with a positive or negative consequence either reinforces or punishes that behavior.[10] Thorndike's *law of effect* states that behaviors followed by positive consequences are more likely to recur and behaviors followed by negative consequences are less likely to recur.[11] Figure 6.1 shows how positive and negative consequences may be applied or withheld in the strategies of reinforcement and punishment.

Reinforcement Reinforcement is a strategy to cultivate desirable behavior by either bestowing positive consequences or withholding negative ones. Positive reinforcement occurs when a positive consequence (like a bonus) follows a desirable behavior (like a successful business year). Marriott International provides positive reinforcement by honoring ten to twenty employees each year with its J. Willard Marriott Award of Excellence. Each recipient receives a medallion engraved

> **positive consequences** Results of a behavior that a person finds attractive or pleasurable.
>
> **negative consequences** Results of a behavior that a person finds unattractive or aversive.
>
> **reinforcement** A strategy to cultivate desirable behavior by either bestowing positive consequences or withholding negative consequences.

Figure 6.1 Reinforcement and Punishment Strategies

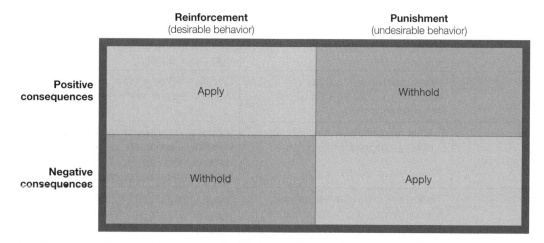

Source: Table from Organizational Behavior Modification by Fred Luthans and Robert Kreitner. Copyright © 1985, p. 58 by Scott Foresman and Company and the authors. Reprinted by permission of the authors.

with the words that express the basic values of the company: dedication, achievement, character, ideals, effort, and perseverance. A recent field experiment examining the reward practices of an Israeli high-tech manufacturing factory sought to better understand the type of short-term bonus (monetary or nonmonetary) with the most positive effect on worker productivity and the circumstances under which short-term bonuses reinforced employee behavior. One group of employees was incentivized with monetary bonuses in the form of cash and family meal vouchers; the other group, with nonmonetary bonuses in the form of a note providing them with positive feedback. Employees who received monetary and nonmonetary bonuses increased their productivity by over 5%. Similarly, productivity decreased for both sets of employees once they were no longer being incentivized for their performance. However, the performance decrease took longer for the employees who had been incentivized with a simple note acknowledging their good performance than those who received cash or the meal voucher.[12]

Negative reinforcement occurs when managers withhold a negative consequence after an employee demonstrates a desirable behavior. For example, a manager who reduces an employee's pay (negative consequence) if the employee comes to work late (undesirable behavior) refrains from doing so when the employee is on time (desirable behavior). The employee avoids the negative consequence (a reduction in pay) by exhibiting the desirable behavior (being on time to work).

When managers design organizational reward systems, they consider not only the type of reinforcement but also how often to provide it, according to continuous or intermittent schedules, as shown in Table 6.1.

Table 6.1 Schedules of Reinforcement

Schedule	Description	Effects on Responding
Continuous	Reinforcer follows every response.	Steady, high rate of performance as long as reinforcement follows every response. High frequency of reinforcement may lead to early satiation. Behavior weakens rapidly (undergoes extinction) when reinforcers are withheld. Appropriate for newly emitted, unstable, low-frequency responses.
Intermittent	Reinforcer does not follow every response.	Capable of producing high frequencies of responding. Low frequency of reinforcement precludes early satiation. Appropriate for stable or high-frequency responses.
Fixed ratio	A fixed number of responses must be emitted before reinforcement occurs.	A fixed ratio of 1:1 (reinforcement occurs after every response) is the same as a continuous schedule. Tends to produce a high rate of response that is vigorous and steady.
Variable ratio	A varying or random number of responses must be emitted before reinforcement occurs.	Capable of producing a high rate of response that is vigorous, steady, and resistant to extinction.
Fixed interval	The first response after a specific period of time has elapsed is reinforced.	Produces an uneven response pattern varying from a very slow, unenergetic response immediately following reinforcement to a very fast, vigorous response immediately preceding reinforcement.
Variable interval	The first response after varying or random periods of time have elapsed is reinforced.	Tends to produce a high rate of response that is vigorous, steady, and resistant to extinction.

Source: F. Luthans and R. Kreitner, *Organizational Behavior Modification* (Glenview, Ill.: Scott, Foresman, 1985). Copyright © by Scott Foresman and Company and the authors. Reprinted by permission of the authors.

6-1d Punishment

Punishment is a strategy to discourage undesirable behavior. One way to punish a person is to follow an undesirable behavior with a negative consequence. For example, a professional athlete who is excessively offensive to an official (undesirable behavior) may be ejected from the game (negative consequence). The other way to punish a person is to withhold a positive consequence following an undesirable behavior. For example, a salesperson who puts little effort into their pitch (undesirable behavior) won't likely receive a large commission check (positive consequence).

Punishment sometimes has unintended results. Because punishment is discomforting to the individual being punished, it can bring about negative psychological, emotional, performance, or behavioral consequences (such as workplace deviance), especially when applied too often. Being aware of this potential consequence of a generalized negative response and decreased motivation to work better, some managers use the threat of punishment—rather than actually applying the punishment—to scare workers into greater effort whenever possible.[13]

Extinction An alternative to punishing undesirable behavior is **extinction**—a strategy to weaken a behavior by attaching no consequences (either positive or negative) to it. This strategy may require time and patience, but the absence of consequences eventually weakens a behavior. Extinction may be most effective when used in conjunction with the positive reinforcement of desirable behaviors. For example, complimenting a sarcastic colleague for constructive comments (reinforcing desirable behavior) while ignoring sarcastic comments (extinguishing undesirable behavior) may prove doubly effective. Extinction is not always the best strategy, however. In cases of dangerous or seriously undesirable behavior, punishment might better deliver a swift, clear lesson.

6-2 Social and Cognitive Theories of Learning

In addition to behaviorist theory, social and cognitive theories of learning have been proposed.

6-2a Bandura's Social Learning Theory

Albert Bandura's social learning theory offers a complementary alternative to Pavlov's and Skinner's behaviorist approaches.[14] Bandura asserts that learning occurs when we observe other people and model their behavior. Because employees look to their supervisors for acceptable norms of behavior, they are likely to pattern their own actions after the supervisor's. Central to Bandura's social learning theory is the notion of **task-specific self-efficacy**, an individual's internal expectancy to perform a specific task effectively. Individuals with high self-efficacy believe that they have the ability to get things done. Self-efficacy is higher in a learning context than in a performance context, especially for individuals with a high learning orientation.[15] There are four sources of task-specific self-efficacy: prior experiences, behavior models (witnessing the success of others), persuasion from other people, and assessment of current physical and emotional capabilities.[16] Evidence suggests that self-efficacy leads to high performance on a wide variety of physical and mental tasks.[17] Employees with high self-efficacy are more likely to learn new things and seek out variety in conducting their job tasks.[18] Prior success can also enhance one's self-efficacy. For example, women who trained in physical self-defense increased their self-efficacy in self-defense and new tasks.[19]

Alexander Stajkovic and Fred Luthans drew on Bandura's ideas of self-efficacy and social learning to expand their original work in behavioral management and OBM into a comprehensive framework for performance management.[20] Bandura saw the power of social reinforcement, recognizing that financial and material rewards often follow or coincide with the approval of others, whereas punishments often follow social disapproval. Thus, Stajkovic and Luthans saw that self-efficacy and social reinforcement influence behavior and

punishment A strategy to discourage undesirable behavior by either bestowing negative consequences or withholding positive consequences.

extinction A strategy to weaken a behavior by attaching no consequences to it.

task-specific self-efficacy An individual's internal expectancy to perform a specific task effectively.

> Managers can empower employees and help them develop self-efficacy by providing job challenges, offering coaching and counseling, and rewarding employees' achievements.

performance at work and have suggested that managers can be confident that employees with high self-efficacy will perform well.

Managers can empower employees and help them develop self-efficacy by providing job challenges, offering coaching and counseling for improved performance, and rewarding employees' achievements. Managers can also remove organizational barriers that stand in the way of employees making progress in meaningful work.[21] Given the increasing diversity of the workforce, managers may want to target their efforts toward women and minorities, who tend to have lower than average self-efficacy.[22]

6-2b Cognitive Theories of Learning

The cognitive approach to learning is based on the *Gestalt* school of thought and draws on Jung's theory of personality differences, discussed in Chapter 3. Recall the distinction between introverts (who need to study, concentrate, and reflect) and extraverts (who need to interact with other people). Introverts

goal setting The process of establishing desired results that guide and direct behavior.

learn best alone, whereas extraverts learn best by exchanging ideas with others.

The personality functions of intuition, sensing, thinking, and feeling all have learning implications, which are listed in Table 6.2. Each person has a preferred mode of gathering information and a preferred mode of evaluating and making decisions about that information. For example, an intuitive thinker may want to skim research reports about implementing total quality programs and then, based on hunches, decide how to apply the research findings to the organization. A sensing feeler may prefer viewing videos of interviews with people in companies that implemented total quality programs and then identify people in the organization most likely to be receptive to the approaches presented.

6-3 Goal Setting at Work

Goal setting is the process of establishing desired results that guide and direct behavior. Goal-setting theory is based on laboratory studies, field research experiments, and comparative investigations by Edwin Locke, Gary Latham, John M. Ivancevich, and others.[23] Goals crystallize the sense of purpose and mission that drives success.

6-3a Characteristics of Effective Goals

Various organizations define the characteristics of effective goals differently. As one example, Sanger-Harris, a former retail organization, used SMART goals. SMART stands for *Specific, Measurable,*

Table 6.2 Personality Functions and Learning

Personality Preference	Implications for Learning by Individuals
Information gathering	
Intuitors	Prefer theoretical frameworks. Look for the meaning in material. Attempt to understand the grand scheme. Look for possibilities and interrelations.
Sensors	Prefer specific, empirical data. Look for practical applications. Attempt to master details of a subject. Look for what is realistic and doable.
Decision making	
Thinkers	Prefer analysis of data and information. Work to be fair-minded and evenhanded. Seek logical, just conclusions. Do not like to be too personally involved.
Feelers	Prefer interpersonal involvement. Work to be tenderhearted and harmonious. Seek subjective, merciful results. Do not like objective, factual analysis.

Source: From Type Talk at Work by Otto Kroeger and Janet Theusen, copyright © 1992 by Janet Theusen and Otto Kroeger. Used by permission of Delacorte Press, an imprint of The Random House Publishing Group, a division of Random House, Inc.

Attainable, *Realistic*, and *Time-bound*. Specific and challenging goals focus attention on exactly what will be accomplished and inspire peak performance. People who set specific, challenging goals consistently outperform those with easy or unspecified goals, as Figure 6.2 shows. Subconscious thought may have a positive effect as well. Two studies of subconscious motivation found that goals that were ingrained but not explicitly expressed significantly enhanced task performance for difficult conscious goals, though not for easy goals.[24]

Measurable, quantitative goals provide opportunities for feedback about goal progress. Qualitative goals are also valuable. The Western Company of North America (now part of BJ Services Company) allows about 15% of a manager's goals to be of a qualitative nature.[25] An example of a qualitative goal is improving customer relations. To assess its progress, this qualitative goal might be quantified using measures like the number of complaints or the frequency of compliments.

Time-bound goals enhance measurability. Many organizations work on standardized cycles of time, such as quarters or years. If there is any uncertainty about the time period of the goal effort, the time limit should be explicitly stated.

The prioritizing of goals allows efficient resource allocation. As time, energy, or other resources become available, a person can work through their list of goals in order of importance.[26] Priority helps direct a person's efforts and behavior.

Goal setting can serve three functions. First, it can increase work motivation and task performance.[27]

Second, it can reduce stress caused by conflicting or confusing expectations.[28] Third, it can improve the accuracy and validity of performance evaluation.[29] Let's look at each of these functions in some detail.

6-3b Goals Increase Work Motivation and Task Performance

Goals often increase employee effort and motivation, which in turn improve task performance. The higher the goal is, the better the performance. People work harder to reach difficult goals. Figure 6.2 depicts this positive relationship.

Managers who use goal setting should ensure employee participation, supervisory commitment, and useful performance feedback. Participation encourages employees to accept and commit to the goal, two prerequisites to goal accomplishment. Employee participation is especially important in the accomplishment of difficult goals.[30] And when a difficult goal is assigned, acceptance and commitment are considered essential prerequisites to accomplishment.

Supervisory goal commitment reflects an organization's commitment to goal setting. Indeed, organizational commitment is a prerequisite for successful goal-setting programs such as *management by objectives (MBO)*, discussed shortly.[31] The organization commits to the program, and the supervisors and employees commit to its specific work goals.

Figure 6.2 Goal Level and Task Performance

The supervisor also provides employees with interim performance feedback on their progress toward goals. Such performance feedback is most useful for goals that are specific, and specific goals improve performance most when interim feedback is given.[32] When approached correctly, even negative performance feedback can improve performance.[33] For example, assume an insurance salesperson has a goal of selling $500,000 worth of insurance in six months but has sold only $200,000 after three months. During an interim performance feedback session, the supervisor helps the salesperson identify their problem—that they are not focusing their calls on the likeliest prospects—and gets them back on track to achieve their goal. Feedback is most helpful when it provides practical advice and is timely.

6-3c Goals Reduce Role Stress, Conflict, and Ambiguity

Goal setting also reduces the *role stress* associated with conflicting and confusing expectations because it clarifies the task–role expectations for employees. Supervisors, coworkers, and employees all provide task-related information. A fourteen-month evaluation found that goal setting reduced conflict, confusion, and absenteeism.[34]

Because goal setting improves role clarity, it generally improves communication between managers and employees.[35] This is why FedEx encourages managers to include communication-related targets in their annual MBO goal-setting process.[36]

6-3d Goals Improve Performance Evaluation

The third major function of goal setting is improving the accuracy and validity of performance evaluation. One of the best methods for this is **management by objectives (MBO)**—a goal-setting program based on interaction and negotiation between employees and managers.

According to Peter Drucker, who developed the concept of MBO over fifty years ago, the

Reward Employee

Provide Feedback

Define Organizational Goals

MBO Process

Evaluate Performance

Define Employee Objectives

Monitor Performance

marigranula/123RF

objectives-setting process begins with the employee writing a so-called employee's letter to the manager. The letter explains the employee's general understanding of the scope of the manager's job as well as the scope of the employee's own job. The employee lays out a set of specific objectives to be pursued over the next six to twelve months, and after some discussion and negotiation, the manager and the employee finalize these items into a performance plan.

Drucker considers MBO a participative and interactive process. This does not mean that goal setting begins at the bottom of the organization. It means that goal setting is applicable to all employees; both lower-level organizational members and professional staff influence the goal-setting process.[37] Most goal-setting programs are designed to enhance performance, especially when incentives are associated with goal achievement.[38]

The two central ingredients in goal-setting programs are planning and evaluation. The *planning* component consists of organizational and individual goal setting, two essential and interdependent processes.[39] In planning, individuals and departments usually develop operational and tactical plans to support the corporate objectives. The idea is to formulate a clear, consistent, measurable, and ordered set of goals to articulate *what* to do. Operational support planning then determines *how* to do it. The concept of *intention* encompasses both the goal

management by objectives (MBO) A goal-setting program based on interaction and negotiation between employees and managers.

Hot Trend

Avoiding the Pitfalls of Goal-Setting

Setting specific, challenging goals can be very useful for both employers and employees. A long line of work supports this idea and the general tenets of goal-setting theory. Yet recent work in organizational behavior has uncovered concerning downsides to goal setting. There appear to be at least two "side effects" of goal setting that can be harmful.

First, because goals narrow attention, they can prevent employees from recognizing and responding to ethical dilemmas. This can occur because employees' resources (time, energy, focus) drain when working towards a challenging goal. As a result, they have fewer resources available to appropriately identify and respond to ethical concerns. Second, working towards very specific goals can sometimes demotivate employees from learning new strategies. That is, a narrow focus on achieving an outcome can prevent employees from developing novel solutions to the problem.

Fortunately, the same research that has uncovered these downsides has begun to identify potential solutions. For instance, the risk of unethical behavior in pursuit of a challenging goal can be limited by having leaders who model ethical behaviors. Learning and innovation can be encouraged via the setting of learning-based, as opposed to outcome-based, goals. In this case, employees set a goal to learn something like a new skill or a new strategy, which can then be used to achieve desired outcomes.

In sum, goal-setting, while a powerful tool for organizations, does have the potential to cause some harmful "side-effects." Emerging research is identifying these risks and developing potential solutions that managers and leaders can consider.

Sources: L. D. Ordóñez., M. E. Schweitzer., A. D. Galinsky., & M. H. Bazerman. "Goals Gone Wild: The Systematic Side Effects of Overprescribing Goal Setting." Academy of Management Perspectives, 23 (2009): 6–16.
D. Welsh., J. Bush., C. Thiel., J. & Bonner. "Reconceptualizing goal setting's dark side: The ethical consequences of learning versus outcome goals." Organizational Behavior and Human Decision Processes, 150 (2019): 14–27.
D. Welsh., M. D. Baer., H. Sessions., & N. Garud. "Motivated to disengage: The ethical consequences of goal commitment and moral disengagement in goal setting." Journal of Organizational Behavior, 41 (2020): 663–677.

(*what*) and the pathways that lead to goal attainment (*how*).[40] This part of the planning process ensures that individual employee goals are aligned with organizational objectives.[41]

The *evaluation* component of goal setting consists of interim reviews conducted by managers and employees and formal performance evaluation. The interim reviews are designed to help employees take self-corrective action. The formal performance evaluation occurs at the close of a reporting period, usually once a year. Based on goal orientation theory, four types of feedback seeking were developed: self-positive, self-negative, other-positive, and other-negative.[42] If the goal was improved performance, the following feedback seeking patterns worked best. Self-negative feedback seeking was positively related to job performance, role clarity, and social integration, while self-positive feedback seeking was negatively related, and other-positive feedback seeking was positively related to job performance. Interim and formal performance evaluations can both be optimized via advances in machine learning and AI. Self-corrective feedback loops can be built via such technologies to help employees improve continually.[43] Big data techniques can help keep track of trends in employee engagement and prove useful in making organizational policy changes related such engagement.

Because goal-setting programs are somewhat mechanical by nature, they are most valuable and easily implemented in stable, predictable industrial settings. They are less useful in small, unpredictable organizations. Neither individual personality differences nor gender nor cultural differences appear to threaten the success of goal-setting programs, making them useful tools for a large, diverse workforce.[44]

Goal setting can increase work motivation and task performance, reduce stress, and improve the accuracy of performance evaluation.

6-4 Performance: A Key Construct

Performance is most often called *task accomplishment*, the term *task* coming from Frederick W. Taylor's conception of a worker's required activity.[45] Since

Taylor's time in the early 1900s, there has been an extensive body of applied research on the constructs of performance management and performance appraisal.[46] Principal concerns over the past century have included purposes for evaluating performance, training, and reactions to appraisals, as well as demographic differences and cognitive processes. Hence, outcomes and effort are both important to good performance.

Predicting job performance has also been a concern for over a century. Early World War I–era theories focused on intelligence and *general mental ability (GMA)*. Research has found GMA highly predictive of job knowledge in both civilian and military jobs.[47] Researchers have found mixed EI (emotional intelligence) to be a valid predictor of job performance. Mixed EI consists of personality traits, such as extraversion and conscientiousness, as well as affect and self-perceived abilities.[48] But before job performance can be predicted, it must be defined.

6-4a Performance Management

Performance management is a process of defining, measuring, appraising, providing feedback on, and improving performance.[49] Defining performance in behavioral terms is an essential first step in the process. Done well, the performance management process leads to increased employee engagement, whereby workers know exactly what's expected of them and have the skills and abilities to meet those expectations.[50] Once defined, performance can be measured and assessed so that workers can receive feedback and managers can set goals to improve performance. Positive performance behaviors should be rewarded, and poor performance behaviors should be corrected.

6-4b Defining Performance

Managers must clearly define performance if their employees are to perform well at work. Most work performance is multidimensional. For example, a sales executive's performance will require administrative,

financial, and interpersonal skills. Knowing the skills and behaviors needed to succeed in a position is a prerequisite to measuring and evaluating job performance.

Although different jobs require varying skills and behaviors, *organizational citizenship behavior (OCB)* spans many jobs. Recall from Chapter 4 that OCB is behavior above and beyond the call of duty. Employee involvement programs enhance OCB by engaging employees in the work environment.[51] OCB emphasizes collective performance rather than individual performance. It is but one of many dimensions to consider when defining the requirements of a specific job.

Performance appraisal is the evaluation of a person's performance. Accurate appraisals help supervisors fulfill their dual roles as evaluators and coaches. As the latter, a supervisor encourages growth and development. As the former, a supervisor makes judgments about employees' roles in the organization. Keeping an employee's position within the company in mind lends greater contextual significance to the appraisal process.[52]

Performance appraisals give employees feedback on performance, identify their developmental needs, and influence promotion, demotion, termination, selection and placement decisions.

6-4c Measuring Performance

Ideally, actual performance matches measured performance, but this is actually seldom the case. Since operational performance generates more quantifiable data, it is easier to measure than managerial performance. Recent research measuring motivation for task performance has found that wording and context may influence the validity of direct self-reports.[53] Accuracy of self-performance evaluations is also important. The more accurately individuals evaluate their performance on a task, the better their performance will be on a subsequent task.[54]

Performance appraisal systems should improve the accuracy of measured performance and increase its parity with actual performance. The extent of their agreement is called the *true assessment*, as Figure 6.3 shows. Performance measurement problems such as deficiency, unreliability, and invalidity contribute to inaccuracy. *Deficiency* occurs when important aspects of a person's actual performance are overlooked. Unreliability results from poor-quality performance measures. *Invalidity* stems from inaccurate definition of the expected job

performance management A process of defining, measuring, appraising, providing feedback on, and improving performance.

performance appraisal The evaluation of a person's performance.

Figure 6.3 Actual and Measured Performance

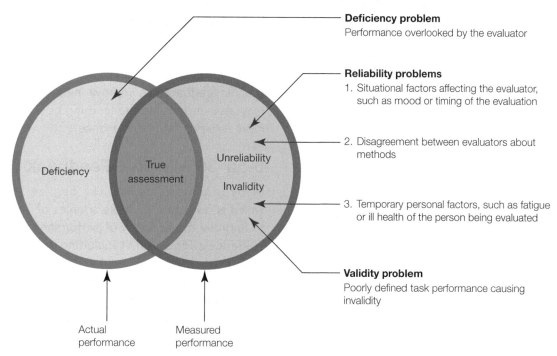

Deficiency problem
Performance overlooked by the evaluator

Reliability problems
1. Situational factors affecting the evaluator, such as mood or timing of the evaluation

2. Disagreement between evaluators about methods

3. Temporary personal factors, such as fatigue or ill health of the person being evaluated

Validity problem
Poorly defined task performance causing invalidity

Source: Table from The *Air Officer's Guide*, 6th ed. Copyright © 1952 Stackpole Books. Used with permission.

performance. Further, when performance appraisals are done so that they are fair, consistent, and valid, they improve employee motivation, job satisfaction, and performance while also resulting in lower turnover.[55]

Table 6.3, a sample of officer effectiveness reports from a nineteenth-century infantry company, demonstrates the bias of early performance appraisals. Even contemporary executive appraisals have a dark side, arousing the defenses of managers and executives. Addressing emotions and defenses is important to the effectiveness of appraisal sessions.[56] Some performance review systems lead to forced rankings of employees, which may be controversial or counterproductive. Although a recent study found that supervisors were reluctant to give negative feedback overall, they were more likely to emphasize social factors when describing the performance of ethnic minorities.[57]

Many performance-monitoring systems use modern electronic technology to measure the performance of vehicle operators, computer technicians, and customer service representatives. For example, such systems might record the rate or the total number of keystrokes for a computer technician.

Sometimes employees are unaware that their performance is being measured. What constitutes

Table 6.3 Officer Effectiveness Reports, CIRCA 1813

Alexander Brown, Lt. Col., Comdg.—A good-natured man.

Clark Crowell, 1st Major—A good man, but no officer.

Jess B. Wordsworth, 2nd Major—An excellent officer.

Captain Shaw—A man of whom all unite in speaking ill. A knave despised by all.

Captain Thomas Lord—Indifferent, but promises well.

Captain Rockwell—An officer of capacity, but imprudent and a man of violent passions.

1st Lt. Jas. Kearns—Merely good, nothing promising.

1st Lt. Robert Cross—Willing enough, has much to learn, with small capacity.

2nd Lt. Stewart Berry—An ignorant unoffending fellow.

Ensign North—A good young man who does well.

Source: J. C. Benton, The Air Officer's Guide, 6th ed. (Mechanicsburg, Penn.: Stackpole Books 1952). Copyright © 1952 Stackpole Books. Used with Permission.

inappropriate electronic monitoring of an employee? The ethics of monitoring performance differ by culture. For example, firms in the United States and Sweden generally respect individual privacy more than those in Japan or China.

Goal setting and MBO are results-oriented performance appraisal methods that do not necessarily rely on modern technology. Like performance-monitoring systems, they focus on observable, verifiable results, instead of subjective, judgmental performance dimensions. Goals established during planning serve as the standard for measuring subsequent performance. However, managers who adhere rigidly to a results-oriented approach risk overlooking performance opportunities.

6-5 Performance Feedback

Feedback sessions create stress for both supervisors and employees. Early research at General Electric found, not surprisingly, that employees responded constructively to positive feedback but often responded defensively to critical or negative feedback. In response to negative feedback, they shifted responsibility for the problem, denied it outright, or provided a wide range of excuses.[58] In a study of 499 Chinese supervisor–subordinate pairs, supervisors responded positively to employees who sought performance feedback if their motive was performance enhancement or improvement but not so positively if the employee's motive was to influence how their supervisor perceived them.[59]

Employee responses to negative feedback may be consequential. Role congruity theory suggests that there may be a gender bias in the performance feedback process related to some behaviors, such as the act of crying. The argument goes that a male employee crying in response to negative performance feedback will be seen as atypical behavior by the feedback provider, often the supervisor. This result then biases evaluations of the employee on a number of dimensions, such as performance evaluations, assessments of leadership capability, and written recommendations. In fact, the evidence suggests that men who cry in response to negative performance feedback will experience biased evaluations from the feedback provider.[60] Hence, the message "boys, don't cry" has positive value in the performance feedback context.

Supervisors should start performance feedback sessions with something positive. Once the session is

under way and rapport is established, the evaluator can introduce more difficult and negative material. No one is perfect, so everyone can learn and grow through performance feedback and review sessions. Critical feedback is the basis for improvement. Managers should be aware, however, that although specific feedback can improve initial performance, it may also undermine the learning needed for later, more independent performance.[61]

6-5a 360-Degree Feedback

Many organizations use **360-degree feedback**, which is based on multiple sources of information, to improve the accuracy of performance appraisals. Evidence suggests that including self-evaluations in this process makes evaluation interviews more satisfying, more constructive, and less defensive.[62] Some dislike the fact that self-evaluations often conflict with supervisory evaluations.[63] However, these disagreements are part of the full picture of the person's performance. The 360-degree feedback method provides a well-rounded view of performance from superiors, peers, followers, and customers.[64]

As an illustration of the benefits of a 360-degree feedback evaluation, consider a mid-level civilian executive working in a large military organization. The executive is positive, compliant, and deferential toward superiors but largely indifferent toward peers. With followers, he is tough and demanding, bordering on abusive. Without each of these perspectives, the executive's performance cannot be accurately assessed.

Adding a systematic coaching component can improve 360-degree feedback.[65] By focusing on enhanced self-awareness and behavioral

360 degree evaluations can help improve accuracy in performance appraisal.

360-degree feedback A process of self-evaluation and evaluations by a manager, peers, direct reports, and possibly customers.

iStock.com/AndreyPopov

management, feedback coaching improves performance, satisfaction, and commitment, and reduces turnover. Separating the performance feedback component from the management development component also improves the 360-degree method.[66] The feedback component contains quantitative feedback and performance measures, while the management development component emphasizes qualitative feedback and competencies for development.

6-5b Developing People and Enhancing Careers

Good performance appraisal systems develop people and enhance careers. They should explore individual growth needs and future performance.

However, in order to coach and develop employees successfully, the supervisor must establish mutual trust. This means she must be vulnerable and open to challenge from the subordinate while maintaining responsibility for the subordinate's best interests.[67] Good supervisors are skilled, empathetic listeners who encourage employees to discuss their aspirations.[68] Recent advances in technology-based feedback systems such as AI suggest that ongoing, interactive performance feedback and coaching can help people develop over a period of time rather than annual performance meetings.[69,70,71]

Employees must also take active responsibility for future development and growth. This might mean challenging the supervisor's ideas about future development and expressing their own goals. Passive,

Inclusive Conversations

Racial Disparities in Performance Evaluations at *The New York Times*

The New York Times (*The Times*) has won more Pulitzer Prizes than any other media company in U.S. history and is widely known for its investigative reports involving the dynamics of race and gender dynamics in the United States. According to its own figures, people of color represent a third of the company's employees and 23% of its leadership positions.

A recent study commissioned by The Guild, the newspaper's labor union, revealed racial disparities in performance ratings. Black and Latino newsroom employees were less likely to receive strong job performance ratings than their white counterparts. According to the report, "Being Hispanic reduced the odds of receiving a high score by about 60%, and being Black cut the chances of high scores by nearly 50%." A former *Times* reporter who is Asian-American told a story about her weeping after receiving a mediocre performance rating despite receiving positive performance assessments. She saw no future with the paper and took a job with a competitor. Frances Robles, an investigative reporter with the *Times* complained about the racial disparities and saw her performance ratings increase. She points to her being a "Puerto Rican girl from Queens" to her ability to obtain important information on cases that her white colleagues were unable to obtain. Performance evaluation ratings at *The Times*, as in many organizations, are often tied to the size of monetary bonuses and promotional opportunities. More importantly, racial disparities in performance evaluations can signal deeper underlying issues that lead to feelings of inequity among employees and stalled efforts by decision-makers to build and maintain a diverse workforce.

1. How do you explain the lower performance ratings for employees of color at *The Times*?

   Students will have a variety of responses ranging from the Guild's data collection and analysis to discrimination based on race and ethnicity. Instructors should guide students to the need for performance evaluations to be equitable and non-biased.

2. What steps can organizations take to increase the performance ratings for all employees, specifically employees of color?

   Organizations should follow guidelines outlined in the chapter for measuring performance and providing performance feedback.

Source: Folkenflik, D. (2022, August 23). People of Color at New York Times Get Lower Ratings in Job Reviews, Union Says. *NPR News*, https://www.npr.org/2022/08/23/1118817023/new-york-times-race-employees-job-review-union; Watson, A. (2023, June 14). Credibility of the New York Times in the U.S. 2022. *Statista*, https://www.statista.com/statistics/239749/credibility-of-the-new-york-times-in-the-united-states/#:~:text=In%20addition%20to%20generally%20high,be%20accurate%20in%20its%20reporting.

Adobe's "Check-in" Replaces Formal Annual Reviews

Annual performance reviews have long been a staple of organizational performance management. In recent years, however, some companies have been re-thinking the necessity and usefulness of this tradition. Consider Adobe's transition from annual performance reviews to what they call "Check-in": a system encouraging on-going, less formal development conversations between managers and employees. The company referenced employee frustration at the infrequent and structured yearly performance reviews as a motivator for this change, and they tout the new system as having a large amount of employee buy-in.

Adobe has not stopped making adjustments either. Adjusting to an increasingly hybrid and virtual work environment, the company has moved Check-in to a centralized digital space. Doing so has allowed managers and employees alike to share documents, collaborate using online tools, and maintain more regular feedback. Adobe, like other companies, is continually adjusting its performance management system instead of hewing exclusively to traditional methods.

Source: Adobe. "Check-in" (2022). https://www.adobe.com/check-in.html

compliant employees cannot accept responsibility for themselves or achieve full emotional development. Individual responsibility is a key characteristic of the culture of the steel manufacturer Gerdau Ameristeel. The company joke is that the company manages by "adultry" (pun intended). Gerdau Ameristeel treats people like adults and expects adult behavior from them.

6-5c Key Characteristics of an Effective Appraisal System

Effective performance appraisal systems have five key characteristics: validity, reliability, responsiveness, flexibility, and equitability. *Validity* means capturing multiple dimensions of a person's job performance. *Reliability* means collecting evaluations from multiple sources and at different times throughout the evaluation period. *Responsiveness* means allowing the person being evaluated to have some input. *Flexibility* means staying open to modification based on new information such as federal requirements. *Equitability* means evaluating fairly against established criteria, regardless of individual differences. High-quality performance appraisals with these characteristics have a positive effect on employee participation in voluntary informal learning activities.[72]

FedEx has incorporated a novel and challenging approach to evaluation in its blueprint for service quality. All managers at FedEx are evaluated by their employees through a survey-feedback-action system. Employees, in turn, evaluate their managers using a five-point scale on twenty-nine standard statements

and ten local option ones. Low ratings suggest problem areas requiring management attention. One year the survey revealed that employees thought upper management was not paying attention to ideas and suggestions from people at their level. In response, CEO Fred Smith developed a biweekly employee newsletter to correct the problem.

6-6 Rewarding Performance

Performance appraisals can provide input for reward decisions. If companies celebrate teamwork, values, and customer focus, they must reward behaviors demonstrating these ideas. Despite their importance, reward decisions are among the most difficult and complicated decisions managers make. There is abundant research documenting a gender pay gap, with women earning less than men, all else being equal. However, the "all else being equal" caveat does not always hold. Theory and research evidence show that high-potential women are more valuable for achieving organizational diversity goals than high-potential men, thus challenging the assumption that the gender pay gap uniformly disadvantages women.[73] High-potential women are those with the abilities needed to reach the upper echelons of organizations. Their advantage over high-potential men ends up reversing the gender pay gap and enables them to receive a pay premium. While pay and rewards for performance have value, so too do trust, fun, and meaningful work. In fact, some

> Reward and punishment decisions affect entire organizations, not just the people receiving the consequence.

compensation professionals have advanced the idea of Total Rewards that include extrinsic rewards like compensation and benefits as well as intrinsic ones like work-life benefits, performance and recognition, and career-development opportunities.

Reward and punishment decisions affect entire organizations, not just the people receiving the consequence. Reward allocation involves sequential decisions about which people to reward, how to reward them, and when to reward them. These decisions shape all employees' behavior, either directly or through vicarious learning, especially when new programs are implemented. People watch what happens to peers who make mistakes and adjust their own behavior accordingly.

6-6a Individual versus Team Reward Systems

While motivation and reward systems outside the United States are often group focused, many U.S. organizations use systems that are focused on rewarding employees as individuals.[74] These systems foster independent behavior and encourage creativity, problem solving, and distinctive contributions to the organization. Different types of employees may prefer different rewards. For example, adventure seekers may prefer travel awards, while nesters prefer days off.[75]

Individual reward systems directly affect individual behavior and encourage competition within a work team.[76] Too much competition, however, may create a dysfunctional work environment. At the Western Company of North America (now part of BJ Services Company), individual success in the MBO program was tied too tightly to rewards, and individual managers became divisively competitive. Some managers took last-minute interdepartmental financial actions to meet their objectives. By doing so, they caused other managers to miss their objectives. These actions raise ethical questions about how far individual managers should go in serving their own self-interest at the expense of their peers.

Team reward systems solve the problems caused by individual competitive behavior in that they encourage cooperation, joint efforts, and the sharing of information and expertise. The collectivist orientations of Japanese and Chinese cultures position the individual as an element of the team, not as a separate individual.

Some organizations have experimented with individual and group alternative reward systems. At the individual level, these include skill-based and pay-for-knowledge systems that emphasize skills or knowledge possessed by an employee beyond the requirements for the basic job. At the group level, gain-sharing plans emphasize collective cost reduction by allowing workers to share in the gains achieved by reducing production costs. In such plans, everyone shares equally in the collective gain. Avnet, Inc. found that collective profit sharing improved performance. The most effective incentives are those that celebrate the group's accomplishments collectively rather than those that single out individuals.[77]

6-6b The Power of Earning

Both individual and team reward systems can shape productive behavior, so effective performance management boosts both individual and team achievements in an organization. Performance management and reward systems assume a demonstrable connection between performance and rewards; that is, organizations get the performance they reward, not the performance they say they want.[78]

When there is no apparent link between performance and rewards, people may begin to believe they are entitled to rewards regardless of their performance. The notion of entitlement at work counteracts the *power of earning*.[79] People who believe they are entitled to rewards without earning them are not motivated to behave constructively. Merit raises in

iStock.com/Blue Planet Studio

Managers play a critical role in helping to establish the link between employee performance and rewards.

some organizations, for example, have come to be viewed as entitlements, thus reducing their positive value in the organizational reward system. Entitlement engenders passive, irresponsible behavior, whereas earning engenders active, responsible behavior. The power of earning rests on a direct link between performance and rewards. Managers play a critical role in helping to establish this link by establishing performance goals, providing employees with feedback and assistance toward goal completion, evaluating their performance, then recommending rewards based on performance. These "contingent reward leadership" behaviors strengthen the line-of-sight that helps employees more clearly see the connection between the pay they receive and their performance of established goals.[80]

6-7 Correcting Poor Performance

Often a challenge for supervisors, correcting poor performance can be conceived as a three-step process. First, supervisors must identify the cause or primary responsibility for the poor performance. Second, if the primary responsibility is the employee's (and not the organization's) supervisors must determine the source of the personal problem. Third, they must develop a plan for correcting the poor performance.

A number of problems trigger poor performance. These include poorly designed work systems, poor selection processes, inadequate training and skills development, lack of personal motivation, and personal problems intruding on the work environment. Not all poor performance is self-motivated, though; some is induced by the work system. Therefore, a good diagnosis should precede corrective action, and work systems should be the

consensus An informational cue indicating the extent to which peers in the same situation behave in a similar fashion.

distinctiveness An informational cue indicating the degree to which an individual behaves the same way in other situations.

consistency An informational cue indicating the frequency of behavior over time.

first factor considered. It may be that an employee is subject to a work design or selection system that keeps him from exhibiting good performance.

If the poor performance can't be attributed to work design or organizational process problems, then supervisors should examine the employee. The problem may lie in (1) some aspect of the person's relationship to the organization or supervisor, (2) some area of the employee's personal life, or (3) a training or developmental deficiency. In the latter two cases, poor performance can be treated as a symptom rather than as a motivated consequence. In such cases, identifying financial problems, family difficulties, or health disorders may help the employee solve problems before they become too extensive.

Poor performance may also stem from an employee's displaced anger or conflict with the organization or supervisor. In such cases, the employee may be unaware of the internal reactions causing the problem. Such angry motivations can generate sabotage, work slowdowns, and work stoppages. The supervisor might be attributing the cause of the problem to the employee while the employee is attributing it to the supervisor or organization. Supervisors must treat the poor performance as a symptom with a deeper cause and resolve the underlying anger or conflict.

6-7a Performance and Kelley's Attribution Theory

Recall from Chapter 3 that humans want to know why people behave the way they do. The same is true for managers. According to Harold Kelley's *attribution theory*, managers make attributions, or inferences, concerning employees' behavior and performance.[81] The attributions may not always be accurate. Supervisors and employees who share perceptions and attitudes tend to evaluate each other highly.[82] Those who do not share perceptions and attitudes are more likely to blame each other for performance problems.

Kelley's attribution theory proposes that individuals make attributions based on information gathered in the form of three informational cues: consensus, distinctiveness, and consistency.[83] **Consensus** is an informational cue indicating the extent to which peers in the same situation behave in a similar fashion. **Distinctiveness** is a cue indicating the degree to which an individual behaves the same way in other situations. **Consistency** is a cue indicating the

Correcting Poor Performance

At one time or another, each of us has had a poor performance of some kind. It may have been a poor test result in school, a poor presentation at work, or a poor performance in an athletic event. Think of a poor performance event you have experienced and work through the following three steps.

Step 1. Briefly describe the specific event in some detail. Include why you label it a poor performance (bad score? someone else's evaluation?).

Step 2. Analyze the Poor Performance

a. List all the possible contributing causes to the poor performance. Be specific, such as the room was too hot, you did not get enough sleep, you were not told how to perform the task, etc. You might ask other people for possible ideas, too.

1. _____
2. _____
3. _____
4. _____
5. _____
6. _____
7. _____

b. Is there a primary cause for the poor performance? What is it?

Step 3. Plan to Correct the Poor Performance

Develop a step-by-step plan of action that specifies what you can change or do differently to improve your performance the next time you have an opportunity. Include seeking help if it is needed. Once your plan is developed, look for an opportunity to execute it.

The notion of entitlement at work is counterproductive when taken to the extreme because it counteracts the power of earning. People who believe they are entitled to rewards regardless of their behavior or performance are not motivated to behave constructively. Some view merit raises as entitlements, thus reducing their positive value in the organizational reward system. People believe they have a right to be taken care of by someone, whether that is the organization or a specific person. Entitlement engenders passive, irresponsible behavior, whereas earning engenders active, responsible, adult behavior. If rewards depend on performance, people must perform responsibly to receive them. The power of earning rests on a direct link between performance and rewards.

frequency of behavior over time. We form attributions based on whether these cues are low or high.

Certain combinations of cues suggest an internal attribution, while other combinations suggest that the cause of the poor performance is external. Suppose you have received several complaints from customers regarding one of your customer service representatives, Niki. You have not received complaints about your other service representatives (low consensus). Reviewing Niki's records, you find that she also received customer complaints during her previous job as a sales clerk (low distinctiveness). The complaints have been coming in steadily for three months (high consistency). In this case, you would most likely make an internal attribution and conclude that the complaints must stem from Niki's behavior. The combination of low consensus, low distinctiveness, and high consistency suggests internal attributions.

Other combinations of these cues, however, point to external attributions. High consensus, high distinctiveness, and low consistency, for example, produce external attributions. Suppose one of your employees, Sanjay, is performing poorly on collecting overdue accounts. You find that the behavior is widespread within your work team (high consensus) and that Sanjay is performing poorly only on this aspect of the job (high distinctiveness), and that most of the time he handles this aspect of the job well (low consistency). You will probably decide that something about the work situation caused the poor performance.

On the basis of the informational cues, the supervisor makes either an internal (personal) attribution or an external (situational) attribution. Internal attributions might include low effort, lack of commitment, or lack of ability. External attributions are outside the employee's control and might include equipment failure or unrealistic goals. These examples are illustrated visually in Figure 6.4. Be warned, however, that the process of determining the cause of a behavior is not always as simple and clear-cut as these examples suggest, because biases sometimes interfere.

Figure 6.5 presents an attribution model of supervisors' responses to poor performance. Supervisors may choose from a wide range of responses. They can, for example, express personal concern, reprimand the employee, or provide training. Supervisors who attribute the cause of poor performance to a person (an internal cause) will respond more harshly than supervisors who blame the work situation (an external cause). Supervisors should avoid both common attribution errors discussed in

Chapter 3: the fundamental attribution error and the self-serving bias.

6-7b Coaching, Counseling, and Mentoring

Supervisors and coworkers are often more effective guides than formally as-signed mentors from higher up in the organizational hierarchy.[84] Consequently, they have important coaching, counseling, and mentoring responsibilities to their subordinates. Success in the mentoring relationship depends on openness and trust.[85] This relationship may help address performance-based deficiencies or personal problems.[86] In either case, supervisors can play a helpful role in employee problem-solving activities

Figure 6.4 Informational Cues and Attributions

Figure 6.5 Attribution Model

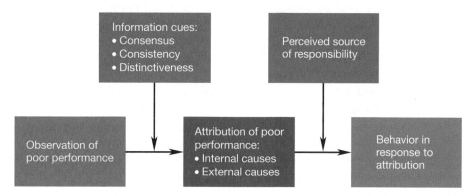

without accepting responsibility for the employees' problems. They may refer the employee to trained professionals.

Coaching and counseling are among the career and psychosocial functions of a mentoring relationship.[87] **Mentoring** is a work relationship that encourages development and career enhancement for people moving through the career cycle. Research has found a positive relationship between supervisory mentoring and OCBs. Employees who receive mentoring from their immediate supervisors are more likely to engage in individually focused OCBs (OCB-Is). OCB-Is are those helping behaviors that directly benefit coworkers as opposed to those that benefit the organization as a whole.[88] Mentor relationships typically go through four phases: initiation, cultivation, separation, and redefinition.

Mentoring offers protégés many career benefits.[89] The relationship can significantly enhance the early development of a newcomer and the midcareer development of an experienced employee. Some companies, such as IBM, offer mentoring at all levels of employment.[90] Peer relationships can also enhance career development.[91] Executive coaching is increasingly used to outsource the business mentoring functions. Informational, collegial, and special peers aid the individual's development by sharing information, career strategies, job-related feedback, emotional support, and friendship.

mentoring A work relationship that encourages development and career enhancement for people moving through the career cycle.

Experiential Exercise

Positive and Negative Reinforcement

Purpose: To examine the effects of positive and negative reinforcement on behavior change.

1. Two or three volunteers are selected to receive reinforcement from the class while performing a particular task. The volunteers leave the room.

2. The instructor identifies an object for the student volunteers to locate when they return to the room. (The object should be unobtrusive but clearly visible to the class. Objects that have worked well are a small triangular piece of paper left behind when a notice was torn

off a classroom bulletin board, a smudge on the chalkboard, or a chip in the paint of a classroom wall.)

3. The instructor specifies the reinforcement contingencies to be used when the volunteers return to the room. For negative reinforcement, students should hiss, boo, or throw (harmless) things when the first volunteer is moving away from the object; cheer and applaud when the second volunteer is getting closer to the object; and if a third volunteer is used, use negative and positive reinforcement.

4. The instructor should assign a student to keep a record of the time it takes each of the volunteers to locate the object.

5. Volunteer number one is brought back into the room and is instructed: "Your task is to locate and touch a particular object in the room, and the class has agreed to help you. You may begin."

6. Volunteer number one continues to look for the object until it is found while the class is giving negative reinforcement.

7. Volunteer number two is brought back into the room and is instructed: "Your task is to locate and touch a particular object in the room, and the class has agreed to help you. You may begin."

8. Volunteer number two continues to look for the object until it is found while the class is giving positive reinforcement.

9. Volunteer number three is brought back into the room and is instructed: "Your task is to locate and touch a particular object in the room, and the class has agreed to help you. You may begin."

10. Volunteer number three continues to look for the object until it is found while the class is giving positive and negative reinforcement.

11. In a class discussion, answer the following questions:
    a. How did the behavior of the volunteers differ when the three kinds of reinforcement (positive, negative, or both) were used?
    b. What were the emotional reactions of the volunteers to the different kinds of reinforcement?
    c. Which type of reinforcement, positive or negative, is most common in organizations? What effect do you think this has on motivation and productivity?

Learning Objectives

6-1 **Describe behavioral theories of learning.** The behaviorist approach to learning assumes that observable behavior is a function of its consequences. Behaviorists argue that learning stems from classical and operant conditioning. *Classical conditioning* is the process of modifying behavior so that pairing a conditioned stimulus with an unconditioned stimulus elicits an unconditioned response. *Operant conditioning* is the process of modifying behavior by following specific behaviors with positive or negative consequences. Reinforcement enhances desirable behavior, while punishment and extinction diminish undesirable behavior.

6-2 **Describe social and cognitive theories of learning.** The social learning theory occurs when we observe other people and model their behavior. Central to the theory is the notion of *task-specific self-efficacy*, an individual's beliefs and expectancies about his or her ability to perform a task effectively. In the cognitive theory, the personality functions of intuition, sensing, thinking, and feeling have learning implications. Each person has a preferred mode of gathering, evaluating, and making decisions about information.

6-3 **Explain how goal setting can be used to direct learning and performance.** *Goal setting* is the process of establishing desired results that guide and direct behavior. Goals often increase employee effort and motivation, which in turn improve task performance. Goal setting also reduces the role of stress associated with conflicting and confusing expectations because it clarifies the task-role expectations for employees. The third major function of goal setting is improving the accuracy and validity of performance evaluation.

6-4 **Define performance and identify the tools used to measure it.** Performance is most often called task accomplishment. *Performance management* is a process of defining, measuring, appraising, providing feedback on, and improving performance. Performance appraisals give employees feedback on performance, identify the employees' developmental needs, and influence promotion and reward decisions, demotion and termination decisions, and information about selection and placement decisions. Electronic performance monitoring systems, goal setting, and MBO are performance appraisal methods.

6-5 **Explain the importance of performance feedback and how it can be delivered effectively.** Good performance appraisal systems develop people, enhance careers, and boost individual and team achievements in an organization. Effective performance appraisal systems have five key characteristics: validity, reliability, responsiveness, flexibility, and equitability. The supervisor must establish mutual trust, be vulnerable and open to challenge, and be a skilled, empathetic listener who encourages employees to discuss their aspirations.

6-6 **Identify ways managers can reward performance.** Performance rewards can be pay, rewards, trust, fun, and meaningful work. Individual reward systems foster autonomous, independent behavior; and encourage creativity, problem solving, and distinctive contributions. At the individual level, these include skill-based and pay-for-knowledge systems. Team reward systems encourage cooperation, joint efforts, and the sharing of information and expertise. At the group level, gain-sharing plans emphasize collective cost reduction by allowing workers to share in the gains achieved by reducing production costs.

6-7 **List several strategies for correcting poor performance.** Harold Kelley's attribution theory aims to explain behavior based on shared perceptions and attitudes between supervisors and employees. Internal attributions might include low effort, lack of commitment, or lack of ability. External attributions might include equipment failure or unrealistic goals. Supervisors may express personal concern, reprimand the employee, or provide training. They may provide coaching, counseling, mentoring, or refer the employee to trained professionals

Key Terms

360-degree feedback A process of self-evaluation and evaluations by a manager, peers, direct reports, and possibly customers. (p. 122)

classical conditioning Modifying behavior by pairing a conditioned stimulus with an unconditioned stimulus to elicit an unconditioned response. (p. 112)

consensus An informational cue indicating the extent to which peers in the same situation behave in a similar fashion. (p. 126)

consistency An informational cue indicating the frequency of behavior over time. (p. 126)

distinctiveness An informational cue indicating the degree to which an individual behaves the same way in other situations. (p. 126)

extinction A strategy to weaken a behavior by attaching no consequences to it. (p. 115)

goal setting The process of establishing desired results that guide and direct behavior. (p. 116)

learning A change in behavior acquired through experience. (p. 112)

management by objectives (MBO) A goal-setting program based on interaction and negotiation between employees and managers. (p. 118)

mentoring A work relationship that encourages development and career enhancement for people moving through the career cycle. (p. 129)

negative consequences Results of a behavior that a person finds unattractive or aversive. (p. 113)

operant conditioning Modifying behavior through the use of positive or negative consequences following specific behaviors. (p. 112)

performance appraisal The evaluation of a person's performance. (p. 120)

performance management A process of defining, measuring, appraising, providing feedback on, and improving performance. (p. 120)

positive consequences Results of a behavior that a person finds attractive or pleasurable. (p. 113)

punishment A strategy to discourage undesirable behavior by either bestowing negative consequences or withholding positive consequences. (p. 115)

reinforcement A strategy to cultivate desirable behavior by either bestowing positive consequences or withholding negative consequences. (p. 113)

task-specific self-efficacy An individual's internal expectancy to perform a specific task effectively. (p. 115)

Ethical Dilemma

Isaac works for Creative Works, an agency that writes copy for marketing firms. Isaac loves his job. He is well paid, and he gets to work on many different campaigns and enjoys learning about a lot of new products and services.

Lately, however, he has developed a concern. Several people have resigned, and Creative Works does not seem to be in a rush to replace them. The reduced workforce is significantly increasing the workload on those people who remain with the company.

When Isaac was given four new accounts last week, he realized that he could not take on any more additional work. Then today he was given two new accounts, one of which is going to require him to learn details about a product he has never seen before. He is happy that Creative Works is doing well but he is beginning to feel like they are taking advantage of him.

There are several urgent deadlines on Monday, but Isaac has plans for the weekend that he has been looking forward to for a while. He contemplates how he can manage to both meet the deadlines and keep his weekend plans. When he realizes it is impossible to do both, he begins to consider what his options might be. He could just cancel his personal plans but he has grown really tired of doing that. He could miss the deadlines but that would go against his personal work ethic.

Then he thinks about AI. Maybe he could use one of the artificial intelligence sites to write the first draft of the ad copy for the product with which he is not familiar. He could always make it better later if the client does not like it. This plan would allow him to keep his plans and meet the deadlines.

1. Using consequential, rule-based, and character theories, evaluate Isaac's options.
2. What should Isaac do? Why?

Chapter 7

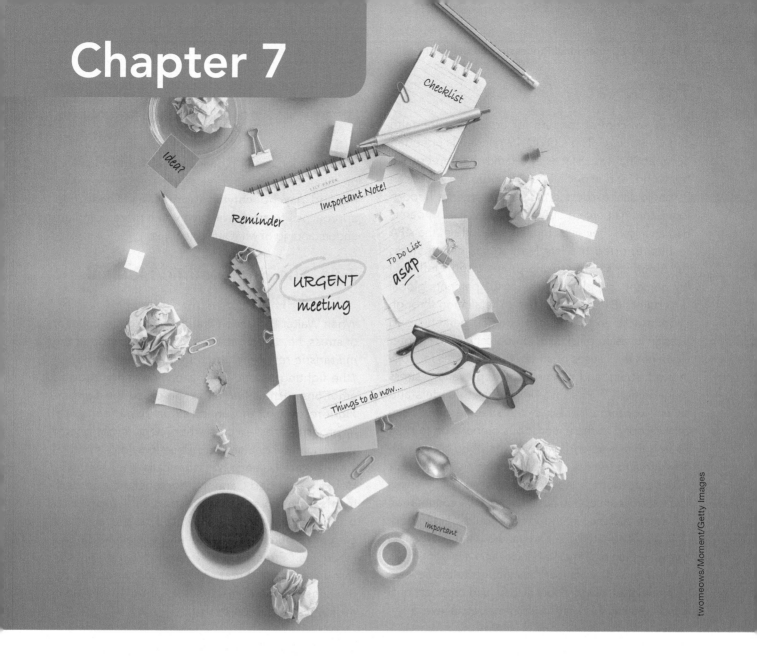

twomeows/Moment/Getty Images

Stress and Well-Being at Work

Learning Objectives

7-1 Define stress, distress, and strain.

7-2 Compare four different approaches to stress.

7-3 Explain the psychophysiology of the stress response.

7-4 Identify work and nonwork causes of stress.

7-5 Describe the consequences of stress.

7-6 Discuss individual factors that influence a person's response to stress and strain.

7-7 Identify the stages and elements of preventive stress management for individuals and organizations.

7-1 What Is Stress?

Stress is a central concern for occupational health and well-being.[1] The COVID-19 pandemic upended occupational workplaces and family life throughout the world, and especially in America. The American Psychological Association's *Stress in America Report*[2] found that 63 percent of American said the pandemic had changed their lives forever. In addition, the APA results reported the five leading sources of stress for Americans to be: rising prices due to inflation (87 percent), supply chain issues (81 percent), global uncertainty (81 percent), Russian retaliation through cyberattacks and nuclear threats (80 percent), and Russian invasion of Ukraine (80 percent). This chapter examines the causes of stress, the antidotes for coping with stress, and the methods of preventive stress management.™ First, it is important to understand several key terms. **Stress**, or the *stress response*, can be described as the unconscious preparation to fight or flee that a person experiences when faced with any demand.[3] A **stressor**, or demand, is a person or event that triggers the stress response. While stress is a neutral concept, it carries a negative connotation for some people, as though it should be avoided. This is unfortunate because eustress is a great asset in managing legitimate emergencies and achieving peak performance. **Distress**, or **strain**, refers to the adverse psychological, physical, behavioral, and organizational consequences that may result from stressful events.

7-2 Four Approaches to Stress

The *stress response* was discovered by Walter B. Cannon, a medical physiologist, early in the twentieth century.[4] Later, however, researchers defined stress differently than Cannon did, so we will review four

stress The unconscious preparation to fight or flee that a person experiences when faced with any demand.

stressor The person or event that triggers the stress response.

distress The adverse psychological, physical, behavioral, and organizational consequences that may arise as a result of stressful events.

strain Distress.

homeostasis A steady state of bodily functioning and equilibrium.

> Stress is a great asset in managing legitimate emergencies and achieving peak performance.

different approaches to define stress: the homeostatic/medical, cognitive appraisal, person–environment fit, and psychoanalytic approaches. These four approaches to stress will give you a more complete understanding of what stress really is.

7-2a The Homeostatic/Medical Approach

When Walter B. Cannon first developed the concept of stress, he called it the *emergency response* or the *militaristic response*, arguing that it was rooted in "the fighting emotions." His early writings showed emotions such as fear and rage cause the *fight-or-flight* response.[5] In Cannon's *homeostatic/medical approach*, stress occurs when deep emotions or environmental demands upset an individual's natural steady state balance, what he calls **homeostasis**.[6] Hobfoll extended Cannon's homeostatic approach in his Conservation of Resources Theory that proposes people are motivated to protect their current resources while investing to gain additional resources.[7] Stress primarily results from the loss of resources or the threat of loss of resources; hence, the conservation of resources is central to people in avoiding stressful conditions.

7-2b The Cognitive Appraisal Approach

Richard Lazarus was more concerned with the psychology of stress, emphasizing the psychological and cognitive aspects of the stress response in his *cognitive appraisal approach*.[8] Like Cannon, Lazarus saw stress as a result of a person–environment interaction, yet he emphasized the individual's cognitive appraisal in classifying persons or events as stressful or not. When appraising stressful workplace events, an important distinction can be made between "hindrance" and "threat" stressors. Whereas hindrance stressors tend to block goal achievement, threat stressors pose immediate personal harm or loss.[9] Individuals differ in their appraisals of events and people. Perception and cognitive appraisal are important processes in determining what is stressful. One study found higher instances of major depression when job demands were objectively assessed.[10] Another study found culture-specific differences in the perception of job stress between China and the United States.[11] American employees reported lack of control as a source of stress, while Chinese employees reported job evaluations as a significant source. In addition to cognitive appraisal, Lazarus introduced the ideas of problem-focused and emotion-focused coping. The former emphasizes managing the stressor, while the latter emphasizes managing the response. Whether individuals use problem-or emotion-focused coping strategies depends on motivation. For example, students planning and preparing for exams would more likely use problem-focused coping.[12] Those who evaluate themselves positively and consider themselves capable and in control of their own lives tend to favor emotion-focused coping when faced with stressors.[13]

7-2c The Person–Environment Fit Approach

Robert Kahn was concerned with the social psychology of stress, so his *person–environment fit* approach emphasized the idea that confusing and conflicting expectations of a person in a social role create stress for that person.[14] He extended the approach to consider a person's fit in the environment. A good person–environment fit occurs when one's skills and abilities match a clearly defined, consistent set of role expectations. Stress occurs when the role expectations are confusing and/or conflict with one's skills and abilities. After a period of this type of stress,

one can expect to experience symptoms of strain such as depression.

7-2d The Psychoanalytic Approach

Freudian psychoanalytic theory can help us understand the role of unconscious personality factors as causes of stress within a person.[15] Applying this *psychoanalytic* approach, Harry Levinson argued that two elements of the personality interact to cause stress. The first element is the **ego-ideal**—the embodiment of a person's perfect self. The second element is the **self-image**—how the person really sees themself both positively and negatively. Although not sharply defined, the ego-ideal encompasses admirable attributes of parental personalities, desired and/or imaginable qualities, and the absence of any negative or distasteful qualities. Stress results from the discrepancy between the idealized self (ego-ideal) and the real self-image; the greater the discrepancy, the more stress a person experiences.

7-3 The Stress Response

Whether activated by an ego-ideal/self-image discrepancy, a poorly defined social role, a cognitive appraisal suggesting threat, or a lack of balance,

ego-ideal The embodiment of a person's perfect self.

self-image How a person sees themself, both positively and negatively.

The Psychophysiology of Stress

In preparing to fight or flee, the body:

1. redirects blood to the brain and large muscle groups.
2. increases alertness through improved vision, hearing, and other sensory processes.
3. releases glucose (blood sugar) and fatty acids into the bloodstream to sustain the body during the stressful event.
4. suppresses the immune system as well as restorative and emergent processes (such as digestion).

Fight ⟷ Flight

sangoiri/123RF

Hot Trend

A Scientific Approach to Stress Recovery

When stressed out and anxious at work, our energy and resources are at a low ebb.

That is not the time to double-down on longer work hours and time-pressured deadlines. Rather, that is the time to engage in the paradox of stress recovery by following some scientific practices.

1. Psychologically detach from work by engaging in a totally non-work-related activity, maybe a videogame or drawing.

2. Harness the power of micro-breaks during the workday, taking a time out at the water cooler or for a chair stretch.

3. Consider your preference for recovery activity, choosing to engage in what is fun for _you_.

4. Prioritize high-effort recovery activities that call for activity, like the gym.

5. Shape your environment for optimal recovery; the design of your workspace and your personal space does matter.

There is a time to work hard and expend energy, there is a time to de-stress and recover energy.

Source: A. Meister, B. H. Cheng, N. Dael, and F. Krings, How to Recover from Work Stress, According to Science. _Harvard Business Review_, July 5 (2022).

the resulting stress response is characterized by a predictable sequence of mind and body events. The stress response begins with the release of chemical messengers, primarily adrenaline, into the bloodstream. These messengers activate the sympathetic nervous system and the endocrine (hormone) system. These two systems work together to trigger four mind–body changes that prepare the person for fight or flight.

The Hot Trend discusses the paradox, anchored in science, that calls for a balance between the stress of hard work and the practice of stress recovery.

As the body responds, the person shifts from a neutral posture to an offensive posture. The stress response can be very effective in preparing a person to handle legitimate emergencies through peak performance. Thus, it is neither inherently bad nor necessarily destructive. Perceptions of interactional injustice in the workplace can trigger the physiological stress response, with high levels of cortisol being released into the bloodstream of individuals who perceive they are being treated unfairly.[16]

7-4 Sources of Work Stress

Work stress is caused by factors in the work environment as well as by nonwork (external) pressures that spill over into the workplace. The two

major categories of sources of both types of work stress are shown in Table 7.1. An example of an external pressure is when a working mother or father is called at work to come pick up a sick child from day care. Job insecurity can be a pervasive source of work stress. Job insecurity can trigger employee responses that are very costly for organizations, such as workplace deviance and developing intentions to leave.[17] The reasoning behind these dysfunctional behaviors is that employees morally disengage. A positive relationship with leadership and the supervisor can help mitigate against these dysfunctional employee responses.

7-4a Work Demands

The four major categories of on-the-job work demands that trigger stress for employees in organizations are task demands, role demands, interpersonal demands, and physical demands. Table 7.1 does not present an exhaustive list of work demands but rather aims to show major causes of work stress in each of the four major domains of the work environment.

Task Demands Dramatic changes at work lead to uncertainty in a person's daily tasks and activities, provoking on-the-job pressure and stress. Globalization and large-scale business trends lead to change, as do smaller-scale shifts in company policy. In recent years, a global economic recession led

Table 7.1 Work and Nonwork Demands

Work Demands	
Task Demands	**Role Demands**
Change	Role conflict:
Lack of control	Interrole
Career progress	Intrarole
New technologies	Person–role
Temporal pressure	Role ambiguity
Interpersonal Demands	**Physical Demands**
Emotional toxins	Extreme environments
Sexual harassment	Strenuous activities
Poor leadership	Hazardous substances Global travel

Nonwork Demands	
Home Demands	**Personal Demands**
Family expectations	
Child-rearing/day care arrangements	Civic and volunteer work
Parental care	Traumatic events

many companies to make stressful changes, such as downsizing. At least 20 million jobs were lost by the end of 2009 due to the crisis.[18] Even during periods of growth, when hundreds of thousands of jobs are created every month, there may be significant numbers of jobs lost within certain sectors of the U.S. economy. For those who do not lose their jobs, underemployment, monotony, and boredom may be problematic.

Technological innovation creates change and uncertainty for many employees, requiring additional training, education, and skill development. New technologies create both career stress and so-called technostress for those who wonder if smart machines will replace them.[19] Although they enhance the organization's productive capacity, new technologies may be viewed as the enemy by workers who must ultimately learn to use them. This creates a real dilemma for management. Intended to make work easier and more convenient, information technology may have the paradoxical effect of incurring stress rather than relieving it.

Lack of control is another major task-related source of stress, especially in positions that are difficult and psychologically demanding. The lack of control may be caused by the inability to

- influence the timing of tasks and activities;
- select tools or methods for accomplishing the work;
- make decisions that influence work outcomes; or
- exercise direct action to affect the work outcomes.

Concerns over career progress and time pressures (or work overload) are two additional task demands triggering stress at work. Career stress has occurred in many organizations over the past two decades as middle-manager ranks have been thinned by mergers, acquisitions, and downsizing.[20] Leaner organizations, unfortunately, mean overload for the retained employees. Fewer people doing the same amount of work or more creates time pressure, a leading cause of stress often associated with work overload. Time pressure may also result from poor time-management skills. But not all task demands are negative. Challenge stressors that promote personal growth and achievement are positively related to job satisfaction and organizational commitment.[21]

Role Demands The social–psychological demands of the work environment may be every bit as stressful as task demands. Role stress may be particularly harmful to the job satisfaction and affective commitment of newcomers to the organization.[22] People encounter two major categories of role stress at work: role conflict and role ambiguity.[23] *Role conflict* results from inconsistent or incompatible expectations. The conflict may be an interrole, intrarole, or person–role conflict.

Interrole conflict is caused by opposing expectations related to two separate roles assumed by the same individual, such as employee and parent. For example, the employee with a major sales presentation due on Monday and a sick child at home Sunday night is likely to experience interrole conflict. Companies benefit from having policies and practices that address this work-nonwork, interrole interface.[24] Improved work-nonwork balance can both reduce interrole conflict and improve employee well-being.[25] The accompanying Inclusive Conversation on page 139 addresses the mental health crisis triggered by interrole conflict for working mothers.

Effects of Stress on the Body

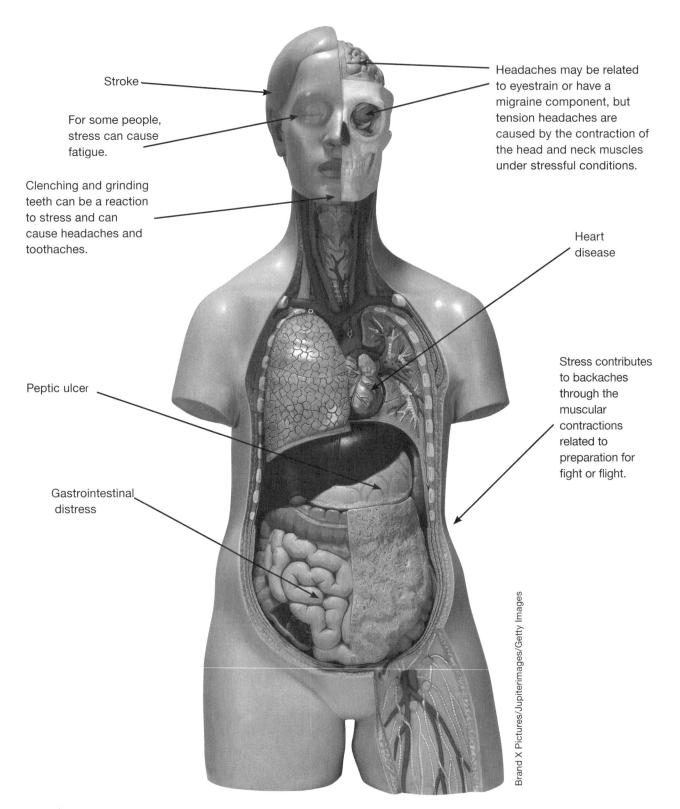

Stroke

For some people, stress can cause fatigue.

Clenching and grinding teeth can be a reaction to stress and can cause headaches and toothaches.

Headaches may be related to eyestrain or have a migraine component, but tension headaches are caused by the contraction of the head and neck muscles under stressful conditions.

Heart disease

Stress contributes to backaches through the muscular contractions related to preparation for fight or flight.

Peptic ulcer

Gastrointestinal distress

Brand X Pictures/Jupiterimages/Getty Images

Intrarole conflict is caused by opposing expectations related to a single role. For example, the manager who presses employees for both very fast and high-quality work may be viewed at some point as creating a conflict for employees.

Ethics violations are likely to cause *person–role conflicts*. Employees expected to behave in ways that violate personal values, beliefs, or principles experience this type of conflict. Person–role conflicts and ethics violations create a sense of divided loyalty for an employee. For example, if a distributor tells an organic farmer to cut costs by using a synthetic pesticide, the farmer may find that their personal beliefs are compromised by their role as a producer. Organizations with high ethical standards are less likely to create ethical conflicts for employees.

The second major cause of role stress is *role ambiguity*, which is the confusion a person experiences in relation to the expectations of others. Role ambiguity may be caused by misunderstanding what is expected, not knowing how to do it, or not knowing the result of failure to do it. For example, a new magazine employee asked to copyedit a manuscript may experience confusion because the new

> New technologies create both career stress and so-called technostress for those who wonder if smart machines will replace them.

employee mistakes copyediting for proofreading, doesn't know what formatting style to use, or doesn't know what will happen if they miss their deadline.

A twenty-one-nation study examined middle managers' experiences in role conflict, role ambiguity, and role overload. The results indicated that role stress varies more by country than it does by demographic and organizational factors. For example, non-Western managers experience less role ambiguity and more role overload than do their Western counterparts.[26] Another study, this time of 2,273 Norwegian employees, found that role conflict, role ambiguity, and conflict with coworkers increased under laissez-faire leadership, suggesting that a hands-off leadership style is destructive.[27] On the other hand, a study of U.S. military personnel found that when role clarity was high in a supportive work group, psychological strain was low.[28]

Inclusive Conversations

Interrole Conflict Leads to a Mental Health Crisis for Working Mothers

Can women have it all? Working women have been asking that question since 1982 when Helen Gurley Brown literally wrote the book. Today women struggle to have a vibrant career, a supportive partner, and thriving, well-behaved children. The struggle that women experience is often one with their mental health. Even women believe they have the areas of their lives under control, the conflict between work and family can take its toll on the mental health of working women. A Harris poll found that 42 percent of working mothers surveyed had been diagnosed with anxiety and/or depression compared with 28 percent of the entire population and 25 percent of their co-workers with children. It has been common for some time for women to serve as the primary caregivers for their families, but what is new is that working mothers are ignoring their own mental health needs to take care of the mental health needs of those they love. This has led to a mental health crisis for working moms.

1. What strategies can working mothers take to reduce the interrole conflict they experience?

   Students should be guided to consider the strategies suggested in the preventive stress management model—meditation apps (e.g., Calm). Employees can also set boundaries. For instance, establish a time to turn off their telephone at a specific time and/or remove work email from their personal phone.

2. What actions can employers take to reduce the anxiety of working mothers and parents?

   Employers can provide paid-leave policies for all parents and flexible work schedules, encourage employees to establish clear boundaries between work and home, and offer employee assistance programs (EAPs) and mental health services.

Sources: M. Chappet, Seriously, Why Are We Still Asking if Women Can "Have It All"? *Glamour Magazine*, March 20 (2019), accessed at https://www.glamourmagazine.co.uk/article/can-women-have-it-all#:~:text=Today%2C%20it%20is%20more%20commonly,Having%20It%20All'%20in%201982; L. T. Payton and K. Crowley, 42% of Working Moms Struggle with Depression and Anxiety – I'm One of Them. *Fortune*, March 17 (2023), accessed at *https://fortune.com/2023/04/07/working-moms-depression-anxiety/*; A. Slaughter, Why Women Still Can't Have It All. *The Atlantic*, July–August (2012), accessed at https://www.theatlantic.com/magazine/archive/2012/07/why-women-still-cant-have-it-all/309020/.

Interpersonal Demands *Emotional toxins*, such as sexual harassment and poor leadership in the organization, are examples of interpersonal demands, often generated at work by abrasive personalities.[29] Employees' ability to recharge and replace physical and psychological resources depleted during the work day is necessary for well-being. This recovery of resources often takes place once employees leave the workplace. Though considered less severe than other forms of interpersonal demands, workplace incivility experienced one day often remains with the individual and negatively affects the employee's ability to detach from the work and replenish resources needed for the next work day.[30] Another consequence of interpersonal demands can be *emotional dissonance*, which can spread through a work environment and cause a range of disturbances and stress.[31] Organizations are increasingly less tolerant of sexual harassment, a damaging interpersonal demand that creates a stressful working environment for both the person being harassed and for others. The vast majority of sexual harassment is directed at women in the workplace and is a chronic yet preventable problem.[32]

Poor organizational leadership and demanding managerial styles are leading causes of work stress for employees. But much depends on an employee's individual characteristics. Employees who feel secure under strong, directive leadership may be anxious under an open, self-directed style of management. Those comfortable with participative leaders may feel restrained by a directive style. In every case, however, trust is an important characteristic of the leader–follower interpersonal relationship, so a threat to a worker's reputation with their supervisor may be especially stressful.[33] Organizational trust is composed of management trust, supervisor trust, and coworker trust. Building supervisor trust and coworker trust can reduce job stress, especially, for example, among police officers in this high threat profession.[34]

Physical Demands Extreme environments, strenuous activities, hazardous substances, and global travel create physical demands for people at work. One cross-cultural study that examined the effects of ambient temperature on role stress concluded that uncomfortable temperatures diminish human well-being, leading to the development of the term *sweatshop* for inhumane working conditions.[35] The unique physical demands of work are often

Office work has frustrations and physical hazards, such as eyestrain, neck stiffness, and lower back pain.

occupation-specific, such as the gravitational forces on military pilots flying high-performance fighters or jet lag and loss of sleep for globetrotting CEOs. Even though there are many positive aspects to business travel, the associated demands are increasingly recognized as sources of stress,[36] as well as health risk since COVID-19.

Office work has its physical hazards as well. Noisy, crowded offices, such as those of some stock brokerages, can prove stressful, and even harmful. Working with a computer can also be stressful, especially if the ergonomic design of the workstation is not correct. Eyestrain, neck stiffness, and arm and wrist problems may result. Office designs that use partitions rather than full walls may create stress by offering little privacy and little protection from interruptions. *Stress audits* provide companies with detailed assessments of possible workplace stressors. Identification and alleviation of overlooked stress factors can save a company money and boost productivity.

7-4b Nonwork Demands

Nonwork demands are stressful, too, and can carry over into the work environment. *Nonwork demands* may broadly be identified as impositions from an individual's personal life environment (home) and self-imposed restrictions.

Home Demands The wide array of home and family arrangements in contemporary American society has created great diversity in the arena of home demands. Traditional and nontraditional families may experience demands that create role conflicts or overloads that are difficult to manage. For example, the loss of good day care for children may be especially stressful for dual-career and single-parent families.[37] The tension between work and family may lead to a real struggle for balance in life. This struggle led Rocky Rhodes, cofounder of Silicon Graphics, to establish four priorities for his life: God, family, exercise, and work.[38] These priorities helped him reallocate his time for better balance in his life. Moreover, as a result of the maturing of the American population, an increasing number of people face the added demand of parental care. Even when a person dedicates themself to reducing stress by integrating opposing social and work-related roles into a balanced, "whole" identity, the process is not an easy one.[39]

Personal Demands Self-imposed personal demands are the second major category of nonwork demands identified in Table 7.1. **Workaholism**, a form of addiction, may be the most notable of these stress inducing demands.[40] Some of the early warning signs of workaholism include overcommitment to work, inability to enjoy vacations and respites from work, preoccupation with work problems when away from the workplace, and insistence on working at home over weekends.

Another type of personal demand comes from civic activities, volunteer work, and organizational commitments to religious or public service organizations. These demands become more or less stressful depending on their compatibility with work and family life, and their capacity to provide alternative satisfactions for the individual. Finally, traumatic events, such as the devastating earthquake and tsunami in Japan in March 2011, are stressful for people who experience them.[41] Not all traumatic events are as catastrophic as natural disasters, of course, but job loss, failed exams, and romantic break-ups are all traumatic and may lead to distress if not addressed and resolved.

7-5 **The Consequences of Stress**

Stress may be positive or negative. Positive stress can create a healthy, thriving work environment, while negative stress, or distress, can erode morale and performance.

7-5a Eustress

Some managers and executives thrive under pressure because they practice what world-class athletes already know—that bringing mind, body, and spirit to peak condition requires recovering energy, which is as important as expending energy.[42] Hence, world-class athletes and managers get high marks on any stress test because they use stress-induced energy in positive, healthy, and productive ways. As we saw in Chapter 5, *eustress* is healthy, positive, normal stress that accrues a number of performance and health benefits.[43] An organization striving for high-quality products and services needs a healthy workforce to support the effort. Eustress is a characteristic of healthy people; distress is not.

The *Yerkes-Dodson law*, shown in Figure 7.1, indicates that stress leads to improved performance up to an optimum point.[44] Beyond that point, stress has a detrimental effect on performance. Therefore, healthy amounts of stress are desirable to improve performance by arousing a person to action. The greatest performance benefits from stress are achieved in the midrange of the Yerkes-Dodson curve, and after that, as Joseph McGrath has suggested, increasing difficulty of the task is probably what causes performance to decline.[45] Thus, the stress response invokes heightened strength and physical force for limited periods of exertion. This is how stress provides a basis for peak performance in athletic competition, and it can do the same for any type of job performance. Employee psychological well-being has additional primary and secondary effects on performance and can be bolstered by leadership.[46]

Specific stressful activities, including aerobic exercise, weight training, and flexibility training, improve health and enhance a person's ability to manage stressful demands or situations. Cannon argued that the stress response better prepares soldiers for combat.[47] In the outdoors, in survival or combat situations, stress provides one with the necessary energy boost to manage the situation successfully.

The various individual and organizational forms of distress often associated with the word *stress*

workaholism An imbalanced preoccupation with work at the expense of home and personal life satisfaction.

Figure 7.1 Yerkes-Dodson Law

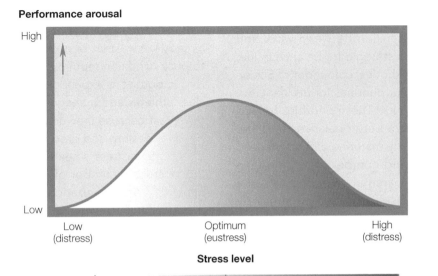

Performance arousal

High

Low

Low (distress) Optimum (eustress) High (distress)

Stress level

Boredom from understimulation   Optimum stress load   Conditions perceived as stressful   Distress from overstimulation

are the result of prolonged activation of the stress response, mismanagement of the energy induced by the response, or unique vulnerabilities in a person. We next examine the forms of individual distress and then the forms of organizational distress.

7-5b Individual Distress

An extreme preoccupation with work may result in acute individual distress. In its most extreme form, individual distress can lead to a phenomenon described by the Japanese word *karoshi*, or death by overwork.[48] Work-related psychological disorders are among the ten leading health disorders and diseases in the United States, according to the National Institute for Occupational Safety and Health.[49] The most common symptoms of psychological distress are depression, burnout, and psychosomatic disorders—physical ailments with psychological origins. These psychological distresses usually lead to *emotional exhaustion*, a form of psychological fatigue caused by energy depletion.[50] Emotional exhaustion may also be caused by the requirement for sustained emotional expression on the job.[51] A recent study of 257 Australian police officers found that emotional exhaustion at work had the potential to spill over to home life, causing work–family conflict.[52]

Burnout is among the most significant on-the-job hazards, whose signs are most often exhaustion, cynicism, and ineffectiveness. Maslach and Leiter shine a light on dysfunctional work environments as a key cause of employee burnout, versus thinking that burnout is a personal problem requiring therapy or relaxation training.[53] While burnout is a form of individual distress, the individual is not the cause of the burnout. When employees interact with an unhealthy work environment, burnout may well result. There is an important distinction between burnout and clinical depression, the latter being an important mental health condition requiring professional treatment. The distinction is best made through clinical diagnosis by a qualified professional.[54]

Flickr/Official U.S. Navy Page

Evidence suggests that the stress response better prepares soldiers for the experience of combat.

Burnout is not the same as *rust-out*, which is a form of psychological distress caused by a lack of challenge, inspiration, and/or opportunity on the job.[55] For example, a fast-food line cook who has flipped burgers at minimum wage for three years may experience rust-out for all the previously mentioned reasons, resulting in apathy, resentment, and diminished performance.

A number of medical illnesses have a stress-related component.[56] The most significant are heart disease, strokes, backaches, peptic ulcers, and headaches. Ford Motor Company found that cardiovascular diseases, the leading cause of death in the United States since 1910, constituted only 1.5 percent of the medical incidents among 800 salaried employees at its headquarters but accounted for 29 percent of the reported medical costs.[57]

Behavioral problems are another form of individual distress. These problems include workplace aggression, insomnia, substance abuse, and accidents. Workplace aggression may be triggered by perceptions of injustice in the workplace.[58] Interpersonal conflicts can be a form of nonphysical aggression. Insomnia is a nonaggressive behavioral problem that does have harmful effects on work outcomes such as job satisfaction, interpersonal deviance, and self-control.[59] The use of Internet-based cognitive behavior therapy has been found to be a partial solution to mitigate the harmful effect of insomnia.

Substance abuse ranges from legal behaviors such as alcohol abuse, excessive smoking, and the overuse of prescription drugs to illegal behaviors such as heroin and cocaine use. The abuse of certain substances, such as tobacco and heroin, can lead to addiction—a physical and/or psychological dependency. Abuse and addiction are behavioral problems that can impair job performance and often lead to significant individual distress.

Accidents, both on and off the job, are still another behavioral form of distress that can sometimes be traced to work-related stressors. For example, an unresolved problem at work may preoccupy or distract an employee, causing an accident either at the office or on the road. These three forms of individual distress—psychological disorders, medical illnesses, and behavioral problems—cause a burden of personal suffering. They also cause a collective burden of suffering reflected in organizational distress.

7-5c Organizational Distress

Studies performed at the University of Michigan on *organizational stress* identified a variety of indirect costs of mismanaged stress for an organization, such as low morale, dissatisfaction, breakdowns in communication, and disruption of working relationships. The direct costs of organizational distress include the high cost of turnover, the often hidden costs of absenteeism, and poor performance on the job.[60] Research suggests that even positive performance stereotypes can have an adverse effect on organizational health.[61] Three major costs of organizational distress are participation problems, performance decrements, and compensation awards.

Participation problems include absenteeism, tardiness, strikes and work stoppages, and turnover. In the case of absenteeism, the organization may compensate by hiring temporary personnel who take the place of the absentee, possibly elevating personnel costs. When considering turnover, a distinction should be made between dysfunctional and functional turnover. *Dysfunctional turnover* occurs when an organization loses a valuable employee. Replacement costs, including recruiting and retraining, range from five to seven months of the individual monthly salary. *Functional turnover*, in contrast, benefits the organization by creating opportunities for new members, new ideas, and fresh approaches. Functional turnover occurs when an organization loses an employee who has little or no value to the organization; thus, the loss of that employee is considered a positive result. The up-or-out promotion policy for members of some organizations is designed to create functional turnover.

Performance decrements are the costs resulting from poor quality or low quantity of production, grievances, and unscheduled machine downtime and repair. As in the case of medical illness, stress is not the only causal agent in these performance decrements. Stress does play a role, however, whether the poor quality or low quantity of production is motivated by distressed employees or by an unconscious response

participation problem A cost associated with absenteeism, tardiness, strikes and work stoppages, and turnover.

performance decrement A cost resulting from poor quality or low quantity of production, grievances, and unscheduled machine downtime and repair.

to stress on the job. Some employees in California have the option of taking a "stress leave" rather than filing a grievance against the boss.

Compensation awards are the organizational costs resulting from court awards for job distress.[62] In a federal lawsuit against Allstate, Frank Deus claimed that the company created a high-strain job for him that resulted in incapacitating depression.[63] A jury awarded him a $1.5 million judgment that was later overturned. Job stress-related claims have skyrocketed and threaten to bankrupt the workers' compensation system in some states, although claims and costs are down in other states.[64] Employers need not panic because fair procedures go a long way toward avoiding legal liability, and legal rulings are setting realistic limits on employers' obligations.[65]

7-6 Individual Differences in the Stress–Strain Relationship

Individual differences play a central role in the stress–strain relationship. The *weak organ hypothesis* in medicine, also known as the *Achilles' heel phenomenon*, suggests that a person breaks down at their weakest point. Individual differences, such as sex and Type A behavior pattern, enhance vulnerability to strain under stressful conditions. Other individual differences, such as personality hardiness and self-reliance, reduce vulnerability to strain under stressful conditions. One study of personality and emotional performance found that individuals high on extraversion experienced elevated heart rates when asked to express personality-incongruent emotions such as anger and that neuroticism was more generally associated with increased heart rate and poor performance.[66] Extraversion and neuroticism thus seem to affect the stress–strain relationship.

compensation award An organizational cost resulting from court awards for job distress.

Type A behavior pattern A complex of personality and behavioral characteristics, including competitiveness, time urgency, social status insecurity, aggression, hostility, and a quest for achievements.

7-6a Sex Differences and Biobehavioral Responses

There is substantive evidence that vulnerabilities constitute the important differences between the sexes.[67] Males are more vulnerable at an earlier age to fatal health problems such as cardiovascular disease, whereas females report more nonfatal but long-term and disabling health problems. Although we can conclude that sex indeed creates a differential vulnerability to stress between males and females, it may actually be more important to examine the differences *among* females or *among* males as well as revisit the binary nature of sex as an individual difference. Some literature suggests that there are differences in the stressors to which the two sexes are subject.[68] For example, sexual harassment is a sex-related source of stress for many working women, women in the military, and college women.[69] Men experience sexual harassment as well but nowhere near at the level to which females are exposed to harassment and abuse. Sex discrimination and disparate treatment based on sex fall in the category of differential stress exposure based on sex.[70]

Despite the disparate treatment on the basis of sex, females have a longer life expectancy by almost six years compared to the American male. This may be in part attributable to research findings that females' biobehavioral responses to stress are healthier than male responses.[71] Specifically, females characteristically display a Tend-and-Befriend response that is a protective factor found much less commonly in males.

7-6b Type A Behavior Pattern

Type A behavior pattern is a combination of personality and behavioral characteristics that include competitiveness, time urgency, social status insecurity, aggression, hostility, and a quest for achievements. Type A behavior pattern is also labeled *coronary-prone behavior* because it is linked with coronary heart disease.[72] There are two primary hypotheses concerning which part of the Type A behavior pattern is lethal. One suggests that the problem is time urgency, while the other suggests that it is hostility and aggression. The weight of evidence suggests that hostility and aggression, not time urgency, are the lethal agents.[73]

The alternative to the Type A behavior pattern is the Type B behavior pattern. People with Type B personalities are relatively free of Type A behaviors and characteristics. Type B people are less coronary prone, but if they do have a heart attack, they do not appear to recover as well as those with Type A personalities.

Type A behavior can be modified. The first step is for Type A people to recognize that they are prone to the Type A pattern and possibly to spend time with Type B individuals. Type B people often recognize Type A behavior and can help Type A individuals judge situations realistically. Type A individuals can also pace themselves, manage their time well, and try not to do multiple things at once. Focusing only on the task at hand and its completion rather than worrying about other tasks can help Type A individuals cope more effectively.

7-6c Personality Hardiness

People who have hardy personalities resist strain reactions when subjected to stressful events more effectively than do people who are not hardy.[74] The components of **personality hardiness** are commitment, control, and challenge. Commitment is an engagement with one's environment that leads to the experience of activities as interesting and enjoyable. Employees with high levels of commitment are less likely to leave the organization or experience promotion-related stress.[75] Control is an ability to influence the processes and outcomes of events that lead to the experience of activities as personal choices. Challenge is the conception of change as a stimulus to personal development, which leads to the welcome experience of new activities.

Time urgency is a key component of Type A Behavior Pattern.

The hardy personality appears to use these three components actively to engage in transformational coping when faced with stressful events.[76] **Transformational coping** is the active process of modifying one's perception of an event in order to reduce stress. This is accomplished by viewing the event in broader terms, by altering the course and outcome through action, and/or by achieving greater understanding of the process. The alternative to transformational coping is *regressive coping*, characterized by a passive avoidance of events and decreased interaction with the environment. Regressive coping may lead to short-term stress reduction at the cost of healthy, long-term life adjustment.

Hardy	Not Hardy
Commitment	Alienation
Control	Powerlessness
Challenge	Threat

7-6d Self-Reliance

There is well established scientific evidence that social relationships have positive effects on health and life expectancy.[77] **Self-reliance**, a healthy, secure interdependent pattern of behavior, is a personality attribute strongly related to social relationships. The concept of self-reliance was originally based on *attachment theory*, a psychological approach to normal human development that identifies three distinct patterns of attachment.[78] Research suggests that these patterns become behavioral strategies during adulthood in professional as well as personal relationships.[79] A secure pattern of attachment and *interdependent* behavior results in self-reliance. The connection between self-reliance and the word *interdependent* may appear paradoxical because a person appears independent while maintaining a host of supportive attachments.[80] But self-reliant people respond to stressful, threatening situations

personality hardiness A personality characterized by commitment, control, and challenge and, hence, resistant to distress.

transformational coping A way of managing stressful events by changing them into less subjectively stressful events.

self-reliance A healthy, secure, interdependent pattern of behavior related to how people form and maintain supportive attachments with others.

Dima Sob-xo/Shutterstock.com

iStock.com/Maica

Self-reliance individuals are secure in their own strengths and abilities.

by reaching out to others appropriately. Indeed, self-reliance is a flexible, responsive strategy of forming and maintaining multiple, diverse relationships. Self-reliant people are confident, enthusiastic, and persistent in facing challenges. A secure attachment style can help people initiate and maintain friendships, a valuable resource and buffer to stress.[81]

Interpersonal attachment is emotional and psychological connectedness to another person. In contrast, the two insecure patterns of attachment are counterdependence and overdependence. **Counterdependence** is an unhealthy, insecure pattern of behavior that leads to separation in relationships with other people. When faced with stressful and threatening situations, counterdependent people withdraw. Counterdependence may be characterized as a rigid, dismissing denial of the need for other people in difficult and stressful times. Counterdependent people exhibit a fearless, aggressive, and active response to challenges, but they are not truly self-reliant.

counterdependence An unhealthy, insecure pattern of behavior that leads to separation in relationships with other people.

overdependence An unhealthy, insecure pattern of behavior that leads to preoccupied attempts to achieve security through relationships.

preventive stress management An organizational philosophy according to which people and organizations should take joint responsibility for promoting health and preventing distress and strain.

primary prevention The stage in preventive stress management designed to reduce, modify, or eliminate the demand or stressor causing stress.

Overdependence is also an unhealthy, insecure pattern of behavior. Overdependent people respond to stressful and threatening situations by clinging to other people in any way possible. Overdependence may be characterized as a desperate, preoccupied attempt to achieve a sense of security through relationships. Overdependent people exhibit an active but disorganized and anxious response to challenges. This quality prevents a person from being able to organize and maintain healthy relationships; therefore, it creates distress. Interestingly, both counterdependence and overdependence can be exhibited by military personnel who are experiencing adjustment difficulties during the first thirty days of basic training.[82] The recruits who have the most difficulty adjusting to new jobs demonstrate severe overdependence. They often find it difficult to function on their own during training.

The YOU feature on page 147 provides an opportunity to examine your self-reliance, counterdependence, and overdependence.

7-7 Preventive Stress Management

Stress is an inevitable part of work and personal life. **Preventive stress management** is an organizational philosophy encouraging people and organizations to take joint responsibility for promoting health and preventing distress and strain. This philosophy is rooted in public health practices first used in preventive medicine. A framework for understanding preventive stress management is presented in Figure 7.2, which includes three stages of prevention that apply in a preventive medicine context as well as an organizational context. Johnson & Johnson has a long history of health promotion and disease prevention. The company set out over four decades ago to make Johnson & Johnson employees the healthiest in the world.[83] The Organizational Example on page 148 discusses how Johnson & Johnson Health and Wellness Solutions, with its J&J Human Performance Institute, has pursued that goal.

Primary prevention is intended to reduce, modify, or eliminate the stress-causing demand or stressor. The idea behind primary prevention is to eliminate or alleviate the source of a problem. True organizational stress prevention is largely primary in nature because it reduces the demands the organization places on the employee. **Secondary prevention** is intended to modify the individual's or the organization's response to a demand or stressor. Employees must learn to manage the inevitable, unalterable work stressors and demands to avert distress and strain while improving health and well-being. **Tertiary prevention** is intended to heal individual or organizational symptoms of distress and strain. The symptoms may range from early warning signs (such as headaches or absenteeism) to more severe forms of distress (such as hypertension, work stoppages, and strikes). An innovative approach used by the data recovery company DriveSavers bolsters treatment

> **secondary prevention** The stage in preventive stress management designed to alter or modify the individual's or the organization's response to a demand or stressor.
>
> **tertiary prevention** The stage in preventive stress management designed to heal individual or organizational symptoms of distress and strain.

YOU

Are You Self-Reliant?

Each of the following questions relates to how you form relationships with people at work, at home, and in other areas of your life. Read each statement carefully and rate each on a scale from 0 (strongly disagree) to 5 (strongly agree) to describe your degree of disagreement or agreement with the statement.

Answer all 16 questions.

_____ 1. I feel secure in my ability to meet life's challenges.

_____ 2. It is difficult to make a decision without consulting others.

_____ 3. I can perform high quality work with little support from others.

_____ 4. Friends are a waste of time because in the end they will desert you.

_____ 5. On some tasks I can work effectively without other people.

_____ 6. It is difficult for me to delegate works to others.

_____ 7. Life would be much easier if I didn't have to deal with other people.

_____ 8. I put myself at risk if I ever let anyone know I need them.

_____ 9. Difficult situations can be overcome.

_____ 10. I'm more comfortable being a follower than a leader.

_____ 11. I am successful at what I do.

_____ 12. There is no one who can understand things in my life.

_____ 13. People will always reject you when they find out what you are really like.

_____ 14. The actions that I take are usually right.

_____ 15. I don't like it when people try to find out too much about me.

_____ 16. Needing someone is a sign of weakness.

Scoring:

Follow the instructions to determine your score for each subscale of the Self-Reliance Inventory.

Counterdependence

Step 1: Total your responses to Questions 4, 7, 8, 12, 13, 15 and 16 _____

The score range for counterdependence is 0 to 35. Scores above 22 suggest counterdependence.

Self-Reliance

Step 2: Total your responses to Questions 1, 3, 5, 9, 11 and 14 _____

The score range for self-reliance is 0 to 30. Scores above 17 suggest self-reliance.

Overdependence

Step 3: Total your responses to Questions 2, 6 and 10 _____

The score range for overdependence is 0 to 15. Scores above 9 suggest overdependence.

A set of scores less than 13 in Step 1, greater than 17 in Step 2, and less than 7 in Step 3 indicate self-reliance.

Source: J. R. W. Joplin, D. L., Nelson, J. C. Quick, and J. D. Quick, *The Self-Reliance Inventory* (Arlington, TX: The University of Texas at Arlington), 1992.

Figure 7.2 A Framework for Preventive Stress Management

Source: J. D. Quick, R. S. Horn, and J. C. Quick, "Health Consequences of Stress," *Journal of Organizational Behavior Management* 8, No. 2 (Fall 1986): 21. Reprinted by permission of (Taylor & Francis Ltd, http://www.tandf.co.uk/journals).

and prevention with a full-time grief counselor.[84] The stages of prevention can be applied to organizational prevention, individual prevention, and comprehensive health promotion.

7-7a Organizational Stress Prevention

Some organizations maintain low-stress, healthy environments, while others cultivate high-stress environments that may place their employees' health

at risk. The experience of organizational justice and fairness is emerging as one contextual factor that leads to a positive, low-stress work environment.[85] One comprehensive approach to organizational health and preventive stress management was pioneered in the U.S. Air Force by Colonel Joyce Adkins, who developed an Organizational Health Center (OHC) with the Air Force Materiel Command.[86] The OHC's goal is to keep workers happy, healthy, and on the job while increasing efficiency and productivity to their highest levels. This goal is achieved by focusing

Organizational Example

Johnson & Johnson Health and Wellness

The Johnson & Johnson approach to employee health and wellness focuses on the combination of health promotion, such as increased aerobic physical activity, and disease prevention, such as reducing health risk factors noted in Figure 7.2. Key health risk factors include tobacco use, obesity, high blood pressure, high cholesterol levels, and alcohol consumption associated with driving. Additional health risk factors are poor nutrition, diabetes risk, and failure to use seat belts. Johnson & Johnson's health promotion combined with their disease prevention has had evidence-based impact in reducing many of these known health risk factors, leading to improved employee health and well-being. The J&J Health Promotion Institute unit relies on Jim Loehr's high performance professional skill of managing energy, not just time, to advance mental, emotional, physical, and spiritual well-being.

Sources: J. A. Quelch, Johnson & Johnson: The Promotion of Wellness, *Harvard Business School Teaching Note 515-021*, July 2014 (Revised February 2015); A. Janin, How to Build your Professional Skills, *Wall Street Journal*, April 2 (2021).

on workplace stressors, organizational and individual forms of distress, and managerial and individual strategies for preventive stress management. Adkins's comprehensive, organizational health approach addresses primary, secondary, and tertiary prevention. Most organizational prevention, however, is primary prevention, including job redesign, goal setting, role negotiation, and career management.

Two organizational stress prevention methods—team building and social support at work—are secondary prevention. We discuss team building in Chapter 9, but we should note here that under stress, team structure may influence team effectiveness. Specifically, teams experiencing quantitative demands are more effective when more tightly structured, while teams experiencing qualitative demands are more effective when more loosely structured.[87] Finally, the U.S. Department of Labor,

Occupational Safety and Health Administration offers guidance on preventing workplace violence, especially for high risk occupations. Violence in organizations is a category of dysfunctional behaviors that is often motivated by stressful events and whose negative consequences need to be prevented.[88] Ethical decision-making may also be affected by worker anxiety. Studies have shown that anxiety increases threat perception, which in turn often leads individuals to focus narrowly on their own self-interests rather than ethical principles.[89]

Job Redesign The job strain model illustrated in Figure 7.3 suggests that the combination of stringent demands and restricted control leads to a high-strain job. A major goal in job redesign should be to increase worker control. In many cases, this reduces distress and strain without reducing

Figure 7.3 Job Strain Model

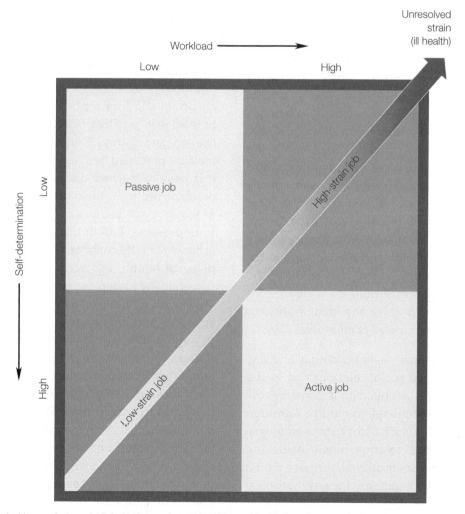

productivity. The direct costs of organizational distress include the high cost of turnover, the often hidden costs of absenteeism, and poor performance on the job.

Increasing worker control is a strategy of preventive stress management that can be accomplished in a number of ways, the most common being to increase job decision latitude. Increased latitude might include greater authority over the sequencing of work activities, the timing of work schedules, the selection and sequencing of work tools, or the selection of work teams. A second objective of job redesign should be to reduce uncertainty and increase predictability in the workplace.

Goal Setting Preventive stress management can also be achieved through goal-setting activities. These activities are designed to increase task motivation while reducing role conflict and ambiguity. Goal setting focuses a person's attention while directing energy into a productive channel. Implicit in much of the goal-setting literature is the assumption that people participate in determining their work goals.

Role Negotiation The organizational development technique of role negotiation has value as a stress-management method because it allows individuals to modify their work roles.[90] Role negotiation begins with the definition of a focal role within the organizational context. The person in the focal role identifies the expectations understood for the role, and organizational supervisors specify their own expectations of the person in the focal role. A negotiation of integrated role expectation follows. In the process of such negotiation, points of confusion and conflict become opportunities for clarification and resolution. The final result of the role negotiation process should be a clear, well-defined focal role with which the incumbent and organizational members are all comfortable.

Social Support Systems Team building is one way to develop supportive social relationships in the workplace. However, team building is primarily task oriented, not socioemotional, in nature. Although employees may receive much of their socio-emotional support from personal relationships outside the workplace, some socioemotional support within the workplace is also necessary for psychological well-being.

Social support systems can be enhanced through the work environment in a number of ways. Implementing support systems that help employees identify with the company may buffer the negative effects of workplace stressors and improve employees' ability to adjust.[91] Interpersonal communication is the key to unlocking social support for preventive stress management.[92] Figure 7.4 identifies key elements in a person's work and nonwork social support system. These relationships provide emotional caring, information, evaluative feedback, modeling, and instrumental support.

7-7b Individual Prevention

Clinical research shows that individuals may use a number of self-directed interventions to help prevent distress and enhance positive well-being.[93] Such individual prevention can be of a primary, secondary, or tertiary nature. The *primary prevention* activities we discuss are learned optimism, time management, and leisure time activities. The *secondary prevention* activities we discuss are physical exercise, relaxation, and diet. The *tertiary prevention* activities we discuss are opening up and professional help.

Positive Thinking The power of *positive thinking* too often goes unappreciated. When one cultivates an optimistic frame of mind, bad life events are bathed in a positive light, preventing future and healing past distress.[94] An optimistic style of thought must be practiced habitually in order to be effective. It is usually learned over time, though some are predisposed to it. *Pessimism* is an alternative style of thought that focuses on the negative. It can lead to depression, health problems, and low levels of achievement. By contrast, positive thinking enhances physical health and achievement and decreases susceptibility to depression.

Positive thinking does not mean ignoring stressors and challenges. It means viewing them through a different lens. Optimistic people avoid distress by framing the difficult times in their lives as temporary, limited in scope, and often unavoidable. They face adversity with hope and take credit for the good events in their lives, which they see as more pervasive and generalized. Optimists are also more motivated and more likely to use proactive coping skills to achieve goals and pursue development opportunities.[95] *Learned optimism* begins with identifying pessimistic thoughts and then distracting

Figure 7.4 Social Support At Work and Home

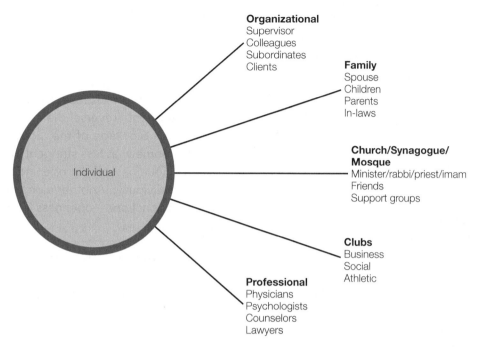

Source: J. C. Quick, J. D. Quick, D. L. Nelson, and J. J. Hurrell Jr., *Preventive Stress Management in Organizations* (Washington, D.C.: American Psychological Association, 1997), 198. Reprinted with permission.

oneself from these thoughts or disputing them with evidence and alternative thoughts. Psychological capital (PsyCap) is an evidence-based positive approach that extends from positive psychology and positive organizational behavior (POB). The positive psychological resources that make up PsyCap include **h**ope, **e**fficacy, **r**esilience and **o**ptimism, or the HERO within. A review suggests that PsyCap has scientific, evidence-based rigor and practical relevance.[96]

Time Management Temporal pressure is one of the major sources of stress, as listed in Table 7.1. It applies to people both at work and in school. Symptoms of poor time management include constant rushing, missed deadlines, work overload, the sense of being overwhelmed, insufficient rest time, and indecision. Effective time managers employ the macro-level *GP³ method* of time management.[97] The GP³ method is to (1) set *goals* that are challenging yet attainable; (2) *prioritize* these goals in terms of their relative importance; (3) *plan* for goal attainment through specific tasks, activities, scheduling, and delegation; and (4) *praise* oneself for specific achievements along the way. Setting concrete goals and prioritizing these goals are the most important first steps in time-management skills, ensuring that the most important work and study activities receive enough time and attention. This system of time management enables a person to track their success over time and goes a long way toward reducing unnecessary stress and confusion.

Leisure Time Activities People with a high need for achievement are often characterized by an unremitting urge to strive for excellence. Leisure time provides employees an opportunity for rest and recovery from strenuous activities at home and work. When asked what they do with their leisure time, many individuals say that they clean the house or mow the lawn. These activities are fine, as long as the individual gets the stress-reducing benefit of pleasure from them. Some say our work ethic is a cultural barrier to pleasure. We work longer hours, and two-income families are the norm. Leisure is increasingly a luxury among working people. The key to the effective use of leisure time is enjoyment. Leisure time can be used for spontaneity, joy, and connection with others in our lives. Although vacations can be a relief from job burnout, they may incur fade-out effects.[98] Hence, leisure time and vacations must be periodic, recurring activities.

Physical Exercise Different types of physical exercise are important secondary stress prevention activities for individuals. Kenneth Cooper is the pioneer in aerobic exercise to improve a person's responsiveness to stressful activities.[99] Research at the Aerobics Center in Dallas has found that aerobically fit people (1) have lower levels of adrenaline in their blood at rest; (2) have a slower, stronger heart beat; and (3) recover from stressful events more quickly. Steady exercisers display five habits, which are exercising at the same time most days; widening their definition of exercise, such as climbing stairs; having pre-exercise routines with visual cues; being flexible about how long and vigorously they exercise; and being more likely to exercise for pleasure, versus for weight loss or health goals.[100]

Flexibility training is an important type of exercise because muscular contractions are associated with the stress response. One component of the stress response is the contraction of the flexor muscles, which prepares a person to fight or flee. Flexibility training enables a person to stretch and relax these muscles to prevent the accumulation of unnecessary muscular tension.[101] In addition, flexibility exercises help maintain joint mobility, increase strength, and play an important role in the prevention of injury.

Relaxation Training Herbert Benson was one of the first people to identify the relaxation response as the natural counterresponse to stress.[102] In studying Western and Eastern peoples, Benson found that Jews and Christians have elicited this response through their time-honored traditions of prayer, whereas those with backgrounds in Eastern religions have elicited it through meditation. The relaxation response does not require a theological or religious component, however. Reading, massage, and secular yoga practice can all elicit the relaxation response. The yoga discipline of breathing has been found to have beneficial impacts on work and well-being.[103] If you have an unwinding ritual, you may already elicit the relaxation response regularly.

DIET Diet may play an indirect role in stress and stress management. Large amounts of sugar in one's diet can stimulate the stress response, and foods high in cholesterol can adversely affect blood chemistry. Good dietary practices contribute to overall health.

> Mental and physical health improves through self-disclosure.

In his nonsurgical, nonpharmacological approach to reversing heart disease, Dean Ornish proposes a very stringent "reversal diet" for individuals with identifiable blockage of the arteries.[104] He recommends a somewhat less stringent "prevention diet" as one of four methods for opening up the arteries of healthy individuals. Another element in his program is an emotional one—openness in relationships with other people.

Opening Up Traumatic, distress-inducing events are an unfortunate fact of life. One of the most therapeutic responses to such events is to confide in other people.[105] Discussing difficult experiences with another person is not always easy, but mental and physical heath improves through self-disclosure. Confessions need not be made in person, or to another person at all. Writing in a private diary and posting anonymously on the Internet are also therapeutic. In a study comparing those who wrote once a week about traumatic events with those who wrote about nontraumatic events, significant health benefits and reduced absenteeism were found in the first group.[106] Whatever form it takes, the process of opening up and confessing appears to counter the detrimental effects of stress.

Professional Help Confession and opening up may occur in professional healing relationships. Psychological counseling, career counseling, physical therapy, medical treatment, surgical intervention, and other therapeutic techniques are available to people who need help. *Employee assistance programs (EAPs)* may be very helpful in referring employees to appropriate caregivers. Even soldiers who experience battle stress reactions severe enough to take them out of action can experience healing through EAPs and then participate in subsequent combat missions.[107] The early detection of distress and strain reactions, coupled with prompt professional treatment, can be instrumental in averting permanent physical and psychological damage, such as posttraumatic stress disorder.

7-7c Comprehensive Health Promotion

Whereas organizational stress prevention programs are aimed at eliminating health risks at work, wellness, and well-being approaches aim at enhancing a "strong and resistant host" in the case of individuals, organizations, and their communities.[108] Physical fitness and exercise programs characterize corporate health promotion programs in the United States and Canada.[109] A health and wellness survey of accredited medical schools in the United States, Canada, and Puerto Rico found that these programs place significant emphasis on physical well-being and minor emphasis on spiritual well-being.[110] A new approach to comprehensive health promotion places emphasis on the organization and *organizational wellness*.[111] Still, social and cognitive processes are key considerations in the successful implementation of stress prevention programs.[112]

Johnson & Johnson developed a comprehensive health promotion program with a wide array of educational modules for individuals and groups. Each of these educational modules addresses a specific topic, such as Type A behavior, stress, diet (through cooperative activities with the American Heart Association), and risk assessment (through regular health evaluations for participants). Upon implementation of this health promotion program, Johnson & Johnson found that the health status of employees improved, even if they didn't participate in the program.

Experiential Exercise

Workplace Stress Diagnosis

The following exercise gives you an opportunity to work within a group to compare the work demands and job stressors found in different work settings. Intervention for preventive stress management must be based on a good diagnosis. This exercise points you in this direction.

Step 1. Rate the degree to which each of the following work demands is a source of stress for you and your coworkers at work. Use a seven-point rating scale for assigning the stressfulness of the work demand, with 7 (high source of stress), 4 (moderate source of stress), and 1 (little source of stress).

_____ Uncertainty about various aspects of the work environment

_____ Lack of control over people, events, or other aspects of work

_____ Lack of career opportunities and progress

_____ The implementation of new technologies

_____ Work overload; that is too much to do and not enough time

_____ Conflicting expectations from one or more people at work

_____ Confusing expectations from one or more people at work

_____ Dangerous working conditions and/or hazardous substances

_____ Sexual harassment by supervisors, coworkers, or others

_____ Abrasive personalities and/or political conflicts

_____ Rigid, insensitive, unresponsive supervisors or managers

Step 2. Write a brief description of the most stressful event that has occurred in your work environment during the past twelve-month period.

Step 3. The class will form into groups of approximately six members each. Each group elects a spokesperson and compares the information developed by each person in Steps 1 and 2. In the process of this comparison, answer the following questions:

a. What are the similarities between work environments in terms of their most stressful work demands?

b. What are the differences among work environments in terms of their most stressful work demands?

c. Are there similarities in the descriptions of the most stressful events? If so, what are they?

Step 4. Each group will share the results of its answers to the questions in Step 3. Cross-team questions and discussion follow.

Step 5 (Optional). Your instructor may ask you to choose one or another of the work environments in which to develop some preventive stress management strategies. Complete parts a and b below in your group.

a. Identify one to three preventive stress management strategies that you think are the best to use in the work environment. Why have you chosen them?

b. How should the effectiveness of these strategies be evaluated?

Learning Objectives

7-1 Define stress, distress, and strain. *Stress,* or the stress response, is the unconscious preparation to fight or flee experienced when faced with any demand. A *stressor,* or demand, is the person or event triggering the stress response. *Distress* or *strain* refers to adverse psychological, physical, behavioral, and organizational consequences that may occur as a result of stressful events.

7-2 Compare four different approaches to stress. There are four principal approaches to stress. Walter B. Cannon developed the homeostatic/medical approach because he believed stress resulted when an external, environmental demand upset the *homeostasis.* Richard Lazarus's cognitive appraisal approach saw stress as a result of a person-environment interaction, yet emphasized cognitive appraisal in classifying persons or events as stressful. Robert Kahn's person-environment fit approach claimed that confusing and conflicting expectations of social roles create stress. Harry Levinson's psychoanalytic approach believed the *ego-ideal* and the *self-image* interact to cause stress.

7-3 Explain the psychophysiology of the stress response. The stress response begins with the release of chemical messengers, primarily adrenaline, into the bloodstream. These messengers activate the sympathetic nervous system and endocrine (hormone) system to trigger mind-body changes to prepare the person for fight or flight. As the body responds, the person shifts from a neutral posture to an offensive posture.

7-4 Identify work and nonwork causes of stress. Major categories of work demands that cause stress are role conflict, role ambiguity, task demands, role demands, interpersonal demands, and physical demands. Nonwork demands may broadly be identified as home demands from an individual's personal life environment and personal demands that are self-imposed

7-5 Describe the consequences of stress. Positive stress can create *eustress,* while negative stress, or distress, can erode morale and performance. Three forms of individual distress are: *psychological distress, medical illnesses,* and *behavioral problems.* The symptoms of *organizational stress* are: low morale, dissatisfaction, communication breakdowns, and disruption of working relationships. Three major costs of *organizational distress* are: participation problems, performance decrements, and compensation awards.

7-6 Discuss individual factors that influence a person's response to stress and strain. Individual differences, such as gender and Type A behavior pattern, enhance vulnerability to strain under stressful conditions. Other individual differences, such as personality hardiness and self-reliance, reduce vulnerability to strain under stressful condition.

7-7 Identify the stages and elements of preventive stress management for individuals and organizations. The three stages of prevention are primary, secondary, and tertiary prevention. *Primary prevention* is intended to reduce, modify, or eliminate the demand or stressor causing stress. *Secondary prevention* is intended to alter or modify the individual's or the organization's response to a demand or stressor. *Tertiary prevention* is intended to heal individual or organizational symptoms of distress and strain.

Key Terms

compensation award An organizational cost resulting from court awards for job distress. (p. 144)

counterdependence An unhealthy, insecure pattern of behavior that leads to separation in relationships with other people. (p. 146)

distress The adverse psychological, physical, behavioral, and organizational consequences that may arise as a result of stressful events. (p. 134)

ego-ideal The embodiment of a person's perfect self. (p. 135)

homeostasis A steady state of bodily functioning and equilibrium. (p. 134)

overdependence An unhealthy, insecure pattern of behavior that leads to preoccupied attempts to achieve security through relationships. (p. 146)

participation problem A cost associated with absenteeism, tardiness, strikes and work stoppages, and turnover. (p. 143)

performance decrement A cost resulting from poor quality or low quantity of production, grievances, and unscheduled machine downtime and repair. (p. 143)

personality hardiness A personality characterized by commitment, control, and challenge and, hence, resistant to distress. (p. 145)

preventive stress management An organizational philosophy according to which people and organizations should take joint responsibility for promoting health and preventing distress and strain. (p. 146)

primary prevention The stage in preventive stress management designed to reduce, modify, or eliminate the demand or stressor causing stress. (p. 146)

secondary prevention The stage in preventive stress management designed to alter or modify the individual's or the organization's response to a demand or stressor. (p. 147)

self-image How a person sees themself, both positively and negatively. (p. 135)

self-reliance A healthy, secure, interdependent pattern of behavior related to how people form and maintain supportive attachments with others. (p. 145)

strain Distress. (p. 134)

stress The unconscious preparation to fight or flee that a person experiences when faced with any demand. (p. 134)

stressor The person or event that triggers the stress response. (p. 134)

tertiary prevention The stage in preventive stress management designed to heal individual or organizational symptoms of distress and strain. (p. 147)

transformational coping A way of managing stressful events by changing them into less subjectively stressful events. (p. 145)

Type A behavior pattern A complex of personality and behavioral characteristics, including competitiveness, time urgency, social status insecurity, aggression, hostility, and a quest for achievements. (p. 144)

workaholism An imbalanced preoccupation with work at the expense of home and personal life satisfaction. (p. 141)

Ethical Dilemma

Berta's decision and Juan's burnout risk

Berta is a manager at Professional Partners, LLC, an accounting firm that works with small or family-owned businesses to provide their auditing needs. In the post COVID world, finding accountants has become exceedingly difficult. Berta has been trying to hire additional auditors for months but has had no success. She knows that her staff is overworked and the extra bonuses she has been giving them are not enough to keep them from burning out given the workload.

On Thursday, Berta got a notice that Professional Partners had retained several new clients. One of the new clients is the biggest the company has ever attracted. This client would be given to her department and the audit should begin immediately. Berta is happy for the organization as Professional Partners is a great employer. But she is very concerned about who is going to take this assignment.

Juan is an awesome employee and person. He is very smart and has an amazing work ethic. He is also a very nice person with great interpersonal skills. Clients give Juan incredible evaluations. He is the best employee in the department.

As Berta considers whom to give the new client, she realizes that there is no one she would trust with this new client more than Juan. However, no one in the department is more overworked than Juan. She knows that her duty to the company and the new client is to put the best possible person on the account. She also knows that Juan is quickly approaching burnout, and that she has a duty to Juan and his current clients. She could give some of Juan's current clients to someone else so he can take on the new client, but that would anger those clients as they would not want to lose Juan as their auditor. She is so confused as to what she should do.

1. Using consequential, rule-based, and character theories, evaluate Berta's options.

2. What should Berta do? Why?

iStock.com/Tomozina

Communication

Learning Objectives

8-1 Describe the interpersonal communication process and the role of listening in the process.

8-2 Describe the five communication skills of effective supervisors.

8-3 Explain five communication barriers and the gateways through them.

8-4 Distinguish between civility and incivility, and defensive and nondefensive communication.

8-5 Explain the impact of nonverbal communication.

8-6 Explain positive, healthy communication.

8-7 Identify how new communication technologies and social media affect the communication process.

8-8 Describe how organizational communication is disrupted by crises.

8-1 Interpersonal Communication

Communication evokes a shared, or common, meaning in another person. Interpersonal communication occurs between two or more people in an organization. It is central to health and well-being, both at home and on the job. In crises like the COVID-19 pandemic, it is essential to prioritize listening in interpersonal communications.[1] In Chapter 7, we noted that interpersonal communication is the key to unlocking social support for preventive stress management.[2] Interpersonal communication is essential to building and sustaining human relationships at work. Recent advances in information technology and data management cannot replace interpersonal communication. Figure 8.1 illustrates the key elements of interpersonal communication: the communicator, the receiver, the perceptual screens, and the message.

communication The evoking of a shared or common meaning in another person.

interpersonal communication Communication between two or more people in an organization.

communicator The person sending a message.

receiver The person accepting a message.

perceptual screen A window through which one interacts with others. It influences the quality, accuracy, and clarity of the communication.

message The thoughts and feelings that the communicator is attempting to evoke in the receiver.

> Interpersonal communication is central to health and well-being, both at home and on the job.

8-1a An Interpersonal Communication Model

The **communicator** is the person sending the message. The **receiver** is the person accepting the message. **Perceptual screens** are the windows through which we interact. The communicator's and the receiver's respective perceptual screens influence the quality, accuracy, and clarity of the message. They can allow the message to transmit smoothly, or they can cause static and distortion. Perceptual screens are built upon the sender's and receiver's individual attributes, such as age, gender, values, beliefs, past experiences, cultural influences, and individual needs. The degree to which these screens are open significantly influences both sent and received messages.

The **message** contains the thoughts and feelings that the communicator intends to evoke in the receiver. The message has two primary components. The *thought*, or conceptual component, of the message (its content) is contained in the words, ideas, symbols, and concepts chosen to relay the message. The *feeling*, or emotional component, of the message (its affect) is contained in the intensity, demeanor, and gestures of the communicator. The emotional component of the message adds overtones of joy, anger, fear, or pain to the conceptual component. This addition often enriches and clarifies the message.

Figure 8.1 A Basic Interpersonal Communication Model

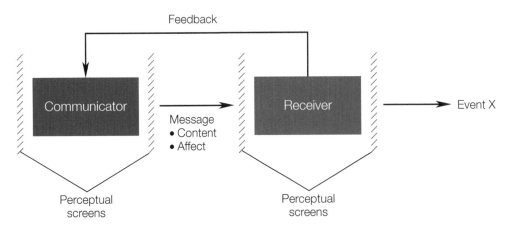

Feedback may or may not be activated in communication. It occurs when the receiver provides the communicator with a response to the message. More broadly, feedback occurs when information is fed back to the sender that completes two-way communication.

The language of the message is important. *Language* is a broad term denoting the words, their pronunciations, and the methods of combining them used and understood by a group of people. Culture and situation dictate the specific language utilized in a message.

Data are the uninterpreted, unanalyzed elements of a message. Information is data with meaning to the person who interprets or analyzes them. Since messages are conveyed through a *medium*, such as a telephone or face-to-face discussion, they differ in richness according to the ability of that medium to transmit meaning to a receiver.[3] Despite the popularity of text messaging as a communication medium, e-mail remains the preferred method of workplace communication. A recent survey found that workers are almost three times as likely to send an e-mail to a colleague rather than a text message to communicate work-related as well as non-work-related information.[4] Table 8.1 compares different media with regard to data capacity and richness. Such attributes of communication media affect how influence-seeking behavior is generated and perceived in organizations.[5]

8-1b Employee Voice Behavior

Employees may communicate and give voice through their behavior. Employee voice behavior refers to the behavior that proactively challenges the status quo and makes constructive changes in the workplace. Research shows that core employee self-evaluations can influence voice behavior, especially when moderated by personal control and approach motivation, especially when procedural justice is perceived to be high.[6] While some aspects of the status quo may be good, other aspects need to be challenged and constructively changed. It takes courage to challenge the status quo, and speaking up is one of the best ways for leaders and followers to display courage.[7] Courageous

feedback Information fed back that completes two-way communication.

language The words, their pronunciations, and the methods of combining them used and understood by a group of people.

data Uninterpreted and unanalyzed elements of a message.

information Data that have been interpreted, analyzed, and have meaning to some user.

richness The ability of a medium to convey meaning to a receiver.

employee voice behavior Communication of suggestions, concerns, information about problems, or work-related opinions to effect constructive changes in the workplace.

Table 8.1 Communication Media: Information Richness and Data Capacity

Medium	Information Richness	Data Capacity
Face-to-face discussion	Highest	Lowest
Video conferencing	High	Low
Telephone	High	Low
Electronic mail	Moderate	Moderate
Blog	Moderate	Moderate
Individualized letter	Moderate	Moderate
Personalized note or memo	Moderate	Moderate
Chat-based collaboration (e.g., Slack, Microsoft Teams)	Moderate	Moderate
Formal written report	Low	High
Flyer or bulletin	Low	High
Formal numeric report	Lowest	Highest

Source: Adapted from E. A. Gerloff, "Information Richness: A New Approach to Managerial Behavior and Organizational Design," by R. L. Daft and R. H. Lengel in *Research in Organizational Behavior* 6 (1984): 191–233. Reprinted by permission of JAI Press Inc.

communication is best when in *constructive voice*, which refers to employees' upward communication of ideas or suggestions intended to improve the work unit or the organization. Constructive voice is best conceptualized as a dyadic exchange between employees and managers.[8]

8-1c Reflective Listening

One skill essential for communication in the work-place is listening. The Fast Fact on this page below suggests why there is so much miscommunication and why listening may be a difficult skill to master. **Reflective listening** is the skill of carefully listening to a message and immediately repeating it back to the speaker. This technique helps the communicator clarify the intended message and correct inaccuracies or misunderstandings. Reflective listening emphasizes the role of the receiver, or audience, in interpersonal communication. Reflective listening better enables the listener to comprehend the communicator's meaning, reduce perceptual distortions, and overcome interpersonal barriers that lead to communication failures. Especially useful in problem solving, reflective listening can be learned in a short time. Given its positive effects on behavior and emotion in the corporate environment, reflective listening is a valuable skill to possess.[9]

Reflective listening can be characterized as personal, feeling oriented, and responsive.[10] First, it emphasizes the *personal* elements of the communication process. The reflective listener demonstrates empathy and concern for the communicator as a person, not an object. Second,

reflective listening emphasizes the *feelings* communicated in the message—the receiver must pay special attention to the feeling component as she repeats the message. Third, reflective listening emphasizes a rational and considerate *response*. Receivers should distinguish their own feelings and thoughts from those of the speaker. In other words, the conversation's focus must remain at all times on the ideas and emotions of the speaker in order for the receiver to effectively respond to them. Empathy and emotional self-control are key emotional competencies in good reflective listening.

Reflective listening necessitates four levels of verbal response: affirming contact, paraphrasing expressed thoughts and feelings, clarifying implicit thoughts and feelings, and reflecting core feelings not fully expressed. Nonverbal behaviors, such as eye contact and silence, are also important in reflective listening. Each of these responses can be illustrated through an example: the interaction between a software engineer, who has just discovered a major problem in a large information system they are building for a difficult customer, and their supervisor.

Affirming Contact The receiver (in this case, the supervisor of the software engineer) affirms contact with the communicator (the software engineer) by making periodic statements such as "I see," "Okay," and "Yes, I understand." The purpose of an affirmation response is to communicate attentiveness, not necessarily agreement. Affirming contact is especially reassuring to a speaker in the early stages of expression, and even more so when there may be some associated anxiety or discomfort. As the problem is more fully explored and expressed, it is increasingly important for the receiver to employ other reflective responses.

reflective listening Carefully listening to message and immediately repeating it back to the speaker.

Fast Fact

Why Is There so Much Miscommunication?

Many people have difficulty being understood at work. Why is that? Some estimates suggest that people speak about 7,000 words per day. The research suggests that the average person hears between 20,000 and 30,000 words per day. Now add to that hundreds of texts, messages, emails, and social media inputs for a significant communication load. In addition to volume, language is complex. Miscommunication at work is more than an inconvenience, it can be detrimental to the work and, in some cases, dangerous, even lethal. Therefore, to accurately understand the message, it is important to become a good reflective listener. To be understood, first know the audience to whom you are communicating, using 10 words clearly rather than 100 or 1,000.

Source: T. Chamorro-Premuzic, "The Science of Miscommunication at Work," *Fast Company*, December 5 (2022).

Paraphrasing The Expressed After an appropriate length of time, the receiver (the supervisor in our example) might paraphrase the expressed thoughts and feelings of the speaker (the engineer). Paraphrasing is useful because it tells the speaker what the receiver heard and what the receiver's thoughts and feelings are about what they heard. This verbal response enables the speaker and receiver to build greater empathy, openness, and acceptance into their relationship while ensuring the accuracy of the communication process.

In the case of the software engineer, the supervisor may find paraphrasing the engineer's message particularly useful for both of them in developing a clearer understanding of the system problem. They might say, "I can tell that you're very upset about this problem. Even though you're not quite sure how it happened, it sounds like you have a few good leads." It is difficult to solve a problem until it is clearly understood.

Clarifying The Implicit People often communicate *implicit* thoughts and feelings—that is, thoughts and feelings that are not clearly or fully expressed—along with their explicitly expressed message. The receiver may or may not assume that this implicit component of the message is within the awareness of the speaker. For example, the software engineer may be anxious about how to approach a difficult customer with the system problem. This may be implicit in their discussion with their supervisor because of a previous discussion about this customer. If their feelings of anxiety are not expressed, the supervisor may want to clarify them. The supervisor might say, "You seem particularly stressed . . . were you worried about the client's reaction?" This would help the engineer shift the focus of their attention from the main problem, which is in the software, to the important issue of discussing the matter with the customer.

Reflecting Core Feelings Next, the receiver should look beyond the speaker's explicit and implicit messages to understand the speaker's *core feelings*, the speaker's deepest and most important emotions, beliefs, and values. If the software engineer had not been aware of any anxiety in their relationship with the difficult customer, their supervisor's ability to sense the tension and bring it to the engineer's awareness would exemplify the reflection of core feelings. Emotional intelligence is especially important here.

However, the receiver runs a risk of overreaching if a secure, empathetic relationship with the speaker has not already been established or if strongly repressed feelings are reflected back. Even if the receiver is correct, the speaker may not want those feelings brought to their awareness. Therefore, it is important to exercise caution and care in reflecting core feelings to a speaker.

Silence Long periods of silence may cause discomfort or embarrassment, but a certain amount of silence can help both speaker and listener in reflective listening. From the speaker's perspective, silence may be useful in moments of thought or confusion about how to express difficult ideas or feelings. The software engineer may need some patient silence from their supervisor as they think through what to say next. Listeners can use brief periods of silence to sort their own thoughts and feelings from those of the speaker. In the case of the software engineer's supervisor, any personal feelings toward the difficult customer should not intrude on the engineer's immediate problem. Silence provides time to identify and isolate the listener's personal responses and exclude them from the dialogue.

Eye Contact Eye contact is a nonverbal behavior that may promote openness in communication between two people. During a dialog, the absence of appropriate eye contact tends to close communication. However, the presence of inappropriate eye contact can also hinder a relationship. Cultural and individual differences influence what constitutes appropriate and inappropriate eye contact. For example, direct eye contact initiated by women and children is discouraged in India. In fact, too much direct eye contact, regardless of the individual or culture, can have an intimidating effect.

Moderate direct eye contact communicates openness and affirmation without causing either speaker or listener to feel intimidated. Periodic aversion of the eyes allows for a sense of privacy and control, even in intense interpersonal communication. The software engineer and the supervisor make eye contact throughout their discussion, though each looks away periodically to ease the tension of intimacy.

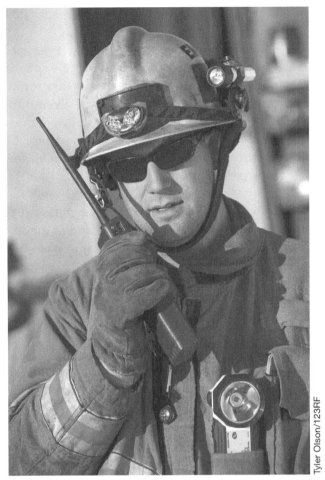

Tyler Olson/123RF

Law enforcement, firefighters, and military personnel rely on abbreviated one-way communication in emergency situations.

One-Way Versus Two-Way Communication Reflective listening encourages **two-way communication**, an interactive form of communication in which there is an exchange of thoughts, feelings, or both, and through which shared meaning often occurs. Problem solving and decision-making are often examples of two-way communication. **One-way communication** occurs when a person sends a message to another person and no feedback, questions, or interaction follows. Giving instructions and giving directions are examples of one-way communication.

One-way communication tends to be efficient, although how efficient it is depends on the amount

two-way communication An interactive form of communication in which there is an exchange of thoughts, feelings, or both.

one-way communication Communication in which a person sends a message to another person and no feedback, questions, or interaction follows.

and complexity of information communicated and the medium chosen. Even though it is faster than two-way communication, one-way communication is often less accurate. This is especially true for complex tasks that require clarification for completion. When time and accuracy are both important to the successful completion of a task and two-way communication is not an option (such as in combat or emergency situations), extensive training prior to execution enhances accuracy and efficiency.[11] Firefighters and military combat personnel engage extensively in such training to minimize the need for communication during emergencies. These highly trained professionals rely on abbreviated one-way communication as shorthand for more complex information. However, this communication works only within the range of situations for which the professionals are specifically trained.

It is difficult to draw generalizations about individual preference for one-way or two-way communication. Communicators with a stronger need for feedback or who are comfortable with conflict or confusing questions may find two-way communication more satisfying. By contrast, receivers who believe that a message is straightforward may be satisfied with one-way communication and be impatient with lengthy two-way communication.

8-2 Communication Skills for Effective Managers

Interpersonal communication is a critical foundation for effective performance and individual well-being in organizations. Power is intertwined in the language of communication between managers and their employees.[12] This power dynamic is especially critical when leaders are articulating an organizational vision and attempting to achieve buy-in from employees.[13] One large study of managers in a variety of industries found that those with the most effective work units engaged in routine communication with their employees, whereas the managers with the highest promotion rates engaged in networking activities with superiors.[14] A study of banking managers found that higher performing managers were more effective, less apprehensive communicators than lower performing managers.[15] Oral communication and managerial cooperation are important contextual performance skills that have positive effects on the psychosocial quality of the work environment.[16]

Research on manager–employee communication identifies five communication skills that distinguish good supervisors from bad ones.[17] A good supervisor is an expressive speaker, an empathetic listener, a persuasive leader, a sensitive person, and an informative manager. Some supervisors are effective without possessing all of these skills, however, and some organizations value one or two skills over the others. But because dyadic relationships are at the core of much organization-based communication, possessing all five skills makes a supervisor that much more effective in communicating to employees.[18]

8-2a Expressiveness

Effective supervisors express their thoughts, ideas, and feelings openly and aren't afraid to voice opinions in meetings. They tend toward extroversion. Supervisors who are not talkative or who tend toward introversion may at times leave their employees wondering what they're thinking about certain issues. Supervisors who speak out let the people they work with know where they stand, what they believe, and how they feel.

8-2b Empathy and Sensitivity

In addition to being expressive speakers, good supervisors are willing, empathetic, reflective listeners. Empathetic listeners are able to hear the emotional dimensions of the messages people send them, as well as the content of the ideas and issues. Good supervisors are approachable and willing to listen to suggestions and complaints. In a recent study of physicians, those with higher perceptions of control were more open in their communication, and patients found them more empathetic.[19] Good supervisors are emotionally intelligent.

Good supervisors are also sensitive to the feelings, self-images, and psychological defenses of their employees. They know how and when to communicate with employees to maximize psychological health. For example, employees' accomplishments, honors, and achievements should be announced in public, while criticism should be delivered in private. The best supervisors are sensitive to the self-esteem of others.

8-2c Persuasiveness

All supervisors must exercise power and influence in organizations if they want to ensure high performance and achieve positive results. Effective supervisors tend to be persuasive leaders, distinguished by their

> Good supervisors keep their employees well informed by appropriately and selectively disseminating information.

use of persuasive language to influence others. They are not deceitful or autocratic; they encourage results earnestly instead of manipulating others.

Of course, sometimes emergencies and high-risk situations necessitate the abandonment of sensitive and subtle persuasion. In cases such as a fire at an oil rig or a life-threatening trauma in an emergency room, a supervisor must be direct and assertive.

8-2d Informative Managing Style

Finally, good supervisors keep their employees well informed by appropriately and selectively disseminating information. Failing to effectively filter information may lead to either information overload or a lack of sufficient information for task accomplishment. Good supervisors give advance notice of organizational changes and explain the rationale for organizational policies. Good supervisors are also transparent, communicating openly and honestly with employees. Such transparency leads to increased trust among employees, which, in turn, results in increased employee engagement.[20]

A person may become a good supervisor even in the absence of one of these communication skills. For example, a manager with special talents in planning, organizing, or decision-making may compensate for a shortcoming in expressiveness or sensitivity. No matter their perceived skill level or effectiveness, when supervisors and employees engage in open communication and forward planning, they have a greater number of agreements about the employee's performance and behavior.[21]

8-3 Barriers and Gateways to Communication

Barriers to communication are factors that distort, disrupt, or even halt successful communication. They may be temporary and easily resolved or long-lasting and deeply rooted. Roughly 20 percent of all such barriers to communication can be prevented or solved

---

barriers to communication Factors that distort, disrupt, or even halt successful communication.

by communication policy guidelines.[22] **Gateways to communication** are the openings that break down communication barriers. Awareness and recognition of communication barriers are the first steps in opening the gateways. Obvious barriers are physical separation (employees in different geographic locations or buildings) and status differences (related to the organizational hierarchy). One apparent gateway for the separation of geographically dispersed teams is to improve the frequency of face-to-face interaction. Geographically dispersed teams can also increase their performance by targeting their use of information and communication technologies (ICTs) to address specific coordination needs. For example, if teams are responsible for performing nonroutine tasks, their performance can be enhanced by using ICTs to provide task knowledge.[23] Not so obvious are the barriers caused by gender differences, cultural diversity, and language.

8-3a Gender Differences

Communication barriers can be attributed in part to differences in conversational styles.[24] When individuals of different economic backgrounds converse, the receiver's understanding may not be the same as the speaker's meaning. In a similar vein, men and women tend to have different conversational styles. For example, women often prefer to converse face to face, whereas men are comfortable conversing while sitting side by side, concentrating on a focal point in front of them. Hence, conversational differences may result in a barrier of communication between men and women. Male–female conversation is really cross-cultural communication. In a work context, one study found that female employees sent less information to their supervisors and experienced less information overload than did male employees.[25] The Inclusive Conversation on page 165 addresses the question: are gender communication differences biological in origin? There is emerging research on genders beyond binary but no evidence yet on communication preferences among genders beyond the binary.

gateways to communication Openings that break down communication barriers.

An important gateway through the gender barrier is the development of an awareness and appreciation of gender-specific differences in conversational style. These differences can enrich organizational communication and empower professional relationships.[26] A second gateway is to actively seek clarification of the person's meaning rather than freely interpreting meaning from one's own frame of reference.

8-3b Cultural Diversity

Culturally influenced values and patterns of behavior can be very confusing barriers to communication. Significant differences in work-related values exist among people in the United States versus those in Germany, the United Kingdom, Japan, and other nations.[27] These differences in value impact motivation, leadership, and teamwork in work organizations.[28] Habitual patterns of interaction can obstruct communication in any given culture. For example, the German culture places greater value on authority and hierarchical differences than does the United States. It is therefore more difficult for German workers to engage in open communication with their supervisors than it is for U.S. workers.[29]

When a person from one culture views people from another culture through the lens of a stereotype, they discount the individual differences that exist within that foreign culture. For example, a stereotype of Americans common throughout Asia is that they are aggressive and arrogant, and thus insensitive and unapproachable. Stereotypes of Asians common throughout America are that they are studious, subservient, and assimilative. Individuals who depend on the accuracy of cultural stereotypes may unknowingly create barriers in communicating with people from other cultures.

One gateway through the barrier of diversity is increasing cultural awareness and sensitivity. Part of that knowledge is paying attention to message context when communicating cross-culturally. Whereas Westerners are categorized as being low-context communicators who emphasize message content, Easterners, such as Japanese, Korean, and Chinese, are categorized as high-context communicators who focus more on the context of the message rather than the explicit content.[30] Further, companies can provide support for expatriate managers as part

Inclusive Conversations

Can Gender Communication Differences Be Biological?

There is much evidence, both empirical and anecdotal, to support the existence of gender differences in the ways men and women communicate. Much of this evidence points to how both genders are socialized over time. There is some support, however, for the idea that gender communication differences could be explained by biology, specifically the way the brain is structured and the assignment of estrogen and testosterone, sex hormones typically assigned to females and males respectively, at birth. According to this view, language skills, such as women having complicated conversations and including feelings and men communicating more literally, are attributed to how "female" and "male" brains are wired and the assignment of sex hormones. While this view may have some scientific appeal, it does not explain the stability of communication patterns when sex hormones change, such as after hormone replacement therapy or gender reassignment surgery. In fact, in the role of nature versus nurture, much of the research in this area supports the view that communication skills and styles are learned—by watching and mimicking how others communicate and adopting those behaviors. According to one expert, "nature and nurture are not equally responsible for gendered communication differences. Nature plays almost no role, with the minor exception of vocal pitch (higher or lower voice)."

1. Discuss how attributing communication differences between men and women to biological factors can affect workplace diversity issues.

   It is important for students to recognize that women and men communicate differently, but these differences are primarily based on how both genders are socialized from birth. Attributing communication differences to biology—brain formation and hormones—ignores nonbinary, transgender, or intersex individuals. It also ignores individuals who have had gender reassignment surgery or HRT (hormone replacement therapy). Instructors should suggest empathy as a "gateway" to this communications barrier.

2. Describe how models have affected your current style of communication. Were these models personal, professional, or both?

Source: D. Valenzuela, "Do Men and Women Actually Communicate Differently? Experts Weigh In," *Katie Couric Media*, September 3 (2022), accessed at https://katiecouric.com/lifestyle/relationships/gender-differences-in-communication-style/.

of their training for overseas assignments. Cultural intelligence (CQ) can be a key component of training and preparation for cross-cultural adaptation and performance, on the job and within the new culture.[31] A second gateway is developing or acquiring a guide for understanding and interacting with members of other cultures. For example, Irish pubs, the Spanish bullfight, and American football are consensually derived metaphors for culturally specific conversational styles that can enable those outside the culture to understand members within.

8-3c Language

Language can be another barrier to communication. Growing numbers of businesspeople are bilingual or multilingual, but even subtle distinctions in dialects within the same language can be barriers. For example, the word *chemist* means a molecular scientist in the United States and a drugstore worker in Great Britain. Language barriers are created across disciplines and professional boundaries by technical terminology. Although acronyms and professional jargon may be very useful tools of communication within a discipline, they may serve only to confuse and derail any attempt at clear understanding by those unfamiliar with the profession. When doing business, it's best to use simple, direct, declarative language. One should speak in brief sentences and employ terms or words already used by one's audience. As much as possible, one should speak in the language of the listener. Above all else, one should not use jargon or technical language except with those who are already familiar with it.

8-4 Civility and Incivility

While **incivility** can create a barrier between people and jar people's emotions, **civility** may be a gateway to communication that smooths troubled waters at work. Workplace incivility is low-intensity deviant workplace behavior with an ambiguous intent to harm. A review of the literature suggests that there are three types of incivility: experienced, witnessed, and instigated.[32] In worst case scenarios, incivility results in harm and is damaging. In this section, we examine the full range of consequences of incivility, the role of forgiveness, and the blessings of civility. The YOU feature on this page below gives you an opportunity to test your own verbal incivilities.

8-4a Consequences of Incivility

Workplace incivility can jar the emotions and cause a range of adverse outcomes both in the workplace and at home. Discourteousness, rudeness, impatience, and lack of respect are very common forms of incivility. The consequences of incivility depend on its source. Research suggests that vulnerability to the negative effects of workplace civility may also depend on ethnicity and cultural values.[33] Much incivility originates with superiors and those in powerful positions within the organization. This type of incivility is often tolerated even though it leads to a decline in satisfaction with the supervisor. Coworkers may display incivility too. As we would expect, someone subject to coworker incivility experiences less satisfaction with the coworker and that may generalize to all coworkers. In fact, observing incivility at work may destroy perceptions of professional conduct and cause the observer concern about whether they or other coworkers will receive similar treatment.[34] In addition, coworker incivility can trigger the perception of being treated unfairly at work and may even lead to depression. So the emotional and psychological adverse effects of coworker incivility are quite real along with additional costs from unfair treatment and depression. Understanding the dynamics of workplace incivility can enable incivility change with positive secondary effects in reducing burnout and turnout cognitions.[35] These positive effects may vary across time and individuals.

Forgiveness is a positive choice in responding to incivility and the emotional or psychological harm it may trigger.[36] Forgiveness is a powerful and healing force in relationships but should be carefully

incivility Discourteous communication and rude behavior that are disrespectful, hurtful, or injurious.

civility Communication and behavior that respect the integrity and dignity of the individual.

YOU

Test Your Verbal Incivilities

Common everyday incivilities are those behaviors that are thought of as rude or inconsiderate. Incivilities generally fall into one of two categories: physical and verbal.

Think about the range of interpersonal communications in which you participate on a weekly basis. In the first column, indicate how often you have experienced any of these behaviors. In the second column, indicate how often you have engaged in any of these behaviors.

Behavior	Others	You
Use of inappropriate language (swearing, making sexual remarks)		
Display of verbal aggression (using abusive or threatening language)		
Use of mobile phones in an inappropriate way (answering calls during funerals, church services, meetings, interviews, or other similar social settings)		

Look at the number of marks in the "You" column. If you notice a lot of marks, consider making a conscience effort to reduce or eliminate these uncivil behaviors.

Source: Adapted from T. Phillips and P. Smith, "Everyday Incivility: Towards a Benchmark," *The Sociological Review* 51 (2003): 85–105.

distinguished from what it is not. Forgiveness should not be confused with pardoning, condoning, excusing, forgetting, denying, minimizing, or trusting. Forgiveness does not necessarily lead to reconciliation, nor does it preclude formal complaints when warranted. Finally, forgiveness cannot be decoupled from the need for uncivil offenders to take responsibility for their words and actions.

8-4b Benefits of Civility

The benefits of civility are found in its gracious and positive nature. Civil communication and behavior carry the potential to avoid hurt feelings, prevent harm and damage to working relationships, and contribute to well-being in the workplace. There are several ways to create a more civil workplace: bring difficult issues out in the open, write things down before speaking, set enforcement guidelines for incivility, and be consistent in enforcing those guidelines. Civility ensures respect for the integrity and dignity of every member of the workplace.

8-5 Defensive and Nondefensive Communication

In the workplace, defensive language creates barriers between people, whereas nondefensive communication helps to open and deepen relationships.[37] **Defensive communication** includes aggressive, malevolent messages as well as passive, withdrawn messages. **Nondefensive communication** is assertive, direct, and powerful. Though it can be misinterpreted as aggressiveness, assertiveness is indeed nondefensive. Corporations today are increasingly engaged in situations such as courtroom battles and media exchanges that are fertile ground for defensive communication yet benefit greatly from nondefensive language and emotionally intelligent communication.

Defensive communication leads to a wide range of problems, including injured feelings, communication barriers, alienation in working relationships, destructive and retaliatory behaviors, nonproductive efforts, and problem-solving failures. Defensive reactions such as counterattack and sheepish withdrawal derail communication. These responses tend to lend

> Civility should not be confused with the avoidance of difficult or complicated workplace issues, which must be confronted and addressed.

heat, not light, to the process of communication. Defensive communication often evokes still more defensive communication.

Nondefensive communication, in contrast, provides a positive and productive basis for asserting and defending oneself against aggression without further damaging the communication process. An assertive, nondefensive style restores order, balance, and effectiveness in working relationships. Further discussion of nondefensive communication and defensive communication in the workplace follows.

8-5a Defensive Communication at Work

The two basic patterns of defensiveness are dominant defensiveness and subordinate defensiveness. Subordinate defensiveness is characterized by passive or submissive behavior. The psychological attitude of the subordinately defensive person is "You are right, and I am wrong." People with low self-esteem may be prone to this form of defensive behavior, as may people at lower organizational levels. Individuals who are subordinately defensive do not adequately assert their thoughts and feelings. Their input is likely to be lost, even if it is critical to organizational performance.[38] Passive-aggressive behavior is a form of defensiveness that begins as subordinate defensiveness and ends up as dominant defensiveness. It is behavior that appears very passive, though it actually masks underlying aggression and hostility.

In contrast, dominant defensiveness is characterized by overtly aggressive and domineering behavior. It is offensive in nature, sometimes culminating in verbal or physical harassment. The psychological

defensive communication Messages that are aggressive, malevolent, passive, or withdrawn.

nondefensive communication Messages that are assertive, direct, and powerful.

attitude of the dominantly defensive person is "I am right, and you are wrong." People who are egotistical or overcompensating for low self-esteem may exhibit this pattern of behavior, as may people in higher-level positions within the organizational hierarchy.

8-5b Defensive Tactics

Defensive tactics are subversive actions that employ defensive communication. Unfortunately, these tactics are common in many work organizations. Until defensiveness and defensive tactics are recognized for what they are at an organizational level, it is difficult to address them or respond to them in nondefensive ways. In many cases, defensive tactics raise ethical dilemmas for victims and their supervisors. At what point does simple defensiveness become unethical behavior? Consider the following defensive tactics.

Power plays are tactics used to control and manipulate others. Restricting the choices of employees, enforcing either/or conditions, intentionally ignoring or insulting others, bullying, and displaying overt aggression are all power plays. The underlying dynamic in power plays is that of domination and control, the aggressor makes the victim feel inferior and thus vulnerable.

Labeling is often used to portray another person as abnormal or deficient. Medical and legal labels are often used out of context for this purpose. The words *paranoid*, *narcissistic*, and *insane* have specific, clinical meanings that are discarded in defensive labeling. Similar to labeling is publicly raising doubts about a person's abilities, values, sexual orientation, or other personal aspects, which breeds confusion and uncertainty.

Disseminating misleading information, a form of deception, is the selective presentation of information intentionally designed to produce an inaccurate impression in the listener's mind. This obfuscated information can be used to scapegoat, or pass the buck, which shifts responsibility for an error or problem to the wrong person. Or, defensive individuals may simply blame others for their own wrongdoing.

Finally, *hostile jokes* are a passive-aggressive defensive tactic. While a jocular framing is used to mask aggressive and even overtly mean sentiments, hostile jokes do harm. They should not be confused with good humor, which is both therapeutic and

> An individual who consistently communicates nondefensively may be characterized as centered, assertive, controlled, informative, realistic, and honest.

nondefensive. Jokes made at the expense of others are damaging and disruptive.

8-5c Nondefensive Communication

Nondefensive communication is a healthy alternative to defensive communication in working relationships. An individual who consistently communicates nondefensively may be characterized as centered, assertive, controlled, informative, realistic, and honest. Nondefensive communication is powerful because the speaker exhibits self-control and self-possession without rejecting the listener. It should be self-affirming without being self-aggrandizing—a sometimes difficult balance to maintain.

Converting defensive patterns of communication to nondefensive ones builds relationships at work. Behaviors that build relationships simultaneously reduce adverse responses, such as blame and anger, when negative events occur at work.[39]

To strengthen nondefensive patterns, the subordinately defensive person must learn to be more assertive. One way to do this is to report what one intends to do and invite confirmation instead of asking for permission to do something. Another way is to stop using self-deprecating phrases such as "I'm just following orders." One should drop the *just* and thereby convert the message into a self-assertive, declarative statement.

To strengthen nondefensive patterns, the dominantly defensive person must learn to be less aggressive. This may be especially difficult because it requires overcoming the sense of certitude. Those who are working to overcome dominant defensiveness should be particularly sensitive to feedback from others about their behavior. To change this behavior, one can stop giving and denying permission. Instead, one should give others free rein (except in situations where permission is essential to clearance or the security of the task). Alternatively, instead of becoming inappropriately angry, one should provide information about the adverse consequences of a particular course of action. Communication should be healthy and productive.

8-6 Healthy, Productive Communication

The absence of heartfelt communication in relationships leads to loneliness and social isolation, a condition labeled **communicative disease** by James Lynch.[40] Communicative disease has adverse effects on the heart and cardiovascular system that can ultimately lead to premature death. According to Lynch, the only cure for communicative disease is to reengage in thoughtful, heartwarming conversation with friends, colleagues, and loved ones. While heartfelt conversations are important, productive conversations are equally important in the workplace.

8-6a Heartfelt Communication

Heartfelt conversations are an important aspect of *working together*—that is, cooperating to reach a shared goal—in both the interpersonal and intrapersonal settings.[41] Such communication requires trust and truthfulness. However, it does not exclude honest competition within the workplace, which in fact is consistent with the concept of working together. Sincere, well-managed competition can bring out the best in all those involved.

Healthy communication is at the core of personal integrity and managerial success, as is evident in the lives of most successful executives, including those in the executive branch of the U.S. government.[42] President Ronald Reagan was nicknamed "the great communicator" for his ability to connect with the American people. He conveyed strong ethical character, personal integrity, and simplicity in his communication. Reagan exemplified Lynch's concept of heartfelt communication because his language in speeches and interviews seemed to stem from core values and sincere aspirations. Communication from the heart is communication anchored in personal integrity and ethical character.

8-6b Productive Conversations

Silence and voice are both important aspects of productive workplace conversations.[43] Edmondson and Besieux propose a productive conversation, two-dimensional matrix as shown in Figure 8.2. One dimension is voice, and the other dimension is type of contribution. Unproductive conversations can occur in one of two ways: either a person is speaking up in a disruptive way or they are withholding information by being silent. Alternatively, productive conversations occur when a person is speaking up and contributing in a courageous, constructive voice, adding value to the discussion. Another way of being productive in conversation is making space for silence. During silent reflection, one person quietly processes or reflects upon what is being or has been said. Productive conversations are ones in which constructive voice is used and ones that occur in a psychologically safe work environment; that is, a work environment free of incivility, fear, retribution, and retaliatory or punitive responses.

Healthy, productive conversations are at the center of courageous, constructive communication in a workplace. Emotionally healthy and psychologically safe workplaces are ones in which employees and managers can engage in open, honest exchanges about subjects that are professionally and personally important. In addition to voice and silence, nonverbal communication is a key feature of the workplace.

communicative disease Loneliness and social isolation resulting from the absence of heartfelt communication in relationships.

Figure 8.2 The Productive Workplace Conversation Matrix

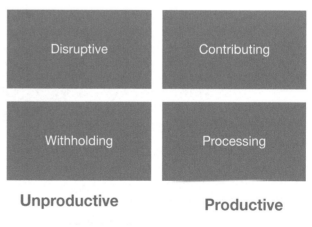

Disruptive	Contributing
Withholding	Processing
Unproductive	**Productive**

Type of Contribution

8-7 Nonverbal Communication

Whereas defensive and nondefensive communication focus on the language used in delivering a message, most of the meaning in a message is nonverbal or behavioral. Rudeness is an example of low-intensity negative behavior that may communicate an ambiguous message but more importantly be contagious in organizations.[44] Mindfulness of both the verbal and nonverbal elements of communication are therefore important. **Nonverbal communication** includes all elements of communication that do not involve words or language such as gestures and the use of space.[45] The four basic types of nonverbal communication that managers need to understand are proxemics, kinesics, facial and eye behavior, and paralanguage.

nonverbal communication All elements of communication that do not involve words or language.

proxemics The study of an individual's perception and use of space.

territorial space Bands of concentric space radiating outward from the body.

Managers also need to understand that nonverbal communication is influenced by both psychological and physiological processes.[46]

The interpretation of nonverbal communication is specific to the context of the interaction and the actors. That is, the particular meaning of any nonverbal cue relies on its sender, receiver, and the environment in which the cue occurs. For example, some federal and state judges attempt to curb nonverbal communication in the courtroom. Though it may mean nothing outside the courtroom, some nonverbal behavior may unfairly influence jurors' decisions if displayed during a trial. Beyond the contextual element, nonverbal behavior is also culturally bound. (Recall from Chapter 2 the difference in meaning the "thumbs-up" sign has in Australia versus the United States.)

8-7a Proxemics

The study of an individual's perception and use of space, including territorial space, is called **proxemics**.[47] **Territorial space** refers to bands of concentric space radiating outward from the body. These bands are commonly known as *comfort zones*. Figure 8.3 illustrates the four zones of territorial space common to U.S. culture.

Figure 8.3 Zones of Territorial Space in U.S. Culture

—12— —4— —1½—
feet feet feet   a   b   c   d →

Zone a, **intimate space:** spouses, significant others, family members, and others with whom one has an intimate relationship
Zone b, **personal distance:** friends
Zone c, **social distance:** business associates and acquaintances
Zone d, **public distance:** strangers

ESB Basic/Shutterstock.com

Territorial space varies greatly around the world. Both the sizes of comfort zones and their acceptable modes of interaction are culturally defined. And people often become uncomfortable when operating in territorial spaces different from those with which they are familiar.

According to leading proxemics researcher Edward Hall, Americans working in the Middle East tend to back away to a comfortable distance when conversing with Arabs because Arabs' comfortable conversation distance is closer than that of Americans. As a result, Arabs sometimes perceive Americans as cold and aloof. One Arab wondered, "What's the matter? Does he find me somehow offensive?"[48] The circumference of personal space tends to be larger in cultures with cool climates, such as the United States, Great Britain, and northern Europe, and smaller in cultures with warm climates, such as southern Europe, the Caribbean, India, and South America.[49]

Our relationships shape our use of territorial space. For example, we hold hands with or put an arm around significant others to pull them into *intimate space*. Conversely, we can use territorial space to shape our interactions. A four-foot-wide desk pushes business interactions into the *social distance* zone. Not comfortable with that definition of space, one SBC manager met with her seven first-line supervisors crowded around her four-foot desk, putting them elbow to elbow with each other. As a result of being placed in one another's intimate space, they appeared to act more like friends and frequently talked about their children, favorite television shows, and other personal concerns. When the manager moved the staff meetings to a larger room and thus relocated the supervisors into each others' social distance zones, the personal exchanges ceased, and they acted more like business associates again.

Seating dynamics, another aspect of proxemics, is the art of seating people in certain positions according to their purpose in communication. Figure 8.4 depicts some common seating dynamics. To encourage cooperation, one should seat the adjoining party beside oneself, facing the same direction. To facilitate direct and open communication, one should seat the other party across a corner of one's desk or in another place where they will be at right angles. This allows for more honest disclosure. To take a competitive stand with someone, one must position the person directly across from oneself. Suppose a manager holds a meeting around a conference table, and two of the attendees are disrupting the meeting by chatting loudly. Where should they be seated? If the manager places the two disruptive attendees on either side of themselves, the talking should be stifled (unless one is so bold as to lean in front of the manager to keep chatting).

8-7b Kinesics

Kinesics is the study of body movement and posture.[50] Like proxemics, kinesics is bound to culture. With this in mind, we can interpret some common U.S. gestures. Rubbing one's hands together while inhaling sharply indicates anticipation. Stress is indicated by balled fists, clenched teeth, hand wringing, and rubbing the temples. Nervousness may be indicated by drumming fingers, pacing, or jingling coins in one's pocket. Kinesics also includes insulting gestures like giving someone "the finger."

8-7c Facial and Eye Behavior

The face is a rich source of nonverbal communication. Facial expression and eye behavior are used to communicate an emotional state, reveal behavioral intentions, and cue the receiver. It may even give unintended clues to emotions the sender is trying to hide.[51] Unintended facial movements can undermine the illusion of truthfulness, especially in stressful situations.[52]

kinesics The study of body movement and posture.

Figure 8.4 Seating Dynamics

Culture, environment, and specific actors must be taken into consideration when interpreting smiles, frowns, raised eyebrows, and other expressions. One study of Japanese and U.S. students illustrated the point. The students were shown a stress-inducing film, and their facial expressions were videotaped. When alone, the students had almost identical expressions. When in the presence of others, however, the Japanese students masked their facial expressions of unpleasant feelings much better than the American students did.[53]

As mentioned earlier, eye contact can enhance reflective listening. Along with smiling, eye contact is an easy way to express honesty and positive emotion.[54] However, eye contact must be understood in a cultural context. A direct gaze indicates dedication, truthfulness, and forthrightness in the United States. The eyes not only communicate to another person, they are the pathways for receiving significant messages. What is seen cannot be unseen, which may be very troubling in traumatic contexts. However, seeing war traumas is not universally injurious psychologically. A person's organizational context can give meaning to what is seen, therefore determining in part whether the outcome is psychological growth or psychological injury.[55]

8-7d Paralanguage

Paralanguage consists of variations in speech, such as pitch, loudness, tempo, tone, duration, laughing, and crying.[56] People make assumptions about the communicator by deciphering paralanguage cues. A man who uses extensive profanity in the workplace may be stereotyped as "uneducated" or "lacking in refinement." Rapid, loud speech may be taken as a sign of nervousness or anger. Interruptions such as "mmm" and "okay" may be used to speed up the speaker so that the receiver can get in a few words. Clucking of the tongue and the tsk-tsk sound are used to shame someone. All these cues relate to how something is said.

8-8 Organizational Communication

Organizational communication is an encompassing term for all forms of communication within an organization. This final section of the chapter addresses crisis communication, written communication, communication technologies, and how communication technologies affect behavior. Organizational communication is the key interpersonal process for linking all of the individuals, groups, and teams within a cohesive organization to accomplish the mission.

8-8a Crisis Communication

The COVID-19 pandemic demonstrated how important **crisis communication** is for an organization. In response, organizations adopted technology-driven solutions through which managers communicated time-critical information via multiple channels.[57] These channels included but were not limited to email, intranet, video conferencing, and other tools. By adopting an attributional lens, organizations were better able to get critical information through to employees who were operating as 'naïve' psychologists. When the information communicated was distinctive (i.e., stood out in the environment), consistent (i.e., was the same across situations), and consensual (i.e., multiple sources sent the same message), then employees better 'got it' and acted on the information. Zoom, Slack, and Microsoft Teams really took off during the pandemic as digital platforms through which dyads, triads, and larger teams could communicate.

A study of 3,143,270 knowledge workers' digital communication patterns during the pandemic in 16 large metropolitan areas in North America, Europe, and the Middle East found notable pre-pandemic to post-pandemic shifts.[58] While there was a 13 percent increase in meetings per person and number of attendees per meeting, there was a 20 percent decrease in average meeting length. The net effect was 11 percent less time in meetings per day. Interestingly, there was a durable increase of 8 percent, or 48+ minutes per day, in the length of the average workday. How sustained these organizational communication shifts are will take time to determine.

8-8b Written Communication

Even though many organizations are working toward paperless offices and paperless interfaces with their customers, written communication is still an essential skill—many types of written communication are still necessary to business. The

crisis communication A communication strategy to defend an organization under threat.

Grammarly's AI Can Smooth Out Your Prose

Grammarly was a Kiev-based startup that is now headquartered in San Francisco with venture capital funding. The company has won Time 100 and Fast Company honors for innovation, using artificial intelligence (AI) to edit the written word. In addition, Grammarly has been recognized among Inc.'s Best Workplaces while doing good in the world, sending $5,000,000 in aid to the Ukrainian people. Grammarly helps companies fine-tune how their staffers write, going beyond style preferences that companies might have to brand tones they prefer and vocabulary they use. More than 30 million people and 30,000 teams use Grammarly's free and paid versions. The written word continues to be an essential element of organizational communication.

Source: H. McCracken, "Grammarly Writes a New Corporate Playbook," *Fast Company*, May 9 (2022).

Organizational Example on this page above focuses on an awarding winning company that can improve the written word. Manuals and reports are generally the longest forms of written communication found in the office. Policy manuals are important in organizations because they establish guidelines for decision-making and codes of conduct. Operations and procedures manuals explain how to perform various tasks and resolve problems that may occur at work. Reports, such as annual company finance reports, may summarize the results of a committee's or department's work or provide information on progress toward certain objectives.

Letters and memorandums (memos) are briefer than manuals and reports and are more frequently used in larger organizations. Letters are still sometimes used to communicate formally with individuals and businesses outside the organization. They vary substantially in length and topic. Memos and emails are also used for formal, internal communication within an organization. They are sometimes used as historical records of specific events or occurrences that individuals within the organization can refer back to later.

One of the shortest kinds of written communication is the form, which may be used to collect information inside or outside the organization. Technologies like Slack or Microsoft Teams are also known for facilitating concise and time-sensitive information.

8-8c Communication Technologies

Computer-mediated communication influences virtually all behavior in the work environment. E-mail, voice mail, instant messaging, and facsimile (fax) machines have been common in the business world for decades., Large information databases have become commonplace. These databases provide a tremendous amount of information at the push of a button. An example of an information database is the electronic card catalog system used in university libraries throughout the world. These systems, sometimes linked with each other to form massive networks of data, store information about books' and journals' contents, distributions, and availability.

One of the newest technologies to impact the work environment (though no longer new) is the smartphone. Smartphones combine the capabilities of advanced cell phones with computer-like applications and connectivity. Examples include the Apple iPhone, Samsung Galaxy devices, and the Google Pixel. The smartphone's introduction was particularly transformative for sales jobs involving travel. While they are widely used, not all reactions to smartphones are positive. For example, one oil producer did not want his daily commute disturbed by outside interference; he used driving as a time for thought and relaxation. Some estimates suggest that using a phone while driving is as risky as driving while under the influence of alcohol. For this reason, some states have outlawed cell phone talking or texting while driving a motor vehicle.

Cell phones are an ubiquitous form of communication technology.

8-8d How Do Communication Technologies Affect Behavior?

Information communication technology (ICT) is an extensive category of new developments in interpersonal communication that allow fast, even immediate, access to information. E-mail, teleconferencing, and Wi-Fi are all classified as ICT. It can facilitate the instant exchange of information in minutes or seconds across geographic boundaries and time zones. With adequate ICT implementation, schedules and office hours become irrelevant in that considerations of time and distance that once beleaguered international and intranational business become far less important in the exchange. Given its impact on the way business is done, ICT has a significant influence on people's behavior.

Computer-mediated communication is impersonal in nature. Instant messaging, e-mail, and other forms of online communication can therefore depreciate the richness of personal interaction. Studies show that using these technologies may increase one's likelihood to flame—that is, to make rude, needlessly argumentative or obscene comments by means of computer-mediated communication.[59] Employees' interpersonal skills such as tact and graciousness may subside online, and managers tend to be more blunt when using electronic media. People who normally participate in discussions quietly and politely may become more intimate, impolite, or uninhibited when they communicate using computer conferencing or electronic mail.[60]

Another effect of computer-mediated communication is that the nonverbal cues we rely on to decipher a message are absent. Gesturing, touching, facial expressions, and eye contact are not possible, so the emotional aspect of the message is difficult to discern. Even in teleconferencing, where users can see each others' faces, it is often difficult to perceive nonverbal cues.[61] Clues to power such as organizational position and departmental membership may not be available, so the social context of the exchange is often altered.

---

information communication technology (ICT) An extensive category of new developments in interpersonal communication that allow fast, even immediate, access to information.

Communication via technology also changes group dynamics by equalizing participation. As a result, charismatic or higher-status members may lose some power.[62] Studies of group decision-making have shown that computer-mediated groups took longer to reach consensus than face-to-face groups. In addition, they were less cooperative, more uninhibited, and there was less influence from any one dominant person. Another study found that ICTs, especially e-mail and e-meetings, reduce tension caused by intercultural communication.[63] Groups that communicate via computer seem to experience a breakdown of social and organizational barriers.

The potential for information overload is particularly great when individuals are first introduced to new communication technologies. Both the sheer volume of information available and its speed of delivery are staggering. An individual can easily become overwhelmed by information and must learn to be selective about its access.

While modern ICT may make work easier and increase employees' productivity, it can also prove precarious for managers. In the wake of mobile e-mail, instant messaging, and texting, managers are more accessible to coworkers, subordinates, and the boss today than they've ever been. Researchers coined the term *workplace telepressure* to describe the pressure employees feel when they perceive asynchronous communication methods as having the same requirements for response time as synchronous communication methods have. Typically, sending an e-mail will give individuals flexibility and additional time to respond, unlike communicating face-to-face. Face-to-face communications require an immediate response. Viewing ICTs as having the same properties as face-to-face communication may cause employees to prioritize these communication methods similarly, making it more difficult for employees to disengage.[64]

Further, many new technologies encourage *polyphasic activity*, or multitasking (i.e., doing more than one thing at a time). Managers can simultaneously make phone calls, send instant messages, and work on memos. Polyphasic activity has its advantages in terms of getting more done—but only up to a point. Paying attention to more than one thing at a time splits a person's attention and may reduce effectiveness at individual tasks. At its extreme, focusing on multiple tasks can become a destructive habit, making it psychologically difficult for a person to let go of work.

New technologies encourage multitasking

StockLite/Shutterstock.com

Finally, new technologies may make people less patient with face-to-face communication. The speed of electronic media may lead to expectations of acceleration in all forms of communication. However, if they spend too much time communicating online, individuals may come to miss social interaction with others, and may find their social needs unmet. Communicating via computer often means the end of small talk. In the name of speed, amenity is sacrificed for efficiency. Managers can use new technologies more efficiently and effectively by keeping in mind the suggestions presented in Table 8.2.

Table 8.2 Channel Etiquette

Meta	Twitter	YouTube	LinkedIn
• Take sensitive queries into a private sphere online or offline • Remember all wall posts are public; don't write anything there that is not for wider consumption. • Ensure that all updates are frequent and relevant but not too frequent. • Use language relevant to the channel and to the target demographics • Show appreciation, and acknowledge positive comments • Follow up and respond to any feedback.	• Begin with an introduction if used for outreach or active engagement • Develop a tone of voice and personality • Keep requests for re-tweets to a minimum. • Keep tweets as short and sweet as possible (less than 140 characters) • Avoid pure self-promotion. Twitter is a knowledge-sharing and conversation channel.	• Develop a thick skin. Many comments are not constructive, so do not take such comments to heart or argue; defensive reactions only fan the flames. • Use video replies because these can be powerful and a good way to spread a message • Acknowledge comments, and thank those who are being positive about a brand.	• Join groups and contribute information about relevant experience. • Answer questions, and contribute to share pages and communities. • Avoid asking for references unless the person is someone already known or if the company has genuinely delivered great service. • Support unsolicited contacts with a full explanation of who is contacting and why; don't assume that contacts will view the underlying profile.

Experiential Exercise

Communicate, Listen, Understand

The following exercise gives you an opportunity to work within a three-person group to do a communication skill-building exercise. You can learn to apply some of the reflective listening and two-way communication materials from the early sections of the chapter, as well as some of the lessons managing difficult communication in a nondefensive manner.

Step 1. The class is formed into three-person groups and each group designates its members "A," "B," and "C." There will be three five- to seven-minute conversations among the group members: first, between A and B; second, between B and C; third, between C and A. During each conversation, the nonparticipating group member is to observe and make notes about two communicating group members.

Step 2. Your instructor will give you a list of controversial topics and ask A to pick a topic. A is then asked to discuss his or her position on this topic, with the rationale for the position, with B. B is to practice reflective listening and engage in listening checks periodically by paraphrasing what he or she understands to be A's position. C should observe whether B is practicing good listening skills or becoming defensive. C should also observe whether A is becoming dominantly defensive in the communication. This should be a two-way communication.

Step 3. Repeat Step 2 with B as communicator, C as listener, and A as observer.

Step 4. Repeat Step 2 with C as communicator, A as listener, and B as observer.

Step 5. After your instructor has had all groups complete Steps 1 through 4, your three-person group should answer the following questions.

   a. Did either the listener or the communicator become visibly (or internally) angry or upset during the discussion?
   b. What were the biggest challenges for the listeners and the communicator in the controversial communication?
   c. What are the most important skill improvements (e.g., better eye contact or more patience) the listener and communicator could have made to improve the quality of understanding achieved through the communication process?

Learning Objectives

8-1 Describe the interpersonal communication process and the role of listening in the process. Interpersonal communication is reflective, objective, and perceptual. The conceptual and emotional component of messages is affected by verbal and nonverbal communication and is key to understanding and verifying the message. Reflective listening enables the listener to understand the communicator's meaning, reduce perceptual distortions, and overcome interpersonal barriers that lead to communication failures.

8-2 Describe the five communication skills of effective supervisors. Five communication skills that distinguish "good" from "bad" supervisors include being expressive speakers, empathetic listeners, persuasive leaders, sensitive people, and informative managers.

8-3 Explain five communication barriers and the gateways through them. Barriers to communication in the workplace are physical separation, status differences, gender differences, cultural diversity, and language. Awareness and recognition are the first steps to overcoming barriers. Other gateways are recognizing differences in gender-specific conversation style, understanding cultural differences, and avoiding technical terms and jargon.

8-4 **Distinguish between civility and incivility, and defensive and nondefensive communication.** *Civility* is communication that respects the integrity and dignity of the individual. It carries the potential to avoid hurt feelings, prevent harm and damage to working relationships, and contribute to well-being in the workplace. *Incivility* is communication that does not respects the integrity and dignity of the individual. It can create a barrier between people and jar emotions, though the consequences of incivility depend on its source. *Defensive communication* includes aggressive and angry communication as well as passive, withdrawing communication. *Nondefensive communication* is an assertive, direct, powerful form of communication.

8-5 **Explain the impact of nonverbal communication.** Most meaning in a message is conveyed nonverbally. *Nonverbal communication* includes all elements of communication, such as gestures and the use of space, that do not involve words or language. The four basic kinds of nonverbal communication that managers need to understand and read are proxemics, kinesics, facial and eye behavior, and paralanguage.

8-6 **Explain positive, healthy communication.** James Lynch suggests that heartfelt communication may be equally or more important than cognition in the communication process. According to Lynch, positive, healthy communication is exemplified by trust and truthfulness, core values and beliefs, strong ethical character, personal integrity, openness, and simplicity in communication.

8-7 **Identify how new communication technologies and social media affect the communication process.** Technologies such as cell phones, e-mail, voice mail, faxes, computers, and informational databases provide instant exchange of volumes of information and render geographic boundaries and time zones irrelevant. Lack of personal interaction and nonverbal cues alter the social context of exchange and remove organizational barriers. The potential for information overload, constant accessibility to work, and multitasking also affects behavior.

8-8 **Describe how organizational communication is disrupted by crises.** Organizational communication is disrupted by crises that break lines of communication, introduce noise, confusion, and increase time urgency. In addition, crises raise anxiety levels, thus straining both the ability to speak clearly as well as to hear and understand accurately. When information is communicated in a crisis, it should be distinctive, consistent, and consensual. Digital platforms help in a crisis too.

Key Terms

barriers to communication Factors that distort, disrupt, or even halt successful communication. (p. 163)

civility Communication and behavior that respect the integrity and dignity of the individual. (p. 166)

communication The evoking of a shared or common meaning in another person. (p. 158)

communicative disease Loneliness and social isolation resulting from the absence of heartfelt communication in relationships. (p. 169)

communicator The person sending a message. (p. 158)

crisis communication A communication strategy to defend an organization under threat. (p. 172)

data Uninterpreted and unanalyzed elements of a message. (p. 159)

defensive communication Messages that are aggressive, malevolent, passive, or withdrawn. (p. 167)

employee voice behavior communication of suggestions, concerns, information about problems, or work-related opinions to effect constructive changes in the workplace. (p. 159)

feedback Information fed back that completes two-way communication. (p. 159)

gateways to communication Openings that break down communication barriers. (p. 164)

incivility Discourteous communication and rude behavior that are disrespectful, hurtful, or injurious. (p. 166)

information Data that have been interpreted, analyzed, and have meaning to some user. (p. 159)

information communication technology (ICT) An extensive category of new developments in interpersonal communication that allow fast, even immediate, access to information. (p. 174)

interpersonal communication Communication between two or more people in an organization. (p. 158)

kinesics The study of body movement and posture. (p. 171)

language The words, their pronunciations, and the methods of combining them used and understood by a group of people. (p. 159)

message The thoughts and feelings that the communicator is attempting to evoke in the receiver. (p. 158)

nondefensive communication Messages that are assertive, direct, and powerful. (p. 167)

nonverbal communication All elements of communication that do not involve words or language. (p. 170)

one-way communication Communication in which a person sends a message to another person and no feedback, questions, or interaction follows. (p. 162)

perceptual screen A window through which one interacts with others. It influences the quality, accuracy, and clarity of the communication. (p. 158)

proxemics The study of an individual's perception and use of space. (p. 170)

receiver The person accepting a message. (p. 158)

reflective listening Carefully listening to message and immediately repeating it back to the speaker. (p. 160)

richness The ability of a medium to convey meaning to a receiver. (p. 159)

territorial space Bands of concentric space radiating outward from the body. (p. 170)

two-way communication An interactive form of communication in which there is an exchange of thoughts, feelings, or both. (p. 162)

Ethical Dilemma

Advanced Technologies

Advanced Technologies is an Internet company that provides a search engine and other Internet applications to consumers. Advanced competes with the major players in the industry like Google and Microsoft Edge. Matt is the CEO of Advanced and has been struggling with his company's profitability. Revenues are down and Matt has accepted that he must face layoffs. This is something that is very difficult for Matt as his previous experiences with releasing people has not been positive. He has been trying to begin the layoffs for the last two weeks and has been unable to bring himself to face the 20 individuals that he has decided to layoff.

He realized that he cannot put this off any longer but is unsure how he is going to bring himself to face this difficult task. He decides that he simply is unable to do this and takes the easy way out. He begins emailing the 20 people who will be let go to tell them they no longer have a job.

Geoff has worked for Advanced Technologies for just over four years. He is having a great weekend with his family and is looking forward to the coming week as he will begin implementing a new program at work that he been involved with for two years. He checks his email on Saturday afternoon to find that he has been laid off. Geoff is devastated as he never saw this coming. How is he going to support his family?

1. Using consequential, rule-based, and character theories, evaluate Matt's decision to use email to deliver this news instead of a face-to-face meeting.

2. What should Matt have done? Why?

Chapter 9

Morsa Images/DigitalVision/Getty Images

Work Teams and Groups

Learning Objectives

9-1 Define group and work team.

9-2 Explain the benefits that organizations and individuals derive from working in teams.

9-3 Identify the factors that influence group behavior.

9-4 Describe how groups form and develop.

9-5 Explain how task and maintenance functions influence group performance.

9-6 Discuss the factors that influence group effectiveness.

9-7 Describe how empowerment relates to self-managed and remote teams.

9-8 Explain the importance of upper echelons and the top management team.

9-1 Groups and Work Teams

A **group** is formed when two or more people have common interests, objectives, and continuing interaction. A **work team** is a group of people with complementary skills who are committed to a common mission. COVID-19 upended many social bonds, connections, and collaborations through social distancing and strained relationships. Despite this, the deep human need for connection endured through and beyond the pandemic, both in the workplace and in personal spaces. Groups and teams are where individuals form the secure relationships that are essential to mental, physical, and psychological health.[1] Groups emphasize individual leadership, personal accountability, and exclusive work products. Work teams emphasize shared leadership, mutual accountability, and collective work products.

Work teams are task-oriented groups, though in some organizations the word *team* has a negative connotation for union members. Work teams make valuable contributions to the organization and are important to the need satisfaction of members.

Several kinds of work teams exist. Some are like baseball teams in that members have set responsibilities, others are like football teams in that members have coordinated action, and still others are like doubles tennis teams in that members have primary yet flexible responsibilities. Another analogy for work teams is that some operate like groundskeeping crews in that all members work synergistically toward a single goal.[2] All work teams need to attend to knowledge-based processes and interactions as well as contextual factors if they are to improvise effectively, such as in R&D environments.[3]

Teams and groups do not all work face-to-face. Advanced computer and telecommunications technologies enable organizations to be more flexible

> Work teams emphasize shared leadership, mutual accountability, and collective work products.

through the use of *virtual teams*.[4] Organizations use virtual teams to access expertise and the best employees around the world. Whether traditional or virtual, groups and teams continue to play a vital role in organizational behavior and performance at work.

9-2 Why Work Teams?

Teams are very useful in performing work that is complicated, fragmented, and/or more voluminous than one person can handle. Harold Geneen, while chairman of ITT, said, "If I had enough arms and legs and time, I'd do it all myself." Obviously, no one person in an organization can do everything by themselves, not only because of the limitations of arms, legs, and time, but also expertise, knowledge, and other resources. However, individual limitations can be overcome through teamwork and collaboration. In a global economy, organizations need to enable virtual and dispersed teams that work effectively. Some of the same principles that work for in-person teams can be applied in dispersed teams. Global teams that are geographically dispersed work best when members display empathy, refrain from domineering behavior, maintain frequent contact, and offer feedback on interactions while allowing for some unstructured time for informal exchanges.[5]

9-2a Benefits to Organizations

Teams make the most significant contributions to organizations when members can put aside individual interests in favor of unity. This joint action is called

Rawpixel.com/Shutterstock.com

Integrated involvement in the workplace results in enjoyment of work and being valued for one's skills and abilities.

group Two or more people with common interests, objectives, and continuing interaction.

work team A group of people with complementary skills who are committed to a common mission, performance goals, and approach for which they hold themselves mutually accountable.

Inclusive Conversations

DEI Teams are a "Need-to-Have," Especially During an Economic Downturn

Diversity, equity, inclusion initiatives became a common and necessary part of many organizational plans following the murder of George Floyd in 2020, serving as a reminder that diversity and inclusion are the key drivers behind teamwork and productivity. Companies spent nearly $7.5 billion on diversity, equity, and inclusion (DEI) efforts after George Floyd's murder, including creating chief diversity officer roles and staffs.

With signs of financial decline across many industries, many of those same organizations who made a commitment to DEI efforts are scaling back those efforts. In addition to reported layoffs in the tech industry, especially, DEI teams have taken a hit. X (formerly Twitter) reportedly cut its DEI team from 30 employees to 2, and job postings for DEI positions worldwide in 2023 are down 19 percent compared to 2022. Abi Williams, founder of Lead Not Lag, believes that teams made up of people with different perspectives, whether the result of race, ethnicity, or gender differences, are key to the most engaged and highest-performing employees.

Companies must respond to economic challenges in ways that will strengthen their financial positions. While some respond by cutting so-called "nice-to-have" initiatives, such as DEI, many more respond by demonstrating how vital to business growth attracting and retaining top talent really is.

1. How can organizations demonstrate the value of DEI initiatives, especially during periods of economic uncertainty?
   Some companies are using evidence to substantiate DEI initiatives. They are moving away from training as a compliance exercise and one that emphasizes outcomes that are connected to organizational values. Others are moving to an ESG (environmental, social, and governance) model that will allow them to be proactive rather than reactive.

2. Explain the value of diversity on top-level teams?
   Heterogeneity in executive-level teams helps to sustain CEO vitality and performance by providing diversity of information and points of view. Note: Students will have additional responses (See also Benefits and Problems of Diversity in Chapter 2).

Source: C. A. Brennan, "Your Business Needs Diversity, Inclusion, Equity, and Belong Now More Than Ever: Why Leaders Shouldn't Lose Sight of DEIB Work in a Downturn," Forbes, February 23 (2023), accessed at https://www.forbes.com/sites/carabrennanallamano/2023/02/23/your-business-needs-diversity-inclusion-equity-and-belonging-now-more-than-ever-why-leaders-shouldnt-lose-sight-of-deib-work-in-a-downturn/?sh=802f054562bd; K. Davis, "What Happened to Companies' Commitment to DEI?" *FastCompany*, March 6 (2023), accessed at https://www.fastcompany.com/90855309/what-happened-companies-commitment-dei.

teamwork. Complex, collaborative work tasks and activities tend to require considerable amounts of teamwork. When knowledge, talent, and abilities are dispersed across numerous workers and require an integrated effort for task accomplishment, teamwork is often the only solution. The Inclusive Conversation on this page above addresses the essential nature of DEI (diversity, equity, inclusion) teams in organizations.

A movement toward team-oriented work environments has championed empowerment through collaboration rather than self-reliance and competition. Teams with experience working together may produce valuable innovations, and individual contributions within teams are valuable as well.[6] A team-oriented work environment aligns with a significantly more empowered workforce in the industrial sectors of the American economy than does a command-and-control work environment. Table 9.1 compares the team environment to the

command-and-control environment. In the environment, teams must bring together members with different specialties and knowledge to work on complex problems. The ability to do so improves team performance and psychological well-being.[7]

9-2b Psychosocial Benefits to Individuals

On an individual level, team or group members derive benefits from the collective experience of teamwork. These individual benefits are best organized into two categories. One set of benefits accrues from achieving psychological intimacy, while the other comes from

teamwork Joint action by a team of people in which individual interests are subordinated to team unity.

Fast Fact

The Connection Between Respect Among Coworkers and Loneliness

Millions of people transitioned to working at home in 2020 and early 2021. For some who worked remotely 100 percent of the time, loneliness became an issue. Over time as people accommodated, the loneliness of remote workers began to drop. However, a deeper look into the work environment revealed that there appeared to be a relationship between respect among coworkers and loneliness. Gallup's research revealed that 16 percent of employees who *strongly agree* that their coworkers are committed to quality work reported feeling lonely. However, the research revealed that 40 percent of those who *strongly disagree* that their coworkers are committed to quality work reported feeling lonely. For those who only disagree, the number was 28 percent who reported feeling lonely. Respect among coworkers appears to have psychosocial benefits for employees and mitigates feelings of loneliness.

Source: J. Harter, "The Loneliest Employees," *GALLUP*, November 15 (2021).

Table 9.1 Team Environment Versus Command-And-Control Environment

Team Environment	Command-and-Control Environment
Person comes up with initiatives. Team has considerable authority to chart its own steps.	Person follows orders. Team depends on the manager to chart its course.
Members form a team because people learn to collaborate in the face of their emerging right to think for themselves. People both rock the boat and work together.	Members were a team because people conformed to direction set by the manager. No one rocked the boat.
People cooperate by using their thoughts and feelings. They link up through direct talk.	People cooperated by suppressing their thoughts and feelings. They wanted to get along.

Source: L. Hirschhorn, *Managing in the New Team Environment: Skills, Tools, and Methods* (San Jose: Authors Choice Press). © 2002. Reprinted with permission.

achieving integrated involvement.[8] The COVID-19 pandemic disrupted some of these benefits due to social distancing and remote work. In the Fast Fact on this page above, Gallup reports on respect among coworkers and the loneliest employees.

Psychological intimacy is emotional and psychological closeness to other team or group members. It results in feelings of affection and warmth, unconditional positive regard, opportunity for expression, security and emotional support, and nurturing. Failure to achieve psychological intimacy may result in feelings of emotional isolation and loneliness. This can be especially problematic for chief executives, who sometimes report experiencing loneliness at the top. However, although psychological intimacy is valuable for emotional health and well-being, it need not necessarily be achieved in the work setting. Many executives satisfy their need for intimacy with a rich home life.

Integrated involvement is closeness achieved through tasks and activities. It results in enjoyment of work, social identity and self-definition, being valued for one's skills and abilities, opportunities for power and influence, conditional positive regard, and support for one's beliefs and values. Failure to achieve integrated involvement may result in social isolation. Whereas psychological intimacy is based more in emotion, integrated involvement is based in behavior and activity. Integrated involvement contributes to social psychological health and well-being.

9-3 Group Behavior

Group behavior has been a subject of interest in social psychology for a long time, and many different aspects of group behavior have been studied over the years. We now look at four of those aspects: norms of behavior, group cohesion, social loafing, and loss of individuality. Group behavior topics related to decision-making, such as polarization and groupthink, are addressed in Chapter 10.

9-3a Norms of Behavior

The standards that a work group uses to evaluate the behavior of its members are its **norms of behavior**. These norms may be written or unwritten, verbalized

psychological intimacy Emotional and psychological closeness to other team or group members.

integrated involvement Closeness achieved through tasks and activities.

norms of behavior The standards that a work group uses to evaluate the behavior of its members.

or not verbalized, implicit or explicit. As long as individual members of the group understand them, the norms can be effective in influencing behavior. They may specify what members of a group should do (such as a specified dress code) or not do (such as executives not behaving arrogantly with employees).

Norms may exist in any aspect of work group life. They may evolve informally or unconsciously, or they may arise in response to specific challenges, such as firefighters' disciplined behavior in responding to a three-alarm fire in a manner that protects the group.[9] *Morality norms* are more important than *competence norms* when it comes to making decisions about improving the status of one's work group.[10] *Performance norms* are among the most important group norms from the organization's perspective. Even when group members work in isolation on creative projects, they display conformity to group norms.[11] Group norms of cooperative behavior within a team can lead to members working for mutual benefit, which in turn facilitates team performance.[12] On the other hand, verbal expressions of negativity can be detrimental to team performance and a violation of group norms.[13] Organizational culture and corporate codes of ethics, such as Johnson & Johnson's credo (recall Figure 2.3), reflect behavioral norms expected within work groups. Finally, norms that create awareness of and help regulate emotions are critical to groups' effectiveness.[14]

9-3b Group Cohesion

The interpersonal glue that makes the members of a group stick together is **group cohesion**. Group cohesion can enhance job satisfaction for members and improve organizational productivity.[15] Highly cohesive groups are able to manage their membership better than work groups low in cohesion. In one study of 381 banking teams in Hong Kong and the United States, increased job complexity and task autonomy led to increased group cohesiveness, which translated into better performance.[16] A recent study found that when there is a fit between the group's values and those of the organization, groups will report more cohesion and exhibit higher levels of organizational citizenship behavior (OCB).[17] In addition to improved performance, highly cohesive groups can lead to the maintenance of close relationships among the members. We will discuss group cohesion in further detail when we examine the common characteristics of well-developed groups.

9-3c Social Loafing

Social loafing occurs when one group member comes to rely on the efforts of other group members and fails to contribute their time, effort, thoughts, or other resources to a group.[18] This may create a real drag on the group's efforts and achievements. Some scholars argue that social loafing, also known as *free riding*, is a rational response to feelings of inequity or situations in which individual efforts are hard to observe. Team member personality factors may mitigate the negative effects of social loafing on team performance. Team members who possess high levels of conscientiousness and agreeableness tend to compensate for social loafers so that team performance is not reduced.[19] However, social loafing shortchanges the group, which loses potentially valuable resources possessed by individual members.[20]

One method for countering social loafing is a member self-evaluation system. If members must formally review their contributions to the group, they are less likely to loaf. Identifying individual contributions to the group product also counters loafing. If each group member is responsible for a specific input, an individual's failure to contribute will be noticed by everyone.

9-3d Loss of Individuality

Social loafing may be detrimental to group achievement, but it does not have the potentially explosive effects of loss of individuality. **Loss of individuality** is a social process through which group members lose self-awareness and its accompanying senses of accountability, inhibition, and responsibility for individual behavior.[21] People may engage in morally reprehensible acts and even violent behavior as committed members of their group or organization when their individuality is lost. Loss of individuality was one of several contributing factors to the riot that destroyed sections of Los Angeles following the

---

group cohesion The interpersonal glue that makes members of a group stick together.

Social loafing The failure of a group member to contribute personal time, effort, thoughts, or other resources to the group.

loss of individuality A social process in which individual group members lose self-awareness and its accompanying sense of accountability, inhibition, and responsibility for individual behavior.

Rodney King verdict in April 1992. Yet, loss of individuality is not always negative or destructive. The loosening of normal ego control mechanisms in the individual sometimes leads to prosocial behavior and even heroic acts in dangerous situations.[22]

9-4 Group Formation and Development

After its formation, a group goes through predictable stages. According to one group development model, a group addresses three issues: interpersonal issues, task issues, and authority issues.[23] The *interpersonal issues* include matters of trust, personal comfort, and security. Trust, in particular, is a key issue for any company in its working relationships. The *task issues* include the mission or purpose of the group, the methods the group employs, and the outcomes expected of the group. The *authority issues* include decisions about who is in charge, how power and influence are managed, and who has the right to tell whom to do what. This section addresses group formation, each stage of group development, and the characteristics of a mature group.

9-4a Group Formation

Formal and informal groups coalesce in organizations for different reasons. Formal groups are sometimes called *official* or *assigned* groups, and informal groups may be called *unofficial* or *emergent* groups. Formal groups such as project task forces, boards of directors, and temporary committees come together to

Groups and teams in organizations take a variety of shapes and forms.

mattjeacock/E+/Getty Images

perform specific tasks. An example of a formal group was the task force assembled by the University of Texas at Arlington to design the Goolsby Leadership Academy. Chaired by the associate dean of business, the task force was composed of seven members with diverse academic expertise and business experience. The task force established a five-year plan to inaugurate the select undergraduate program, which cultivates advanced leadership skills in its Goolsby Scholars and celebrated its twentieth anniversary in 2023.

Informal groups evolve in the work setting to gratify a variety of member needs not met by formal groups. For example, organizational members' inclusion and affirmation needs might be satisfied through informal athletic or specialized interest groups. Corporate sports leagues and corporate sports teams are a popular way for building informal team dynamics while getting valuable physical activity. Golf is among the most popular corporate sports and the Tomahawk Hills Golf League in Kansas is among the venues that host corporate teams.

Diversity is an important consideration in the formation of groups, as it can enhance performance and lead to new ways of thinking. Team members will defer more often to members with task-related diversity, such as education and tenure, for their expertise and perceived contributions to task performance.[24] One study of gender diversity among U.S. workers found that men and women in gender-balanced groups had higher job satisfaction than those in homogeneous groups.[25] Organizations have been challenged to blend culturally and linguistically diverse peoples into effective work groups since America's founding. This task was especially demanding during the early years of the 1900s, when waves of immigrant workers arrived from numerous European nations. In addition to ethnic, gender, and cultural diversity, there is interpersonal diversity, which may be indicated by different needs for inclusion, control of people and events, and affirmation from others. Successful interpersonal relationships are made stronger when group members are emotionally intelligent. The YOU on page 185 provides an opportunity to consider your group's diversity.

9-4b Stages of Group Development

All groups go through stages of development, some more successfully than others. Mature groups are able to work through the interpersonal, task, and

YOU

How Much Diversity Is on Your Team?

This exercise allows you to explore the level of diversity on your team. Listed below are words that describe a variety of individual differences in the workplace.

Categories and Types of Diversity	
Surface-Level	**Deep-Level**
Social category differences	*Differences in knowledge or skills*
Race	Education
Ethnicity	Functional knowledge
Gender	Information or expertise
Age	Training
Religion	Experience
Sexual orientation	Abilities
Physical abilities	*Differences in values or beliefs*
	Cultural background
	Ideological beliefs
	Personality differences
	Cognitive style
	Affective disposition
	Motivational factors
	Organizational- or community-status differences
	Tenure or length of service
	Position title
	Differences in social and network ties
	Work-related ties
	Friendship ties
	Community ties
	In-group memberships

Think about the level of diversity you have on your team.

1. Which of the above attributes are in your team?
2. What attributes contribute to team effectiveness/performance?
3. What diversity characteristics need to be added to your team to make it more effective?

Source: Adapted from E. Mannix and M. A. Neale, "What Differences Make a Difference?" *Psychological Science in the Public Interest* 6 (2005): 31–55.

authority issues inevitable at the highest echelons of the business world. The path to maturity does not always go smoothly, however. Immature groups often experience personality clashes and other fault lines (i.e., potential breaking points within the group) at various stages of development.[26]

Bruce Tuckman's five-stage model of group development proposes that team behavior progresses through five stages: forming, storming, norming, performing, and adjourning.[27] These stages and their properties are illustrated in Figure 9.1.

Dependence on guidance and direction is the defining characteristic of the *forming* stage. At this point, team members are unclear about individual roles and responsibilities and tend to rely heavily on the leader to answer questions about the team's purpose, objectives, and external relationships. Moving from this stage requires that team members feel they are part of the team. During this time, it may also be beneficial for leaders to encourage team members to get to know each other on an interpersonal level before focusing on task performance.[28]

Team members compete for position in the *storming* stage. As the name suggests, this is a period of considerable conflict as power struggles, cliques, and factions within the group begin to surface. Clarity

Figure 9.1 Tuckman's Five-Stage Model of Group Development

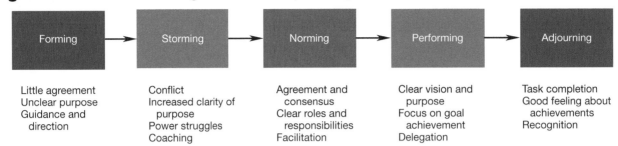

Forming	Storming	Norming	Performing	Adjourning
Little agreement Unclear purpose Guidance and direction	Conflict Increased clarity of purpose Power struggles Coaching	Agreement and consensus Clear roles and responsibilities Facilitation	Clear vision and purpose Focus on goal achievement Delegation	Task completion Good feeling about achievements Recognition

of purpose increases, but uncertainties still exist. This is also the stage in which members assess one another with regard to trustworthiness, emotional comfort, and evaluative acceptance. The group leader's coaching style is key during this stage of development, as team members may challenge her. The supervisor's ability to control her own emotions is important during this phase.

Agreement and consensus are characteristic of team members in the *norming* stage. It is during this period that roles and responsibilities become clear and are accepted. The group's focus will turn from interpersonal relations to decision-making and task accomplishment. Insignificant decisions may be delegated to individuals or small teams, while larger decisions will be discussed and decided by the entire group. The group may address questions of authority, such as the necessity of a primary spokesperson and the delegation of roles within the group. Wallace Supply Company, an industrial distributor of pipes, valves, and fittings, found employee teams particularly valuable in raising and answering questions of authority.[29] The teams concluded that leadership ought to be facilitative and that certain responsibilities could be delegated to teams themselves.

As a team moves into the *performing* stage, it becomes more strategically aware of its mission and purpose. In this stage of development, the group has successfully worked through interpersonal, task, and authority issues and can stand on its own with little interference from the leader. Disagreements are resolved positively with necessary changes to structure and processes attended to by the team. A mature group is able to control its members through the judicious application of positive and negative sanctions based on the evaluation of specific behaviors. Research shows that evaluation biases stemming from liking someone operate in face-to-face groups but not in electronic groups, such as virtual

teams.[30] Members at this stage do not need to be instructed but may ask for assistance from the leader in regard to personal or interpersonal development.

The final stage of group development is the *adjourning* stage. When the task is completed, everyone on the team can move on to new and different things. Team members retain a sense of accomplishment and feel-good knowing that their purpose was fulfilled. The leader's role at this point is primarily to recognize the group's achievements. But unless the group is a task force or other informal team, most groups in organizations remain at the performing stage and do not disband as the adjourning stage suggests.

9-4c Characteristics of a Mature Group or Team

A mature group or team has four characteristics: a clear purpose and mission, well-understood norms and standards of conduct, a high level of group cohesion, and a flexible status structure. The Organizational Example on page 187 discusses a mature set of teams including a NASA Launch Crew and a SpaceX team collaborating to send SpaceX Crew-5 to the International Space Station.

Purpose and Mission The group's purpose and mission may be assigned (as in the example of the Goolsby Leadership Academy task force) or emerge from within the group (as in the example of the American Airlines Running Club). In the case of an assigned mission, the group may embrace the mission as stated or reexamine, revise, or question it. The importance of mission is exemplified by IBM's Process Quality Management, which requires that a process team of no more than twelve people develop a clear understanding of the group's mission as the first step in the process.[31] The IBM approach demands that all members agree to go in

Organizational Example

NASA Launch Crew, SpaceX Crew-5, and *Endurance*

On 5 October 2022, SpaceX launched the Crew Dragon *Endurance* spacecraft from the Kennedy Space Center with a NASA launch crew, sending four astronauts to the International Space Station. SpaceX Crew-5 was composed of Nicole Mann, Josh Cassada, Koichi Wakata, and Anna Kikina. In a demonstration of international teamwork and collaboration, Wakata was from the Japan Aerospace Exploration Agency and Kikina was a cosmonaut from the Russian space agency Roscomos. Mann was the first Native American woman in space. While Crew-5 flew high, SpaceX had a mission control team on the ground, including webcast coverage producer Kyle Schember who documented the launch into orbit. The SpaceX team and the NASA team collaborate to insure a Crew-5 successful mission.

Source: M. Maidenberg, "Elon Musk's SpaceX, NASA Launch Crew, Including Russian Cosmonaut, to Space Station," *Wall Street Journal*, October 5 (2022).

the same direction. The mission statement is converted into a specific agenda, clear goals, and a set of critical success factors. Stating the purpose and mission in the form of specific goals enhances productivity and performance far more effectively than individual goal setting.[32]

Behavioral Norms *Behavioral norms*, which evolve over time, are well-understood standards of behavior within a group.[33] They are benchmarks against which team members are evaluated by other team members. For example, team altruism is the result of norms established as a result of one or more individual team members engaging in altruistic behaviors, often with different motivations ranging from prosocial to impression management.[34] Although some norms become written rules, such as an attendance policy or an ethical code, other norms remain informal, such as dress codes and norms about after-hours socializing. Additionally, behavioral norms may evolve around performance and productivity.[35] For example, productivity norms can influence the performance of sports teams in office leagues as well as in the professional realm.[36]

A group's productivity norm may or may not be consistent with the organization's productivity standards. A high-performance team sets productivity standards above organizational expectations, average teams set productivity standards consistent with organizational expectations, and noncompliant or counterproductive teams set productivity standards below organizational expectations, sometimes with the intent of damaging the organization or creating change. Usually, however, behavioral norms affect organizational culture in a beneficial way for all.

Group Cohesion Group cohesion enables a group to exercise effective control over its members in relation to its behavioral norms and standards. Mature teams have the capacity to share the deep acting strategies employed by individual team members, resulting in members behaving more similarly when expressing emotions.[37] Among the threats to a group's cohesion are goal conflict, unpleasant experiences, and domination of a subgroup. Groups with low levels of cohesion have greater difficulty exercising control over their members and enforcing their standards of behavior; hence, they are more vulnerable to such threats. Specifically, work-related tensions and anxieties decrease in highly cohesive teams and increase in teams low in cohesion, as depicted in Figure 9.2. This relationship suggests that cohesion has a calming effect on team members.

In addition, actual productivity was found to vary significantly less in highly cohesive teams, making them much more predictable. The actual productivity

The U.S. Air Force Thunderbirds are a high precision, prestigious, highly cohesive team.

epicprints/iStock/Getty Images

Figure 9.2 Cohesiveness and Work-Related Tension*

Group cohesiveness	1 (Low)	2	3	4	5	6	7 (High)
Mean tension	3.50	3.53	3.67	3.78	3.82	3.77	3.95
Number of groups	7	16	52	65	57	19	12

Note: Product–moment correlation is 0.28, and critical ratio is 4.20; the group cohesion–tension relationship is highly significant at the .001 level.

*The measure of tension at work is based on group mean response to the question "Does your work ever make you feel 'jumpy' or nervous?" A low numerical score represents relatively high tension.

Source: S. E. Seashore, *Group Cohesiveness in the Industrial Work Group*, 1954. Research conducted by Stanley E. Seashore at the Institute for Social Research, University of Michigan. Reprinted by permission.

levels, though, were primarily determined by the productivity norms within each work group. Thus, highly cohesive groups with high production standards were very productive, but highly cohesive groups with low productivity standards were unproductive despite their high level of cohesion. Nevertheless, no matter what the productivity was, member satisfaction, commitment, and communication were greater in highly cohesive groups.

Group cohesion is influenced by a number of factors, most notably time, size, the prestige of the team, external pressure, and internal competition. Usually, cohesion evolves gradually throughout group development. In other words, the more time a group spends together, the more cohesive it will be. Also, smaller groups—those of five or seven members, for example—tend to be more cohesive than those of more than twenty-five, although cohesion does not decline much with size after forty or more members.

Prestige or social status may enhance a group's cohesion as well. More prestigious groups, such as the U.S. Air Force Thunderbirds or the U.S. Navy Blue Angels, are highly cohesive. However, even groups of very low prestige may be highly cohesive as a result of other factors tending toward cohesion, such as the aforementioned factors of longer time together and smaller group size. Finally, external pressure and internal competition are two other factors influencing group cohesion. Although the mechanics' union, pilots, and other internal constituencies at Eastern Airlines had various differences of opinion, they all pulled together in a cohesive fashion in resisting Frank Lorenzo when he came in to reshape the airline before the airline went out of business. (The Eastern name has been twice purchased but the airline never returned competitively.) Whereas external pressures tend to enhance it, internal competition usually decreases cohesion within a team. One study found that company-imposed pressure disrupted group cohesion by increasing internal competition and reducing cooperative interpersonal activity.[38]

Status Structure Status structure is the set of authority and task relations among a group's members. It may be hierarchical or egalitarian, depending on the group. Successful resolution of the authority issue within a team results in a well-understood status structure of leader–follower relationships. Positive leadership facilitates a team getting into flow, resulting in innovative, harmonious, and productive outcomes with IMPACT.[39] Although groups usually have just one leader, teams tend to share leadership. For example, one person may be the team's taskmaster, who sets the agenda, initiates much of the work activity, and ensures that the team meets its deadlines. Another team member may take a leadership role in maintaining effective interpersonal relationships in the group. Hence, shared leadership is very feasible in teams. An effective status structure results in role interrelatedness among group members.[40] Bill Perez and Bill Wrigley have promoted interrelatedness through a tag-team style of cooperation in leadership that has served the Wm. Wrigley Jr. Company well.

9-5 Task and Maintenance Functions

An effective group or team carries out various task functions to perform its work successfully and various maintenance functions to ensure member satisfaction and a sense of team spirit.[41] Teams that successfully fulfill these functions afford their members the potential for the psychosocial benefits of psychological intimacy and integrated involvement we discussed at the beginning of the chapter. Task functions are rooted in exploratory and mastery behaviors while maintenance functions are rooted in attachment and relationship behaviors (see attachment theory, Chapter 7). Table 9.2 presents nine task and nine maintenance functions in teams or groups.

Task functions are those activities directly related to the effective completion of the team's work. For example, the task of initiating activity involves suggesting ideas, defining problems, and proposing approaches and/or solutions to problems. The task of seeking information involves asking for ideas, suggestions, information, or facts. A study of security analysts found that the quality of colleagues' work helped to improve and maintain the quality of individual member performance.[42] Effective teams have members who fulfill various task functions as they are required.

Table 9.2 Task and Maintenance Functions in Teams or Groups

Task Functions	Maintenance Functions
Initiating activities	Supporting others
Seeking information	Following others' leads
Giving information	Gatekeeping communication
Elaborating concepts	Setting standards
Coordinating activities	Expressing member feelings
Summarizing ideas	Testing group decisions
Testing ideas	Consensus testing
Evaluating effectiveness	Harmonizing conflict
Diagnosing problems	Reducing tension

Different task functions vary in importance throughout the life cycle of a group. For example, during the engineering test periods for new technologies, the engineering team needs members who focus on testing the practical applications of suggestions and those who diagnose problems and suggest solutions. The effective use of task functions leads to the success of the group. In one case, the successful initiation and coordination of an emergency room team's activities by the senior resident saved the life of a knife wound victim.[43] The victim was stabbed one-quarter inch below the heart, and the team acted quickly to stem the bleeding,

status structure The set of authority and task relations among a group's members.

task function An activity directly related to the effective completion of a team's work.

Humor and joking behavior have been found to enhance social relationships in work groups.

begin intravenous fluids, and monitor the victim's vital signs. A recent study found that team member familiarity increases team performance up to a point by reducing team coordination errors (TCEs). Too much team familiarity may lead to increased TCEs as teams begin to rely on habitual routines and implicit coordination rather than explicit coordination methods. The relationship between team familiarity and the occurrence of TCEs is moderated by leader experience.[44]

Maintenance functions are those activities essential to the effective, satisfying interpersonal relationships within a group or team. Following another group member's lead may be as important as being a leader. Communication gatekeepers within a group ensure balanced contributions from all members. Because task activities build tension within teams or groups, tension-reduction activities are important to drain off negative or destructive feelings. In a study of twenty-five work groups over a five-year period, humor and joking behavior were found to enhance the social relationships in the groups.[45] The researchers concluded that performance improvements in the twenty-five groups indirectly resulted from improved relationships attributable to the humor and joking behaviors. Maintenance functions enhance togetherness, cooperation, and teamwork, enabling members to achieve psychological intimacy while furthering the success of the team. Emotional competencies such as empathy self-control are beneficial for maintaining group relationships. Jody Grant's supportive attitude and comfortable demeanor as chair and CEO of Texas Capital Bancshares enabled him to build a vibrant bank in the aftermath of the great Texas banking crash. As Chair *Emeritus* of TCB, Grant went on to be honored with a Horatio Alger Award in 2010 as a Distinguished American, a 2013 Distinguished Alumnus Award from Southern Methodist University, and a 2014 Distinguished Goolsby Leader Award from The University of Texas at Arlington, all while being the driving force behind Klyde Warren Park in Dallas, Texas. Both task and maintenance functions are important for successful groups and teams.

maintenance function An activity essential to effective, satisfying interpersonal relationships within a team or group.

9-6 Factors that Influence Group Effectiveness

Work team effectiveness in the new team environment requires management's attention to both work team structure and work team process.[46] In addition to how the team is structured and what the team does, diversity and creativity are emerging as two areas with significant impact on team performance.

9-6a Work Team Structure

Work team structure issues include goals and objectives, operating guidelines, performance measures, and role specification. A work team's goals and objectives specify what must be achieved, while the operating guidelines set the organizational boundaries and decision-making limits within which the team must function. The goal-setting process discussed in Chapter 6 applies to work teams, too. In addition to these two structural elements, the work team needs to know what performance measures are being used to assess its task accomplishment. For example, a medical emergency team's performance measures might include the success rate in saving critically injured patients and the average number of hours a patient is in the emergency room before being transferred to a hospital bed.

Finally, work team structure requires a clearly specified set of roles for the executives and managers who oversee the work of the team, for the work team leaders who exercise influence over team members, and for team members. These role specifications should include information about required role behaviors, such as decision-making and task performance, as well as restrictions or limits on role behaviors, such as the limitations on managerial interventions in work team activities and decision-making. Expectations as well as experience may be especially important for newcomer role performance in work teams.[47]

9-6b Work Team Process

Work team process is the second important dimension of effectiveness. Two of the important process issues in work teams are the managing of cooperative behaviors and the managing of competitive behaviors. Both sets of behaviors are helpful in task accomplishment, and they should be viewed as complementary. *Cooperative teamwork skills* include open communication, trust, personal integrity, positive interdependence, and mutual support. On the other hand, *positive competitive teamwork skills* include the ability to enjoy competition, play fair, and be a good winner or loser; to have access to information for monitoring where the team and members are in the competition; and not to overgeneralize or exaggerate the results of any specific competition. In a study of reward structures in seventy-five four-member teams, competitive rewards enhanced speed of performance, while cooperative rewards enhanced accuracy of performance.[48]

Work team process issues have become more complex in the global workplace, where teams are composed of members from many cultures and backgrounds. This complexity is increased by the presence of remote and virtual work teams operating on the global landscape. The effects of member experience, expertise, and reward power are important considerations in a work team's process and decision-making.[49] In addition to the process issues of cooperation, competition, and diversity, three other process issues are related to topics we discuss elsewhere in the text. These are empowerment, which is discussed in the next major section of this chapter; team decision-making, which is discussed in Chapter 10; and conflict management and resolution, which are discussed in Chapter 13.

9-6c Diversity

Diversity also plays a large role in how effective work groups and teams are. Diversity in a group is healthy, and members may contribute to the collective effort through one of four basic styles: the contributor, the collaborator, the communicator, or the challenger.[50] The *contributor* is data driven, supplies necessary information, and adheres to high performance standards. The *collaborator* sees the big picture and is able to keep a constant focus on the mission and urge other members to join efforts for mission accomplishment. The *communicator* listens well, facilitates the group's process, and humanizes the collective effort. The *challenger* is the devil's advocate who questions everything from the group's mission, purpose, and methods to its ethics. Members may exhibit one or more of these four basic styles over a period of time. In addition, an effective group must have an *integrator*, especially when the group is a cross-functional one, where different perspectives carry the seeds of conflict.[51] However, cross-functional teams are not necessarily a problem. Effectively managing cross-functional teams of artists, designers, printers,

and financial experts enabled Hallmark Cards to cut its new product development time in half.[52]

Dissimilarity There is research in diversity that focuses on the effect of dissimilarity within a team. This issue is often studied in relation to social identity theory and self-categorization theory. Since creativity concerns new ideas, some amount of dissimilarity is necessary within a team so that creativity, novelty, and innovation can blossom. Although creativity is discussed in some detail in Chapter 10, we address it briefly here in the context of teams.

We defined diversity in Chapter 1 in terms of individual differences. Recent relational demography research finds that demographic dissimilarity influences employees' absenteeism, commitment, turnover intentions, beliefs, work group relationships, self-esteem, and OCB.[53] Thus, dissimilarity may have positive or negative effects in teams and on team members. Racial dissimilarity may also impact the extent to which team members communicate with each other and develop a sense of group identity.[54] While value dissimilarity may be positively related to task and relationship conflict, it is negatively related to team involvement.[55] This fact highlights the importance of managing dissimilarity in teams, being open to diversity, and turning conflicts about ideas into positive outcomes.

Functional background is one way to look at dissimilarity in teams. One study of 262 professionals in thirty-seven cross-functional teams found that promoting social identification with functional background helped individuals perform better as team members.[56] Another study of multifunctional management teams in a *Fortune* 100 company found that functional background predicted team involvement.[57] Finally, in a slightly different study of 129 members on twenty multidisciplinary project teams, informational dissimilarity had no adverse effects when there was member task and goal congruence.[58]

Structural Diversity Structural diversity concerns the number of *structural holes*, or disconnections between members, within a work team. One research study examined structural diversity and performance of nineteen teams in a wood-products company. The investigators were interested in demographic diversity among team members as well as the structural diversity, or presence of structural holes, in the teams. Neither race nor gender was a demographic factor that influenced the proportion of structural

Diversity in a group is healthy.

holes within the teams. However, age diversity significantly improved structural integrity. Hence, greater variance in age within a team leads to more member-to-member connections and fewer member-to-member disconnections.

Are disconnections of team members good or bad for the team? What are the consequences of having more or fewer structural holes between team members? Teams with few structural holes may have problems with creativity, while teams with a high proportion of structural holes may have difficulty coordinating. These observations led the researchers to conclude that there is a curvilinear relationship between structural diversity, or structural integrity, and team performance. The teams with moderate structural diversity achieve the best performance. This research is important because it points out that managers should look at the overall structure and network of relationships within their work teams in addition to the individual characteristics of team members in attempting to achieve the best performance from these teams.[59]

9-6d Creativity

Creativity is often thought of in an individual context rather than a team context. However, there is such a thing as team creativity. In a study of fifty-four research and development teams, team creativity scores were explained by aggregation processes across both people and time.[60] Finding creative

solutions to workplace problems may require teamwork, collaboration, and a set of seven practices for effectively reframing the problem, as seen in the accompanying Hot Trend.

Some think that the deck is stacked against teams as agents of creativity. Leigh Thompson, a management and organizations professor at Northwestern University, thinks differently and suggests that team creativity and divergent thinking can be enhanced through greater diversity in teams, electronic brainstorming, training facilitators, membership change in teams, and building a playground.[61] Human capital diversity in teams can be a source of team social capital, which has the potential to enhance the level of team creativity through increased access to a variety of individuals with varying knowledge and experiences.[62] These practices can overcome social loafing, conformity, and downward norm setting in teams and organizations. Team members might exercise care in timing the insertion of their novel ideas into the team process so as to maximize the positive impact and benefits.[63]

9-7 Empowerment and Teams

Successful teams are empowered by their organizational culture. This is especially true of *self-managed teams* and *remote teams* discussed later in this section, which are often given greater decision latitude by management.

As an individual attribute, empowering leadership positively affects employee psychological empowerment, thus reducing employee cynicism and time theft, when the quality of the relationship with the boss is a good one.[64] As an organizational culture attribute, empowerment encourages participation, an essential ingredient for teamwork.[65] *Quality-Driven Management (QDM)* at FedEx begins with teams and teamwork. be Teamwork is actually an advanced level of empowerment in organizations.[66] Empowerment and team processes both play an important role in team effectiveness and outcomes.[67]

9-7a Empowerment Skills

Empowerment skills needed by individuals working in groups and teams within organizations fall into four categories. These are competence skills, process skills, cooperative and helping behaviors, and communication skills. When developed in the context of a psychologically safe work environment, psychological empowerment reduces emotional exhaustion.[68] However, if the work environment hinders employees from using these skills to perform well, empowerment may backfire and trigger unethical behavior.[69]

Competence skills are the first set of skills required for empowerment. Mastery and experience in one's chosen discipline and profession provide an essential foundation for empowerment. New employees and trainees should experience only limited empowerment until they demonstrate the capacity to accept more responsibility.

Empowerment also requires certain *process skills*. The most critical process skills include negotiating skills, especially with allies, opponents, and adversaries.[70] Allies are the easiest people to negotiate with because they agree with you about the team's mission and you can trust their actions and behavior. Opponents require a different negotiating strategy; although you can predict their actions and behavior, they do not agree with your concept of the team's mission. Adversaries are dangerous, difficult people to negotiate with because you cannot predict their actions or behaviors and they do not agree with your concept of the team's mission.

A third set of empowerment skills involves the development of *cooperative and helping behaviors*.[71] Cooperative people engage in encouraging, helpful behavior to maximize the gains for everyone on the team. The alternative orientations to cooperation are competitive, individualistic, and egalitarian approaches. *Competitive people* are motivated to maximize their personal gains regardless of the expense to other people. This motivation can be very counterproductive to the team. *Individualistic people* are motivated to act autonomously, though not necessarily to maximize their personal gains. They are less prone to contribute to the efforts of the team. *Egalitarian people* are motivated to equalize the outcomes for each team member, which may or may not be beneficial to the team's well-being. Paradoxically, the team members who need the most help often get the least help because helping behaviors often target the most expert team members, a dynamic that actually compromises overall team performance.[72]

Communication skills are a final set of essential empowerment skills.[73] These skills include self-expression skills and skills in reflective listening. Empowerment cannot occur in a team unless members are able to express themselves in emotionally intelligent ways as well as listen carefully to one another.

9-7b Self-Managed Teams

Self-managed teams, also called *self-directed teams* or *autonomous work groups*, are teams that make decisions that were once reserved for managers. Self-managed teams are one way to implement empowerment in organizations. Even though self-managed teams are self-directed, that fact does not negate the influence of managers. In fact, managers have an important role in providing leadership and influence. There is strong support for the use of soft-influence tactics in managers' communication with self-directed teams, which yields more positive results.[74]

A one-year study of self-managed teams suggests that they have a positive impact on employee attitudes but not on absenteeism or turnover.[75] Evaluative research is helpful in achieving a better understanding of this relatively new way of approaching teamwork and the design of work. Such research helps establish expectations for self-managed teams. Nevertheless, there are risks, such as groupthink in self-managed teams, that must be prevented or managed if the team is to achieve full development and function.[76]

self-managed team A team that makes decisions that were once reserved for managers.

The dramatic success of Chrysler during the early 1980s was later followed by struggle and accommodation, raising the question of how long a CEO and top management team can sustain organizational success.

9-7c Remote Teams

Remote teams are comprised of team members with shared responsibilities and common objectives yet perform from a flexible mix of stationary, mobile, and/or remote work environments.[77] They often use digital platforms, such as Zoom or Microsoft Teams, as modes of communication and collaboration. COVID-19 has been a driving force for the rise of remote teams in many organizations. Remote teams may work across cities, states, countries, and even continents because they do not require a central or common location in which to meet. Rather, they are connected through a variety of digital platforms, which may include audio and/or video. In addition to the empowerment skills discussed above, remote team members may require a variety of technical and technological skills for operating in a digital environment. Remote teams operate in remote and hybrid work environments that are discussed in Chapter 14.

It is noteworthy that one evaluation of empowerment, teams, and *Total Quality Management (TQM)* programs found that companies associated with these popular management techniques did not have higher economic performance.[78] Other evaluations of self-managed teams are more positive. Southwest Industries, a high-technology aerospace manufacturing firm, embarked on a major internal reorganization in the early 1990s that included the creation of self-managed teams to fit its high-technology production process. Southwest's team approach resulted in a 30 percent increase in shipments, a 30 percent decrease in lead time, a 40 percent decrease in total inventory, a decrease in machinery downtime, and almost a one-third decrease in production costs.[79] An overall positive history has resulted in U.S.-based multinational corporations increasingly using self-managed teams in their global operations.

remote team A team that works from a mix of stationary, mobile, and/or remote work environments.

upper echelon A top-level executive team in an organization.

9-8 Upper Echelon: The Top Management Team (TMT)

The **upper echelon** is *the top management team (TMT)* of the organization. *Upper echelon theory* argues that the background characteristics of the top management team can predict organizational characteristics and set standards for values, competence, ethics, and unique characteristics throughout the organization. In addition, the distributed cognition and transactive memory systems in top teams affect the ability of the organization to be both explorative with regard to the future and exploitive of present opportunities.[80] The central premise of upper echelon theory is that executives' experiences, values, and personalities greatly influence their interpretations of the situations they face and, in turn, affect their choices.[81] The ability to exert power and influence throughout the entire organization makes the top management team (TMT) a key to the organization's success. However, a review of the Financial Times 50 (FT50) journals found a lack of consistency in the definition of what the TMT is.[82] In addition, the ability of the TMT to exert power and influence may be compromised if the top team sends mixed signals about teamwork and if executive pay systems foster competition, politics, and individualism.[83]

For example, Indra Nooyi has held executive positions at major companies all over the world and is a role model for women and immigrants with her empowering message of inclusivity. At the peak of her career from 2006 to 2019, Nooyi was chairperson and CEO of PepsiCo where she was the architect of Performance with Purpose, a corporate strategy that grew net revenue more than 80 percent and total shareholder return 162 percent, beating the S&P over that period.[84]

Hambrick and Fukutomi addressed this question by examining the dynamic relationship between a CEO's tenure and the success of the organization.[85] They found five *seasons* in a CEO's tenure: (1) response to a mandate, (2) experimentation, (3) selection of an enduring theme, (4) convergence, and (5) dysfunction. A summary of each season is shown in Table 9.3. All else being equal, the seasons model has significant implications for organizational performance. Specifically, organizational performance increases during a CEO's tenure to a peak, after which performance declines. This relationship is depicted in Figure 9.3. The peak has been found to come at about seven years— somewhere in the middle of the executive's seasons.

Table 9.3 The Five Seasons of a CEO's Tenure

Critical CEO Characteristics	1 Response to Mandate	2 Experimentation	3 Selection of an Enduring Theme	4 Convergence	5 Dysfunction
COMMITMENT TO A PARADIGM	Moderately strong	Could be strong or weak	Moderately strong	Strong; increasing	Very strong
TASK KNOWLEDGE	Low but rapidly increasing	Moderate; somewhat increasing	High; slightly increasing	High; slightly increasing	High; slightly increasing
INFORMATION DIVERSITY	Many sources; unfiltered	Many sources but increasingly unfiltered	Fewer sources; moderately filtered	Few sources; highly filtered	Very few sources; highly filtered
TASK INTEREST	High	High	Moderately high	Moderately high but diminishing	Moderately low and diminishing
POWER	Low; increasing	Moderate; increasing	Moderate; increasing	Strong; increasing	Very strong; increasing

Source: D. Hambrick and G. D. S. Fukutomi, "The Seasons of a CEO's Tenure," *Academy of Management Review* (1991): 729. Permission conveyed through Copyright Clearance Center, Inc.

Figure 9.3 Executive Tenure and Organizational Performance

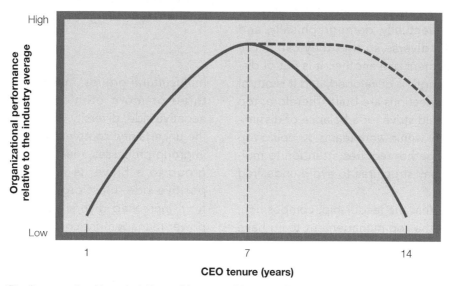

Source: D. Hambrick, "The Seasons of an Executive's Tenure," keynote address, the Sixth Annual Texas Conference on Organizations, Lago Vista, Texas, April 1991.

As indicated by the dotted lines in the figure, the peak may be extended, depending on several factors, such as diversity in the executive's support team.

9-8a Diversity at the Top

From an organizational health standpoint, diversity and depth in the top management team enhance the CEO's well-being.[86] From a performance standpoint, the CEO's top management team can influence the timing of the performance peak, the degree of dysfunction during the closing season of the CEO's tenure, and the rate of decline in organizational performance. Thus, diversity and heterogeneity in the top management team help sustain high levels of organizational performance at the peak and help maintain the CEO's vitality. Despite successes like Indra Nooyi, diversity statistics in the C-suite overstate the likelihood of increased diversity in coming years, based on a study of the size, structure, and demographics of the C-suite.[87]

> Most organizations report benefits from increased diversity.

The presence of a so-called wild turkey in the top management team can be a particularly positive force. The wild turkey is a devil's advocate who challenges the thinking of the CEO and other top executives and provides a counterpoint during debates. If not shouted down or inhibited, the wild turkey helps the CEO and the team sustain peak performance and retard the CEO's dysfunction and decline. For example, former Secretary of State Colin Powell enhanced President George W. Bush's administration by exercising an independent voice. Often taking a more moderate position on policy issues than either the secretary of defense or the vice president, Powell brought variance and value to President Bush's administration.

Leaders must develop communication strategies to bring together team members who are functionally, intellectually, demographically, and temperamentally diverse so that they can act in ways that complement one another. It is out of dissimilarity that strength is developed, and it is out of similarity that connections are built. Therefore, top management should strive for a balance of dissimilarity and similarity within work teams. Keeping top teams working together requires attention to multiple concurrent pay structures to avoid undesired top-team turnover.[88]

We conclude that the leadership, composition, and dynamics of the top management team have an important influence on the organization's performance, leading, in some cases, to a change from having only one CEO to having more than one. While more common in Europe than in the United States, a historical U.S. example of a co-CEO arrangement includes a three-member team created by Walter Wriston while he was chairman at Citicorp (now part of Citigroup).

9-8b Multicultural Top Teams

Homogeneous groups, in which all members share similar backgrounds, are giving way to *token groups*, in which all but one member come from the same background; *bicultural groups*, in which two or more members represent each of two distinct cultures; and

Mike Neale/Shutterstock.com

The wild turkey is a devil's advocate who challenges the thinking of the CEO and provides a counterpoint during debates.

multicultural groups, in which members represent three or more ethnic backgrounds.[89] On the negative side, diversity within a group may increase the uncertainty, complexity, and inherent confusion in group processes, making it more difficult for the group to achieve its full productivity.[90] On the positive side, most organizations report benefits from increased diversity. Eaton is a Fortune 500 power management company established in 1911 that is led by Craig Arnold, one of a handful of Black CEOs. Arnold takes inclusion and diversity in the C-Suite seriously and has a board of directors that is two-thirds women and minorities.[91] Diversities of age and educational specialization within top management teams were found in other studies to have a positive effect on team performance, especially when members needed to participate in cognitive tasks.[92] One study found that the performance of top management teams was greatly increased when the CEO had numerous shared experiences with executives from other companies and cultures.[93] The advantages of culturally diverse groups appear to include the generation of more and better ideas while limiting the risk of groupthink, to be discussed in Chapter 10.

Experiential Exercise

Design a Team

The following exercise gives you an opportunity to design a team. Working in a six-person group, address the individual characteristics, team composition, and norms for an effective group whose task is to make recommendations on improving customer relations. The president of a small clothing manufacturer is concerned his customers are not satisfied enough with the company's responsiveness, product quality, and returned orders process. He has asked your group to put together a team to address these problems.

Step 1. The class will form into groups of approximately six members each. Each group elects a spokesperson and answers the following questions. The group should spend an equal amount of time on each question.

   a. *What characteristics should the individual members of the task team possess?* Members may consider professional competence, skills, department, and/or personality and behavioral characteristics in the group's discussion.

   b. *What should the composition of the task team be?* Once your group has addressed individual characteristics, consider the overall composition of the task team. Have special and/or unique competencies, knowledge, skills, and abilities been considered in your deliberations?

   c. *What norms of behavior do you think the task team should adopt?* A team's norms of behavior may evolve, or they may be consciously discussed and agreed upon. Take the latter approach.

Step 2. Each group will share the results of its answers to the questions in Step 1. Cross-team questions and discussion follow.

Learning Objectives

9-1 **Define group and work team.** A *group* is two or more people having common interests, objectives, and continuing interaction. A *work team* is a group of people with complementary skills who are committed to a common mission, performance goals, and approach for which they hold themselves mutually accountable.

9-2 **Explain the benefits that organizations and individuals derive from working in teams.** Teams are very useful in performing work that is complicated, complex, interrelated, and/ or more voluminous than one person can handle. Teams combine the knowledge, talent, skills, and abilities of individual members and integrate effort for task accomplishment. On an individual level, members benefit from psychological intimacy and achieving integrated involvement.

9-3 **Identify the factors that influence group behavior.** *Group norms* of cooperative behavior facilitate team performance and effectiveness. *Group cohesion* can enhance job satisfaction and improve productivity. Social loafing— member failure to contribute time, effort, thoughts, or other resources to a group—may negate the group's efforts and achievements. With loss of individuality, members may lose their sense of accountability, inhibition, and responsibility for individual behavior.

9-4 **Describe how groups form and develop.** Groups, formal and informal, go through stages of development to become mature and productive units. Mature groups work through the necessary interpersonal, task, and authority issues to achieve at high levels. According to this group development model, a group addresses three issues: interpersonal issues, task issues, and authority issues.

9-5 **Explain how task and maintenance functions influence group performance.** Effective groups carry out various task functions to perform work successfully and do maintenance functions to ensure member satisfaction and a sense of team spirit. Teams that successfully fulfill these functions afford members the potential for the social benefits of psychological intimacy and integrated involvement.

9-6 **Discuss the factors that influence group effectiveness.** Work team effectiveness in the new team environment requires management's attention to both work team structure and work team process. In addition to how the team is structured and what the team does, diversity and creativity are two areas with significant impact on team performance.

9-7 **Describe how empowerment relates to self-managed and remote teams.** Empowerment, an organizational attribute, encourages participation, an essential ingredient for teamwork. Empowered *self-managed teams,* designed to take on responsibilities and address issues traditionally reserved for management, succeed through development of competence skills, process skills, communication skills, and cooperative and helping behaviors.

9-8 **Explain the importance of upper echelons and the top management team.** Self-managed teams at the top of the organization are referred to as *upper echelons.* Organizations are often a reflection of these *upper echelons.* Upper echelon theory argues that background characteristics of the top management team can predict organizational characteristics and set standards for values, competence, ethics, and unique characteristics throughout the organization.

Key Terms

group Two or more people with common interests, objectives, and continuing interaction. (p. 180)

group cohesion The interpersonal glue that makes members of a group stick together. (p. 183)

integrated involvement Closeness achieved through tasks and activities. (p. 182)

loss of individuality A social process in which individualgroup members lose self-awareness and its accompanying sense of accountability, inhibition, and responsibility for individual behavior. (p. 183)

maintenance function An activity essential to effective, satisfying interpersonal relationships within a team or group. (p. 190)

norms of behavior The standards that a work group uses to evaluate the behavior of its members. (p. 182)

psychological intimacy Emotional and psychological closeness to other team or group members. (p. 182)

remote team A team that works from a mix of stationary, mobile, and/or remote work environments. (p. 194)

self-managed team A team that makes decisions that were once reserved for managers. (p. 193)

Social loafing The failure of a group member to contribute personal time, effort, thoughts, or other resources to the group. (p. 183)

status structure The set of authority and task relations among a group's members. (p. 189)

task function An activity directly related to the effective completion of a team's work. (p. 189)

teamwork Joint action by a team of people in which individual interests are subordinated to team unity. (p. 181)

upper echelon A top-level executive team in an organization. (p. 194)

work team A group of people with complementary skills who are committed to a common mission, performance goals, and approach for which they hold themselves mutually accountable. (p. 180)

Ethical Dilemma

Robin at United Media

Robin is employed at United Media, an advertising firm that believes in a team-based approach to all client accounts. Robin used to enjoy her job but lately she does not look forward to going to work. She is on a great team with a lot of high performers.

Recently Robin got sick, and her team did a great job picking up her piece of the project. Returning to work after her illness, she realized that the team would be fine without her putting in 100 percent effort. She would do nothing more than what was minimally required to keep her job. This would free up her time to look for another job she would enjoy more. And, she would not have to worry about rushing to find this new job, as this solution could last as long as necessary.

Robin feels good about her decision to quietly quit because no one is being hurt. The company will not be hurt as all accounts will be well managed. None of her colleagues will be hurt because they are more than capable of picking up the slack and if they spread it out, no one will even notice.

1. Using consequential, rule-based, and character theories, evaluate Robin's plan.

2. What should Robin's teammates do? Why?

Chapter 10

Morsa Images/DigitalVision/Getty Images

Decision Making by Individuals and Groups

Learning Objectives

10-1 Identify the steps in the decision making process.

10-2 Describe various models of decision making.

10-3 Discuss the individual influences that affect decision making.

10-4 Explain how groups make decisions.

10-5 Describe the role culture plays in decision making.

10-6 Explain how organizations can improve the quality of decisions through participation.

10-7 Describe two new applications of decision making in organizations.

10-1 The Decision Making Process

Decision making is a critical activity in the lives of managers. The decisions a manager faces can range from very simple, routine matters for which the manager has an established decision rule (**programmed decisions**) to new and complex decisions that require creative solutions (**nonprogrammed decisions**).[1] Scheduling lunch hours for one's work group, for example, is a programmed decision. The manager performs this programmed decision activity daily, using an established procedure with the same clear goal in mind each time. In contrast, decisions like buying out another company are nonprogrammed, providing a unique, unstructured situation and requiring considerable judgment. Regardless of the type of decision made, it is helpful to understand as much as possible about how individuals and groups make decisions.

Decision making is a process involving a series of steps, as shown in Figure 10.1. The first step is recognizing the problem; that is, the manager realizes that a decision must be made. Identifying the real problem is important; otherwise, the manager may be reacting to symptoms rather than dealing with the root cause of the problem. Next, a manager must identify the objective of the decision. In other words, the manager must determine what is to be accomplished by the decision. The third step in the decision making process is gathering information relevant to the problem. The manager must accumulate sufficient information about why the problem occurred. This involves conducting a thorough diagnosis of the situation and going on a fact-finding mission.

The fourth step is listing and evaluating alternative courses of action. During this step, a thorough "what-if" analysis should be conducted to determine the various factors that could influence the outcome. It is important to generate a wide range of options and creative solutions in order to be able to move on to the next step. Next, the manager selects the alternative that best meets the decision objective.

programmed decision A simple, routine matter for which a manager has an established decision rule.

nonprogrammed decision A new, complex decision that requires a creative solution.

> The first step is recognizing the problem; that is, the manager realizes that a decision must be made.

If the problem has been diagnosed correctly and sufficient alternatives have been identified, this step is much easier. After the solution is implemented, the situation must then be monitored to see whether the decision met its objective. Consistent monitoring and periodic feedback are essential parts of the follow-up process.

Decision making can be stressful. Managers must make decisions with significant risk and uncertainty, and often without all of the necessary information. They must trust and rely on others in their decision making process, yet they are ultimately responsible for the final decision. Sometimes

Figure 10.1 The Decision Making Process

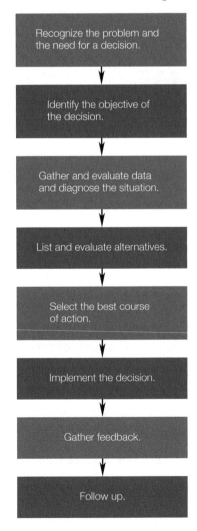

Recognize the problem and the need for a decision.

Identify the objective of the decision.

Gather and evaluate data and diagnose the situation.

List and evaluate alternatives.

Select the best course of action.

Implement the decision.

Gather feedback.

Follow up.

Hot Trend

Tips for Managing Cognitive Fatigue

"I'm too tired to think!" We've all felt it. Mental fatigue makes it difficult to make decisions. New research shows that heavy cognitive work physically alters the brain, and fatigue is a signal that makes us stop working in order to preserve our brain function. So how do we avoid burnout and poor decisions from cognitive fatigue? Here are some tips:

- *Simplify your life by limiting your decisions*. Why add to your decisions by having to think about what to wear or what to eat? Steve Jobs famously wore a black turtleneck and jeans every day, and others create routines like eating the same thing to avoid having to make so many choices.
- *Make a to-do list the night before your workday*. This way, you don't have to decide where to start.
- *Manage your energy wisely*. Make important decisions when your energy is at its highest. If you're a morning person, make decisions early in your day. If you're more of an afternoon person, wait until then. The key is knowing your energy rhythms.
- *Use willpower with social media*. Get your news fix of scan your social media first if you must, but put a time limit on it. Or, only allow yourself time on social media after you complete a cognitively demanding task.

(Sources: A. Wiehler, F. Branzoli, I. Adanyeguh, F. Mochel, and M. Pessiglione, "A Neuro-Metabolic Account of Why Daylong Cognitive Work Alters the Control of Economic Decisions," *Current Biology* 32 (2002): 3564–3575; A. Millson, "Thinking Too Hard Can Make You Tired," *Fortune*, August 11 (2022), accessed at https://fortune.com/2022/08/11/thinking-too-hard-brain-mental-fatigue-scientists-paris-study/).

decisions are painful and involve exiting businesses, firing people, and admitting wrong.

Netflix saw great success during the pandemic, with people staying home and creating a boom in streaming entertainment. Post-pandemic, however, Netflix suffered losses of subscribers and its stock plummeted. Competition increased from Amazon Prime, HBO Max, and Disney+, among others. Leadership style at Netflix moved to a fear-based, reactionary model focused on cost-cutting and laying off employees. Surviving employees are stretched thin, and Netflix is making good on its promise to expand into video games. Did the company over-hire due to the rapid growth during the pandemic? Is adding video games the right decision during a downturn in business? Only time will tell if these decisions pay off once the post-COVID hangover passes.[2]

10-2 Models and Limits of Decision Making

The success of any organization depends on managers' abilities to make **effective decisions**. An effective decision is timely, is acceptable to the individuals affected by it, and meets the desired objective.[3] This section describes three models of decision making: the rational model, the bounded rationality model, and the Z model. The section will conclude with a discussion of the limits of decision making techniques.

10-2a Rational Model

Rationality refers to a logical, step-by-step approach to decision making with a thorough analysis of alternatives and their consequences. The *rational model*

Too many decisions can lead to cognitive fatigue.

alphaspirit.it/Shutterstock.com

effective decision A timely decision that meets a desired objective and is acceptable to those individuals affected by it.

rationality A logical, step-by-step approach to decision making, with a thorough analysis of alternatives and their consequences.

Managers often satisfice because of time constraints.

of decision making comes from classic economic theory and assumes the following:

1. The outcome will be completely rational.
2. The decision maker has a consistent system of preferences, which is used to choose the best alternative.
3. The decision maker is aware of all the possible alternatives.
4. The decision maker can calculate the probability of success for each alternative. [4]

In the rational model, the decision maker strives to *optimize*, that is, to select the best possible alternative through purposeful effort.[5]

Given the assumptions of the rational model, it is sometimes unrealistic. There are time constraints and limits to human knowledge and information-processing capabilities. In addition, a manager's preferences and needs change often. The rational

bounded rationality A theory that suggests that there are limits to how rational a decision maker can actually be.

satisfice To select the first alternative that is "good enough," because the costs in time and effort are too great to optimize.

heuristics Shortcuts in decision making that save mental activity.

model is thus an ideal that managers strive for in making decisions, and it captures the way a decision should be made, but it may not reflect the reality of managerial decision making.

10-2b Bounded Rationality Model

Recognizing the deficiencies of the rational model, Herbert Simon suggested that there are limits on how rational a decision maker can actually be. His decision theory, the *bounded rationality model*, earned a Nobel Prize in economics in 1978. Simon's theory rests on the idea that there are constraints that force a decision maker to be less than completely rational. The bounded rationality model has four assumptions:

1. Managers select the first alternative that is satisfactory.
2. Managers recognize that their conception of the world is simple.
3. Managers are comfortable making decisions without determining all the alternatives.
4. Managers make decisions by rules of thumb, or heuristics.

Bounded rationality assumes that managers **satisfice**; that is, they select the first alternative that is "good enough," because the costs of optimizing in terms of time and effort are too great.[6] Further, the theory assumes that managers develop shortcuts, called **heuristics**, to make decisions in order to save mental activity. Heuristics are rules of thumb that allow managers to make decisions based on what has worked in past experiences. In medicine, heuristics are a part of physician training. Doctors are taught simple decision strategies that ignore some of the available information and focus only on the most relevant predictors. If, for example, a patient shows a certain abnormality on an electrocardiogram, they're sent immediately to cardiac care. If not, a second parameter is considered and they're asked about chest pain. If the answer is no, the patient is sent to a regular nursing unit. Research shows that the heuristic approach has a remarkable success rate and provides a faster diagnosis and treatment plan.[7]

Does the bounded rationality model portray the managerial decision process more realistically? Research indicates that it does. One of the reasons managers face limits to their rationality is that they must make decisions under risk and time pressure. The situation they find themselves in is highly uncertain, and the probability of success is not known.

Herbert Simon felt his theory would be incomplete until the role of emotion in decision making was understood, and researchers are beginning to untangle the complex role that emotion plays in the process.[8]

10-2c Z Model

Isabel Briggs Myers, co-creator of the Myers-Briggs Type Indicator, also developed the *Z problem-solving model*, which capitalizes on the strengths of the four separate preferences (Sensing, Intuiting, Thinking, and Feeling). By using the Z problem-solving model, managers can use both their preferences and nonpreferences to make decisions more effectively. The Z model is presented in Figure 10.2. According to this model, good problem solving has four steps:

1. *Examine the facts and details.* Use Sensing to gather information about the problem.

2. *Generate alternatives.* Use Intuiting to develop possibilities.

3. *Analyze the alternatives objectively.* Use Thinking to logically determine the effects of each alternative.

4. *Weigh the impact.* Use Feeling to determine how the people involved will be affected.

Using the Z model can help an individual develop their nonpreferences. Another way to use the Z model is to rely on others to perform nonpreferred activities. For example, an individual who is an NF (Intuition-Feeling person) might want to turn to a trusted NT (Intuition-Thinking person) for help in analyzing alternatives objectively.

We have seen that there are limits to how rational a manager can be in making decisions. One reason is that individual characteristics affect the decision making process, a subject we address in the next section.

Figure 10.2 The Z Problem-Solving Model

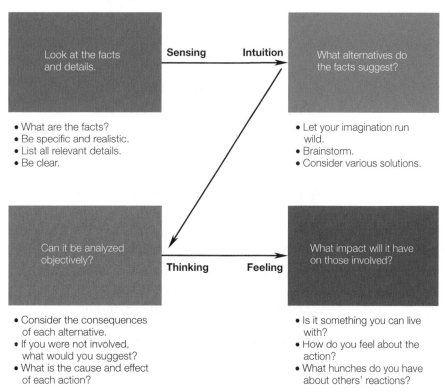

Source: From *Type Talk at Work* by Otto Kroeger and Janet Theusen, copyright © 1992 by Janet Theusen and Otto Kroeger. Used by permission of Delacorte Press, an imprint of The Random House Publishing Group, a division of Random House, Inc.

10-3 Individual Influences on Decision Making

No decision is made in a vacuum. In many ways, decisions reflect the people who make them, so it is appropriate to examine the individual influences on decision making: personality, **cognitive biases**, intuition, and creativity.

10-3a Personality, Attitudes, and Values

In addition to all of the individual differences variables (discussed in Chapters 3 and 4)—personality characteristics, attitudes, and values—managers must use both their logic and their creativity to make effective decisions. Most of us are more comfortable using either logic or creativity, and we show that preference in everyday decision making.

Cognitive biases Subconscious errors in thinking that occur from attempts to conserve cognitive effort.

Our brains have two lateral halves (Figure 10.3). The right side is the center for creative functions, while the left side is the center for logic, detail, and planning. There are advantages to both kinds of thinking, so the ideal situation is to be brain-lateralized, that is, be able to use either logic or creativity or both, depending on the situation.[9] There are ways to develop the side of the brain that you use less often. To develop your right side, or creative side, you can ask what-if questions, engage in play, and follow your intuition. To develop the left side, you can set goals for completing tasks and work to attain those goals. For managers, it is important to see the big picture, craft a vision, and plan strategically, all of which require right-brain skills. But it is equally important to be able to understand day-to-day operations and flowchart work processes, which are left-hemisphere brain skills.

Three particular individual influences that can influence decision making effectiveness will be highlighted next: cognitive biases, intuition and creativity.

10-3b Cognitive Biases

The sheer number of decisions individuals face each day is staggering, and humans seek to simplify the demands on their cognition. To accomplish this,

Figure 10.3 Functions of the Left and Right Brain Hemispheres

Two Brains,
Two Cognitive Styles

Left hemisphere	Right hemisphere
Verbal	Nonverbal, visuospatial
Sequential, temporal, digital	Simultaneous, spatial, analogical
Logical, analytic	Gestalt, synthetic
Rational	Intuitive
Western thought	Eastern thought

Source: Based on ideas from S. P. Springer and G. Deutsch, *Left Brain, Right Brain* (New York: W. H. Freeman and Company, 1993): 272.

we use shortcuts, and predictable errors in decision making called cognitive biases occur.[10] There are many cognitive biases that have been identified; here we concentrate on the biases that often plague managers.

- **Anchoring**: basing our judgments or decisions on the first pieces of information we encounter. An example would be accepting the first solution a team offers. To avoid anchoring, encourage the team to question all solutions, even those from managers or experts.
- **Availability**: relying on information that is easily accessible (available in memory). Often such information is frequently seen or extreme in nature. To avoid availability bias, take a step back from the decision and cast a wider net for data that might contradict the easy choice.
- **Confirmation** bias: searching for or interpreting information as evidence to confirm one's pre-existing beliefs, while discounting evidence that supports a different viewpoint. Bosses may show a pattern of praising ideas that support their views. If this is the case, decisions may reflect what the boss believes, but not what is best for the company. To avoid confirmation bias, seek out opposing viewpoints and encourage open discussion of alternatives.
- **Commitment**: Also known as escalation of commitment, this bias involves continuing to support a failing course of action. Individuals are often unwilling to abandon bad decisions, even when the decisions are costly. One way to prevent commitment bias is to give people graceful exits from failing projects, and to destigmatize failure by treating it as a learning experience. Reward individuals for cutting their losses rather than continuing to invest in a losing course of action.
- **Dunning-Kruger effect**: the tendency for experts to underestimate their abilities and for less qualified individuals to overestimate their abilities. Experts often realize that the more they know, the more there is to learn. Unskilled people, however, seldom recognize their ignorance. To manage employees in this latter category, it is important to give candid, frequent feedback and offer ways to develop their capabilities.[11]
- **Framing**: choices or decisions are influenced by the way they are presented (framed) by different words or contexts. Choices can be framed as losses or gains, positive or negative. Consider milk, for example. Would you rather have milk with 15 percent fat, or milk that is 85 percent fat free? As a manager, you can present a change in the company in terms of what team members stand to gain, or what they will lose from the changes. To overcome the framing bias, learn as much about the issue or choice at hand as possible. Think carefully about the decision and examine information from multiple perspectives, not just one presentation of the issue.
- **Optimism/overconfidence**: the tendency to be overly optimistic and see situations as slightly more positive than they really are. Optimism is generally a good thing, but persistently being overconfident can lead a manager to take unnecessary risks. No one likes a pessimist; but evaluating projects both critically and realistically can help to avoid optimism bias.

Managers should take concrete steps to mitigate the impact of cognitive biases on their decisions. A first step is to recognize your own tendencies and biases. Research has looked at different professions to determine if patterns of biases exist. One study compared professionals in management, finance, medicine and law. For managers, the most frequently seen biases were framing and overconfidence, especially among CEOs. Financiers also exhibited overconfidence. Doctors committed availability bias, and judges experienced confirmation bias and anchoring

Anchoring Basing our decisions on the first piece of information we encounter.

Availability Relying on information that is easily accessible at the expense of further information search.

Confirmation Seeking out or interpreting information that confirms one's beliefs or viewpoints.

Commitment Hanging onto a losing course of action. Also called escalation of commitment.

Dunning-Kruger effect Experts tend to underestimate their abilities whereas less skilled individuals overestimate their abilities.

Framing Affecting a choice or decision by the way the information is presented (framed).

Optimism/Overconfidence The tendency to see situations as more positive than they really are.

Inclusive Conversations

Unconscious Bias in Employment Selection

The most important decisions an organization will make are whom to hire, fire, promote, and reward. There is a good chance that these decisions could be influenced by bias that many decision makers may not be aware they hold. Unconscious bias is a phenomenon that is activated in our minds when we make quick decisions about people and situations without realizing we are doing it. This bias is shaped by the ways in which we have been socialized from an early age throughout our lives and includes beliefs and attitudes toward others. Because these beliefs and attitudes are below the cognitive surface, it becomes difficult to understand how they can affect the choices we make. In short, these unconscious biases can become hidden prejudices with the potential to create unintentional discrimination that creates a barrier to diverse and inclusive workplaces. For instance, a recruiter prides themselves on their ability to treat everyone equally but fails to consider a fat person for a job opening based on an unconscious bias favoring thin people.

The best solution for hidden biases is to reveal them. Though it may be uncomfortable for some, decision makers should recognize that everyone has biases and seek to raise awareness of them through training, such as the Harvard Implicit Association Test (IAT), which operates by measuring the speed with which an individual prefers one characteristic over another (e.g., thin versus fat). Organizations can also reduce unconscious bias during the employment selection process by anonymizing candidate information and using structured interviews.

1. How can organizations use the Harvard IAT to reduce unconscious bias in decision making processes other than employment selection?

   In addition to age, race, gender, and disability bias to select certain employees over others, unconscious bias may be activated when people gravitate towards others who are like them (similarity or affinity bias), which could affect group development, decision making, and conflict management. IATs would be valuable in this instance. There may be other instances, such as negating stereotypes and reducing confirmation bias. Students may test their own implicit biases here: https://implicit.harvard.edu/implicit/iatdetails.html.

2. Why is it important to reveal biases even when they are occurring beneath the surface?

   Known biases typically come from known stereotypes about certain groups of people, such as 'old people are afraid of technology.' These beliefs are above the surface and hidden for fear of being inappropriate. Biases that occur beneath the surface are likely to reveal themselves in ways that are unintentional but similarly inappropriate. The results of both can be equally harmful to the organization.

Source: N. Kakabadse and A. Kakabadse, "Unconscious Bias—The Blind Spot Threatening Organizational Performance," *Financier Worldwide*, March (2023), accessed at Unconscious bias – the blind spot threatening organisational performance — Financier Worldwide.

bias. Taking all four professions together, the number one bias was overconfidence.[12]

10-3c Intuition

There is evidence that managers often use their **intuition** to make decisions.[13] Henry Mintzberg, in his work on managerial roles, found that in many cases managers do not appear to use a systematic, step-by-step approach to decision making. Rather,

Mintzberg argued, managers make judgments based on "hunches."[14] Daniel Isenberg studied the way senior managers make decisions and found that intuition was used extensively, especially as a mechanism to evaluate decisions made more rationally.[15] Robert Beck studied the way managers at Bank of America made decisions about the future direction of the company following the deregulation of the banking industry. Beck described their use of intuition as an antidote to analysis paralysis, or the tendency to analyze decisions rather than developing innovative solutions.[16]

Dr. Gary Klein, a renowned cognitive psychologist, has written a book on the power of intuition. Dr. Klein and colleagues insist that skilled decision makers rely on patterns of learned information in

intuition A fast, positive force in decision making that is utilized at a level below consciousness and involves learned patterns of information.

making quick and efficient decisions. In a series of studies conducted with the U.S. Navy, firefighters, and the U.S. Army, they found that decision makers normally rely on intuition in unfamiliar, challenging situations. These decisions were superior to those made after careful evaluation of information and potential alternatives.[17]

Just what is intuition? In Jungian theory, intuiting (N) is a preferred method used for gathering data. This is only one way that the concept of intuition has been applied to managerial decision making, but it is perhaps the most widely researched form of the concept of intuition. There are, however, many definitions of *intuition* in the managerial literature. Chester Barnard, one of the early influential management researchers, argued that intuition's main attributes were speed and the inability of the decision maker to determine how the decision was made.[18] Other researchers have contended that intuition occurs at an unconscious level and that this is why the decision maker cannot verbalize how the decision was made.[19]

Intuition has been variously described as follows:

- The ability to know or recognize quickly and readily the possibilities of a situation.[20]
- Smooth automatic performance of learned behavior sequences.[21]
- Simple analyses frozen into habit and into the capacity for rapid response through recognition.[22]

These definitions share some common assumptions. First, there seems to be a notion that intuition is fast. Second, intuition is used at a level below consciousness. Third, there seems to be agreement that intuition involves learned patterns of information. Fourth, intuition appears to be a positive force in decision making.

The use of intuition may lead to more ethical decisions as intuition allows an individual to take on another's role with ease, and role taking is a fundamental part of developing moral reasoning. You may recall from Chapter 4 the role of cognitive moral development in ethical decision making. One study found a strong link between cognitive moral development and intuition. The development of new perspectives through intuition leads to higher moral growth, and thus to more ethical decisions.[23]

One question that arises is whether managers can be taught to use their intuition. Weston Agor, who has conducted workshops on developing intuitive skills in managers, has attained positive results in organizations such as the city government of Phoenix and entertainment powerhouse Walt Disney Enterprises. After giving intuition tests to more than 10,000 executives, he has concluded that in most cases, higher management positions are held by individuals with higher levels of intuition. But, just as the brain needs both hemispheres to work, Agor cautions that organizations need both analytical and intuitive minds to function at their peak. Agor suggests relaxation techniques, using images to guide the mind, and taking creative pauses before making a decision.[24] A review of the research on intuition suggests that, although intuition itself cannot be taught, managers can be trained to rely more fully on the promptings of their intuition.[25]

Intuition, with its many definitions, is an elusive concept. Some researchers view so-called rational methods as preferable to intuition, yet satisfaction with a rational decision is usually determined by how the decision feels intuitively.[26] Intuition appears to have a positive effect on managerial

inguldima/Shutterstock.com

Illumination is essential to the creative process.

decision making, but it is not without controversy. Some writers argue that intuition has its place and that instincts should be trusted, but not as a substitute for reason. With new technologies, managers can analyze a lot more information in a lot less time, making the rational method less time-consuming than it once was.[27]

10-3d Creativity

In some ways, creativity is as elusive a concept as intuition. (We know it when we encounter it and when we feel its absence.) Even though creativity is highly individual, it is also collective. Personal creativity plays a role in the decisions made in organizations every day. For our purposes in this text, we can define **creativity** as a process influenced by individual and organizational factors that results in the production of novel and useful ideas, products, or both.[28]

The four stages of the creative process are preparation, incubation, illumination, and verification.[29] *Preparation* means seeking out new experiences and opportunities to learn because creativity grows from a base of knowledge. *Incubation* is a process of reflective thought and is often conducted subconsciously. During incubation, the individual engages in other pursuits while the mind considers the problem and works on it. *Illumination* occurs when the individual senses an insight for solving the problem. Finally, *verification* is conducted to determine if the solution or idea is valid. Verification is accomplished by thinking through the implications of the decision, presenting the idea to another person, or trying out the decision. Momentary quieting of the brain through relaxation can increase coherence, or the ability of different parts of the brain to work together.[30] Both individual and organizational influences affect the creative process.

Individual Influences Several individual variables are related to creativity. One group of factors involves the cognitive processes that creative individuals tend to use. One such cognitive process is *divergent thinking*, meaning the individual's ability to generate several potential solutions to a problem.[31]

In addition, associational abilities and the use of imagery are associated with creativity.[32] Unconscious processes such as dreams are also essential cognitive processes related to creative thinking.[33]

Personality factors have also been related to creativity in studies of individuals from several different occupations. These characteristics include intellectual and artistic values, breadth of interests, high energy, concern with achievement, independence of judgment, intuition, and self-confidence.[34] Creative self-efficacy, the belief that one can perform creative work effectively, is an important predictor of creativity.[35] Not surprisingly, people who have a high level of motivation are more creative, since they are more likely to try to think of different ways to get things done. Also, people who can see and understand others' perspectives are more creative since they have skills at seeing situations from more than one viewpoint.[36]

There is evidence that people who are in a good mood are more creative.[37] Positive affect is related to creativity in work teams because being in a positive mood allows team members to explore new ways of thinking.[38] Positive emotions enhance creativity by broadening one's cognitive patterns and resources. These positive emotions initiate thoughts and actions that are novel and unscripted.[39] Moreover, it is a cyclical process: thinking positively makes us more creative, and being more creative makes us think positively.

Neurodiverse individuals can be very creative. Nikola Tesla, the inventor, was likely autistic, and he invented the remote control in 1898. Research supports the link between neurodiversity and creativity.[40] Adults with dyslexia exhibit nonverbal creativity and often seek out creative occupations. Children and adults with autism outperform non-autistic individuals on creative metaphor generation and verbal creativity.[41] University students with ADHD excel at thinking outside the box.[42] When inclusion is embedded within an organization, the organization reaps the benefits of creativity.

Organizational Influences The organizational environment in which people work can either support creativity or impede creative efforts. Creativity killers include focusing on how work is going to be evaluated, being closely monitored while you are working, and competing with other people in win–lose situations. In contrast, creativity facilitators

creativity A process influenced by individual and organizational factors that results in the production of novel and useful ideas, products, or both.

YOU

Creative or Logical Problem Solving: What Is Your Preference?

Try the following creative problem-solving challenge. Each of the following problems is an equation that can be solved by substituting the appropriate words for the letters. Have fun with them!

Examples: 3F = 1Y (3 feet = 1 yard.)
4LC = GL (4 leaf clover = Good luck.)

1. M + M + NH + V + C + RI = NE.
2. "1B in the H = 2 in the B."
3. 8D − 24H = 1W.
4. 3P = 6.
5. HH & MH at 12 = N or M.
6. 4J + 4Q + 4K = All the FC.
7. S & M & T & W & T & F & S are D of W.
8. A + N + AF + MC + CG = AF.
9. T = LS State.
10. 23Y − 3Y = 2D.

11. E − 8 = Z.
12. Y + 2D = T.
13. C + 6D = NYE.
14. Y − S − S − A = W.
15. A & E were in the G of E.
16. My FL and South P are both MC.
17. "NN = GN."
18. N − P + SM = S of C.
19. 1 + 6Z = 1M.
20. "R = R = R."
21. AL & JG & WM & JK were all A.
22. N + V + P + A + A + C + P + I = P of S.
23. S + H of R = USC.

Source: Roger Von Oech, *A Whack on the Side of the Head* (Warner Books, 1983, 1990, 1998). By permission of Warner Books, New York.

Now try the following logical problem-solving exercise, entitled "Who Owns the Fish?", which is attributed to Albert Einstein.

There are five houses in a row and in five different colors. In each house lives a person from a different country. Each person drinks a certain drink, plays a certain game, and keeps a certain pet. No two people drink the same drink, play the same game, or keep the same pet.

- The Brit lives in a red house.
- The Swede keeps dogs.
- The Dane drinks tea.
- The green house is on the left of the white house.
- The green house owner drinks coffee.
- The person who plays tennis rears birds.

- The owner of the yellow house plays chess.
- The man living in the house right in the center drinks milk.
- The Norwegian lives in the first house.
- The man who plays poker lives next to the man who keeps cats.
- The man who keeps horses lives next to the one who plays chess.
- The man who plays billiards drinks beer.
- The German plays golf.
- The Norwegian lives next to the blue house.
- The man who plays poker has a neighbor who drinks water.

Question: Who owns the fish?
Answer: Your instructor can provide the solutions to this exercise.

Source: From A Whack on the Side of the Head by Roger Von Oech. Copyright © 1983, 1990, 1998 by Roger Von Oech. By permission of Grand Central Publishing. All Rights Reserved.

include feelings of autonomy, being part of a team with diverse skills, and having creative supervisors and coworkers.[43] High-quality, supportive relationships with supervisors are related to creativity.[44] Some individuals are catalysts for the creative performance of others. Catalysts contribute to coworkers' creative thinking process through interactions about a specific project. Individuals who are highly creative can be great resources for others, and managers can place catalysts on teams to fulfill the role. The key is providing time and space for individual work, along with interaction, in a balance. Too much interference from creative catalysts can be a distraction.[45]

An organization can present impediments to creativity by means of internal political problems, harsh criticism of new ideas, destructive internal competition, and avoidance of risk.[46] Even the physical environment can hamper creativity. Companies like Oticon, a Danish hearing aid manufacturer, and Ethicon Endo-Surgery, a division of Johnson & Johnson, use open-plan offices that eliminate walls and cubicles so that employees can interact more frequently. When people mix, ideas mix as well.[47] Organizations can therefore enhance individuals' creative decision making by providing a supportive environment, participative decision making, and a flexible structure.

Individual–Organization Fit Research has indicated that creative performance is highest when there is a match, or fit, between the individual and organizational influences on creativity. When individuals who desire to be creative are matched with an organization that values creative ideas, the result is more creative performance.[48]

A common mistaken assumption regarding creativity is that either you have it or you do not. Research refutes this myth and has shown that individuals can be trained to be more creative.[49] The Disney Institute, for example, features a wide range of programs offered to companies, and one of their best sellers is creativity training. Part of creativity training involves learning to open up *mental locks* that keep us from generating creative alternatives to a decision or problem. Following are some mental locks that diminish creativity:

- Searching for the "right" answer
- Trying to be logical
- Following the rules
- Avoiding ambiguity
- Striving for practicality
- Being afraid to look foolish
- Avoiding problems outside our own expertise
- Fearing failure
- Believing we are not really creative
- Not making play a part of work[50]

synergy A positive force that occurs in groups when group members are stimulated to produce new solutions to problems through the process of mutual influence and encouragement within the group.

Note that many of these mental locks stem from values within organizations.

Organizations can facilitate creative decision making in many ways. Rewarding creativity, allowing employees to fail, making work more fun, and providing creativity training are a few suggestions. Another way companies can encourage creativity is by exposing employees to new ideas through job rotation. As employees move through different jobs, they can be exposed to different information, projects, and teams, either within or outside the company. Finally, managers can encourage employees to surround themselves with stimuli that they have found to enhance their creative processes. These may be music, artwork, books, or anything else that encourages creative thinking.[51]

We have seen that both individual and organizational factors can produce creativity. Leaders can play key roles in modeling creative behavior. One of the most critical skills that determines leader performance is creative thinking.[52] Sir Richard Branson, founder and chair of the U.K.-based Virgin Group, believes that if you do not use your employees' creative potential, you are doomed to failure. At Virgin Group, the culture encourages risk taking and rewards innovation rather than following rules and regulations. Branson says an employee should be able to have an idea in the morning and implement it that afternoon.

Culture also affects creativity. Tight cultures are those with strong social norms and strong sanctions for violating the norms. Pakistan, Norway, and Malaysia are culturally tight. Loose cultures are less predictable and lack clear norms and enforcement of behavior. Hungary, Brazil, and Australia are looser cultures. Individuals from loose cultures are more likely to take on and succeed in foreign, unfamiliar creative tasks than individuals from tight cultures. However, tight cultures are more successful with innovation within their own cultures.[53]

10-4 The Group Decision Making Process

Managers use groups to make decisions for several reasons. One is **synergy**, which occurs when group members stimulate new solutions to problems through the process of mutual influence and encouragement within the group. Another reason for using a group is to gain commitment to a decision. Groups also bring more knowledge and experience to the problem-solving situation.

Group decisions can sometimes be predicted by comparing the views of the initial group members with the final group decision. These simple relationships are known as **social decision schemes**. One social decision scheme is the *majority-wins rule*, in which the group supports whatever position is taken by the majority of its members. Another scheme, the *truth-wins rule*, predicts that the correct decision will emerge as an increasing number of members realize its appropriateness. The *two-thirds-majority rule* means that the decision favored by two-thirds or more of the members is supported. Finally, the *first-shift rule* states that members support a decision represented by the first shift in opinion shown by a member.

Research indicates that these social decision schemes can predict a group decision as much as 80 percent of the time.[54] Current research is aimed at discovering which rules are used in particular types of tasks. For example, studies indicate that the majority-wins rule is used most often in judgment tasks (i.e., when the decision is a matter of preference or opinion), whereas the truth-wins rule predicts decisions best when the task is an intellective one (i.e., when the decision has a correct answer).[55]

10-4a Advantages and Disadvantages of Group Decision Making

Group decision making has advantages and disadvantages. The advantages of group decision making include (1) more knowledge and information through the pooling of group member resources, (2) increased acceptance of and commitment to the decision because the members had a voice in it, and (3) greater understanding of the decision because members were involved in the various stages of the decision process. The disadvantages of group decision making include (1) pressure within the group to conform and fit in, (2) domination of the group by one forceful member or a dominant clique who may ramrod the decision, and (3) the amount of time required because a group makes decisions more slowly than an individual.[56]

Given these advantages and disadvantages, should decisions be made by an individual or a group? Substantial empirical research indicates that effectively making that determination depends on the type of task involved. For judgment tasks requiring an estimate or a prediction, groups are usually superior to individuals because of the breadth of experience that multiple individuals bring to the problem.[57] On tasks that have a correct solution, other studies have indicated that the most competent individual outperforms the group.[58] This finding has been called into question, however. Much of the previous research on groups was conducted in the laboratory, where group members interacted only for short periods of time. Researchers wanted to know how a longer group experience would affect decisions. Their study showed that groups who worked together for longer periods of time outperformed the most competent member 70 percent of the time. As groups gained experience, the best members became less important to the group's success.[59] This study demonstrated that experience in the group is an important variable to consider when evaluating the individual versus group decision making question.

Given the emphasis on teams in the workplace, many managers believe that groups produce better decisions than individuals, yet the evidence is mixed. More research needs to be conducted in organizational settings to help answer this question.

10-4b Limits of Group Decision Making

There are two potential liabilities in group decision making: groupthink and group polarization.

Groupthink One liability of a cohesive group is its tendency to develop the dysfunctional process of **groupthink**. Irving Janis, the originator of this concept, describes groupthink as "a deterioration of mental efficiency, reality testing, and moral judgment" resulting from pressures within the group.[60]

social decision schemes Simple rules used to determine final group decisions.

groupthink A deterioration of mental efficiency, reality testing, and moral judgment resulting from pressures within the group.

Hybrid Group Meetings at Microsoft

When decisions are made in teams, the meeting attendees are often a combination of in-office employees and at-home workers. Microsoft managers noticed that the at-home workers felt disconnected, and the creative minds at the company invested a year figuring out how to design the meeting for optimal participation.

Dysfunctional ✕	Functional ✓	Functional ✓
In-office workers at a rectangular table speak among themselves. The camera captures the profiles of six of the eight people in the room.	The camera captures everyone in the room, thanks to the triangular table's shape. Remote attendees are at eye level and are at least as large as in-person ones.	The half-oval table inhibits in-person participants from clustering together and talking. Remote and in-person employees are at the same eye level.

Another key suggestion is to keep the digital chat open on conference room screens. This is another way to facilitate full participation in the meeting and decision making process.

(Sources: Microsoft, accessed at https://www.microsoft.com/en-us/worklab/designing-the-new-hybrid-meeting-experience; A. Cohen, "Improving Hybrid Meetings," *Bloomberg BusinessWeek*, accessed at https://www.bloomberg.com/news/articles/2022-04-07/zoom-meeting-table-change-can-improve-hybrid-work?leadSource=uverify%20wall.)

One of the conditions that leads to the development of groupthink is high cohesiveness. Cohesive groups tend to favor solidarity because members identify strongly with the group.[61] High-ranking teams that make decisions without outside help are especially prone to groupthink because they are likely to have shared mental models; that is, they are more likely to think alike.[62] Homogeneous groups (ones with little to no diversity among members) are more likely to suffer from groupthink.[63]

Two other conditions that encourage groupthink are (1) having to make a highly consequential decision and (2) time constraints.[64] A highly consequential decision is one that will have a great impact on the group members and on outside parties. Time restraints may cause group members to rush through the decision making process. Both conditions can influence members to desire concurrence in decisions so much that they fail to evaluate one another's suggestions critically. A group suffering

from groupthink shows recognizable symptoms. Table 10.1 presents these symptoms and makes suggestions on how to avoid groupthink.

An incident cited as a prime example of groupthink is the 1986 space shuttle *Challenger* disaster, in which the shuttle exploded, killing all seven crew members. A presidential commission concluded that flawed decision making was the primary cause of the accident. In 2003, the shuttle *Columbia* exploded over Texas upon reentering the earth's atmosphere, killing all seven crew members. Within days of the *Columbia* disaster, questions began to surface about the decision making process that led flight engineers to assume that damage caused to the shuttle upon take-off was minor and to continue the mission. The subsequent investigation of the disaster led observers to note that NASA's decision making process appeared just as flawed in 2003 as it was in 1986, exhibiting all the classic symptoms of groupthink. The final accident report blamed the NASA

Table 10.1 Symptoms of Groupthink and How to Prevent It

Symptoms of Groupthink

- *Illusions of invulnerability.* Group members feel that they are above criticism. This symptom leads to excessive optimism and risk taking.
- *Illusions of group morality.* Group members feel they are moral in their actions and therefore above reproach. This symptom leads the group to ignore the ethical implications of their decisions.
- *Illusions of unanimity.* Group members believe there is unanimous agreement on the decisions. Silence is misconstrued as consent.
- *Rationalization.* Group members concoct explanations for their decisions to make them appear rational and correct. The results are that other alternatives are not considered, and there is an unwillingness to reconsider the group's assumptions.
- *Stereotyping the enemy.* Competitors are stereotyped as evil or stupid. This leads the group to underestimate its opposition.
- *Self-censorship.* Members do not express their doubts or concerns about the course of action. This prevents critical analysis of the decisions.
- *Peer pressure.* Any members who express doubts or concerns are pressured by other group members who question their loyalty.
- *Mindguards.* Some members take it upon themselves to protect the group from negative feedback. Group members are thus shielded from information that might lead them to question their actions.

Guidelines for Preventing Groupthink

- Ask each group member to assume the role of the critical evaluator who actively voices objections or doubts.
- Have the leader avoid stating his or her position on the issue prior to the group decision.
- Create several groups that work on the decision simultaneously.
- Bring in outside experts to evaluate the group process.
- Appoint a devil's advocate to question the group's course of action consistently.
- Evaluate the competition carefully, posing as many different motivations and intentions as possible.
- Once consensus is reached, encourage the group to rethink its position by reexamining the alternatives.

Source: From Breckler/Wiggins/Olson. *Social Psychology Alive!*, 1E. © 2008 Nelson Education Ltd. Reproduced by permission. www.cengage.com/permissions

culture that downplayed risk and suppressed dissent for the decision.[65]

Consequences of groupthink include an incomplete survey of alternatives, failure to evaluate the risks of the preferred course of action, biased information processing, and a failure to work out contingency plans. Consequences like these can be devastating in medicine, where artificial intelligence (AI) is used more and more for diagnostic assistance, therapy critiquing, and image interpretation. Advances in AI are narrowing the gap with human intelligence, emphasizing creativity, empathy, and judgment. If AI can include positive human decision making attributes, it may also fall prey to negative human decision processes such as groupthink, which in the case of AI is called "loopthink." AI is limited by the biases and assumptions of its programming and may exclude moral principles such as human dignity and ethical reasoning. One avenue for preventing loopthink would be to program AI in medicine to be more self-critical and self-correcting, along the lines of ways of preventing groupthink in humans.[66]

Zoom meetings are perfect storms for groupthink. Often Zoom meetings are dominated by one or two participants, and body language cues are less evident. The assumption that everyone is on the same page brings a sense of complacency. Zoom meetings are sometimes rushed and scheduled too frequently, leaving participants burned out. The "Zoomthink" that results can lead to bad decisions.[67]

Table 10.1 presents Janis's guidelines for avoiding groupthink. Many of these suggestions center around ensuring that decisions are evaluated completely, with opportunities for discussion from all group members. This strategy encourages members to evaluate one another's ideas critically. Groups that are educated about the value of diversity tend to perform better as a result. Less successful are groups that are homogenous and not educated about the value of diversity.[68]

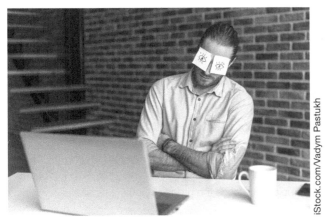

iStock.com/Vadym Pastukh

Too many Zoom meetings, or lengthy Zoom meetings, can contribute to Zoomthink.

Janis has used the groupthink framework to conduct historical analyses of several political and military fiascoes, including the Bay of Pigs invasion, the Vietnam War, and Watergate. One review of the decision situation in the *Challenger* incident proposed that two variables, time and leadership style, are important to include.[69] When a decision must be made quickly, there is more potential for groupthink. Leadership style can either promote groupthink (if the leader makes their opinion known up front) or avoid groupthink (if the leader encourages open and frank discussion).

A more recent example of groupthink occurred at eBay. The e-commerce company's chief executive and a group of employees are being accused of stalking, intimidating, and harassing a couple who ran a niche publication about e-commerce that allows merchants to express their opinions about companies like eBay and Amazon. At eBay's Silicon Valley headquarters, a comment from the CEO to "take them down" was taken literally and a hand-picked group of eBay staff made the couple's life miserable. The couple's home was inundated with live cockroaches and spiders, and they were harassed on Twitter with crude and violent threats. Their address was published, and they were stalked. eBay employees egged each other on, rather than de-escalating their behavior. They rationalized that the illegal activity was done in an effort to please their

boss. Seven people have been indicted, and the court cases continue.[70]

Group Polarization Another group phenomenon was discovered by a graduate student. His study showed that groups and individuals within the group made riskier decisions and accepted greater levels of risk following a group discussion of the issue. Subsequent studies uncovered another shift—toward caution. Thus, group discussion produced shifts both toward more risky positions and toward more cautious positions.[71] Further research revealed that individual group member attitudes simply became more extreme following group discussion. Individuals who were initially against an issue became more radically opposed, and individuals who were in favor of the issue became more strongly supportive following discussion. These shifts came to be known as **group polarization**.[72]

The tendency toward polarization has important implications for group decision making. Groups whose initial views lean a certain way can be expected to adopt more extreme views following interaction between members. Several ideas have been proposed to explain why group polarization occurs. One explanation is the *social comparison approach*. Prior to group discussion, individuals believe they hold better views than the other members. During group discussion, they see that their views are not so far from average, so they shift to more extreme positions.[73] A second explanation is the *persuasive arguments view*. It contends that group discussion reinforces the initial views of the members, so they take a more extreme position.[74] Both explanations are supported by research. It may be that both processes, along with others, cause the group to develop more polarized attitudes.

In sum, group polarization leads groups to adopt extreme attitudes. In some cases, this can be disastrous. For instance, if individuals are leaning toward a dangerous decision, they are likely to support it more strongly following discussion. A recent study found that after discussing hiring decisions as a group, employers were less accurate in their ratings and were more susceptible both to contrast effects and halo effects.[75]

Both groupthink and group polarization are potential liabilities of group decision making, but several techniques can be used to help prevent or control these two liabilities.

group polarization The tendency for group discussion to produce shifts toward more extreme attitudes among members.

10-4c Techniques for Group Decision Making

Once a manager has determined that a group decision approach should be used, they can determine the technique that is best suited to the decision situation. There are several techniques for group decision making. These include brainstorming, nominal group technique, devil's advocacy and dialectical inquiry.

Brainstorming Brainstorming is one technique for generating alternatives in a group. The idea behind **brainstorming** is to generate as many ideas as possible, suspending evaluation until all the ideas have been suggested. Participants are encouraged to build on the suggestions of others, and imagination is emphasized.

Evidence suggests, however, that group brainstorming is less effective than a comparable number of individuals working alone. This may be because in groups, participants engage in discussions that can make them lose their focus. Also, individuals may censor themselves in groups or simply agree with the ideas of the most senior person in the room. There are a couple of techniques that can help avoid the drawbacks of brainstorming. Brainwriting is an idea generation technique in which individuals independently write down ideas and then come together as a group to discuss and refine their ideas. It's effective because individuals are more likely to generate creative ideas when working alone.

Another technique for overcoming the limitations of group brainstorming is electronic brainstorming. In this technique, group members use computers to simultaneously produce as many ideas as possible during a short period of time.[76] Studies show that electronic brainstorming is slightly more effective than traditional brainstorming. One of the limitations of electronic brainstorming is that people may spend more time generating their own ideas rather than looking at the ideas of others. This limitation can be overcome if participants are told in advance that others in the brainstorming group are creative. This entices them to pay attention to others' ideas and can improve the quality and quantity of ideas produced in electronic brainstorming.[77]

Nominal Group Technique A structured approach to decision making that focuses on generating

Individuals tend to outperform groups when it comes to generating creative ideas.

alternatives and choosing one is called **nominal group technique (NGT)**, which involves the following discrete steps:

1. Individuals silently list their ideas.
2. Ideas are written on a chart one at a time until all ideas are listed.
3. Discussion is permitted but only to clarify the ideas. No criticism is allowed.
4. A written vote is taken.

NGT is a good technique to use when group members fear criticism from others.

Devil's Advocacy In the **devil's advocacy** decision method, a group or individual is given the role of critic. This devil's advocate has the task of coming up with the potential problems of a proposed decision. By identifying potential pitfalls in advance, organizations can often avoid costly mistakes in decision making.[78] As we discussed in Chapter 9, a devil's advocate who challenges the CEO and top management team can help sustain the vitality and performance of the upper echelon.

brainstorming A technique for generating as many ideas as possible on a given subject while suspending evaluation until all the ideas have been suggested.

nominal group technique (NGT) A structured approach to group decision making that focuses on generating alternatives and choosing one.

devil's advocacy A technique for preventing groupthink in which a group or individual is given the role of critic during decision making.

Dialectical Inquiry **Dialectical inquiry** is essentially a debate between two opposing sets of recommendations. Although it sets up a conflict, it is a constructive approach because it brings out the benefits and limitations of both sets of ideas.[79] However, when using this technique, it is important to guard against a win–lose attitude and to concentrate on reaching the most effective solution for all concerned. Research has shown that the way a decision is framed (i.e., win–win versus win–lose) is very important. A decision's outcome could be viewed as a gain or a loss depending on the way the decision is framed.[80]

10-4d Factors in Selecting the Appropriate Technique

Before choosing a group decision making technique, the manager should carefully evaluate the group members and the decision situation. Only then can the best method for accomplishing the objectives of the group decision making process be selected. If the goal is generating a large number of alternatives, for example, brainstorming would be a good choice. If group members are reluctant to contribute ideas, the nominal group technique would be appropriate. The need for expert input would be best facilitated by the Delphi technique, which uses a panel of experts. To guard against groupthink, devil's advocacy or dialectical inquiry would be effective. Decisions that concern quality or production would benefit from the advice of quality circles or the empowered decisions of quality teams. Moreover, recent research results suggest that if individuals within a team are made accountable for the process of decision making (rather than the end decision itself), then such teams are more likely to gather diverse information, share information, and eventually make better decisions.[81] Finally, a manager who wants to provide total empowerment to a group should consider self-managed teams.

10-5 Diversity and Culture in Decision Making

Styles of decision making vary greatly among cultures. Many of the dimensions proposed by Hofstede that were presented in Chapter 2 affect

decision making. Uncertainty avoidance, for example, can affect the way people view decisions. In the United States, a culture with low uncertainty avoidance, decisions are seen as opportunities for change. In contrast, cultures such as those of Indonesia and Malaysia attempt to accept situations as they are rather than try to change them.[82] Power distance also affects decision making. In more hierarchical cultures, such as India, top-level managers make nearly all decisions. In countries with low power distance, lower-level employees make many decisions. The Swedish culture exemplifies this type.

The individualist/collectivist dimension has implications for decision making. Japan, with its collectivist culture, favors group decisions. The United States has a more difficult time with group decisions because it is an individualistic culture. Time orientation affects the frame of reference of the decision. In China, with its long-term view, decisions are made with the future in mind. In the United States, many decisions are made considering only the short term.

The masculine/feminine dimension can be compared to the Jungian thinking/feeling preferences for decision making. Masculine cultures, as in many Latin American countries, value quick, assertive decisions. Feminine cultures, as in many Scandinavian countries, value decisions that reflect concern for others.

Recent research examining the effects of cultural diversity on decision making has found that when individuals in a group are racially dissimilar, they engage in more open information sharing, encourage dissenting perspectives, and arrive at better decisions than racially similar groups.[83] Other kinds of diversity, such as functional background, have been studied as well. Top management teams that have members who come from a variety of functional backgrounds (e.g., marketing, accounting, information systems) engage in greater debate in decision making than top management teams in which the members come from similar backgrounds. This diversity results in better financial performance for the firm.[84] To capitalize on diversity in decision making, leaders may need to deal with inherent biases. One such bias is toward nonnative accents. Often, individuals will choose new companies, products, or employees based on accents and are more favorable toward accents that are similar to their own. Biases like this have serious

---

dialectical inquiry A debate between two opposing sets of recommendations.

implications for companies engaging in global business, and managers can provide training to reduce biases and stereotypes regarding accents different from one's own.[85]

10-6 Participation in Decision Making

Effective management of people can improve a company's economic performance. Firms that capitalize on this fact share several common practices. Chief among them is participation of employees in decision making.[86] Many companies do this through highly empowered self-managed teams. Even in situations where formal teams are not feasible, decision authority can be handed down to front-line employees who have the knowledge and skills to make a difference. At Hampton Inn hotels, for example, guest services personnel are empowered to do whatever is necessary to make guests happy—without consulting their superiors.

10-6a The Effects of Participation

Participative decision making occurs when individuals who are affected by decisions influence the making of those decisions. Participation buffers employees from the negative experiences of organizational politics.[87] Participation in decisions such as how technology is developed has also been found to affect employee's attitudes toward the technology and how they use it.[88] In addition, participative management has been found to increase employee creativity, job satisfaction, and productivity.[89] GE Capital is one company that believes in participation. Each year it holds so-called dreaming sessions, in which employees from all levels of the company attend strategy and budget meetings to discuss where the company is heading.

As our economy becomes increasingly based on knowledge work and as new technologies make it easier for decentralized decision makers to connect, participative decision making will undoubtedly increase.[90] Consider the city and county of San Francisco, a combined city/county government organization. Needing to adopt a single messaging system to meet the requirements of more than 20,000 employees, it faced a huge challenge in getting all

the users to provide input into the decision. Technology helped craft a system that balanced the needs of all the groups involved, and IT planners developed a twenty-eight-page spreadsheet to pull together the needs and desires of all sixty departments into a focused decision matrix. Within two years, 90 percent of the users had agreed on and moved to a single system, reducing costs and complexity.[91]

10-6b Foundations for Participation and Empowerment

What conditions must be in place in order for participative decision making to work? The organizational foundations include a supportive organizational culture and a team-oriented work design. A supportive work environment is essential because of the uncertainty within the organization. Lower-level organizational members must be able to make decisions and take action on them. As operational employees are encouraged to take part in making decisions, however, fear, anxiety, or even terror can be created among middle managers in the organization.[92] Thus, senior leadership must create an organizational culture that is supportive and reassuring for these middle managers as the power dynamics of the system change.

A second organizational foundation for participative decision making concerns the design of work. A team-oriented work design is a key organizational foundation because it leads to broader tasks and a greater sense of responsibility. For example, Volvo builds cars using a team-oriented work design in which each person does many different tasks; therefore, each person retains direct responsibility for the finished product.[93] These work designs create a context for effective participation.

The three individual prerequisites for participative decision making are

1. the capability to become psychologically involved in participative activities,
2. the motivation to act autonomously, and
3. the capacity to see the relevance of participation for one's own well-being.[94]

participative decision making Decision making in which individuals who are affected by decisions influence the making of those decisions.

First, people must be psychologically equipped to become involved in participative activities if they are to be effective team members. Not all people are so predisposed. For example, Germany has an authoritarian tradition that runs counter to participative decision making at the individual and group levels. As a result, General Motors encountered significant difficulties implementing participative decision making in its German plants because workers expected to be directed by supervisors, not to engage in participative problem solving. New initiatives to establish supervisory/worker boards in German corporations are intended to change this authoritarian tradition.

The second individual prerequisite is the motivation to act autonomously. People with dependent personalities are predisposed to be told what to do and to rely on external motivation rather than internal, intrinsic motivation.[95] These dependent people are not often effective contributors to decision making.

Finally, if participative decision making is to work, employees must be able to comprehend how it provides a personal benefit to them. The personal payoff for the individual need not be short term. It may be a long-term benefit that results in workers receiving greater rewards through enhanced organizational profitability.

10-6c Self-Managed Teams

An example of a fully empowered team is the self-managed teams discussed in Chapter 9. Self-managed teams make many of the decisions that were once reserved for managers, such as work scheduling, job assignments, and staffing. Self-managed teams were being used long before the pandemic of 2020, which necessitated remote work. The old "command and control" management style made way for "trust and verify." In today's hybrid environment, many workers essentially self-manage. Teams can do the same, with technologies that provide good data and feedback so they can gauge how they're performing at any time.[96]

Design thinking A human-centric, non-linear approach to complex problems.

Empathy map A problem-solving tool used in design thinking to better understand people affected by the problem or decision.

Many organizations have claimed success with self-managed teams, including Google, Zappos, and General Electric. At Riot Games, teams are coached to say "I intend to do this…" rather than to ask permission. Managers are coached not to make decisions for others, but to give opinions when asked.[97]

Self-managed teams, like any cohesive group, can fall victim to groupthink, especially if a lot of peer pressure exists. The key to stimulating innovation and better problem solving in these groups is welcoming dissent among members. Dissent breaks down complacency and sets in motion a process that results in better decisions. Team members must know that dissent is permissible so that they won't fear embarrassment or ridicule.[98]

10-7 Emerging Trends in Decision Making

Organizations are exploring innovative ways of problem solving and decision making. Two of these approaches are design thinking and choice architecture. Each offers advantages for improving decisions in organizations.

10-7a Design Thinking

Managers can be seen as more than decision makers; they are also designers whose work goes beyond analysis. Design thinking involves creative responses to human needs (see Figure 10.4).[99] Originating in product design at Stanford University, the concept of design thinking has migrated into the management space.[100] Leaders are essentially designers of the work experience for themselves and others. **Design thinking** is a human-centric, nonlinear process for solving complex problems. It seeks to understand the people involved and affected by the problem, challenges old ways of thinking, and creates new solutions that can be implemented, tested, and refined.[101] The focus of design thinking is on people and innovation. It is a continuous, iterative process in which constant learning occurs.

A hallmark of design thinking is empathy, which helps managers get a full picture of what people need and feel in terms of the problem to be solved or decision to be made. It helps set aside the manager's biases or assumptions. To accomplish this step, empathy maps are used. A traditional **empathy map** has four quadrants, focusing on what people say,

Figure 10.4 Design Thinking Steps

Empathize   Define   Ideate   Prototype   Test

Source: Interaction Design Foundation, interaction-design.org.

think, do, and feel (see Figure 10.5). It is a visual tool to help managers understand the human side of problem solving. Empathy maps can be used by decision makers to better understand their team members. Questions that emerge from empathy maps might be: What are my team members thinking and feeling? What do they say about their workplace? Does their experience change when working remotely? What are their pain points during times of change? Whose work life can I improve today? In essence, design thinking is about generating a holistic, empathic understanding about the problems people face.[102]

Design thinking has been adopted at many companies, including IDEO, Apple, and Samsung. Apple is an example of exceptional design thinking. Apple's physical products are constantly the focus of innovations that put users' needs at the center of the design process, earning the company millions of devotees. Steve Jobs' vision included focusing on real people's needs and building empathy for Apple customers. Continuous improvement and innovation through constant iterations of its product means that Apple products constantly evolve. What can managers learn from Apple's design thinking? First, to integrate users' (employees') experiences into every decision. Employee input and feedback is essential. Second, decisions or solutions are never static; they need continuous improvement and revision. Finally, design thinking can produce a culture in which innovation is

the norm. Design thinking can be especially helpful in successfully managing large scale changes in the organization because of the explicit focus on employees' experiences and the awareness that continuous feedback and tweaks will be a part of the process.[103]

10-7b Choice Architecture

Human beings often make poor decisions for a host of reasons, including falling prey to the cognitive biases we discussed earlier in the chapter. To help people make better decisions, managers can use **choice architecture**, originating in behavioral economics.[104] Choice architecture is a tool for improving decisions by structuring how information and alternatives are presented to people. Central to this idea is that people can be "nudged' in a direction without taking away their freedom to make their own decisions.[105]

A simple example of **nudging** can be seen in the retail industry. Certain products or brands are placed on the shelves directly at eye level, which is "buy level" because it's the first place consumers look when they're shopping. Competition is fierce for the prized shelf space. Companies that seek to encourage healthy behaviors at work can also use nudges. If a company wants to encourage employees to take the stairs rather than the elevator, they might place signs around that say "Taking the stairs means gaining fitness," or "enjoy your mindfulness while taking the stairs." Of course, nudges can be used for good, but they can be used for evil, aka "sludges." In some cases of buying products online, you're automatically subscribed to their email list, or the box to subscribe is automatically checked when you order. In this type

Figure 10.5 Empathy Mapping

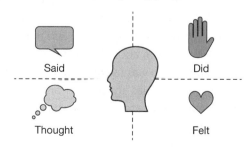

Said   Did

Thought   Felt

Source: Interaction Design Foundation, interaction-design.org.

Choice architecture A tool for improving decisions by structuring how information and alternatives are presented.

Nudging Guiding people toward the better choice in decision making without restricting their freedom to choose.

Uber and Lyft use "nudges" to manage their workforce.

of "sludge" or evil nudge, your decision freedom is actually limited or taken away altogether.

When nudges are used to enhance productivity at work, are they good or evil? Ride share services Uber and Lyft use nudges to manage their freelance workforces. You may remember the allure (being your own boss, ultimate flexibility) of these jobs for drivers. In reality, drivers must decide whether to take on a rider without actually knowing where the pickup or dropoff points will be; therefore, they can't decipher how much money a particular trip will pay. The app that matches drivers and riders governs the rules of the game, and rules are constantly changing. When drivers log on, the app tracks every move including the percentage of pickups they accept, the times they're working, the neighborhoods they prefer, and their ratings by riders. During peak periods or busy areas, flashing spots show up on the map that offer bonuses, or the ability to unlock features on the app.

The companies say that the information helps them track performance and prevents drivers from cherry-picking high dollar rides. Drivers feel like the app is rigged to make bonuses harder to claim and pay difficult to decipher, and yields the company (rather than the driver) more profits. Some drivers try to beat the app by figuring out and overcoming the nudges.

Choice architecture and nudging are ways in which managers try to shape employee decisions. Given that the average adult makes approximately 35,000 decisions per day, influencing employee decision making is a huge challenge.

Experiential Exercise

Making a Layoff Decision

Purpose

In this exercise, you will examine how to weigh a set of facts and make a difficult personnel decision about laying off valued employees during a time of financial hardship. You will also examine your own values and criteria used in the decision making process.

The Problem

Walker Space Institute (WSI) is a medium-sized firm located in Connecticut. The firm essentially has been a subcontractor on many large space contracts that have been acquired by firms like Alliant Techsystems and others.

With the cutback in many NASA programs, Walker has an excess of employees. Stuart Tartaro, the head of one of the sections, has been told by his superior that he must reduce his section of engineers from nine to six. He is looking at the following summaries and pondering how he will make this decision.

1. *Roger Allison*, age twenty-six, married, two children. Allison has been with WSI for a year and a half. He is a very good engineer, with a degree from Rensselaer Polytech. He has held two prior jobs and lost both of them because of cutbacks in the space program. He moved to Connecticut from California to take this job. Allison is well liked by his coworkers.

2. *Dave Jones*, age twenty-four, single. Jones is an African American, and the company looked hard to get him because of affirmative action pressure. He is not very popular with his coworkers. Because he has been employed less than a year, not much is known about his work. On his one evaluation (which was average), Jones accused his supervisor of bias against African Americans. He is a graduate of the Detroit Institute of Technology.

3. *William Foster*, age fifty-three, married, three children. Foster is a graduate of "the school of hard knocks." After serving in Desert Storm, he started to go to school but dropped out because of high family expenses. Foster has worked at the company for twenty years. His ratings were excellent for fifteen years. The last five years they have been average. Foster feels his supervisor grades him down because he does not "have sheepskins covering his office walls."

4. *Donald Boyer*, age thirty-two, married, no children. Boyer is well liked by his coworkers. He has been at WSI five years, and he has a B.S. and M.S. in engineering from Purdue University. Boyer's ratings have been mixed. Some supervisors rated him high and some average. Boyer's wife is an M.D.

5. *Ann Shuster*, age twenty-nine, single. Shuster is a real worker but a loner. She has a B.S. in engineering from the University of California. She is working on her M.S. at night, always trying to improve her technical skills. Her performance ratings have been above average for the three years she has been at WSI.

6. *Sherman Soltis*, age thirty-seven, divorced, two children. Soltis has a B.S. in engineering from Ohio State University. He is very active in community affairs: Scouts, Little League, and United Way. He is a friend of the vice president through church work. His ratings have been average although some recent ones indicate that he is out of date. He is well liked and has been employed at WSI for fourteen years.

7. *Warren Fortuna*, age forty-four, married, five children. Fortuna has a B.S. in engineering from Georgia Tech. He headed this section at one time. He worked so hard that he had a heart attack. Under doctor's orders, he resigned from the supervisory position. Since then he has done good work, though because of his health, he is a bit slower than the others. Now and then he must spend extra time on a project because he did get out of date during the eight years he headed

the section. His performance evaluations for the last two years have been above average. He has been employed at WSI for fourteen years.

8. *Robert Treharne*, age forty-seven, single. Treharne began an engineering degree at MIT but had to drop out for financial reasons. He tries hard to stay current by regular reading of engineering journals and taking all the short courses the company and nearby colleges offer. His performance evaluations have varied, but they tend to be average to slightly above average. He is a loner, and Tartaro thinks this has negatively affected Treharne's performance evaluations. He has been employed at WSI for sixteen years.

9. *Sandra Rosen*, age twenty-two, single. Rosen has a B.S. in engineering technology from the Rochester Institute of Technology. She has been employed less than a year. She is enthusiastic, is a very good worker, and well liked by her coworkers. She is well regarded by Tartaro.

Tartaro does not quite know what to do. He sees the good points of each of his section members. Most have been good employees. They all can pretty much do one another's work. No one has special training.

He is fearful that the section will hear about the downsizing and morale will drop. Work would fall off. He does not even want to talk to his wife about it, in case she would let something slip. Tartaro has come to you, Edmund Graves, personnel manager at WSI, for some guidelines on this decision—legal, moral, and best personnel practice.

Assignment

You are Edmund Graves. Write a report with your recommendations for termination and a careful analysis of the criteria for the decision. You should also carefully explain to Tartaro how you would go about the terminations and what you would consider reasonable termination pay. You should also advise him about the pension implications of this decision. Generally, fifteen years' service entitles you to at least partial pension.

Source: W. F. Glueck, *Cases and Exercises in Personnel* (Dallas, TX: Business Publications, 1978): 24–26.

Learning Objectives

10-1 **Identify the steps in the decision making process.** The decision making process involves *programmed decisions* and *nonprogrammed decisions*. The first step is recognizing the problem or realizing a decision must be made. Second, the objective of the decision is identified. The third step is gathering information relevant to the problem. The fourth step is listing and evaluating alternative courses of action. Finally, the manager selects the alternative that best meets the decision objective.

10-2 **Describe various models of decision making.** The *rational model* of decision making contends that the decision maker is completely rational in his or her approach. *Bounded rationality* theory suggests that constraints force decision makers to be less rational and assumes that managers satisfice and develop heuristics. The *Z problem-solving model* capitalizes on the strengths of four separate preferences (Sensing, Intuiting, Thinking, and Feeling), allowing managers to use preferences and nonpreferences to make decisions.

10-3 **Discuss the individual influences that affect decision making.** Decisions reflect the people who make them. The individual influences that affect decision making are comfort with risk, cognitive style, personality, intuition, and creativity.

10-4 **Explain how groups make decisions.** Group decisions are utilized for several reasons: to achieve *synergy*, to gain commitment to a decision, and to maximize knowledge and experience in problem-solving situations. Seven techniques utilized in group decisions are brainstorming, nominal group technique, devil's advocacy, dialectical inquiry, quality circles and quality teams, and self-managed teams.

10-5 **Describe the role culture plays in decision making.** Styles of decision making vary greatly among cultures and affect the way people view decisions. The dimensions proposed by Hofstede in Chapter 2 that affect decision making are: uncertainty avoidance, power distance, individualism/collectivism, time orientation, masculinity/femininity, cultural diversity, functional background, and strategic decision making.

10-6 **Explain how organizations can improve the quality of decisions through participation.** *Participative decision making* can include employees identifying problems, generating alternatives, selecting solutions, planning implementations, and/or evaluating results. Participative management can increase employee creativity, job satisfaction, and productivity, and improve a company's economic performance.

Key Terms

anchoring Basing our decisions on the first piece of information we encounter. (p. 205)

availability Relying on information that is easily accessible at the expense of further information search. (p. 205)

bounded rationality A theory that suggests that there are limits to how rational a decision maker can actually be. (p. 202**)**

brainstorming A technique for generating as many ideas as possible on a given subject while suspending evaluation until all the ideas have been suggested. (p. 215)

choice architecture A tool for improving decisions by structuring how information and alternatives are presented. (p. 219)

cognitive biases Subconscious errors in thinking that occur from attempts to conserve cognitive effort. (p. 204)

commitment Hanging onto a losing course of action. Also called escalation of commitment. (p. 205)

confirmation Seeking out or interpreting information that confirms one's beliefs or viewpoints. (p. 205)

creativity A process influenced by individual and organizational factors that results in the production of novel and useful ideas, products, or both. (p. 208)

design thinking A human-centric, non-linear approach to complex problems. (p. 218)

devil's advocacy A technique for preventing groupthink in which a group or individual is given the role of critic during decision making**.** (p. 215)

dialectical inquiry A debate between two opposing sets of recommendations. (p. 216)

Dunning-Kruger effect Experts tend to underestimate their abilities whereas less skilled individuals overestimate their abilities. (p. 205)

effective decision A timely decision that meets a desired objective and is acceptable to those individuals affected by it. (p. 201)

empathy map A problem-solving tool used in design thinking to better understand people affected by the problem or decision. (p. 218)

framing Affecting a choice or decision by the way the information is presented (framed). (p. 205)

group polarization The tendency for group discussion to produce shifts toward more extreme attitudes among members. (p. 214)

groupthink A deterioration of mental efficiency, reality testing, and moral judgment resulting from pressures within the group. (p. 211)

heuristics Shortcuts in decision making that save mental activity. (p. 202)

intuition A fast, positive force in decision making that is utilized at a level below consciousness and involves learned patterns of information. (p. 206)

nominal group technique (NGT) A structured approach to group decision making that focuses on generating alternatives and choosing one. (p. 215)

nonprogrammed decision A new, complex decision that requires a creative solution. (p. 200)

nudging Guiding people toward the better choice in decision making without restricting their freedom to choose. (p. 219)

Optimism/Overconfidence The tendency to see situations as more positive than they really are. (p. 205)

participative decision making Decision making in which individuals who are affected by decisions influence the making of those decisions. (p. 217)

programmed decision A simple, routine matter for which a manager has an established decision rule. (p. 200)

rationality A logical, step-by-step approach to decision making, with a thorough analysis of alternatives and their consequences. (p. 201)

satisfice To select the first alternative that is "good enough," because the costs in time and effort are too great to optimize. (p. 202)

social decision schemes Simple rules used to determine final group decisions. (p. 211)

synergy A positive force that occurs in groups when group members are stimulated to produce new solutions to problems through the process of mutual influence and encouragement within the group. (p. 210)

Ethical Dilemma

David is the president of Allied Industries, a medium sized farm equipment manufacturing firm. He has been in his position for just over a year. A close friend, John, approaches him and asks if Allied could possibly help with a problem he was having. John owns a ranch that is having a lot of financial problems. He has considered closing the ranch, but it serves a need in the community by providing animal therapy for troubled adolescents.

John asks David to please have Allied buy the ranch. Allied has deep enough pockets to make the ranch financially solvent, and it will keep this important community service alive. David struggles with the idea but knows that it will be hard to justify his idea to the Board of Directors of Allied.

After much pressure, David agrees for Allied to purchase the ranch. At the next board meeting, David explains Allied's new acquisition. He develops an explanation as to why this addition makes good business sense.

Joan, chairman of the board, is surprised by this new acquisition made by the president. The board and David have had a great working relationship and she does not want to cause trouble, but this decision has her greatly concerned. Why would he go so far outside of Allied's business sector without discussing it with the board? The financial investment is not that large, but this decision should have been discussed.

1. Using consequential, rule-based, and character theories, evaluate David's actions.

2. What should Joan do? Why?

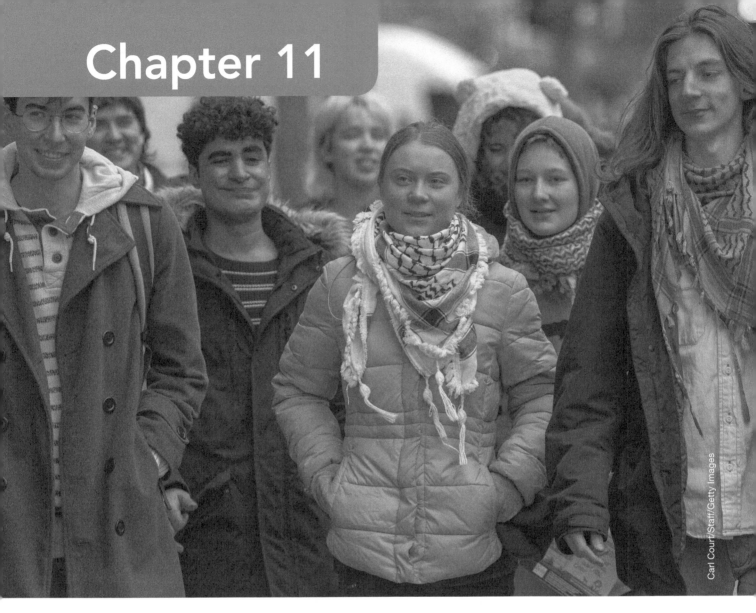

Chapter 11

Carl Court/Staff/Getty Images

Power and Political Behavior

Learning Objectives

11-1 Describe the concept of power.

11-2 Identify forms and sources of power in organizations.

11-3 Describe the role of ethics in using power.

11-4 Identify symbols of power and powerlessness in organizations.

11-5 Define organizational politics through an understanding of the role of political skill, influence tactics and political capital.

11-6 Identify political behavior and how to navigate it in organizations.

11-1 The Concept of Power

Power is the ability to influence another person. As an exchange relationship, it occurs in transactions between an agent and a target. The agent is the person using the power, and the target is the recipient of the attempt to use power.[1] Because power is an ability, individuals can learn to use it effectively, employing either influence or authority or both. **Influence** is the process of affecting the thoughts, behavior, and feelings of another person. **Authority** is the right to influence another person.[2] It is important to understand the subtle differences among these terms. For instance, a manager may have authority but no power. They may have the right, by virtue of their position as boss, to tell someone what to do. But they may not have the skill or ability to influence other people.

In a relationship between the agent and the target, there are many influence attempts that the target will consider legitimate. Working forty hours per week, greeting customers, solving problems, and collecting bills are actions that, when requested by the manager, are considered legitimate by a customer service representative. Requests such as these fall within the employee's **zone of indifference**—the range in which attempts to influence the employee are perceived as legitimate and are acted on without a great deal of thought.[3] The employee accepts that the manager has the authority to request such behaviors and complies with the requests. Some requests, however, fall outside the zone of indifference, so there the manager must work to enlarge the employee's zone of indifference. Enlarging the zone is accomplished with power (an ability) rather than with authority (a right).

Suppose the manager asks an employee to purchase a birthday gift for the manager's wife or to overcharge a customer for a service call. The employee may think that the manager has no right to ask these things. These requests fall outside the zone of indifference. They're viewed as extraordinary, and the manager has to operate from outside the authority base to induce the employee to fulfil them. In some cases, no power base is enough to induce the employee to comply, especially if the employee considers the behaviors requested by the manager to be unethical.

Individuals have many forms of power to use in their work settings.

11-2 Forms and Sources of Power in Organizations

Individuals have many forms of power to use in their work settings. Some of them are interpersonal, that is, used in interactions with others. One of the earliest and most influential theories of power comes from John French and Bertram Raven, who tried to determine both the forms and the sources of power managers use to influence other people.

11-2a Interpersonal Forms of Power

French and Raven identified five forms of interpersonal power that managers use: reward, coercive, legitimate, referent, and expert power.[4]

Reward power is power based on an agent's ability to control rewards that a target wants, such as salary increases, bonuses, and promotions. Reward power can lead to better performance, but only as long as the employee sees a clear and strong link between performance and rewards. To use reward power effectively, then, the manager should be explicit about the behavior being rewarded and should make the connection clear between the behavior and the reward.

Coercive power is power that is based on an agent's ability to cause the target to have an unpleasant experience. To coerce someone into

---

power The ability to influence another person.

influence The process of affecting the thoughts, behavior, and feelings of another person.

authority The right to influence another person.

zone of indifference The range in which attempts to influence a person will be perceived as legitimate and will be acted on without a great deal of thought.

reward power Power based on an agent's ability to control rewards that a target wants.

coercive power Power that is based on an agent's ability to cause an unpleasant experience for a target.

doing something means to force the person to do it, often with threats of punishment. Managers using coercive power may verbally abuse employees or withhold support from them.

Legitimate power, which is similar to authority, is power that is based on position and mutual agreement. The agent and target agree that the agent has the right to influence the target. Just because a manager thinks they have the right to influence their employees doesn't mean that they will have legitimate power in their eyes. For legitimate power to be effective, the employees must also believe the manager has the right to tell them what to do.

Referent power is an elusive power that is based on interpersonal attraction. The agent has referent power over the target because the target identifies with or wants to be like the agent. Charismatic individuals are often thought to have referent power. Interestingly, the agent need not be superior to the target in any way. People who use referent power well are most often individualistic and respected by the target.

Expert power is the power that exists when an agent has specialized knowledge or skills that the target needs. For expert power to work, three conditions must be in place. First, the target must trust that the expertise given is accurate. Second, the knowledge involved must be relevant and useful to the target. Third, the target's perception of the agent as an expert is crucial. Using easy-to-understand language signals the target that the expert has an appreciation for real-world concerns and increases the target's trust in the expert.[5]

Which type of interpersonal power is most effective? Research has focused on this question since French and Raven introduced their five forms of power. Some of the results are surprising. Reward power and coercive power have similar effects.[6] Both lead to compliance. That is, employees will do what the manager asks them to, at least temporarily, if the manager offers a reward or threatens them with

Dario Pignatelli/Bloomberg/Getty Images

Indra Nooyi has referent and expert power as a leader.

punishment. Reliance on these sources of power is dangerous, however, because it may require the manager to be physically present and watchful in order to apply rewards or punishment when the behavior occurs. Constant surveillance creates an uncomfortable situation for managers and employees and eventually results in a dependency relationship: employees will not work unless the manager is present.

Legitimate power also leads to compliance. When told "Do this because I'm your boss," most employees will comply. However, the use of legitimate power has not been linked to organizational effectiveness or to employee satisfaction.[7] In organizations where managers rely heavily on legitimate power, organizational goals are not necessarily met.

Referent power is linked with organizational effectiveness. It is the most dangerous power, however, because it can be too extensive and intensive in altering the behavior of others. Charismatic leaders need an accompanying sense of responsibility for

legitimate power Power that is based on position and mutual agreement; agent and target agree that the agent has the right to influence the target.

referent power An elusive power that is based on interpersonal attraction.

expert power The power that exists when an agent has specialized knowledge or skills that the target needs.

others. Actor Michael J. Fox puts referent power to good use. Diagnosed with Parkinson's disease in 1991, he has written three books, done voiceover work in films, and continued his acting on television. He created the Michael J. Fox Foundation, which focuses on finding a cure for Parkinson's.

Expert power has been called the power of the future.[8] Of the five forms of power, it has the strongest relationship with performance and satisfaction. It is through expert power that vital skills, abilities, and knowledge are passed on within the organization. Employees internalize what they observe and learn from managers they perceive to be experts.

The results on the effectiveness of these five forms of power pose a challenge in organizations. The least effective power bases—legitimate, reward, and coercive—are the ones most likely to be used by managers.[9] Managers inherit these power bases as part of the position when they take a supervisory job. In contrast, the most effective power bases—referent and expert—are ones that must be developed and strengthened through interpersonal relationships with employees. Indra Nooyi, CEO of Pepsi, has both referent and expert power. Her expertise lies not only in leading the company and exceeding analyst's expectations, but also in her emotional intelligence. Nooyi wrote the parents of each of her direct reports so that they would know they had succeeded as a parent, thanking them for the gift of their children. She believes leaders should work hard to bond the employees to the company and to win hearts as well as minds.[10] Expert power and social networks help CEOs influence their top management teams in ways that are profitable for the firm.

11-2b Intergroup Sources of Power

Groups or teams within an organization can also use power from several sources. One source of intergroup power is control of *critical resources*.[11] When one group controls an important resource that another group desires, the first group holds power. Controlling resources needed by another group allows the power-holding group to influence the actions of the less powerful group. This process can continue in an upward spiral. Groups seen as powerful tend to be given more resources from top management.[12]

Groups also have power to the extent that they control **strategic contingencies**—activities that other groups depend on in order to complete their tasks.[13] The dean's office, for example, may control the number of faculty positions to be filled in each department of a college. The departmental hiring plans are thus contingent on approval from the dean's office. In this case, the dean's office controls the strategic contingency of faculty hiring, and thus has power.

Three factors can give a group control over a strategic contingency.[14] One is the *ability to cope with uncertainty*. If a group can help another group deal with uncertainty, it has power. One group that has gained power in recent years in most organizations is the legal department. Faced with increasing government regulations and fears of litigation, many other departments seek guidance from the legal department.

Another factor that can give a group control power is a *high degree of centrality* within the organization. If a group's functioning is important to the organization's success, it has high centrality. The sales force in a computer firm, for example, has power because of its immediate effect on the firm's operations and because other groups (accounting and servicing groups, for example) depend on its activities.

The third factor that can give a group power is *nonsubstitutability*—the extent to which a group performs a function that is indispensable to an organization. A team of computer specialists may be powerful because of its expertise with a system. It may have specialized experience that another team cannot provide.

The strategic contingencies model thus shows that groups hold power over other groups when they can reduce uncertainty, when their functioning is central to the organization's success, and when the group's activities are difficult to replace.[15] The key to all three of these factors, as you can see, is dependency. When one group controls something that another group needs, it creates a dependent relationship—and gives one group power over the other.

strategic contingencies Activities that other groups depend on in order to complete their tasks.

11-3 Using Power Ethically

Managers can work at developing all five forms of power for future use. The key to using them well is to use them ethically, as Table 11.1 shows. Coercive power, for example, requires careful administration if it is to be used in an ethical manner. Employees should be informed of the rules in advance, and any punishment should be used consistently, uniformly, and privately. The key to using all five types of interpersonal power ethically is to be sensitive to employees' concerns and to communicate well.

To French and Raven's five power sources we can add a source that is very important in today's

organizations. **Information power** is access to and control over important information. Consider, for example, the CEO's administrative assistant. They have information about the CEO's schedule that people need in order to get in to see the CEO. Central to the idea of information power is the person's position within the communication networks in the organization, both formal and informal. Also important is the idea of *framing*, which is the "spin" that managers put on information. Managers not only pass information on to subordinates, they also interpret this information and influence the subordinates' perceptions of it. Information power may flow upward from subordinates to managers as well as downward from managers to subordinates. For instance, in manufacturing plants, database operators often control information about plant metrics and shipping performance that is vital to managerial decision-making. Information power can

information power Access to and control over important information.

Table 11.1 Guidelines for the Ethical Use of Power

Form of Power	Guidelines for Use
Reward power	Verify compliance. Make feasible, reasonable requests. Make only ethical requests. Offer rewards desired by subordinates. Offer only credible rewards.
Coercive power	Inform subordinates of rules and penalties. Warn before punishing. Administer punishment consistently and uniformly. Understand the situation before acting. Maintain credibility. Fit punishment to the infraction. Punish in private.
Legitimate power	Be cordial and polite. Be confident. Be clear and follow up to verify understanding. Make sure request is appropriate. Explain reasons for request. Follow proper channels. Exercise power consistently. Enforce compliance. Be sensitive to subordinates' concerns.
Referent power	Treat subordinates fairly. Defend subordinates' interests. Be sensitive to subordinates' needs and feelings. Select subordinates similar to oneself. Engage in role modeling.
Expert power	Maintain credibility. Act confident and decisive. Keep informed. Recognize employee concerns. Avoid threatening subordinates' self-esteem.

Source: G. A. Yuki, *Leadership in Organizations*, 1st ed., © 1981. Reprinted by permission of Pearson Education, Inc., Upper Saddle River, N.J.

also flow laterally. Salespeople convey information from the outside environment (their customers) that is essential for marketing efforts.

Determining whether a power-related behavior is ethical is complicated. One helpful method for establishing criteria in this respect is to ask three questions:[16]

1. *Does the behavior produce a good outcome for people both inside and outside the organization?* This question represents the criterion of *utilitarian outcomes*. The behavior should result in the greatest good for the greatest number of people. If the power-related behavior serves only the individual's self-interest and fails to help the organization reach its goals, it is considered unethical. A salesperson might be tempted to deeply discount a product in order to make a sale that would win a contest. Doing so would be in their self-interest but would not benefit the organization.

2. *Does the behavior respect the rights of all parties?* This question emphasizes the criterion of *individual rights*. Free speech, privacy, and due process are individual rights that are to be respected, and power-related behaviors that violate these rights are considered unethical.

3. *Does the behavior treat all parties equitably and fairly?* This question represents the criterion of *distributive justice*. Power-related behavior that treats one party arbitrarily or benefits one party at the expense of another is unethical. Granting a day of vacation to one employee in a busy week in which coworkers must struggle to cover for them might be considered unethical.

To be considered ethical, power-related behavior must meet all three criteria. If the behavior fails to meet the criteria, then alternative actions should be considered.

Unfortunately, most power-related behaviors are not easy to analyze. Conflicts may exist among the criteria; for example, a behavior may maximize the greatest good for the greatest number of people but may not treat all parties equitably. Individual rights may need to be sacrificed for the good of the organization. A CEO may need to be removed from power for the organization to be saved. Still, these

Hot Trend

Recognizing Bullying in the Workplace

One form of unethical power use is workplace bullying. Researchers define workplace bullying as repetitive and ongoing acts of harassment and/or social exclusion in the workplace. While management researchers have been aware of workplace bullying for decades, systemic research on the topic is a more recent phenomenon. Workplace bullying can be considered a particular kind of coercive power, where one or multiple people have the ability to cause an unpleasant experience for another. Recent work has uncovered a few key insights on the process of workplace bullying.

First, while anyone can engage in workplace bullying, it appears that its effects are more pronounced when the bully is a supervisor. This may be because supervisors have additional power bases like reward power: they can grant or withhold things like promotions and raises. As a result, being bullied by a supervisor can be particularly threatening to employees.

Second, research has shown that witnessing bullying also creates detrimental organizational outcomes. For instance, an observer may be more likely to engage in subsequent workplace bullying when they see others do it. In addition, witnessing workplace bullying can damage employees' perceptions of the organization and its culture even when they are not the target of the harassment.

Fortunately, researchers are also developing interventions that organizations can consider when addressing workplace bullying. These include things like awareness training and coaching as well as more system-level interventions for cases where organizations have wider, cultural issues with bullying.

Sources: C. Caponecchia, S. Branch, and J. P. Murray, "Development of a Taxonomy of Workplace Bullying Intervention Types: Informing Research Directions and Supporting Organizational Decision Making," *Group & Organization Management* 45 (2020): 103–133.
P. Gupta, U. Gupta, and S. Wadhwa, "Known and Unknown Aspects of Workplace Bullying: A Systematic Review of Recent Literature and Future Research Agenda," *Human Resource Development Review* 19 (2020): 263–308.

criteria can be used on a case-by-case basis to sort through the complex ethical issues surrounding the use of power. The ethical use of power is one of the hottest topics in the current business arena due to the abuse of power by top executives such as Bernie Madoff, who was convicted of running a $50 billion Ponzi scheme that financially ruined people and businesses around the world.

11-3a Positive Versus Negative Power

We turn now to a theory of power that takes a strong stand on the "right" versus "wrong" kind of power to use in organizations. David McClelland has spent a great deal of his career studying the need for power and the ways managers use power. As was discussed in Chapter 5, he believes that there are two distinct faces of power, one negative and one positive.[17] The negative face of power is **personal power**—power used for personal gain. Managers who use personal power are commonly described as "powerhungry." Sexual harassment is an abuse of personal power. One of Uber's top executives was asked to resign after others learned he was accused of sexual harassment at his former employer, Google. Amit Singhal did not disclose the allegations when he was hired. Uber is now facing an internal investigation into alleged sexual harassment after a former engineer blogged about problems within Uber's culture. People who approach relationships with an exchange orientation often use personal power to ensure that they get at least their fair share—and often more—in the relationship. They are most interested in their own needs and interests. One way to encourage ethical behavior in organizations is to encourage *principled dissent*. This term refers to valid criticism that can benefit the organization rather than mere complaints about working conditions. Much like whistle-blowers, who can serve as checks on powerful people within the organization, dissenters can pinpoint wrongdoings, encourage employee

voice in key issues, and create a climate conducive to the ethical use of power.[18]

Individuals who rely on personal power at its extreme might be considered *Machiavellian*—willing to do whatever it takes to get one's own way. Niccolo Machiavelli was an Italian statesman during the sixteenth century who wrote *The Prince*, a guide for acquiring and using power.[19] Among his methods for using power was manipulating others, believing that it was better to be feared than loved. Machiavellians (or high Machs) are willing to manipulate others for personal gain and are unconcerned with others' opinions or welfare.

The positive face of power is **social power**—power used to create motivation or to accomplish group goals. McClelland clearly favors the use of social power by managers. People who approach relationships with a communal orientation focus on the needs and interests of others. In other words, they rely on social power.[20] McClelland has found that managers who use power successfully have four power-oriented characteristics:

1. *Belief in the authority system.* They believe that the institution is important and that its authority system is valid. They are comfortable influencing and being influenced. The source of their power is the authority system of which they are a part.

2. *Preference for work and discipline.* They like their work and are very orderly. They have a basic value preference for the Protestant work ethic, believing that work is good for a person over and beyond its income-producing value.

3. *Altruism.* They publicly put the company and its needs before their own needs. They are able to do this because they see their own well-being as integrally tied to the company's well-being.

4. *Belief in justice.* They believe justice is to be sought above all else. People should receive that to which they are entitled and that which they earn.

McClelland takes a definite stand on the proper use of power by managers. When power is used for the good of the group, rather than for individual gain, it is positive.

personal power Power used for personal gain.

social power Power used to create motivation or to accomplish group goals.

Inclusive Conversations

The Role of a "Playing Politics" Culture on Career Advancement for Men and Women

Understanding the politics of an organization is necessary for getting things done. However, "playing politics" is often viewed as toxic and guided by self-interest. Given these negative views of playing politics, how important is this type of culture to employee advancement? Does it matter if the employee is a man or a woman? Researchers examined these questions by comparing indicators of lack of fit in two organizational cultures, cultures in which playing politics was important for advancement to higher positions and cultures in which competence was the most important factor for advancement to higher positions. Lack of fit was measured by the degree to which career advancement strategies (particularly playing politics) conflicted with the individual's concept of who they were, the extent to which they believed colleagues would dislike them if they engaged in political behavior, the extent to which they wanted to advance to a high-level position, and the degree to which they possessed the self-efficacy to play politics well. The study revealed that both men and women had negative views of cultures in which playing politics was important. However, women were more likely than men to be deemed as having a lack of fit in cultures in which playing politics, rather than demonstrating competence was important to advance to high-level positions. Practically, this research suggests that organizations should build cultures where competence, rather than politics, is important for advancement especially if the focus is to attract and retain women to leadership positions.

1. What is your experience with playing politics in organizations in which you have worked? If you do not have work experience, discuss your experience with political behavior in a school project or another group.

   Students will have different experiences with political behavior. Instructors should guide students to distinguish between politics and political behavior (e.g., playing politics) when discussing their experiences.

2. What might leaders do to create and/or maintain cultures that discourage politics and encourage competence?

   All organizations are inherently political. Given that, leaders should emphasize the importance of developing the four dimensions of political skill. Modeling behaviors associated with effective political skill and basing rewards on competence will demonstrate to employees the importance of both.

Source: M. Salwender, C. Schoel, H. Bless, and D. Stahlberg, "The Politics Hurdle: Joint Effect of Organizational Culture and Gender on Lack of Fit Experiences," *Social Psychology and Personality Science* 14, No. 1 (2023): 84–92.

11-4 Symbols of Power

Organization charts show who has authority, but they do not reveal much about who has power. Two very different ideas about the symbols of power come from Rosabeth Moss Kanter and Michael Korda.

11-4a Kanter's Symbols of Power

Kanter offers a scholarly approach to determining who has power and who feels powerless, providing several characteristics of powerful people in organizations:[21]

1. *Ability to intercede for someone in trouble.* An individual who can pull someone out of a jam has power.

2. *Ability to get placements for favored employees.* Getting a key promotion for an employee is a sign of power.

3. *Exceeding budget limitations.* A manager who can go above budget limits without being reprimanded has power.

4. *Procuring above-average raises for employees.* One faculty member reported that her department head distributed 10 percent raises to the most productive faculty members although the budget allowed for only 4 percent increases. "I don't know how he did it; he must have pull," she said.

5. *Getting items on the agenda at meetings.* If a manager can raise issues for action at meetings, it's a sign of power.

The ability to get action items on a meeting's agenda is one symbol of power.

6. *Access to early information.* Having information before anyone else does is a signal that a manager is plugged into key sources.

7. *Having top managers seek out their opinion.* When top managers have a problem, they may ask for advice from lower-level managers. The managers they turn to have power.

A theme that runs through Kanter's list is doing things for others—for people in trouble, for employees, for bosses. There is an active, other-directed element in her symbols of power. You can use Kanter's symbols of power to identify powerful people in organizations. They can be particularly useful in finding a mentor who can effectively use power.

11-4b Kanter's Symbols of Powerlessness

Kanter also wrote about symptoms of **powerlessness**—a lack of power—in managers at different levels of the organization. First-line supervisors, for example, often display three symptoms of powerlessness: overly close supervision, inflexible adherence to the rules, and a tendency to do the job themselves rather than training their employees to do it. Staff professionals such as accountants and lawyers display different symptoms of powerlessness. When

powerlessness A lack of power.

> By identifying powerful people and learning from their modeled behavior, you can learn the keys to power use in the organization.

they feel powerless, they tend to resist change and try to protect their turf. Top executives can also feel powerless. They show symptoms such as focusing on budget cutting, punishing others, and using dictatorial, top-down communication. Acting in certain ways can lead employees to believe that a manager is powerless. By making *external attributions* (blaming others or circumstances) for negative events, a manager looks as if they have no power.[22]

11-4c Korda's Symbols of Power

Michael Korda offers a semiserious look at some tangible symbols of power: office furnishings, time power, and standing by.[23] Furniture is not just physically useful; it also conveys a message about power. Locked file cabinets are signs that the manager has important and confidential information in the office. A rectangular (rather than round) conference table enables the most important person to sit at the head of the table. The size of one's desk may convey the amount of power, too, as most executives prefer large, expensive desks.

Time power means using clocks and watches as power symbols. Korda says that the biggest compliment a busy executive can pay a visitor is to remove their watch and place it facedown on the desk, thereby communicating "my time is yours." He also notes that the less powerful the executive, the more intricate the watch. Moreover, managers who are really secure in their power wear no watch at all, since they believe nothing important can happen without them. A full calendar is also proof of power. Personal planners are left open on the desk to display busy schedules.

Standing by is a game in which people are obliged to keep their cell phones, pagers, and so forth with them at all times so executives can reach them. The idea is that the more you can impose your schedule on other people, the more power you have. In fact, Korda defines *power* as follows: there are more people who inconvenience themselves on your behalf than there are people on whose behalf you would inconvenience yourself. Closely tied to this is the ability to make others perform simple tasks for you, such as getting your coffee or fetching the mail.

While Kanter's symbols focus on the ability to help others, Korda's symbols focus on status—a person's relative standing in a group based on prestige and having other people defer to him.[24] By identifying powerful people and learning from their modeled behavior, you can learn the keys to power use in the organization.

11-5 Political Behavior in Organizations

Like the word *power*, the phrase *politics in organizations* may conjure up negative images. However, **organizational politics** is not necessarily negative; it is the use of power and influence in organizations. Because organizations are arenas in which people have competing interests, effective managers must reconcile competing interests. Organizational politics are central to managing. Some research suggests that political behavior fuels innovation and support for change.[25] The advances in social media and technology can further supercharge political activities in organizations. As people try to acquire power and expand their power base, they use various tactics and strategies. Some are sanctioned (acceptable to the organization); others are not. **Political behavior** refers to actions not officially sanctioned by an organization that are taken to influence others in order to meet one's personal goals.[26] Sometimes personal goals are aligned with team or organizational goals, and they can be achieved in support of others' interests. But other times personal goals and the interests of others collide, and individuals pursue politics at the expense of others' interests.[27]

Politics is a controversial topic among managers. Some managers take a favorable view of political behavior; others see it as detrimental to the organization. Some workers who perceive their workplace as highly political actually find the use of political tactics more satisfying and report greater job satisfaction when they engage in political behavior. Some people may therefore thrive in political environments, while others may find office politics distasteful and stressful.[28] It's important to remember, however,

that political behavior is not inherently constructive or destructive.

Most people are also amazingly good at recognizing political behavior at all levels of the firm. Employees are not only keenly aware of political behavior at their level but can also spot political behavior at both their supervisor's level and the topmost levels of the organization.[29]

Many organizational conditions encourage political activity. Among them are unclear goals, autocratic decision-making, ambiguous lines of authority, scarce resources, and uncertainty.[30] Moreover, even supposedly objective activities may involve politics. One such activity is the performance appraisal process. A study of sixty executives who had extensive experience in employee evaluation indicated that political considerations were nearly always part of the performance appraisal process.[31]

The effects of political behavior in organizations can be quite negative when the political behavior is strategically undertaken to maximize self-interest. If people within the organization are competitively pursuing selfish ends, they're unlikely to be attentive to the concerns of others. As a consequence, the workplace can seem less helpful, more threatening, and more unpredictable. When people focus on their own concerns rather than on organizational goals, we see the negative face of power described earlier by David McClelland as personal power. And when employees view the organization's political climate as extreme, they experience more anxiety, tension, fatigue, and burnout. They are also dissatisfied with their jobs and are more likely to leave.[32]

However, not all political behavior is destructive. Though positive political behavior still involves self interest, when it is aligned with organizational goals, the self-interest is perceived positively by employees. Political behavior is also viewed positively when it is seen as the only means by which to accomplish something. Job satisfaction and satisfaction with coworkers and supervisors are affected by any kind of political behavior.[33]

organizational politics The use of power and influence in organizations.

political behavior Actions not officially sanctioned by an organization that are taken to influence others in order to meet one's personal goals.

The Consequences of Letting Political Behavior Run Amok

Office politics can have serious ramifications for a company and its performance. Take Activision Blizzard, the video game company behind popular titles like Call of Duty and World of Warcraft. In recent years, the company has come under fire for what was reported to be a toxic culture that allowed harassment and political behavior to run rampant. A lawsuit was filed against the company, creating a major public relations scandal and forcing the company to face up to serious allegations of misconduct and negligence.

The company has since taken steps to address their culture by, for instance, creating a zero-tolerance policy for employees who are found to have harassed another. For large companies like Activision Blizzard, it is especially important to address political behavior and unethical uses of power; allowing these behaviors to spread has the potential to lead to serious and long-term consequences.

Source: K. Browning, "Activision Blizzard Commits to Improving Diversity and Workplace Culture," *New York Times*, October 28 (2021).

11-5a Influence Tactics

Influence is the process of affecting the thoughts, behavior, or feelings of another person. That other person could be the boss (upward influence), an employee (downward influence), or a coworker (lateral influence). There are eight basic types of influence tactics. They are listed and described in Table 11.2.[34] Research has shown that the four tactics used most frequently are consultation, rational persuasion, inspirational appeals, and ingratiation. Upward appeals and coalition tactics are used moderately. Exchange tactics are used least often.

Influence tactics are used for *impression management*, which was described in Chapter 3. In impression management, individuals use influence tactics to control others' impressions of them. One way in which people engage in impression management is through image building. The interview is a prime example of image building being used by all parties. Job candidates are trying to create favorable impressions with the interviewer through firm handshakes, strong eye contact, and confident posture. Similarly, interviewers are trying to make a good impression with the candidates by displaying warmth, referring to the candidates by name, and portraying themselves as similar to the candidates.[35]

Ingratiation is an example of one tactic often used for impression management. Ingratiation can take many forms, including flattery, opinion conformity, and subservient behavior. *Exchange* is another influence tactic that may be used for impression management. Offering to do favors for someone in an effort to create a favorable impression is an exchange tactic.

Which influence tactics are most effective? It depends on the target of the influence attempt and the objective. Individuals use different tactics for different purposes, and they use different tactics for different people. Influence attempts with subordinates, for example, usually involve assigning tasks or changing behavior. With peers, the objective is often to request help. With superiors, influence attempts are often made to request approval, resources, political support, or personal benefits. *Rational persuasion* and *coalition tactics* are used most often to get support from peers and superiors to change company policy. *Consultation* and *inspirational appeals* are particularly effective for gaining support and resources for a new project.[36] Overall, the most effective tactic in terms of achieving objectives is rational persuasion. *Pressure* is the least effective tactic.

Influence tactics are often used on bosses to get them to evaluate employees more favorably or to give the employees a promotion. Two tactics— rational persuasion and ingratiation—appear to work effectively in this way. Employees who use these tactics receive higher performance evaluations than employees who don't.[37] When supervisors believe an employee's motive for doing favors for the boss is simply to be a good citizen, they are likely to reward that employee. However, when the motive is seen as "brownnosing" (ingratiation), supervisors respond negatively.[38] And, as it becomes more obvious that the employee has something to gain by impressing the boss, the likelihood that ingratiation will succeed decreases. So, how does one use ingratiation effectively?

Table 11.2 Influence Tactics Used in Organizations

Tactics	Description	Examples
Pressure	The person uses demands, threats, or intimidation to convince you to comply with a request or to support a proposal.	"If you don't do this, you're fired. You have until 5:00 to change your mind, or I'm going without you."
Upward appeals	The person seeks to persuade you that the request is approved by higher management or appeals to higher management for assistance in gaining your compliance with the request.	"I'm reporting you to my boss. My boss supports this idea."
Exchange	The person makes an explicit or implicit promise that you will receive rewards or tangible benefits if you comply with a request or support a proposal or reminds you of a prior favor to be reciprocated.	"You owe me a favor. I'll take you to lunch if you'll support me on this."
Coalition	The person seeks the aid of others to persuade you to do something or uses the support of others as an argument for you to agree also.	"All the other supervisors agree with me. I'll ask you in front of the whole committee."
Ingratiation	The person seeks to get you in a good mood or to think favorably of them before asking you to do something.	"Only you can do this job right. I can always count on you, so I have another request."
Rational persuasion	The person uses logical arguments and factual evidence to persuade you that a proposal or request is viable and likely to result in the attainment of task objectives.	"This new procedure will save us $150,000 in overhead. It makes sense to hire John; he has the most experience."
Inspirational appeals	The person makes an emotional request or proposal that arouses enthusiasm by appealing to your values and ideals or by increasing your confidence that you can do it.	"Being environmentally conscious is the right thing. Getting that account will be tough, but I know you can do it."
Consultation	The person seeks your participation in making a decision or planning how to implement a proposed policy, strategy, or change.	"This new attendance plan is controversial. How can we make it more acceptable? What do you think we can do to make our workers less fearful of the new robots on the production line?"

Source: First two columns from G. Yukl and C. M. Falbe, "Influence Tactics and Objectives in Upward, Downward, and Lateral Influence Attempts," *Journal of Applied Psychology* 75 (1990): 132–140. Copyright © 1990 by the American Psychological Association. Reprinted with permission.

Results from a study conducted among supervisors and subordinates of a large state agency indicate that subordinates with higher scores on political skill used ingratiation regularly and received higher performance ratings, whereas individuals with lower scores on political skill who used ingratiation frequently received lower performance ratings.[39]

Managers and other people with high social status and power are often the most difficult to ingratiate successfully. One technique for success is to reflect on genuine positive feelings such as admiration for the high-status colleague, which translates into ingratiation that feels more genuine to the receiver and less like a blatant attempt to gain favors.[40]

CEOs are often the targets of ingratiation attempts such as flattery or opinion conformity, and they often respond to these attempts with positive affect toward the ingratiator. Falling for ingratiation often, though, can backfire. Top managers who feel they need to use ingratiation with their CEO can become resentful. The resentment can escalate into social undermining of the CEO with important other people such as journalists who are writing about the company.[41]

There is evidence that men and women view politics and influence attempts differently. Men tend to view political behavior more favorably than do women. When both men and women witness political behavior, they view it more positively if the agent is of their gender and the target is of the opposite gender.[42] Some women executives may view politics with distaste, and may expect to be recognized and promoted solely on the merit of their work. A lack of awareness of organizational politics is a barrier that holds women back in terms of moving into senior executive ranks.[43] Moreover, women may have fewer opportunities to develop political skills because of a lack of mentors and role models and because they are often excluded from informal networks.[44]

Different cultures prefer different influence tactics at work. One study found that American managers dealing with a tardy employee tended to rely on pressure tactics such as, "If you don't start reporting on time for work, I will have no choice but to start docking your pay." In contrast, Japanese managers relied on influence tactics that either appealed to the employee's sense of duty ("It is your duty as a responsible employee of this company to begin work on time.") or emphasized a consultative approach ("Is there anything I can do to help you overcome the problems that are preventing you from coming to work on time?").[45]

Influence can also stem from the way a person's personality fits into their work environment. A recent study found that extraverts have more influence in team-oriented work environments, whereas conscientious employees have more influence in environments where individuals work alone on technical tasks.[46]

It is important to note that influence tactics do have some positive effects. When investors form coalitions and put pressure on firms to increase their research and development efforts, it works.[47] However, some influence tactics, including pressure, coalition building, and exchange, can have strong ethical implications. There is a fine line between being an impression manager and being seen as a manipulator.

How can a manager use influence tactics well? First, a manager can develop and maintain open lines of communication in all directions: horizontally, vertically, and laterally. Then, the manager can treat the targets of influence attempts—whether managers, employees, or peers—with basic respect. Finally, the manager can understand that influence relationships are reciprocal—they are two-way relationships. As long as the influence attempts are directed toward organizational goals, the process of influence can be advantageous to all involved.

political skill The ability to get things done through favorable interpersonal relationships outside formally prescribed organizational mechanisms.

11-5b Political Skill

Researchers at Florida State University have generated an impressive body of research on political skill.[48] They have found that political skill is a distinct interpersonal attribute that is important for managerial success. Researchers suggest therefore that political skill should be considered in hiring and promotion decisions. Leaders' political skills have a positive effect on team performance, trust for the leader, and support for the leader.[49] Furthermore, political skill buffers the negative effects of stressors such as role conflict in work settings. This set of research findings points to the importance of developing political skill for managerial success.[50]

So what exactly is **political skill**? It is the ability to get things done through positive interpersonal relationships outside the formal organization. Politically skilled individuals have the ability to accurately understand others and use this knowledge to influence others in order to meet personal or organizational goals. Political skill is made up of four key dimensions: social astuteness, interpersonal influence, networking ability, and sincerity.

Social astuteness refers to the accurate perception and evaluation of social situations. Socially astute individuals manage social situations in ways that present them in the most favorable light. *Interpersonal influence* refers to a subtle and influential personal style that is effective in getting things done. Individuals with interpersonal influence are very flexible in adapting their behavior to differing targets of influence or differing contexts in order to achieve one's goals. *Networking ability* is an individual's capacity to develop and retain diverse and extensive social networks. Individuals with political skills can thrive in the challenging central position of a network in which colleagues turn to you for information. Finally, *sincerity* refers to an individual's ability to portray forthrightness and authenticity in all of their dealings. Individuals who have behavioral integrity inspire more confidence and trust, making them more successful in influencing others.[51] These four dimensions of political skill can each be learned.

High self-monitors and politically savvy individuals score higher on an index of political skill. Individuals who are emotionally intelligent are better able to develop political skills at work.[52] Recruiting new members to the organization is important,

YOU

Using the following seven-point scale, choose the number that best describes how much you agree with each statement about yourself.

1 = *strongly disagree*
2 = *disagree*
3 = *slightly disagree*
4 = *neutral*
5 = *slightly agree*
6 = *agree*
7 = *strongly agree*

1. _____ I spend a lot of time and effort at work networking with others.

2. _____ I am able to make most people feel comfortable and at ease around me.

3. _____ I am able to communicate easily and effectively with others.

4. _____ It is easy for me to develop good rapport with most people.

5. _____ I understand people very well.

6. _____ I am good at building relationships with influential people at work.

7. _____ I am particularly good at sensing the motivations and hidden agendas of others.

8. _____ When communicating with others, I try to be genuine in what I say and do.

9. _____ I have developed a large network of colleagues and associates at work who I can call on for support when I really need to get things done.

10. _____ At work, I know a lot of important people and am well connected.

11. _____ I spend a lot of time at work developing connections with others.

12. _____ I am good at getting people to like me.

13. _____ It is important that people believe I am sincere in what I say and do.

14. _____ I try to show a genuine interest in other people.

15. _____ I am good at using my connections and I network to make things happen at work.

16. _____ I have good intuition or savvy about how to present myself to others.

17. _____ I always seem to instinctively know the right things to say or do to influence others.

18. _____ I pay close attention to people's facial expressions.

A higher score indicates better political skill.

Source: G. Ferris, S. L. Davidson, and P. L. Perrewe, *Political Skill at Work: Impact on Work Effectiveness* (Boston, MA: Davies-Black Publishing, 2005).

and political skill can make a better recruiter. Even in college football, the recruiter's political skill, combined with the head coach's winning record, leads to more success in recruiting NCAA football players.[53] Individuals who have political skill have been shown to be more likely to engage in organizational citizenship behaviors, have more total promotions, have higher perceived career success, and greater life satisfaction.[54]

11-5c Political Capital

The continued use of political skill, different forms of interpersonal power, and influence tactics can lead to accumulation of a resource known as political capital. Having such capital in organizations helps in accessing resources, and elicits trust and professional respect. Individuals within an organization can derive such political capital in several different ways. For example, their position in a social network could lead to accrual of this valuable resource. Or their reputation for dependability and integrity could help build political capital. Their position within an organization (i.e., legitimate power) or their expertise (i.e., expert power) can help build political capital. **Political capital** is thus not a static resource, it can be gained or lost over a period of time.[55]

political capital The ability to command power and influence in organizations.

11-6 Managing Political Behavior in Organizations

Politics cannot and should not be eliminated from organizations. Managers should, however, take a proactive stance and manage the political behavior that inevitably occurs.[56] The first step in managing political behavior is to recognize it. Some behaviors to watch for include networking, finding key players to support initiatives, making friends with powerful people, bending the rules, and self-promoting. Lesser-used tactics include misinformation, spreading rumors, and blackmailing.[57]

To diffuse these behaviors, open communication is an important tool. Uncertainty tends to increase political behavior, and communication that reduces uncertainty is important. One way to open communication is to clarify the sanctioned and nonsanctioned political behaviors in the organization. For example, managers may want to encourage social power as opposed to personal power.[58]

Another key is to clarify expectations regarding performance. This can be accomplished through the use of specific, quantifiable goals and through the establishment of a clear connection between goal accomplishment and rewards.[59] Participative management is yet another key. Often, people engage in political behavior when they feel excluded from decision-making processes in the organization. By including them, managers will encourage positive input and eliminate behind-the-scenes maneuvering. Also, encouraging cooperation among work groups is helpful in managing political behavior. Managers can instill a unity of purpose among work teams by rewarding cooperative behavior and by implementing activities that emphasize the integration of team efforts toward common goals.[60]

Managing scarce resources well is also important. An obvious solution to the problem of scarce resources is to increase the resource pool, but few managers have this luxury. However, clarifying the resource allocation process and making the connection between performance and resources (e.g., office space, budgets) explicit can discourage dysfunctional political behavior. Providing a supportive organizational climate allows employees to discuss controversial issues promptly and openly, thus preventing an issue from festering and potentially causing friction among employees.[61]

Managing political behavior at work is important, since the perception of dysfunctional political behavior can lead to job dissatisfaction.[62] When employees perceive that there are dominant interest groups or cliques at work, they are less satisfied with pay and promotions. When they believe that the organization's reward practices are influenced by who you know rather than how well you perform, they are less satisfied.[63] Furthermore, when employees believe that their coworkers are exhibiting increased political behavior, they are less satisfied with their coworkers. Open communication, clear expectations about performance and rewards, participative decision-making practices, work group cooperation, effective management of scarce resources, and a supportive organizational climate can help managers prevent the negative consequences of political behavior.

11-6a Managing Up: Managing the Boss

One of the least discussed aspects of power and politics is the relationship between you and your boss. This is a crucial relationship because your boss is your most important link with the rest of the organization.[64] The employee–boss relationship is one of mutual dependence; you depend on your boss to give you performance feedback, provide resources, and supply critical information. Your boss depends on you for performance, information, and support. Because it's a mutual relationship, you should take an active role in managing it. Too often, the management of this relationship is left to the boss; but if the relationship doesn't meet the employee's needs, chances are the employee hasn't taken the responsibility to manage it proactively.

Table 11.3 shows the basic steps to take in managing your relationship with your boss. The first step

alphaspirit/Shutterstock.com

Table 11.3 Managing Your Relationship with Your Boss

Make sure you understand your boss and their context, including:
Their goals and objectives.
The pressures on them.
Their strengths, weaknesses, and blind spots.
Their preferred work style.
Assess yourself and your needs, including:
Your own strengths and weaknesses.
Your personal style.
Your predisposition toward dependence on authority figures.
Develop and maintain a relationship that:
Fits both your boss's and your own needs and styles.
Is characterized by mutual expectations.
Keeps your boss informed.
Is based on dependability and honesty.
Selectively uses your boss's time and resources.

Source: Reprinted with permission of *Harvard Business Review.* From "Managing Your Boss", by J. J. Gabarro and J. P. Kotter (May–June 1993): 155.

is to try to understand as much as you can about your boss. What are their goals and objectives? What kind of pressures do they face in the job? Many individuals naively expect the boss to be perfect and are disappointed when they find that this is not the case. What are the boss's strengths, weaknesses, and blind spots? Because this is an emotionally charged relationship, it is difficult to be objective; but this is a critical step in forging an effective working relationship. What is the boss's preferred work style? Do they prefer everything in writing or hate detail? Does the boss prefer that you make appointments or is dropping in acceptable? The point is to gather as much information about your boss as you can and to try to put yourself in their shoes.

The second step in managing this important relationship is to assess yourself and your own needs much in the same way you analyzed your boss's. What are your strengths, weaknesses, and blind spots? What is your work style? How do you normally relate to authority figures? Some of us have tendencies toward counterdependence; that is, we rebel against the boss as an authority and view them as a hindrance to our performance. Or, in contrast, we might take an overdependent stance, passively accepting the employee–boss relationship and treating the boss as an all-wise, protective parent. What is your tendency? Knowing how you react to authority figures can help you understand your interactions with your boss.

Once you have done a careful self-analysis and tried to understand your boss, the next step is

to work to develop an effective relationship. Both parties' needs and styles must be accommodated. A fundraiser for a large volunteer organization related a story about a new boss, describing him as cold, aloof, unorganized, and inept. She made repeated attempts to meet with him and clarify expectations, and his usual reply was that he didn't have the time. Frustrated, she almost looked for a new job. "I just can't reach him!" was her refrain. Then she stepped back to consider her boss's and her own styles. Being an Intuitive-Feeling type of person, she prefers constant feedback and reinforcement from others. Her boss, an Intuitive-Thinker type, works comfortably without feedback from others and has a tendency to fail to praise or reward others. She sat down with him and cautiously discussed the differences in their needs. This discussion became the basis for working out a comfortable relationship. "I still don't like him, but I understand him better," she said.

Another aspect of managing the relationship involves working out mutual expectations. One key activity is to develop a plan for work objectives and have the boss agree to it.[65] It is important to do things right, but it is also important to do the right things. Neither party to the relationship is a mind reader, so clarifying the goals is a crucial step. Keeping the boss informed is also a priority. No one likes to be caught off guard.

The employee–boss relationship must be based on dependability and honesty. This means giving and receiving positive and negative feedback. Most of us are reluctant to give any feedback to the boss, but positive feedback is welcomed at the top. Negative feedback, while tougher to initiate, can clear the air. If given in a problem-solving format, it can even bring about a closer relationship.[66]

Finally, remember that your boss is on the same team you are. The golden rule is to make your boss look good because you expect the boss to do the same for you.

11-6b Sharing Power: Empowerment

As modern organizations grow flatter, eliminating layers of management, empowerment becomes more and more important. Jay Conger defines **empowerment** as "creating conditions for heightened motivation through the development of a strong sense of personal self efficacy."[67] This means sharing power in such a way that individuals learn to believe in their ability to do the job. The driving idea of empowerment is that the individuals closest to the work and to the customers should make the decisions and that this makes the best use of employees' skills and talents. You can empower yourself by developing your sense of self-efficacy.

Four dimensions comprise the essence of empowerment: meaning, competence, self-determination, and impact.[68] *Meaning* is a fit between the work role and the employee's values and beliefs. It is the engine of empowerment through which employees become energized about their jobs. If employees' hearts are not in their work, they cannot feel empowered. *Competence* is the belief that one has the ability to do the job well. Without competence, employees will feel inadequate and lack a sense of empowerment. *Self-determination* is having control over the way one does work. Employees who feel they're just following orders from the boss cannot feel empowered. *Impact* is the belief that one's job makes a difference within the organization. Without a sense of contributing to a goal, employees cannot feel empowered. Effective empowerment results in employees with better job performance, strong organizational commitment, and lower levels of job stress. One way to make individuals feel more empowered is to empower their work units or teams. Individuals who work in empowered groups feel more psychologically empowered, and this enhances both individual and team performance.[69]

> The driving idea of empowerment is that the individuals closest to the work and to the customers should make the decisions and that this makes the best use of employees' skills and talents.

Empowerment is easy to advocate for but difficult to put into practice. Conger offers some guidelines on how leaders can empower others in the organization. First, managers should express confidence in employees and set high performance expectations. Positive expectations can go a long way toward enabling good performance, as the Pygmalion effect shows (Chapter 3). Second, managers should create opportunities for employees to participate in decision-making. This means participation in the forms of both voice and choice. Employees should not just be asked to contribute their opinions about an issue; they should also have a vote in the decision that is made. One method for increasing participation is using *self-managed teams*, which, as discussed in Chapter 9, are the ultimate in empowered teams because they take on decisions and activities that traditionally belong to managers.

Third, managers should remove bureaucratic constraints that stifle autonomy. Often, companies have antiquated rules and policies that prevent employees from managing themselves. An example is a collection agency, where a manager's signature was once required to approve long-term payment arrangements for delinquent customers. Collectors, who spoke directly with customers, were the best judges of whether the payment arrangements were workable, and having to consult a manager made them feel closely supervised and powerless. The rule was dropped, and collections increased. Fourth, managers should set inspirational or meaningful goals. When individuals feel they "own" a goal, they are more willing to take personal responsibility for it.

Empowerment is a matter of degree. Jobs can be thought of in two dimensions: job content and job context. *Job content* consists of the tasks and procedures necessary for doing a particular job. *Job context* is broader. It is the reason the organization needs the job and includes the way the job fits into the organization's mission, goals, and objectives. These two dimensions are depicted in Figure 11.1, the employee empowerment grid.

Both axes of the grid contain the major steps in the decision-making process. As shown on the

empowerment Sharing power in such a way that individuals learn to believe in their ability to do the job.

Figure 11.1 Employee Empowerment Grid

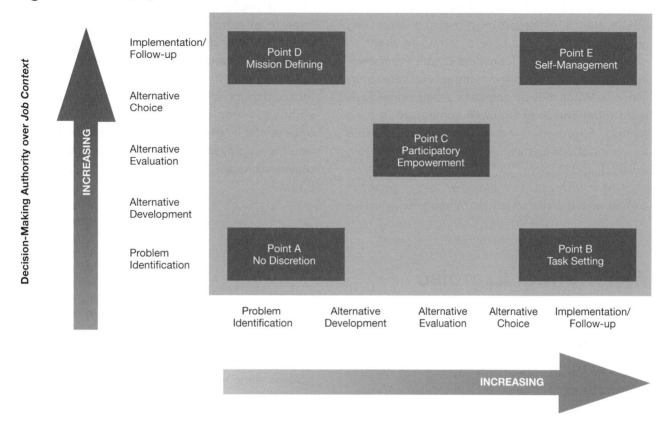

Decision-Making Authority over *Job Content*

horizontal axis, decision-making authority over job content increases in terms of greater involvement in the decision-making process. Similarly, the vertical axis shows that authority over job context increases with greater involvement in that decision-making process. Combining job content and job context authority in this way produces five points that vary in terms of the degree of empowerment.[70]

No Discretion (point A) represents the traditional, assembly-line job—highly routine and repetitive with no decision-making power. Recall from Chapter 7 that if these jobs have a demanding pace and if workers have no discretion, distress will result.

Task Setting (point B) is the essence of most empowerment programs in organizations today. In this case, the worker is empowered to make decisions about the best way to get the job done but has no decision responsibility for the job context.

Participatory Empowerment (point C) represents a situation that is typical of autonomous work groups that have some decision-making power over both job content and job context. Their involvement is in identifying problems, developing alternatives,

and evaluating alternatives, but the actual choice of alternatives is often beyond their power. Participatory empowerment can lead to job satisfaction and productivity.

Mission Defining (point D) is an unusual case of empowerment and is seldom seen. Here, employees have power over job context but not job content. An example would be a unionized team that is asked to decide whether their jobs could be better done by an outside vendor. Deciding to outsource would dramatically affect the mission of the company but would not affect job content, which is specified in the union contract. Assuring these employees of continued employment regardless of their decision would be necessary for this case of empowerment.

Self-Management (point E) represents total decision-making control over both job content and job context. It is the ultimate expression of trust. One example is TXI Chaparral Steel (part of Texas Industries), where employees redesign their own jobs to add value to the organization.

Empowerment should begin with job content and proceed to job context. Because the workforce is so diverse, managers should recognize that some employees are more ready for empowerment than others. Hence, managers must diagnose situations and determine the degree of empowerment to extend to employees. Managers can also empower entire teams of employees with appropriate interventions. When they do empower a team, individuals learn more and they are more committed to their teams.[71] Empowered individuals are also valuable to organizations because they are more motivated, satisfied, and creative.[72]

Unfortunately, the empowerment process carries with it a risk of failure. When you delegate responsibility and authority, you must be prepared to allow employees to fail, and failure is not something most managers tolerate well. Although the airline industry gets criticized for poor customer service, Southwest Airlines has maintained its loyal following for fifty years by providing excellent service through empowering employees. Southwest empowers employees to bend the rules if they believe it's in the customer's best interest. The result is employees who go the extra mile to make customers happy, because it's within their power to do so.[73]

Experiential Exercise

Empowerment in the Classroom

1. Divide the class into groups of six people.

2. Each group is to brainstorm ways in which students might be more empowered in the classroom. The ideas do not have to be either feasible or reasonable. They can be as imaginative as possible.

3. Each group should now analyze each of the empowerment ideas for feasibility, paying attention to administrative or other constraints that may hamper implementation. This feasibility discussion might include ideas about how the college or university could be altered.

4. Each group should present its empowerment ideas along with its feasibility analysis. Questions of clarification for each group should follow each presentation.

5. Discuss the following questions as a class:
   a. Who is threatened by the power changes caused by empowerment?
   b. Are there unintended or adverse consequences of empowerment? Explain.

Learning Objectives

11-1 **Describe the concept of power.** Power is the ability to influence others. Influence is the process of affecting the thoughts, behavior, and feelings of others. Authority is the right to influence others. Power is an exchange relationship.

11-2 **Identify forms and sources of power in organizations.** Power in organizations can be categorized simply as interpersonal or intergroup. French and Raven's five forms of interpersonal power are reward, coercive, legitimate, referent, and expert power. Information power is another form of interpersonal power. Intergroup power derives from control of critical resources and of strategic contingencies. To have control over contingencies, a group must be able to cope with uncertainty, have a high degree of centrality, and perform a function indispensable to the organization.

11-3 **Describe the role of ethics in using power.** The key to using all of these types of power well is to use them ethically. McClelland believes personal power is negative and social power is positive. That is, when power is used for the good of the group rather than for individual gain, the power is positive.

11-4 **Identify symbols of power and powerlessness in organizations.** Two theorists examine symbols of power: Rosabeth Moss Kanter's list of symbols is grounded in doing things for others: for people in trouble, for employees, for bosses. There is an active, other-directed element in her symbols. Michael Korda's list focuses on status and whether there are more people for whom you would inconvenience yourself than people who would inconvenience themselves for you.

11-5 Define organizational politics through an understanding of the role of political skill, influence tactics and political capital. Organizational politics is an inevitable feature of work life. Political behavior consists of actions not officially sanctioned that are taken to influence others in order to meet personal goals. Managers should take a proactive role in managing politics. Political skill is the ability to get things done through favorable interpersonal relationships outside formally prescribed organizational mechanisms.

11-6 Identify political behavior and how to navigate it in organizations. To manage political behavior in their employees, managers can: use open communication; clarify expectations regarding employee performance; use participative management techniques; encourage cooperation among work groups; manage scarce resources well; and provide a supportive organizational climate. Individuals must also manage up—that is, manage the boss. The biggest trump to political behavior is empowerment.

Key Terms

authority The right to influence another person. (p. 225)

coercive power Power that is based on an agent's ability to cause an unpleasant experience for a target. (p. 225)

empowerment Sharing power in such a way that individuals learn to believe in their ability to do the job. (p. 240)

expert power The power that exists when an agent has specialized knowledge or skills that the target needs. (p. 226)

influence The process of affecting the thoughts, behavior, and feelings of another person. (p. 225)

information power Access to and control over important information. (p. 228)

legitimate power Power that is based on position and mutual agreement; agent and target agree that the agent has the right to influence the target. (p. 226)

organizational politics The use of power and influence in organizations. (p. 233)

personal power Power used for personal gain. (p. 230)

political behavior Actions not officially sanctioned by an organization that are taken to influence others in order to meet one's personal goals. (p. 233)

political capital The ability to command power and influence in organizations. (p. 237)

political skill The ability to get things done through favorable interpersonal relationships outside formally prescribed organizational mechanisms. (p. 236)

power The ability to influence another person. (p. 225)

powerlessness A lack of power. (p. 232)

referent power An elusive power that is based on interpersonal attraction. (p. 226)

reward power Power based on an agent's ability to control rewards that a target wants. (p. 225)

social power Power used to create motivation or to accomplish group goals. (p. 230)

strategic contingencies Activities that other groups depend on in order to complete their tasks. (p. 227)

zone of indifference The range in which attempts to influence a person will be perceived as legitimate and will be acted on without a great deal of thought. (p. 225)

Ethical Dilemma

Frank is an architect with Design Solutions. He enjoys his work but is committed to work-life balance. His designs are good, and clients really like him. But Frank is very clear that work should never get in the way of his enjoying his life. He clearly works to live and does not live to work.

Zahir is also an architect and a recent graduate. When he joined Design Solutions, Frank was assigned as his mentor to help him get acclimated to the organization. Zahir really likes Frank and looks up to him as a role model.

Frank was recently given a new assignment on which he has been diligently working. His first draft is due in two weeks, and he feels he should make this deadline easily. On Thursday morning, Frank gets a call from his supervisor informing him that the client is going to be in town a week early and would like to see the first draft early the following week.

This is not good news for Frank. He has big family plans for the weekend. The only way he can meet this accelerated deadline is to cancel his plans and work all weekend. This is not something Frank is willing to do if he can help it.

While Frank is considering his options, Zahir walks into his office. Frank knows that Zahir looks up to him and is always trying to impress him. He knows that Zahir would jump at the chance to work on a project with him. Zahir is a talented architect and Frank could give him a piece of the design to finish for him.

Frank considers taking advantage of Zahir's desire to impress him to resolve his weekend conflict. He feels like he has paid his dues, Zahir should do the same. Zahir wants to make a good impression, and this will give him that opportunity.

1. Using consequential, rule-based, and character theories, evaluate Frank's options.

2. What should Frank do? Why?

Chapter 12

Ringo Chiu/Shutterstock.com

Leadership and Followership

Learning Objectives

12-1 Discuss the differences between leadership and management and between leaders and managers.

12-2 Explain the role of trait theory in describing leaders.

12-3 Describe the role of foundational behavioral research in the development of leadership theories.

12-4 Compare and contrast the four contingency theories of leadership.

12-5 Discuss contemporary leadership frameworks such as leader–member exchange and inspirational styles.

12-6 Discuss emerging issues in leadership, including gender and the use of artificial intelligence.

12-7 Define followership and identify different types of followers.

12-8 Synthesize historical leadership research into key guidelines for leaders.

Leadership in organizations is the process of guiding and directing the behavior of people in the work environment. In the first section, we discuss the ways that leadership differs from *management*. **Formal leadership** is officially sanctioned leadership based on the authority of a formal position. **Informal leadership** is unofficial leadership accorded to a person by other members of the organization. Though one of the most researched topics in organizational behavior, leadership remains one of the least understood social processes in organizations.

12-1 Leadership Versus Management

John Kotter describes leadership and management as two distinct yet complementary systems of action in organizations.[1] Specifically, he believes that effective leadership produces useful change in organizations while good management controls complexity in the organization and its environment.

The *management process* involves (1) planning and budgeting, (2) organizing and staffing, and (3) controlling and problem solving. Done effectively, the management process reduces uncertainty and stabilizes an organization. Alfred P. Sloan's integration and stabilization of General Motors after its early years of growth are an example of good management. In contrast, the *leadership process* involves (1) setting a direction for the organization; (2) aligning people with that direction through communication; and (3) motivating people to action, partly through empowerment and partly through basic need gratification. The leadership process creates uncertainty and change in an organization.

> **Healthy organizations need both effective leadership and good management.**

Effective leaders not only control the future of the organization but also act as enablers of change in organizations. They disturb existing patterns of behaviors, promote novel ideas, and help organizational members make sense of the change process.[2] Sheryl Sandberg, chief operating officer of Facebook, knows about creating change. Since joining the company in 2007, she has helped lead the company to great success by creating an advertising platform that's attracted the world's largest brands.[3]

Abraham Zaleznik proposes that leaders have distinct personalities that stand in contrast to the personalities of managers.[4] Therefore, although both leaders and managers make valuable contributions to an organization, their contributions are different. Whereas **leaders** agitate for change and new approaches, **managers** advocate stability and the status quo. As a result, there is a dynamic tension between leaders and managers that makes it difficult for each to understand the other. Leaders and managers differ along four separate dimensions of personality: attitudes toward goals, conceptions of work, relationships with other people, and sense of self. The differences between these two personality types are summarized in Table 12.1.

It has been proposed that some people are *strategic leaders* who combine the stability of managers with the visionary abilities of leaders in a synergistic way.

leadership The process of guiding and directing the thoughts, feelings, and behavior of people in the work environment.

formal leadership Officially sanctioned leadership based on the authority of a formal position.

informal leadership Unofficial leadership accorded to a person by other members of the organization.

leaders An advocate for change and new approaches to problems.

managers An advocate for stability and the status quo.

Ian Tuttle/Getty Images Entertainment/Getty Images

Everette Taylor, CEO of Kickstarter, leads the funding platform with an emphasis on supporting creative projects.

Table 12.1 Leaders and Managers

Personality Dimension	Manager	Leader
Attitudes toward goals	Has an impersonal, passive, functional attitude; believes goals rise out of necessity and reality	Has a personal and active attitude; believes goals arise from desire and imagination
Conceptions of work	Views work as an enabling process that combines people, ideas, and things; seeks moderate risk through coordination and balance	Looks for fresh approaches to old problems; seeks high-risk positions, especially with high payoffs
Relationships with others	Avoids solitary work activity, preferring to work with others; avoids close, intense relationships; avoids conflict	Is comfortable in solitary work activity; encourages close, intense working relationships; is not conflict averse
Sense of self	Is once born; makes a straightforward life adjustment; accepts life as it is	Is twice born; engages in a struggle for a sense of order in life; questions life

Source: Reprinted by permission of *Harvard Business Review*. From "Managers and Leaders: Are They Different?" by A. Zaleznik (January 2004).

PepsiCo's CEO Indra Nooyi shifted the company's strategy toward healthier options, and it has paid off. Less than 25 percent of sales come from soda, and the emphasis now is on water and noncarbonated beverages, along with Frito-Lay and Quaker products.[5]

12-2 Early Trait Theories

The first studies of leadership attempted to identify what physical attributes, personality characteristics, and abilities distinguished leaders from other members of a group.[6] The physical attributes that were considered were height, weight, physique, energy, health, appearance, and age. Although this line of research yielded some interesting findings, it provided insufficient evidence for concluding that leaders can be distinguished on the basis of physical attributes.

Leader *personality* characteristics that have been examined include originality, adaptability, introversion–extroversion, dominance, self-confidence, integrity, conviction, mood optimism, and emotional control. There is some evidence that leaders may be more adaptable and self-confident than the average group member. With regard to leader *abilities*, attention has been devoted to such constructs as social skills, intelligence, scholarship, speech fluency, cooperativeness, and insight. In this area, there is some evidence that leaders are more intelligent, verbal, and cooperative and have a higher level of scholarship than the average group member.

Nonetheless, these findings are neither strong nor uniform. For each attribute or trait claimed to distinguish leaders from followers, there were always at least one or two studies with contradictory findings. For some, the trait theories are invalid, though interesting and intuitively of some relevance. It is generally agreed that the trait theories have had very limited success in being able to identify universal, distinguishing attributes of leaders.

12-3 Behavioral Theories

Behavioral theories emerged as a response to the deficiencies of the trait theories. Trait theories attempted to tell us who leaders are, but didn't address how leaders behaved or what they did on a daily basis. Moreover, trait research did not provide much information on the trainability of leadership. That is, we cannot change/develop or train personality or physical attributes. But we can train people to act more leader-like.[7] Three research studies built the foundations of many modern leadership theories: the Lewin, Lippitt, and White studies; the Ohio State studies; and the Michigan studies.

12-3a Foundational Behavioral Research

The earliest research on leadership style, conducted by Kurt Lewin and his students, identified three basic styles: autocratic, democratic, and laissez-faire.[8] A leader uses one of these three basic styles when approaching a

People First at Marriott International

What should leadership prioritize: the tasks or the people? While research supports the idea that leaders can be both task- and relationship-oriented, sometimes one approach takes priority over the other. For leaders at Marriott International, the answer is clear: put the people first.

Ty Breland, Marriott's chief human resource officer, calls their approach a "people first mindset." For him, that starts with the hiring process. Breland explains that being people-oriented means hiring "the whole person" and investing in all aspects of their life, not just their work life. In addition, he believes it is important to allow employees to be their whole selves at work.

Breland also sees this people-first mindset in the way that the leadership team makes decisions. He notes that the first question the team asks is how a decision will impact employees: "It's the very first question we ask...And we wrestle through that. We think through that. And then we move on to other elements of the strategy. But it always starts with that putting people first mindset."

The people-first mindset that Breland describes at Marriott is a good example of a relationship-focused (consideration) style of leadership. While this orientation can have downsides, it has worked well for Marriott: the hotel chain has maintained a spot in the top 100 Best Companies to Work For list for 25 years.

Source: R. Amire. "People-First Culture Vital to Marriott's 25-Year Run as One of the 100 Best Companies." *Great Place to Work*. April 11, 2022.

group of followers in a leadership situation. The specific situation is not an important consideration because the leader's style does not vary with the situation. The leader with an **autocratic style** uses strong, directive actions to control the rules, regulations, activities, and relationships in the work environment. Followers have little discretionary influence over the nature of the work, its accomplishment, or other aspects of the work environment. The leader with a **democratic style** uses interaction and collaboration with followers to direct work and the work environment. Followers have a high degree of discretionary influence, although the leader has ultimate authority and responsibility. The leader with a **laissez-faire style** entails a hands-off approach. A laissez-faire leader abdicates the authority and responsibility of the position, and this style often results in chaos. Laissez-faire leadership also causes role ambiguity for followers because the leader fails to clearly define goals, responsibilities, and outcomes. It leads to higher interpersonal conflict at work.[9]

The leadership research program at The Ohio State University also measured specific leader behaviors. The initial results suggested that there were two important underlying dimensions of leader behaviors—initiating structure and consideration.[10] **Initiating structure** is leader behavior aimed at defining and organizing work relationships and roles, as well as establishing clear patterns of organization, communication, and ways of getting things done. **Consideration** is leader behavior aimed at nurturing friendly, warm working relationships, as well as encouraging mutual trust and interpersonal respect within the work unit. These two leader behaviors are independent of each other; that is, a leader may be high on both, low on both, or high on one and low on the other.[11]

Finally, studies conducted at the University of Michigan suggest that the leader's style has very important implications for the emotional atmosphere of the work environment and, therefore, for the followers who work under that leader. Two styles of leadership were identified: production oriented and employee oriented.[12]

A *production-oriented style* leads to a work environment where the focus is on getting things done.

autocratic style A style of leadership in which the leader uses strong, directive actions to control the rules, regulations, activities, and relationships in the work environment.

democratic style A style of leadership in which the leader uses interaction and collaboration with followers to direct the work and work environment.

laissez-faire style A style of leadership in which the leader has a hands-off approach.

initiating structure Leader behavior aimed at defining and organizing work relationships and roles, as well as establishing clear patterns of organization, communication, and ways of getting things done.

consideration Leader behavior aimed at nurturing friendly, warm working relationships as well as encouraging mutual trust and interpersonal respect within the work unit.

The leader in this environment uses direct, close supervision or many written and unwritten rules and regulations to control behavior.

In contrast, an *employee-oriented leadership* style leads to a work environment that focuses on relationships. The leader exhibits less direct, or less close, supervision and establishes fewer written or unwritten rules and regulations for behavior. Employee-oriented leaders display concern for people and their needs.

Taken together, these three groups of studies (the Lewin studies, the Ohio State studies, and the Michigan studies) form the building blocks of many recent leadership theories. What the studies have in common is that two basic leadership styles were identified, with one focusing on *tasks* (autocratic, production oriented, initiating structure) and one focusing on *people* (democratic, employee oriented, consideration). Now, after the global COVID-19 pandemic and normalization of virtual work, one might wonder if these task- and people-focused leader behaviors still are useful? Research is emerging on these topics but early evidence indicates that when crises strike, leaders have to focus on stability and a return to status quo engaging in task- and people-oriented behaviors.[13]

12-4 Contingency Theories

Contingency theories involve the belief that leadership style must be appropriate for the particular situation. By their nature, contingency theories are if-then theories: If the situation is *x*, then the appropriate leadership behavior is *y*. We examine four such theories, including Fiedler's contingency theory, path–goal theory, normative decision theory, and situational leadership theory.

12-4a Fiedler's Contingency Theory

Fiedler's contingency theory of leadership proposes that the fit between the leader's need structure and the favorableness of the leader's situation determines the team's effectiveness in work accomplishment. This theory assumes that leaders are either task oriented or relationship oriented, depending upon how the leaders obtain their primary need gratification.[14] Task-oriented leaders are primarily gratified by accomplishing tasks and getting work done. Relationship-oriented leaders are primarily gratified by developing good, comfortable interpersonal relationships. Accordingly, the effectiveness of both types of leaders depends on the favorableness of their situation. The theory classifies the favorableness of the leader's situation according to the leader's position power, the structure of the team's task, and the quality of the leader–follower relationships.

The Least Preferred Coworker Fiedler classifies leaders using the Least Preferred Coworker (LPC) Scale, a projective technique in which a leader is asked to choose the person they least prefer to work with (the **least preferred coworker**, or **LPC**).[15] The leader is asked to describe this LPC using sixteen eight-point bipolar adjective sets. Two of these bipolar adjective sets follow (the leader marks the one most descriptive of the LPC):

> Efficient : : : : : : : : : Inefficient
> Cheerful : : : : : : : : : Gloomy

Leaders who describe their LPC in positive terms (i.e., pleasant, efficient, cheerful, and so on) are classified as high LPC, or relationship-oriented, leaders. Those who describe their LPC in negative terms (i.e., unpleasant, inefficient, gloomy, and so on) are classified as low LPC, or task-oriented, leaders.

The LPC score is a controversial element in contingency theory.[16] It has been critiqued conceptually and methodologically because it is a projective technique with low measurement reliability.

Situational Favorableness The leader's situation has three dimensions: task structure, position power, and leader–member relations. Based on these three dimensions, the situation is either favorable or unfavorable for the leader. **Task structure** refers to the degree of clarity, or ambiguity, in the work activities assigned to the group. **Position power** refers to the authority associated with the leader's formal position in the organization.

Leader–member relations, the quality of interpersonal relationships among a leader and the group

---

least preferred coworker (LPC) The person a leader has least preferred to work with.

task structure The degree of clarity, or ambiguity, in the work activities assigned to the group.

position power The authority associated with the leader's formal position in the organization.

leader–member relations The quality of interpersonal relationships among a leader and the group members.

> Recent research has shown that relationship-oriented leaders encourage team learning and innovation, which helps products get to market faster.

	Favorable	
	Moderate	**Unfavorable**
Task structure	Structured	Unstructured
Position power	Strong	Weak
Leader–member relations	Good	Poor

members, is measured by the *Group-Atmosphere Scale*, composed of nine eight-point bipolar adjective sets. Two of these bipolar adjective sets follow:

Friendly : : : : : : : : Unfriendly
Accepting : : : : : : : : Rejecting

A favorable leadership situation, according to Fiedler, is one with a structured task for the work group, strong position power for the leader, and good leader–member relations. In contrast, an unfavorable leadership situation is one with an unstructured task, weak position power for the leader, and moderately poor leader–member relations. Between these two extremes, the leadership situation has varying degrees of moderate favorableness for the leader.

Leadership Effectiveness The contingency theory suggests that low LPC and high LPC leaders are both effective if placed in the right situation.[17] Specifically, low LPC (task-oriented) leaders are most effective in either very favorable or very unfavorable leadership situations. In contrast, high LPC (relationship-oriented) leaders are most effective in situations of intermediate favorableness. Figure 12.1 shows the nature of these relationships and suggests that leadership effectiveness is determined by the degree of fit between the leader and the situation. Recent research has shown that relationship-oriented leaders encourage team learning and innovation, which helps products get to market faster. This means that

Figure 12.1 Leadership Effectiveness in the Contingency Theory

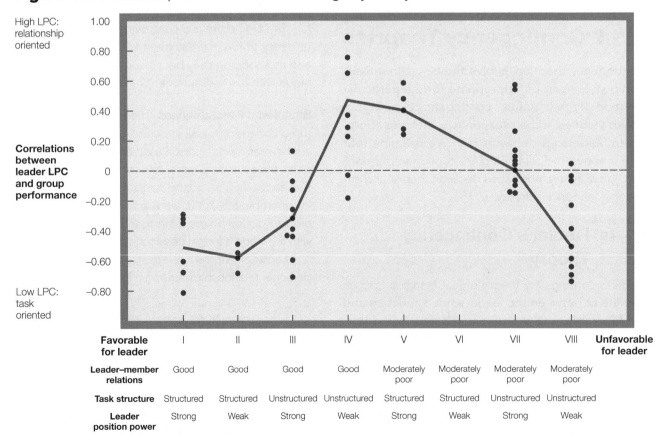

Source: F. E. Fiedler, *A Theory of Leader Effectiveness* (New York: McGraw-Hill, 1964). Reprinted with permission of the author.

most relationship-oriented leaders perform well in leading new product development teams. In short, the right team leader can help get new products out the door faster, while a mismatch between the leader and the situation can have the opposite effect.[18]

What, then, is to be done if there is a misfit? What happens when a low LPC leader is in a moderately favorable situation or when a high LPC leader is in a highly favorable or highly unfavorable situation? It is unlikely that the leader can be changed, according to the theory, because the leader's need structure is an enduring trait that is hard to change. Fiedler recommends that the situation be changed to fit the leader's style.[19] A moderately favorable situation would be reengineered to be more favorable and therefore more suitable for the low LPC leader. A highly favorable or highly unfavorable situation would be changed to one that is moderately favorable and more suitable for the high LPC leader.

12-4b Path–Goal Theory

Robert House developed a path–goal theory of leader effectiveness based on an expectancy theory of motivation.[20] From the perspective of path–goal theory, the basic role of the leader is to clear the follower's path to the goal. The leader uses the most appropriate of four leader behavior styles to help followers clarify the paths that lead them to work and personal goals. The key concepts in the theory are shown in Figure 12.2.

A leader selects from the four leader behavior styles, shown in Figure 12.2, the one that is most helpful to followers at a given time. The directive style is used when the leader must give specific guidance about work tasks, schedule work, and let followers know what is expected. The *supportive style* is used when the leader needs to express concern for followers' well-being and social status. The *participative style* is used when the leader must engage in joint decision-making activities with followers. The *achievement-oriented style* is used when the leader must set challenging goals for followers and show strong confidence in those followers.

In selecting the appropriate leader behavior style, the leader must consider both the followers and the work environment. A number of characteristics are included in Figure 12.2. Let us consider two scenarios. In scenario one, the followers are inexperienced and are working on an ambiguous, unstructured task. The leader in this situation might best use a directive style. In scenario two, the followers are highly trained professionals, and the task is difficult but achievable. The leader in this situation might best use an achievement-oriented style.

In path–goal theory, the leader always chooses the leader behavior style that helps followers achieve their goals. The theory assumes that leaders adapt their behavior and style to fit the characteristics of the followers and the environment in which they work. Actual tests of the path–goal theory and its propositions provide conflicting evidence.[21] The path–goal theory does have intuitive appeal and reinforces the idea that the appropriate leadership style depends on both the work situation and the followers. Research is focusing on which style works best in specific situations. For example, in small organizations, leaders

Figure 12.2 The Path–Goal Theory of Leadership

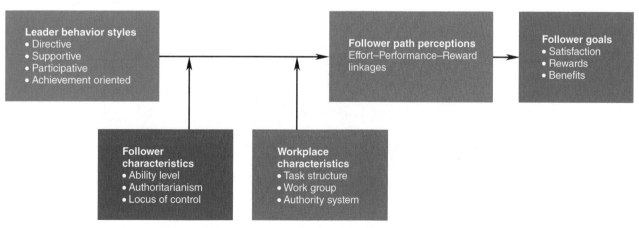

who used visionary, transactional, and empowering behaviors, while avoiding autocratic behaviors, were most successful.[22]

12-4c The Situational Leadership® Model

The Situational Leadership model, developed by Paul Hersey and Kenneth Blanchard, suggests that the leader's behavior should be adjusted to the maturity level of the followers.[23] The model employs two dimensions of leader behavior as used in the Ohio State studies; one dimension is task oriented, and the other is relationship oriented. Follower maturity is categorized into four levels, as shown in Figure 12.3. Follower readiness is determined by the follower's ability and willingness to complete a specific task. Readiness can therefore be low or high depending on the particular task. In addition, readiness varies within a single person according to the task. One person may be willing and able to satisfy simple requests from customers (high readiness) but less able or willing to give highly technical advice to customers (low readiness). It is important that the leader be able to evaluate the readiness level of each follower for each task. The four styles of leader behavior associated with the four readiness levels are depicted in Figure 12.3.

According to the Situational Leadership model, a leader should use a *telling style* (S1) when a follower is unable and unwilling to do a certain task. This style involves providing instructions and closely monitoring performance. As such, the telling style involves considerable task behavior and low relationship behavior. When a follower is unable but willing and confident to do a task, the leader can use the *selling style* (S2), in which there is high task behavior and high relationship behavior. In this case, the leader explains decisions and provides opportunities for the employee to seek clarification or help. Sometimes a follower will be able to complete a task but may seem unwilling or insecure about doing so. In these cases, a *participating style* (S3) is warranted, which involves high relationship but low task behavior. The leader here encourages the follower to participate in decision-making. Finally, for tasks in which a follower is able and willing, the leader is able to use a *delegating style* (S4), characterized by low task behavior and low relationship behavior. In this case, follower readiness is high, and low levels of leader involvement (task or relationship) are needed.

One key limitation of the situational leadership model is the absence of central hypotheses that could be tested and would therefore make it a more valid, reliable theory of leadership.[24] However, the theory has intuitive appeal and is widely used for training and development in corporations. In addition, the theory focuses attention on follower maturity as an important determinant of the leadership process.

Figure 12.3 The Situational Leadership Model

FOLLOWER READINESS			
LOW	**MODERATE**	**MODERATE**	**HIGH**
Unwilling and unable followers	Willing and unable followers	Unwilling but able followers	Willing and able followers

TELLING	**SELLING**	**PARTICIPATING**	**DELEGATING**
Give specific instructions and supervise closely	Clarify and explain decisions as needed	Share ideas with followers and facilitate their decision-making	Empower followers to make the decisions
Task Behaviors	High	High	Low	Low
Relationship Behaviors	Low	High	High	Low

12-5 Contemporary Leadership Frameworks

Many contemporary and cutting edge developments in leadership merit discussion here, specifically, leader–member exchange and inspirational leadership styles, which includes transformational and charismatic leadership [25] as well as the dark side of leadership, abusive supervision.

12-5a Leader–Member Exchange

Leader–member exchange theory, or *LMX*, recognizes that leaders may form different relationships with followers. LMX is defined as the quality of the relationship between a leader and follower.[26] Higher quality relationships with the leader lead to being in the *in-group*, with greater responsibilities, more rewards, and more attention. Those in the in-group work within the leader's inner circle of communication. As a result, in-group members are more satisfied, have lower turnover, and have higher organizational commitment. In contrast, lower quality relationships or simply low LMX leads to being in the *out-group* and receiving less attention and fewer rewards. They are managed by formal rules and policies.[27]

Research on LMX is fascinating. Amongst all of the leadership frameworks discussed until now, LMX has the most scientific support in predicting important follower outcomes such as performance, job satisfaction, and commitment.[28,29] These findings are intuitive and simply boil down to: An employee's relationship with the boss is a key predictor of their performance, in deciding to stay or leave, and in going above and beyond for the company. What explains the differences in work relationships though? Two theories have tried to explain how LMX relationships develop into high or low quality. First is role theory: This suggests that the leader–follower relationship goes through three phases: strangers, acquaintance, and a mature friendship phase. Leaders test followers in each successive phase and progression through all phases is not guaranteed. For example, a follower who excels at tasks assigned might quickly progress into an acquaintance or friend stage wherein the boss trusts them with increasing responsibilities, allows decision-making latitude and such.

> Employees who enjoy more frequent contact with the boss also have a better understanding of what the boss's expectations are.

From here, if they deliver, role theory suggests that the follower then moves into a friendship phase with the leader based on trust, affection and a concern for the followers' career and forward progression.

Second is social exchange theory that extends the explanation above and suggests that LMX develops based on reciprocal social and task related interactions. These interactions could be subsumed under the different stages per role theory above. Do you have such a social exchange-based relationship with your boss? Take You 12.1 below to find out.

Relationships are a cornerstone of leadership. Creating and cultivating high-quality relationships is critical. But LMX has drawn severe critiques as well. One such critique is that much of what we know about LMX is drawn from follower reports of their LMX with the leader. Yet, any relationship involves two parties. When the leader and follower both are surveyed, studies have found that the positive benefits ascribed to LMX (e.g., follower performance, satisfaction) are only evident when both parties have similar perceptions of their LMX. When leader and follower do not share such perceptions of their relationship, such positive benefits do not ensue. Thus, this line of studies suggests that developing high-quality relationships is a two-party effort.[30,31,32]

12-5b Inspirational Leadership

Leadership is an exciting area of organizational behavior, one in which new research is constantly emerging. Many scientists have noted that our collective fascination with great leaders and how they lead dates back to the ancient Greeks. In addition, implicitly and explicitly, we routinely cast leaders as being inspirational and somewhat superhuman.[33] Two key frameworks fall under this school of inspirational leader styles: transformational leadership and charismatic leadership. These theories can be called *inspirational leadership theories* because in each one, followers are inspired by the leader to perform beyond expectations.

Transformational Leadership *Transactional leaders*, you will recall, are those who use rewards and

LMSX

Think about your overall relationship with your supervisor. Please rate the extent to which you agree with the statements below using the scale provided.

LMSX	Strongly disagree (1)	Disagree (2)	Neither Agree nor Disagree (3)	Agree (4)	Strongly Agree (5)
My supervisor and I had a two-way exchange relationship. (1)	◯	◯	◯	◯	◯
I did not have to specify the exact conditions to know my supervisor would return a favor. (2)	◯	◯	◯	◯	◯
If I did something for my supervisor, they would eventually repay me. (3)	◯	◯	◯	◯	◯
I had a balance of inputs and outputs with my supervisor. (4)	◯	◯	◯	◯	◯
My supervisor reciprocated my efforts. (5)	◯	◯	◯	◯	◯
My relationship with my supervisor was composed of comparable exchanges of giving and receiving. (6)	◯	◯	◯	◯	◯
When I gave effort at work, my supervisor would return it. (7)	◯	◯	◯	◯	◯
Voluntary actions on my part would be returned in some way by my supervisor. (8)	◯	◯	◯	◯	◯

Source: J. B. Bernerth, A. A. Armenakis, H. S. Field, W. F. Giles, and H. J. Walker, "Leader-Member Social Exchange (LMSX): Development and Validation of a Scale," *Journal of Organizational Behavior* 28 (2007): 979–1003.

Interpretation: Higher scores represent better LMX. These scores develop over time and as a function of investments in the relationship by both parties.

punishment to strike deals with followers and shape their behavior. In contrast, *transformational leaders* inspire and excite followers to high levels of performance.[34] They rely on their personal attributes instead of their official position to manage followers. There is some evidence that transformational leadership can be learned.[35] Transformational leadership consists of the following four subdimensions: charisma, individualized consideration, inspirational motivation, and intellectual stimulation. We describe *charisma* in detail shortly. *Individualized consideration* refers to how much concern the leader displays for each follower's individual needs and acts as a coach or a mentor. *Inspirational motivation* is the extent to which the leader is able to articulate a vision that is appealing to followers.[36]

Transformational leadership has been shown to increase firm performance. U.S. corporations increasingly operate in a global economy, so there is a greater demand for leaders who can practice transformational leadership by converting their visions into reality and by inspiring followers to perform "above and beyond the call of duty."[37] Howard Schultz, founder and chair of Starbucks Coffee, is the transformational leader and visionary heart of Starbucks. After two stints as CEO, Schultz will remain as executive chair and turns his attention to building Starbucks' new premium Roasteries and high-end Reserve coffee.[38]

Transformational leadership is very important for individual followers as well. Transformational leadership that is focused on individuals increases task performance and initiative. Employees who work for a transformational leader are more satisfied, motivated, and perform better than those who do not.[39] Leaders can be both transformational and transactional.[40] However, whereas transformational leadership adds to the effects of transactional leadership, even exceptional transactional leadership cannot substitute for transformational leadership.[41] Questions have been raised about whether transformational leadership is effective with Millennials. Because Millennials are individualistic and see work as less central to their lives, transformational leadership may be less effective at motivating them to put the company's needs first. The inspirational nature of transformational leadership and intrinsic rewards may not be effective for Millennials, who are more interested in extrinsic rewards such as rapid recognition and advancement.[42]

Charismatic Leadership Steve Jobs, the pioneer behind Apple, had an uncanny ability to create a vision and convince others to become part of it. Jobs's unique ability was so powerful that Apple employees coined a term in the 1980s for it—the *reality-distortion field*. This expression is used to describe the persuasive ability and peculiar charisma of managers like Steve Jobs. His reality-distortion field allowed Jobs to convince even skeptics that his plans were worth supporting, no matter how unworkable they may appear. Those close to charismatic managers become passionately committed to possibly insane projects without regard to the practicality of their implementation or competitive forces in the marketplace.[43]

Charismatic leadership results when a leader uses the force of personal abilities and talents to have profound and extraordinary effects on followers.[44] Charismatic leadership falls to those who are chosen (are born with the "gift" of charisma) or who cultivate that gift. Charismatic leadership has been sharply criticized for its lack of scientific validity and tautological definitions. That is, charisma and to an extent transformational leadership are both defined in terms of their effects on followers. To remedy this issue, Antonakis and colleagues created a new definition of charismatic leadership below.[45]

Charisma can be taught in the form of charismatic leadership tactics (CLTs).[46] The evidence on the efficacy of such CLTs is still emerging but thus far it appears to be a promising path in the training and development of charismatic leadership. Curious about what these CLTs are? See Table 12.2 below.[47]

Charismatic leadership carries with it not only great potential for high levels of achievement and performance on the part of followers but also shadowy risks of destructive courses of action that might harm followers or other people.[48] The ugly face of charisma is revealed in the personalized power motivations of Adolf Hitler in Nazi Germany and David Koresh of the Branch Davidian cult in Waco, Texas. Both men led

charismatic leadership A leader's values-based, emotion-laden signaling.

Table 12.2 Charismatic Leadership Tactics (CLTs)

CLTs: 12 Total = 9 Verbal + 3 Non-Verbal

Verbal	Non-Verbal
Metaphors or Similes	Animated Voice
Stories and Anecdotes	Facial Expressions
Setting High Expectations	Gestures
Create Confidence that Goals can be Achieved	
Contrasts	
Moral Conviction	
Sentiment of the Collective	
Lists and Repetition	
Rhetorical Questions	

Source: J. Antonakis, M. Fenley, and S. Liechti, "Learning Charisma. Transform Yourself into the Person Others Want to Follow," *Harvard Business Review* 90, No. 6 (2012): 127–130.

their followers into struggle, conflict, and death. The brighter face of charisma is revealed in the socialized power motivations of former presidents Bill Clinton and Ronald Reagan. While worlds apart in terms of their political beliefs, were actually quite similar in their use of personal charisma to inspire followers and motivate them to pursue a specific vision. In each case, followers perceived the leader as imbued with a unique vision for America and unique abilities to lead the country there.

Despite the tremendous volume of research on the two inspirational styles of leadership noted above, several critiques have emerged.[49] For example, most studies in these domains are correlational, and making causal connection between such inspirational styles and follower or workgroup outcomes is erroneous.[50] Moreover, most of these studies capture follower perceptions rather than actual inspirational leader behaviors.[51] Finally, they cast leaders in a positive light, and such romantic notions of leadership do not quite fit with the changed world we live in today.

Abusive Supervision Research has investigated not only what makes leaders effective but also negative leadership behaviors. The most common include sexual harassment, physical violence, angry outbursts, public ridicule, taking credit for employees' successes, and scapegoating employees.[52] *Abusive supervision*, as these behaviors are called, is estimated to affect about 13 percent of U.S. workers and leads to many negative consequences. Abused workers report diminished well-being along with increased deviance behavior, problem drinking, psychological distress, and emotional exhaustion.[53] In addition, abusive supervision increases absenteeism and reduces productivity. In fact, the cost of abusive supervision to U.S. corporations has been estimated at $23.8 billion.[54] It is not clear why supervisors abuse others. Some research suggests that injustice experienced by supervisors increases the likelihood that they will, in turn, abuse others. Other studies suggest that abuse stems from the failure of managers to control themselves and handle stress.[55] One type of stress that leads to abusive supervision is family-work conflict. Supervisors who experience high levels of conflict between family and work display more abusive behaviors toward direct reports.[56]

Hot Trend

The What and How of Leadership Vision

Visions play an important role in both transformational and charismatic leadership. But what are visions and what makes them capture (or fail to capture) the attention of followers? Research is beginning to focus on these questions, defining visions as *images of the future of a collective* (e.g., an organization, a country). Charismatic and transformational leadership often involves coming up with and communicating a vision—an image of the future of a collective—to others. Unlike concrete goals (e.g., "we will sell X number of items this month"), visions are abstract and represent a bigger-picture aspirational goal. They aren't usually something that can be achieved overnight.

Visions can be highly effective at motivating people. They provide followers with an image of what the collective is trying to achieve, thus promoting behavior that is oriented towards realizing the imaged future. When are visions effective? So far, research has identified at least two factors. First, visions are effective at motivating followers when leaders engage in charismatic behaviors. Communicating a vision in a charismatic manner appears more likely to get followers on board with the vision. Second, visions are more effective when the content of the vision matches the values of the follower. If followers value the things that a leader communicates in their vision, they are more motivated to help pursue that vision.

When are visions most useful? Emerging research suggests that visions are particularly helpful in the context of change. When leaders want to promote changes, particularly big changes, they need to share a vision of what the future of the collective will (or should) look like. But leaders need to be careful; communicating a vision only of what will change can make people resistant. Thus, leaders also need to communicate a vision of what about the collective will be preserved. That is, they need to communicate a vision of change *and* a vision of continuity to get people fully on board.

Source: X.-L. Fan, D. van Knippenberg, and X.-H. (Frank) Wang, "Vision–Value Match: Leader Communication of Visions, Follower Values, Meaningfulness, and Creativity," *European Journal of Work and Organizational Psychology* 31, No. 4 (2022): 550–566; N. Meslec, P. L. Curseu, O. C. Fodor, and R. Kenda, "Effects of Charismatic Leadership and Rewards on Individual Performance," *The Leadership Quarterly* 31, No. 6 (2020): 1–12; M. Venus, D. Stam, and D. van Knippenberg, "Visions of Change as Visions of Continuity," *Academy of Management Journal* 62, No. 3 (2019): 667–690.

12-6 Emerging Issues in Leadership

Along with the recent developments in theory, some exciting issues have emerged of which leaders should be aware. These include moral approaches to leadership, the rise of women leaders, and the use of artificial intelligence in leadership.

12-6a Moral Approaches to Leadership

Three approaches fall under the moral approaches umbrella and have steadily gained momentum: **servant**, **ethical**, and **authentic leadership**.

Servant Leadership Robert Greenleaf, director of management research at AT&T for many years, believed that leaders should serve employees, customers, and the community, and his essays are the basis for today's view of *servant leadership*. His personal and professional philosophy was that leaders lead by serving others. Other tenets of servant leadership are that work exists for the person as much as the person exists for work and that servant leaders try to find out the will of the group and lead based on that. Servant leadership leads to higher team performance and increased organizational citizenship behaviors in the organization.[57] Servant leaders consider themselves stewards who regard leadership as a trust and desire to leave the organization in better shape for future generations.[58] Although Greenleaf's writings were completed thirty years ago, many have now been published and are becoming more popular.

Authentic Leadership A new form of leadership emerged in the early 2000s thanks to the ethical scandals rocking the business environment. In response to concerns about the potential negative side of inspirational forms of leadership, researchers have called for authentic leadership, which includes four key concepts: self-awareness and staying true to one self, balanced processing of information, transparency in interactions with followers, and acting in accordance with the leader's conscious and well-developed sense of values.[59] Because authentic leaders act in ways that are consistent with their value systems, they have a highly evolved sense of moral right and wrong. Authentic leaders are self-aware, confident, optimistic, and resilient. They have

Inclusive Conversations

The Effect of Psychology Diversity Climate (PDC) on Leadership Style

Abusive supervision costs U.S. businesses $23.8 billion annually in terms of increased absenteeism, health care costs, and lost productivity. In fact, leaders are the *primary* reason workers quit their jobs. According to Gallup, 50% of over 7,200 U.S. employees surveyed quit their job because of their boss. Psychological Diversity Climate (PDC) is a term that reflects the extent to which individuals perceive their work environments as fair and inclusive as opposed to abusive and unfair. Much of the existing research on PDC has been focused on understanding the impact of PDC on front-line, non-supervisory employees. Professor Darryl Rice and colleagues extended this research to understanding leaders' own perceptions of PDC and the likelihood that their subordinates will perceive them as having an ethical or abusive leadership style. In addition to other hypotheses, the researchers predicted that supervisors with positive PDC would display an ethical leadership style, and supervisors with negative PDC would display an abusive leadership style. Across three studies (one experimental; the other two using a survey method), the researchers found support for their predictions. These findings are consistent with the idea that leaders are often an extension of the organizations they lead and serve as models for desired employee behavior.

1. In behavioral terms, describe your level of PDC at your current organization, whether school or work.
   Encourage students to describe their PDC in behavioral terms (e.g., What have you done to indicate how fair and inclusive you are?).

2. Speculate on whether and to what extent your supervisor's PDC affects your PDC. In small groups compare your responses to your classmates'.

Sources: D. B. Rice, P. Prosper, and C. Scott, "Leading with DEI on My Mind: Examining the Interactive Effects of Supervisor Perceptions of Psychological Diversity Climate and Supervisor Characteristics on Leadership Style," *Journal of Leadership & Organizational Studies* 30, No. 2 (2023): 239–258; M. Schwantes, "The No. 1 Reason Why Employees Quit Their Managers," *The Future of Leadership*, July 18 (2022), accessed at https://www.linkedin.com/pulse/1-reason-why-employees-quit-managers-marcel-schwantes/.

fizkes/Shutterstock.com

Authentic leaders motivate followers to perform better by developing their hope, optimism, resilience, and self-efficacy.

a deep sense of self and act as role models to others by conveying what they believe and stand for.[60]

Authentic leaders arouse and motivate followers to higher levels of performance by building a workforce characterized by high levels of hope, optimism, resiliency, and self-efficacy.[61] Followers also experience more positive emotions and trust as a result of the authentic leader's transparency and the collective caring climate engendered by such a leader. Researchers contend that this is the kind of leadership embodied by Gandhi, Nelson Mandela, and others like them throughout history. Does authentic leadership sound too good to be true? Can a leader be authentic and yet toxic or abusive? Some authors have argued authenticity is not a necessary condition for effective leadership and further feeds into the positivity trap that pervades leadership science.[62] Time will tell if authenticity in leadership is here to say.[63]

Ethical Leadership A new leadership style was introduced at about the same time as authentic leadership (2005) and for the same reasons. The inspirational leadership styles did not prioritize the goodness of leadership, rather, they simply focused on inspiration which can be deployed for personal or societal good. Ethical leadership is the display of appropriable moral conduct by leaders who also serve as role models for followers' ethical behaviors via such role modeling, reinforcing normative conduct and engaging on communication regarding such norms.[64]

All three moral approaches to leadership have been linked to follower and workgroup outcomes such as job satisfaction, follower ethical behaviors, leader effectiveness, and values that promote a focus on the environment. The empirical evidence for these approaches also suggests that they overlap to a large extent and might not contribute anything unique beyond established leadership theories discussed above. The promise of these approaches, however, is in their focus on leaders and followers doing the right thing. More science is needed before we could draw strong conclusions, however.[65]

12-6b Gender and Leadership

An important, emergent leadership question is whether women and men lead differently. Historical stereotypes persist, and people characterize successful managers as having more male-oriented attributes than female-oriented attributes.[66] Although legitimate gender differences may exist, the same leadership traits may be interpreted differently in a man and a woman because of stereotypes. The real issue should be leader behaviors that are not bound by gender stereotypes.

Early evidence shows that women tend to use a more people-oriented style that is inclusive and empowering. Women managers excel in positions that demand strong interpersonal skills.[67] Even though more and more women are assuming positions of leadership in organizations, interestingly, much of what we know about leadership is based on studies that were conducted on men. We need to know more about the ways women lead.

Recent research looks at the phenomenon of the *glass cliff* (as opposed to the *glass ceiling* effect discussed in Chapter 2). The *glass cliff* represents a trend in organizations wherein more women are placed in difficult leadership situations. Women perceive these assignments as necessary to accept due to the difficulty of attaining leadership positions and lack of alternate opportunities combined with male in-group favoritism. On the other hand, men perceive that women are better suited to difficult leadership positions because women are better decision-makers.[68]

Making matters more complex, all of the leadership theories were fundamentally formulated via followers' observations of predominantly men leaders

Evidence shows that women tend to use a more people-oriented style that is inclusive and empowering. Women managers excel in positions that demand strong interpersonal skills.

during the two world wars and when we lived in a manufacturing, industrialized context. With the shift towards more women in the workforce, and a knowledge- and service-oriented economy, we need new definitions of leadership itself. For example, one study found that when asked to describe their leadership behaviors during the COVID-19 crisis women leaders reported more emotion-focused behaviors, empathy, having limited agency, explaining, and managing conflicts than a comparable group of men leaders. These authors suggested that women leaders approach the leader role differently—they more readily admit their limits, are comfortable with the experience, expression, and management of emotion, and appear more human than the superhuman stereotypes we ascribe to leaders.[69,70]

12-6c Artificial Intelligence and Leadership

Artificial intelligence (AI) is quickly emerging as the new frontier in leadership. AI allows leaders to tap into insights from big data sources, use machine learning algorithms to predict future trends, and enhance their decision-making effectiveness.[71] This is an exciting new avenue, and more findings emerge every day. While most of the existing leadership science has focused on how humans work with each other, the future of leadership includes a focus on how human-robot collaborations could function. For example, could we teach robots to enact task- and people-oriented leadership behaviors? What are the boundaries of such robotic leadership? How might we use algorithms to predict leadership emergence and effectiveness?[72]

Leaders increasingly use social media such as Twitter, Instagram, Facebook, and Tik-Tok to communicate with their followers. The speed and frequency of leader communications is quite different and faster than ever before in history. Social media usage provides another new avenue for studying leader influence.[73]

12-7 Followership

In contrast to leadership, the topic of followership has not been extensively researched. Much of the leadership literature suggests that leader and follower roles are highly differentiated. The traditional view casts followers as passive, whereas a more contemporary view casts the follower role as an active one with potential for leadership.[74] The follower role has alternatively been cast as one of self-leadership in which the follower assumes responsibility for influencing his own performance.[75] This approach emphasizes the follower's individual responsibility and self-control. Self-led followers perform tasks that are naturally motivating and also do work that must be done but is not naturally motivating. Self-leadership enables followers to be disciplined and effective, essential first steps if one is to become a leader. Organizational programs such as empowerment and self-managed work teams may be used to further activate the follower role.[76]

12-7a Types of Followers

Contemporary work environments are ones in which followers recognize their interdependence with leaders and learn to challenge them while at the same time respecting the leaders' authority.[77] Effective followers are active, responsible, autonomous in their behavior, and critical in their thinking without being insubordinate or disrespectful—in essence, they are highly engaged at work.

Effective followers and four other types of followers are identified based on two dimensions: (1) activity versus passivity and (2) independent, critical thinking versus dependent, uncritical thinking.[78] Figure 12.4 shows these follower types.

Alienated followers think independently and critically, yet are very passive in their behavior. As a result, they become psychologically and emotionally distanced from their leaders. These alienated followers are potentially disruptive and a threat to the health of the organization. *Sheep* are followers who do not think independently or critically and are passive in

followership The process of being guided and directed by a leader in the work environment.

Figure 12.4 Five Types of Followers

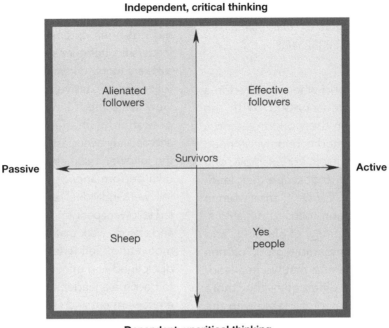

their behavior. *Yes people* are followers who do not think independently or critically, yet are very active in their behavior. They uncritically reinforce the thinking and ideas of their leaders with enthusiasm, never questioning or challenging the wisdom of the leaders' ideas and proposals. Yes people are the most dangerous to a leader because they are the most likely to give a false positive reaction and give no warning of potential pitfalls. *Survivors* (see the center of the figure) are the least disruptive and the lowest-risk followers in an organization. They perpetually sample the wind, and their motto is "better safe than sorry."

Effective followers are the most valuable to a leader and an organization because of their active contributions. Effective followers share four essential qualities. First, they practice self-management and self-responsibility. A leader can delegate to an effective follower without anxiety about the outcome. Second, they are committed both to the organization and a purpose, principle, or person outside themselves. Effective followers are not self-centered or self-aggrandizing. Third, effective followers invest in their own competence and professionalism and focus

their energy for maximum impact. Effective followers look for challenges and ways in which to add to their talents or abilities. Fourth, they are courageous, honest, and credible. Companies can support such qualities among followers by providing training in mindfulness.[79]

Effective followers might be thought of as self-leaders who do not require close supervision. The notion of *self-leadership*, or *superleadership*, blurs the distinction between leaders and followers. Caring leaders are often able to encourage the development of self-leadership in their employees, creating effective, dynamic followers.

12-8 Guidelines for Leadership

Leadership is a key to influencing organizational behavior and achieving organizational effectiveness. When artifacts are eliminated, studies of leadership succession show a moderately strong leader influence on organizational performance.[80] With this said, it is important to recognize that other factors also influence organizational performance. These include environmental factors (such as general economic conditions) and technological factors (such as efficiency).

Corporate leaders play a central role in setting the ethical tone and values for their organizations. While many corporate leaders talk about ethics, many never have to actually risk the firm's fortune on an ethical decision. In 1976, when James Burke, then head of Johnson & Johnson, challenged his management team to reaffirm the company's historic commitment to ethical behavior, he had no idea he would be asked to demonstrate that commitment in action. But six years later, when poisoned packages of Tylenol appeared on store shelves, Burke did not hesitate to act on what he had pledged. The company pulled the product from the shelves at a cost of $100 million. It also offered a reward for a new design that would revamp the product's packaging. In the end, Tylenol recovered and is once again the leading pain medication in the United States.

Five useful guidelines appear to emerge from the extensive leadership research of the past sixty years:

1. Leaders and organizations should appreciate the unique attributes, predispositions, and talents of each leader. No two leaders are the same, and there is value in this diversity.

2. Although there appears to be no single best style of leadership, there are organizational preferences in terms of style. Leaders should be chosen who challenge the organizational culture, when necessary, without destroying it.

3. Participative, considerate leader behaviors that demonstrate a concern for people appear to enhance the health and well-being of followers in the work environment. This does not imply, however, that a leader must ignore the team's work tasks.

4. Different leadership situations call for different leadership talents and behaviors. Leaders must know when to give advice, when to counsel, when to coach, and when to mentor.[81,82] To meet the needs of their followers, they must be good diagnosticians.

5. Good leaders are likely to be good followers. Although there are distinctions between their social roles, the attributes and behaviors of leaders and followers may not be as distinct as is sometimes thought.

Experiential Exercise

National Culture and Leadership

Effective leadership often varies by national culture, as Hofstede's research has shown. This exercise gives you the opportunity to examine your own and your group's leadership orientation compared to norms from ten countries, including the United States.

Exercise Schedule

1. Preparation (before class)
   Complete the 29-item questionnaire.

2. Individual and Group Scoring
   Your instructor will lead you through the scoring of the questionnaire, both individually and as a group.

3. Comparison of Effective Leadership Patterns by Nation
   Your instructor leads a discussion on Hofstede's value system and presents the culture dimension scores for the ten countries.

In the questionnaire below, indicate the extent to which you agree or disagree with each statement. For example, if you strongly agree with a particular statement, circle the 5 next to the statement.

1 = strongly disagree

2 = disagree

3 = neither agree nor disagree

4 = agree

5 = strongly agree

QUESTIONNAIRE	STRONGLY DISAGREE				STRONGLY AGREE
1. It is important to have job instructions spelled out in detail so that employees always know what they are expected to do.	1	2	3	4	5
2. Managers expect employees to closely follow instructions and procedures.	1	2	3	4	5
3. Rules and regulations are important because they inform employees what the organization expects of them.	1	2	3	4	5
4. Standard operating procedures are helpful to employees on the job.	1	2	3	4	5
5. Instructions for operations are important for employees on the job.	1	2	3	4	5
6. Group welfare is more important than individual rewards.	1	2	3	4	5
7. Group success is more important than individual success.	1	2	3	4	5
8. Being accepted by the members of your work group is very important.	1	2	3	4	5
9. Employees should pursue their own goals only after considering the welfare of the group.	1	2	3	4	5
10. Managers should encourage group loyalty even if individual goals suffer.	1	2	3	4	5
11. Individuals may be expected to give up their goals in order to benefit group success.	1	2	3	4	5
12. Managers should make most decisions without consulting subordinates.	1	2	3	4	5
13. Managers should frequently use authority and power when dealing with subordinates.	1	2	3	4	5
14. Managers should seldom ask for the opinions of employees.	1	2	3	4	5
15. Managers should avoid off-the-job social contacts with employees.	1	2	3	4	5
16. Employees should not disagree with management decisions.	1	2	3	4	5
17. Managers should not delegate important tasks to employees.	1	2	3	4	5
18. Managers should help employees with their family problems.	1	2	3	4	5
19. Managers should see to it that employees are adequately clothed and fed.	1	2	3	4	5
20. A manager should help employees solve their personal problems.	1	2	3	4	5
21. Management should see that all employees receive health care.	1	2	3	4	5
22. Management should see that children of employees have an adequate education.	1	2	3	4	5
23. Management should provide legal assistance for employees who get into trouble with the law.	1	2	3	4	5
24. Managers should take care of their employees as they would their children.	1	2	3	4	5
25. Meetings are usually run more effectively when they are chaired by a man.	1	2	3	4	5
26. It is more important for men to have a professional career than it is for women to have a professional career.	1	2	3	4	5
27. Men usually solve problems with logical analysis; women usually solve problems with intuition.	1	2	3	4	5
28. Solving organizational problems usually requires an active, forceful approach, which is typical of men.	1	2	3	4	5
29. It is preferable to have a man, rather than a woman, in a high-level position.	1	2	3	4	5

Sources: P. Dorfman, *Advances in International Comparative Management*, vol. 3 (1988): 127–150. Reprinted by permission of JAI Press Inc.; D. Marcic and S. M. Puffer, "Dimensions of National Culture and Effective Leadership Patterns: Hofstede Revisited," *Management International* (Minneapolis/St. Paul: West Publishing, 1994): 10–15. All rights reserved. May not be reproduced without written permission of the publisher.

Learning Objectives

12-1 **Discuss the differences between leadership and management and between leaders and managers.** Leadership is the process of guiding and directing behavior of people in the work environment. The management process reduces uncertainty and stabilizes an organization. *Leaders* agitate for change and new approaches; in contrast, *managers* advocate stability and the status quo. They differ along four separate dimensions of personality: attitudes toward goals, conceptions of work, relationships with other people, and sense of self.

12-2 **Explain the role of trait theory in describing leaders.** The first studies of leadership attempted to identify what physical attributes, personality characteristics, and abilities distinguished leaders from other members of a group. The trait theories have had very limited success in being able to identify the universal, distinguishing attributes of leaders.

12-3 **Describe the role of foundational behavioral research in the development of leadership theories.** Behavioral theories address how leaders behave. The Lewin, Lippitt, and White studies identified three basic leadership styles: autocratic, democratic, and laissez-faire. Ohio State University measured specific leader behaviors—initiating structure and consideration. The University of Michigan studies suggested two styles of leadership: employee oriented and production oriented.

12-4 **Compare and contrast the four contingency theories of leadership.** Fiedler's contingency theory proposes that the fit between the leader's need structure and the favorableness of the leader's situation determine the team's effectiveness in work accomplishment. The role of the leader in path–goal theory is to clear the follower's path to the goal. In normative decision theory, leaders and managers determine the appropriate level of employee participation in decision-making, and the Situational Leadership theory suggests that the leader's behavior should be adjusted to the maturity level of the followers.

12-5 **Discuss contemporary leadership frameworks such as leader–member exchange and inspirational styles.** With leader–member exchange theory (LMX), leaders form *in-groups* whose members work within the leader's inner circle and *out-groups* whose members are outside the circle. In-group members receive greater responsibilities, more rewards, and more attention. Inspirational leadership theories—*transformational leadership, charismatic leadership*, and *authentic leadership*—can result in positive, productive member behavior because followers are inspired by the leader to perform well.

12-6 **Discuss emerging issues in leadership, including gender and the use of artificial intelligence.** All workers must be aware of emerging leadership issues such as emotional intelligence, trust, women leaders, and servant leadership. These trait studies can affect leaders' decision-making skills, strategy implementation, and ability to build organizational citizenship behaviors. For women as leaders, the focus is shifting to behaviors and style rather than gender stereotypes.

12-7 **Define followership and identify different types of followers.** The follower role has alternatively been cast as one of self-leadership in which the follower assumes responsibility for influencing his or her own performance. Five types of followers are *effective, alienated, sheep, yes people*, and *survivors*. They are identified based on two dimensions: (1) activity versus passivity and (2) independent, critical thinking versus dependent, uncritical thinking.

12-8 **Synthesize historical leadership research into key guidelines for leaders.** Leaders and organizations appreciate the unique attributes, predispositions, and talents of each leader. Leaders challenge the organizational culture, when necessary, without destroying it. Participative, considerate leader behaviors demonstrate a concern for people. Different leadership situations call for different leadership talents and behaviors. Good leaders are likely to be good followers.

Key Terms

autocratic style A style of leadership in which the leader uses strong, directive actions to control the rules, regulations, activities, and relationships in the work environment. (p. 248)

charismatic leadership A leader's values-based, emotion-laden signaling. (p. 255)

consideration Leader behavior aimed at nurturing friendly, warm working relationships as well as encouraging mutual trust and interpersonal respect within the work unit. (p. 248)

democratic style A style of leadership in which the leader uses interaction and collaboration with followers to direct the work and work environment. (p. 248)

followership The process of being guided and directed by a leader in the work environment. (p. 259)

formal leadership Officially sanctioned leadership based on the authority of a formal position. (p. 246)

informal leadership Unofficial leadership accorded to a person by other members of the organization. (p. 246)

initiating structure Leader behavior aimed at defining and organizing work relationships and roles, as well as establishing clear patterns of organization, communication, and ways of getting things done. (p. 248)

laissez-faire style A style of leadership in which the leader has a hands-off approach. (p. 248)

leader–member relations The quality of interpersonal relationships among a leader and the group members. (p. 249)

leaders An advocate for change and new approaches to problems. (p. 246)

leadership The process of guiding and directing the thoughts, feelings, and behavior of people in the work environment. (p. 246)

least preferred coworker (LPC) The person a leader has least preferred to work with. (p. 249)

managers An advocate for stability and the status quo. (p. 246)

position power The authority associated with the leader's formal position in the organization. (p. 249)

task structure The degree of clarity, or ambiguity, in the work activities assigned to the group. (p. 249)

Ethical Dilemma

Red River Manufacturing produces motors for small household appliances and has been in business since the 1920s. Business has been good, but the supply chain issues since COVID has made things difficult. Getting parts has become almost impossible. This has resulted in a lot of delayed orders, causing many unhappy customers.

Mary is the CEO of Red River. She is preparing the annual report for investors. This report will also be distributed to employees. She is struggling with exactly what to include in the report. Industry reports keep saying that the supply chain is recovering, and supply distributions will return to pre-COVID levels. However, industry experts have been saying this for a while, and Mary has not seen that happen.

The financial position of the company is still very positive. So, reporting the facts is not a problem. It is the climate of Red River's customers that concerns Mary the most. Because of all of the delays in fulfilling orders, Mary fears that customers will be looking for other suppliers. If this happens, things will change quickly for Red River.

Mary has always been completely forthcoming in the annual report. It is not in her nature to hide anything from any stakeholder. However, she is not sure that being completely transparent this year is the best thing to do. It may hurt more than it helps. If others find out she knew things she did not share, it may affect the trusting relationships she has with both investors and employees.

1. Using consequential, rule-based, and character theories, evaluate Mary's options.

2. What should Mary do? Why?

Chapter 13

iStock.com/MediaProduction

Conflict and Negotiation

Learning Objectives

13-1 Describe the nature of conflicts in organizations.

13-2 Explain the role structural and personal factors play in causing conflict in organizations.

13-3 Discuss the nature of group conflict in organizations.

13-4 Describe the factors that influence conflict between individuals in organizations.

13-5 Describe effective and ineffective techniques for managing conflict.

13-6 Identify five styles of conflict management.

13-1 The Nature of Conflicts in Organizations

All of us have experienced conflict of various types, yet we probably fail to recognize the variety of conflicts that occur in organizations. *Conflict* is defined as any situation in which incompatible goals, attitudes, emotions, or behaviors lead to disagreement or opposition between two or more parties.[1] Today, organizations may face greater potential for conflict than ever before in history. The marketplace, with its increasing competition and globalization, magnifies differences among people in terms of personality, values, attitudes, perceptions, languages, cultures, and national backgrounds.[2] With the increasing diversity of the workforce comes the potential for incompatibility and conflict.

13-1a Importance of Conflict Management Skills for the Manager

Estimates show that managers spend about 21 percent of their time, or one day every week, dealing with conflict.[3] Not surprisingly, then, conflict management skills are a major predictor of managerial success.[4] A critical indicator of a manager's ability to manage conflict is their *emotional intelligence (EI)*, which is the power to control one's emotions and perceive emotions in others, adapt to change, and manage adversity. (Conflict management skills may be more a reflection of EI than of IQ.) People who lack emotional intelligence, especially empathy, or the ability to see life from another person's perspective, are more likely to be causes of conflict than managers of conflict. Management development programs that focus on EI competencies such as impulse control can help with conflict management skills.[5]

Conflict can be very costly for organizations. Grievances, complaints, and lawsuits result when conflict that should have been handled at an earlier stage spirals out of control. Absenteeism increases

Estimates show that managers spend about 21 percent of their time, or one day every week, dealing with conflict.

when employees stay away from the office to avoid conflict or take time off to address the emotional and physical stress produced by conflict.[6] All in all, workplace conflict can breed distrust and the feeling that the workplace is not a psychologically safe environment.

The largest costs of conflict may be associated with ending the employment relationship through resignation or firing. This means there are expenses of recruiting new employees, bringing them onboard, and training them. The overall total annual cost of conflict to employers in the United Kingdom is estimated at 28.5 billion pounds.[7] In the United States, costs of conflict are estimated to exceed $359 billion.

13-1b Functional Versus Dysfunctional Conflict

Not all conflict is bad. In fact, some types of conflict encourage new solutions to problems and enhance creativity in the organization. In these cases, managers will want to encourage the conflicts. Thus, the key to conflict management is to stimulate functional conflict and prevent or resolve dysfunctional conflict. The difficulty, however, is distinguishing between dysfunctional and functional conflicts. The consequences of conflict can be positive or negative, as shown in Table 13.1.

Functional conflict is a healthy, constructive disagreement between two and more people. New ideas, learning, and growth among individuals can result from functional conflict. Such conflict is constructive conflict; individuals can develop a better awareness of themselves and others through it. In addition, functional conflict can improve working relationships because when two parties work through disagreements, they feel they have accomplished something together. By releasing tensions and solving problems in working together this way, they experience improved morale.[8] Functional conflict can lead to innovation and positive change for the organization.[9] Because it tends to encourage creativity among individuals, this positive form of conflict often translates into increased productivity.[10]

functional conflict A healthy, constructive disagreement between two or more people.

Table 13.1 Consequences of Conflict

Positive Consequences	Negative Consequences
• Leads to new ideas	• Diverts energy from work
• Stimulates creativity	• Threatens psychological well-being
• Motivates change	• Wastes resources
• Promotes organizational vitality	• Creates a negative climate
• Helps individuals and groups establish identities	• Breaks down group cohesion
• Serves as a safety valve to indicate problems	• Can increase hostility and aggressive behaviors

A key to recognizing functional conflict is that it is often cognitive in origin; that is, it arises from someone challenging old policies or thinking of new ways to approach problems. In fact, managers should work to stimulate this type of conflict when they suspect their group is suffering from groupthink.[11]

Dysfunctional conflict is an unhealthy, destructive disagreement between two or more people. Its danger is that it takes the focus away from the work to be done and places it on the conflict itself and the parties involved. Excessive conflict drains energy that could be used more productively. A key to recognizing a dysfunctional conflict is that its origin is often emotional or behavioral. For example, disagreements that involve personalized anger and resentment directed at specific individuals rather than specific ideas are dysfunctional.[12] Individuals involved in dysfunctional conflict tend to act before thinking, and they often rely on threats, deception, and verbal abuse to communicate. Moreover, dysfunctional conflict can often lead to aggressive acts or retaliation directed at supervisors, peers, subordinates, or even service providers.[13] In dysfunctional conflict, losses to both parties may exceed any potential gain from the conflict.

13-1c Diagnosing Conflict

Diagnosing conflict as functional or dysfunctional is not easy. The manager must look at the issue, the context of the conflict, and the parties involved. Once the manager has diagnosed the type of conflict, they can either work to resolve it (if it is dysfunctional) or to stimulate it (if it is functional).

It is easy to make mistakes in diagnosing conflicts. Sometimes task conflict, which is functional, can be misattributed as being personal, and dysfunctional conflict can follow. Developing trust within the work group can keep this misattribution from occurring.[14]

A study of group effectiveness found that decision-making groups made up of friends were able to engage more openly in disagreement than groups made up of strangers, allowing the friends' groups to make more effective decisions. Relationship conflict, in contrast with task conflict, is more likely to become dysfunctional, especially if it persists over time. Prolonged, unresolved relationship conflict depletes employees' energy, and they become burned out. Burned-out employees perform poorly and may want to leave the organization to get away from the dysfunctional conflict.[15]

13-2 Causes of Conflict in Organizations

Conflict is pervasive in organizations. To manage it effectively, managers should understand its many sources. These can be classified into two broad categories: *structural factors*, which stem from the nature of the organization and the way in which work is organized, and *personal factors*, which arise from differences among individuals. Figure 13.1 summarizes the causes of conflict within each category.

13-2a Structural Factors

The causes of conflict related to the organization's structure include specialization, interdependence, common resources, goal differences, authority relationships, status inconsistencies, and jurisdictional ambiguities.

dysfunctional conflict An unhealthy, destructive disagreement between two or more people.

Figure 13.1 Causes of Conflict in Organizations

Tsurukame Design/Shutterstock.com

Specialization When jobs are highly specialized, employees become experts at certain tasks. For example, one software company has one specialist for databases, one for statistical packages, and another for expert systems. Highly specialized jobs can lead to conflict because people have little awareness of the tasks that others perform.

A classic conflict of specialization often occurs between salespeople and engineers. Engineers are technical specialists responsible for product design and quality. Salespeople are marketing experts and liaisons with customers. Salespeople are often accused of making delivery promises to customers that engineers cannot keep because the sales force lacks the technical knowledge necessary to develop realistic delivery deadlines.

Interdependence Work that is interdependent requires groups or individuals to depend on one another to accomplish goals.[16] Depending on other people to get work done is fine when the process works smoothly. When there is a problem, however, it becomes very easy to blame the other party, and conflict escalates. In a garment manufacturing plant, for example, when the fabric cutters get behind in their work, the workers who sew the garments are delayed as well. Considerable frustration may result when the workers at the sewing machines feel their efforts are being blocked by the cutters' slow pace and their pay is affected because they are paid piece-rate.

Common Resources Anytime multiple parties must share resources, there is potential for conflict.[17] This potential is enhanced when the shared resources become scarce. For example, managers often share administrative support. Not

uncommonly, one administrative assistant supports ten or more managers, each of whom believes their work is most important. This puts pressure on the administrative assistant and leads to potential conflicts in prioritizing and scheduling work.

Goal Differences When work groups have different goals, these goals may be incompatible. For example, in one cable television company, the salesperson's goal was to sell as many new installations as possible. This created problems for the service department because its goal was timely installations. With increasing sales, the service department's workload became backed up, and orders were delayed. Often these types of conflicts occur because individuals do not have knowledge of another department's objectives.

Authority Relationships A traditional boss–employee relationship is hierarchical in nature, with a boss who is **seen as superior** to the employee. For some employees, such a relationship is not a comfortable one; they don't like another person telling them what to do. There are people who resent authority, and obviously this creates conflicts. In addition, some bosses are more autocratic than others, compounding the potential for conflict in the relationship. As organizations move toward the team approach and empowerment, there should be less potential for conflict from authority relationships.

Status Inconsistencies Some organizations have a strong status difference between management and nonmanagement workers. Managers may enjoy privileges—such as flexible schedules, reserved parking spaces, and longer lunch hours—that are

Dragon Images/Shutterstock.com

not available to nonmanagement employees and that may result in resentment and conflict.

Jurisdictional Ambiguities Have you ever called a company with a problem and had your call transferred through several different people and departments? This situation illustrates **jurisdictional ambiguity**, that is, unclear lines of responsibility within an organization.[18] The classic situation here involves the hardware/software dilemma. You call the company that made your computer, and it informs you that the problem is caused by the software. You call the software division, and it tells you it's the hardware....

13-2b Personal Factors

Not all conflicts arise out of structural factors in the organization. Some conflicts arise out of differences among individuals. The causes of conflict that arise from individual differences include skills and abilities, personalities, perceptions, values and ethics, emotions, communication barriers, and cultural differences.

Skills and Abilities Diversity in skills and abilities may be positive for the organization, but it also holds potential for conflict, especially when jobs are interdependent. Experienced, competent workers may find it difficult to work alongside new and unskilled recruits. Workers can become resentful when their new boss, fresh from college, knows a lot about managing people but is unfamiliar with the technology with which they are working.

Personalities Individuals do not leave their personalities at the doorstep when they enter the workplace. Personality conflicts are thus realities in organizations. It is naïve to expect that you will like all of your coworkers, just as it is naïve to expect that they will all like you.

One personality trait that many people find difficult to deal with is abrasiveness.[19] An abrasive person ignores the interpersonal aspects of work and the feelings of colleagues. These types of people are often achievement oriented and hardworking, but their perfectionist, critical style can leave others feeling unimportant. The working style of abrasive individuals causes stress and strain for those around them.[20]

Perceptions Differences in perception can also lead to conflict. For example, managers and workers may not have a shared perception of what motivates people. In this case, the reward system can create conflicts if managers provide what they *think* employees want rather than what they actually want.

Values and Ethics Differences in values and ethics can be sources of disagreement. Older workers, for example, value company loyalty and probably would not take a sick day when they were not really ill. Younger workers, valuing work/life balance, may be quicker to take time off for a wider variety of reasons beyond physical illness. This may not be true for all workers, but it illustrates that differences in values can lead to conflict.

Most people have their own sets of values and ethics, although the extent to which they apply these ethics in the workplace varies. Some people have strong desires for approval from others and will work to meet others' ethical standards. Others are relatively unconcerned about approval from others and strongly apply their own ethical standards. Still others operate seemingly without regard to ethics or values.[21] When conflicts about values or ethics do arise, heated disagreement is common because of the personal nature of the differences.

jurisdictional ambiguity The presence of unclear lines of responsibility within an organization.

Personality conflicts are realities in organizations; it is naive to expect that you will like all of your coworkers or to expect that they will all like you.

Emotions Conflict is by nature an emotional interaction, and the emotions of the parties involved in conflict play a pivotal role in how they perceive any type of negotiation and therefore how they respond to one another.[22] In fact, emotions are now considered critical elements of negotiation and must be included in an examination of the process and how it unfolds.[23] When negotiators begin to act based on emotions rather than on cognitions, they become much more likely to reach an impasse.[24]

Communication Barriers Communication barriers such as physical separation and language can create distortions in messages, and these can lead to conflict. Another communication barrier is value judgment, in which a listener assigns worth to a message before it is received. For example, suppose a team member is a chronic complainer. When this individual enters the manager's office, the manager is likely to devalue the message before it is even delivered. Conflict can then emerge.

Cultural Differences Although cultural differences are assets in organizations, sometimes they can be sources of conflict. Often, these

conflicts stem from a lack of understanding of another culture. In one MBA class, for example, Indian students were horrified when American students challenged the professor. Meanwhile, the American students thought the students from India were too passive. Subsequent discussions revealed that professors in India expect to be treated deferentially and with great respect. While students might challenge an idea vigorously, they would rarely challenge the professor. Diversity training that emphasizes education on cultural differences can make great strides in preventing misunderstandings.

13-3 Forms of Group Conflict in Organizations

Conflict in an organization can take on any of several different forms that can mainly be sorted into two core groups: conflicts that occur at the group level and conflicts that occur at the individual level. Conflicts at each level can be further classified as either *inter* or *intra*. It is important to note that the prefix *inter* means "between," whereas the prefix *intra* means "within." Conflict at the group level can occur between organizations (interorganizational), between groups (intergroup), or within a group (intragroup).

13-3a Interorganizational Conflict

Conflict that occurs between two or more organizations is called **interorganizational conflict**. Competition can heighten interorganizational conflict. Corporate takeovers, mergers, and acquisitions can also produce interorganizational conflict. What about the interorganizational conflict between the National Football League's players unions and team owners, which was often characterized as a battle between millionaires and billionaires? The players who regularly go on strike may be seen as doing so to extract more of the profits from the owners, and in response the owners claim they are not making a reasonable profit.

interorganizational conflict Conflict that occurs between two or more organizations.

13-3b Intergroup Conflict

When conflict occurs between groups or teams, it is known as **intergroup conflict**. Conflict between groups can have positive effects within each group, such as increased group cohesiveness, increased focus on tasks, and increased loyalty to the group. There are, however, negative consequences as well. Groups in conflict tend to develop an us-against-them mentality whereby each sees the other team as the enemy, becomes more hostile, and decreases its communication with the other group. Groups are even more competitive and less cooperative than individuals. The inevitable outcome is that one group gains and the other group loses.[25]

Competition between groups must be managed carefully so that it does not escalate into dysfunctional conflict. Research has shown that when multiple groups compete for a goal that only one group can achieve, negative consequences such as territoriality, aggression, and prejudice toward other groups can result.[26] Commitment also plays a role in intergroup conflict. When employees are more committed to their own groups or teams than to the organization as a whole, dysfunctional conflict handling strategies are likely to result. To prevent this, managers should encourage both team commitment and organizational commitment among employees.[27] In addition, managers should encourage social interactions across groups so that trust can be developed. Trust allows individuals to exchange ideas and resources with members of other groups and results in innovation when members of different groups cooperate.[28]

13-3c Intragroup Conflict

Conflict that occurs within groups or teams is called **intragroup conflict**. Some conflict within a group is functional, since it can help prevent groupthink, as discussed in Chapter 10.

Even virtual teams are not immune to conflict. The nuances and subtleties of face-to-face communication are often lacking in these teams, and misunderstandings can result. Face-to-face and telephone interactions early on can eliminate later conflicts and allow virtual teams to move on to use electronic communication because trust has been developed. When top management teams make strategic decisions, conflicts within the team frequently arise because so much is at stake. If a crisis occurs, however, intragroup conflicts may be superseded by the need for urgent decisions and collaboration among the team members.[29]

13-4 Individual Conflict in Organizations

As with groups, conflict can occur between individuals (interpersonal) or within a single individual (intrapersonal).

13-4a Types of Intrapersonal Conflict

When conflict occurs within an individual, it is called **intrapersonal conflict**. There are several types of intrapersonal conflict, including interrole, intrarole, and person–role conflicts. A *role* is a set of expectations placed on an individual by others.[30] The person occupying the focal role is the *role incumbent*, and the individuals who place expectations on the person are *role senders*. Figure 13.2 depicts a set of role relationships.

Interrole conflict occurs when a person experiences conflict among the multiple roles in their life. One interrole conflict that many employees experience is *work–home conflict*, in which their role as worker clashes with their role as spouse or parent.[31] Work–home conflict can arise from time constraints, strain, and having responsibilities for people in the workplace and at home.[32] This type of conflict has become even more common with the rise of work-at-home professionals and

---

intergroup conflict Conflict that occurs between groups or teams in an organization.

intragroup conflict Conflict that occurs within groups or teams.

intrapersonal conflict Conflict that occurs within an individual.

interrole conflict A person's experience of conflict among the multiple roles in their life.

Figure 13.2 An Organization Member's Role Set

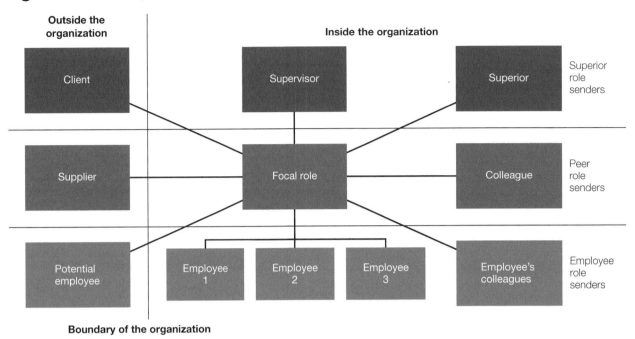

Source: J. C. Quick, J. D. Quick, D. L. Nelson, and J. J. Hurrell Jr., *Preventive Stress Management in Organizations* (Washington, DC: American Psychological Association, 1997). Copyright © 1997 by the American Psychological Association. Reprinted with permission.

telecommuting, in which the home becomes the office and the boundary between work and family life is blurred.[33] Ambitious and highly involved employees use office communications (e.g., texting, e-mail, and so on) nights and weekends. After-hours communication usage is associated with increased work–life conflict as reported by the employee and a significant other.[34] Work–home conflict reduces personal well-being, decreases organizational citizenship behavior, and increases stress. People also tend to drink more alcohol on days they experience work–home conflict.[35] Work–home conflicts make it difficult to concentrate at work, and job performance suffers.[36]

Intrarole conflict is conflict within a single role. It often arises when a person receives conflicting messages from role senders about how to perform a certain role. Suppose a manager receives counsel from their department head that they need to socialize less with nonmanagement employees. They are

also told by their project manager that they need to be a better team member and to accomplish this by socializing more with other nonmanagement team members. This situation is one of intrarole conflict.

One intrapersonal conflict that many employees experience is work-home conflict.

intrarole conflict Conflict that occurs within a single role, such as when a person receives conflicting messages from role senders about how to perform a certain role.

Hot Trend

Don't Contact Me Outside of Business Hours

The new reality of the home office brought with it an explosion of work–home conflict and the inability to get away from the office. What rights do employees have when they work from home? Must they accept 24/7 access by managers, coworkers, and customers?

Portugal is taking steps to improve work-life balance by making it illegal to text employees after work. Companies will face fines for contacting employees after hours, and monitoring employees who work from home is prohibited. Companies also must help with work-from-home expenses like electricity and Internet. Portugal is not alone in changing its labor laws. France's "right to disconnect" policy allows employees to ignore emails sent outside office hours, and the entire EU may follow suit.

Sources: "Reimagining the Workplace in a COVID World," *Real-Leaders*, Summer (2022), 61, J. Kelly, "Belgium, Portugal and Other European Countries Prohibit Managers from Contacting Employees Outside of Working Hours," *Forbes*, February 3 (2022), accessed at https://www.forbes.com/sites/jackkelly/2022/02/03/belgium-portugal-and-other-european-countries-are-ahead-of-the-us-prohibiting-managers-from-contacting-employees-outside-of-working-hours/?sh=446265001d00.

Person–role conflict occurs when an individual in a particular role is expected to perform behaviors that clash with their personal values.[37] Salespeople, for example, may be required to offer the most expensive item in the sales line first to the customer, even when it is apparent that the customer does not want or cannot afford it. A computer salesperson may be required to offer a large, elaborate system to a student they know is on a tight budget. This may conflict with the salesperson's values, and they may experience person–role conflict.

Intrapersonal conflicts can have positive consequences. Often, professional responsibilities clash with deeply held values. A budget shortfall may force you to lay off a loyal, hardworking employee. Your child may have a piano recital on the same day your largest client is scheduled to be in town visiting the office. In such conflicts, we often have to choose between right and right; that is, there's no wrong response, only one that is better than the other. These decisions pose what may be thought of as *defining moments* that challenge individuals to choose between two or more things in which they believe.[38] Character is formed in defining moments because they cause individuals to shape their identities. They help people crystallize their values and serve as opportunities for personal growth.

Three actions in particular can help prevent or resolve intrapersonal conflicts. First, when seeking a new job, you should find out as much as possible about the values of the organization.[39] Many person–role conflicts center around differences between the organization's values and the individual's values. Research has shown that when there is a good fit between the values of the individual and the organization, the individual is more satisfied and committed and is less likely to leave the organization.[40]

Second, *role analysis* is a good tool for managing intrarole or interrole conflicts.[41] In role analysis, the individual asks the various role senders what is expected of them The outcomes are clearer work roles and the reduction of conflict and ambiguity.[42] Role analysis is a simple tool that clarifies the expectations of both parties in a relationship and reduces the potential for conflict within a role or between roles.

Third, political skills can help buffer the negative effects of stress that stem from role conflicts. Effective politicians can negotiate role expectations when conflicts occur. All these forms of conflict can be managed. An understanding of the many forms is a first step.

13-4b Managing Intrapersonal Conflict

Intrapersonal conflict can be managed with careful self-analysis and diagnosis of the situation.

person–role conflict Conflict that occurs when an individual in a particular role is expected to perform behaviors that clash with their personal values.

13-4c Managing Interpersonal Conflict

Conflict that occurs between two or more individuals, or **interpersonal conflict**, can arise from many individual differences, including personalities, attitudes, values, and perceptions. To manage interpersonal conflict, it is essential to understand incivility, **microaggressions**, and defense mechanisms exhibited by individuals when they are in conflict situations.

Incivility is discourteous communication and rude behaviors that are disrespectful, hurtful, or injurious, as discussed in Chapter 8. Unfortunately, incivility is on the rise in the workplace.[43] During the pandemic, frontline workers who came to be known as "essential workers" were often the targets of uncivil behavior. Ignoring people, undermining them, mocking, teasing, and belittling are all examples of incivility. An example would be berating a server because they did not get your order exactly correct, sending a nasty note to a colleague, or insulting someone in public.

Why is there so much incivility at work? Several factors contribute to increased incivility, including stress, negative emotions, weakened sense of community, and heavy use of social media. One of the challenges with incivility is that it is contagious and can spread like wildfire within organizations. Interruptions, condescension, and lack of courtesy can take a toll on mental and physical health. Merely witnessing uncivil behavior takes a cognitive toll and decreases performance at work.[44]

How can organizations manage incivility? First, be creating a culture of psychological safety and mutual respect. When incivility is counter to the norms of the company, it becomes the exception rather than the rule. Second, train employees to handle uncivil behavior, paying special attention to frontline, customer-facing employees. Two essential elements in the training should be empathy and mindfulness. Mindful individuals seldom exhibit uncivil behavior, and when they do, their guilt leads them to make amends.[45] Finally, coach employees on de-escalation skills. This can prevent incivility from spiraling into aggressive behavior.

What if you are the target of rude or uncivil behavior at work? There are several things to keep in mind when responding. First, acknowledge your emotional reaction. Uncivil or rude behaviors like being insulted, yelled at, or rejected can elicit a brain response that is very similar to the experience of physical pain.[46] Second, take a breath. Assess the risks of responding, and whether it's worth it. Also assess the risks of not speaking up. Third, use "I" or "It" statements. For example, "I felt dismissed by your comment," "It would be helpful if we took the heat out of this conversation," or "That comment is not productive for either of us." Sometimes just an "ouch" will get the point across.[47] Finally, ask questions. Ask the individual to clarify their intent or repeat what they said, which may give them an

interpersonal conflict Conflict that occurs between two or more individuals.

microaggressions Insensitive statements, questions, and assumptions directed toward marginalized identity groups.

Organizational Example

No Tolerance for Incivility at Dick's Sporting Goods

No doubt retail employees experience their share of uncivil behavior. Dick's Sporting Goods, cited as one of the Great Places to Work in Retail, has a zero tolerance approach to incivility. With more than 850 stores and 50,000 employees, disrespectful behavior increased during the pandemic with mask and vaccination rules.

The company has a hotline number for employees to call if they feel they've not been treated with dignity and respect. Customers can use the same hotline to report uncivil behavior by team members. Store managers are empowered to remove customers from the store if conflicts can't be de-escalated, resulting in some customers being asked not to return.

Protecting frontline workers during challenging times has helped Dick's Sporting Goods attract and keep its talent pool.

Sources: C. Hastwell, "How the Best Workplaces in Retail Are Retaining Employees Amid the Great Resignation," *Fortune*, November 4 (2021), accessed at https://fortune.com/2021/11/04/best-workplaces-retail-dicks-sporting-goods-abercrombie-fitch-bombas-great-resignation/.

opportunity to rethink their comment. Have an exit plan for ending the conversation or moving on, especially so you don't return incivility with your own uncivil behavior.

Microaggressions are insensitive statements, questions, and assumptions directed toward marginalized identity groups. Such[48] statements feel offensive and hostile, yet often the perpetrator may not realize the harm caused. Many times, microaggressions stem from unconscious biases, as we discussed in Chapter 3. Although incivility and microaggressions are similar, the distinguishing feature of microaggression is that it is a violation based on the target's identity. Microaggressions reported by women in the workplace reached an all-time high in 2022, and women in hybrid jobs reported the greatest frequency of microaggressions.[49]

Women report that being interrupted and having their judgment questioned are the top microaggressions they encounter. Being excluded from interactions and meetings, having someone take credit for their ideas, and being given fewer opportunities to speak up in meetings are also among the microaggressions faced by women.[50] Organizations with non-inclusive cultures can be fraught with these behaviors even when workers are not physically present, such as in hybrid work environments.

Women in minority racial groups and LGBTQ+ women are even more likely to be targets of microaggressions.[51] Being underestimated or undermined and being the target of disparaging remarks about one's gender, race, or ethnicity are examples of these behaviors. Statements like "You don't look Mexican," "Where are you really from?" "That's so gay!" and "You can work late since you don't have kids," are a few of the offensive comments. When an organization does not promote an inclusive culture, microaggressions can proliferate, and they are costly. Targets of microaggressions have lower job satisfaction, higher burnout, higher stress levels, and are likely to leave the organization due to these indignities.

When you experience a microaggression, it is challenging to know how to respond. If you feel comfortable with the person, you might consider saying something like "Hey, regarding the comment you made earlier—it didn't sit well with me." Sometimes, educating the individual about why the comment was insensitive can bring about a fruitful dialogue.[52] What if you commit a microaggression? In this case, it is important to ask for clarification, learn, and apologize.

Organizations that create a more inclusive and culturally competent environment can work to minimize microaggressions at work. Encouraging more intentional communication and awareness of unconscious biases can help. Creating a norm of listening for understanding and open, non-defensive dialogue can help keep microaggressions from becoming dysfunctional conflicts.

13-4d Defense Mechanisms

When individuals are involved in conflict with another human being, frustration often results.[53] Conflicts can often arise within the context of a performance appraisal session. Most people do not react well to negative feedback, as was illustrated in a classic study in which more than 50 percent of employees reacted defensively when given criticism about their work.[54]

When individuals are frustrated, as they often are in interpersonal conflict, they respond by exhibiting *defense mechanisms*.[55] Aggressive mechanisms, such as fixation, displacement, and negativism, are aimed at attacking the source of the conflict. In **fixation**, an individual fixates on the conflict, or keeps up a dysfunctional behavior that obviously will not solve the conflict. An example of fixation occurred in a university where a faculty member became embroiled in a battle with the dean because the faculty member felt he had not received a large enough salary increase. He persisted in writing angry letters to the dean, whose hands were tied because of a low budget allocation to the college. Another aggressive defense mechanism is **displacement**, which means directing anger toward someone who is not the source of the conflict. For example, a manager may respond harshly to an employee after a telephone confrontation with an angry customer. **Negativism** is an aggressive mechanism in which a person responds

fixation An aggressive mechanism in which an individual keeps up a dysfunctional behavior that obviously will not solve the conflict.

displacement An aggressive mechanism in which an individual directs their anger toward someone who is not the source of the conflict.

negativism An aggressive mechanism in which a person responds with pessimism to any attempt at solving a problem.

with pessimism to any attempt at solving a problem. Negativism is illustrated by a manager who, when appointed to a committee on which she did not want to serve, made negative comments throughout the meeting.

Compromise mechanisms, such as compensation, identification, and rationalization, are used by individuals to make the best of a conflict situation. **Compensation** is a compromise mechanism in which an individual attempts to make up for a negative situation by devoting themselves to another pursuit with increased vigor. Compensation can be seen when a person makes up for a bad relationship at home by spending more time at the office. **Identification** is a compromise mechanism whereby an individual patterns her behavior after another's. One supervisor at a construction firm, not wanting to acknowledge consciously that she was not likely to be promoted, mimicked the behavior of her boss, even going so far as to buy a car just like the boss's. **Rationalization** is trying to justify one's behavior by constructing bogus reasons for it. Employees may rationalize unethical behavior like padding their expense accounts with the argument that "everyone else does it."

Withdrawal mechanisms are exhibited when frustrated individuals try to flee from a conflict using either physical or psychological means. Flight, conversion, and fantasy are examples of withdrawal mechanisms. Physically escaping a conflict is **flight**. An employee taking a day off after a blowup with

Withdrawal mechanisms are exhibited when frustrated individuals try to flee from a conflict.

Kaspars Grinvalds/Shutterstock.com

the boss is an example. **Withdrawal** may take the form of emotionally leaving a conflict, such as exhibiting an "I don't care anymore" attitude. **Conversion** is a process whereby emotional conflicts become expressed in physical symptoms. Most of us have experienced the conversion reaction of a headache following an emotional exchange with another person. **Fantasy** is a withdrawal mechanism that provides an escape from a conflict through daydreaming. In the Internet age, fantasy as an escape mechanism has found new meaning. A study conducted by International Data Corporation (IDC) showed that 30 to 40 percent of all Internet surfing in the office is nonwork-related and that more than 70 percent of companies have had sex sites accessed from their networks, suggesting that employees' minds aren't always focused on their jobs.[56]

When employees exhibit withdrawal mechanisms, they often pretend to agree with their bosses or coworkers in order to avoid facing an immediate conflict. Many employees fake a positive response this way because the firm informally rewards agreement and punishes dissent. The long-term consequence of withdrawal and faking a positive response is emotional distress for the employee.[57]

Knowledge of these defense mechanisms can be extremely beneficial to a manager. By understanding the ways in which people typically react to interpersonal conflict, managers can be prepared for employees' reactions and help them uncover their feelings about a conflict.

compensation A compromise mechanism in which an individual attempts to make up for a negative situation by devoting themselves to another pursuit with increased vigor.

identification A compromise mechanism whereby an individual patterns their behavior after another's.

rationalization A compromise mechanism characterized by trying to justify one's behavior by constructing bogus reasons for it.

flight/withdrawal A withdrawal mechanism that entails physically escaping (flight) or psychologically escaping (withdrawal) a conflict.

conversion A withdrawal mechanism in which emotional conflicts are expressed in physical symptoms.

fantasy A withdrawal mechanism that provides an escape from a conflict through daydreaming.

13-5 Conflict Management Strategies and Techniques

The overall approach (or strategy) you use in a conflict is important in determining whether the conflict will have a positive or negative outcome. Overall strategies to deal with conflict can be classified as competitive versus cooperative strategies. Table 13.2 depicts the two strategies and four different conflict scenarios. The *competitive strategy* is founded on assumptions of win–lose and entails dishonest communication, mistrust, and a rigid position from both parties.[58] The *cooperative strategy* is founded on different assumptions: the potential for win–win outcomes, honest communication, trust, openness to risk and vulnerability, and the notion that the whole may be greater than the sum of the parts.

To illustrate the importance of the overall strategy, consider the case of two groups competing for scarce resources. Suppose budget cuts have to be made at an insurance company. The claims manager argues that the sales training staff should be cut because agents are fully trained. The sales training manager argues that claims personnel should be cut because the company is processing fewer claims. This could turn into a dysfunctional brawl, with both sides refusing to give ground. The result would be a win–lose, lose–win, or lose–lose scenario. Personnel cuts could be made in one department or the other, or in both departments. In all three cases, the organization winds up in a losing position with the competitive approach.

Even in such intense conflicts as those over scarce resources, a win–win strategy can lead to an overall win for the organization. In fact, conflicts over scarce resources can be productive if the parties have cooperative goals—a strategy that seeks a winning solution for both parties. To achieve a win–win outcome, the conflict must be approached with open-minded discussion of opposing views. Through open-minded discussion, both parties integrate views and create new solutions that facilitate productivity and strengthen their relationship; the result is feelings of unity rather than separation.[59]

In the example of the conflict between the claims manager and sales training manager, open-minded discussion might reveal that there are ways to achieve budget cuts without cutting personnel. Sales support might surrender part of its travel budget, and claims might cut overtime. This represents a win–win situation for the company. The budget has been reduced, and relationships between the two departments have been preserved. Both parties have given up something (note the "Win–" in Table 13.2), but the conflict has been resolved with a positive outcome.

You can see the importance of the broad strategy used to approach a conflict. We now move from broad strategies to more specific techniques.

Effective conflict management techniques include appealing to superordinate goals, expanding resources, changing personnel, changing structure, and confronting and negotiating.

13-5a Ineffective Techniques

There are many specific techniques for dealing with conflict. Before turning to techniques that work, it should be recognized that some actions commonly taken in organizations to deal with conflict are not effective.[60]

Nonaction is doing nothing in hopes that the conflict will disappear. Generally, this is not a good technique because most conflicts do not go away, and the individuals involved in the conflict react with frustration.

nonaction Doing nothing in hopes that a conflict will disappear.

Table 13.2 Win–Lose Versus Win–Win Strategies

Strategy	Department A	Department B	Organization
Competitive	Lose	Lose	Lose
	Lose	Win	Lose
	Win	Lose	Lose
Cooperative	Win 2	Win 2	Win

Secrecy, attempting to hide a conflict or an issue that has the potential to create conflict, only creates suspicion. An example is an organizational policy of pay secrecy. In some organizations, discussion of salary is grounds for dismissal. When this is the case, employees suspect that the company has something to hide. **Administrative orbiting** is delaying action on a conflict by buying time, usually by telling the individuals involved that the problem is being worked on or that the boss is still thinking about the issue. Like nonaction, this technique leads to frustration and resentment.

Due process nonaction is a procedure set up to address conflicts that is so costly, time-consuming, or personally risky that no one will use it. Some companies' sexual harassment policies are examples of this technique. To file a sexual harassment complaint, the accuser must complete detailed paperwork, has to go through appropriate channels, and may be branded a troublemaker. Thus, the company has a procedure for handling complaints (due process), but no one uses it (nonaction).

Character assassination is the deliberate destruction of a person's reputation or credibility through character attacks.[61] Character assassination can backfire and make the individual who uses it appear dishonest and cruel. It often leads to name-calling and accusations by both parties, who both end up losers in the eyes of those who witness the conflict.

The pandemic brought considerable conflict in the public health arena, and Dr. Anthony Fauci was a target of character assassination attempts.[62] As the director of the National Institute of Allergy and Infectious Diseases and a trusted advisor to seven U.S. presidents, his role was to guide the public through the pandemic. Dr. Fauci was seen as a hero by some, emphasizing science and evidence-based medicine as the guides to managing the pandemic. Others,

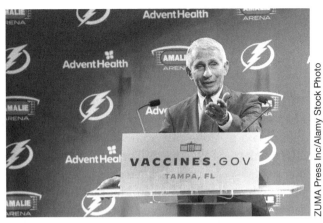

Dr. Anthony Fauci faced character assassination attempts during the COVID pandemic.

however, portrayed him as a threat to their personal freedom. He became the figurehead for the things people hated about the government's response to the pandemic. The Internet gave rise to multiple conspiracy theories attempting to discredit and vilify him.[63] As the character assassination escalated, Dr. Fauci faced death threats and required Secret Service outside his house for protection.[64]

13-5b Effective Techniques

Fortunately, there are effective conflict management techniques. These include appealing to superordinate goals, expanding resources, changing personnel, changing structure, and confronting and negotiating.

Superordinate Goals An organizational goal that is more important to both parties in a conflict than their individual or group goals is a **superordinate goal**.[65] Superordinate goals cannot be achieved by an individual or by one group alone. The achievement of these goals requires cooperation by both parties. One effective technique for resolving conflict is to appeal to this superordinate goal—in effect, to focus the parties on a larger issue on which they both agree. This helps them realize their similarities rather than their differences.

In the conflict between service representatives and cable television installers that was discussed earlier, appealing to a superordinate goal would be an effective technique for resolving the conflict. Both departments can agree that superior customer service is a goal worthy of pursuit and that this goal cannot be achieved unless cables are installed properly and in a timely manner, and customer complaints are handled effectively. Quality service requires that both departments cooperate to achieve the goal.

secrecy Attempting to hide a conflict or an issue that has the potential to create conflict.

administrative orbiting Delaying action on a conflict by buying time.

due process nonaction A procedure set up to address conflicts that is so costly, time-consuming, or personally risky that no one will use it.

character assassination The deliberate destruction of a person's reputation or credibility through character attacks.

superordinate goal An organizational goal that is more important to both parties in a conflict than their individual or group goals.

Expanding Resources One conflict resolution technique is so simple that it may be overlooked. If the conflict's source is common or scarce resources, providing more resources may be a solution. Of course, managers working with tight budgets may not have the luxury of obtaining additional resources. Nevertheless, it is a technique to be considered. In the example of shared administrative support presented earlier in this chapter, one solution to the conflict among managers over administrative support would be to hire more administrative assistants.

Changing Personnel In some cases, long-running severe conflict may be traced to a specific individual. For example, managers with lower levels of emotional intelligence demonstrate more negative work attitudes, exhibit less altruistic behavior, and produce more negative work outcomes. A chronically disgruntled manager who exhibits low emotional intelligence might not only frustrate their employees but also impede the department's performance. In such cases, transferring or firing an individual could be the best solution, but only after due process.[66]

Changing Structure Another way to resolve a conflict is to change the structure of the organization. One way of accomplishing this is to create an integrator role. An *integrator* is a liaison between groups with very different interests. In severe conflicts, it may be best that the integrator be a neutral third party.[67] Creating the integrator role is a way of opening dialogue between groups that have difficulty communicating.

Using *cross-functional teams* is another way of changing the organization's structure to manage conflict. In the old methods of designing new products in organizations, many departments had to contribute, and delays resulted from difficulties in coordinating the activities of the various departments. Using a cross-functional team made up of members from different departments improves coordination and reduces delays by allowing many activities to be performed at the same time rather than sequentially.[68] The team approach allows members from different departments to work together and reduces the potential for conflict. However, recent research also suggests that such functional diversity can lead to slower informational processing in teams due to differences in members' perceptions of what might be required to achieve group goals. When putting together cross-functional teams, organizations should emphasize superordinate goals and train team members on resolving conflict. One such training technique could involve educating individual members in other functional areas so that everyone on the team can have a shared language.[69] In teamwork, it is helpful to break up a big task so that it becomes a collection of smaller, less complex tasks and to have smaller teams work on the smaller tasks. This helps to reduce conflict, and organizations can potentially improve the performance of the overall team by improving the outcomes in each subteam.[70]

Confronting and Negotiating Some conflicts require confrontation and negotiation between the parties. Both of these strategies require skill on the part of the negotiator and careful planning before engaging in negotiations. The process of negotiating involves an open discussion of problem solutions, and the outcome often is an exchange in which both parties work toward a mutually beneficial solution.

Negotiation is a joint process of finding a mutually acceptable solution to a complex conflict. There are two major negotiating approaches: distributive bargaining and integrative negotiation.[71] **Distributive bargaining** is an approach in which the goals of one party are in direct conflict with the goals of the other party. Resources are limited (fixed-pie thinking), and each party wants to maximize its share of the resources (piece of the pie). It is a competitive, or win–lose, approach to negotiations. Sometimes, distributive bargaining causes negotiators to focus so much on their differences that they ignore their common ground. In these cases, distributive bargaining can become counterproductive. The reality is, however, that some situations are distributive in nature, particularly when the parties are interdependent.

Greg Brave/Shutterstock.com

Changing the structure of an organization is one way to resolve conflict.

distributive bargaining A negotiation approach in which the goals of the parties are in conflict, and each party seeks to maximize its resources.

Golden Brown/Shutterstock.com

Golden Brown/Shutterstock.com

If a negotiator wants to maximize the value of a single deal and is not worried about maintaining a good relationship with the other party, distributive bargaining may be an option.

In contrast, **integrative negotiation** is an approach in which the parties' goals are not seen as mutually exclusive, but the focus is on both sides achieving their objectives. Integrative negotiation focuses on the merits of the issues and is a win–win approach. (How can we make the pie bigger?) For integrative negotiation to be successful, certain preconditions must be present. These include having a common goal, faith in one's own problem-solving abilities, a belief in the validity of the other party's position, motivation to work together, mutual trust, and clear communication. It also helps if both parties are good at perspective taking, which is the

integrative negotiation A negotiation approach in which the parties' goals are not seen as mutually exclusive, but the focus is on both sides achieving their objectives.

ability to see the other person's point of view.[72] One tactic for achieving integrative negotiations is the deliberate use of silence in interacting with the other party. When one or both parties take a silent pause of at least 3 seconds, the silence leads to a more deliberative mindset, and to less fixed-pie thinking. In this way, silent pauses in negotiations can be a very effective tool for creating valuable solutions.[73]

Cultural differences play a role in negotiation styles. For example, negotiation strategies differ among dignity cultures (e.g., the United States), face cultures (China), and honor cultures (Qatar). In dignity cultures, people derive their self-worth intrinsically and see each individual as having inherent self-worth. Independence and choosing one's own goals are valued. In face cultures, people derive their self-worth from social interactions. A premium is placed on saving face, showing humility, and preserving social harmony. In honor cultures, people are tough in protecting self and family, but polite and warm in social interactions depending on the context. Researchers have shown that individuals from face and honor cultures use more competitive negotiation strategies than individuals from dignity cultures when negotiating a new business relationship. The finding that honor cultures produce more competitive negotiation styles is not surprising, but the finding that face cultures such as China use competitive styles is interesting. It is a reminder that not all face cultures are alike. In China, reform policies have placed more emphasis on competition, which may lead to tougher negotiation styles. This may not be the case in other face cultures such as Korea or Japan, and this is a reminder that we shouldn't assume that negotiators in a particular cultural prototype (dignity, face, or honor) share the same negotiation behavior. Even among prototypes there may be subtle differences.[74]

Gender may also play a role in negotiation. There appears to be no evidence that men are better negotiators than women or vice versa. It depends on the context of the negotiation. Men achieve better economic outcomes when negotiating for themselves. In contrast, women achieve better outcomes when they are negotiating on behalf of another individual. Often, women lack experience when it comes to negotiating and can benefit from training in negotiation skills.[75]

Inclusive Conversations

The Key to Negotiation for Women—Experience

Barbara Corcoran is no ordinary negotiator. As an entrepreneur and investor on ABC's "Shark Tank," Corcoran has learned a few lessons on negotiating successfully. One of those lessons is to realize that negotiation is ultimately about ego and timing. Corcoran tells the story of her failure to sell her real estate business by taking too long to submit a counteroffer and failing to consider the prospective buyer's personality. When she returned with her counteroffer after two days of mulling it over, the prospective buyer rejected it outright and pulled out of negotiations altogether. Corcoran realized that by waiting too long to respond with her counteroffer, the buyer felt disrespected.

Managing egos more than numbers is a lesson Corcoran has taught to her mostly female real estate brokers who she describes as "phenomenal" and "much better than my men." Women are perceived to lack negotiating skills compared to men, often cited as one of the factors used to explain the gender wage gap. Why then are Corcoran's real estate brokers so successful? These brokers have experience getting up and trying again after being rejected. According to Corcoran, "Negotiation is the second-most important skill...Unfortunately, the only way to really learn is ...by tripping up and making many, many mistakes."

1. Barbara Corcoran suggests that employees be able to make mistakes to gain experience negotiating. How can organizations support all employees, both women and men, as they "learn"?

   Companies can create a culture that supports an open and growth mindset, emphasized by creativity and innovation. This kind of mindset may unfortunately include mistakes, which should not punished but rather viewed as important parts of the learning process.

2. Society tends to view men as better negotiators than women, which may discourage women from negotiating. What ways can organizations encourage women to negotiate more often?

   Women and men should learn the value and basics of negotiating as a management conflict technique. They should be encouraged to take negotiating courses whether offered by their organizations or external to their organizations—many of these courses are online.

Source: M. Sauer, "Barbara Corcoran Shares Her Simple Yet Effective Negotiating Strategy: It's About 'Ego and Timing,' Not 'Price,'" *CNBC*, March 9 (2023), Accessed at Barbara Corcoran: Mistake Taught Me That Secret to Negotiating Is Ego (cnbc.com).

13-6 Conflict Management Styles

Managers have at their disposal a variety of conflict management styles: avoiding, accommodating, competing, compromising, and collaborating. One way of classifying styles of conflict management is to examine the styles' *assertiveness* (the extent to which you want your goals met) and *cooperativeness* (the extent to which you want to see the other party's concerns met).[76] Figure 13.3 graphs the five conflict management styles using these two dimensions. Table 13.3 lists appropriate situations for using each conflict management style.

13-6a Avoiding

Avoiding is a style low on both assertiveness and cooperativeness. Avoiding is a deliberate decision to take no action on a conflict or to stay out of a conflict situation. One common case of conflict avoidance occurs when managers avoid giving difficult feedback to employees. The problem with avoiding this, or any difficult conversation, is that the issues may escalate and the conflict may blow up. Some relationship conflicts, such as those involving political norms and personal tastes, may distract team members from their tasks, in which case, avoiding may be an appropriate strategy.[77] When the parties are angry and need time to cool down, it may be best to use avoidance. There is a potential danger in using an avoiding style too often, however. Research shows that overuse of this style results in negative evaluations from others in the workplace.[78]

13-6b Accommodating

A style in which you are concerned that the other party's goals be met but relatively unconcerned with getting your own way is called accommodating.

Figure 13.3 Conflict Management Styles

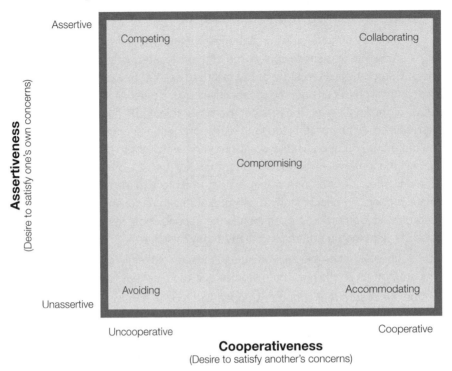

Source: K. W. Thomas, "Conflict and Conflict Management," in M. D. Dunnette, ed., *Handbook of Industrial and Organizational Psychology* (Chicago: Rand McNally, 1976): 900. Used with permission of M. D. Dunnette.

It is cooperative but unassertive. Appropriate situations for accommodating include times when you find you are wrong, when you want to let the other party have their way so that that individual will owe you similar treatment later, or when the relationship is important. One of the skills essential when you find you're wrong is how to make a sincere apology. In conflict resolution, apologies are essential for preserving relationships. High-quality apologies are comprehensive, non-defensive, and characterized by humility.[79] Figure 13.4 shows a simple method for constructing an effective apology.

There are also things you should avoid when making an apology. Be as specific as possible rather than saying "I apologize for whatever went wrong," Use active voice rather than passive voice that avoids responsibility. "I made a mistake" is preferable to "Mistakes were made." Don't shift blame back on the other person by saying "I'm sorry you feel that way," or "I didn't know you were so sensitive." Finally, focus on impact, not intent. Saying "That wasn't my intention" fails to acknowledge the negative impact of words or actions.[80]

Overreliance on accommodating has its dangers. Managers who constantly defer to others may find that others lose respect for them. In addition, accommodating managers may become frustrated because their own needs are never met, and they may lose self-esteem.[81] Research has also shown that individuals will overestimate the importance of the relationship and accommodate at the expense of actual outcomes. Research has shown that two females involved in conflict or negotiation overuse accommodation more than two males involved in similar situations.[82]

13-6c Competing

Competing is a style that is very assertive and uncooperative. You want to satisfy your own interests and are willing to do so at the other party's expense. In an emergency or in situations where you know you are right, it may be appropriate to put your foot down. Starbucks management and its employees who want to unionize appear to be mired in a competitive conflict. Former CEO Howard Schultz returned to lead the company in 2022 and respects the workers' rights to organize. He does not, however, feel that Starbucks needs a union, given its status as a model employer

Table 13.3 Uses of Five Styles of Conflict Management

Conflict-Handling Style	Appropriate Situation
Competing	When quick, decisive action is vital (e.g., emergencies). On important issues for which unpopular actions need implementing (e.g., cost cutting, enforcing unpopular rules, discipline). On issues vital to company welfare when you know you are right. Against people who take advantage of noncompetitive behavior.
Collaborating	To find an integrative solution when both sets of concerns are too important to be compromised. When your objective is to learn. To merge insights from people with different perspectives. To gain commitment by incorporating concerns into a consensus. To work through feelings that have interfered with a relationship.
Compromising	When goals are important but not worth the effort or potential disruption of more assertive modes. When opponents with equal power are committed to mutually exclusive goals. To achieve temporary settlements to complex issues. To arrive at expedient solutions under time pressure. As a backup when collaboration or competition is unsuccessful.
Avoiding	When an issue is trivial or more important issues are pressing. When you perceive no chance of satisfying your concerns. When potential disruption outweighs the benefits of resolution. To let people cool down and regain perspective. When gathering information supersedes immediate decision. When others can resolve the conflict more effectively. When issues seem tangential or symptomatic of other issues.
Accommodating	When you find you are wrong—to allow a better position to be heard, to learn, and to show your reasonableness. When issues are more important to others than to yourself—to satisfy others and maintain cooperation. To build social credits for later issues. To minimize loss when you are outmatched and losing. When harmony and stability are especially important. To allow employees to develop by learning from mistakes.

Source: K. W. Thomas, "Toward Multidimensional Values in Teaching: The Example of Conflict Behaviors," *Academy of Management Review* 2 (1977): 309–325. Reproduced by permission of the publisher via Copyright Clearance Center, Inc.

Figure 13.4 A Two-Step Model for Effective Apologies

Step 1: "I apologize for…"	Step 2: "Moving forward, I will…"
Be specific about the transgression and take ownership.	*Ask for guidance for moving on in reconciliation.*
"I apologize for misgendering you."	"Please share with me how you'd like for me to refer to you and I will do that moving forward.
"I am sorry I took credit for our work."	"I will immediately contact the team and make it clear that this was a dual effort. Moving forward, I will ensure that your name is on the author credits."

Adapted from A. Cabral, "This Is How to Make a Sincere Apology," *Fast Company*, January 6 (2022), accessed at https://www.fastcompany.com/90710657/this-is-how-to-make-a-sincere-apology?partner=rss&utm_source=rss&utm_medium=feed&utm_campaign=rss+fastcompany&utm_content=rss.

YOU

What Is Your Conflict-Handling Style?

Instructions:

For each of the fifteen items, indicate how often you rely on that tactic by circling the appropriate number.

	Rarely	Always
1. I argue my case with my coworkers to show the merits of my position.	1—2—3—4—5	
2. I negotiate with my coworkers so that a compromise can be reached.	1—2—3—4—5	
3. I try to satisfy the expectations of my coworkers.	1—2—3—4—5	
4. I investigate an issue with my coworkers to find a solution acceptable to us.	1—2—3—4—5	
5. I am firm in pursuing my side of the issue.	1—2—3—4—5	
6. I attempt to avoid being "put on the spot" and try to keep my conflict with my coworkers to myself.	1—2—3—4—5	
7. I hold on to my solution to a problem.	1—2—3—4—5	
8. I use "give and take" so that a compromise can be made.	1—2—3—4—5	
9. I exchange accurate information with my coworkers to solve a problem together.	1—2—3—4—5	
10. I avoid open discussion of my differences with my coworkers.	1—2—3—4—5	
11. I accommodate the wishes of my coworkers.	1—2—3—4—5	
12. I try to bring all our concerns out in the open so that the issues can be resolved in the best possible way.	1—2—3—4—5	
13. I propose a middle ground for breaking deadlocks.	1—2—3—4—5	
14. I go along with the suggestions of my coworkers.	1—2—3—4—5	
15. I try to keep my disagreements with my coworkers to myself in order to avoid hard feelings.	1—2—3—4—5	

Scoring Key:

Collaborating		Accommodating		Competing		Avoiding		Compromising	
Item	Score	Item	Score	Item	Score	Item	Score	Item	Score
4.	___	3.	___	1.	___	6.	___	2.	___
9.	___	11.	___	5.	___	10.	___	8.	___
12.	___	14.	___	7.	___	15.	___	13.	___
Total	=___	Total	=___	Total	=___	Total	=___	Total	=___

Your primary conflict-handling style is: _____
(The category with the highest total.)

Your backup conflict-handling style is: _____
(The category with the second highest total.)

Source: Republished with permission from M.A. Rahim, "A Measure of Styles of Handling Interpersonal Conflict," *Academy of Management Journal* (1983), adapted and republished with permission. Permission conveyed through Copyright Clearance Center, Inc.

who treats staff like a family. Since his return, he has improved pay, benefits, and work conditions for employees. Still, over 300 Starbucks locations have unionized. Meanwhile, Starbucks has closed several stores for reasons of employee safety. It seems that Starbucks and its "partners" (workers) are each relying on a competing style of conflict management and seem more like adversaries.[83] Relying solely on competing strategies is dangerous, though. Managers who do so may become reluctant to admit when they are wrong and may find themselves surrounded by people who are afraid to disagree with them. As noted earlier, task conflict and relationship conflict could occur together in team settings, although task conflict is seen as functional and relationship conflict as dysfunctional for the team. In a recent study, dyads of participants were exposed to task-based conflict. One of the two members of the dyads was trained on using either the competing conflict-handling style or the collaborative style. Results indicated that the competing style led to the most relationship conflict, whereas the collaborative style led to the least relationship conflict.[84]

13-6d Compromising

The compromising style is intermediate in both assertiveness and cooperativeness because each party must give up something to reach a solution to the conflict. Compromises are often made in the final hours of union–management negotiations when time is of the essence. Compromise may be an effective backup style when efforts toward collaboration are not successful.[85]

It is important to recognize that compromises are not optimal solutions. Return to work policies, for example, are often a source of conflict between different leaders within the same organization. Chief executive officers (CEOs), for example, may prefer bringing everyone back into the office full-time, because of concerns about productivity and collaboration. In contrast, chief human resource officers (CHROs), who may be more aware of employees' wishes, may believe that employees should have the ultimate say in where and how they should work. What results is horse-trading between the CEO and CHRO and a compromise that is somewhere in the middle ground, like a three day in the office policy hybrid model.[86] One of the problems with the hybrid model is that when workers are at the office, they are on Zoom calls that could be done at home. Another is desk-sharing arrangements, which employees say make it hard to focus and stay productive. When the hybrid work model is the result of a compromise, and not a well-considered conscious choice that best fits the organization, it may not be optimal.

13-6e Collaborating

A win–win style that is high on both assertiveness and cooperativeness is known as collaborating. Working toward it involves an open and thorough discussion of the conflict and arriving at a solution that is satisfactory to both parties. Situations where collaboration may be effective include times when both parties need to be committed to a final solution or when a combination of different perspectives can be formed into a solution. Long-term collaboration leads to improved relationships and effective performance.[87] Teams that use collaboration effectively view conflict as a mutual problem that needs common consideration to achieve resolution.

Understanding this, team members have confidence that other members will work toward mutually beneficial solutions and ultimately generate diverse ideas to facilitate team performance.[88] When team members are trained in mindfulness practices, they gravitate toward collaborative conflict management styles and away from competitive approaches.[89]

Research on the five styles of conflict management indicates that although most managers favor a certain style, they have the capacity to change styles as the situation demands.[90] When supervisors are a third party to a conflict, using collaboration rather than competing or accommodating, and intervening early in the conflict, minimizes anxiety and bullying among team members.[91]

Experiential Exercise

Conflict and Mindful Listening

Sometimes the root of a conflict is feeling that you are not being heard. Sometimes it is also helpful to prepare for a difficult conversation by seeing the conflict from other perspectives. This exercise will give you experience of both verbalizing a conflict situation, examining a conflict from other perspectives, and practicing mindful listening skills.

This exercise will be done in pairs. There will be two rounds, with each person playing the speaker and then the listener.

Instructions for the speaker: This will be a monologue, and you get to speak uninterrupted for five minutes. Think of an unresolved conflict in your life. It could be a conflict with a friend, family member, coworker, or boss. First, describe the conflict as specifically as you can from your perspective. Second, take on the perspective of the other person in the conflict. How would they view the situation? Third, take on the perspective of an uninvolved person. How would they see the conflict?

If you run out of things to say, it's fine. Sit in silence for a few minutes to see what arises and then speak again. The entire five minutes is yours.

Instructions for the listener: Your job is to give your full attention to the speaker and to practice your mindful listening skills. You may not ask questions or give advice. You can acknowledge with facial expressions, body language, or by saying "I hear you," "I see," or "I understand." Try not to over-acknowledge. If the speaker runs out of things to say, make space for the silence and be prepared to listen again.

Let one person speak and one listen for five minutes and then reverse roles for another five minutes. After that, engage in the following conversation in which you both discuss what this experience was like for you.

Source: Adapted from C.-M. Tan, Search Inside Yourself (New York, NY: Harper Collins, 2012).

Discussion questions:

For both the speaker and the listener: What are you feeling right now?

For the speaker:

- How did the experience feel to you? Were you comfortable describing the conflict?
- What did you learn about the conflict you described? What did you learn from the three different perspectives?
- What actions will you take moving forward?

For the listener:

- How would you evaluate your mindful listening skills? Did you feel a desire to interrupt? To advise?
- What was the most difficult part of being the listener?
- What lessons will you take moving forward?

Learning Objectives

13-1 **Describe the nature of conflicts in organizations.** *Conflict* is defined as any situation in which incompatible goals, attitudes, emotions, or behaviors lead to disagreement or opposition between two or more parties. *Functional conflict* is a healthy, constructive disagreement between two or more people. *Dysfunctional conflict* is an unhealthy, destructive disagreement between two or more people.

13-2 **Explain the role structural and personal factors play in causing conflict in organizations.** Conflict can be classified into categories: *structural factors* and *personal factors*. Structural factors include specialization, interdependence, common resources, goal differences, authority relationships, status inconsistencies, and jurisdictional ambiguities. The causes of conflict that arise from individual differences include skills and abilities, personalities, percept.

13-3 **Discuss the nature of group conflict in organizations.** *Interorganizational conflict* occurs between two or more organizations. Conflict

occurring between groups or teams is known as *intergroup conflict*. Possible positive effects include increased group cohesiveness, task focus, and group loyalty. Possible negative consequences include extreme competition, hostility, and decreased communication between groups. *Intragroup conflict* is within groups or teams and can serve to avoid groupthink.

13-4 **Describe the factors that influence conflict between individuals in organizations.** *Intrapersonal conflict* occurs within an individual. Tips for managing intrapersonal conflict are to analyze and match your values with the organization's, understand expectations, and develop political skills. Conflict between two or more people, or *interpersonal conflict*, can arise from individual differences. To manage interpersonal conflict, it is helpful to understand power networks in organizations, defense mechanisms exhibited by individuals, and ways to cope with difficult people.

13-5 **Describe effective and ineffective techniques for managing conflict.**
Effective conflict management techniques include appealing to superordinate goals, expanding resources, changing personnel, changing structure, and confronting and negotiating. Ineffective techniques include nonaction, secrecy, administrative orbiting, due process nonaction, and character assassination.

13-6 **Identify five styles of conflict management.** Managers have at their disposal a variety of conflict management styles: avoiding, accommodating, competing, compromising, and collaborating. One way of classifying styles of conflict management is to examine the styles' assertiveness (the extent to which you want your goals met) and cooperativeness (the extent to which you want to see the other party's concerns met).

Key Terms

administrative orbiting Delaying action on a conflict by buying time. (p. 278)

character assassination The deliberate destruction of a person's reputation or credibility through character attacks. (p. 278)

compensation A compromise mechanism in which an individual attempts to make up for a negative situation by devoting themselves to another pursuit with increased vigor. (p. 276)

conversion A withdrawal mechanism in which emotional conflicts are expressed in physical symptoms. (p. 276)

displacement An aggressive mechanism in which an individual directs their anger toward someone who is not the source of the conflict. (p. 275)

distributive bargaining A negotiation approach in which the goals of the parties are in conflict, and each party seeks to maximize its resources. (p. 279)

due process nonaction A procedure set up to address conflicts that is so costly, time-consuming, or personally risky that no one will use it. (p. 278)

dysfunctional conflict An unhealthy, destructive disagreement between two or more people. (p. 267)

fantasy A withdrawal mechanism that provides an escape from a conflict through daydreaming. (p. 276)

fixation An aggressive mechanism in which an individual keeps up a dysfunctional behavior that obviously will not solve the conflict. (p. 275)

flight/withdrawal A withdrawal mechanism that entails physically escaping (flight) or psychologically escaping (withdrawal) a conflict. (p. 276)

functional conflict A healthy, constructive disagreement between two or more people. (p. 266)

identification A compromise mechanism whereby an individual patterns their behavior after another's. (p. 276)

integrative negotiation A negotiation approach in which the parties' goals are not seen as mutually exclusive, but the focus is on both sides achieving their objectives. (p. 280)

intergroup conflict Conflict that occurs between groups or teams in an organization. (p. 271)

interorganizational conflict Conflict that occurs between two or more organizations. (p. 270)

interpersonal conflict Conflict that occurs between two or more individuals. (p. 274)

interrole conflict A person's experience of conflict among the multiple roles in their life. (p. 271)

intragroup conflict Conflict that occurs within groups or teams. (p. 271)

intrapersonal conflict Conflict that occurs within an individual. (p. 271)

intrarole conflict Conflict that occurs within a single role, such as when a person receives conflicting messages from role senders about how to perform a certain role. (p. 272)

jurisdictional ambiguity The presence of unclear lines of responsibility within an organization. (p. 269)

microaggressions Insensitive statements, questions, and assumptions directed toward marginalized identity groups. (p. 274)

negativism An aggressive mechanism in which a person responds with pessimism to any attempt at solving a problem. (p. 275)

nonaction Doing nothing in hopes that a conflict will disappear. (p. 277)

person–role conflict Conflict that occurs when an individual in a particular role is expected to perform behaviors that clash with their personal values. (p. 273)

rationalization A compromise mechanism characterized by trying to justify one's behavior by constructing bogus reasons for it. (p. 276)

secrecy Attempting to hide a conflict or an issue that has the potential to create conflict. (p. 278)

superordinate goal An organizational goal that is more important to both parties in a conflict than their individual or group goals. (p. 278)

Ethical Dilemma

Jack was excited to see the Mill Furniture delivery van pull into his driveway. He had been waiting for his new sofa to arrive for almost three weeks. The sofa had arrived just in time for him to host a couple of friends for the Super Bowl happening in a few days.

On Sunday, Jack and his friends take their places and begin to watch the game. Shortly after half time, Jack and one of his friends who was sitting on the new sofa with him begin to itch. After closer inspection, both men notice they have bites on them, and the sofa is infested with small black bugs.

The next day, Jack calls Mill Furniture. He tells them he wants his money back. Customer service states that he is not eligible for a refund and offers to send a new sofa. At this point, Jack is totally frustrated and he asks to speak with Robert Mill, owner of the company. He speaks to Mr. Mill who also only offers him a replacement item and refuses to do a refund. Jack tells him that he will sue to get his money back. Mr. Mill informs Jack that he has put a binding arbitration clause into all of Mill Furniture contracts. This clause prohibits Jack from suing.

Jack is speechless. How can they do this? He looks at his six-page contract and finds the clause hidden in the middle of page four. He wants a fair resolution to this conflict but does not feel that binding arbitration will provide this.

1. Using consequential, rule-based, and character theories, evaluate Mr. Mill's decision to insert the binding arbitration clause.

2. What should Mr. Mill do? Why?

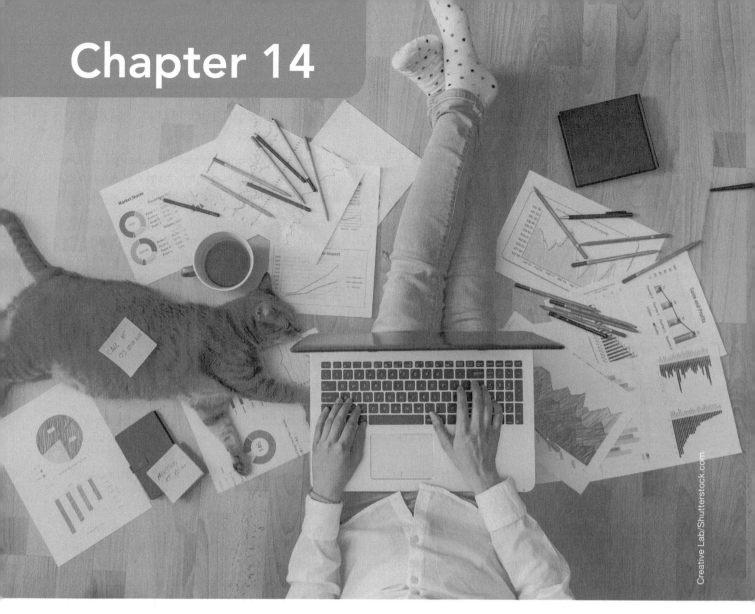

Creative Lab/Shutterstock.com

Chapter 14

Jobs and the Design of Work

Learning Objectives

14-1 Differentiate between job and work.

14-2 Discuss the traditional approaches to job design.

14-3 Describe alternative approaches to job design.

14-4 Describe contemporary issues facing organizations in the design of work.

14-1 Work in Organizations

A **job** can be defined as a set of specified work and task activities that engage an individual in an organization. A job is not the same as an organizational position or a career. *Organizational position* identifies a job in relation to other parts of the organization; *career* refers to a sequence of job experiences over time. A job is also not the same as *work*, at least not in relation to an organization. **Work**, which can be defined as mental or physical activity that has productive results, is organized into jobs. Thus, a *job* is composed of a set of specific tasks, each of which is an assigned piece of *work* to be done in a specific time period.

Work is one important reason organizations exist. Plus, work is an especially important human endeavor because through work, people become securely attached to reality and securely connected in human relationships. However, the COVID-19 pandemic has upended many of the established patterns of both where we work and how we work.[1] The research that preceded the pandemic spans the design of work systems and the study of work groups as well as the study of job design and job redesign. Jobs and the design of work are the key subjects of Chapter 14. Chapter 15 focuses on the larger issue of organizational design. Together, these two chapters emphasize the set of task and authority relationships in organizations through which people get work done.

14-1a The Meaning of Work

The **meaning of work** differs by person, by culture, by country, and by profession. It is not uncommon for contemporary workers to describe their work and careers as a calling, a sense of fulfilling life's purpose.[2] In an increasingly global workplace, it is important to understand and appreciate differences among individuals and cultures with regard to the meaning of work. One study found six patterns that people follow in defining *work*, and these help explain the cultural differences in people's motivation to work.[3]

- *Pattern A* people define *work* as an activity in which value comes from performance and for which a person is accountable. It is generally self-directed and devoid of negative affect.
- *Pattern B* people define *work* as an activity that provides a person with positive personal affect and identity. Work contributes to society and is not unpleasant.
- *Pattern C* people define *work* as an activity from which profit accrues to others by its performance and that may be done in various settings other than a working place. Work is usually physically strenuous and somewhat compulsive.
- *Pattern D* people define *work* as primarily a physical activity a person must do that is directed by others and generally performed in a working place. Work is usually devoid of positive affect and is unpleasantly connected to performance.
- *Pattern E* people define *work* as a physically and mentally strenuous activity. It is generally unpleasant and devoid of positive affect.
- *Pattern F* people define *work* as an activity constrained to specific time periods that does not bring positive affect through its performance.

These six patterns were studied in six different countries: Belgium, Germany, Israel, Japan, the Netherlands, and the United States. Table 14.1 summarizes the percentage of workers in each country who defined work according to each of the six patterns. An examination of the table shows that a small percentage of workers in all six countries used either Pattern E or Pattern F to define *work*. Furthermore, there are significant differences among countries in how *work* is defined. In the Netherlands, *work* is defined most positively and with the most balanced personal and collective reasons for doing it. *Work* is defined least positively and with the most collective reason for doing it in Germany and Japan. Belgium, Israel, and the United States represent a middle position between these two poles.

job A set of specified work and task activities that engage an individual in an organization.

work Mental or physical activity that has productive results.

meaning of work The way a person interprets and understands the value of work as part of life.

Table 14.1 Work Definition Patterns By Nation

SAMPLE	Pattern[a]					
	A	B	C	D	E	F
Total Sample (*N* × 4,950)	11%	28%	18%	22%	11%	12%
NATION						
Belgium	8%	40%	13%	19%	11%	9%
Germany	8%	26%	13%	28%	11%	14%
Israel	4%	22%	33%	23%	9%	9%
Japan	21%	11%	13%	29%	10%	17%
The Netherlands	15%	43%[5]	12%	11%	9%	9%
United States	8%	30%	19%	19%	12%	11%

Note: $X^2 = 680.98$ (25 degrees of freedom). $P < 0.0001$ Significance level.

[a]In Pattern A, work is valued for its performance. The person is accountable and generally self-directed. In Pattern B, work provides a person with positive affect and identity. It contributes to society. In Pattern C, work provides profit to others by its performance. It is physical and not confined to a working place. In Pattern D, work is a required physical activity directed by others and generally unpleasant. In Pattern E, work is physically and mentally strenuous. It is generally unpleasant. In Pattern F, work is constrained to specific time periods. It does not bring positive affect through performance.

Source: From G. W. England and I. Harper, "How Working Is Defined: National Contexts and Demographic and Organizational Role Influences," *Journal of Organizational Behavior* 11 (1990): 253–266. This material is used by permission of John Wiley & Sons, Inc.

In another international study, 5,550 people across ten occupational groups in twenty different countries completed the *Work Value Scales (WVS)*.[4] The WVS is composed of thirteen items measuring various aspects of the work environment, such as responsibility and job security. The study found two common basic work dimensions across cultures: *work content*, measured by items such as "the amount of responsibility on the job," and *job context*, measured by items such as "the policies of my company." This finding suggests that people in many cultures distinguish between the nature of the work itself and elements of the context in which work is done. The idea of two work dimensions supports Herzberg's two-factor theory of motivation (see Chapter 5) and his job enrichment method discussed later in this chapter. Although the meaning of *work* differs among countries, new theorizing about crafting a job also suggests that individual employees can alter work meaning and work identity by changing task and relationship configurations in their work.[5]

14-1b Jobs in Organizations

Task and authority relationships define an organization's structure. Jobs, being the basic building blocks of this task–authority structure, are considered the micro-structural element to which employees most directly relate. Jobs are usually designed to complement and support other jobs in the organization. A new trend is flexible jobs that are a better fit for the emerging agile workforce. These new flexible jobs have less rigidity and less structure than did many of the manufacturing jobs of earlier eras in U.S. work life.

Jobs in organizations are interdependent and designed to make a contribution to the organization's overall mission and goals. For salespeople to be successful, the production people must be effective. For production people to be effective, the material department must be effective. These interdependencies require careful planning and design so that all of the pieces of work fit together into a whole. Suppose an envelope salesperson wants to take an order for 1 million envelopes from John Hancock Financial Services. He must coordinate that order with the production department to establish an achievable delivery date. Failure to incorporate this interdependence into his planning could create conflict, resulting in late delivery to John Hancock.

The central concerns of this chapter are designing work and structuring jobs to prevent such problems and to ensure employee well-being. Inflexible jobs that are rigidly structured have an adverse effect, as they cause stress to employees and limit their career growth. In contrast, so-called smart jobs stimulate learning and growth and thus serve as building blocks for a person's career.[6]

The larger issues in the design of organizations are the competing processes of differentiation and integration (see Chapter 15). *Differentiation* is the process of subdividing and departmentalizing the work of an organization. Jobs result from differentiation, which is necessary because no one can do it all (contrary to the famous statement made by Harold Geneen, former chair of ITT: "If I had enough arms and legs and time, I'd do it all myself"). Even small organizations must divide work so that each person is able to accomplish a manageable piece of the whole. At the same time that the organization divides up the work, however, it must also integrate those pieces back into a whole. *Integration* is the process of connecting jobs and departments into a coordinated, cohesive whole. For example, if the envelope salesperson coordinates his order from John Hancock with the production manager, the company will meet the customer's expectations because integration will have occurred.

14-2 Traditional Approaches to Job Design

Failure to differentiate, integrate, or both may result in badly designed jobs, which in turn cause a variety of performance problems in organizations. Good job design helps avoid these problems, improves productivity, and enhances employee well-being. Approaches to job design that were developed during the twentieth century are job enlargement/ job rotation, job enrichment, and the job characteristics theory. Each approach offers unique benefits to the organization, the employee, or both, but each also has limitations and drawbacks. Furthermore, an unthinking reliance on a traditional approach can be a

work simplification The standardization and the narrow, explicit specification of task activities for workers.

job enlargement A method of job design that increases the number of activities in a job to overcome the boredom of overspecialized work.

serious problem in any company. The later job design approaches were developed to overcome the limitations of traditional job design approaches. For example, job enlargement was intended to overcome the problem of boredom associated with scientific management's narrowly defined approach to jobs.

14-2a Scientific Management

Scientific management, an approach to work design first advocated by Frederick Taylor, emphasizes work simplification. **Work simplification** is the standardization and the narrow, explicit specification of task activities for workers.[7] Jobs designed through scientific management have a limited number of tasks, and each task is scientifically designed so that the worker is not required to think or deliberate. According to Taylor, the role of management and the industrial engineer is to calibrate and define each task carefully. The role of the worker is to execute the task. Elements of scientific management, such as time and motion studies, differential piece-rate systems of pay, and the scientific selection of workers, all focus on the efficient use of labor to the economic benefit of the corporation.

14-2b Job Enlargement/Job Rotation

Job enlargement is a method of job design that increases the number of activities in a job to overcome the boredom of overspecialized work. It is a

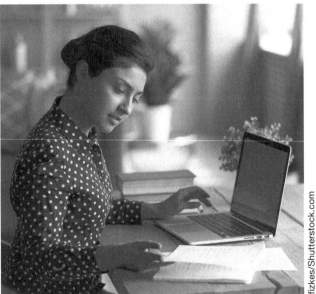
fizkes/Shutterstock.com

Work simplification can give an employee a renewed sense of confidence in his or her work.

traditional approach to solving not only the problem of boredom but also the difficulty of coordinating work.[8] **Job rotation**, a variation of job enlargement, exposes a worker to a variety of specialized job tasks over time. Both of these approaches came into being to solve the perceived problems of overspecialization that arose from lack of variety. In other words, jobs designed by scientific management were too narrow and limited in the number of tasks and activities assigned to each worker. The lack of variety led to understimulation and underutilization of the worker.

Variety can be increased by adding to a worker's activities by means of job enlargement or by giving a worker different activities by means of job rotation. For example, job enlargement for a lathe operator in a steel plant might include selecting the steel pieces to be turned and performing all of the maintenance work on the lathe in addition to running it. As an example of job rotation, an employee at a small bank might take new accounts one day, serve as a cashier another day, and process loan applications on a third day.

One of the first studies of the problem of repetitive work was conducted at IBM after World War II. The company implemented a job enlargement program during the war and evaluated the effort after six years.[9] The two most important results were a significant increase in product quality and a reduction in idle time, both for people and for machines. Less obvious and measurable benefits were enhanced worker status and improved manager–worker communication. The IBM study concluded that job enlargement countered the problems of work specialization. A contemporary study in a Swedish electronics assembly plant used physiological measures of muscle tension.[10] Job enlargement had a positive effect on mechanical exposure variability.

A later study examined the effects of mass production jobs on assembly line workers in the automotive industry.[11] The Hot Trend below discusses electric cars, the latest thing, or is it? Mass production jobs have six characteristics: mechanically controlled work pace, repetitiveness, minimum skill requirements, predetermined tools and techniques, minute division of the production process, and a requirement for surface mental attention rather than thoughtful concentration. The researchers conducted 180 private interviews with assembly line workers and found generally positive attitudes toward pay, security, and supervision. They concluded that job enlargement and job rotation would improve other job aspects, such as repetition and a mechanical work pace.

Job rotation and **cross-training** programs are variations of job enlargement. Pharmaceutical company Eli Lilly has found that job rotation can be a proactive means for enhancing work experiences for career development and can have tangible benefits for employees in the form of salary increases and promotions.[12] In cross-training, workers are trained in different specialized tasks or activities of different jobs. While job rotation may be common practice for high-potential employees, they should remain in a position long enough to see the consequences of their decisions.[13]

> **job rotation** A variation of job enlargement in which workers are exposed to a variety of specialized jobs over time.
>
> **cross-training** A variation of job enlargement in which workers are trained in different specialized tasks or activities.

Hot Trend

Jay Leno on Electric Cars

Electric cars are a hot trend in automotive manufacturing and there are government subsidies aimed at encouraging the mass production of electric cars. But are electric cars really all that new? Apparently, this latest hot trend predates the gas turbine engine of the early 1900s. Car lover Jay Leno owns both a 1909 Baker Electric and a 1914 Detroit Electric, each of which has been converted to modern electrics. In the case of the Detroit Electric, Leno has added air conditioning, Bluetooth, and all kinds of things. In the early 1900s, only the wealthy could afford electric cars because electricity was not widely available in most homes. Leno is very impressed with American manufacturing and drove the new electric Ford F-150 as a work vehicle. So, out with the old...and in with the old! Electric cars are a current hot trend.

Source: J. Leno, "Jay Leno on Electric Cars" *Wall Street Journal*, December 15 (2022), R2.

All three kinds of programs—job enlargement, job rotation, and cross-training horizontally—enlarge jobs; that is, the number and variety of an employee's tasks and activities are increased. Graphic Controls Corporation (now a subsidiary of Tyco International) used cross-training to develop a flexible workforce that enabled the company to maintain high levels of production.[14] The predictions are that global productivity will rise over the next 50 years. Engaged workers are often productive workers, but over focus does have its limitations. Therefore, it is important that employees be able to disengage from one task before moving on to another to achieve high levels of performance.[15]

14-2c Job Enrichment

Job enrichment is designing or redesigning a job by incorporating motivational factors into it. Whereas job enlargement increases the number of job activities through horizontal loading, job enrichment increases the amount of job responsibility through vertical loading. Both approaches to job design are intended, in part, to increase job satisfaction for employees. A study to test whether job satisfaction results from characteristics of the job or of the person found that an interactionist approach is most accurate and that job redesign can contribute to increased job satisfaction for some employees. Another two-year study found that intrinsic job satisfaction and job perceptions are reciprocally related to each other.[16]

Job enrichment builds on Herzberg's two-factor theory of motivation, which distinguished between motivational and hygiene factors for people at work. Whereas job enlargement recommends increasing and varying the number of activities a person does, job enrichment recommends increasing the recognition, responsibility, and opportunity for achievement. For example, enlarging the lathe operator's job means adding maintenance activities, and enriching the job means having the operator meet with customers who buy the products.

Herzberg believed that only certain jobs should be enriched and that the first step is to select the jobs appropriate for job enrichment.[17] He recognized

job enrichment Designing or redesigning a job by incorporating motivational factors into it.

that some people prefer simple jobs. Once jobs are selected for enrichment, management should brainstorm about possible changes, revise the list to include only specific changes related to motivational factors, and screen out generalities and suggestions that would simply increase activities or numbers of tasks. Those whose jobs are to be enriched should not participate in this process, as doing so would present a conflict of interest.

A seven-year implementation study of job enrichment at AT&T found that approach beneficial.[18] Job enrichment required a big change in management style, and AT&T found that it could not ignore hygiene factors in the work environment just because it was enriching existing jobs. One problem with job enrichment as a strategy for work design is that it is based on an oversimplified motivational theory. Another problem is the lack of consideration for individual differences among employees. Job enrichment, like scientific management's work specialization and job enlargement/job rotation, is a universal approach to the design of work and thus does not differentiate among individuals. Many chief marketing officers (CMOs) appear to believe they do not have enriched jobs. The average tenure of a CMO was found to be 4.1 years, which compares to 8 years for CEOs, 5.1 years for CFOs, 5 years for CHROs, and 4.3 years for CIOs.[19] Just getting to the C-Level does not guarantee an enriched job, nor job satisfaction.

14-2d Job Characteristics Theory

The job characteristics theory, which was initiated during the mid-1960s, is a traditional approach to the design of work that makes a significant departure from the three earlier approaches. It emphasizes the interaction between the individual and specific attributes of the job; therefore, it is a person–job fit model rather than a universal job design model. It originated in a research study of 470 workers in forty-seven different jobs across eleven industries.[20] The study measured and classified relevant task characteristics for these forty-seven jobs and found four core job characteristics: job variety, autonomy, responsibility, and interpersonal interaction. The study also found that core job characteristics did not affect all workers in the same way. A person's values, religious beliefs, and ethnic background influenced how the worker responded to the job. Specifically, workers with rural values and workers with strong religious beliefs preferred jobs high in core characteristics, and workers with urban values and those with weaker religious beliefs preferred jobs low in core characteristics. Another study tested the effect of job and work characteristics on employee turnover intentions and found that employees consider both when deciding to leave a company.[21]

Richard Hackman and his colleagues modified the original model by including three critical psychological states of the individual and refining the measurement of core job characteristics. The result is the **Job Characteristics Model** shown in Figure 14.1.[22] The **Job Diagnostic Survey (JDS)**, the most commonly used job design measure, was developed to diagnose jobs by measuring the five core job characteristics and three critical psychological states shown in the model. The core job characteristics stimulate the critical psychological states in the manner shown in Figure 14.1. This results in varying personal and work outcomes, as identified in the figure. A new proposal to modify the job characteristics model suggests that psychological ownership is an important factor in job design.[23]

Hackman and his colleagues say that the five core job characteristics interact to determine an overall *Motivating Potential Score (MPS)* for a specific job. The MPS indicates a job's potential for motivating incumbents. An individual's MPS is determined by the following equation:

$$MPS = \frac{\left[\begin{array}{c}Skill\\variety\end{array}\right] + \left[\begin{array}{c}Task\\identity\end{array}\right] + \left[\begin{array}{c}Task\\significance\end{array}\right]}{3}$$

$$[Autonomy] \times [Feedback]$$

The Job Characteristics Model includes *growth need strength* (the desire to grow and fully develop one's abilities) as a moderator. People with high growth

Job Characteristics Model A framework for understanding person–job fit through the interaction of core job dimensions with critical psychological states within a person.

Job Diagnostic Survey (JDS) The survey instrument designed to measure the elements in the Job Characteristics Model.

Figure 14.1 The Job Characteristics Model

Source: J. R. Hackman and G. R. Oldham, "The Relationship Among Core Job Dimensions, the Critical Psychological States, and On-the-Job Outcomes," in *The Job Diagnostic Survey: An Instrument for the Diagnosis of Jobs and the Evaluation of Job Redesign Projects* (New Haven, Conn.: Department of Administrative Services, Yale University, 1974). Reprinted by permission of Greg R. Oldham.

need strength respond favorably to jobs with high MPSs, and individuals with low growth need strength respond less favorably to such jobs. The job characteristics theory further suggests that core job dimensions stimulate three critical psychological states according to the relationships specified in the model. These critical psychological states are defined as follows:

1. *Experienced meaningfulness of the work*, or the degree to which the employee experiences the job as one that is generally meaningful, valuable, and worthwhile.

2. *Experienced responsibility for work outcomes*, or the degree to which the employee feels personally accountable and responsible for the results of the work they do.

3. *Knowledge of results*, or the degree to which the employee knows and understands, on a continuous basis, how effectively they are performing the job.

In one early study, Hackman and Oldham administered the JDS to 658 employees working on sixty-two different jobs in seven business organizations.[24] The JDS was useful for job redesign efforts through one or more of five implementing concepts: (1) combining tasks into larger jobs, (2) forming natural work teams to increase task identity and task significance, (3) establishing relationships with customers, (4) loading jobs vertically with more responsibility, and/or (5) opening feedback channels for the job incumbent. For example, if an automotive mechanic received little feedback on the quality of repair work performed, one redesign strategy would be to solicit customer feedback one month after each repair.

A recent sequence of two studies conducted in Egypt aimed to disaggregate *work autonomy*, an important component in job design theory.[25] Study 1 included 534 employees in two Egyptian organizations. Study 2 involved 120 managers in four organizations. The results indicated that separate work method, work schedule, and work criteria autonomy were three separate facets of work autonomy.

An alternative to the Job Characteristics Model is the *Job Characteristics Inventory (JCI)* developed by Henry Sims and Andrew Szilagyi.[26] The JCI primarily

measures core job characteristics. It is not as comprehensive as the JDS because it does not incorporate critical psychological states, personal and work outcomes, or employee needs. The JCI does give some consideration to structural and individual variables that affect the relationship between core job characteristics and the individual.[27] One comparative analysis of the JCI and JDS found similarities in the measures and in the models' predictions.[28] The comparative analysis also found two differences. First, the variety scales in the two models appear to have different effects on performance. Second, the autonomy scales in the two models appear to have different effects on employee satisfaction. Overall, the JCI and JDS both support the usefulness of a person–job fit approach to the design of work over the earlier, universal theories.

Engagement Psychological conditions related to job design features are a particular concern of the Job Characteristics Model.[29] One study of more than 200 managers and employees in a Midwestern insurance company found that meaningfulness, safety, and availability were three important psychological conditions that affected employees' **engagement** in their jobs and work roles. The extent to which employees are engaged in their jobs has an impact on workplace behaviors. Employees who identify with supervisor goals are less likely to engage in counterproductive behaviors in the workplace, and this relationship operates through employee engagement. The degree to which work engagement functions as a bridge between goal congruence and deviant behaviors depends on the emotional intelligence of employees. Employees with highly developed emotional intelligence skills will be more likely to respond positively to goal congruence.[30] Gallup's Q12 survey was used to improve engagement for a clinical nutrition group at St. Mary's/Duluth Clinic Health System with successful results.[31] Despite its importance to company success, however, only one-third of employees in a recent study reported that they were engaged in their work.[32]

Full engagement requires the strategic management of one's energy in response to the environment.[33] Being fully engaged in one's work role and job can be highly appropriate and yet demand energy, time, and effort. To achieve balance and afford opportunity for recovery, there is

engagement The expression of oneself as one performs in work or other roles.

a commensurate need to strategically and appropriately disengage from one's job and work role on a periodic basis. The effective management of energy in response to one's job and work role leads to both high performance and personal renewal. Thus, while the design of work is important, the human spirit's response to job characteristics and work design features is equally important.

14-3 Alternative Approaches to Job Design

Because each of the traditional job design approaches has limitations, several alternative approaches have emerged over the past couple of decades. This section examines four alternatives that are in the process of being tried and tested. First, it examines the social information-processing model. Second, it reviews ergonomics and the interdisciplinary framework of Michael Campion and Paul Thayer. Their framework builds on traditional job design approaches. Third, this section examines the international perspectives of the Japanese, Germans, and Scandinavians. Finally, it focuses on the health and well-being aspects of work design. Healthy work enables individuals to adapt, function well, and balance work with private life activities.[34] An emerging fifth approach to the design of work through teams and autonomous work groups was addressed in Chapter 9.

14-3a Social Information Processing

The traditional approaches to the design of work emphasize objective core job characteristics. In contrast, the **social information-processing (SIP) model** emphasizes the interpersonal aspects of work design. Specifically, the SIP model says that what others tell us about our jobs is important.[35] The SIP model has four basic premises about the work environment.[36] First, other people provide cues we use to understand the work environment. Second, other people help us judge what is important in our jobs. Third, other people tell us how they see our jobs. Fourth, other people's positive and negative feedback helps us understand our feelings about our jobs. This is very consistent with the dynamic model

of the job design process that views it as a social one involving job-holders, supervisors, and peers.[37]

The COVID-19 pandemic, especially with the demands for social distancing, introduced an existential threat into many social networks and strained interpersonal ecosystems. This pandemic distress not only reshaped many people's work and social connections but added emotional distance to many relationships.[38] One of the job-related consequences of this was that advice seeking behavior was constrained and social information-processing was compromised. The dynamism of this approach to job design was curtailed in degrees by pandemic coping behaviors. However, all employees are unlikely to be impacted equally by an exogenous shock to the work environment such as the pandemic. In many work systems there are core and peripheral employees in social networks. Research suggests that those in the core have information advantages that are not enjoyed by those in the periphery.[39] Zoom and Microsoft Teams as communication media do not quite replicate the level of information richness that is available in face-to-face discussion. In addition to the job design impact of COVID-19, the pandemic introduced a range of mental health challenges for job incumbents, such as social isolation. Building on the SIP model of interpersonal work design, a mitigating approach to pandemic distress might be playful work design.[40] A process that proactively introduces fun or competition into the design of work helps lighten the load for everyone.

14-3b Ergonomics and Interdisciplinary Framework

Michael Campion and Paul Thayer used **ergonomics** based on engineering, biology, and psychology to develop an interdisciplinary framework for the design of work. Actually, they say that four approaches—the mechanistic, motivational, biological, and perceptual/motor approaches—are necessary because no one approach can solve all performance problems caused by poorly designed jobs. Table 14.2

social information-processing (SIP) model A model that suggests that the important job factors depend in part on what others tell a person about the job.

ergonomics The science of adapting work and working conditions to the employee or worker.

Table 14.2 Summary of Outcomes From Various Job Design Approaches

Job Design Approach (Discipline)	Positive Outcomes	Negative Outcomes
Mechanistic Approach (mechanical engineering)	Decreased training time Higher personnel utilization levels Lower likelihood of error Less chance of mental overload Lower stress levels	Lower job satisfaction Lower motivation Higher absenteeism
Motivational Approach (industrial psychology)	Higher job satisfaction Higher motivation Greater job involvement Higher job performance Lower absenteeism	Increased training time Lower personnel utilization levels Greater chance of errors Greater chance of mental overload and stress
Biological Approach (biology)	Less physical effort Less physical fatigue Fewer health complaints Fewer medical incidents Lower absenteeism Higher job satisfaction	Higher financial costs because of changes in equipment or job environment
Perceptual Motor Approach (experimental psychology)	Lower likelihood of error Lower likelihood of accidents Less chance of mental stress Decreased training time Higher personnel utilization levels	Lower job satisfaction Lower motivation

Source: Reprinted from Michael A. Campion and Paul W. Thayer, "Job Design: Approaches, Outcomes, and Trade-Offs," *Organizational Dynamics*, 15, No. 3 (1987). Copyright © 1987, with permission from Elsevier.

describes the benefits and limitations of each approach; we will take a closer look at the biological and perceptual/motor approaches below. One ergonomics study of eighty-seven administrative municipal employees found lower levels of upper body pain along with other positive outcomes thanks to the workstation redesign.[41]

The interdisciplinary framework allows the job designer or manager to consider trade-offs and alternatives among the approaches based on

Ergonomically designed work stations aim to optimize health, well-being, and productivity.

desired outcomes. If a manager finds poor performance a problem, for example, the manager should analyze the job to ensure a design aimed at improving performance. The interdisciplinary framework is important because badly designed jobs cause far more performance problems than managers realize.[42]

The *biological approach* to job design emphasizes the person's interaction with physical aspects of the work environment and is concerned with the amount of physical exertion, such as lifting and muscular effort, required by the position. For example, an analysis of medical claims at TXI's Chaparral Steel Company identified lower back pain as the most common physical problem experienced by steel workers and managers alike. As a result, the company instituted an education and exercise program under expert guidance to improve employees' lower back care. Program graduates received back cushions for their chairs with "Chaparral Steel Company" embossed on them.[43]

The *perceptual/motor approach* to job design also emphasizes the person's interaction with physical aspects of the work environment and is based on engineering that considers human factors such as strength or coordination, ergonomics, and experimental psychology. It places an important emphasis on human interaction with computers, information, and other operational systems. This approach addresses how people mentally process information acquired from the physical work environment through perceptual and motor skills. The approach emphasizes perception and fine motor skills as opposed to the gross motor skills and muscle strength emphasized in the *mechanistic approach*. The perceptual/motor approach is more likely to be relevant to operational and technical work, such as keyboard operations and data entry jobs, which may tax a person's concentration and attention, than to managerial, administrative, and custodial jobs, which are less likely to strain concentration and attention.

One study using the interdisciplinary framework to improve jobs evaluated 377 clerical, 80 managerial, and 90 analytical positions.[44] The jobs were improved by combining tasks and adding ancillary duties. The improved jobs provided greater motivation for the incumbents and were better from a perceptual/motor standpoint. The jobs were poorly designed from a mechanical engineering standpoint, however, and they were unaffected from a biological standpoint. Again, the interdisciplinary framework considers trade-offs and alternatives when evaluating job redesign efforts. Table 14.2 presents a summary of the positive and negative outcomes of redesign.

14-3c International Perspectives on the Design of Work

Each culture has a unique way of understanding and designing work.[45] As organizations become more global and international, an appreciation of the perspectives of others is increasingly important. A study of 2,359 call centers in sixteen countries found that an organization's management strategy and operational context influences variation in work design.[46] The Japanese, Germans, and Scandinavians in particular have distinctive perspectives on the design and organization of work.[47] Each of these cultures has a perspective forged within its unique cultural and economic system, and each is distinct from the approaches used in North America.

The Japanese Approach The Japanese began harnessing their productive energies during the 1950s by drawing on the product quality ideas of

> A study of 2,359 call centers in sixteen countries found that an organization's management strategy and operational context influences variation in work design.

W. Edwards Deming.[48] In addition, the central government became actively involved in the economic resurgence of Japan, and it encouraged companies to conquer industries rather than to maximize profits.[49] Such an industrial policy, built on the Japanese cultural ethic of collectivism, has implications for how work is done. Whereas Frederick Taylor and his successors in the United States emphasized the job of an individual worker, the Japanese system emphasizes the strategic level and encourages collective and cooperative working arrangements.[50] Also, the Japanese emphasize performance, accountability, and other-or self-directedness in defining work, whereas Americans emphasize the positive affect, personal identity, and social benefits of work.

Japanese success with lean production has drawn the attention of managers. **Lean production** methods are similar to the production concept of **sociotechnical systems (STS)**, although there are some differences.[51] In particular, STS gives greater emphasis to (1) teamwork and self-managed and autonomous work groups, (2) the ongoing nature of the design process, and (3) human values in the work process. The approaches are similar, however, in that both differ from Taylor's scientific management and both emphasize job variety, feedback to work groups and teams, support of human resources, and control of production variance close to the point of origin. One three-year evaluation of lean teams, assembly lines, and workflow formalization as lean production practices conducted in Australia found that employees in all lean production groups were negatively affected, with the assembly line employees experiencing the worst effects.[52]

lean production Using committed employees with ever expanding responsibilities to achieve zero waste and 100 percent good product, delivered on time, every time.

sociotechnical systems (STS) Giving equal attention to technical and social considerations in job design.

The German Approach The German approach to work has been shaped by Germany's unique educational system, cultural values, and economic system. The Germans are a highly educated and well-organized people. For example, their educational system has a multitrack design with technical and university alternatives. The German economic system puts a strong emphasis on free enterprise, private property rights, and management–labor cooperation. A comparison of voluntary and mandated management–labor cooperation in Germany found that productivity was superior under voluntary cooperation.[53] The Germans value hierarchy and authority relationships and, as a result, are generally disciplined.[54] Germany's workers are highly unionized, and their discipline and efficiency have enabled Germany to be highly productive while its workers labor substantially fewer hours than do Americans.

The traditional German approach to work design was **technocentric**, an approach that placed technology and engineering at the center of job design decisions. Also, German industrial engineers have a more **anthropocentric** approach, which places human considerations at the center of job design decisions. The former approach uses a natural scientific process in the design of work, whereas the latter relies on a more humanistic process, as shown in Figure 14.2. In the anthropocentric approach, work is evaluated using the criteria of practicability and worker satisfaction at the individual level and the criteria of endurability and acceptability at the group level. Figure 14.2 also identifies problem areas and disciplines concerned with each aspect of the work design. Can technology in the workplace be overdone? The above feature discusses this possibility.

The Scandinavian Approach The Scandinavian cultural values and economic system stand in contrast to the German system. The social democratic tradition in Scandinavia has emphasized social concern rather than industrial efficiency. Accordingly, the Scandinavians place great emphasis on a work design model that encourages a high degree of worker control and good social support systems for workers.[55] Lennart Levi believes that circumstantial and inferential scientific evidence provides a sufficiently strong basis for legislative and policy actions

technocentric Placing technology and engineering at the center of job design decisions.

anthropocentric Placing human considerations at the center of job design decisions.

Figure 14.2 Hierarchical Model of Criteria for the Evaluation of Human Work

Scientific approaches of labor sciences	Levels of evaluation of human work	Problem areas and assignment to disciplines
View from natural science	Practicability	Technical, anthropometric, and psychophysical problems (ergonomics)
	Endurability	Technical, physiological, and medical problems (ergonomics and occupational health)
Primarily oriented to individuals / Primarily oriented to groups	Acceptability	Economical and sociological problems (occupational psychology and sociology, personnel management)
View from cultural studies	Satisfaction	Sociopsychological and economic problems (occupational psychology and sociology, personnel management)

Source: H. Luczak, "'Good Work' Design: An Ergonomic, Industrial Engineering Perspective," in J. C. Quick, L. R. Murphy, and J. J. Hurrell, eds., Stress and Well-Being at Work (Washington, D.C.: American Psychological Association, 1997). Copyright © 1997 by the American Psychological Association. Reprinted with permission.

for redesigns aimed at enhancing worker well-being. An example of such an action for promoting good working environments and occupational health was Swedish Government Bill 1976/77:149, which stated, "Work should be safe both physically and mentally *but also* provide opportunities for involvement, job satisfaction, and personal development." In 1991, the Swedish Parliament set up the Swedish Working Life Fund to fund research, intervention programs, and demonstration projects in work design. For example, a study of Stockholm police on shift schedules found that going from a daily, counterclockwise rotation to a clockwise rotation was more compatible with human biology and resulted in improved sleep, less fatigue, lower systolic blood pressure, and lower blood levels of triglycerides and glucose.[56] Hence, the work redesign improved the police officers' health.

14-3d Work Design and Well-Being

An international, interdisciplinary collaboration of psychologists, organizational scholars, industrial engineers, and occupational health and medical scientists is concerned about designing work and jobs that are both healthy and productive.[57] For example, the effort-reward imbalance model emphasizes the adverse effects of demands and obligations when the work exceed the rewards provided, such as salary, esteem, and security.[58] Health and well-being accompany the restoration of balance. The job demands-resources (JD-R) model is a second imbalance model that emphasizes the strain and well-being effects of the imbalance.[59] The American Psychological Association suggests that organizations should design jobs to increase

worker control and reduce worker uncertainty, while at the same time managing conflict and task/job demands. **Job crafting** is one high-control job redesign strategy in which the incumbent proactively manages the tasks, relationships, and personal perceptions of the work. These are often then aligned with the incumbent's skills, abilities, and knowledge.[60]

In addition to these effects of work and job design on well-being, there are also direct effects of sleep on well-being.[61] Actually, the well-being concern with sleep is when individuals fail to get enough sleep, or sleep deprivation. Sleep disorders can increase cardiovascular disease risk along with less server medical and psychological problems. Shift work is one place where work and sleep have interactive effects on well-being. Beyond the individual adverse well-being effects of sleep deprivation, there can be spillover effects into the workplace, influencing emotions, perceptions of work, as well as workplace (and even non-worksite) injuries and accidents. On the positive side, achieving sufficient and restful sleep carries well-being benefits that may have positive spillover effects into the workplace. See Table 14.3 for more information on increasing control, reducing uncertainty, and managing conflict. The YOU on page 302 provides an opportunity to evaluate how psychologically healthy your work environment is.

Job crafting is a work redesign strategy in which an incumbent proactively manages job tasks, relationships and perceptions to achieve better person-job fit.

Table 14.3 Adjusting Work Design Parameters

Increase control by:	Reduce uncertainty by:	Manage conflict through:
• Giving workers the opportunity to control several aspects of the work and the workplace	• Providing employees with timely and complete information needed for their work	• Participative decision-making
• Designing machines and tasks with optimal response times and/or ranges	• Making clear and unambiguous work assignments	• Supportive supervisory styles
• Implementing performance-monitoring systems as a source of relevant feedback to workers	• Improving communication at shift change time	• Having sufficient resources available to meet work demands, thus preventing conflict
	• Increasing employee access to information sources	

Is your work environment a healthy one?

To determine whether your work environment is a healthy one, read the text section on "Work Design and Well-Being," and then complete the following four steps. Answer each question in the five steps "yes" or "no."

Step 1. Control and Influence

_____ Do you have influence over the pace of your work?

_____ Are system response times neither too fast nor too slow?

_____ Do you have a say in your work assignments and goals?

_____ Is there an opportunity for you to comment on your performance appraisal?

Step 2. Information and Uncertainty

_____ Do you receive timely information to complete your work?

_____ Do you receive complete information for your work assignments?

_____ Is there adequate planning for changes that affect you at work?

_____ Do you have access to all the information you need at work?

Step 3. Conflict at Work

_____ Does the company apply policies clearly and consistently?

_____ Are job descriptions and task assignments clear?

_____ Are there adequate policies and procedures for the resolution of conflicts?

_____ Is your work environment an open, participative one?

Step 4. Job Scope and Task Design

_____ Is there adequate variety in your work activities and/or assignments?

_____ Do you receive timely, constructive feedback on your work?

_____ Is your work important to the overall mission of the company?

_____ Do you work on more than one small piece of a big project?

Scoring

Count the number of "yes" answers in Steps 1 through 4: _____

If you have 10 to 16 "yes" answers, this suggests that your work environment is a psychologically healthy one.

If you have 7 or fewer "yes" answers, this may suggest that your work environment is not as psychologically healthy as it could be.

14-4 Contemporary Issues in the Design of Work

COVID-19 generated a wide range of threats to occupational health, safety, well-being, and economic security.[62] For jobs and the design of work, COVID-19 created job insecurity, drove remote work arrangements and hybrid work, and led to lack of information, all of which posed threats to many people's work lives and economic well-being. In addition, COVID-19 spawned innovations to cope with the crisis and **gig workers** seemed to thrive during the pandemic, especially among essential workers. Gig workers, sometimes called digital nomads, represent one form of flexible work arrangement between the organization and those doing the work Flexible work arrangements have been linked to increased employee retention in developing countries. For example, one study of Malaysian banking employees found that allowing workers to participate in flexible work arrangements increased the likelihood that they would remain in their jobs once minimum salary requirements had been met.[63] Companies have found it necessary to respond to COVID-19

Gig workers are independent contractors, online platform workers, contract firm workers, on-call workers, and temporary workers.

Inclusive Conversations

Glass Escalators in the Teaching Profession

The *glass escalator* is a term that describes a man's rapid ascension to higher levels in occupations dominated by women. Three-quarters of K–12 teachers are women, so why do male teachers make more on average than female teachers? According to data from a national survey of teachers and principals, male teachers tend to take on extra responsibilities for which they receive extra pay. As a result, male teachers made $2,200 more than female teachers even after accounting for differences in subject taught and student characteristics. Michael Hansen, senior fellow at Brookings' Brown Center on Education Policy and colleagues, suggests that while teachers work under a compensation system that does not favor one gender over another, male teachers between the ages of 21 to 30 are more likely than their female counterparts to take on additional duties, such as coaching or teaching summer school, duties that come with additional compensation. The potential for male teachers to be paid for taking on additional duties increases when the principal is also male, which may be an indicator of gender-based discrimination.

1. Why might male teachers be more willing to take on additional job duties than female teachers?
   Students may suggest that males, especially in the age ranges indicated, may be unlikely to have families, which gives them extra time after school to take on additional responsibilities. Other reasons may include similarity bias in which male leaders provide opportunities to like members of their in-group.

2. Think about other occupations where glass escalators may exist. Why might men be considered for high level positions in occupations where women are the majority?
   Due to gender role socialization, men may be perceived as possessing leadership characteristics despite the occupation. Whether teaching or nursing, where women make up the majority, decision-makers (whether men or women) may view men as leaders and steer them to leadership roles.

Source: A. Wong, "Equal Pay Day? Not for Teachers. Why Men Make More Than Women in Female-Dominated Positions," *USAToday*, March 14 (2023), accessed at Why Teachers' Pay Gap Persists, Women Still Earn Less on Equal Pay Day (usatoday.com).

with **remote work** arrangements, **hybrid work** arrangements, and other innovations that lead to redesigns in many workplaces. Transcending these COVID-19 coping issues is the glass escalator, discussed in the Inclusive Conversation above.

14-4a Remote Work

Remote work encompasses a range of remote working arrangements that include work from home (WFH), work from anywhere, remote job, distance work, mobile work, and telework. As remote work rose during COVID-19, researchers were concerned about several aspects of the arrangement, such as its effect on employees personally, effect on employees' careers, family life and gender roles, and health, well-being and safety.[64] As with any job and work design strategy, there are pros and cons for the job incumbent as well as the organization. For remote workers, relationships and the use of social media were important resources during the pandemic.[65] Remote work-from-home arrangements were an accommodation to the COVID-19 pandemic but were accompanied by work design considerations that had

significant impact on the work-family interface. For example, the interruption landscape is different when working in a corporate office versus in the home.[66] Family-to-work interruptions in the home can interfere with productivity and contribute to emotional exhaustion from competing demands for employees. Having a dedicated home office space, to include a physical boundary such as a wall and door, can help reduce interference with work from home interruptions. However, both work and family roles got upended because of COVID-19 and virtually everyone found their established patterns of work-family conflict and enrichment fundamentally altered.[67] The process of reestablishing functional boundaries to ensure productive work time and happy family time did not come with a playbook,

remote work is any work done by employees without their commuting to a central location, such as an office, for the purpose of working.

hybrid work is a flexible work model that divides working hours between a company location and elsewhere, such as remote location or on-the-go.

thus leaving employees and family members in a position to renegotiate boundaries to manage conflicts and enhance enrichment. For leaders, supervisors, and human resource professionals, the dynamics between remote work and work-life balance are important for employee well-being and workplace productivity.[68] There are some undesirable realities of remote work and the misfits between expectations and reality seem to fall into four categories. These are (1) flextime vs. work intensity, (2) flexplace vs. space limitation, (3) technologically feasible work arrangements, technostress, and isolation, and (4) family-friendly work arrangement vs. housework and care intensity. Giving consideration to these four dimensions in designing a successful remote work strategy is important. There is a compelling argument for returning to the office as a way of mitigating the mental health consequences of social isolation in the work domain.

In conclusion, is remote work a blessing or a burden?[69] There is evidence on both sides of the question. On the negative side, remote work triggered by the pandemic increased levels of stress and anxiety for many employees, having an adverse impact on their mental health and overall well-being. Employees expressed concerns about increased meetings and less cyber security from work-from-home arrangements. On the positive side, remote work resulted in many employees experiencing more support from their supervisors and companies as well as having greater discretionary latitude about work and experiencing a slower pace to the work process, maybe less intensity. Employees and organizations benefit from weighing the pros and cons, thoughtfully considering both sides of the ledger.

While hybrid work is flexible, designing time and place tradeoffs can optimize mutual benefits and productivity at the same time.

The *four-day workweek* is a variation on hybrid work that has been around for some time. However, a six-month trial of the four-day workweek in the UK called 4 Day Week Global showed that for many it is a fairly smooth transition and with some understandable hurdles, mostly among those with fixed or inflexible practices, systems or cultures that date back well into the last century and is catching on in the United States.[71] Overall, there was no productivity loss associated with a four-day work week and some companies reported significant improvements, supporting earlier findings. Additional benefits found were freed up employee personal time, boosting employee well-being, and improved productivity during working hours.

The Boston Consulting Group sees hybrid work as the work of the future, but not in a cookie cutter mold.[72] They encourage employees and organizations to use the COVID-19 pandemic as a lever for reimagining work and redesigning the workplace. This requires attention to four building blocks central to the reimagining process. The first is leadership, culture, and purpose. Leaders must revisit the organization's purpose and culture. The second is structure and roles. This goes to job and organizational design. The third is ways of working. Engage employees in the redesign, reimagining process. Finally, the fourth is systems and spaces. Use the time and place principles discussed above to reimagine office redesigns and work-at-home opportunities. When following this reimagining

14-4b Hybrid Work

Hybrid work is a flexible work model that divides working hours between a company location and elsewhere, such as home location. The two key dimensions of a successful hybrid work arrangement are time and place tradeoffs to ensure productivity. Using four principles along these two dimensions enables employees and organizations to optimize results.[70] The two time principles are: let asynchronous time boost focus and enable synchronous time to be the opportunity for coordination. In essence, there are times to work alone and times to work together, cooperatively. The two place principles are: design the office space for cooperation and make the work time at home a source of energy. Energy and coordination are the key ingredients to productive work.

Employees who are the most satisfied with telecommuting are those who are comfortable with technology and have more experience within an organization.

process for hybrid work, be sure to factor in individual human concerns as well as institutional ones.[73]

Hybrid work does have potential downsides for two domains of work that are, beyond most others, inherently social.[74] These two domains are innovation and culture. There is some anecdotal evidence that hybrid work is causing damage in these two domains but no substantial evidence beyond that. If the threat is there, the best approach for leaders and managers is to be proactive so as to prevent any possible damage to the innovation process or to the organization's culture. This can be achieved to ensure that the hybrid work design has sufficient 'together' work time.

14-4c Innovation

Innovation is an essential element of advances in a wide range of work and professional life. Innovation is a double-edged sword that can be used for good or for ill. The increases in remote and hybrid work have led to accompanying increases, and innovations, in how many organizations, especially large organizations, engage in monitoring their employees.[75] Before COVID-19, about 30 percent of large employers engaged in some form of employee monitoring whereas by 2022 that number doubled, with 60 percent of large employers engaged in some form of employee monitoring. Using employee-monitoring software, organizations measure and/or capture: software used, websites visited, devices used, logins/logouts, documents/data accessed, active and idle time, key logging, technology that reviews e-mails, messaging, and voice and screen captures. Federal law generally prohibits employers from intercepting personal phone calls; however, federal and state laws do not provide effective protection against dominant forms of employee monitoring. While these innovations are generally legal, have employers gone too far? On a cautionary note, increased monitoring may have an unintended effect of increasing employee deviance because of a reduced sense of moral responsibility and agency on their part.[76]

On a creative and more positive note, Boeing-backed Wisk Aero is using innovation to invent new ways to get there by designing and testing the flying taxi.[77] Flying taxis? Yes, they are for real and there are large regulatory authorities with strong initiative to bring these flying taxis to market. Wisk Aero is one of several entrants in this space. Developing the air taxi is only one element of the innovation challenge, and it requires developing an air taxi that can take off and land like a helicopter while flying like an airplane at altitude. The other elements of the system needed are takeoff and landing sites, air traffic control regulations. One idea is using helipads and vertiports on top of buildings, many of these sites are not fully utilized. Being in the flying taxi business startup now may be like being in the early days of the automobile or the early days of flight, thrilling and risky all at once.

For innovations to thrive requires an innovation ecosystem with at least five major stakeholders.[78] These major stakeholders are the entrepreneur who drives the innovation, such as CEO Gary Gysin of Wisk Aero, investors who provide risk capital, major research universities with wide ranges of professional expertise, government agencies, and large corporations. These stakeholders must be linked by a strong social fabric of mutual interest, complementary needs and resources, and trust. Silicon Valley is a key example of an innovation hub that has the necessary ecosystem for supporting, nurturing, sustaining, and launching innovations. Austin, Texas is an emergent innovation hub with a strong ecosystem for entrepreneurs that is linked by a strong social fabric of mutual

Organizational Example

Amazon, Five-Star Innovator

Peter Drucker is the Father of Management and the namesake for the Drucker Institute that annually ranks the best managed companies. The Drucker Institute evaluates companies on five dimensions, one of which is innovation. Amazon gets a five-star rating on innovation. Amazon achieves this level of excellence in six ways. First, every single employee is empowered to innovate. Second, failure is more than embraced, it is expected. Third, decisions are not seen as irreversible. Fourth, employees are helped to move toward their passions and ideas. Fifth, creativity is nurtured, which in turn fosters innovation. Sixth, Amazon invests in tomorrow's innovators. Amazon's five-star excellence in innovation is no accident, rather that level of excellence comes from their systematic process of cultivating innovation.

Source: M. Borrowsky, "The Best-Managed Companies of 2022," *Wall Street Journal*, December 12 (2022), R1–R10.

interest, complementary needs, resources, and trust. Amazon is a company that excels in innovation as seen in the Organizational Example on page 305.

14-4d Skill Development

Employees need a range of technical and soft skills to meet the demands of emerging jobs and innovative work opportunities. Technical skills alone are insufficient for the new economy. The top ten in-demand skills over the next decade are: digital literacy, data literacy, critical thinking, emotional intelligence, creativity, collaboration, flexibility, leadership skills, time management, and curiosity and continuous learning.[79] In addition, managers need a wide range of nontechnical skills, such as communication skills, to be effective in their work.[80] Therefore, any discussion of jobs and the design of work must recognize the importance of incumbent skills and abilities to meet the demands of the work. Organizations must consider the talents and skills of their employees when they engage in job design efforts. The two issues of employee skill development and job design are interrelated. The knowledge and information requirements for jobs of the future are especially high.

Experiential Exercise

Chaos and the Manager's Job

Managers' jobs are increasingly chaotic as a result of high rates of change, uncertainty, and turbulence. Some managers thrive on change and chaos, but others have a difficult time responding to high rates of change and uncertainty in a positive manner. This questionnaire gives you an opportunity to evaluate how you would react to a manager's job that is rather chaotic.

Exercise Schedule

1. Preparation (preclass)
   Complete the questionnaire.

2. Individual Scoring
   Give yourself 4 points for each A, 3 points for each B, 2 points for each C, 1 point for each D, and 0 points for each E. Compute the total, divide by 24, and round to one decimal place.

3. Group Discussion
   Your instructor may have you discuss your scores in groups of six students. The higher your score, the more you respond positively to change and chaos; the lower your score, the more difficulty you would have responding to this manager's job in a positive manner. In addition, answer the following questions.

   a. If you could redesign this manager's job, what are the two or three aspects of the job that you would change first?
   b. What are the two or three aspects of the job that you would feel no need to change?

Source: "Chaos and the Manager's Job" in D. Marcic, "Option B. Quality and the New Management Paradigm," *Organizational Behavior: Experiences and Cases*, 4th ed. (Minneapolis/St. Paul: West Publishing, 1995): 296–297. Reprinted by permission.

A Manager's Job

Below are some statements a thirty-seven-year-old manager made about his job at a large and successful corporation. If your job had these characteristics, how would you react to them? After each statement are letters A through E. Circle the letter that best describes how you would react according to the following scale:

A. I would enjoy this very much; it's completely acceptable.

B. This would be enjoyable and acceptable most of the time.

C. I'd have no reaction one way or another, or it would be about equally enjoyable and unpleasant.

D. This feature would be somewhat unpleasant for me.

E. This feature would be very unpleasant for me.

1. I have difficulty understanding how the quality of my work and my compensation are related.   A B C D E

2. Remaining current in my job requires that I receive at least two weeks of management training per year.   A B C D E

3. My job regularly provides an opportunity for me to interact closely with a variety of different people who represent a variety of demographic groups, including race, nationality, sex, and ethnicity.

   A B C D E

4. At least 30 percent of my work day is spent in meetings.

   A B C D E

5. When I started my job, I was given little direction on how to perform it.

   A B C D E

6. I have to absorb nearly 200 pages of technical material per week in order to be successful on my job.

   A B C D E

7. Finding a time where all of my direct reports are available to meet is a nightmare for my administrative assistant; very often, at least one of my direct reports cannot attend a meeting.

   A B C D E

8. It is very difficult to measure my job's effectiveness using purely objective measures.

   A B C D E

9. More than one person is responsible for evaluating different aspects of my performance.

   A B C D E

10. The management concepts that I learned to earn my current degree have become outdated; I should probably return to college to earn another degree.

    A B C D E

11. The departments in my company are so interdependent that it is difficult to distinguish which departments are responsible for which tasks.

    A B C D E

12. I do not see myself rising to the top levels of my company.

    A B C D E

13. I have a number of ideas about business or personnel policies that will make my company better, but I have no direct influence to enact them.

    A B C D E

14. The technology in my company is constantly evolving which has required me to be more proactive to learn on my own.

    A B C D E

15. My boss can monitor the content on my office computer without my knowledge.

    A B C D E

16. My job requires that I spend at least one night a week out of town.

    A B C D E

17. I have limited authority to perform the tasks for which I am responsible.

    A B C D E

18. It seems that I can never catch up on the number of telephone calls I have to return during the day.

    A B C D E

19. At least a third of my work day is spent dealing with unexpected emergencies that throw me off schedule.

    A B C D E

20. It is likely that I will be promoted to a job in another division with most of the same characteristics that this job has.

    A B C D E

21. Either one department or the entire company has reorganized while I've worked at this company.

    A B C D E

22. While there is a real possibility that I will be promoted, I cannot say that I have a real career path.

    A B C D E

23. My company has recently instituted an assessment center where mine and my other colleagues' management potential is assessed.

    A B C D E

24. My company is currently defending itself in an antitrust suit in which I will probably have to testify about decisions made years ago.

    A B C D E

Learning Objectives

14-1 **Differentiate between job and work.** A *job* is an employee's specific work and task activities in an organization. *Work* is effortful, productive activity resulting in a product or a service. A job is composed of a set of specific tasks, each of which is an assigned piece of work to be done in a specific time period. Work is an especially important human endeavor because it has a powerful effect in binding a person to reality.

14-2 **Discuss the traditional approaches to job design.** Good job design differentiates and integrates tasks, improves productivity, and enhances employee well-being. Approaches to job design that were developed during the twentieth century are job enlargement/job rotation, job enrichment, and the job characteristics theory. Each approach offers unique benefits to the organization, the employee, or both, but each also has limitations and drawbacks.

14-3 **Describe alternative approaches to job design.** Several alternative approaches to job design have emerged over the past couple of decades: the social information-processing model; ergonomics and the interdisciplinary framework of Michael Campion and Paul Thayer; the international perspectives of the Japanese, Germans, and Scandinavians; and the health and well-being aspects of work design. Healthy work enables individuals to adapt, function well, and balance work with private life activities.

14-4 **Describe contemporary issues facing organizations in the design of work.** Contemporary job design issues include telecommuting, alternative work patterns, technostress, and skill development. Work is relationally designed to provide opportunities and increase flexibility for employees. Companies use these and other approaches to the design of work as ways to manage a growing business while contributing to a better balance of work and family life for employees.

Key Terms

anthropocentric Placing human considerations at the center of job design decisions. (p. 300)

cross-training A variation of job enlargement in which workers are trained in different specialized tasks or activities. (p. 293)

engagement The expression of oneself as one performs in work or other roles. p. 296)

ergonomics The science of adapting work and working conditions to the employee or worker. (p. 297)

gig workers are independent contractors, online platform workers, contract firm workers, on-call workers, and temporary workers. (p. 302)

hybrid work is a flexible work model that divides working hours between a company location and elsewhere, such as remote location or on-the-go. (p. 303)

job A set of specified work and task activities that engage an individual in an organization. (p. 290)

Job Characteristics Model A framework for understanding person–job fit through the interaction of core job dimensions with critical psychological states within a person. (p. 295)

job crafting is a work redesign strategy in which an incumbent proactively manages job tasks, relationships and perceptions to achieve better person-job fit. (p. 301)

Job Diagnostic Survey (JDS) The survey instrument designed to measure the elements in the Job Characteristics Model. (p. 295)

job enlargement A method of job design that increases the number of activities in a job to overcome the boredom of overspecialized work. (p. 292)

job enrichment Designing or redesigning a job by incorporating motivational factors into it. (p. 294)

job rotation A variation of job enlargement in which workers are exposed to a variety of specialized jobs over time. (p. 293)

lean production Using committed employees with ever expanding responsibilities to achieve zero waste and 100 percent good product, delivered on time, every time. (p. 299)

meaning of work The way a person interprets and understands the value of work as part of life. (p. 290)

remote work is any work done by employees without their commuting to a central location, such as an office, for the purpose of working. (p. 303)

social information-processing (SIP) model A model that suggests that the important job factors depend in part on what others tell a person about the job. (p. 297)

sociotechnical systems (STS) Giving equal attention to technical and social considerations in job design. (p. 299)

technocentric Placing technology and engineering at the center of job design decisions. (p. 300)

work Mental or physical activity that has productive results. (p. 290)

work simplification The standardization and the narrow, explicit specification of task activities for workers. (p. 292)

Ethical Dilemma

Juan, remote work and the return-to-work dilemma

Juan was having a great day. He loved working from home. While the COVID pandemic was a tragedy for everyone, some good did come from it. When his office closed and he was sent home to work, he enjoyed it so much that he hoped he would never have to go back to the office. Eventually the pandemic eased, the world opened back up, and Juan was still able to work at home. Life was great.

But one day, Juan got an email from Milo, his supervisor, informing him and the rest of the company that in two weeks, everyone was expected to return to the office, and no one would be allowed to work from home any longer. The email went on to say that the reason for the required return to work was because productivity was down and the company was losing money.

Juan is very upset. He knows he has not been less productive. In fact, he believes that he has been more productive given no travel time and shorter lunch breaks. He sends a quick email to Milo asking if there are any exceptions. Milo informed him that the only exceptions will be for those who have strong medical documentation that they are at high risk if exposed to COVID.

This news continues to stress Juan. Why should he have to pay for his co-workers not doing their jobs? He starts to wonder if he might be able to get a doctor to give him the necessary paperwork for a health exemption. He really likes his job but also really does not want to return to an office environment every day. He picks up the phone and calls his physician.

1. Using consequential, rule-based, and character theories, evaluate Juan's decision to seek a health exemption.

2. What should Juan do? Why?

izzuanroslan/Shutterstock.com

Organizational Design and Structure

Learning Objectives

15-1 Summarize differentiation and integration as organizational design processes.

15-2 Discuss the basic design dimensions managers must consider in structuring an organization.

15-3 Describe five structural configurations for organizations.

15-4 Describe four contextual variables that influence organizational structure.

15-5 Explain the forces reshaping organizations.

15-6 Describe emerging organizational structures.

15-7 Identify factors that can adversely affect organizational structure.

Strategic management is the process of formulating and implementing an organization's major goals in a competitive environment.[1] **Organizational design** is the process of constructing and adjusting an organization's structure to achieve its business strategy and goals. The design process begins with the organization's goals. These goals are broken into tasks, or pieces of work, as the basis for jobs, as discussed in Chapter 14. Jobs are grouped into departments, and departments are linked to form the **organizational structure**.

15-1 Key Organizational Design Processes

Differentiation, which will be defined in more detail shortly, can be described as the design process of breaking organizational goals into tasks. *Integration*, also defined in more detail shortly, can then be considered the design process of linking the tasks together to form a structure that supports goal accomplishment. These two processes are the keys to successful organizational design. The organizational structure is designed to prevent chaos through an orderly set of reporting relationships and communication channels. Understanding the key design processes and organizational structure helps a person understand the larger working environment and may prevent confusion in the organization.

The *organization chart* is the most visible representation of the organization's structure and underlying components. Figure 15.1 is the organizational chart for the World Trade Organization. Most organizations have a series of organization charts showing reporting relationships throughout the system. The underlying components are (1) formal lines of authority and responsibility (the organizational structure designates reporting relationships by the way jobs and departments are grouped) and (2) formal systems of communication, coordination, and integration (the organizational structure designates the expected patterns of formal interaction among employees).[2]

15-1a Differentiation

Differentiation occurs in organizations, especially large ones, to structure the work into manageable units. Differentiation ensures that all essential

> Differentiation and integration are the keys to successful organizational design.

organizational tasks are assigned to one or more jobs and that the tasks receive the attention they need. Many dimensions of differentiation have been considered in organizations. Lawrence and Lorsch found four dimensions of differentiation in one study: (1) manager's goal orientation, (2) time orientation, (3) interpersonal orientation, and (4) formality of structure.[3] Three different forms of differentiation are horizontal, vertical, and spatial.

Horizontal Differentiation Horizontal differentiation is the degree of differentiation between organizational subunits and is based on employees' specialized knowledge, education, or training. For example, two university professors who teach specialized subjects in different academic departments are subject to horizontal differentiation. Horizontal differentiation increases with specialization and departmentalization.

Specialization refers to the particular grouping of activities performed by an individual.[4] The degree of specialization, or the division of labor, in the organization gives an indication of how much training is needed for various jobs, what the scope of various jobs is, and what individual characteristics are needed for job holders. Specialization can lead to the development of a specialized vocabulary, as well as other behavioral norms. As the two college professors specialize in their subjects, abbreviations or acronyms take on unique meanings. For example, OB means "organizational behavior" to a professor of management but "obstetrics" to a professor of medicine.

Usually, the more specialized the jobs within an organization, the more departments are differentiated within that organization (in other words, the greater is the *departmentalization*).

organizational design The process of constructing and adjusting an organization's structure to achieve its business strategy and goals.

organizational structure The linking of departments and jobs within an organization.

differentiation The process of deciding how to divide the work in an organization.

Figure 15.1 Organization

WTO structure

All WTO members may participate in all councils, committees, etc., except Appellate Body, Dispute Settlement panels, Textiles Monitoring Body, and plurilateral committees.

Source: WTO Organization Chart, http://www.wto.org/english/thewto_e/whatis_e/tif_e/org2_e.htm.

Departmentalization can be by function, product, service, client, geography, process, or some combination of these. A large organization may departmentalize its structure using some or all of these methods at different levels of the organization. For example, the U.S. Army Reserve changed its departmentalization first from divisional to an operational strategic reserve and then to an operational force structure.[5]

Vertical Differentiation Vertical differentiation is the difference in authority and responsibility in the organizational hierarchy. Vertical differentiation occurs, for example, between a chief executive and a maintenance supervisor. Tall, narrow organizations have greater vertical differentiation, and flat, wide organizations have less vertical differentiation. The height of the organization is also influenced by level of horizontal differentiation and span of control. The *span of control* refers to and defines the number of employees a manager can and should supervise.[6]

Tall structures—those with narrow spans of control—tend to be characterized by closer supervision and tighter controls. In addition, the communication becomes more burdensome, since directives and information must be passed through more layers. The banking industry has often had tall structures. *Flat structures*—those with wider spans of control—have simpler communication chains and reduced promotion opportunities due to fewer levels of management. Google is a famous example of a company with a flat organizational structure. The degree of vertical differentiation affects organizational effectiveness, but there is no strong evidence that flatter or taller organizations are better.[7]

Spatial Differentiation Spatial differentiation is the geographic dispersion of an organization's offices, plants, and personnel. A salesperson who works in New York for a company based in Portland experiences spatial differentiation. An increase in the number of locations increases the complexity of organizational design because of spatial differentiation but may be necessary for organizational goal achievement or organizational protection. For example, if an organization wants to expand into a different country, it may be best to form a separate subsidiary that is partially owned and managed by citizens of that country. Few U.S. citizens think of Shell Oil Company as being a subsidiary of Royal Dutch/Shell Group,

a company whose international headquarters is in the Netherlands. International organizations have the challenge of dealing with cross-cultural issues that impact the work-life interface of their employees, such as differences in public policies and attitudes toward gender equality.[8]

Implications of Differentiation Horizontal, vertical, and spatial differentiation indicate the amount of width, height, and breadth an organizational structure needs. Just because an organization is highly differentiated along one of these dimensions does not mean it must be highly differentiated along the others. The university environment, for example, is generally characterized by great horizontal differentiation but relatively little vertical and spatial differentiation. By contrast, a company such as Coca-Cola is characterized by a great deal of all three types of differentiation.

The more structurally differentiated an organization is, the more complex it is.[9] *Complexity* refers to the number of activities, subunits, or subsystems within the organization. Lawrence and Lorsch suggest that an organization's complexity should mirror the complexity of its environment. As the complexity of an organization increases, its need for mechanisms to link and coordinate the differentiated parts also increases. If these links do not exist, the departments or differentiated parts of the organization can lose sight of the organization's larger mission, and the organization runs the risk of chaos. Chaos is not inevitable, however, as research suggests that environmental complexity may be viewed as a "puzzle" that, if understood correctly, increases competence and increases organizational learning.[10]

15-1b Integration

To be effective, organizations must design and build linkage and coordination mechanisms. This process of coordinating the different parts of the organization is known as **integration**. Integration mechanisms are designed to achieve unity among individuals and groups in various jobs, departments, and divisions in the accomplishment of organizational goals

Integration The process of coordinating the different parts of an organization.

iStock.com/mbbirdy

The Square Mile in the center of London's financial district date to Roman time and includes The Gherkin, a modern architectural design by Sir Norman Foster.

and tasks.[11] Effective integration helps keep the organization in a state of *dynamic equilibrium*, a condition in which all the parts of the organization are interrelated and balanced.

To integrate activities up and down the organizational chain of command, a variety of structural devices can be used to achieve *vertical linkages*. These devices include hierarchical referral, rules and procedures, plans and schedules, positions added to the structure of the organization, and management information systems.[12] On an organization chart, the vertical lines indicate these vertical linkages, showing the lines of hierarchical referral up and down the organization. When employees do not know how to solve a problem, they can refer it upward for consideration and resolution. Work that needs to be assigned is usually delegated downward.

Rules and procedures, as well as plans and schedules, provide standing information for employees without direct communication. These vertical integrators, such as an employee handbook, communicate to employees standard information, or information that they can understand on their own. Such integrators allow managers to have wider spans of control because they do not have to inform each employee of what is expected and when it is expected. Vertical integrators encourage managers to use *management by exception*—to make decisions when employees bring problems up the hierarchy. Military organizations depend heavily on vertical linkages, having a well-defined chain of command. Certain duties are expected to be carried out, and proper paperwork is to be in place. In times of crisis, however, much more information is processed, and the proper paperwork becomes secondary to getting the job done. Vertical linkages help individuals understand their roles in the organization, especially in times of crisis.

Adding positions to the hierarchy is used as a vertical integrator when a manager becomes overloaded by hierarchical referral or problems arise in the chain of command. Positions such as "assistant to" may be added, or another level may be added. Such additions often reflect an organization's growth and increasing complexity. This action tends to reduce the span of control, thus allowing more communication and closer supervision.

Generally, the taller the organization, the more vertical integration mechanisms are needed. This is because the chains of command and communication are longer. Additional length requires more linkages to minimize the potential for misunderstandings and miscommunications.

Horizontal integration mechanisms provide the communication and coordination that are necessary for links across jobs and departments in the organization. The need for horizontal integration mechanisms increases as the complexity of the organization increases. These linkages are built into the design of the organization by including liaison roles, task forces, integrator positions, and teams.

A *liaison role* is created when a person in one department or area of the organization has the responsibility for coordinating with another department (e.g., a liaison between the engineering and production departments). *Task forces* are temporary committees composed of representatives from multiple departments who assemble to address a specific problem affecting these departments.[13]

A stronger device for integration is to develop a person or department designed to be an *integrator*. In most organizations, the integrator has a good deal of responsibility but not much authority. Such an individual must have the ability to get people together to resolve differences within the perspective of organizational goals.[14]

The strongest method of horizontal integration is through *teams*. Horizontal teams cut across existing lines of organizational structure to create new entities that make organizational decisions. An example of this may occur in product development with the formation of a team that includes marketing, research, design, and production personnel. Ford used such a cross-functional team to develop the Taurus automobile, which was designed to restore the company's market share in the United States. The information exchanged by such a product development team should lead to a product that

Getmilitaryphotos/Shutterstock.com

Military organizations have a well-defined chain of command and depend heavily on strong leader-follower bonds.

is acceptable to a wider range of organizational groups, as well as to customers.[15]

The use of these linkage mechanisms varies from organization to organization, as well as within areas of the same organization. In general, the flatter the organization, the more necessary are horizontal integration mechanisms.

15-2 Basic Design Dimensions

Differentiation, then, is the process of dividing work in the organization, and integration is the process of coordinating work in the organization. From a structural perspective, every manager and organization looks for the best combination of differentiation and integration for accomplishing the goals of the organization. There are many ways to approach this process. One way is to establish a desired level of each structural dimension on a high-to-low continuum and then develop a structure that meets the desired configuration. These structural dimensions include the following:

1. **Formalization.** The degree to which an employee's role is defined by formal documentation (procedures, job descriptions, manuals, and regulations).

2. **Centralization.** The extent to which decision-making authority has been delegated to lower levels of an organization. An organization is centralized if the decisions are made at the top of the organization and decentralized if decision-making is pushed down to lower levels in the organization.

3. **Specialization.** The degree to which organizational tasks are subdivided into separate jobs. The division of labor and the degree to which formal job descriptions spell out job requirements indicate the level of specialization in the organization.

4. **Standardization.** The extent to which work activities are described and performed routinely in the same way. Highly standardized organizations have little variation in the defining of jobs.

5. **Complexity.** The number of activities within the organization and the amount of differentiation needed within the organization.

6. **Hierarchy of authority.** The degree of vertical differentiation through reporting relationships and the span of control within the structure of the organization.[16]

An organization that is high in formalization, centralization, specialization, standardization, and complexity and has a tall hierarchy of authority is said to be highly *bureaucratic*. Bureaucracies are not inherently bad; however, they are often tainted by abuse and red tape. There are cases, however, where centralized structures can be beneficial. For example, one study found that a more centralized structure is effective for increased job satisfaction when perceptions of interactional and procedural justice are present.[17] study of 1,000 U.S. firms found that centralized firms had the highest levels of research investments and owned more patents per R&D dollars.[18]

An organization that is on the opposite end of each of these continua is very flexible and loose. Control is very hard to implement and maintain in such an organization, but at certain times such a structure is appropriate. The research and development departments in many organizations are often more flexible than other departments in order to stimulate creativity. Flexibility may be a key in **business model innovation**. For example, Google became a powerhouse through business model innovation, an emergent phenomenon on the organizational landscape.[19]

Another approach to the process of accomplishing organizational goals is to describe what is and is not important to the success of the organization rather than worry about specific characteristics. Henry

formalization The degree to which the organization has official rules, regulations, and procedures.

centralization The degree to which decisions are made at the top of the organization.

specialization The degree to which jobs are narrowly defined and depend on unique expertise.

standardization The degree to which work activities are accomplished in a routine fashion.

complexity The degree to which many different types of activities occur in the organization.

hierarchy of authority The degree of vertical differentiation across levels of management.

business model innovation The innovative processes and rationale for how an organization creates, delivers, and captures value.

Mintzberg argued that the following questions can guide managers in designing formal structures that fit each organization's unique set of circumstances:

1. How many tasks should a given position in the organization contain, and how specialized should each task be?

2. How standardized should the work content of each position be?

3. What skills, abilities, knowledge, and training should be required for each position?

4. What should be the basis for the grouping of positions within the organization into units, departments, divisions, and so on?

5. How large should each unit be, and what should the span of control be (i.e., how many individuals should report to each manager)?

6. How much standardization should be required in the output of each position?

7. What mechanisms should be established to help individuals in different positions and units adjust to the needs of other individuals?

8. How centralized or decentralized should decision-making power be in the chain of authority? Should most of the decisions be made at the top of the organization (centralized) or be made down in the chain of authority (decentralized)?[20]

The manager who can answer these questions has a good understanding of how the organization should implement the basic structural dimensions. These basic design dimensions act in combination with one another and are not entirely independent characteristics of an organization. In the post-COVID-19 world, centralization is an especially relevant dimension. The YOU offers an opportunity to consider how centralized versus decentralized your company is.

YOU

How Decentralized Is Your Company?

Decentralization is one of the key design dimensions in an organization. It is closely related to several behavioral dimensions of an organization, such as leadership style, degree of participative decision making, and the nature of power and politics within the organization. In addition, decentralization has been linked to increased safety in organizations.[24]

The following questionnaire allows you to get an idea about how decentralized your organization is. (If you do not have a job, have a friend who does work complete the questionnaire to see how decentralized his or her organization is.) Which level in your organization has the authority to make each of the following eleven decisions? Answer the questionnaire by circling one of the following:

0 = The board of directors makes the decision.

1 = The CEO makes the decision.

2 = The division/functional manager makes the decision.

3 = A subdepartment head makes the decision.

4 = The first-level supervisor makes the decision.

5 = Operators on the shop floor make the decision.

Decision Concerning:		Circle Appropriate Level					
a.	The number of workers required.	0	1	2	3	4	5
b.	Whether to employ a worker.	0	1	2	3	4	5
c.	Internal labor disputes.	0	1	2	3	4	5
d.	Overtime worked at shop level.	0	1	2	3	4	5
e.	Delivery dates and order priority.	0	1	2	3	4	5
f.	Production planning.	0	1	2	3	4	5
g.	Dismissal of a worker.	0	1	2	3	4	5
h.	Methods of personnel selection.	0	1	2	3	4	5
i.	Method of work to be used.	0	1	2	3	4	5
j.	Machinery or equipment to be used.	0	1	2	3	4	5
k.	Allocation of work among workers.	0	1	2	3	4	5

15-3 Five Structural Configurations

Differentiation, integration, and the basic design dimensions combine to yield various structural configurations. Very early organization structures were often either based on product or function. The *matrix organization* structure merged these two ways of organizing.[21] Mintzberg moved beyond these early approaches and proposed five structural configurations: the simple structure, the machine bureaucracy, the professional bureaucracy, the divisionalized form, and the adhocracy.[22] Table 15.1 shows the prime coordinating mechanism, the key part of the organization, and the type of decentralization for each of these structural configurations. The five basic parts of the organization, for Mintzberg, are the upper echelon, or strategic apex; the middle level, or middle line; the operating core, where work is accomplished; the technical staff, or technostructure; and the support staff. Figure 15.2 depicts these five basic parts with a small strategic apex, connected by a flaring middle line to a large, flat operating core. Each configuration affects people in the organization somewhat is differently,

Figure 15.2 Mintzberg's Five Basic Parts of an Organization

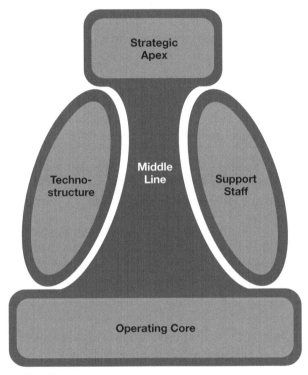

Source: From H. Mintzberg, *The Structuring of Organizations* (Upper Saddle River, N.J.: Pearson, 1979): 20. Reprinted by permission of Pearson Education, Inc., Upper Saddle River, N.J.

Table 15.1 Five Structural Configurations of Organizations

Structural Configuration	Prime Coordinating Mechanism	Key Part of Organization	Type of Decentralization
Simple structure	Direct supervision	Upper echelon	Centralization
Machine bureaucracy	Standardization of work processes	Technical staff	Limited horizontal decentralization
Professional bureaucracy	Standardization of skills	Operating level	Vertical and horizontal decentralization
Divisionalized form	Standardization of outputs	Middle level	Limited vertical decentralization
Adhocracy	Mutual adjustment	Support staff	Selective decentralization

Source: H. Mintzberg, *Structuring of Organizations*, 1st ed., © 1979. Reprinted by permission of Pearson Education, Inc., Upper Saddle River, N.J.

Organizational Example

Microsoft Ranked #1 in 2022

The Drucker Institute, named for Peter Drucker, the Father of Management, annually ranks the best managed companies on five dimensions: customer satisfaction; employee engagement and development; financial strength; innovation; and social responsibility. Microsoft was the #1 ranked of 250 companies in 2022, earning 5-star scores on four of the five dimensions. In innovation, Microsoft earned a 5-star-plus ranking. The company earned 3 stars in customer satisfaction. The company's overall score was 99, the top score. To be a top, best managed company requires excellence along more than one dimension of the business. Microsoft ranked #1 in innovation while ranking in the top 10 companies for employee engagement and development, financial strength, and social responsibility.

Source: M. Borrowsky, "The Best-Managed Companies of 2022," *Wall Street Journal*, December 12 (2022), R1–R10.

and all organizational structures should support the firm's strategic goals. Microsoft is an organization that excels on several dimensions of management as shown in the Organizational Example above.

15-3a Simple Structure

The **simple structure** is a centralized form of organization that emphasizes a small technical and support staff, strong centralization of decision-making in the upper echelon, and a minimal middle level. This structure has a minimum of vertical differentiation of authority and minimal formalization. It achieves coordination through direct supervision, often by the chief executive in the upper echelon. An example of a simple structure is a small, independent landscape practice in which one or two landscape architects supervise the vast majority of work with no middle-level managers.

15-3b Machine Bureaucracy

The **machine bureaucracy** is a moderately decentralized form of organization that emphasizes a support staff differentiated from the line operations of the organization, limited horizontal decentralization of decision-making, and a well-defined hierarchy of authority. The technical staff is powerful in a machine bureaucracy. There is strong formalization through policies, procedures, rules, and regulations. Coordination is achieved through the standardization of work processes. An example of a machine bureaucracy is an automobile assembly plant with routinized operating tasks. The strength of the machine bureaucracy is efficiency of operation in stable, unchanging environments. The weakness of the machine bureaucracy is its slow responsiveness to external changes and to individual employee preferences and ideas.

15-3c Professional Bureaucracy

The **professional bureaucracy** is a decentralized form of organization that emphasizes the expertise of the professionals in the operating core of

> **simple structure** A centralized form of organization that emphasizes a small technical and support staff, strong centralization of decision-making in the upper echelon, and a minimal middle level.
>
> **machine bureaucracy** A moderately decentralized form of organization that emphasizes support staff differentiated from the line operations of the organization, limited horizontal decentralization of decision-making, and a well-defined hierarchy of authority.
>
> **professional bureaucracy** A decentralized form of organization that emphasizes the expertise of the professionals in the operating core of the organization.

Hospitals exemplify professional bureaucracies; the expertise of doctors, nurses, and technicians is emphasized as the operating core of the organization.

Peakstock/Shutterstock.com

the organization. The technical and support staffs serve the professionals. There is both vertical and horizontal differentiation in the professional bureaucracy. Coordination is achieved through the standardization of the professionals' skills. Examples of organizations, where professional bureaucracies can be found, are hospitals and universities. The doctors, nurses, and professors are given wide latitude to pursue their work based on professional training and indoctrination through professional training programs. Large accounting firms may also fall into the category of professional bureaucracies.

15-3d Divisionalized Form

The **divisionalized form** is a loosely coupled, composite structural configuration composed of divisions, each of which may have its own structural configuration.[23] Each division is designed to respond to the market in which it operates. McDonald's and Disney are examples of divisionalized companies. There is vertical decentralization from the upper echelon to the middle of the organization, and the middle level of management is the key part of the organization. This form of organization may have one division that is a machine bureaucracy, one that is an *adhocracy* (discussed next), and one that is a simple structure. The divisionalized organization uses standardization of outputs as its coordinating mechanism.

15-3e Adhocracy

The **adhocracy** is a selectively decentralized form of organization that emphasizes the support staff and mutual adjustment among people. It is designed to fuse interdisciplinary experts into smoothly functioning ad hoc project teams. Liaison devices are the primary mechanism for integrating the project teams through a process of mutual adjustment. There is a high degree of horizontal specialization

---

> Competitive pressures in many industries led to outsourcing, labeled one of the greatest shifts in organization structure in a century.

based on formal training and expertise. Selective decentralization of the project teams occurs within the adhocracy. An example of this form of organization is the National Aeronautics and Space Administration (NASA), which is composed of many talented experts who work in small teams on a wide range of projects related to America's space agenda. New high-technology businesses also often select an adhocracy design.

15-4 Contextual Variables

The basic design dimensions and the resulting structural configurations play out in the context of the organization's internal and external environments. Four **contextual variables** influence the success of an organization's design: size, technology, environment, and strategy and goals. These variables provide a manager with key considerations for the right organizational design, although they do not determine the structure. Competitive pressures in many industries led to *outsourcing*, labeled one of the greatest shifts in organization structure in a century.[24] The maturity of capital markets may be an instrumental contextual factor for organizations as they engage in restructuring and resizing, especially following economic shocks in the environment.[25]

15-4a Size

The total number of employees is the appropriate definition of size when discussing the design of organizational structure. This is logical because people and their interactions are the building blocks of structure. Other measures, such as net assets, production rates, and total sales, are usually highly correlated with the total number of employees. However, these may not reflect the actual number of interpersonal relationships that are necessary to effectively structure an organization.

Although there is some argument over the degree of influence that size has on organizational structure, there is no argument that it does influence design options. In one study, Meyer found the size of the

---

divisionalized form A loosely coupled, composite structural configuration composed of divisions, each of which may have its own structural configuration.

adhocracy A selectively decentralized form of organization that emphasizes the support staff and mutual adjustment among people.

contextual variables A set of four characteristics that influence the success of an organization's design: size, technology, environment, and strategy and goals.

organization to be the most important of all variables influencing the organization's structure and design, whereas other researchers argue that the decision to expand the organization's business causes an increase in size as the structure is adjusted to accommodate the planned growth.[26] Downsizing is a planned strategy to reduce the size of an organization, and it is often accompanied by related restructuring and revitalization activities.[27] Researchers predicted and found that firms experienced the most significant post-downsizing performance improvements when they downsized their workforces on either a large or small scale. Intermediate downsizing led to the least positive performance improvements.[28]

How much influence size exerts on the organization's structure is not as important as the relationship between size and the design dimensions of structure. In other words, when exploring structural alternatives, the manager needs to know certain facts about designing structures for large versus small organizations. For example, formalization, specialization, and standardization all tend to be greater in larger organizations because they are necessary to control activities within the organization. Larger organizations are more likely to use documentation, rules, written policies and procedures, and detailed job descriptions than to rely on personal observation by the manager. McDonald's has several volumes of manuals that describe how to make all its products, how to greet customers, how to maintain facilities, and so on. This level of standardization, formalization, and specialization helps McDonald's maintain the same quality of product no matter where a restaurant is located. In contrast, at a small, locally owned café, your hamburger and French fries may taste a little different every time you visit—evidence of a lack of standardization.

Formalization and specialization also help large and growing organizations decentralize decision-making. For example, when Australian management consulting firm Nous Group's staff grew from 20 employees in the early 2000s to 150 employees in 2014, the organization pushed decision-making down to lower-level managers and to other personnel according to their job descriptions, policies, standard operating procedures, and norms.[29] Because of the complexity and number of decisions in a large organization, formalization and specialization are used to set parameters for decision-making at lower levels. Can you imagine the chaos if the president of the United States, commander-in-chief of all military forces, had to make operational-level decisions in the war on terrorism? By decentralizing decision-making, a large organization adds horizontal and vertical complexity, but not necessarily spatial complexity. However, it is more common for a large organization to have more geographic dispersion. For example, the San Diego County Government in California created a regionalized structure to decentralize decision-making, share common resources and competencies, and meet its unique client needs.[30]

Hierarchy of authority is another dimension of design related to complexity. As size increases, complexity increases; thus, more levels are added to the hierarchy of authority. This keeps the span of control from getting too large. However, there is a balancing force because formalization and specialization are added. The more formalized, standardized, and specialized the roles within the organization, the wider the span of control can be.

15-4b Technology

An organization's technology is an important contextual variable in determining the organization's structure.[31] Technology is defined as the tools, techniques, and actions used by an organization to transform inputs into outputs.[32] The inputs of the organization include human resources, machines, materials, information, and money. The outputs are the products and services that the organization offers to the external environment. Determining the relationship between technology and structure is complicated because different departments may employ very different technologies. As organizations become larger, there is greater variation in technologies across units in the organization. Joan Woodward, Charles Perrow, and James Thompson developed ways to understand traditional organizational technologies. Modern and digital technologies continue to shape organizations in new ways.

Woodward introduced one of the best-known classification schemes for technology, identifying three types: unit, mass, or process production. *Unit technology* is small-batch manufacturing technology and, sometimes, made-to-order production. Examples include the arms manufacturer Smith & Wesson and the production of fine furniture. *Mass technology* is large-batch manufacturing technology.

Examples include automotive assembly lines and latex glove production. *Process production* is a continuous-production process. Examples include oil refining and beer making. Woodward classified unit technology as the least complex, mass technology as more complex, and process technology as the most complex. The more complex the organization's technology, the more complex the administrative component or structure of the organization needs to be.

Perrow proposed an alternative to Woodward's scheme based on two variables: task variability and problem analyzability. *Task variability* considers the number of exceptions encountered in doing the tasks within a job. *Problem analyzability* examines the types of search procedures followed to find ways to respond to task exceptions. For example, for some exceptions encountered while doing a task, the appropriate response is easy to

find. If you are driving down a street and see a sign that says, "Detour—Bridge Out," it is very easy to respond to the task variability, so analyzability is low (i.e., limited analysis is needed). By contrast, when Thomas Edison was designing the first electric light bulb, the problem analyzability was very high for his task.

Perrow went on further to identify the four key aspects of structure that could be modified to technology: (1) the amount of discretion that an individual can exercise to complete a task, (2) the power of groups to control the unit's goals and strategies, (3) the level of interdependence among groups, and (4) the extent to which organizational units coordinate work using either feedback or planning. Figure 15.3 summarizes Perrow's findings about types of technology and basic design dimensions.[33]

Thompson offered yet another view of technology and its relationship to organizational design. This view is based on the concept of **technological interdependence**, which is the degree of interrelatedness of the organization's various technological elements, and the pattern of an organization's work flows. Thompson's research suggests that greater

technological interdependence The degree of interrelatedness of the organization's various technological elements.

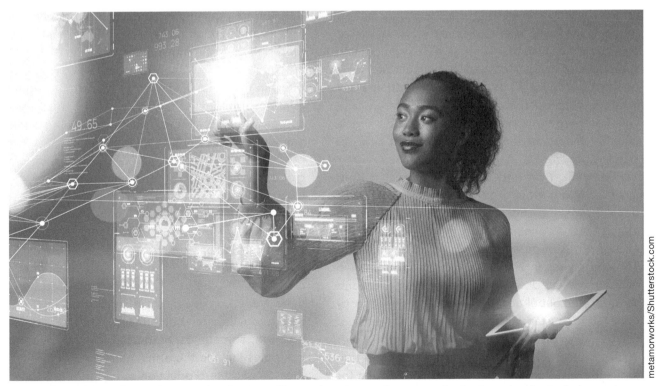

metamorworks/Shutterstock.com

Technological interdependence is the degree of interrelatedness of an organization's technological elements.

Figure 15.3 Summary of Perrow's Findings

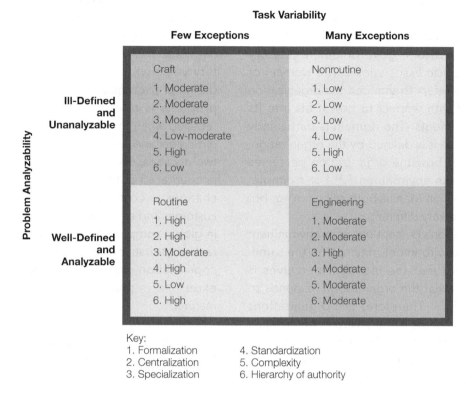

Source: Built from C. Perrow, "A Framework for the Comparative Analysis of Organizations," *American Sociological Review* (April 1967): 194–208.

technological interdependence leads to greater organizational complexity and that the problems of greater complexity may be offset by decentralized decision-making.[34]

The research of these three early scholars on the influence of technology on organizational design can be combined into one integrating concept—*routineness* in the process of changing inputs into outputs in an organization. This routineness has a very strong relationship with organizational structure. The more routine and repetitive the tasks of the organization, the higher the degree of formalization that is possible, the more centralized, specialized, and standardized the organization can be, and the more hierarchical levels with wider spans of control that are possible.

15-4c Environment

The third contextual variable for organizational design is **environment**. The environment of an organization is most easily defined as anything outside the boundaries of that organization. Different aspects of the environment have varying degrees of

influence on the organization's structure. In one study of 318 CEOs, strategic decision speed was found to moderate the relationship between the environment, the structure of an organization, and performance.[35] The general environment includes all conditions that might have an impact on the organization, such as economic factors, political considerations, ecological changes, sociocultural demands, and governmental regulation. Where the demands of the central or federal government and local or state government conflict, this can adversely impact the firms' corporate social responsibility (CSR).[36]

Task Environment When aspects of the general environment become more focused in areas of direct interest to the organization, those aspects become part of the **task environment**, or specific

environment Anything outside the boundaries of an organization.

task environment The part of the environment that is directly relevant to the organization.

environment. The task environment is that part of the environment that is directly relevant to the organization. Typically, this level of environment includes stakeholders such as unions, customers, suppliers, competitors, government regulatory agencies, and trade associations. The *domain* of the organization refers to the area the organization claims for itself with respect to how it fits into its relevant environments. The domain is particularly important because it is defined by the organization, and it influences how the organization perceives and acts within its environments.[37] For example, Walmart and Neiman Marcus both sell clothing, but their domains are very different.

The organization's perceptions of its environment and the actual environment may not be the same. The environment that the manager perceives is the environment that the organization responds to and organizes for.[38] Therefore, two organizations may be in relatively the same environment from an objective standpoint, but if the managers perceive differences, the organizations may enact very different structures to deal with this same environment. For example, one company may decentralize and use monetary incentives for managers that lead it to be competitively aggressive, while another company may centralize and use incentives for managers that lead it to be less intense in its rivalry.[39]

Environmental Uncertainty Environmental uncertainty is the amount and rate of change in the organization's environment. The perceived level of environmental uncertainty is the environmental variable that most influences organizational design. The level of environmental uncertainty can also impact the degree to which internal practices are standardized to match multinational firm policies and practices. For instance, customization of HRM practices in high uncertainty environments led to increased financial performance and customer

satisfaction.[40] Some organizations have relatively static environments with little uncertainty, whereas others are so dynamic that no one is sure what tomorrow may bring. Binney & Smith, for example, has made basically the same product for more than fifty years with very few changes in the product design or packaging. The environment for its Crayola products is relatively static. In fact, customers rebelled when the company tried to get rid of some old colors and add new ones. In contrast, in the last two decades, competitors in the airline industry have encountered deregulation, mergers, bankruptcies, changes in cost and price structures, changes in customer and employee demographics, and changes in global competition. In such uncertain conditions, fast-response organizations must use expertise coordination practices to ensure that distributed expertise is managed and applied in a timely manner.[41]

The amount of uncertainty in the environment influences the structural dimensions. Burns and Stalker labeled two structural extremes that are appropriate for the extremes of environmental uncertainty: **mechanistic structure** and **organic structure**.[42] The mechanistic and organic structures occupy opposite ends of a continuum of organizational design possibilities. Although the general premise of environmental uncertainty and structural dimensions has been upheld by research, the organization must make adjustments for the realities of its perceived environment when designing its structure.[43] Some research suggests that the type of structure, either mechanistic or organic, depends on a manager's level of organizational design experience and formal training.[44]

If the organization's environment is uncertain, dynamic, and complex and resources are scarce, the manager needs an organic structure that is better able to adapt to its environment. Managerial risk taking is a critical aspect of strategic management and must often be taken under conditions of environmental uncertainty. Despite the uncertainty, managers must take risks to improve competitive advantage and performance.[45]

15-4d Strategy and Goals

Strategies and goals are the fourth contextual variable that influences how the design dimensions of structure should be enacted. Strategies and goals

---

environmental uncertainty The amount and rate of change in the organization's environment.

mechanistic structure An organizational design that emphasizes structured activities, specialized tasks, and centralized decision-making.

organic structure An organizational design that emphasizes teamwork, open communication, and decentralized decision-making.

provide legitimacy to the organization, as well as employee direction, decision guidelines, and criteria for performance.[46] In addition, strategies and goals help the organization fit into its environment.

For example, when Apple introduced its line of personal computers to the market, its strategies were very innovative. The structure of the organization was relatively flat and very informal. Apple had Friday afternoon beer and popcorn discussion sessions, and eccentric behavior was easily accepted. As the personal computer market became more competitive, however, the structure of Apple changed to help it differentiate its products and to help control costs. The innovative strategies and structures devised by Steve Jobs, one of Apple's founders, were no longer appropriate. So the board of directors recruited John Scully, a marketing expert from PepsiCo, to help Apple better compete in the market it had created. In 1996 and 1997, Apple reinvented itself again and brought back Jobs to try to restore its innovative edge. After his return, Apple became a major player in the digital music market with its introduction of several models of the iPod and the iPhone.

Limitations exist, however, on the extent to which strategies and goals influence structure. Because the structure of the organization includes the formal information-processing channels in the organization, it stands to reason that the need to change strategies might not be communicated throughout the organization without going through those formal channels. In such a case, the organization's structure influences its strategic choice. Changing the organization's structure might not unlock value but instead drive up costs and difficulties. Therefore, strategic success may hinge on choosing an organization design that works reasonably well, then fine-tuning the structure through a strategic system.[47] The link between strategy and structure extends to acquisitions. Different acquisition strategies, whether unrelated, vertical, or related, will require different levels of centralization and integration. Acculturation processes will also depend on the type of acquisition strategy the organization implements.[48]

The inefficiency of the structure to perceive environmental changes can even lead to organizational failure. In the airline industry, several carriers failed to adjust quickly enough to deregulation and the highly competitive marketplace. Only those airlines that were generally viewed as lean structures with good information-processing systems have flourished in the turbulent years since deregulation. Examples of how different design dimensions can affect the strategic decision process are listed in Table 15.2.

The four contextual variables—size, technology, environment, and strategy and goals—combine to influence the design process. However, the existing structure of the organization influences how the

Table 15.2 Examples of How Structure Affects the Strategic Decision Process

Formalization

As the level of formalization increases, so does the probability of the following:

1. The strategic decision process will become reactive to crisis rather than proactive through opportunities.
2. Strategic moves will be incremental and precise.
3. Differentiation in the organization will not be balanced with integrative mechanisms.
4. Only environmental crises that are in areas monitored by the formal organizational systems will be acted upon.

Centralization

As the level of centralization increases, so does the probability of the following:

1. The strategic decision process will be initiated by only a few dominant individuals.
2. The decision process will be goal-oriented and rational.
3. The strategic process will be constrained by the limitations of top managers.

Complexity

As the level of complexity increases, so does the probability of the following:

1. The strategic decision process will become more politicized.
2. The organization will find it more difficult to recognize environmental opportunities and threats.
3. The constraints on good decision processes will be multiplied by the limitations of each individual within the organization.

Source: Republished with permission of Academy of Management, from J. Fredrickson, "The Strategic Decision Process and Organizational Structure (Table)," *Academy of Management Review* (1986): 284; permission conveyed through Copyright Clearance Center, Inc.

Figure 15.4 The Relationship Among Key Organizational Design Elements

the best structural design. Because of the difficulty in studying the interactions of the four contextual dimensions and the complexity of organizational structures, the argument about which variable is most important continues.

What is apparent is that there must be some level of fit between the structure and the contextual dimensions of the organization. The better the fit, the more likely the organization will achieve its short-run goals. In addition, the better the fit, the more likely the organization will process information and design appropriate organizational roles for long-term prosperity, as indicated in Figure 15.4. Some design elements are theorized to fit better during different phases of firm operations. For instance, existing firms engaged in entrepreneurial activities have traditionally favored decentralization and formalization only during opportunity discovery. Recent research suggests that these design elements may also facilitate entrepreneurship during opportunity realization.[49]

15-5 Forces Reshaping Organizations

Managers and researchers traditionally examine organizational design and structure within the framework of basic design dimensions and contextual variables. In recent decades, though, several forces reshaping organizations are causing managers to go beyond the traditional frameworks to examine ways to make organizations more responsive to customer needs. Some of these forces include shorter organizational life cycles, globalization, artificial intelligence (AI) and cybersecurity, and high reliability organizing. These four forces increase the demands for organizations to change and adapt in design and structure. To retain their health and vitality, organizations must function as open systems that are responsive to their task environment.[50]

15-5a Life Cycles in Organizations

Organizations are dynamic entities. As such, they ebb and flow through different stages. Usually, researchers think of these stages as **organizational life cycles**. The whole organization has a life cycle that begins at birth, moves through growth and maturity to a stage of decline, and possibly

organization interprets and reacts to information about each of the variables. Each of the contextual variables has management researchers who claim that it is the most important variable in determining

organizational life cycle The differing stages of an organization's life from birth to death.

Inclusive Conversations

Startups Designed with Diversity in Mind

Startups are entrepreneurial ventures created to bring unique products or services to a private market in ways that are scalable and ultimately attractive for public investment. The most successful startups often cater to needs that have historically been unaddressed by existing organizations. In Pakistan, women own 1 percent of such businesses compared with 21 percent of men who are business owners.

There has been a rise in startups led by women, however, designed to address the specific needs of women in the region. These businesses have taken the form of an online kitchen prep that reduces the time and effort required to prepare healthy meals, a women-only ride service to ensure women can commute safely and reliably to their destinations, and an educational platform designed to educate women in rural areas who do not have access to smartphone technology, among others. Pakistani startups, designed with women in mind, are not only a source of opportunity to start and grow women-owned businesses, but they are also an important source of empowerment to Pakistani women and to the society, giving everyone the opportunity to achieve their full potential.

1. Why is it important for businesses, large and small, to address the needs of diverse groups?

   The more businesses can meet the needs of diverse groups, the more likely they are to reach unlikely or underdeveloped markets, ultimately leading to healthier financial positions. For startups especially, a healthier financial position may lead to longer survival and ultimate purchase in the broader market.

2. What are some potential challenges for women-led businesses?

   Small businesses, and startups in particular, require initial capital which can be a challenge for every potential business owner. In addition to funding, they may also experience issues finding technical expertise. Finally, ideas suggesting that women should not own businesses (e.g., gender role socialization) may present challenges.

Sources: R. Baldridge, "What Is a Startup? The Ultimate Guide," *Forbes Advisor*, accessed at https://www.forbes.com/advisor/business/what-is-a-startup/; N. Tahir, "Empowered Women, Empowering Startups," *The Express Tribune*, March 19 (2023), accessed at https://tribune.com.pk/story/2406971/empowered-women-empowering-startups Empowered women, empowering startups (tribune.com.pk).

---

experiences revival.[51] The Inclusive Conversation above opens the issue of considering diversity as a design issue in startups.

Organizational subunits may have very similar life cycles. Because of changes in technology and product design, many organizational subunits, especially those that are product based, are experiencing shorter life cycles. Hence, the subunits that compose the organization are changing more rapidly than in the past. These shorter life cycles enable the organization to respond quickly to external demands and changes.

When a new organization or subunit is born, the structure is organic and informal. If the organization or subunit is successful, it grows and matures. This usually leads to formalization, specialization, standardization, complexity, and a more mechanistic structure. If the environment changes, however, the organization must be able to respond. A mechanistic structure is not able to respond to a dynamic environment as well as an organic one. If the organization

or subunit does respond, it becomes more organic and revives; if not, it declines and possibly dies. New research suggests that it may be wise to temporarily cycle through mechanistic and organic designs in order to meet the often conflicting demands of organizations.[52]

Shorter life cycles put more pressure on the organization to be both flexible and efficient at the same time. Further, as flexible organizations use design to their competitive advantage, discrete organizational life cycles may give way to a kaleidoscope of continuously emerging, efficiency-seeking organizational designs.[53] The manager's challenge in this context becomes one of creating congruency among various organizational design dimensions to fit continuously changing markets and locations. Many fast-growing organizations face critical transition points through their life cycles that present growth and structural challenges. The organization should attempt to resolve these before moving on to the next phase of growth and development.[54]

Likee68/Shutterstock.com

The current era of globalization began following the end of the Cold War in 1991 and is currently complicated by international tensions.

15-5b Globalization

Another force that is reshaping organizations is the process of globalization, in which organizations operate worldwide rather than in just one country or region. One potential problem with globalization is that corporations can become pitted against sovereign nations when rules and laws conflict across national borders. Globalization makes spatial differentiation even more of a reality for organizations. Besides the obvious geographic differences, there may be deep cultural and value-system differences between the various countries that an organization operates in. This adds another type of complexity to the structural design process and necessitates the creation of integrating mechanisms so that people are able to understand and interpret one another, as well as coordinate with one another.

The choice of structure for managing an global business is generally based on choices concerning the following three factors:

1. *The level of vertical differentiation.* A hierarchy of authority must be created that clarifies the responsibilities of both domestic and foreign managers.

2. *The level of horizontal differentiation.* Foreign and domestic operations should be grouped in such a way that the company effectively serves the needs of all customers.

3. *The degree of formalization, specialization, standardization, and centralization.* The global structure must allow decisions to be made in the most appropriate area of the organization. However, controls must be in place that reflect the strategies and goals of the parent firm.[55]

The COVID-19 pandemic has introduced a range of complications into the globalization process that took off circa 1990, but business remains in a global context.

15-5c Artificial Intelligence (AI) and Cybersecurity

AI may be on the edge of a boom; one estimate is that it can add $13 trillion to the global economy. However, there are challenges to realizing the potential in AI for a company, and culture rather than technology may be the most important.[56] The organizational design to exploit AI comes from a governing coalition within the organization: a team of business, IT, and analytics leaders with shared accountability for the AI transformation. The governing coalition operates a hub-and-spoke system with the hub being a central group headed by a C-level analytics executive who aligns strategy. The spokes are the business units, functions, or geographical units that assign a manager to the AI product owner and a business analyst to assist them. There is an inevitable gray area of work that could be owned

---

Fast Fact

The Knowledge Gap in Cybersecurity

Less the 15 percent of companies in a random sample of one-third of the Russell 3000 report have a cybersecurity expert on the board. This is consequential because cybersecurity has emerged as a key business risk that threatens an organization's ability to operate, or even to survive. Corporate directors do not currently have the knowledge required to oversee this cybersecurity aspects of the organization. This lack of expertise, this knowledge gap, is a form of ignorance that is a risk to the business. Boards often compensate by relying on the chief information security officer (CISO), which puts directors in an overdependent position for oversight. Corporate boards certainly need to work in concert with CISOs while at the same time having their own cybersecurity expertise within the board itself, enabling them to discharge their oversight and regulatory responsibilities.

Source: A. Vance and M. Lowry, "Why Corporate Boards Need More Cybersecurity Expertise," *Wall Street Journal*, September 9 (2022), R5.

---

by the hub, the spoke, or shared with IT. This design offers the potential for exploiting the potential and power of AI.

While AI offers upside potential for organizations, cyber threats are a danger to many organizations. Therefore, cybersecurity programs are a critical design element in contemporary organizations. Cybersecurity awareness (CSA) is knowing and then transforming what is learned into practice.[57] CSA is a continuous process that is adjusted in subsequent iterations to improve the usability and sustainability of the system. Therefore, CSA programs need review and evaluation in a timely way. To do this, four indicators or metrics are recommended, which are: impact, sustainability, accessibility, and monitoring. By measuring all four indicators, organizations can ensure a systemic, complete, and replicable evaluation as a basis for continuous improvement. The organization's cybersecurity may well depend upon CSA. The Fast Fact above shows that there is a knowledge gap in corporate boards who often lack cybersecurity expertise.

15-5d High Reliability Organizing

Disasters, such as the COVID-19 pandemic, mass workplace gun violence, and technological errors, are an increasing threat to organizations' design and function, if not survival.[58] Disasters damage both individuals and organizations, sometimes fatally. For organizations, disasters compromise functioning and profitability, and can lead to organizational failure. Disaster exposure depletes, or prompts investment of, organizational resources, thus having impacts on organizational well-being. and subsequently impacts organizational outcomes. Organizations cannot control all disasters that may befall them, either from the environment or from within the organization. Disasters may fall in the category of unexpected events; however, this does not mean they cannot be anticipated or guarded against. High reliability organizing is a systemic way of engaging in disaster preparedness.

Weick and Sutcliff studied diverse organizations that must maintain structure and function in uncertainty and where the potential for error and disaster can lead to catastrophe.[59] They found these high reliability organizations (HRO) have a unique structure while also thinking and acting differently from other organizations. HROs are mindful, are conscious, are attentive to the unexpected as well as the expected. What is unique about HROs is that they anticipate the unexpected and they contain events when the unexpected occurs. HROs anticipate by being preoccupied with failure, looking for it to avoid it. Being reluctant to simplify, rather they deeply analyze unexpected events, and they are sensitive to operations as dynamic, nonlinear processes. HROs contain unexpected events through a commitment to resilience and a deference to expertise, in contrast to hierarchical position. As a result, HROs thrive by avoiding unexpected events or disasters when they are able and then learn from them when they do occur. Maintaining and/or recovering health and wellbeing following a disaster or other unexpected event is a real twenty-first century challenge.[60]

15-6 Emerging Organizational Structures

The demands placed on managers and on process capabilities in turn place demands on structures. Consequently, the emphasis in organizations is shifting to organizing around processes (see Table 15.3). For example, Procter & Gamble increased its level of innovation by creating teams dedicated to conducting market research, developing technology, creating business plans, and testing assumptions for specific projects.[61] This process orientation emerges from the combination of three streams of applied organizational design: high-performance, self-managed teams; managing processes rather than functions; and the evolution of information technology. Information technology and advanced communication systems have in turn led to *internetworking*. In a study of 469 firms, deeply internetworked firms were found to be more focused and specialized, less hierarchical, and more engaged in external partnering.[62] Three emerging organizational structures associated with these changes are network organizations, distributed organization design, and the circle organization. In addition, the concept of craft offers alternative models for organizing work.[63]

Network organizations are weblike structures that contract some or all of their operating functions to other organizations and then coordinate their activities through managers and other employees at their headquarters. Information technology is the basis for building the weblike structure of the network organization and business unit managers that are essential to the success of these systems. This type of organization has arisen in the age of electronic commerce and brought into practice transaction-cost economics, interorganizational collaborations, and strategic alliances. Network organizations can be global in scope.[64]

> Trust—a complex phenomenon involving ethics, morals, emotions, values, and natural attitudes—can be particularly challenging for virtual organizations.

Distributed organization design is where at least 50 percent of the organization is working remotely; many distributed organizations have no central office at all. Distributed organization design puts managers at the center of the design/redesign process and delivers better results by empowering them to shape their teams.[65] The four key advantages of distributed design are: (1) empowering managers to act according to their direct experience; (2) improving the odds of finding the best talent for each role; (3) encouraging engagement which improves morale; and (4) strengthening horizontal alignment by providing managers with opportunities to clarify responsibilities with their peers. Distributed organization design fits well with a remote workplace culture as discussed in Chapter 14.[66]

The *circle organization* is a third emerging structure, crafted by Harley-Davidson in its drive to achieve teamwork without teams.[67] The three organizational parts, shown in Figure 15.5, are those that (1) create demand, (2) produce product, and (3) provide support. As the figure indicates, these three parts are linked by the *leadership and strategy council (LSC)*. The circle organization is a more open system than most and an organic structure for customer responsiveness. One innovation in this organizational scheme

Table 15.3 Structural Roles of Managers Today Versus Managers of the Future

Roles of Managers Today	1. Strictly adhering to boss–employee relationships. 2. Getting things done by giving orders. 3. Carrying messages up and down the hierarchy. 4. Performing a prescribed set of tasks according to a job description. 5. Having a narrow functional focus. 6. Going through channels, one by one by one. 7. Controlling subordinates.
Roles of Future Managers	1. Having hierarchical relationships subordinated to functional and peer relationships. 2. Getting things done by negotiating. 3. Solving problems and making decisions. 4. Creating the job by developing entrepreneurial projects. 5. Having broad cross-functional collaboration. 6. Emphasizing speed and flexibility. 7. Coaching their workers.

Source: T. R. Horton and P. C. Reid, "What Fate for Middle Managers?" *Management Review* 80, No. 1 (1991): 22. © 1991. Thomas R. Horton. American Management Association, New York. All rights reserved.

Figure 15.5 Harley-Davidson's Circle Organization

is the so-called circle coach, who possesses acute communication, listening, and influencing skills so as to be highly respected by circle members and the company's president.

15-7 Factors That Can Adversely Affect Structure

This chapter has identified the purposes of structure, the processes of organizational design, and the dimensions and contexts that must be considered in structure. In addition, it has looked at forces and trends in organizational design. Two cautionary notes are important for the student of organizational behavior. First, an organizational structure may be weak or deficient if it is out of alignment with its contextual variables, in which case one or more of the following four symptoms appears:

- Decision-making is delayed because the hierarchy is overloaded and too much information is being funneled through one or two channels.
- Decision-making is of poor quality because information linkages are not providing the correct information to the right person in the right format.
- The organization does not respond innovatively to a changing environment, especially when coordinated effort is lacking across departments.
- A great deal of conflict is evident as some departments work against one another rather than for the strategies and goals of the organization as a whole; the structure is often at fault.

Second, the personality of the chief executive may adversely affect the structure of the organization.[68] Managers' personal, cognitive biases and political ideologies may affect their good judgment and decision-making.[69] The mental health of senior executives may serve as primary prevention of mental health problems for tens, hundreds, and even thousands of employees throughout an organization. Mental distress is no accident and is preventable when risk factors and early warning signs are managed. Organizations with a skilled chief clinical officer, such as an organizational clinical psychologist, who identifies and then helps the 1 to 3 percent of employees who fall in the high risk or dangerous category are able to prevent most mental health or behavioral crises in the workplace.[70]

Experiential Exercise

Design and Build a Castle

This exercise is intended to give your group an opportunity to design an organization and produce a product.

Your group is one of three product-development teams working within the research and development division of the General Turret and Moat Corporation (GTM). GTM has decided to enter new markets by expanding the product line to include fully designed and produced castles rather than selling components to other companies as it has in the past.

Each of the three teams has been asked to design a castle for the company to produce and sell. Given its limited resources, GTM cannot put more than one design on the market. Therefore, it will have to decide which of the three designs it will use and will discard the other two designs.

Your task is to develop and design a castle. You will have forty-five minutes to produce a finished product. At the end of this period, several typical consumers, picked by scientific sampling techniques, will judge which is the best design. Before the consumers make their choice, each group will have one to two minutes to make a sales presentation.

Step 1. Each group is designated 1, 2, or 3. The instructor will provide group members a memorandum appropriate for their group. One observer (or two for larger groups) is selected for each group. Observers read their materials.

Step 2. Groups design their organization in order to complete their goal.

Step 3. Each group designs its own castle and draws it on newsprint.

Step 4. "Typical consumers" (may be observers) tour building locations and hear sales pitches. Judges caucus to determine winner.

Step 5. Groups meet again and write up their central goal statement. They also write the organization chart on newsprint with the goal written beneath. These are posted around the room.

Step 6. Instructor leads a class discussion on how the different memos affected organization design. Which design seemed most effective for this task?

Note: Your instructor may allow more time and actually have you *build* the castles.

Source: "Design and Build a Castle" from Dorothy Marcic and Richard C. Housley, *Organizational Behavior: Experiences and Cases* (St. Paul: West, 1989): 221–225. Reprinted by permission.

Learning Objectives

15-1 **Summarize differentiation and integration as organizational design processes.**
Differentiation is the design process of breaking the organizational goals into tasks. Three different forms of differentiation are horizontal, vertical, and spatial. *Integration* is the design process of linking the tasks together to form a structure that supports goal accomplishment. Vertical linkage devices include hierarchical referral, rules and procedures, plans and schedules, added positions, and management information systems. The horizontal linkages are liaison roles, task forces, integrator positions, and teams.

15-2 **Discuss the basic design dimensions managers must consider in structuring an organization.** Basic design dimensions combine to yield various structural configurations. Structural dimensions include the following: formalization, centralization, specialization, standardization, complexity, and hierarchy of authority. Levels of structural dimensions determine bureaucratic (high) or flexible and loose (low) organizations. Henry Mintzberg's alternative approach is to describe what is and is not important to the success of the organization and design structures that fit each organization's unique set of circumstances.

15-3 **Describe five structural configurations for organizations.** Henry Mintzberg proposed five structural configurations: the simple structure, the machine bureaucracy, the professional bureaucracy, the divisionalized form, and the adhocracy. The five

basic parts of the organization, for Mintzberg, are the upper echelon, and/or strategic apex; the middle level, or middle line; the operating core; the technical staff, or technostructure; and the support staff. The organization's goals and levels of differentiation, integration, and formalization determine the structural configuration.

15-4 **Describe four contextual variables that influence organizational structure.** Four variables influence the success of an organization's design: size, technology, environment, and strategy and goals. These variables provide a manager with key considerations for the right organizational design. The amount of change in the contextual variables throughout the life of the organization influences the amount of change needed in the basic dimensions of the organization's structure.

15-5 **Explain the forces reshaping organizations.** Several forces reshaping organizations are causing managers to go beyond the traditional frameworks and to examine ways to make organizations more responsive to customer needs. Some of these forces include shorter organizational life cycles, globalization, and rapid changes in information technology. These forces together increase the demands on process capabilities within the organization and emerging organizational structures. To successfully retain their health and vitality, organizations must function as open systems that are responsive to their task environment.

15-6 Describe emerging organizational structures. Network organizations are weblike structures that contract some or all of their operating functions to other organizations and then coordinate their activities through managers and other employees at their headquarters. Virtual organizations are temporary network organizations consisting of independent enterprises. The circle organization, crafted by Harley-Davidson in its drive to achieve teamwork without teams, is a more open system and an organic structure for customer responsiveness.

15-7 Identify factors that can adversely affect organizational structure. If organizational structure is out of alignment with its contextual variables, one or more of the following symptoms appears: delayed decision-making, low-quality decision-making, non-response to changing environment, and interdepartmental conflict. Also, managers' personal cognitive biases and political ideologies affect their good judgment and decision-making abilities and may adversely affect the structure of the organization.

Key Terms

adhocracy A selectively decentralized form of organization that emphasizes the support staff and mutual adjustment among people. (p. 320)

business model innovation The innovative processes and rationale for how an organization creates, delivers, and captures value. (p. 316)

centralization The degree to which decisions are made at the top of the organization. (p. 316)

complexity The degree to which many different types of activities occur in the organization. (p. 316)

contextual variables A set of four characteristics that influence the success of an organization's design: size, technology, environment, and strategy and goals. (p. 320)

differentiation The process of deciding how to divide the work in an organization. (p. 311)

divisionalized form A loosely coupled, composite structural configuration composed of divisions, each of which may have its own structural configuration. (p. 320)

environment Anything outside the boundaries of an organization. (p. 323)

environmental uncertainty The amount and rate of change in the organization's environment. (p. 324)

formalization The degree to which the organization has official rules, regulations, and procedures. (p. 316)

hierarchy of authority The degree of vertical differentiation across levels of management. (p. 316)

integration The process of coordinating the different parts of an organization. (p. 313)

machine bureaucracy A moderately decentralized form of organization that emphasizes support staff differentiated from the line operations of the organization, limited horizontal decentralization of decision-making, and a well-defined hierarchy of authority. (p. 319)

mechanistic structure An organizational design that emphasizes structured activities, specialized tasks, and centralized decision-making. (p. 324)

organic structure An organizational design that emphasizes teamwork, open communication, and decentralized decision-making. (p. 324)

organizational design The process of constructing and adjusting an organization's structure to achieve its business strategy and goals. (p. 311)

organizational life cycle The differing stages of an organization's life from birth to death. (p. 326)

organizational structure The linking of departments and jobs within an organization. (p. 311)

professional bureaucracy A decentralized form of organization that emphasizes the expertise of the professionals in the operating core of the organization. (p. 319)

simple structure A centralized form of organization that emphasizes a small technical and support staff, strong centralization of decision-making in the upper echelon, and a minimal middle level. (p. 319)

specialization The degree to which jobs are narrowly defined and depend on unique expertise. (p. 316)

standardization The degree to which work activities are accomplished in a routine fashion. (p. 316)

task environment The part of the environment that is directly relevant to the organization. (p. 323)

technological interdependence The degree of interrelatedness of the organization's various technological elements. (p. 322)

Ethical Dilemma

Jana and the Founder's Dilemma

Jana sat in amazement as she realized that her small start-up company just celebrated 10 years in business and had hired its 100th employee. She was so pleased with her and the company's success. But she also knew that the company's growth and its changing goals were starting to cause some problems.

In the beginning, when the company was small, it could easily respond to changes in technology or market demands. The organic structure worked well then. But with growth and the goal of creating more specialized products to meet customer needs, this structure really needs to change to a more mechanistic one.

The problem that Jana faces is that she is concerned about losing some of her best people if they are suddenly restricted by more levels of authority. She could consider moving these people into the management positions, but they are not really interested in being managers. They are much happier doing the creative work. But Jana knows that she has to do something or the success the company has enjoyed will not last much longer. Is her greater loyalty to the people who helped make the company what it has become or to continuing to make the company successful for everyone?

1. Using consequential, rule-based, and character theories, evaluate Jana's options.

2. What should Jana do? Why?

Chapter 16

Organizational Culture

Learning Objectives

16-1 Evaluate the role that the three levels of organizational culture play in an organization.

16-2 Evaluate the four functions of organizational culture within an organization.

16-3 Explain the relationship between organizational culture and performance.

16-4 Describe five ways leaders reinforce organizational culture.

16-5 Describe the three stages of organizational socialization, including the way culture is communicated in each step.

16-6 Discuss how managers assess their organization's culture.

16-7 Explain actions managers can take to change organizational culture.

16-8 Identify the challenges organizations face developing positive, cohesive cultures.

The concept of organizational culture has its roots in cultural anthropology. Just as there are cultures in larger human society, there are cultures within organizations. Like societal cultures, they are shared, communicated through symbols, and passed down from generation to generation of employees.

The concept of cultures in organizations was alluded to as early as the Hawthorne studies, which described work group culture. The topic came into its own during the early 1970s, when managers and researchers began to search for keys to survival for organizations in a competitive and turbulent environment. Then, in the early 1980s, several books on corporate culture were published, including Terry Deal and Allan Kennedy's *Corporate Cultures*,[1] William Ouchi's *Theory Z*,[2] and Thomas Peters and Robert Waterman's *In Search of Excellence*.[3] These books found wide audiences, and research began in earnest on the elusive topic of organizational cultures. Executives indicated that these cultures were real and could be managed.[4]

16-1 Levels of Organizational Culture

Many definitions of *organizational culture* have been proposed. Most of them agree that there are several levels of culture and that these levels differ in terms of their visibility and their ability to be changed. Culture has been viewed both as what defines the values of the organization and as a toolkit as to how to behave in an organization. As such, culture influences outcomes that an organization desires to achieve, as well as the processes necessary to achieve those outcomes.[5] The definition adopted in this chapter is that **organizational (corporate) culture** is a pattern of basic assumptions that are considered valid and that are taught to new members as the way to perceive, think, and feel in the organization.[6]

> Organizational cultures are shared, communicated through symbols, and passed down from generation to generation of employees.

In his comprehensive book on organizational culture and leadership, Edgar Schein suggests that organizational culture has three levels. His view of culture is presented in Figure 16.1. The levels range from visible *artifacts* and creations to testable *values* to invisible and even preconscious basic *assumptions*. To achieve a complete understanding of an organization's culture, all three levels must be studied.

16-1a Artifacts

Symbols of culture in the physical and social work environments are called **artifacts**. They are the most visible and accessible level of culture. The key to understanding culture through artifacts lies in figuring out their meanings. Artifacts are also the most frequently studied manifestation of organizational culture, perhaps because of their accessibility. Examples of the artifacts of culture include personal enactment, ceremonies and rites, stories, rituals, and symbols.[7]

Figure 16.1 Levels Of Organizational Culture

Artifacts
- Personal enactment
- Ceremonies and rites
- Stories
- Ritual
- Symbols

Visible but often not decipherable

Values
- Testable in the physical environment
- Testable only by social consensus

Greater level of awareness

Basic assumptions
- Relationship to environment
- Nature of reality, time, and space
- Nature of human nature
- Nature of human activity
- Nature of human relationships

Taken for granted
Invisible
Preconscious

Source: From Edgar H. Schein, *Organizational Culture and Leadership: A Dynamic View*. Copyright © 1985 Jossey-Bass, Inc. Reprinted by permission of John Wiley & Sons, Inc.

---

organizational (corporate) culture A pattern of basic assumptions that are considered valid and that are taught to new members as the way to perceive, think, and feel in the organization.

artifacts Symbols of culture in the physical and social work environments.

The corporate culture of Google is apparent in the offices of Google headquarters located in Mountain View, California. The lobby is replete with lava lamps, pianos, and displays of live searches on the Google search engine from around the world. The hallways house bikes and exercise machines, while office spaces are laid back, with couches and dogs who follow their owners to work.[8] The artifacts at Google reinforce the notion that the company cares about employees and wants them to be creative and comfortable.

Personal Enactment Culture can be understood, in part, through an examination of the behavior of organization members. When this behavior reflects the organization's values, it is called *personal enactment*. In particular, personal enactment by the top managers provides insight into the organization's values.

Rosalind Brewer, former CEO of Walgreens, believes inclusion and equity means making employees feel seen and heard. Earlier in her career, when she was on the leadership team at Starbucks, she began a practice of never walking into a unit as a leader and having her mobile device out. She continued this practice at Walgreens, telling leaders to leave their phones in their pockets because she wanted them to be fully present and listening to employees[9].

Michele Buck, CEO at Hershey, wants to make the company more agile.

Michele Buck, the first female CEO of The Hershey Company, wanted to change the culture at the company to be more agile and risk-taking. She looked for people within Hershey who were big thinkers at lower levels of the company, those who epitomized the culture and were disruptive thinkers. She formed a group of nine of them, and then empowered them to work on big initiatives. Then, she paired the disruptive thinkers with excellent executors, so they generated great ideas and executed them flawlessly[10].

Modeled behavior is a powerful learning tool for employees, as Bandura's social learning theory demonstrated.[11] As we saw in Chapter 5, individuals learn vicariously by observing others' behavior and patterning their own behavior similarly. In this way, culture can be an important leadership tool. Managerial behavior can clarify what is important and coordinate the work of employees, in effect negating the need for close supervision.[12]

Ceremonies and Rites Relatively elaborate sets of activities that are repeatedly enacted on important occasions are known as organizational ceremonies and rites.[13] These occasions provide opportunities to reward and recognize employees whose behavior is congruent with the values of the company. Ceremonies and rites send a message that individuals who both espouse and exhibit corporate values are heroes to be admired.

The ceremonies also bond organization members together. Southwestern Bell (now AT&T) emphasized the importance of management training to the company. Training classes were kicked off by a high-ranking executive (a rite of renewal), and completion of the classes was signaled by a

Roz Brewer led culture change at Starbucks and at Walgreens.

graduation ceremony (a rite of passage). Six kinds of rites in organizations have been identified, as shown in Table 16.1.[14]

Berkshire Hathaway, Inc., is an Omaha-based company that owns and operates a number of insurance firms and several other subsidiaries. Chair and CEO Warren Buffett is known for his business acumen and for ensuring good returns on shareholder investments. Berkshire's annual shareholder meeting is a ceremony of celebration and appears more like a major rock music festival than a corporate meeting. Each meeting starts with a short film poking fun at the CEO and his cantankerous sidekick, Charlie Munger. Attendees watch the short film eagerly to see who will make cameo appearances and were rewarded with an appearance by the cast from *Breaking Bad*. Others who have made cameos include Susan Lucci and Jamie Lee Curtis. One year Jimmy Buffett sang "Margaritaville" at the meeting, with some of the lyrics changed to "wasting away in Berkshire-Hathaway-a-ville!" In 2022, the celebration was closed out by "Uptown Funk" by Bruno Mars, with Berkshire Hathaway lyrics. Bill Gates, who is on the board of directors, often makes it to the meeting and has been seen playing ping-pong with Warren Buffett. More than 40,000 shareholders, employees, and Buffett relatives attend the star-studded event annually.[15]

Stories Some researchers have argued that the most effective way to reinforce organizational values is through stories.[16] As they are retold, stories give meaning and identity to organizations and are

Warren Buffett is known for hosting celebrations that serve as ceremonies for his annual shareholders meeting.

especially helpful in orienting new employees. Part of the strength of organizational stories is that the listeners are left to draw their own conclusions—a powerful communication tool.[17]

FedEx employees know the story about the FedEx driver who was out late in snowy weather checking a drop-off box for any packages. When he tried to unlock the box, it was frozen solid and his key broke off inside the lock. He tried every way possible to reach the packages, and then drove to a nearby garage to borrow a torch. Then he cut the legs off the box, took it to the airport, and a maintenance team drilled the box open to retrieve the packages and get them on the airplane en route to their destinations. The story reinforces the message the FedEx will go above and beyond to get your package delivered on time.[18]

Table 16.1 Six Rites in Organizations

Rite	Role	Example
1. *Rites of passage*	Show that an individual's status has changed	Retirement dinners
2. *Rites of enhancement*	Reinforce the achievement of individuals	Awarding certificates to sales contest winners
3. *Rites of renewal*	Emphasize change in the organization and commitment to learning and growth	Opening a new corporate training center
4. *Rites of integration*	Unite diverse groups or teams within the organization and renew commitment to the larger organization	Company functions such as annual picnics
5. *Rites of conflict reduction*	Dealing with conflicts or disagreements that arise naturally in organizations	Grievance hearings and the negotiation of union contracts
6. *Rites of degradation*	Used to visibly punish persons who fail to adhere to values and norms of behavior	Publicly replacing a CEO for unethical conduct or for failure to achieve organizational goals

Research by Joanne Martin and her colleagues has indicated that certain themes appear in stories across different types of organizations[19]:

1. *Stories about the boss.* These stories may reflect whether the boss is "human" or how the boss reacts to mistakes.

2. *Stories about getting fired.* Events leading to employee firings are recounted.

3. *Stories about how the company deals with employees who have to relocate.* These stories relate to the company's actions toward employees who have to move—whether the company is helpful and takes family and other personal concerns into account.

4. *Stories about whether lower-level employees can rise to the top.* Often these stories describe a person who started out at the bottom and eventually became the CEO. QuikTrip is well known for promoting from within, one reason it has been voted one of *Fortune*'s 100 Best Companies to Work For seven years running. In fact, two-thirds of QuikTrip's top 100 managers started at entry-level positions in the organization.[20]

5. *Stories about how the company deals with crisis situations.* These stories show how the company overcomes obstacles. Undoubtedly there will be stories that emerge about how companies survived the pandemic. Whole Foods, for example, turned some of its stores into fulfillment centers. Walgreens pivoted to offer delivery on grocery and personal care items. Chipotle created drive through order pickup lanes called "Chipotlanes" for mobile orders.[21] Often, stories are about CEO behavior. Marriott International's CEO Arne Sorenson donated hotel rooms to front-line workers during the pandemic. He also forfeited his salary for the year. When Marriott's executive staff was asked to sacrifice half of their salaries, many did so.[22]

6. *Stories about how status considerations work when rules are broken.* When Tom Watson, Sr., was the CEO of IBM, he was once confronted by a security guard because he was not wearing an ID badge.

These are the themes that can emerge when stories are passed down. The information from these stories serves to guide the behavior of organization members.

To be effective cultural tools, however, stories must be credible. You can't tell a story about your flat corporate hierarchy and then have reserved parking spaces for managers. Stories that aren't backed by reality can lead to cynicism and mistrust.

Effective stories are not only motivational; they can also reinforce culture and create renewed energy. Storytelling reinforces the culture at Southwest Airlines and reminds employees of their purpose in interactions with customers. Southwest's internal corporate videos are full of stories about employees who go above and beyond to serve customers. In one video, a Southwest customer and her family took her husband to the airport for a six-month deployment in Kuwait. A customer service agent saw the family and asked whether they wanted to go to the departure gate with the soldier. Then, at the departure gate, another employee asked whether the family would like to go onto the plane with him. As passengers cheered, the soldier's children were able to give him one last hug. Stories about employees engaging in behavior consistent with company values motivate other employees to do the same.[23]

Rituals Everyday, repetitive, organizational practices are rituals. They are usually unwritten, but they send a clear message about "the way we do things around here." Rituals enhance the meaningfulness of work and also increase organizational citizenship behaviors, those behaviors that benefit coworkers and the company.[24] While some companies insist that people address each other by their titles and surnames to reinforce a professional image, others prefer that employees operate on a first-name basis—from the top manager on down. Hewlett-Packard values open communication, so its employees address one another by first names only. Global design firm IDEO emphasizes rituals that involve food. Oatmeal is offered every Thursday, and soup served for lunch on Fridays. Tea Time is a weekly ritual that encourages collaboration and deepens relationships and trust.[25]

As everyday practices, rituals reinforce the organizational culture. Insiders who commonly practice the rituals may be unaware of their subtle influence, but outsiders recognize it easily.

Symbols Symbols communicate organizational culture through unspoken messages. They are representative of organizational identity and membership to employees. Some Nike employees proudly display tattoos of the Nike swoosh above their ankles. Symbols are used to build solidarity in the organizational culture.[26] Office design and layout are symbols that reflect the values in the company. An open design and layout communicates that collaboration is important. When individuals' offices are decorated with personal photos and memorabilia, it may indicate the importance of individuality or bringing your authentic self to work.

Personal enactment, rites and ceremonies, stories, rituals, and symbols serve to reinforce the values that are the next level of culture.

16-1b Values

Values are the second, deeper, level of culture. They reflect a person's inherent beliefs of what should or should not be. Values are often consciously articulated, both in conversation and in a company's mission statement or annual report. Among large American companies, 80 percent publish their official corporate values. Clif Bar, the energy bar maker, states its values clearly and calls them their Five Aspirations. The company recognizes that enacting these values is an ongoing journey. The five values are sustaining their business, brands, people, community, and planet. Clif Bar believes the values are like spokes in a wheel, keeping the company in balance.[27] One of the values is Sustaining Our People. This means an emphasis on health, performance, and connecting with nature. Clif Bar's headquarters emphasizes these values, providing a 22-foot climbing wall, massive windows with nature views, and bicycles hanging from the ceiling.

There may be a difference between a company's **espoused values** (what the members say they value) and its **enacted values** (values reflected in the way the members behave). A large study revealed a huge gap between official values and the cultural reality

espoused values What members of an organization say they value.

enacted values Values reflected in the way individuals actually behave.

assumptions Deeply held beliefs that guide behavior and tell members of an organization how to perceive situations and people.

within the organizations. Companies that "walk the talk" (espoused and enacted values match) maximize communication of corporate values and take it a step further by providing behavioral guidelines on how to enact the values. Biogen, a leading biotechnology company, has pioneering as one of its values. To communicate what this means, Biogen provides examples, like "encouraging candor to openly question assumptions," and "being open about what we know and don't know.[28]"

A gap between espoused and enacted values can be particularly evident when it comes to diversity and inclusion efforts. When a company claims it values inclusion, but does not have a diverse workforce, that claim does not ring true. For example, some organizations use gender-diverse images in their recruitment materials in order to attract a diverse set of candidates. When this misrepresents the reality of employee population within the organization, the company is perceived as insincere, and the recruiting strategy can backfire.[29]

16-1c Assumptions

Assumptions are the deeply held beliefs that guide behavior and tell members of an organization how to perceive situations and people. At the deepest and most fundamental level of an organization's culture, according to Edgar Schein, they are the essence of culture. Assumptions are so strongly held that a member behaving in a fashion that would violate them is unthinkable. Another characteristic of assumptions is that they are often unconscious. Organization members may not be aware of their

San Francisco Chronicle/Hearst Newspapers via Getty Images/Hearst Newspapers/Getty Images

At Clif Bar, the values emphasize health and well-being.

assumptions and may be reluctant or unable to discuss them or change them.

While unconscious assumptions often guide a firm's actions and decisions, some companies are quite explicit in their assumptions about employees. Some companies operate under the assumption that work/life balance creates more satisfied and productive companies, and capSpire is a company that makes this explicit. capSpire is a global consulting and technology solutions company that has an unlimited vacation policy. They were awarded the national Alfred P. Sloan Award for their use of creative ideas to promote quality family lives and productive careers.[30]

16-2 Functions of Organizational Culture

In an organization, culture serves four basic functions. First, culture provides a sense of identity to members and increases their commitment to the organization.[31] When employees internalize the values of the company, they find their work intrinsically rewarding and identify with their fellow workers. As a result, motivation is enhanced, and employees are more committed.[32]

Second, culture provides a way for employees to interpret the meaning of organizational events.[33] Leaders can use organizational symbols such as corporate logos to help employees understand the changing nature of their organizational identity. Sometimes symbols should remain the same to ensure that some things stay constant despite changing conditions. Other times symbols may have to change to reflect the new culture in the organization.

Third, culture reinforces the values of the organization.

And, fourth, culture serves as a control mechanism for shaping behavior. Norms that guide behavior are part of culture. Thus, if the norm the company wants to promote is teamwork, then its culture must reinforce that norm. The company's culture must be characterized by open communication, cooperation between teams, and integration of teams.[34] Some norms involve how to show emotion in acceptable or preferred ways. Firefighters, for example, engage in extremely dangerous work. They often have to suppress their emotions and they experience high levels of work-family conflict. When the fire stations where they work have cultures that are jovial and loving, firefighters take fewer unnecessary risks and cope better with their jobs.

16-3 The Relationship of Culture to Performance

The effects of organizational culture are hotly debated by organizational behaviorists and researchers. It seems that although managers attest strongly to the positive effects of culture in organizations, it is difficult to quantify these effects. John Kotter and James Heskett have reviewed three theories about the relationship between organizational culture and performance and the evidence that either supports or refutes these theories.[35] The three are the strong culture perspective, the fit perspective, and the adaptation perspective.

16-3a The Strong Culture Perspective

The strong culture perspective states that organizations with strong cultures perform better than other organizations.[36] A **strong culture** is an organizational culture with a consensus on the values that drive the company and with an intensity that is recognizable even to outsiders. Thus, a strong culture is deeply held and widely shared. It is also highly resistant to change. A good example is IBM, which has a strong culture of conservatism, workforce loyalty, and emphasis on customer service.

Strong cultures are thought to facilitate performance for three reasons. First, these cultures are characterized by goal alignment; that is, all employees share common goals. Second, strong cultures create a high level of motivation because of the values shared by the members. Third, strong cultures provide control without the oppressive effects of a bureaucracy.

Two perplexing questions about the strong culture perspective are (1) what can be said about evidence showing that strong economic performance can create strong cultures, rather than the reverse, and (2) what if the strong culture leads the firm down the wrong path? Sears, for example, is an organization with a strong culture, but since the 1980s, it focused inward, ignoring competition and consumer preferences and damaging its performance.[37]

16-3b The Fit Perspective

The fit perspective argues that a culture is good only if it fits the industry or the firm's strategy. For example, a culture that values a traditional hierarchical structure and stability would not work well in the computer manufacturing industry, which demands fast response and a lean, flat organization. Three particular industry characteristics may affect culture: the competitive environment, customer requirements, and societal expectations.[38]

A study of twelve large U.S. firms indicated that cultures consistent with industry conditions

©Dean Drobot/Shutterstock.com

help managers make better decisions. It also indicated that cultures need not change as long as the industry doesn't change. If the industry does change, however, many cultures change too slowly to avoid negative effects on firms' performance.[39]

The fit perspective is useful in explaining short-term performance but not long-term performance. It also indicates that it is difficult to change culture quickly, especially if the culture is widely shared and deeply held. But it doesn't explain how firms can adapt to environmental change.

16-3c The Adaptation Perspective

The third theory about culture and performance is the adaptation perspective. Its theme is that only cultures that help organizations adapt to environmental change are associated with excellent performance. An **adaptive culture** is a culture that encourages confidence and risk taking among employees,[40] has leadership that produces change,[41] and focuses on the changing needs of customers. To test the adaptation perspective, Kotter and Heskett interviewed industry analysts about the cultures of twenty-two firms. The contrast between adaptive cultures and nonadaptive cultures was striking. The results of the study are summarized in Table 16.2.

Adaptive cultures facilitate change to meet the needs of three groups of constituents: stockholders, customers, and employees. Nonadaptive cultures are characterized by cautious management that tries to protect its own interests. Adaptive firms showed significantly better long-term economic performance in Kotter and Heskett's study. When strong cultures focus intensely on adaptability, they can perform better financially.[42] Given that high-performing cultures are adaptive ones, it is important to know how managers can develop adaptive cultures.

strong culture An organizational culture with a consensus on the values that drive the company and with an intensity that is recognizable even to outsiders.

adaptive culture An organizational culture that encourages confidence and risk taking among employees, has leadership that produces change, and focuses on the changing needs of customers.

Table 16.2 Adaptive Versus Nonadaptive Organizational Cultures

	Adaptive Organizational Cultures	Nonadaptive Organizational Cultures
Core values	Most managers care deeply about customers, stockholders, and employees. They also strongly value people and processes that can create useful change (e.g., leadership up and down the management hierarchy).	Most managers care mainly about themselves, their immediate work group, or some product (or technology) associated with that work group. They value the orderly and risk-reducing management process much more highly than leadership initiatives.
Common behavior	Managers pay close attention to all their constituencies, especially customers, and initiate change when needed to serve their legitimate interests, even if that entails taking some risks.	Managers tend to behave somewhat insularly, politically, and bureaucratically. As a result, they do not change their strategies quickly to adjust to or take advantage of changes in their business environments.

16-4 The Leader's Role in Shaping and Reinforcing Culture

According to Edgar Schein, leaders play crucial roles in shaping and reinforcing culture.[43] The five most important elements in managing culture are (1) what leaders pay attention to, (2) how leaders react to crises, (3) how leaders behave, (4) how leaders allocate rewards, and (5) how leaders hire and fire individuals.

16-4a What Leaders Pay Attention To

Leaders in an organization communicate their priorities, values, and beliefs through the themes that consistently emerge from their focus. These themes are reflected in what they notice, comment on, measure, and control. If leaders are consistent in their focus, employees receive clear signals about what is important in the organization. If, however, leaders are inconsistent, employees spend a lot of time trying to decipher and find meaning in the inconsistent signals. With remote work, there has been an increase in employee monitoring. Digital productivity monitoring means workers are subject to tracking, scoring, and accumulating records. A bad scorecard can lead to a lost job. The use of software to keep tabs on workers not only allows counting keystrokes, but also takes periodic screenshots, records calls, and can even enable complete access to workers' computers. But are leaders measuring the right things? At UnitedHealth, social workers were marked "idle" (a poor rating) due to lack of keyboard activity when they were busy counseling patients. Such systems, intended to facilitate remote

work, can create distrust, anxiety, and burnout if they cause leaders to pay attention to the wrong things.[44]

16-4b How Leaders React to Crises

The way leaders deal with crises communicates a powerful message about culture. Emotions are heightened during a crisis, and learning is intense. Difficult economic times present crises for many companies and illustrate their different values. Some organizations avoid laying off workers at all costs. Others, despite their claim that employees are important, quickly institute major layoffs at the first signal of an economic downturn. Employees may perceive that the company shows its true colors in a crisis and thus pay careful attention to the reactions of their leaders.

16-4c How Leaders Behave

Through role modeling, teaching, and coaching, leaders reinforce the values that support the organizational culture. Employees often emulate leaders' behavior and look to the leaders for cues to appropriate behavior. Many companies encourage employees to be more entrepreneurial, using more initiative and innovation. A study showed that if managers want employees to be more entrepreneurial, they must demonstrate such behaviors themselves.[45] This is the case with any cultural value. Employees observe the behavior of leaders to find out what the organization values.

16-4d How Leaders Allocate Rewards

To ensure that values are accepted, leaders should reward behavior that is consistent with the values. Some companies, for example, may claim that they use a pay-for-performance system that distributes rewards based on performance. When the time comes for raises, however, the increases are awarded according to length of service with the company. Imagine the feelings of a high-performing newcomer who receives only a tiny raise after hearing company leaders espouse the value of rewarding individual performance.

Some companies may claim to value teamwork. They form cross-functional teams and empower these teams to make important decisions. However, when performance is appraised, the criteria for rating employees focus on individual performance. This sends a confusing signal to employees about the company's culture: Is individual performance valued, or is teamwork the key?

Remote and hybrid work brings its own set of challenges when it comes to rewards. Proximity bias is managers' tendency to promote and reward individuals who are most visible to them. This bias existed prior to the pandemic, but it has become more prevalent as the number of people who work remotely is on the rise.[46] One study of remote workers showed that they are given poorer performance ratings, are less likely to be given bonuses, and are not promoted as quickly as in-person workers.[47] Leaders must combat this bias and create equal opportunities for remote workers if they are to be seen as allocating rewards fairly.

16-4e How Leaders Hire and Fire Individuals

A powerful way that leaders reinforce culture is through the selection of newcomers to the organization. With the advent of electronic recruitment practices, applicant perceptions of organizational culture are shaped by what the organization advertises on its recruitment website. Typical perception-shaping mechanisms are organizational values, policies, awards, and goals.[48] Just as newcomers learn culture from perusing corporate websites, leaders shape and communicate culture by the way they hire employees. Many CEOs have a set of questions they like to use in interviews. Barbara Corcoran, CEO of The Corcoran Group, leads New York's largest real estate company. You may have seen her on the television hit "Shark Tank." When interviewing job candidates, she never looks at resumes beforehand, believing that sticking to the resume leads to small talk. Instead, she prefers questions that determine whether the candidate is a happy, positive individual. Some questions she asks include "Tell me about your family?" and "What's your hobby?" Energy

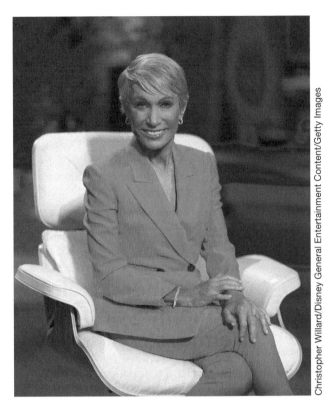

Barbara Corcoran looks for energy and positive attitudes in people she hires.

and a positive attitude are critical to success, according to Corcoran. Who does she love to fire? Complainers![49]

The way a company fires an employee and the rationale behind the firing also communicates the culture. Some companies deal with poor performers by trying to find a place within the organization where they can perform better and make a contribution. Other companies seem to operate under the philosophy that those who cannot perform are out quickly.

The reasons for terminations may not be directly communicated to other employees, but curiosity leads to speculation. Suppose an employee caught in the act of unethical behavior is simply reprimanded, with no other penalty, even though such behavior is clearly against the organization's values. Other employees may view this as a failure to reinforce the values within the organization.

In summary, leaders play a critical role in shaping and reinforcing organizational culture. Managers need to create a positive culture through what they pay attention to, how they react to crises, how they behave, the way they allocate rewards, and how they hire and fire employees. Transformational leaders create a more adaptive culture, which in turn increases business unit performance.[50]

16-5 Organizational Socialization

We have seen that leaders play key roles in shaping an organization's culture. Another process that perpetuates culture is the way it is passed on from generation to generation of employees. Newcomers learn the culture through **organizational socialization**—the process by which newcomers are transformed from outsiders to participating, effective members of the organization.[51] As we saw earlier, cultural socialization begins with the careful selection of newcomers who are likely to reinforce the organizational culture.[52] Once selected, newcomers pass through the stressful socialization process.

16-5a The Stages of the Socialization Process

The organizational socialization process is generally described as having three stages: anticipatory socialization, encounter, and change and acquisition. Figure 16.2 presents a model of the process and the key concerns at each stage of it.[53] It also describes the outcomes of the process, which will be discussed in the next section of the chapter.

Anticipatory Socialization The first stage of the socialization process, **anticipatory socialization**, encompasses all of the learning that takes place prior to the newcomer's first day on the job, including the newcomer's expectations. The two key concerns at this stage are realism and congruence.

Realism is the degree to which a newcomer holds realistic expectations about the job and organization. One thing newcomers should receive information about during entry into the organization is the culture. Information about values at this stage can help newcomers begin to construct a scheme for interpreting their organizational experiences. Later, a deeper understanding of the organization's culture will be possible through time and experience in the organization. When organizations give realistic job previews that not only highlight major stressors but also teach various coping strategies to deal with them, newcomers feel less stressed and report higher levels of adjustment six and nine months postentry.[54] Kansas Child Welfare uses a video for applicants and new recruits that provides a full overview of both the stressors of the job and the ability to make a difference that the job provides.[55]

There are two types of *congruence* between an individual and an organization: congruence between the individual's abilities and the demands of the job, and the fit between the individual's values and the organization's values. Organizations disseminate information about their values through their web pages, annual reports, and recruitment brochures. *Value congruence* is particularly important for organizational culture. It is also important in terms of newcomer adjustment. Newcomers whose values match the company's values are more satisfied with their new jobs, adjust more quickly, and say they intend to remain with the firm longer.[56] Newcomers will cope better throughout the socialization experience if they believe the organization has fulfilled its promises and met the newcomer's expectations.[57]

Figure 16.2 The Organizational Socialization Process: Stages and Outcomes

Stages of socialization

1. Anticipatory socialization — Realism / Congruence

2. Encounter — Job demands
   - Task
   - Role
   - Interpersonal

3. Change and acquisition — Mastery

Outcomes of socialization
- Performance
- Satisfaction
- Mutual influence
- Low levels of distress
- Intent to remain

Source: Reprinted from *Organizational Dynamics*, Autumn 1989, "An Ethical Weather Report: Assessing the Organization's Ethical Climate" by John B. Cullen et al. Copyright © 1989, with permission from Elsevier Science.

organizational socialization The process by which newcomers are transformed from outsiders to participating, effective members of the organization.

anticipatory socialization The first socialization stage, which encompasses all of the learning that takes place prior to the newcomer's first day on the job.

Encounter The second stage of socialization, encounter, is when newcomers learn the tasks associated with the job, clarify their roles, and establish new relationships at work. This stage commences on the first day at work and is thought to encompass the first six to nine months on the new job. Newcomers face task demands, role demands, and interpersonal demands during this period.

Task demands involve the actual work performed. Learning to perform tasks is related to the organization's culture. In some organizations, where creativity is valued, newcomers are given considerable latitude to experiment with new ways to do their job. In others, newcomers are expected to learn the established procedures for their tasks. Early experiences with trying to master task demands can affect employees' entire careers. Auditors, for example, are often forced to choose between being thorough and being fast in completing their work. By pressuring auditors in this way, firms often set themselves up for problems later, when these pressures may lead auditors to make less-than-ethical decisions.

Role demands involve the expectations placed on newcomers. Newcomers may not know exactly what is expected of them (role ambiguity) or may receive conflicting expectations from other individuals (role conflict). The way newcomers approach these demands depends in part on the culture of the organization. Are newcomers expected to operate with considerable uncertainty, or is the manager expected to clarify the newcomers' roles? Some cultures even put newcomers through considerable stress in the socialization process, including humility-inducing experiences, so newcomers will be more open to accepting the firm's values and norms. Long hours, tiring travel schedules, and an overload of work are examples of some socialization practices.

Interpersonal demands arise from relationships at work. Politics, leadership style, and group pressure are interpersonal demands. All of them reflect the values and assumptions that operate within the organization. Most organizations have basic assumptions about the nature of human relationships. For example, the

Korean *chaebol* LG Group strongly values harmony in relationships and in society, and its decision-making policy emphasizes unanimity.

In the encounter stage, the expectations formed in anticipatory socialization may clash with the realities of the job. It is a time of facing the task, role, and interpersonal demands of the new job.

Change and Acquisition In the third and final stage of socialization, change and acquisition, newcomers begin to master the demands of the job. They become proficient at managing their tasks, clarifying and negotiating their roles, and engaging in relationships at work. The time when the socialization process is completed varies widely depending on the individual, the job, and the organization. The end of the process is signaled by newcomers being considered by themselves and others as organizational insiders.

16-5b Outcomes of Socialization

Newcomers who are successfully socialized should exhibit good performance, high job satisfaction, and the intention to stay with the organization. In addition, they should exhibit low levels of distress symptoms.[58] A high level of organizational commitment is also a mark of successful socialization.[59] This commitment is facilitated throughout the socialization process by the communication of values that newcomers can buy into. Successful socialization is also signaled by mutual influence; that is, the newcomers have made adjustments in the job and organization to accommodate their knowledge and personalities. Newcomers are expected to leave their mark on the organization and not be completely conforming.

When socialization is effective, newcomers understand and adopt the organization's values and norms. This ensures that the company's culture, including its central values, survives. Newcomers adopt the company's norms and values more quickly when they receive positive support from organizational insiders. Sometimes this is accomplished through informal social gatherings.[60]

Socialization is not just the responsibility of the organization and the manager but of the employees as well. Newcomers who are more curious and adaptable adjust to their new jobs more effectively, leading to better performance.[61] Additionally, newcomers who have proactive personalities adjust

encounter The second socialization stage, in which newcomers learn the tasks associated with the job, clarify their roles, and establish new relationships at work.

change and acquisition The third socialization stage, in which the newcomer begins to master the demands of the job.

Organizational Example

A Culture of Giving Back at Bombas

Founded in 2013, Bombas is best known for its socks and now offers a full line of comfort-focused apparel. Bombas' founders learned that socks are the most needed item at homeless shelters, so for every item sold, the company donates an item to the homeless community. Very few people spend much time thinking about their socks, and yet socks are perceived as a luxury by the 650,000+ homeless individuals in the United States. The emphasis on giving extends to employees, too. "Hive members" (employees) share a common mission of helping those in need. They are encouraged to do neighborhood sock drop-offs, to join monthly volunteer opportunities, and to welcome new hires into the Hive by taking them out for coffee. Events like paint nights and axe throwing, along with biannual retreats, keep the culture alive.

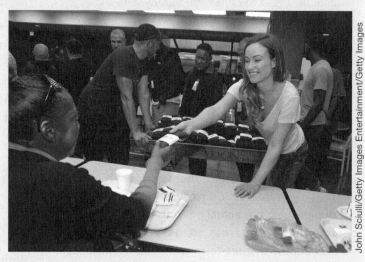

John Sciulli/Getty Images Entertainment/Getty Images

Co-Founder David Health says that the culture attracts people who care, and it's no wonder they like working together because they share the same values. Bombas is a regular on *Fortune*'s Best Workplaces list. The company recently donated its 65 millionth pair of socks.

(Sources: https://www.greatplacetowork.com/certified-company/7005361; B. Morse, "Bombas Co-Founder on Why the Buy-One-Give -One Model Isn't for Everyone," Inc., May 24 (2022), accessed at https://www.inc.com/brit-morse/bombas-david-heath-charity-socks -business-model.html.)

more effectively to the organization because they are more likely to seek out the information they need to become socialized.[62]

16-6 Assessing Organizational Culture

Although some organizational scientists argue for assessing organizational culture with quantitative methods, others say that organizational culture must be assessed with qualitative methods.[63] Quantitative methods, such as questionnaires, are valuable because of their precision, comparability, and objectivity. Qualitative methods, such as interviews and observations, are valuable because of their detail, descriptiveness, and uniqueness.

Two widely used quantitative assessment instruments are the Organizational Culture Inventory (OCI) and the Kilmann–Saxton Culture Gap Survey.

Both assess the behavioral norms of organizational cultures, as opposed to the artifacts, values, or assumptions of the organization.

16-6a Organizational Culture Inventory

The OCI focuses on behaviors that help employees fit into the organization and meet the expectations of coworkers. Using Maslow's motivational need hierarchy as its basis, it measures twelve cultural styles. The two underlying dimensions of the OCI are task/people and security/satisfaction. There are four satisfaction cultural styles and eight security cultural styles.

A self-report instrument, the OCI contains 120 questions. It provides an individual assessment of culture and may be aggregated to the work group and to the organizational level.[64] It has been used in firms throughout North America, Western Europe, New Zealand, and Thailand, as well as in U.S. military units, the Federal Aviation Administration, and nonprofit organizations.

Newcomers who are successfully socialized should exhibit good performance, high job satisfaction, and the intention to stay with the organization.

16-6b Kilmann–Saxton Culture Gap Survey

The Kilmann–Saxton Culture Gap Survey focuses on what actually happens and on the expectations of others in the organization.[65] Its two underlying dimensions are (1) technical/human orientation and (2) short-term versus long-term time. With these two dimensions, the actual operating norms and the ideal norms in four areas are assessed. The areas are *task support* (short-term technical norms), *task innovation* (long-term technical norms), *social relationships* (short-term human orientation norms), and *personal freedom* (long-term human orientation norms). Significant gaps in any of the four areas are used as a point of departure for cultural change to improve performance, job satisfaction, and morale.

Like the OCI, the Gap Survey, as a self-report instrument, provides an individual assessment of culture and may be aggregated to the work group. It has been used in firms throughout the United States and in not-for-profit organizations.

16-6c Triangulation

A study of a rehabilitation center in a 400-bed hospital incorporated **triangulation**—the use of multiple methods to measure organizational culture—to improve inclusiveness and accuracy in measuring the organizational culture.[66] Triangulation has been used by anthropologists, sociologists, and other behavioral scientists to study organizational culture. Its name comes from the navigational technique of using multiple reference points to locate an object. In the rehabilitation center study, the three methods used to triangulate on the culture were (1) obtrusive observations by eight trained observers, which provided an outsider perspective; (2) self-administered questionnaires, which provided quantitative insider

triangulation The use of multiple methods to measure organizational culture.

information; and (3) personal interviews with the center's staff, which provided qualitative contextual information.

The study showed that each of the three methods made unique contributions to the discovery of the rehabilitation center's culture. The complete picture could not have been drawn with just a single technique. Triangulation can lead to a better understanding of the phenomenon of culture and is the best approach to assessing organizational culture.

16-7 Changing Organizational Culture

With rapid environmental changes such as globalization, workforce diversity, and technological innovation, the fundamental assumptions and basic values that drive the organization may need to be altered.

Changing an organization's culture is feasible but difficult.[67] One reason for the difficulty is that assumptions—the deepest level of culture—are often unconscious. As such, they are often resistant to confrontation and debate. Another reason for difficulty is that culture is deeply ingrained and behavioral norms and rewards are well learned.[68] In a sense, employees must unlearn the old norms before they can learn new ones. Managers who want to change the culture should look first to the ways culture is maintained. Research among hospitals found that change was welcomed in private hospitals with a collaborative culture whereas it was met with opposition in public hospitals with an autocratic culture.[69]

A model for cultural change that summarizes the interventions managers can use is presented in Figure 16.3. In this model, the numbers represent the steps managers can take. There are two basic approaches to changing the existing culture: (1) helping current members buy into a new set of values (steps 1, 2, and 3) or (2) adding newcomers and socializing them into the organization while removing current members as appropriate (steps 4 and 5).[70]

The first step is to change behavior in the organization. Even if behavior does change, however, this change is not sufficient for cultural change to occur. Behavior is an artifact (level 1) of culture. Individuals may change their behavior but not the values that

Figure 16.3 Interventions for Changing Organizational Culture

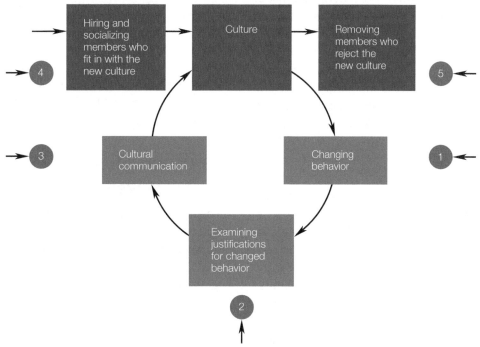

→ Managers seeking to create cultural change must intervene at these points.

Source: From Vijay Sathe, "How to Decipher and Change Corporate Culture," Chap. 13 in *Gaining Control of the Corporate Culture* (R. H. Kilmann et al., eds.), Fig. 1, p. 245. Copyright © 1985 Jossey-Bass, Inc. Reprinted by permission of John Wiley & Sons, Inc.

drive it. They may rationalize, "I'm only doing this because my manager wants me to."

Therefore, managers must use step 2, which is to examine the justifications for the changed behavior. Are employees buying into the new set of values, or are they just complying?

The third step, cultural communication, is extremely important. All of the artifacts (personal enactment, stories, rites and ceremonies, rituals, and symbols) must send a consistent message about the new values and beliefs. It is crucial that the communication be credible; that is, managers must live the new values and not just talk about them. Leaders should pay attention to the informal social networks more so than structural positions in leading organizational change. These informal network communication channels combined with employees' values, and beliefs that managers are highly committed to the change effort, can go a long way in making the change a success.[71]

The two remaining steps (4 and 5) involve shaping the workforce to fit the intended culture. First, the organization can revise its selection strategies to more accurately reflect the new culture. Second,

the organization can identify individuals who resist the cultural change or who are no longer comfortable with the values in the organization. Reshaping the workforce should not involve a ruthless pursuit of nonconforming employees; it should be a gradual and subtle change that takes considerable time. Changing personnel in the organization is a lengthy process; it cannot be done effectively in a short period of time without considerable problems.

Evaluating the success of cultural change may be best done by looking at behavior. Cultural change can be assumed to be successful if the behavior is intrinsically motivated—that is, on "automatic pilot." If the new behavior were to persist even if rewards were not present, and if the employees have internalized the new value system, then the behavior is probably intrinsically motivated. If employees automatically respond to a crisis in ways consistent with the corporate culture, then the cultural change effort can be deemed successful.

When might culture require changing? Mergers and acquisitions present unique challenges for managing organizational culture. The blending of two distinct organizational cultures can be very difficult. Amazon's purchase of Whole Foods may be a mix of cultures like water and oil. Amazon built its culture on being fast, efficient, and cheap, along with imposing strict employee control. Whole Foods built its culture around employee empowerment and customer service, and pricing that reflected the nickname "Whole Paycheck." So far, the results have not been good. Whole Foods employees struggle with new required paperwork and stressful performance metrics. For the first time, Whole Foods failed to make Fortune's best companies to work for list. Clearly, the cultures clashed, and analysts wonder whether Amazon plans to phase out the Whole Foods brand.[72]

In contrast, Disney's merger with Pixar yielded *Frozen*, the world's most successful animated feature film, with an Academy award and $1.3 billion in revenue. Although Pixar employees were concerned about losing their innovative culture and bottom-up approach to creativity, Disney used Pixar as a stimulus for its own culture growth. It took on Pixar's more relaxed culture and tasked Pixar employees with revamping Disney's animation studio. An intentional, employee-driven approach to combining the two cultures was a major factor in the merger's success.[73]

Some organizational cultures could be called "toxic." During what has been called the "Great Resignation" from April 2021 to September 2021, over 24 million employees left their jobs. The strongest predictor of turnover was toxic culture. The leading elements contributing to toxic culture are disrespectful behavior, noninclusive behavior, unethical behavior, cutthroat competition, and abuse such as bullying and harassment.[74] Toxic cultures produce elevated stress, burnout, and mental health issues. They also contribute to high health care costs, and when word gets out about the toxic culture, the company has a hard time attracting talent. Can a toxic culture be fixed? It requires a gargantuan effort focused on all the drivers of culture that we discussed earlier in the chapter.

The transition to remote work also presents opportunities for culture refinement. Unlike in face-to-face work, remote work presents fewer and different interactions for sharing and modeling the behavioral norms that are essential for sustaining culture.[75] It may be a mistake to assume that culture will simply transmit virtually in the same way it did in the traditional workplace. Virtual work requires more intentionality about cultural communication. Research on culture in remote work is emerging.

16-8 Developing a Positive, Cohesive Culture

Organizations that want to develop and sustain positive, cohesive cultures must address many issues. Among these are wellness, ethics, and diversity and inclusion.

16-8a Developing a Culture of Wellness

The pandemic caused many employees to seek out companies that emphasize wellness. The ability to work from anywhere without time boundaries led to burnout, and prompted some companies to re-evaluate their approach to wellness. Physical fitness programs, corporate challenges, and corporate workout centers have been around for a while, whereas a more holistic approach to wellness is evolving. Deloitte's Chief Well-Being Officer Jen Fisher's job is to empower employees to focus on their well-being. She is helping Deloitte create a culture of inclusive well-being that includes physical wellness, mental and emotional health, personal purpose, and financial well-being. Mental Health @ Work is Deloitte's program providing resources and learning opportunities to create a mental health literate culture.[76]

An emphasis on mental health at work is critical, given that large-scale surveys show that 81 percent of workers say that employer support for mental health is an essential consideration for them.[77] Many veterans who enter the civilian workforce struggle with trauma, and one-third of them say the mental health issues in their new work lives are worse than combat. Over half of veterans say their mental health affects their relationships at work.[78] All employees can gain from mental health benefits, and cultures that work to reduce the stigma surrounding mental health can develop cultures that approach wellness in a more complete way.

Comprehensive wellness programs may include paramedic services, telehealth appointments, healthy snack alternatives, and weight/disease management programs. Behavior change programs, therapy subscriptions, and incentives for physical and mental wellness may also be included. As we discussed in Chapter 7, preventive management also focuses on changing the causes of stress.

Inclusive Conversations

When it Comes to Intermountain Healthcare, There is No "One Size Fits All" Culture

Intermountain Healthcare is a network of 60,000 medical providers responsible for serving the needs of diverse populations in the Intermountain West region of the United States, primarily Utah, Idaho, Nevada, Colorado, Montana, Wyoming, and Kansas. Because of the diversity of the communities they serve, Intermountain Healthcare finds it important to confront existing systems of inequity directly to create a more inclusive culture. In practice, this looks like considering one's individual needs, cultures, and customs when providing medical services. For example, many of Intermountain's Native American patients have a custom to carry their newborns on a cradleboard and take the placenta home to return it to the earth. To meet those specific needs, Intermountain provides bassinets that will fit cradleboards and guidelines for taking the placenta home. Other examples of creating an inclusive culture are translating hospice services into Spanish to meet the needs of its Latino population and qualifying one of its hospitals as a Health Care Equity Index facility, which designates the facility as friendly to the LGBTQ+ community. Megan Chepkwurui is the chairperson of the Diversity Equity Inclusion Committee for one of Intermountain Healthcare's regional hospitals. According to Chepkwurui, the focus of their diversity committee is centered on the patient experience—"the different communities, cultures, religions, races, and the sexual orientations of the people we serve." At Intermountain Healthcare, creating a culture of inclusion is not a one-size-fits-all proposition.

1. Why is addressing individual needs, customs, and culture an important diversity issue for healthcare organizations, such as Intermountain Healthcare?

   One of the outcomes of the COVID-19 pandemic was the revelation of healthcare disparities for communities of color and a recognition among many organizations of the benefits of addressing customer needs.

2. What other aspects of culture would you suggest to help Intermountain Healthcare create and maintain a culture of inclusion?

   Students should be guided to consider the levels and aspects of culture discussed in the text.

Sources: Intermountain Healthcare, About Intermountain, https://intermountainhealthcare.org/about; L. Larson, "Intermountain Health: Creating A More Inclusive Culture," *The Spectrum*, July 27 (2023), A1.

Flexible work schedules, caregiver support, diversity and inclusion initiatives, and other interventions that improve the quality of work life and eliminate stressors can also contribute to wellness efforts.

16-8b Developing an Ethical Organizational Culture

The culture of an organization can have profound effects on the ethical behavior of organization members.[79] Organizations in which supervisors and top managers act as role models of ethical behavior and create an openness to discuss ethical issues have fewer incidents of unethical behavior.[80] Employees who work in high-trust cultures enjoy their jobs more, are more aligned with their companies' purpose and values, and treat each other better because they have more empathy for each other.[81] Creating and nurturing a high-trust culture can pay off in higher productivity and more ethical behavior among employees.

Strong ethics and compliance programs also contribute to strong ethics cultures. And in organizations with strong ethics cultures, there is less pressure to compromise ethical standards, less observed misconduct, more reporting when misconduct is observed, and less retaliation for reporting ethics violations.[82]

McDonalds is facing its share of ethical challenges. Former CEO Steve Easterbrook was fired for engaging in sexual relationships with employees. Global Chief People Officer David Fairhurst was also ousted for ignoring and fostering a toxic company culture that condoned impropriety. The new CEO, Chris Kempczinski, has stated that the culture's problems run much deeper, and he vows to bring employee behavior back in line with McDonalds' ethical values.[83]

16-8c Developing an Inclusive Culture

Throughout this book, we have seen that successful organizations promote cultures that value diversity and encourage inclusion. Leader behavior

Hot Trend

Best Practices for Pronouns

Pronouns are an important part of a person's identity and using a person's preferred pronouns shows respect and inclusion. Examples of pronouns are "she/her/hers," "he/him/his," and "they/them/theirs." Here are some tips for promoting inclusion using pronouns:

- Consider including your pronouns in your email signature.
- Use neutral languages in greetings like "Welcome, everyone" rather than "Hey guys."
- If you make a mistake on someone's pronouns and they correct you, thank them.
- You can't tell someone's gender by their appearance, so share your pronouns and then invite others to do the same.

Source: S. Eagan, "Best Practices for Using Pronouns in the Workplace and Everyplace!" *ADP Spark*, accessed at https://www.adp.com/spark/articles/2021/06/best-practices-for-using-pronouns-in-the-workplace-and-everyplace.aspx.

drives an inclusive culture more strongly than policy statements.[84] There are several concrete steps leaders can take to promote an inclusive workplace:

Ensure diversity in every meeting. Diverse views lead to diverse ideas.

Be a role model of inclusive behavior.

Adopt a "no tolerance" position for disrespectful behavior of any kind.

Take quick action to eliminate even subtle behaviors that lead to disrespect.[85]

The Human Rights Campaign foundation publishes a national benchmarking tool called the Corporate Equality Index annually that rates how companies promote inclusion for lesbian, gay, bisexual, transgender, and queer (LGBTQ+) employees. Some of the companies earning a perfect score are Apple, American Airlines, J. P. Morgan Chase, Nike, and Xerox.[86] Eliminating LGBTQ+ discrimination makes a company more competitive by helping it attract and retain top talent, win business from discerning consumers, and capitalize on LGBTQ+ employees' knowledge to drive innovation.

Mondelez International is a global foods company that has three pillars of its diversity, equity, and inclusion commitment. These pillars are colleagues, culture, and community. The company has representation goals that reflect the diversity in the local marketplace and holds 100 percent of managers accountable for delivering on an annual DE&I goal. In addition, it mobilizes its brands to drive change, equity, and inclusion.[87] An example is Oreo, the best-selling cookie in the world. For over 10 years, Oreo has been a strong supporter

of LGBTQ+ pride, and in partnership with PFLAG national, fights for a world in which all families belong. Its original Pride cookie featured rainbow colored filling, and its most recent offering is the Oreo Pride Pack with original Oreos embossed with the word "proud.[88]" The diversity culture at Oreo comes from within the company and extends outside to the community as lifelong allies.

AT&T consistently earns praise for its history of diversity and inclusion. At AT&T every voice matters, and the company supports twenty-six Employee Resource Groups and Employee Networks, with memberships surpassing eighty-nine thousand employees.[89] The groups provide support, mentoring, education, and advocacy to cultural populations, veterans, female employees, the disabled, young professionals, LGBTQ+ community, and others. AT&T also embeds inclusion in its overall business strategy.

UCG/Universal Images Group/Getty Images

Oreo has a history of support for diversity in its cookie and packaging designs.

Experiential Exercise

Identifying Behavioral Norms

This exercise asks you to identify campus norms at your university. Every organization or group has a set of norms that help determine individuals' behavior. A norm is an unwritten rule for behavior in a group. When a norm is not followed, negative feedback is given. It may include negative comments, stares, harassment, and exclusion. These norms are a part of the campus culture.

1. As a group, brainstorm all the norms you can think of in the following areas:

   - Dress
   - Classroom behavior
   - Studying
   - Weekend activities
   - Living arrangements
   - Campus activities
   - Participation in campus traditions
   - Relationships with faculty
   - Eating on campus versus off campus
   - Transportation

2. How did you initially get this information?

3. What happens to students who don't follow these norms?

4. What values can be inferred from these norms?

5. What assumptions do these norms and values reflect?

Source: Adapted from Dorothy Marcic, "Identifying Behavioral Norms," *Organizational Behavior: Experiences and Cases* (St. Paul, MN: West Publishing, 1989). Reprinted by permission.

Learning Objectives

16-1 **Evaluate the role that the three levels of organizational culture play in an organization.** *Organizational culture* is a pattern of basic assumptions considered valid and taught to new members as the way to perceive, think, and feel in the organization. *Artifacts* are cultural symbols in the physical and social work environments, such as personal enactment, ceremonies and rites, stories, rituals, and symbols. Deeper level *values* reflect inherent beliefs, and *assumptions* guide behavior and tell members of an organization how to perceive situations and people.

16-2 **Evaluate the four functions of organizational culture within an organization.** Organizational culture serves four basic functions. First, culture provides a sense of identity to members and increases commitment to the organization. Second, culture provides a way for employees to interpret the meaning of organizational events. Third, culture reinforces the values in the organization. Finally, culture serves as a control mechanism for shaping behavior.

16-3 **Explain the relationship between organizational culture and performance.** A *strong culture* organization acts with a consensus on the values that drive the company and with an intensity that is recognizable even to outsiders. The "fit" perspective (*fit culture*) argues that a culture is good only if it fits the industry or the firm's strategy. Three particular industry characteristics may affect culture: the competitive environment, customer requirements, and societal expectations. An *adaptive culture* is a culture that encourages confidence and risk taking among employees, has leadership that produces change, and focuses on the changing needs of customers.

16-4 **Describe five ways leaders reinforce organizational culture.** Leaders play a critical role in shaping and reinforcing organizational culture. Managers need to create a positive culture through what they pay attention to how they react to crises, how they behave, how they allocate rewards, and how they hire and fire employees. Transformational leaders create a more adaptive culture, which in turn increases business unit performance.

16-5 **Describe the three stages of organizational socialization and the ways culture is communicated in each step.** Newcomers are transformed from outsiders to participating, effective members of the organization through *organizational socialization*. Three stages in the socialization process are *anticipatory socialization, encounter,* and *change and acquisition.* Through positive effective socialization, newcomers understand and adopt values and norms ensuring the company's culture and central values survive. Results can be good performance, high job satisfaction, and the intention to stay with the organization.

16-6 **Discuss how managers assess their organization's culture.** Both qualitative and quantitative methods can be used to assess organizational culture. The Organizational Culture Inventory (OCI) and the Kilmann-Saxton Culture Gap Survey are quantitative tools. In the hopes of generating a more accurate assessment of organizational culture, managers combine multiple instruments, a practice called *triangulation*.

16-7 **Explain actions managers can take to change organizational culture.** Managers can use two approaches to change organizational culture: help current members buy into a new set of values, or add newcomers and socialize them into the organization and remove current members appropriately. Managers must send consistent messages about the new values and beliefs, provide credible communication, and live the new values. Cultural change can be assumed to be successful if new behavior is intrinsically motivated.

16-8 **Identify the challenges organizations face developing positive, cohesive, cultures.** Achieving a positive, cohesive corporate culture may be difficult in mergers, acquisitions, and globalization due to possible conflicts between organizations and cultural diversity on a geographic level. Developing an ethical culture requires management modeling, promoting ethical norms, and trust. Developing a culture of empowerment and quality involves including employees in decision-making, removing obstacles to their performance, and reinforcing the value of product and service.

Key Terms

adaptive culture An organizational culture that encourages confidence and risk taking among employees, has leadership that produces change, and focuses on the changing needs of customers. (p. 342)

anticipatory socialization The first socialization stage, which encompasses all of the learning that takes place prior to the newcomer's first day on the job. (p. 345)

artifacts Symbols of culture in the physical and social work environments. (p. 336)

assumptions Deeply held beliefs that guide behavior and tell members of an organization how to perceive situations and people. (p. 340)

change and acquisition The third socialization stage, in which the newcomer begins to master the demands of the job. (p. 346)

enacted values Values reflected in the way individuals actually behave. (p. 340)

encounter The second socialization stage, in which newcomers learn the tasks associated with the job, clarify their roles, and establish new relationships at work. (p. 346)

espoused values What members of an organization say they value. (p. 340)

organizational (corporate) culture A pattern of basic assumptions that are considered valid and that are taught to new members as the way to perceive, think, and feel in the organization. (p. 336)

organizational socialization The process by which newcomers are transformed from outsiders to participating, effective members of the organization. (p. 345)

strong culture An organizational culture with a consensus on the values that drive the company and with an intensity that is recognizable even to outsiders. (p. 342)

triangulation The use of multiple methods to measure organizational culture. (p. 348)

Ethical Dilemma

Alita is an administrative assistant who works at Legal Partners, a very old and successful law firm. They represent some of the biggest companies and most wealthy people in the area. Almost all the partners are male and have been with the firm for over 40 years.

Alita reports to Martin, the senior partner of the firm. In this position, she is responsible for working with the human resources department in setting up interviews for potential hires and for promotions of current firm attorneys. Because of the firm's growth, there has been a rise in the number of these interviews with Martin.

Recently, Alita has noticed that the number of minorities being offered an interview had diminished and no minorities have been hired. This is very troublesome for Alita. She is a strong proponent of equity, diversity, and inclusion and feels that the firm is doing nothing to address this issue.

When a call comes in from a friend in HR with another candidate, Alita asks her friend why there are so few minority candidates. Her friend replies that most minorities would not fit in with the culture at the firm. After Alita hangs up, she begins to wonder about her friend and the culture of the firm. It does not seem to be the culture of inclusion the firm website claims.

Alita is upset. She is considering going to speak to Martin about her concerns. However, if her concerns are accurate, could Martin support this non-inclusive culture? Could she be jeopardizing her job?

1. Using consequential, rule-based, and character theories, evaluate Alita's options.

2. What should Alita do? Why?

Chapter 17

Sergey Tinyakov/Shutterstock.com

Career Management

Learning Objectives

17-1 Explain occupational and organizational choice decisions.

17-2 Identify foundations for a successful career.

17-3 Explain the career stage model.

17-4 Spell out the major tasks facing individuals in the establishment stage of the career stage model.

17-5 Identify the issues confronting individuals in the advancement stage of the career stage model.

17-6 Describe how individuals can navigate the challenges of the maintenance stage of the career stage model.

17-7 Articulate the ways that individuals withdraw from the workforce.

17-8 Explain how career anchors help form a career identity.

A **career** is a pattern of work-related experiences that spans the course of a person's life.[1] The two elements in a career are the objective element and the subjective element.[2] The *objective element* of the career is the observable, concrete environment. For example, you can manage a career by getting training to improve your skills. In contrast, the *subjective element* involves your perception of the situation. Rather than getting training (an objective element), you might change your aspirations (a subjective element). Thus, both objective events and the individual's perception of those events are important in defining a career.

Career management is a lifelong process of learning about self, jobs, and organizations, setting personal career goals, developing strategies for achieving the goals, and revising the goals based on work and life experiences.[3] Whose responsibility is career management? It is tempting to place the responsibility solely on individuals, but it is also the organization's duty to form partnerships with individuals in managing their careers. Careers are made up of exchanges between individuals and organizations; in other words, give-and-take is a part of the relationship between an organization and an individual when a career is involved.

Whether we approach it as managers or as employees, career management is an integral activity in our lives. It is important to understand careers for three reasons:

1. If we know what to look forward to over the course of our careers, we can take a proactive approach to planning and managing them.

2. As managers, we need to understand the experiences of our employees and colleagues as they pass through the various stages of careers over their life spans.

3. Career management is good business. It makes good financial sense to have highly trained employees keep up with their fields so that organizations can protect valuable investments in human resources.

17-1 Occupational and Organizational Choice Decisions

The time of the fast track to the top of the hierarchical organization is past. Also gone is the idea of lifetime employment in a single organization. Today's

> Whether we approach it as managers or as employees, career management is an integral activity in our lives.

environment demands leaner organizations, and the paternalistic attitude that organizations should take care of employees no longer exists. Individuals now take on more responsibility for managing their own careers. So the concept of the career is undergoing a paradigm shift, as shown in Table 17.1. The old career is giving way to a new career characterized by discrete exchange, occupational excellence, organizational empowerment, and project allegiance.[4] Moreover, one recent study found that both individuals and organizations are actively involved in the management of the new career of employees. As such, the new career involves a type of participatory management technique on the part of the individual, but the organization responds to each individual's needs and thus is more flexible in its career development programs.[5]

Discrete exchange occurs when an organization gains productivity while a person gains work experience. It is a short-term arrangement that recognizes that job skills change in value and that renegotiation of the relationship must occur as conditions change. This idea contrasts sharply with the mutual loyalty contract of the old career paradigm in which employee loyalty was exchanged for job security.

Occupational excellence means continuously honing skills that can be marketed across organizations. The individual identifies more with the occupation ("I am an engineer") than the organization ("I am an IBMer"). In contrast, the old one-employer focus meant that training was company specific and not meant to prepare the person for future job opportunities. A research study that focused on ethnographic data (interviews and stories) was conducted among software engineers in three European firms and two U.S. firms. The study showed that software

> **career** The pattern of work-related experiences that spans the course of a person's life.
>
> **career management** A lifelong process of learning about self, jobs, and organizations; setting personal career goals; developing strategies for achieving the goals; and revising the goals based on work and life experiences.

Table 17.1 The New Versus Old Career Paradigms

New Career Paradigm	Old Career Paradigm
Discrete exchange means: • explicit exchange of specified rewards in return for task performance • basing job rewards on the current market value of the work being performed • engaging in disclosure and renegotiation on both sides as the employment relationship unfolds • exercising flexibility as each party's interests and market circumstances change	**The mutual loyalty contract meant:** • implicit trading of employee compliance in return for job security • allowing job rewards to be routinely deferred into the future • leaving the mutual loyalty assumptions as a political barrier to renegotiation • assuming employment and career opportunities are standardized and prescribed by the firm
Occupational excellence means: • performance of current jobs in return for developing new occupational expertise • employees identifying with and focusing on what is happening in their adopted occupation • emphasizing occupational skill development over the local demands of any particular firm • getting training in anticipation of future job opportunities; having training lead jobs	**The one-employer focus meant:** • relying on the firm to specify jobs and their associated occupational skill base • employees identifying with and focusing on what is happening in their particular firm • forgoing technical or functional development in favor of firm-specific learning • doing the job first to be entitled to new training: making training follow jobs
Organizational empowerment means: • strategic positioning is dispersed to separate business units • everyone is responsible for adding value and improving competitiveness • business units are free to cultivate their own markets • new enterprise, spinoffs, and alliance building are broadly encouraged	**The top-down firm meant:** • strategic direction is subordinated to "corporate headquarters" • competitiveness and added value are the responsibility of corporate experts • business unit marketing depends on the corporate agenda • independent enterprise is discouraged, and likely to be viewed as disloyalty
Project allegiance means: • shared employer and employee commitment to the overarching goal of the project • a successful outcome of the project is more important than holding the project team together • financial and reputational rewards stem directly from project outcomes • upon project completion, organization and reporting arrangements are broken up	**Corporate allegiance meant:** • project goals are subordinated to corporate policy and organizational constraints • being loyal to the work group can be more important than the project itself • financial and reputational rewards stem from being a "good soldier" regardless of results • social relationships within corporate boundaries are actively encouraged

engineers did not have much regard for their immediate supervisors, the organization, or formal dress codes. The only thing they did believe in was occupational excellence so that they could be better at what they do. In this regard, the authors of the study note that software engineers represent a unique group in terms of career development and that they fit well within the model of the "new career."[6]

Organizational empowerment means that power flows down to business units and in turn to employees. Employees are expected to add value and help the organization remain competitive by being innovative and creative. The old top-down approach meant that control and strategizing were done only by the top managers, and individual initiative could even be viewed as disloyalty or disrespect.

Project allegiance means that both individuals and organizations are committed to the successful completion of a project. The firm's gain is the project outcome; the individual's gain is experience and shared success. Upon project completion, the project team breaks up as individuals move on to new projects. Under the old paradigm, *corporate allegiance* was paramount, not project allegiance. The needs of projects were overshadowed by corporate policies and procedures. Work groups were long term, and keeping the group together was often a more important goal than project completion.

A form of work that has emerged from the weakening of the old paradigm is gig work, as was discussed in Chapter 14. "Gig" workers manage their own projects with multiple organizations or "gigs," and this employment arrangement is attractive to some individuals. Many gig workers prefer the freedom and flexibility of this type of work, with its short-term nature and project-based compensation.[7] Companies are increasingly recruiting gig workers because of the advantages of the "on-demand" workforce.[8] Going the freelance hiring route can make it easier to find a wider set of specialized skills and gives flexibility during times of economic uncertainty.

17-1a Preparing for the World of Work

When viewed from one perspective, you might say that we spend our youth preparing for the world of work. Educational and personal life experiences help an individual develop the skills and maturity needed to enter a career. Preparation for work is a developmental process that gradually unfolds over time.[9] As the time approaches for beginning a career, individuals face two difficult decisions: occupational choice and organizational choice.

17-1b Occupational Choice

In choosing an occupation, individuals assess their needs, values, abilities, and preferences and attempt to match them with an occupation that provides a fit. Personality plays a role in the selection of occupation. John Holland's theory of occupational choice contends that there are six types of personalities and that each personality is characterized by a set of interests and values.[10]

Holland also states that occupations can be classified using this typology. For example, realistic occupations include mechanic, restaurant server, and mechanical engineer. Artistic occupations include architect, voice coach, and interior designer. Investigative occupations include physicist, surgeon, and economist. Real estate agent, human resource manager, and lawyer are enterprising occupations. Social occupations include counselor, social worker,

and member of the clergy. Conventional occupations include word processor, accountant, and data entry operator. Holland's typology has been used to predict career choices with a variety of international participants, including Australians, Germans, Indians, Mexicans, New Zealanders, Pakistanis, South Africans, and Taiwanese.[11]

An assumption that drives Holland's theory is that people choose occupations that match their personalities. People who fit Holland's social types are those who prefer jobs that are highly interpersonal in nature. They may see careers in physical and math sciences, for example, as not affording the opportunity for interpersonal relationships.[12] Therefore, to fulfill the desire for interpersonal work, they may gravitate toward jobs in customer service.

Although personality is a major influence on occupational choice, it is not the only influence. There are a host of other influences, including social class, parents' occupations, economic conditions, and geography.[13] Once a choice of occupation has been made, another major decision individuals face is the choice of organizations. Individuals are often attracted to organizations whose mission matches their passions and values.

17-1c Organizational Choice and Entry

There are several theories of how individuals choose organizations, ranging from theories that postulate very logical and rational choice processes to those that offer seemingly irrational processes. *Expectancy theory*, discussed in Chapter 5, can be applied to organizational choice.[14] According to expectancy theory, individuals choose organizations that maximize positive outcomes and avoid negative outcomes. Job candidates calculate the probability that an organization will provide a certain outcome and then compare the probabilities across organizations.

Other theories propose that people select organizations in a much less rational fashion. Job candidates may *satisfice*, that is, select the first organization that meets one or two important criteria and then justify their choice by distorting their perceptions.[15] The method of selecting an organization varies greatly among individuals and may reflect a combination of the expectancy theory and theories that postulate less rational approaches.

> Organizational empowerment means that power flows down to business units and in turn to employees.

Entry into an organization is further complicated by the conflicts that occur between individuals and organizations during the process. Figure 17.1 illustrates these potential conflicts. The arrows in the figure illustrate four types of conflicts that can occur as individuals choose organizations and organizations choose individuals. The first two conflicts (1 and 2) occur between individuals and organizations. The first is a conflict between the organization's effort to attract candidates and the individual's choice of an organization. The individual needs complete and accurate information to make a good choice, but the organization may not provide it. Since the organization is trying to attract many qualified candidates, it presents itself in an overly attractive way.

The second conflict is between the individual's attempt to attract several organizations and the organization's need to select the best candidate. Individuals want good offers, so they do not disclose their faults. They describe their preferred job in terms of the organization's opening instead of describing a job they would really prefer.

The third and fourth conflicts are internal to the two parties. The third is a conflict between the organization's desire to recruit a large pool of qualified applicants and the organization's need to select and retain the best candidate. In recruiting, organizations tend to give only positive information, and this sometimes results in mismatches between the individual and the organization. The fourth conflict is internal to the individual; it concerns their need to make a good choice from among more than one desirable job offer. This situation can occur when individuals present themselves as overly attractive and consequently receive more job offers than they would have otherwise received, some of which might be a poor fit in terms of their skills and career goals.[16]

The organizational choice and entry process is very complex due to the nature of these conflicts. Partial responsibility for preventing these conflicts rests with the individual. Individuals should conduct thorough research of the organization through published reports and industry analyses. In addition, they should conduct a careful self-analysis and be as honest as possible with organizations to ensure a good match. The job interview process can be stressful, but also fun if it is engaged properly. Of course, the organization bears part of the responsibility for avoiding a mismatch by conducting an effective job interview.

Realistic Job Previews The conflicts just discussed may result in unrealistic expectations on the part of the candidate. People entering the world of work may expect, for example, that they will receive explicit directions from their boss, only to find that they are left with ambiguity about how to do the job. They may expect that promotions will be based on performance but find that promotions are based mainly on political considerations. Some new hires also expect to be given managerial responsibilities right away, but they rarely are.

Figure 17.1 Conflicts During Organizational Entry

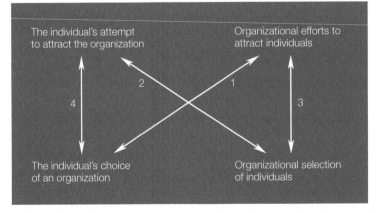

Source: Figure in L. W. Porter, E. E. Lawler III, and J. R. Hackman, *Behavior in Organizations* (New York, NY: McGraw-Hill, Inc., 1975): 134. Reproduced with permission of The McGraw-Hill Companies.

Fast Fact

Interview Mistakes That Sabotage Your Chances of Success

When interviewing for a job, likability is important. While likability can be very subjective, it's easier to agree on what makes a job candidate unlikable. Here are six behaviors that can diminish your likability in interviews:

- *Bragging*. While it is important to sell yourself, it's also important to be genuine and honest. Pick a couple of your strengths and support them with stories and examples.
- *Being self-centered*. Talking about yourself all the time is a turnoff. Asking questions of your interviewer about themselves and their company shows you can build relationships with others and that you are a good listener.
- *Appearing over-confident*. Don't be arrogant; speak with humility and modesty.
- *Being aloof*. Everyone is nervous in an interview, and some people shut down or clam up, which can make you seem distant. Be authentic, and let the interviewer get to know your authentic self.
- *Being too casual*. Show respect by being on time, thanking the interviewer, and dressing professionally. Use professional language and avoid terms like "bro" and "you guys."
- *Failing to read the room*. Make sure you're accurately sizing up your interviewer and the company. Be sensitive to the culture and values of the company you're interviewing with.

Sources: J. Humphrey, "Six Common Mistakes That Sabotage Your Likability in a Job Interview," *Fast Company*, January 9 (2023), accessed at https://www.fastcompany.com/90828134/mistakes-sabotage-likability-job-interview; L. Rivera, "Employer Decision Making," *Annual Review of Sociology* 46 (2020): 215–232.

Giving potential employees a realistic picture of the job they are applying for is known as a **realistic job preview (RJP)**. When candidates are given both positive and negative information, they can make more effective job choices. Traditional recruiting practices often produce unrealistically high expectations, which produce low job satisfaction, whereas RJPs tend to create expectations that are much closer to reality and thus encourage many candidates to withdraw from further consideration.[17]

Spectrum, the broadband company and cable operator, uses "A Day in the Life" videos on its website that show what a typical day is like for employees in customer service, inside sales, credit services, and other departments. Also featured are videos on the career paths that upper-level managers at Spectrum have taken that show realistically how to advance within the company.[18] Netflix has a podcast called "We Are Netflix" with 40 episodes so far, featuring Netflix employees talking about work and life at

realistic job preview (RJP) Both positive and negative information given to potential employees about the job they are applying for, thereby giving them a realistic picture of the job.

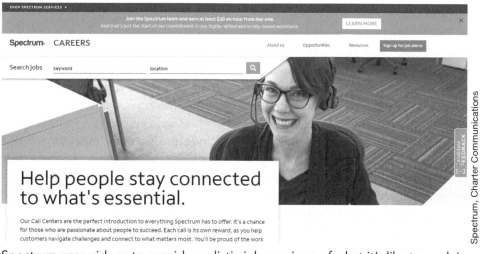

Spectrum uses videos to provide realistic job previews of what it's like to work in customer service.

the organization.[19] Other companies' websites use photo and video tours of their offices and locations, videos of meetings, and testimonials from current employees about what it's like to work there. Often, the RJP is given face-to-face during the candidate's onsite visit.

RJPs can also be thought of as inoculation against disappointment. If new recruits know what to expect in the new job, they can prepare for the experience. Newcomers who are not given RJPs may find that their jobs don't measure up to their expectations. They may then believe that their employer was deceitful in the hiring process, become unhappy and mishandle job demands, and ultimately leave the organization.[20]

Job candidates who receive RJPs view the organization as honest and they also have a greater ability to cope with the demands of the job.[21] RJPs perform another important function: uncertainty reduction.[22] Knowing what to expect, both good and bad, gives a newcomer a sense of control that is important to job satisfaction and performance.

With today's emphasis on ethics, organizations need to do all they can to be seen as operating consistently and honestly. Realistic job previews are one way in which companies can provide ethically required information. Ultimately, RJPs result in more effective matches, lower turnover, and higher organizational commitment and job satisfaction.[23] There is much to gain in providing realistic job information. The U.S. Army hopes to increase its recruitment and retention for Officer Candidate School by using a realistic job preview. By helping potential candidates understand what they will encounter in OCS, the Army looks to establish trust and honesty, reduce role ambiguity, and promote realistic expectations.[24]

In summary, the needs and goals of individuals and organizations can clash during entry into an organization. To avoid potential mismatches, individuals should conduct a careful self-analysis and provide accurate information about themselves to potential employers. They also need to ask appropriate questions. While applicants often focus on asking questions about organizational rewards and not employee contributions, they should seek both in obtaining a realistic job preview.[25] Organizations should present realistic job previews to show candidates both the positive and negative aspects of the job, along with the potential career paths available to the employee.

17-2 Foundations for a Successful Career

In addition to planning and preparation, building a career takes attention and self-examination. One way you can build a successful career is by becoming your own career coach. Another is by developing your emotional intelligence, which is an important attribute if you want to climb the corporate ladder.

17-2a Becoming Your Own Career Coach

The best way to stay employed is to see yourself as being in business for yourself, even if you work for someone else. Know what skills you can package for other employers and what you can do to ensure that your skills are state of the art. Organizations need employees who have acquired multiple skills and are adept at more than one job. Employers want employees who have demonstrated competence in dealing with change.[26] To be successful, think of organizational change not as a disruption to your work but instead as the central focus of your work. You will also need to develop self-reliance, as discussed in Chapter 7, to deal effectively with the stress of change. Self-reliant individuals take an interdependent approach to relationships and are comfortable both giving and receiving support from others.

The people who will be most successful in the new career paradigm are individuals who are flexible, team oriented (rather than hierarchical), energized by change, and tolerant of ambiguity. Those who will become frustrated in the new career paradigm are individuals who are rigid in their thinking and learning styles and who have high needs for control. A commitment to continuous, lifelong learning will prevent you from becoming a professional dinosaur.[27] An intentional and purposeful commitment to taking charge of your professional life will be necessary in managing the new career.

Behaving in an ethical manner, standing by your values, and building a professional image of integrity are also very important. Major corporations such as Google conduct extensive reference checks on their applicants—not just with the references supplied in the application, but also with friends of such references. Behaving ethically is not just a benefit to your job application, since an ethical foundation can also help you withstand pressures that might endanger your career. One study suggests that executives succumb to the temptation of fraud because they feel pressure to keep up with inflated expectations and changes in cultural norms, short-term versus long-term orientations, the composition of the board of directors, and senior leadership in the organization.[28]

17-2b Emotional Intelligence and Career Success

Almost 40 percent of new managers fail within the first eighteen months on the job. What are the reasons for the failure? Newly hired managers flame out because they fail to build good relationships

---

YOU

Check Your Emotional Intelligence

This brief assessment will give you a rough idea of your emotional intelligence, and hopefully encourage you to learn more about EI. Try to see yourself as others would see you in rating the statements below using the following scale:

1 = strongly disagree
2 = disagree somewhat
3 = neither agree nor disagree
4 = agree somewhat
5 = strongly agree

_____ 1. I 'm able to stay cool and calm even under stressful circumstances.

_____ 2. I 'm usually aware of how my emotions are affecting my behavior.

_____ 3. I can often sense how other people are feeling.

_____ 4. In most instances, I handle conflict quite effectively.

_____ 5. I seldom lose my temper in a public setting.

_____ 6. I have an accurate picture of my strengths and weaknesses.

_____ 7. I read other peoples' moods pretty accurately.

_____ 8. I offer feedback to others in order to improve their performance.

_____ 9. I can deal with failure and move on in a productive manner.

_____ 10. I hold positive expectations about other people.

_____ 11. I 'm in tune with what other people need from me.

_____ 12. I work well in teams through cooperation and collaboration.

_____ 13. I behave in an ethical manner even if it may be unpopular.

_____ 14. I welcome feedback from others as a learning tool.

_____ 15. I am a good listener.

_____ 16. I am able to use my influence skills to build consensus.

The assessment reflects four dimensions of Emotional Intelligence, which are self-awareness, self-management, awareness of others' emotions, and managing others' emotions. Calculate your scores for each dimension using the key below.

Self-Awareness: total of items 2, 6, 9, 14: _____
Self-Management: total of items 1, 5, 10, 13: _____
Awareness of Others' Emotions: total of items 3, 7, 11, 15: _____
Management of Others' Emotions: total of items 4, 8, 12, 16: _____
Total all scores: _____

Your lowest-scored dimension is your target for improvement. In general, higher scores suggest greater overall emotional intelligence.

Daniel Goleman, a pioneer in emotional intelligence research, has found emotional intelligence to be the major predictor of career success.

with peers and subordinates, are confused about what their bosses expect, lack internal political skills, or are unable to achieve the two or three most important objectives of the new job.[29] You'll note that these failures are all due to a lack of interpersonal skills.

In Chapter 13, we introduced the concept of *emotional intelligence (EI)* as an important determinant of conflict management skills. Daniel Goleman argues that emotional intelligence is a constellation of the qualities that mark a star performer at work. These attributes include self-awareness, self-control, trustworthiness, confidence, and empathy, among others. Goleman's belief is that emotional competencies are twice as important to people's success today as raw intelligence or technical know-how. He also argues that the further up the corporate ranks you go, the more important emotional intelligence becomes.[30] Employers, either consciously or unconsciously, look for emotional intelligence during the hiring process. And emotional intelligence applies across careers. EI predicts success in medical school and success as a doctor. Physicians who show

interpersonal sensitivity and effective communication skills improve therapeutic outcomes for their patients.[31] Neither gender seems to have dominated the market on EI. Both men and women who can demonstrate high levels of EI are seen as particularly gifted and may be promoted more rapidly.[32]

Emotional intelligence is important to career success in many cultures. A recent study in Australia found that high levels of emotional intelligence are associated with job success. EI improves one's ability to work with other team members and to provide high-quality customer service, and workers with high EI are more likely to take steps to develop their skills. Several U.S. studies have confirmed that high emotional intelligence is an important attribute for the upwardly mobile worker.[33]

The good news is that emotional intelligence can be developed and does tend to improve throughout life. Accordingly, some companies are providing training in emotional intelligence competencies. When American Express began sending managers through an emotional competence training program, it found that trained managers outperformed those who lacked this training. In the year after completing the course, managers trained in emotional competence grew their businesses by an average of 18.1 percent compared to 16.2 percent for those businesses whose managers were untrained.[34]

17-3 The Career Stage Model

A common way of understanding careers is viewing them as a series of stages through which individuals pass during their working lives.[35] Figure 17.2 presents the career stage model, which will form the basis for our discussion in the remainder of this chapter.[36] The career stage model shows that individuals pass through four stages in their careers: establishment, advancement, maintenance, and withdrawal. It is important to note that the age ranges shown are approximations; that is, the timing of the career transitions varies greatly among individuals.

Establishment is the first stage of a person's career. The activities that occur in this stage center around learning the job and fitting into the organization and occupation. **Advancement** is a high achievement-oriented stage in which people focus

establishment The first stage of a person's career in which the person learns the job and begins to fit into the organization and occupation.

advancement The second, high achievement-oriented career stage in which people focus on increasing their competence.

Figure 17.2 The Career Stage Model

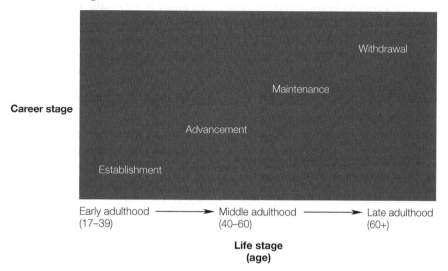

on increasing their competence. The **maintenance** stage finds the individual trying to maintain productivity while evaluating progress toward career goals. The **withdrawal** stage involves contemplation of retirement or possible career change.

Along the horizontal axis in Figure 17.2 are the corresponding life stages for each career stage. These life stages are based on the pioneering research on adult development conducted by Levinson and his colleagues. Levinson conducted extensive biographical interviews to trace the life stages of men and women. He interpreted his research in two books, *The Seasons of a Man's Life* and *The Seasons of a Woman's Life*.[37] Levinson's life stages are characterized by an alternating pattern of stability and transition.[38] Throughout the discussion of career stages that follows, we weave in the transitions of Levinson's life stages. Work and personal life are inseparable, and to understand a person's career experiences, we must also examine the unfolding of the person's personal experiences.

You can see that adult development provides unique challenges for the individual and that there may be considerable overlap between the stages. Now let us examine each career stage in detail.

17-4 The Establishment Stage

During the establishment stage, the individual begins a career as a newcomer to the organization. This is a period of great dependence on others,

as the individual is learning about the job and the organization. The establishment stage usually occurs during the beginning of the early adulthood years (ages eighteen to twenty-five). During this time, Levinson notes, an important personal life transition into adulthood occurs: the individual begins to separate from their parents and becomes less emotionally and financially dependent on them. Following this period is a fairly stable time of exploring the adult role and settling down.

The transition from school to work is a part of the establishment stage. Many graduates find the transition to be a memorable experience. The following description was provided by a new graduate who went to work at a large public utility:

> We all tried to one-up each other about jobs we had just accepted ... bragging that we had the highest salary, the best management training program, the most desirable coworkers, the most upward mobility ... and believed we were destined to become future corporate leaders... .
> Every Friday after work we met for happy hour to visit and relate the events of the week. It is interesting to look at how the mood of those happy

maintenance The third stage in an individual's career in which the individual tries to maintain productivity while evaluating progress toward career goals.

withdrawal The final stage in an individual's career in which the individual contemplates retirement or possible career changes.

hours changed over the first few months ... at first, we jockeyed for position in terms of telling stories about how great these new jobs were, or how weird our bosses were... . Gradually, things quieted down at happy hour. The mood went from "Wow, isn't this great" to "What in the world have we gotten ourselves into?" There began to be general agreement that business wasn't all it was cracked up to be.[39]

Establishment is thus a time of big transitions in both personal and work life. At work, three major tasks face the newcomer: negotiating effective psychological contracts, managing the stress of socialization, and making a transition from organizational outsider to organizational insider.

17-4a Psychological Contracts

A **psychological contract** is an implicit agreement between the individual and the organization that specifies what each is expected to give and receive in the relationship.[40] Individuals expect to receive salary, status, advancement opportunities, and challenging work to meet their needs. Organizations

expect to receive time, energy, talents, and loyalty to meet their goals. Working out the psychological contract with the organization begins with entry, but the contract is modified as the individual proceeds through the career.

Psychological contracts also exist between individuals.[41] During the establishment stage, newcomers form attachment relationships with many people in the organization. This process of working out effective psychological contracts within each relationship is important. Newcomers need social support in many forms and from many sources. Table 17.2 shows the type of psychological contracts, in the form of social support, that newcomers may work out with key insiders in the organization.

One common newcomer concern, for example, is whose behavior to watch for cues to appropriate behavior. Senior colleagues can provide modeling support by displaying behavior that the newcomer can emulate. Newcomers also depend on peers for information they need. Trusted peers can be especially helpful in clarifying the newcomer's role in the team.[42] Broken or breached psychological contracts can have detrimental outcomes. When a breach occurs, employees might experience negative emotional reactions that can lead to loss of trust, reduced job satisfaction, lower commitment to the organization, and higher turnover.[43] Some employees can react strongly to a breach of the psychological

psychological contract An implicit agreement between an individual and an organization that specifies what each is expected to give and receive in the relationship.

Table 17.2 Newcomer–Insider Psychological Contracts for Social Support

Type of Support	Function of Supportive Attachments	Newcomer Concern	Examples of Insider Response/Action
Protection from stressors	Direct assistance in terms of resources, time, labor, or environmental modification	What are the major risks/threats in this environment?	*Supervisor* cues newcomer to risks/threats.
Informational	Provision of information necessary for managing demands	What do I need to know to get things done?	*Mentor* provides advice on informal political climate in organization.
Evaluative	Feedback on both personal and professional role performances	How am I doing?	*Supervisor* provides day-to-day performance feedback during first week on new job.
Modeling	Evidence of behavioral standards provided through modeled behavior	Whom do I follow?	Newcomer is apprenticed to *senior colleague*.
Emotional	Empathy, esteem, caring, or love	Do I matter? Who cares if I'm here or not?	*Other newcomers* empathize with and encourage individual when reality shock sets in.

Source: From D. L. Nelson, J. C. Quick, and J. R. Joplin, "Psychological Contracting and Newcomer Socialization: An Attachment Theory Foundation," *Journal of Social Behavior and Personality* 6 (1991): 65.

contract with deviant behaviors such as open hostility or chronically being late to work. Mindful employees are less likely to do so because they are better able to cope with adverse work experiences.[44]

17-5 The Advancement Stage

The advancement stage is a period when many individuals strive for achievement. They seek greater responsibility and authority and strive for upward mobility. Usually around age thirty, an important life transition occurs, leading people to reassess their goals and make changes in their career dreams.[45] The transition at age thirty is followed by a period of stability during which the individual tries to find a role in adult society and wants to succeed in the career. During this stage, several issues are important: exploring career paths, finding a mentor, working out dual-career partnerships, and managing conflicts between work and personal life.

17-5a Career Paths and Career Ladders

Career paths are sequences of job experiences along which employees move during their careers.[46] At the advancement stage, individuals examine their career dreams and the paths they must follow to achieve those dreams. For example, suppose a person's dream is to become a top executive in the pharmaceutical industry. She majors in chemistry in college and takes a job with a nationally recognized firm. After she has adjusted to her job as a quality control chemist, she reevaluates her plan and decides that further education is necessary. Now she plans to pursue an MBA degree part time, hoping to gain expertise in management. From there, she hopes to be promoted to a supervisory position within her current firm. If this does not occur within five years, she will consider moving to a different pharmaceutical company. An alternate route would be to try to transfer to a sales position, from which she might advance into management.

The career paths of many women have moved from working in large organizations to starting their own businesses. Currently, there are 9.1 million women-owned firms in the United States. From 1997 to 2014, the number of woman-owned firms grew at 1.5 times the national average. What is the motivation for this exodus to entrepreneurship? The main reasons are to seek additional challenge and self-fulfillment and to have more self-determination and freedom.[47]

A career ladder is a structured series of job positions through which an individual progresses in an organization. For example, at Southwestern Bell, it is customary to move through a series of alternating line and staff supervisory assignments to advance toward upper management. Supervisors in customer service might be assigned next to the training staff and then rotate back as line supervisors in network services to gain experience in different departments.

Some companies use the traditional concept of career ladders to help employees advance in their careers. Other organizations take a more contemporary approach to career advancement. Sony, for instance, encourages creativity from its engineers by using nontraditional career paths in which people have the freedom to move on to interesting and challenging job assignments without notifying their supervisors. If they join a new project team, their current boss is expected to let them move on. This self-promotion philosophy at Sony is seen as a key to high levels of innovation and creative new product designs.

There has been heightened interest in international assignments in response to globalization and global staffing issues. One problem in this regard has been that most expatriate assignments are not successful. Therefore, organizations have been facing the challenge of properly training and preparing individuals for such assignments. One proposed solution is alternative international work assignments such as commuter work assignments, virtual assignments, short-term assignments, and so on, which can be used to help individuals gain international work experience in preparation for higher levels in the organization.[48]

Another approach used by some companies to develop skills is the idea of a *career lattice*—an approach to building competencies by moving laterally through different departments in the

career path A sequence of job experiences that an employee moves along during their career.

career ladder A structured series of job positions through which an individual progresses in an organization.

organization or by moving through different projects. Top management support for the career lattice is essential because in traditional terms an employee who has made several lateral moves might not be viewed with favor. However, the career lattice approach is an effective way to develop an array of skills to ensure one's employability.[49]

17-5b Finding a Mentor

Exploring career paths is one important activity in advancement. Another crucial activity during advancement is finding a mentor. A **mentor** is an individual who provides guidance, coaching, counseling, and friendship to a protégé. Mentors are important to career success because they perform both career and psychosocial functions.[50]

The *career functions* provided by a mentor include sponsorship, facilitating exposure and visibility, coaching, and protection. *Sponsorship* means actively helping the individual get job experiences and promotions. *Facilitating exposure and visibility* means providing opportunities for the protégé to develop relationships with key figures in the organization in order to advance. *Coaching* involves providing advice in both career and job performance. *Protection* is provided by shielding the protégé from potentially damaging experiences. Career functions are particularly important to the protégé's future success. One study found that the amount of career coaching received by protégés was related to more promotions and to higher salaries four years later.[51]

The mentor also performs *psychosocial functions*: role modeling, acceptance and confirmation, counseling, and friendship. *Role modeling* occurs when the mentor displays behavior for the protégé to emulate. Such modeling facilitates social learning. *Acceptance and confirmation* are important to both the mentor and protégé. When the protégé feels accepted by the mentor, it fosters a sense of pride. Likewise, positive regard and appreciation from the junior colleague provide a sense of satisfaction for the mentor. *Counseling* by a mentor helps the protégé explore personal issues that arise and require assistance. *Friendship* is

JuliusKielaitis/Shutterstock.com

At IBM, mentoring isn't optional; it's an important performance metric, and senior managers are evaluated on specific mentoring goals.

another psychosocial function that benefits both mentor and protégé alike.

In effective mentoring relationships, there is regular contact between mentor and protégé that has clearly specified purposes. Mentoring should be consistent with the corporate culture and the organization's goals. Both mentors and protégés alike should be trained in ways to manage the relationship. Mentors should be held accountable and rewarded for their role. They should be perceived (accurately) by protégés as having considerable influence within the organization.[52] While it may be tempting to go after the "top dog" as your mentor, personality compatibility is also an important factor in the success or failure of a mentoring relationship. Thus, mentors who are similar to their protégés in terms of personality traits such as extraversion, and whose expectations are largely met by the relationship, are more likely to show interest in continuing the arrangement.[53]

At IBM, mentoring isn't optional; it's an important performance metric, and senior managers are evaluated on specific mentoring goals. From their first day on the job, employees are told that they are expected to have a mentor and given help on getting a mentor and contracting with a mentor. Senior managers are evaluated on the development of their mentees and their own effectiveness as mentors.[54] KPMG is another company with a formal mentoring program, and accountability metrics for leaders and managers around mentoring.

Mentoring programs may be informal or formal. *Informal mentoring programs* identify pools of mentors and protégés, provide training in the

mentor An individual who provides guidance, coaching, counseling, and friendship to a protégé.

development of effective mentoring and diversity issues, and then provide informal opportunities for the development of mentoring relationships. *Network groups* are another avenue for mentoring. These groups help members identify with a few others who are like them within an organization, build relationships with them, and build social support. Network groups, sometimes called employee resource groups, enhance the chance that employees will find mentors.[55] Nike, for example, has networks that connect teammates and allies around shared interests and experiences. Some of the groups are Ability Network, Black Employee Network and Friends, Latino and Friends Network, Pride Network, and Women of NIKE.[56] Companies are also adding network groups that support mental health. Johnson & Johnson has a Mental Health Diplomats group for those employees who may need support and also those who want to learn to support others. Some companies are creating resource groups specifically focused on neurodiversity. Yahoo's Neurodiversity ERG highlights the strengths of those with neurological differences like autism, ADHD, dyslexia, and OCD. The group's slogan, "Minds of All Kinds," promotes company awareness of neurodiversity.

Some companies have *formal mentoring programs*. At PricewaterhouseCoopers (PwC) each intern is assigned both a peer mentor to help with day-to-day questions and an experienced mentor to help with larger issues such as career path development.[57] Time Warner Cable matches mentors and mentees so that mentees work on professional development, and mentors hone their coaching skills. And mentoring programs do not have to be face-to-face.

Yahoo believes that the power of diversity is awesome.

Virtual mentoring is a necessity in remote and hybrid work situations, which require flexibility in mentor and mentee schedules and locations. It requires more intentionality in mentoring than in traditional office settings where informal, drop-in chats are possible.[58]

In companies without formal mentoring programs, junior employees are often left to negotiate their own mentoring relationships. The barriers to finding a mentor under these circumstances include lack of access to mentors, fear of initiating a mentoring relationship, and fear that supervisors or coworkers might not approve of the mentoring relationship. Individuals may also be afraid to initiate a mentoring relationship because it might be misconstrued as a sexual advance by the potential mentor or by others. Potential mentors may fear this misinterpretation as well. Some are therefore unwilling to develop a relationship because of their own or the protégé's gender. Women report more of these barriers than men, and individuals who lack previous experience report more barriers to finding a mentor.[59]

There are other gender differences found in mentoring relationships. Male protégés report receiving less psychological support than female protégés. Additionally, male mentors report giving more career development support, whereas female mentors report giving more psychological support.[60] Mentoring can be particularly important for women in male-dominated professions. In these environments, women who have male mentors have higher levels of compensation and career progress satisfaction than those without a male mentor.[61] Organizations can encourage junior workers to approach mentors by providing opportunities for them to interact with senior colleagues. The immediate supervisor is not always the best mentor for an individual, so exposure to other senior workers is important. Seminars, multilevel teams, and social events can serve as vehicles for bringing together potential mentors and protégés.

Mentoring relationships go through a series of phases: initiation, cultivation, separation, and redefinition. There is no fixed time length for each phase because each relationship is unique. The *initiation* phase is when the mentoring relationship begins to take on significance for both the mentor and the protégé. In the *cultivation* phase the relationship becomes more meaningful, and the protégé shows rapid progress because of the career support and psychosocial support provided by the mentor. Protégés influence mentors as well. In the *separation* phase the protégé feels the need to assert independence and work more autonomously. Separation can be voluntary, or it can result from an involuntary change (the protégé or mentor may be promoted or transferred). The separation phase can be difficult if it is resisted, either by the mentor (who is reluctant to let go of the relationship) or by the protégé (who resents the mentor's withdrawal of support). Moreover, separation may result from a conflict that disrupts the mentoring relationship rather than proceeding smoothly and naturally.

The *redefinition* phase occurs if separation has been successful. In this phase, the relationship takes on a new identity as the two parties consider each other colleagues or friends. The mentor feels pride in the protégé, and the protégé develops a deeper appreciation for the support from the mentor.

Why are mentors so important? Aside from the support they provide, research shows that mentors are important to the protégé's future success. For example, studies have demonstrated that individuals with mentors have higher promotion rates and higher incomes than individuals who do not have mentors.[62] Individuals with mentors are also better

decision-makers.[63] Mentors can also help protégés make the transition into leadership positions. In addition to an individual being promoted into leadership position, the team members grant leadership; it's a two-way process. Team members are more likely to accept leaders who are older than themselves. Younger individuals, seen as less prototypical leaders, are not automatically accepted and granted status. Mentors can provide advice on how to navigate this challenge.[64]

17-5c Dual-Career Partnerships

During the advancement stage, many individuals face another transition. They settle into a relationship with a life partner. This lifestyle transition requires adjustment in many respects—learning to live with another person, being concerned with someone besides yourself, dealing with an extended family, and many other demands. The partnership can be particularly stressful if both members are career oriented.

The two-career lifestyle has increased in recent years due in part to the need for two incomes to maintain a preferred standard of living. **Dual-career partnerships** are relationships in which both people have important career roles. This type of partnership can be mutually beneficial, but it can also be stressful.

One stressor in a dual-career partnership is time pressure. When both partners work outside the home, there may be a time crunch in fitting in work, family, and leisure time.[65] Demonstrating gender equality at home benefits the next generation in their work lives. When fathers do an equal share of housework, daughters are less likely to limit their career aspirations to female-stereotyped jobs because they see housework as a shared responsibility.[66] Another issue to work out is whose career takes precedence. For example, what happens if one partner is transferred to another city? Must the other partner make a move that might threaten their own career to be with the partner who was transferred? And who, if anyone, will stay home and take care of a new baby?

Working out a dual-career partnership takes careful planning and consistent communication between the partners. Each partner must serve as a source of social support for the other. In addition, couples may need to turn to other family members, friends, and professionals for support.

dual-career partnership A relationship in which both people have important career roles.

17-5d Work–Home Conflicts

A huge stressor that is faced throughout the career cycle but often first encountered in the advancement phase is the conflict between work and personal life. Such conflict negatively affects an individual's overall quality of life and may even lead to emotional exhaustion. Dealing with customer complaints all day, failed sales calls, or missed deadlines can magnify negative events at home, and vice versa.[67]

Responsibilities at home will likely clash at times with responsibilities at work, so these conflicts must be planned for. Suppose a child gets sick at school. Who will pick up the child and stay home with him? Couples must work together to resolve these conflicts.[68] Work–home conflicts can mean taking out work-related frustrations on family. When individuals feel undermined at work, they sleep poorly, have less patience, and vent their anger at home. One way to interrupt this pattern is to exercise, which helps people control their behavior.[69] Sleep is also important for staying healthy at work and at home. After a good night's sleep, people are more positive at work and at home, have more positive interactions with colleagues, and are more engaged at work.[70]

Work–home conflicts are especially stressful for working women. Women have been quicker to share the provider role than men have been to share responsibilities at home.[71] When working women experience work–home conflict, their performance declines, and they suffer more strain. Work–home conflict is a broad topic. It can be narrowed further into work–family conflict, in which work interferes with family, or family–work conflict, in which family or home life interferes with work.[72] Individuals who believe that men and women should share work and home lives equally experience more guilt from work–home conflict than traditionalists, who tend to feel more guilt when home life interferes with work.[73]

Remote and hybrid work arrangements have brought work–home conflicts into the forefront of consciousness. During the pandemic, remote work became a necessity and it has now become the preferred working arrangement for the majority[74] of people. The benefits of remote work are many, but it also blurs the lines between work and personal life.

Ways to Manage Work–Home Conflict To help individuals deal with work–home conflict, companies like Ernst & Young and Cisco Systems offer **flexible work schedules**, programs that give

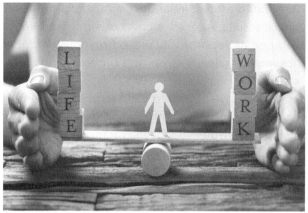

Andrey_Popov/Shutterstock.com

employees the freedom to set their own hours so that they can attend to personal issues.[75] There are multiple ways of achieving flexible work schedules. One is flextime, which allows employees to work when they feel most productive. Some people perform better in the morning, some in the afternoon, and some in the evening. Flextime gives employees the option to customize their schedule and take meal breaks that work best for them. Another flexible work option is the alternative work schedule, which is not confined to the regular Monday-to-Friday workweek. Employees can choose to work any five days of the week.

Another flexible work option is the compressed workweek. Some companies opt for a 9-day, 2-week plan, which compresses two weeks of work into 9 days, freeing up two extra days off each month. There is substantial attention and research currently regarding the 4-day workweek. The concept is 100 percent pay and 100 percent effort in 80 percent of the hours. Some businesses are experimenting with this idea, including Microsoft Japan, which tried the 4-day workweek for a month. Its results were impressive: productivity increased by 40 percent, and 92 percent of the workers were happier with the new schedule. Microsoft also had the benefit of using 23 percent less electricity that month.[76] The company is considering the 4-day workweek and other types of flexible work to roll out company-wide. A large pilot study involving 30 companies in

flexible work schedule A work schedule that allows employees discretion in order to accommodate personal concerns.

the United States, Ireland, and Australia produced similar results. After six months of 4-day workweeks, companies reported increased revenue, reduced absenteeism, lower stress and burnout, and higher satisfaction.[77]

Company-sponsored child care is another way to help. Companies with on-site day-care centers include Johnson & Johnson, Valero, and Campbell Soup. Patagonia has an onsite child-care center at its headquarters in Ventura, California, and another one at its distribution and service center in Reno, Nevada. Patagonia values a broad suite of family-affirming benefits, and believes that they improve productivity and retention, and result in more women in management.[78] Whereas large companies may offer corporate day care, small companies can also assist their workers by providing referral services for locating the type of child care the workers need. For smaller organizations, this is a cost-effective alternative. At the very least, companies can be sensitive to work–home conflicts and handle them on a case-by-case basis with flexibility and concern.

A program of increasing interest that organizations can provide is **eldercare**. Often workers find themselves part of the so-called sandwich generation. They are expected to care for both their children and their elderly parents. In many countries, the need for eldercare is expected to increase dramatically over the next decade.[79] Inclusion in this extremely stressful role is reported more often by women than men.[80] The impact of caring for an aging loved one is often underestimated—17 percent of those who provide such care eventually quit their jobs due to time constraints, and another 15 percent cut back their work hours.[81] Caring for an elderly dependent at home not only creates work–home conflicts for an employee but also takes a toll on the employee's own well-being and performance at work. This is most often the case if the organization is not one that provides a supportive climate for discussion of eldercare issues.[82] Global pharmaceutical company Sanofi has taken steps to help its employees with eldercare issues by contracting with Bright Horizons, a firm that specializes in employer-sponsored eldercare. Fannie Mae's pioneering approach to eldercare began

The need for eldercare is increasing dramatically.

iStock.com/Daisy-Daisy

in 1999. The company, which has more than 6,000 employees, offers an Elderkit planner, reimbursement for emergency backup care, and sessions with a professional eldercare consultant to assist with options for elderly parents.[83]

Almost one-third of U.S. workers say their careers have been impacted by caregiving obligations. There is also a gap between employers who realize that caregiving affects employee performance (24 percent) and employees who say that caregiving affects their performance (80 percent), according to a large study from Harvard Business School.[84] The emotional and physical stress and exhaustion of caregiving leads caregivers to reduce their work hours, or to leave the job, and companies lose talented employees. Caregiving is not limited to children or elderly parents. It could mean caring for a spouse or partner, brother or sister, or any loved one, as COVID and its long-term effects have shown. Companies are beginning to provide caregiver support benefits, including paid and/or unpaid leave, information resources and referrals, and emergency backup care. Kimberly-Clark provides 40 hours of paid time off when a family member has a serious health condition. Intel provides up to eight weeks of paid leave for seriously ill family members. Johns Hopkins University provides webinars every month to help caregivers with diverse topics like self-care, managing your emotions as a caregiver, caring for children with disabilities, and caring for aging relatives. Some companies, like Levi Strauss and Enbridge, have employee resource groups (ERGs) focused on caregivers, allowing them to share experiences and support with other caregivers. Argonne National Laboratory also has a caregiver ERG, and provides a Slack workspace open to any

eldercare Assistance in caring for elderly parents and/or other elderly relatives.

Organizational Example

Team Anywhere at Atlassian

Land on Atlassian's careers webpage, and you'll find the following: "Welcome, we're Atlassian and we work from anywhere." The Australian-based company, which makes collaboration software, believes in the power of teamwork; its stock ticker is T.E.A.M. Much of the teamwork within Atlassian is virtual.

Bloomberg/Getty Images

Employees can choose whether they want to work in the office, at home, or some combination. They can also choose to work in any country where Atlassian has a legal business entity if there is a time zone overlap with their team members. Want to work in a different location during the summer? Atlassian allows 90 days a year of work outside the designated work location. It's all about maintaining a flexible lifestyle.

Annie Dean is Atlassian's Head of Team Anywhere, and she spearheaded the opening of a "team anywhere-focused office" in Austin. Rather than cubicles, there is soft seating, white boards on rollers, and a chef's kitchen. She calls the old way of working "productivity focused" and the new Atlassian model "experience focused."

Other companies are adding titles like vice president of flexible work and head of remote work, similarly focused on improving the flexible work experience.

Sources: https://www.atlassian.com/company/careers, E. Goldberg, "Head of Team Anywhere and Other Job Titles for an Uncertain Time," *The New York Times*, August 4 (2022), accessed at https://www.nytimes.com/2022/08/04/business/job-titles-remote-work .html?action=click&pgtype=Article&state=default&module=styln-rto&variant=show&region=MAIN_CONTENT_1&block=storyline_top _links_recirc.

Argonne-affiliated caregiver, along with their spouses and partners.

Alternative work arrangements such as flextime, compressed workweeks, and remote work, can help employees manage work–home conflicts. Childcare, eldercare, and caregiver support programs constitute another category of benefits to help with work–home conflicts. People have different preferences for managing the work–home boundary. Some people prefer integration, which means they are comfortable with blurred work–family boundaries. Integrators often work after hours at home and take care of family responsibilities during work hours. They are more satisfied and committed when organizations offer benefits like onsite childcare and workout facilities that help them integrate their work and home lives. Other people prefer segmentation, which means keeping work and home life separate, with clear boundaries. Segmentors focus on work during

work hours and family during family time. Segmentors prefer flexible work arrangements that allow them to separate work responsibilities from home responsibilities. Companies need to recognize the diversity of employees' preferences for managing work–home boundaries when providing support.[85]

In remote work, both integrators and segmentors may find themselves challenged. Integrators may have never felt the need to have boundaries between work and home lives until they start working from home. They may have to create schedules and routines more than they have been comfortable with in the past. The workspace for integrators at home could be a central location like the kitchen or living room where they can see what's going on with family members. For segmentors, trying to keep work and home separate when working from home is difficult. Negotiating "work hours" and privacy with family may be important for segmentors to feel productive.

Segmentors may still dress for work when working from home, to preserve the work boundary. Segmentors need a separate space for work and typically choose a room with a door. When team members understand each other's different preferences for managing the work–home boundary, they can navigate officeless work life more effectively.[86]

17-6 The Maintenance Stage

Maintenance may be a misnomer for this career stage because some people continue to grow in their careers, although the growth is usually not at the rate it was earlier. A career crisis at midlife may accompany the midlife transition.

Some individuals who reach a career crisis are burned out, and sabbaticals can be offered as a benefit. Sabbaticals are extended breaks from work, sometimes paid and sometimes unpaid. Zillow, the real estate company, offers six weeks of sabbatical (three weeks paid and three weeks unpaid) for employees with continuous full-time employment.[87] Workers who take sabbaticals can either pursue professional or personal development, or simply rest and recharge. Sabbaticals provide reduced stress and increased well-being for the workers who take them. In addition, the less experienced workers who fill in for those on sabbatical gain valuable skills, often in leadership roles.[88]

Other individuals who reach the maintenance stage experience a sense of achievement and contentment, feeling no need to strive for further upward mobility. Whether the maintenance stage is a time of crisis or contentment, however, there are two issues to grapple with: sustaining performance and becoming a mentor.

17-6a Sustaining Performance

Remaining productive is a key concern for individuals in the maintenance stage. This becomes challenging when one reaches a **career plateau**, a point where the probability of moving further up the hierarchy is low. Some people handle career plateauing fairly well, but

career plateau A point in an individual's career at which the probability of moving farther up the hierarchy is low.

others may become frustrated, bored, and dissatisfied with their jobs. To keep employees productive, organizations can provide challenges and opportunities for learning. *Lateral moves* are one option. Another option is to involve the employee in *project teams* that provide new tasks and skill development. The key is keeping the work stimulating and involving. Individuals at this stage also need continued affirmation of their value to the organization. They need to know that their contributions are significant and appreciated.[89]

Another strategy for remaining happy and productive during maintenance is job crafting, as was presented in Chapter 14.[90] Job crafting makes a job more fulfilling by customizing tasks and relationships with others. Employees can take an inventory of their tasks and increase their challenge demands by pursuing projects to develop new skills. In addition, employees can shed hindrance demands—those tasks that are energy-depleting and low value.[91] Job crafting can also be accomplished by increasing social resources by working outside one's department or team to form relationships that will promote growth and development. One way of increasing social resources is serving as a mentor.

17-6b Becoming a Mentor

During maintenance, individuals can contribute by sharing their wealth of knowledge and experience with others. Opportunities to be mentors to new employees can keep senior workers motivated and involved in the organization. It is important for organizations to reward mentors for the time and energy they expend. Some employees adapt naturally to the mentor role, but others may need training on how to coach and counsel junior workers. Different generations in mentoring relationships can learn a lot from each other. Gen Z, as the first digital native generation, can contribute technological skills, and older generation employees can provide advice when technology is not the answer to the problem. Gen Z's calls for prioritizing mental health and improving work–life balance can benefit all generations in the workforce.[92] Some companies have programs for reverse mentoring, in which younger employees are paired with seasoned employees for two-way opportunities for connection and growth. ADP (Automatic Data Processing), the global provider of HR software solutions, offers its Connect program for traditional mentoring as well as reverse mentoring opportunities.[93] Employees in the maintenance stage can take advantage of both becoming a mentor and being mentored.

Maintenance is a time of transition, like all career stages. It can be managed by individuals who know what to expect and plan to remain productive, as well as by organizations that focus on maximizing employee involvement in work. According to Levinson, during the latter part of the maintenance stage, another life transition occurs. The so-called age-fifty transition is another time of reevaluating the dream and working further on the issues raised in the midlife transition. Following the age-fifty transition is a fairly stable period. During this time, individuals begin to plan seriously for withdrawing from their careers.

17-7 The Withdrawal Stage

The withdrawal stage usually occurs later in life and signals that a long period of continuous employment will soon come to a close. Older workers may face discrimination and stereotyping. They are often viewed by others as less productive, more resistant to change, and less motivated. However, older workers are one of the most undervalued groups in the workforce. They have more experience, can provide continuity in the midst of change, and can serve as mentors and role models to younger generations of employees.

Discrimination against older workers is prohibited under the Age Discrimination in Employment Act (go to eeoc.gov/policy/adea.html to read the provisions of this 1967 act). Organizations should strive to create a culture that values older workers' contributions. With their level of experience, strong work ethic, and loyalty, these workers have much to contribute. In fact, older workers have lower rates of tardiness and absenteeism, are more safety conscious, and are more satisfied with their jobs than are younger workers.[94]

17-7a Planning for Change

The decision to retire is an individual one, but the need for planning is universal. A retired sales executive from Boise Cascade said that the best advice is to "plan no unplanned retirement."[95] This means carefully planning not only the transition but also the activities you will be involved in once the transition is made. All options should be open for consideration. One recent trend is to work as a temporary top-level executive. The qualities of a good temporary

---

Inclusive Conversations

After Retirement, "Unretirement"

NFL player Tom Brady shocked the professional football community when he retired at age 44 and "unretired" one month later to play for another team. Brady is not unlike many other Americans who retired, then returned to work for financial or other reasons. While only 3.2 percent of retirees have "unretired," one in six have considered returning to the workforce, a trend that could upend career stages as we know them.

Uncertainty surrounding the stock market, inflation, and COVID are some of the factors affecting decisions to come out of retirement, but these are not the only factors. Many retirement-aged individuals long for the structure, social contact, and sense of purpose that work provides. For individuals who want to continue helping, supporting, and growing, "unretirement" may be the right career move after retirement.

1. Presently, the number of unretires is considerably small. What factors might impact the number of retirees who decide to return to the workforce?
   Physical requirements of the job; organizational culture (e.g., the extent to which age diversity is valued); individual factors (e.g., health and life spans, knowledge, competency, etc.); students will have a variety of potential factors, both individual and organizational.

2. How is unretirement a diversity issue in organizations?
   Retirement is a "withdrawal" stage process, primarily relevant to older organizational employees. As the unretirement trend increases, decision-makers may design employment retention strategies with unretirement in mind. This will add to the value of age diversity in organizations. Students could potentially view unretirement as having relevance to younger workers also as values change.

Source: H. Dennis, "Why 'Unretirement' Is Bringing Older Workers Back into the Workplace," *Los Angeles Daily News*, March 19 (2023).

executive include substantial high-level management experience, financial security that allows the executive to choose only assignments that really interest her, and a willingness to relocate.[96] Some individuals at the withdrawal stage find this an attractive option.

Planning for retirement should include not only financial planning but also a plan for psychologically withdrawing from work. The pursuit of hobbies and travel, volunteer work, or more time with extended family can all be part of the plan. The key is to plan early and carefully, as well as to anticipate the transition with a positive attitude and a full slate of desirable activities.

17-7b Retirement

There are several retirement trends right now, ranging from early retirement to phased retirement to never retiring. Some adults are choosing a combination of these options, leaving their first career for some time off before reentering the workforce either part time or full time doing something they enjoy. For more and more Americans, the idea of a retirement spent sitting beside the swimming pool sounds, for lack of a better word, boring. Factors that influence the decision of when to retire include company policy, financial considerations, family support or pressure, health, and opportunities for other productive activities.

During the withdrawal stage, the individual faces a major life transition that Levinson refers to as the *late adulthood transition* (ages sixty to sixty-five). One's own mortality becomes a major concern, and the loss of family members and friends becomes more frequent. The person works to achieve a sense of integrity in life; that is, the person works to find the encompassing meaning and value in life.

The average retirement age in the United States is 61, and it has been slowly increasing. In fact, Americans who are still working say they expect to

work until age 66. This may reflect better health and longer life spans, changes in employer-sponsored retirement plans, or lifestyle choices to simply work longer.[97] Retirement need not be a complete cessation of work. Many alternative work arrangements can be considered, and many companies offer flexibility in these options. **Phased retirement** is a popular option for retirement-age workers who want to gradually reduce their hours and/or responsibilities. There are many forms of phased retirement, including reduced workdays or workweeks, job sharing, and consulting and mentoring arrangements. Research has demonstrated that phased retirement contributes to the healthy aging of older workers.[98] Many individuals do not fully retire, but engage in **bridge employment**, which is employment that takes place after a person retires from a full-time position but before the person's permanent withdrawal from the workforce. Bridge jobs "bridge the gap" between career employment and retirement. They might be seasonal jobs, or part-time, or self-employment. Some individuals want a less stressful, more flexible position, or want to work in a non-profit organization they are passionate about. Bridge employment is related to retirement satisfaction and overall life satisfaction.[99]

Some companies are helping employees transition to retirement in innovative ways. For example, retired individuals can continue their affiliation with the organization by serving as mentors to employees who are embarking on retirement planning or other career transitions. This helps diminish the fear of loss some people have about retirement because the retiree has an option to serve as a mentor or consultant to the organization.

Labor shortages are concerning to many organizations, and some are taking steps to bring retirees back into the workforce. UPS, Goldman Sachs, and Blue Cross/Blue Shield are among a growing list of companies that have programs to actively recruit retirees.[100]

Now that you understand the career stage model, you can begin to conduct your own career planning. It is never too early to start.

phased retirement An arrangement that allows employees to reduce their hours and/or responsibilities in order to ease into retirement.

bridge employment Employment that takes place after a person retires from a full-time position but before the person's permanent withdrawal from the workforce.

career anchors A network of self-perceived talents, motives, and values that guide an individual's career decisions.

17-8 Career Anchors

Much of an individual's self-concept rests upon a career. Over the course of the career, **career anchors** are developed—self-perceived talents, motives, and values that guide an individual's career decisions.[101]

Bridge employment takes place after a person retires from full-time work but before a permanent withdrawal from the workforce.

Edgar Schein developed the concept of career anchors based on a 12-year study of MBA graduates from the Massachusetts Institute of Technology (MIT). Schein found great diversity in the graduates' career histories but great similarities in the way they explained the career decisions they had made.[102] From extensive interviews with the graduates, Schein developed the five career anchors. He analyzed 44 MBA students as they started their careers out of graduate school, and he found that these students tended to be driven by one of five things: (1) Managerial competence; (2) Technical-functional competence; (3) Security; (4) Creativity; and (5) Autonomy and independence. Schein called these motivators "career anchors" and suggested that the career anchor that was most important to a person would shape that person's career. In other words, if the managerial competence anchor was most important to you, you would seek out jobs that allowed you to rise up in an organization, while if your primary career anchor was technical-functional competence, you would try to become good at a particular type of work (for example, accounting) without being driven by the need to be a manager. In Schein's later research, he noted that there were eight career anchors: the five mentioned above, plus (6) Sense of service; (7) Pure challenge; and (8) Freedom to organize oneself around one's private life.

Career anchors emerge over time and may be modified by work or life experiences. The importance of knowing your career anchor is that it can help you find a match between you and an organization. For example, individuals with creativity as an anchor may find themselves stifled in bureaucratic organizations. Textbook sales may not be the place for an individual with a security anchor because of the frequent travel and seasonal nature of the business.

Experiential Exercise

The Ethics of Résumés and Recommendations

The purpose of this exercise is to explore ethical issues concerning résumés and recommendations. First, read the following brief introductory scenario. Jason Eckerle returned to his desk from lunch with a single mission in mind: to select the half-dozen best candidates for a regional customer service manager position. As he sat down, Eckerle sized up the stack of résumés and recommendations he'd been dealing with all morning—more than 100 of them.

The work had been slow but steady, gradually forming into three distinct piles: one contained absolute rejects (not enough work experience, wrong academic credentials, or poor recommendations from former employers), the second contained a few definite candidates for personal interviews, and the third held the applications of those about whom he still had questions or reservations.

His task for the afternoon—selecting three applicants to bring to the company headquarters for interviews—was complicated by the résumés and recommendation letters themselves. Some questions were obvious: "This guy lists five years' full-time sales and marketing experience, yet he's only twenty-two years old. How can he go to school full-time and have that kind of experience?" Here's another: "This young lady says she went to school at the Sorbonne in Paris for two years; yet on the application form, under the heading 'Foreign Languages' she's checked 'none.'" Here's one more: "This fella says he has a degree from the University of Texas, yet nowhere on his résumé does he say he lived or spent time there. Did he get that diploma totally online?"

Other issues are even more mysterious: "This young lady's résumé lists education and work experience, but there's a three-year gap from 2016 to 2019. What's that all about? Is she trying to conceal something, or just absentminded?" As Eckerle read through another résumé, he noticed the application form declaring "fluency in Japanese, French, and Spanish." "How do you get to be *fluent* in a language unless you've lived where it's spoken?" he wondered. The résumé didn't list any of those languages as native, nor did the application mention living abroad.

"Some of this stuff is outright fraud," he observed. As he sifted through the "reject" pile, Eckerle pulled out one application with an education block that lists a degree the applicant didn't have. "When we checked," he said, "they told us he was close to finishing a master's degree, but he hadn't yet finished his thesis. The applicant said he had the degree in hand." Another listed work experience no one could verify. "This guy's résumé says he was a client service representative for Litiplex, Inc., of Boston, but the phone book doesn't list any firm by that name, no one in our business has ever heard of it, and we can't check out his claims. I asked the applicant about the company, and he says, 'Maybe they went out of business.'"

Résumés weren't Eckerle's only problem. Recommendations were almost as bad. "Letters of recommendation aren't particularly useful," he said. "In the first place, almost no one is dumb enough to ask for a recommendation from someone who'll give them a bad one. Second, most recommenders write in broad, general, vague terms that don't tell me much about an applicant's work history, aptitude, or potential. They use glowing, nonspecific words that tell me the applicant's a marvelous human being but don't say whether the guy's had any comparable work experience that I could use to help make a decision."

Eckerle mentioned one other recommendation problem. "Most of the people who write letters in support of a job applicant are fairly close friends of the applicant. They'll often say things that are laudatory, but just aren't true. By the time you're done reading the letter, you'd think the young man in question could walk on water. When he comes for an interview, he can't get his own name straight." Excessive praise in letters of recommendation, Eckerle noted, can be expensive for a firm when the recommendation just doesn't reflect the applicant's true potential. "It costs us nearly \$4,000 to bring in an entry-level management candidate for interviews," he said, "and it's my job to make sure we don't bring in someone who's just not competitive." Inflated recommendations, he thought, can make that job much more difficult.

Next, the class should be divided into ten groups. Each group will be assigned one ethical issue. The group should formulate an answer to the dilemma and be ready to present the group's solution to the class.

1. Is a job applicant obligated to list *all employment* or *every work experience* on a résumé? What about jobs in which an applicant has had a bad relationship with a supervisor? Is it fair to "load up" a résumé only with positive work experience?

2. What if an applicant has been fired? Is a résumé *required* to reveal the exact circumstances under which they left the job?

3. Is it ethical to list educational institutions or degree programs that an applicant has attended but not completed? How much detail is necessary? Should an applicant explain *why* they left a degree program or school without finishing?

4. Is a job applicant *obliged* to list offenses against the law on a résumé? What about convictions or incarceration—say, 90 days' jail time for DWI?

5. Under such résumé categories as "Foreign Languages," how does an applicant determine whether they are "fluent," "conversant," or merely "familiar with" a language? Do the same general rules apply to listing technical skills, such as computer languages and software applications?

6. In a letter of recommendation, is it ethical to lavish praise on a young applicant just because you know the person is in need of a job? Conversely, does faint praise mean that a job applicant will likely be refused?

7. Is it better to turn away a student for asking for a letter of recommendation, or should you do what's *honest* and tell a graduate school (or potential employer) exactly what you think of the person?

8. Is a résumé something like a *certificate of authenticity*, listing specifics and details with absolute adherence to honesty and accuracy? Or is it more like a *sales brochure*, offering the best possible picture of a person in search of employment?

9. How well do you have to know someone before you can write an authentic, honest letter of recommendation? Is there a minimum time requirement before you can do so in good conscience?

10. Is the author of a letter of recommendation required to reveal *everything relevant* that they know about an applicant? What about character or integrity flaws that may stand in the way of a job applicant's success? To whom is the author of such letters obligated—the potential employer or the applicant?

Source: Adapted from J. S. O'Rourke, "The Ethics of Résumés and Recommendations: When Do Filler and Fluff Become Deceptions and Lies?" *Business Communication Quarterly* 58 (1995): 54–56. Reprinted with permission by the author.

Learning Objectives

17-1 **Explain occupational and organizational choice decisions.** Today most workers no longer work in one organization for the length of their working lives. The new career model is characterized by discrete exchange, occupational excellence, organizational empowerment, and project allegiance. When building a career, individuals first select an occupation that meets their needs, values, abilities, and preferences.

17-2 **Identify foundations for a successful career.** Two foundations for a successful career are becoming your own career coach and developing your emotional intelligence. To become your own career coach, you must acquire multiple skills, develop self-reliance, and cultivate a flexible, team-oriented attitude. Emotional competencies are of equal or greater importance than technical skills.

17-3 **Explain the career stage model.** The career stage model shows that individuals pass through four stages in their careers: establishment, advancement, maintenance, and withdrawal. Timing of career transitions varies greatly among individuals.

17-4 **Spell out the major tasks facing individuals in the establishment stage of the career stage model.** *Establishment* is the first stage of a person's career. The activities that occur in this stage center around learning the job and fitting into the organization and occupation. Individuals in this stage begin to work out their psychological contract with the organization and form attachment relationships with coworkers.

17-5 **Identify the issues confronting individuals in the advancement stage of the career stage model.** *Advancement* is a high achievement-oriented stage in which people focus on increasing their competence. A hallmark of this stage is the exploration of career paths, or sequences of job experiences along which employees move during their careers. Some companies use career lattices that move employees laterally through the organization in an attempt to build diverse skills. A mentor provides numerous sponsorship, facilitating, and psychosocial functions for the protégé. Dualcareer partnerships are common now and can lead to work–home conflicts.

17-6 **Describe how individuals can navigate the challenges of the maintenance stage of the career stage model.** The *maintenance* stage finds the individual trying to maintain productivity while evaluating progress toward career goals. Individuals sustain their performance and continue to grow, although at a slower rate. Individuals in this stage may also become mentors.

17-7 **Articulate the ways that individuals withdraw from the workforce.** The *withdrawal* stage involves contemplation of retirement or possible career change. Increasingly, individuals in this stage are opting for phased retirement, which is a gradual cessation of work. To help workers at this stage of their careers, organizations should provide opportunities for continued involvement with the organization, such as mentoring to other employees making career transitions.

17-8 **Explain how career anchors help form a career identity.** Career anchors are self-perceived talents, motives, and values that guide an individual's career decisions. Five main anchors are technical/functional competence, managerial competence, autonomy and independence, creativity, and security/stability.

Key Terms

advancement The second, high achievement-oriented career stage in which people focus on increasing their competence. (p. 364)

bridge employment Employment that takes place after a person retires from a full-time position but before the person's permanent withdrawal from the workforce. (p. 376)

career The pattern of work-related experiences that spans the course of a person's life. (p. 357)

career anchors A network of self-perceived talents, motives, and values that guide an individual's career decisions. (p. 376)

career ladder A structured series of job positions through which an individual progresses in an organization. (p. 367)

career management A lifelong process of learning about self, jobs, and organizations; setting personal career goals; developing strategies for achieving the goals; and revising the goals based on work and life experiences. (p. 357)

career path A sequence of job experiences that an employee moves along during their career. (p. 367)

career plateau A point in an individual's career at which the probability of moving farther up the hierarchy is low. (p. 374)

dual-career partnership A relationship in which both people have important career roles. (p. 370)

eldercare Assistance in caring for elderly parents and/or other elderly relatives. (p. 372)

establishment The first stage of a person's career in which the person learns the job and begins to fit into the organization and occupation. (p. 364)

flexible work schedule A work schedule that allows employees discretion in order to accommodate personal concerns. (p. 371)

maintenance The third stage in an individual's career in which the individual tries to maintain productivity while evaluating progress toward career goals. (p. 365)

mentor An individual who provides guidance, coaching, counseling, and friendship to a protégé. (p. 368)

phased retirement An arrangement that allows employees to reduce their hours and/or responsibilities in order to ease into retirement. (p. 376)

psychological contract An implicit agreement between an individual and an organization that specifies what each is expected to give and receive in the relationship. (p. 366)

realistic job preview (RJP) Both positive and negative information given to potential employees about the job they are applying for, thereby giving them a realistic picture of the job. (p. 361)

withdrawal The final stage in an individual's career in which the individual contemplates retirement or possible career changes. (p. 365)

Ethical Dilemma

Jasmine is a software engineer and has been working at Acme Technologies for 15 years. She loves her job and would be happy to stay in it until retirement. Lately she has noticed that her co-workers seem to be getting younger and younger. When she tries to discuss current projects with them, she feels a bit out of touch with the innovations they are discussing. She knows she should have kept up with all the latest developments, but her skills are strong and so far she has been able to do any job that has been given to her. Besides, she finished college a long time ago and does not want to start attending classes again.

At a recent meeting, Jasmine's supervisor gives her a new assignment. At first she was very excited about the job but then notices that the job requires using one of the newer systems that she does not know. She approaches her supervisor to ask permission to do it using the system she knows. He says no because the client wants it done in the way they requested. He also asks if there is a problem. Jasmine says that there is not and returns to her office.

Jasmine sits in her office getting more frustrated by the moment. She does not want to learn new programming systems. She wants to do her job and be left alone. She knows she can do exactly what the client wants using her current knowledge and skills. She contemplates doing the job her own way. Who will know the difference? She closes the door and begins work.

1. Using consequential, rule-based, and character theories, evaluate Jasmine's decision.

2. What should Jasmine do? Why?

Chapter 18

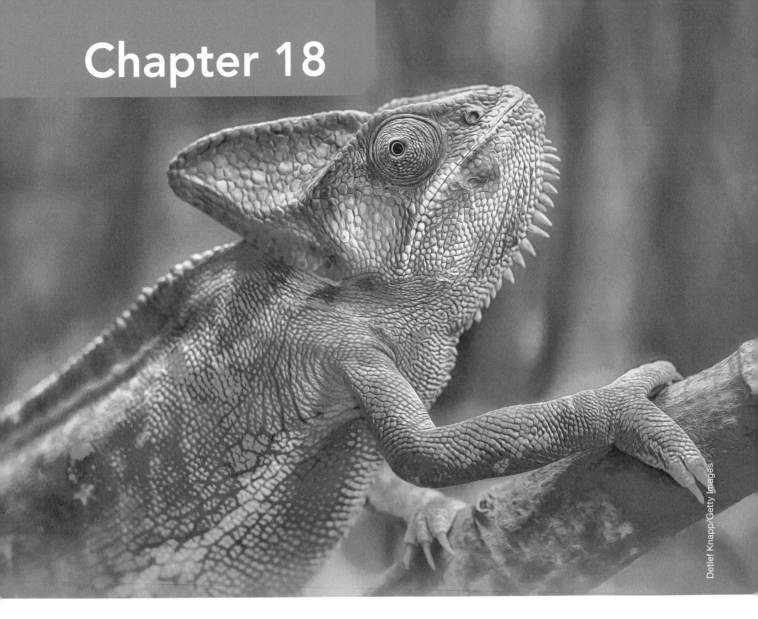

Detlef Knapp/Getty Images

Managing Change

Learning Objectives

18-1 Identify the major external and internal forces for change in organizations.

18-2 Describe how different types of change vary in scope.

18-3 Discuss methods organizations can use to manage resistance to change.

18-4 Explain Lewin's organizational change model.

18-5 Explain how companies determine the need to conduct an organization development intervention.

18-6 Discuss the major group-focused techniques for organization development intervention.

18-7 Discuss the major individual-focused techniques for organization development intervention.

18-1 Forces for Change in Organizations

Change has been the norm in most organizations. Many American companies have experienced plant closings, failures, mergers and acquisitions, and downsizing. *Adaptiveness*, *flexibility*, and *responsiveness* are characteristics of organizations that succeed in meeting the competitive challenges that businesses face.[1] Then, along came COVID-19. The speed and scope of the pandemic was unprecedented in living memory, and its long-term effects on economies, countries, organizations, and families are yet to play out. During the first year of the pandemic, anxiety and depression increased 25 percent worldwide due to stressors like social isolation, fears of infection, suffering and death of loved ones, and financial worries.[2] Employers have grappled with the fact that mental health and well-being must be of paramount concern. Perhaps no industry has suffered more than health care, with thousands of deaths, and survivors experiencing burnout, PTSD, depression, anxiety, and insomnia.[3] Long COVID, a myriad of lingering conditions that some people experience even after recuperating from COVID-19, may be disabling. Approximately 4 million Americans are being kept out of work by long COVID, which may account for 15 percent of the labor shortage, so in addition to the individual suffering, there are economic impacts.[4]

Peloton is one company that has experienced head-spinning changes during and since the pandemic. When COVID-19 hit, demand for Peloton bikes and treads skyrocketed, and so did the company's sales and stock price. When people were able to get outside and get back to gyms, sales plummeted and Peloton incurred massive losses. They hired a new CEO to bring them out of crisis mode and shifted their strategy away from hardware and onto software, using a subscription model. Time will tell whether and how Peloton might recover.

The way we work has been entirely changed by the crisis and its effects. Remote work was the norm of the pandemic, and organizations shifted to remote work without noticeable losses in productivity. Some companies even saw productivity rise during the height of the pandemic.[5] Post-pandemic, hybrid work (a mix of remote and in-office work) has become widespread. Employees now demand greater flexibility and work-life balance, while some

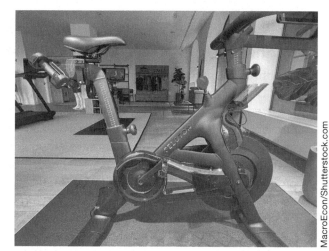

Peloton's sales rocketed during the pandemic but fell sharply in the years following.

MacroEcon/Shutterstock.com

employers want to call workers back into the office. Gig work, or freelance work, has seen a boom among skilled workers. The size of the gig workforce may surpass the size of the full-time workforce by 2027.[6]

The consequences of the pandemic and the changes in the ways we work are not the only global issues on leaders' minds. Poverty, climate changes, and inclusion continue to demand attention.

There are two basic forms of change in organizations. **Planned change** results from a deliberate decision to alter the organization. For example, companies that wish to move from a traditional hierarchical structure to one that facilitates self-managed teams must use a proactive, carefully orchestrated approach. **Unplanned change** is imposed on the organization and is often unforeseen. The pandemic crisis, of course, falls into this category. Changes in government regulations and changes in the economy are two other examples. Responsiveness to unplanned change requires tremendous flexibility and adaptability on the part of organizations. If the crisis is as impactful as the pandemic, crisis management is what is required. Managers must be prepared to handle both planned and unplanned forms of change in organizations.

planned change Change resulting from a deliberate decision to alter the organization.

unplanned change Change that is imposed on the organization and is often unforeseen.

Northwell Health Keeps Staff and Patients Healthy

Health care providers were forced to adapt when COVID-19 hit, and some fared better than others. Northwell Health is New York's largest health care provider, and its culture allowed it to move quickly to manage the change. Employees were empowered to be flexible, creative, and aggressive in developing programs to care for both patients and staff. At the height of the pandemic, Northwell was adding 200 beds per day by converting spaces like auditoriums, lobbies, and conference rooms to care rooms. Northwell's research institute worked with Fitbit to develop wearable technology to detect COVID before

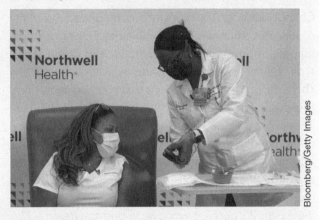

symptoms began. The technology uses algorithms to track variations in heart rate and respiration and other signs of potential infection so employees can test early for the virus.

Northwell also used predictive technology to determine where ambulances were most likely to be needed. The technology tracked emergency calls and allowed the company to position ambulances where there would be a call within 20 minutes. Northwell prides itself on being a learning organization, and the lessons learned from the pandemic underscore its culture of agility, adaptability, and innovation. It has been recognized by *Fast Company* as one of the World's Most Innovative Companies, and by *Fortune* as one of the Best Companies to Work For.

Sources: https://www.northwell.edu/news/in-the-news/northwell-ranks-third-on-fast-company-most-innovative-health-companies-for-2022; Fastco Works, "Rising to the Occasion—and Saving Lives," *Fast Company*, May 10 (2022), accessed at https://www.fastcompany.com/90747913/rising-to-the-occasion-and-saving-lives.

Forces for change can come from many sources. Some of these are external, arising from outside the company, whereas others are internal, arising from sources within the organization.

18-1a External Forces

There are many external forces for change, including crises like the global pandemic. In addition, the managerial challenges described throughout the book are also major external forces for change: globalization, workforce diversity, technological change, and managing ethical behavior.

Globalization The power players in the global market are the organizations that can capitalize on emerging markets throughout the world. The prime example is China, which has become the second largest economy in the world. Predictions are that by 2050, the emerging markets could grow twice as fast as advanced economies on average. Among these emerging economies are not only China, but also India, Indonesia, Brazil, and Russia.[7]

The United States is but one nation in the drive to open new markets. Japan and Germany are responding to global competition in different ways, and the European Union as a powerful trading group is attempting a big impact on world markets. By joining with their European neighbors, companies in smaller countries will begin to make major progress in world markets, thus increasing the fierce competition that already exists. These changes, among others, have led companies to rethink the borders of their markets and to encourage their employees to think globally. You may think of Costco, the big box retailer, solely as a North American company. But in reality, Costco has more than 800 outlets in the United States, Canada, Mexico, Britain, Spain, South Korea, and Japan. Its expansion into Australia has been a big success, with plans to open more stores. Walmart is the world's largest brick and mortar retailer, with 10,500 stores and clubs in 24 countries.

The list of the largest companies in the world today fluctuates depending on what measure is used.

testing/Shutterstock.com

By daily market capitalization, a recent ranking of the top five world's largest was Apple, Microsoft, Alphabet, Amazon, and Tesla.[8] It is notable that currently, all of the top five were in the technology sector. Regardless of industry, global businesses face substantial challenges including language barriers, cultural differences, managing global teams, currency exchange and inflation rates, and the nuances of politics, foreign policy, and international relationships.[9]

Workforce Diversity Related to globalization is the challenge of workforce diversity. As we have seen throughout this book, workforce diversity is a powerful force for change in organizations. Women in the U.S. workforce have made some advancements overall. In terms of education, women have earned more bachelor's, master's, and doctorate degrees than men since 2006. And women now comprise 47 percent of the labor force. However, women's jobs were hit hard by the pandemic, with 579,000 fewer women in the labor force in 2022 than when the pandemic began in 2020. Even though more than half of all management positions are held by women, very few make it to CEO, and the majority of board seats are still occupied by men.[10] Almost 64 percent of the U.S. workers earning the minimum wage or less are women. Women hold 2/3 of the U.S.'s student loan debt.[11] These and other data show that advancing women's inclusion is a multi-faceted challenge and requires bold leadership and a comprehensive approach.[12]

Barilla is a family-owned Italian company that has been on a journey to global inclusion. As a private company, it has no obligation to shareholders, but has emphasized inclusion motivated by passion and the message that exclusion will not be tolerated, regardless of the local culture it is operating in. Barilla achieved gender pay equity in 2020 globally and became the first Italian company to support the United Nations Standards of Conduct for Business against LGBTQ+ Discrimination in the workplace.[13]

Persons with disabilities are the largest underrepresented cohort in the U.S. workforce, and that cohort now includes those with long COVID. Remote work and flexible schedules are particularly beneficial for workers with disabilities. Meta is one company that is increasing its workforce by hiring employees with disabilities and making accommodations. Current progress is an increase from 4.7 percent to 6.2 percent and continuing to climb.[14]

Technological Change Rapid technological innovation is another force for change in organizations. With the advent of remote and hybrid work, emerging technologies will focus on supporting work patterns that are asynchronous, intelligent, and interactive, allowing employees to work autonomously but in connected ways. Electric vehicles will continue to be adopted, and the charging infrastructure will have to gear up to meet the demand. On the horizon is magnetized concrete technology for road surfaces that will charge electric vehicles while they're moving. Another alternative is wireless charging by placing electronic coils beneath the pavement.

One of the biggest drivers of technological changes is artificial intelligence, which has been around for some time in the form of online virtual assistants for customer support. ChatBots like ChatGPT now respond to comments in conversational dialogue,

EvgeniiAnd/Shutterstock.com

Barilla has a strong commitment to global inclusion.

Inclusive Conversations

Investing in DEI Helps Companies Become More Adaptable

In recent years, U.S. businesses have faced a business landscape filled with increased uncertainty because of sociopolitical, geopolitical, and macroeconomic actions. These changes require organizations to measure, quantify, and build their ability to change, a term researchers call "change power." Indeed, every leader would like to improve their ability to capitalize on changes that take place in the external environment. Researchers have found that one important way to build change power is to invest in diversity, equity, and inclusion (DEI). DEI has been linked to increased capacity to change, which correlates with increased employee engagement and subsequent financial performance. The most highly correlated elements of DEI to increased change power are **purpose**—the ability to create a sense of belongingness among employees; **choreography**—the ability to reorder actions and quickly change priorities as needed; and **development**—the ability to help employees build new skills required in the new change state. Diverse teams provide many organizational benefits, among them, the potential to adapt and evolve during times of change and uncertainty. Rather than cut DEI budgets during tough times, which many organizations have done since 2020, companies should continue their investment in DEI to ensure their organizations have the collective power to change.

1. Do you agree that companies benefit from investing in DEI during times of change? Why or why not?

   Students will answer this question in a couple of ways. Some may address bottom line goals that organizations must achieve, especially during downturns. For these students, they should be guided to indirect financial benefits of DEI through the correlates listed. Others may support investment in DEI. For these students, they should realize the dilemma that leaders face in investing in programs that, on the face, are difficult to show a financial, bottom-line benefit. The important takeaway is that leading during tough times is indeed a dilemma that requires considerable thought and communication.

2. One of the correlates listed in the article is choreography, the ability to quickly reorder priorities and move on them. Speculate on how such quick action can occur, given the documented problems of diversity.

   Answering this question requires students to return to the Benefits and Problems of Diversity discussed in Chapter 2 of the text, specifically communication, resistance to change, and slower decision-making.

Sources: K. Davis, "What Happened to Companies' Commitment to DEI?" *Fast Company*, March 6 (2023), accessed at https://www.fastcompany.com/90855309/what-happened-companies-commitment-dei; D. Michels, K. Murphy, and K. Venkataraman, "How Investing in DEI Helps Companies Become More Adaptable," *HBR.org*, May 5 (2023), accessed at https://hbr.org/2023/05/how-investing-in-dei-helps-companies-become-more-adaptable.

---

with the ability to reject inappropriate requests and challenge false assumptions. ChatGPT has been used to write poetry, answer essay questions, and build new apps. OpenAI, the company that developed ChatGPT, has a goal of creating artificial intelligence that matches human intellect.[15] So far ChatGPT has proven to have limitations, so much so that some school districts have banned its use. Vanderbilt University's Peabody School apologized after using ChatGPT to write an email to students addressing the tragedy at Michigan State that killed three students. The end of the email contained the line "Paraphrase from OpenAI's ChatGPT AI language model, personal communication."[16] Students were outraged about the use of AI to address human tragedy.

Although ChatGPT has gained a lot of users, it has also raised concerns about inaccurate information, possible biases, and the ability to help students cheat.

Still, companies like Google and China's Baidu are racing to develop and introduce their own ChatBots.

Technological innovations bring about profound change within organizations because the innovation process promotes associated changes in work relationships and organizational structures.[17] The team approach adopted by many organizations leads to flatter structures, decentralized decision-making, and more open communication between leaders and team members.

Managing Ethical Behavior Recent scandals have brought ethical behavior in organizations to the forefront of public consciousness. Ethical issues, however, are not always public and monumental. Employees face ethical dilemmas in their daily work lives. The need to manage daily ethical behavior has brought about several changes in organizations, most centering around the idea that an organization must create a culture that encourages ethical behavior, as we discussed in Chapter 16.

There are plenty of examples of unethical behavior in organizations. Instead, let's focus on a company that consistently tries to do the right thing. In September of 2022, Patagonia founder Yvon Chouinard announced that he was giving the company away. "Earth is now our only stakeholder," he wrote, giving the $3 billion global outdoor company to a family trust and a not-for-profit called the Holdfast Collective.[18] The goal is to put the money toward fighting climate change and will yield $100 million per year for saving the planet.

Chouinard's decision is in keeping with Patagonia's long focus on sustainability and ethical manufacturing. The company gives 1 percent of its sales to environmental causes every year. Recycled materials are planned to be in 100 percent of their products by 2025. A "buy less, demand more" campaign enlists consumers' help in changing the way clothes are made by having them demand ethically made, mindfully sourced products. Customers are encouraged to buy, sell, and trade their used Patagonia clothing on the company's Worn Wear website, which helps customers reuse, recycle, repair, or resell items and keep them out of the landfill. The company is a founding member of the Sustainable Apparel Coalition, which brings global brands in the apparel and footwear industries together to create a more equitable and sustainable world through positive social and environmental impact.[19]

Society expects organizations to maintain ethical behavior both internally and in relationships with other organizations, as well as with customers, the environment, and society. These expectations may be informal, or they may come in the form of increased regulation. In addition to the pressure from societal expectations, legal developments, changing stakeholder expectations, and shifting consumer demands can also lead to change.[20] And some companies change simply because others are changing.[21] Other powerful forces for change originate from within the organization.

18-1b Internal Forces

Pressures for change that originate inside the organization are generally recognizable by symptoms such as declining effectiveness. A company that experiences its third quarterly loss within a fiscal year undoubtedly experiences a pressure for change. Some companies react by instituting layoffs and massive cost-cutting programs, whereas others look at the bigger picture, view the loss as symptomatic of an underlying problem, and seek out its cause.

A crisis may also stimulate change in an organization. Strikes or walkouts may lead management to change the wage structure. The resignation of a key decision maker may cause the company to rethink the composition of its management team and its role in the organization.

Fast Fact

Burnout Is a Long-Term, Global Issue

The pandemic not only changed the way we work; it also increased everyone's risk of burnout. From long working hours to increasing demands at home, everyone suffers, but human services workers, first responders, and people in health care are especially at risk. Burnout is a syndrome characterized by three facets: feelings of exhaustion, mental distance from or negativity about one's job, and reduced professional efficacy.

Asana's Anatomy of Work Index showed that 63% of employees reported experiencing burnout. Most staggering of their findings about burnout was that 84% of Gen Z workers reported burnout during the last year.

Despite organizations' efforts during and since the pandemic, burnout remains a worldwide problem. U.S. employees reported the highest levels of burnout globally.

iStock.com/lakshmiprasad S

Sources: A. Abramson, "Burnout and Stress Are Everywhere," *APA Monitor on Psychology*, January 1 (2022), accessed at https://www.apa.org/monitor/2022/01/special-burnout-stress; *Asana Anatomy of Work Index 2022*, accessed at https://investors.asana.com/news/news-details/2022/Asana-Anatomy-of-Work-Index-2022-Work-About-Work-Hampering-Organizational-Agility/default.aspx

Changes in employee expectations can trigger change in organizations as well. A company that hires a group of young newcomers may find that their expectations are very different from those of older workers. One reason for changed expectations is that the workforce is more educated than ever before. Although this has its advantages, workers with more education demand more of employers. Furthermore, today's workers are concerned with career and family balance issues, such as dependent care. And the many sources of workforce diversity hold potential for a host of other differing expectations among employees. In general, issues of trust, equity, flexibility, inclusion, and work-life balance are driving employee expectations.

Sometimes external forces for change translate into internal forces for change. A global movement has emerged calling for a 4-day workweek. The idea is to redefine the workweek from 40 hours to 32 hours, maintaining 100 percent productivity. A pilot program in the U.K. produced positive results for businesses and employees. Ninety-two percent of the participating companies said they would continue the 4-day workweek, given that productivity either stayed the same or increased. The effects for employees were also positive, with decreased anxiety, fatigue, and insomnia. By the trial's end, 70 percent of employees said they experienced lower levels of burnout. The movement has spread worldwide, with employees urging companies to convert to the 4-day workweek.[22]

Still another pressure is a change in the work climate that produces a workforce that is lethargic, unmotivated, and dissatisfied. Such symptoms, sometimes called survivor syndrome, are common in organizations that have experienced layoffs. Workers who have escaped a layoff may grieve for those who have lost their jobs and may find it difficult to continue to be productive. They may fear that they will be laid off as well, and many feel insecure in their jobs.

incremental change Change of a relatively small scope, such as making small improvements.

strategic change Change of a larger scale, such as organizational restructuring.

transformational change Change in which the organization moves to a radically different, and sometimes unknown, future state.

18-2 The Scope of Change

Change can be of a relatively small scope, such as a modification in a work procedure (an **incremental change**). Such changes are a fine-tuning of the organization. For example, Intel and other chip producers must continually upgrade their manufacturing equipment just to stay competitive. Intel's conversion of an Arizona fab (a chip-making plant) from older to newer technology cost $3 billion.[23] While radical change is more exciting and interesting to discuss, most organizational change—and therefore most research on organizational change—has focused on evolutionary (incremental) rather than revolutionary change.[24] Change can also be on a larger scale, such as the restructuring of an organization (a **strategic change**).[25] In strategic change, the organization moves from an old state to a known new state during a controlled period of time. Sometimes strategic changes work; sometimes they don't. YouTube was a startup that was acquired by Google for $1.65 billion, and Google altered YouTube's strategy by going after premium content providers such as ABC, NBC, and CBS. In addition, a partner program was launched that allowed popular users to share in the advertising revenue their videos generated. This change in strategy has not worked, however. Although it now has one billion viewers, YouTube has yet to become profitable. Some say that a new strategy is needed that focuses on attracting a broader audience beyond young people.[26]

The most massive scope of change is **transformational change**, in which the organization moves to a radically different, and sometimes unknown, future state.[27] In transformational change, the organization's mission, culture, goals, structure, and leadership may all change dramatically.[28] Of all the tasks a leader undertakes, many say that changing the form and nature of the organization itself may be the most difficult, an observation supported by research.[29]

One of the toughest decisions faced by leaders is the proper pace of change. Some scholars argue that rapid change is more likely to succeed than slower change because it creates momentum,[30] while others argue that these short, sharp changes are actually rare and not experienced by most firms.[31] Still others observe that change in a large organization may occur incrementally in some parts of the firm and quickly in others.[32] In summary, researchers agree that the pace of change is important, but they can't quite agree on which pace of change is most beneficial.

One thing that both researchers and managers alike can agree on is the increasing volatility, interconnection, and uncertainty in business. These changes demand that leaders understand what it takes to lead in a fast-paced and ever-changing world. Complexity leadership means leading both people and organizations so that they handle complex changes with adaptability and resilience.[33]

18-2a The Change Agent's Role

The individual or group that introduces and manages change in an organization is known as the **change agent**. Change agents can be internal, such as managers or employees who are appointed to oversee the change process. In her book *The Change Masters*, Rosabeth Moss Kanter notes that at companies like Hewlett-Packard, managers and employees alike can develop the skills needed to produce change and innovation in the organization.[34]

Internal change agents have certain advantages in managing the change process. First, they know the organization's history, its political system, and its culture. Then, because they must live with the results of their change efforts, internal change agents are likely to be very careful about managing change. There are disadvantages, however, to using internal change agents. They may be associated with certain factions within the organization, be accused of favoritism, or be too close to the situation to have an objective view of what needs to be done.

Change leaders within organizations tend to be young, between twenty-five and forty. A high number of change leaders are women. Also, change agents are more flexible than ordinary general managers and much more people oriented. Using a balance of technical and interpersonal skills, they are tough decision-makers who focus on performance results. Plus, they know how to energize people and get them aligned in the same direction. In addition, they have the ability to operate in more than one leadership style and can shift from a team mode to command and control, depending on the situation. Finally, change agents are comfortable with uncertainty.[35]

If change is large scale or strategic in nature, it may require a team of leaders with a variety of skills, expertise, and influence that can work together harmoniously.[36]

External change agents bring an outsider's objective view to the organization. They may be preferred by employees because of their impartiality. External change agents face certain problems, however. Not only is their knowledge of the organization's history limited, but they may also be viewed with suspicion by organization members. External change agents have more power in directing changes if employees perceive them as being trustworthy, possessing important expertise, having a track record that establishes credibility, and being similar to them.[37]

Different change agent competencies are required at different stages of the change process. Leadership, communication, training, and participation have varying levels of impact as the change proceeds, meaning change agents must be flexible in how they work through the different phases of the process.[38] Effective change leaders build strong relationships within their leadership team, between the team and organizational members, and between the team and key environmental players. Maintaining all three relationships simultaneously is quite difficult, so successful leaders are continually coupling and uncoupling with the different groups as the change process proceeds. Adaptability is a key skill for both internal and external change leaders.[39]

18-3 Resistance to Change

People often resist change in a rational response based on self-interest. However, there are countless other reasons people resist change. Many of these reasons center around the notion of *reactance*—that is, a negative reaction that occurs when individuals feel that their personal freedom is threatened.[40] Let's look at some expressions of reactance and then at some ways of dealing with it.

18-3a Major Reasons People Resist Change

Common reasons people resist change include fear of the unknown, fear of loss, fear of failure, fear of disruption of interpersonal relationships, personality factors, politics, and cultural assumptions and values.

change agent The individual or group that undertakes the task of introducing and managing a change in an organization.

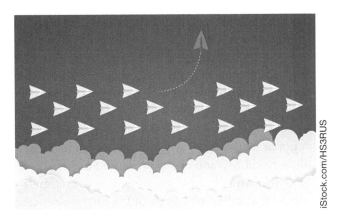

iStock.com/HS3RUS

Fear of the Unknown Change often brings with it substantial uncertainty. Employees facing a technological change may resist the change simply because it introduces ambiguity into what was once a comfortable situation for them.

Fear of Loss Some employees may fear losing their jobs with impending change, especially when an advanced technology like robotics is introduced. Employees may also fear losing their status because of change.[41] Computer systems experts, for example, may feel that their expertise will be less appreciated when a more user-friendly networked information system is installed. Another common fear is that changes may diminish the positive qualities the individual enjoys in the job. Computerizing the customer service positions at Southwestern Bell (now part of SBC Communications), for example, threatened the autonomy that representatives previously enjoyed.

Fear of Failure Some employees fear changes because they fear their own failure because of those changes. They may question their competence to deal with changes that might mean increased workloads or increased task difficulty. They may also fear that performance expectations will be elevated following the change and that they might not measure up.[42]

Resistance can also stem from the fear that change will not really take place. In other words, there can be fear of failure on the part of the organization, not the individual. In one large library that was undergoing a major automation effort, employees were doubtful that the vendor could deliver the state-of-the-art system that was promised. In this case, the implementation never became a reality; the employees' fears were well founded.[43]

Fear of Disruption of Interpersonal Relationships Employees may resist change that threatens to limit meaningful interpersonal relationships on the job. Librarians facing the automation effort feared that once the computerized system was implemented, they would not be able to interact as they did when they had to go to another floor of the library to get help finding a resource.

Personality Individuals with an internal locus of control, high growth needs, strong motivation, and a positive outlook are more likely to embrace changes at work.[44] Personality conflicts may impact workers' acceptance of change. A change agent who appears insensitive to employees' concerns and feelings may meet considerable resistance from those who feel that their needs are not being considered.

Politics Organizational change may also shift the existing balance of power in the organization. Individuals or groups empowered under the current arrangement may be threatened with losing these political advantages in the advent of change.

Cultural Assumptions and Values Sometimes cultural assumptions and values can be impediments to change, particularly if the assumptions underlying the change are alien to employees. Other times, employees might interpret strategic change initiatives from the standpoint of the organization's value system and ideologies of the management team. In fact, research indicates that employees pay attention to the informal sense-making process prevalent in organizations and leading top-down change initiatives to fail.[45] This form of resistance can be very difficult to overcome because some cultural assumptions are unconscious. As discussed in Chapter 2, some cultures tend to avoid uncertainty. In Mexican and Greek cultures, for example, change that creates a great deal of uncertainty may be met with great resistance.

We have described several sources of resistance to change, but the reasons for resistance are as diverse as the workforce itself and vary with different individuals and organizations. Some organizations as a whole may be more change resistant than others.[46] The challenge for managers is introducing change in a positive manner and managing employee resistance.

18-3b Managing Resistance and Developing Resilience

The traditional view of managing resistance to change was to treat it as something to be overcome, and many organizational attempts to reduce the resistance have only served to intensify it. The contemporary view holds that resistance is simply a form of feedback and that this feedback can be used very productively to manage the change process. When individuals, teams, or organizations are not ready for change, it is an opportunity to gather important diagnostic information that can be used to identify weaknesses in the organization's approach to change and to improve the process.[47] In this view,

the idea is to manage resistance by planning for it and being ready with a variety of strategies for using the resistance as feedback and helping employees negotiate the transition. Three key strategies for managing resistance to change are communication, participation, and empathy and support.[48]

Communication about impending change is essential if employees are to adjust effectively.[49] The details and, equally important, the rationale of the

YOU

Tolerance for Ambiguity

Tolerance for Ambiguity Survey Form

Read each of the following statements carefully. Then rate each of them in terms of the extent to which you either agree or disagree with the statement using the following scale:

Completely Disagree			Neither Agree nor Disagree			Completely Agree
1	2	3	4	5	6	7

Place the number that best describes your degree of agreement or disagreement in the blank to the left of each statement.

_____ 1. An expert who doesn't come up with a definite answer probably doesn't know much.

_____ 2. I would like to live in a foreign country for a while.

_____ 3. The sooner we all acquire similar values and ideals, the better.

_____ 4. A good teacher is one who makes you wonder about your way of looking at things.

_____ 5. I like parties where I know most of the people more than ones where all or most of the people are complete strangers.

_____ 6. Teachers or supervisors who hand out vague assignments give a chance for one to show initiative and originality.

_____ 7. A person who leads an even, regular life in which few surprises or unexpected happenings arise really has a lot to be grateful for.

_____ 8. Many of our most important decisions are based upon insufficient information.

_____ 9. There is really no such thing as a problem that can't be solved.

_____ 10. People who fit their lives to a schedule probably miss most of the joy of living.

_____ 11. A good job is one where what is to be done and how it is to be done are always clear.

_____ 12. It is more fun to tackle a complicated problem than to solve a simple one.

_____ 13. In the long run, it is possible to get more done by tackling small, simple problems rather than large and complicated ones.

_____ 14. Often the most interesting and stimulating people are those who don't mind being different and original.

_____ 15. What we are used to is always preferable to what is unfamiliar.

Scoring: For even-numbered questions, add the total points.

For odd-numbered questions, use reverse scoring and add the total points.

Your score is the total of the even- and odd-numbered questions.

Norms Using the Tolerance for Ambiguity Scale

Basis: The survey asks fifteen questions about personal and work-oriented situations with ambiguity. You were asked to rate each situation on a scale from 1 (tolerant) to 7 (intolerant). (Alternating questions have the response scale reversed.) The index scores the items. A perfectly tolerant person would score 15 and a perfectly intolerant person 105. Scores between 20 and 80 are reported, with means of 45. The responses to the even-numbered questions with 7 minus the score are added to the response for the odd-numbered questions.

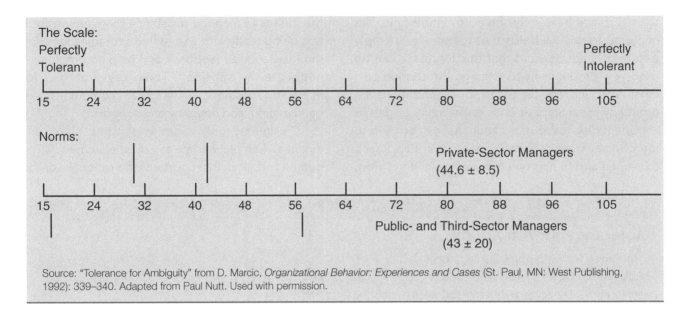

The Scale:

Perfectly Tolerant — Perfectly Intolerant

| 15 | 24 | 32 | 40 | 48 | 56 | 64 | 72 | 80 | 88 | 96 | 105 |

Norms:

Private-Sector Managers
(44.6 ± 8.5)

| 15 | 24 | 32 | 40 | 48 | 56 | 64 | 72 | 80 | 88 | 96 | 105 |

Public- and Third-Sector Managers
(43 ± 20)

Source: "Tolerance for Ambiguity" from D. Marcic, *Organizational Behavior: Experiences and Cases* (St. Paul, MN: West Publishing, 1992): 339–340. Adapted from Paul Nutt. Used with permission.

change should be provided. Accurate and timely information can help prevent unfounded fears and potentially damaging rumors from developing. Conversely, delaying announcements and withholding information can serve to fuel the rumor mill. Open communication in a culture of trust is a key ingredient for successful change.[50] Managers should pay attention to the informal communication networks in an organization because they can serve as power channels for disseminating change-related information.[51] Educating employees on new work procedures and other potential consequences of change is helpful. In addition, both mentors and mentees derive benefits from going through the process of organizational change together. Mentees are assisted by mentors who help them make sense of the change, and mentors experience satisfaction in having helped the mentee through the change process. Another key ingredient that can help employees adjust to change is a supervisor whom they can trust. When employees trust their supervisors, it serves as a social support mechanism, and they are more committed to the organization even if they feel they can't control the change process.[52]

There is substantial research support underscoring the importance of *participation* in the change process. Employees must be engaged and involved for change to work—as supported by the notion "That which we create, we support." Participation helps employees become involved in the change and establishes a feeling of ownership in the process. Mergers and acquisitions are widely prevalent in the current business environment.

Another strategy for managing resistance is to provide *empathy and support* to employees who have trouble dealing with the change. Active listening is an excellent tool for identifying the reasons behind resistance and for uncovering fears. An expression of concerns about the change can provide important feedback that managers can use to improve the change process. Emotional support and encouragement can help an employee deal with the anxiety that is a natural response to change. Employees who experience severe reactions to change can benefit from talking with a counselor. Some companies provide counseling through their employee assistance plans.

Promoting resilience among employees helps them stay healthy and productive during times of change. Resilience is the ability to use positive skills to remain steady and focused when encountering challenges and adversities. Stressful work environments are health risks, and employees who feel appreciated

One key strategy for managing resistance to change is open communication.

and supported at work are more resilient. Resilience has a protective effect on sleep, stress, burnout, depression, and productivity during times of change. Many companies offer resilience training because of these benefits.[53] Among the companies that use resilience training are Aetna, IBM, and Goldman Sachs.

Encouraging growth mindsets is another way to help employees deal with change. A growth mindset is a belief that people can change themselves. This stands in opposition to a fixed mindset, which is the belief that people are largely unchangeable.[54] Employees with growth mindsets approach change with more confidence. Research shows that employees can benefit not only from a growth mindset about themselves, but also a growth mindset about their jobs. The belief that one can change themselves and their jobs during change leads to sustainable happiness at work.[55]

18-4 Lewin's Model for Managing Change

Kurt Lewin developed a model of the change process that has stood the test of time and continues to influence the way organizations manage planned change. Lewin's model is based on the idea of *force field analysis*.[56] Figure 18.1 shows a force field analysis of a decision to engage in exercise behavior. This model contends that a person's behavior is the product of two opposing forces: one force pushes toward preserving the status quo, and the other force pushes for change. When the two opposing forces are approximately equal, current behavior is maintained. For behavioral change to occur, the forces maintaining the status quo must be overcome. This can be accomplished by increasing the forces for change, by weakening the forces for the status quo, or by a combination of these actions.

Lewin's change model is a three-step process, as shown in Figure 18.2. The process begins with **unfreezing**, which is a crucial first hurdle in the change process. Unfreezing involves encouraging individuals to discard old behaviors by shaking up the equilibrium state that maintains the status quo. Change management literature has long advocated that certain

unfreezing The first step in Lewin's change model, in which individuals are encouraged to discard old behaviors by shaking up the equilibrium state that maintains the status quo.

Figure 18.1 Force Field Analysis of a Decision to Engage in Exercise

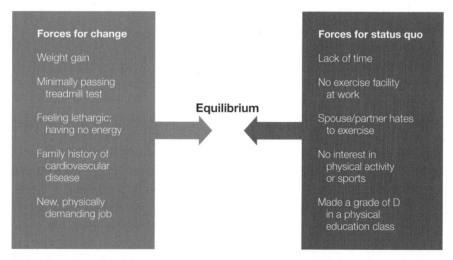

Forces for change	Forces for status quo
Weight gain	Lack of time
Minimally passing treadmill test	No exercise facility at work
Feeling lethargic; having no energy	Spouse/partner hates to exercise
Family history of cardiovascular disease	No interest in physical activity or sports
New, physically demanding job	Made a grade of D in a physical education class

Equilibrium

Figure 18.2 Lewin's Change Model

Unfreezing	Moving	Refreezing
Reducing forces for status quo	Developing new attitudes, values, and behaviors	Reinforcing new attitudes, values, and behaviors

individuals have personalities that make them more resistant to change. However, recent research indicates that only a small portion of a study's respondents (23 percent) displayed consistency in their reactions to three different kinds of change: structural, technological, and office relocation. The majority of respondents (77 percent) reacted differently to these different kinds of change, suggesting that reactions to change might be more situationally driven than was previously thought.[57] Organizations often accomplish unfreezing by eliminating the rewards for current behavior and showing that current behavior is not valued. In essence, individuals surrender by allowing the boundaries of their status quo to be opened in preparation for change.[58]

The second step in the change process is **moving**. In the moving stage, new attitudes, values, and behaviors are substituted for old ones. Organizations accomplish moving by initiating new options and explaining the rationale for the change, as well as by providing training to help employees develop the new skills they need. Employees should be given the overarching vision for the change so that they can establish their roles within the new organizational structure and processes.[59]

Refreezing is the final step in the change process. In this step, new attitudes, values, and behaviors are established as the new status quo. The new ways of operating are cemented in and reinforced. Managers should ensure that the organizational culture and formal reward systems encourage the new behaviors. Changes in the reward structure may be needed to ensure that the organization is not rewarding the old behaviors and merely hoping for the new behaviors. A study by Exxon Research and Engineering showed that framing and displaying a mission statement in managers' offices may eventually change the behavior of 2 percent of the managers. In contrast, changing managers' evaluation and reward systems will change the behavior of 55 percent of the managers almost overnight.[60]

The approach used by Monsanto to increase opportunities for women within the company is an illustration of how to use Lewin's model effectively. First, Monsanto emphasized unfreezing by helping employees debunk negative stereotypes about women in business. This also helped overcome resistance to change. Second, Monsanto moved employees' attitudes and behaviors through diversity training in which differences were emphasized as positive, and supervisors learned ways of training and developing female employees. Third, Monsanto changed its reward system so that managers were evaluated and paid according to how they coached and promoted women, which helped refreeze the new attitudes and behaviors.

One frequently overlooked issue is whether or not the change is consistent with the company's deeply held core values. Value consistency is critical to making a change stick. Organizations whose members perceive the changes to be consistent with the firm's values adopt the changes much more easily and fully. Conversely, organizations whose members' values conflict with the changes may display "superficial conformity," in which members pay lip service to the changes but ultimately revert to their old behaviors.[61]

18-5 Determining the Need for Organization Development Interventions

Related to change is the subject of *organization development*, a method that consists of various programs for making organizations more effective. **Organization development (OD)** is defined as a systematic approach to organizational improvement that applies behavioral science theory and research in order to increase individual and organizational well-being and effectiveness.[62] This definition implies certain characteristics. First, as a systematic approach to planned change, OD is a structured cycle of diagnosing organizational problems and opportunities and then applying expertise to them. Second, OD is grounded in solid research and theory. It involves the application of behavioral science knowledge to the challenges that organizations face. Third, OD recognizes the reciprocal relationship between individuals and organizations. It acknowledges that for organizations to change, individuals must change. Finally, OD is goal

---

moving The second step in Lewin's change model, in which new attitudes, values, and behaviors are substituted for old ones.

refreezing The final step in Lewin's change model, in which new attitudes, values, and behaviors are established as the new status quo.

organization development (OD) A systematic approach to organizational improvement that applies behavioral science theory and research in order to increase individual and organizational well-being and effectiveness.

Figure 18.3 The Organization Development Cycle

oriented. It is a process that seeks to improve both individual and organizational well-being and effectiveness.

Prior to deciding on a method of intervention, managers must carefully diagnose the problem they are attempting to address. Diagnosis and needs analysis is a critical first step in any OD intervention. Following this, an intervention method is chosen and applied. Finally, a thorough follow-up of the OD process is conducted. Figure 18.3 presents the OD cycle, a continuous process of moving the organization and its employees toward effective functioning.

18-5a Diagnosis and Needs Analysis

Before any intervention is planned, a thorough organizational diagnosis should be conducted. Diagnosis is an essential first step for any organization development intervention.[63] The term *diagnosis* comes from two Greek words, *dial* (through) and *gnosis* (knowledge). Thus, the diagnosis should pinpoint specific problems and areas in need of improvement. Six areas to examine carefully are the organization's purpose, structure, reward system, support systems, relationships, and leadership.[64]

Harry Levinson's diagnostic approach asserts that the process should begin by identifying where the pain (the problem) in the organization is, what it is like, how long it has been happening, and what has already been done about it.[65] Then a four-part, comprehensive diagnosis can begin. The first part of the diagnosis involves achieving an understanding of the organization's history. In the second part, the organization as a whole is analyzed to obtain data about its structure and processes. In the third part, interpretive data about attitudes, relationships, and current organizational functioning are gathered. In the fourth part of the diagnosis, the data

are analyzed, and conclusions are reached. In each stage of the diagnosis, the data can be gathered using a variety of methods, including observation, interviews, questionnaires, and archival records.

A *needs analysis* is another crucial step in managing change. This is an analysis of the skills and competencies that employees must have to achieve the goals of the change. A needs analysis is essential because interventions such as training programs must target these skills and competencies.

Hundreds of alternative OD intervention methods exist. One way of classifying these methods is by the target of change, which can be the organization, groups within the organization, or individuals.

18-6 Group-Focused Techniques for OD Intervention

Some OD intervention methods emphasize changing the organization itself or changing the work groups within the organization rather than targeting the employees as individuals. Intervention methods in this category include survey feedback, management by objectives, product and service quality programs, team building, and process consultation.

18-6a Survey Feedback

Survey feedback is a widely used intervention method whereby employee attitudes are solicited using a questionnaire. Once the data are collected,

survey feedback A widely used intervention method whereby employee attitudes are solicited using a questionnaire.

they are analyzed and fed back to the employees to diagnose problems and plan other interventions. Survey feedback is often used as an exploratory tool and then is combined with some other intervention. The effectiveness of survey feedback in improving outcomes (e.g., absenteeism or productivity) increases substantially when this method is combined with other interventions.[66] Furthermore, the effectiveness of this technique is contingent upon trust between management and subordinates, and this can be reinforced through the anonymity and confidentiality of survey responses.

For survey feedback to be an effective method, certain guidelines should be used. Employees must be assured that their responses to the questionnaire will be confidential and anonymous. Feedback should be reported in a group format. Employees must be able to trust that negative repercussions will not result from their responses. Employees should be informed of the purpose of the survey. Failing to do this can set up unrealistic expectations about the changes that might come from the surveys.

In addition, management must be prepared to follow up on the survey results. If some things cannot be changed, the rationale (e.g., prohibitive cost) must be explained to the employees. Without appropriate follow-through, employees will not take the survey process seriously the next time.

18-6b Team Building

Team building programs can improve the effectiveness of work groups. Usually they begin with a diagnostic process through which team members identify problems and continue with the team planning actions to resolve those problems. The OD practitioner in team building serves as a facilitator, and the work itself is completed by team members.[67]

Team building is a very popular OD method. A survey of *Fortune* 500 companies indicated that human resource managers considered team building the most successful OD technique.[68] Managers are particularly interested in building teams that can learn. To build *learning teams*, members must be

encouraged to seek feedback, discuss errors, reflect on successes and failures, and experiment with new ways of performing. Mistakes should be analyzed for ways to improve, and a climate of mutual support should be developed. Leaders of learning teams are good coaches who promote a climate of psychological safety so that team members feel comfortable discussing problems.[69]

One popular technique for team building is the use of creative challenges. One of TeamBonding's culinary challenges takes advantage of the popularity of food trucks. In the Food Truck Challenge, teams design the façade of their tabletop food trucks, along with a logo for their aprons.[70] They create recipes, prepare their signature dishes, and market their creations from one of three cuisines: Southwest, All-American, or Tailgater. A panel of judges does a taste test, and then the teams are evaluated on best taste, best presentation, and culinary champion. The objective of the Food Truck Challenge is to improve teamwork through the power of play. Genentech, Tesla, and American Express have used the Food Truck Challenge for team building.

Outdoor challenges are also popular for team building. Rowing, rock climbing, and group hikes in nature can be catalysts for team growth. The idea is to increase a team's sense of connection and cohesion, by forcing them to work collaboratively and to see these benefits transfer back to the workplace. Aberkyn Wilderness Trails, for example, takes teams on guided trail locations in Europe, Asia, Africa, and North America.[71] Team dynamics during the journey build mutual trust and support. The goal is for team members to gain renewed energy, clarity, and insight. In the absence of technology, competing demands for attention, office politics, and impending deadlines, outdoor challenges place people in unfamiliar environments that require adopting new skills and ways of interacting.[72]

Team building is particularly challenging in virtual teams. Normal processes such as conflict management, decision-making, and communication of emotions are challenges with which virtual teams may need help. It takes time in virtual teams to build relationships, and interventions that help build trust among the geographically dispersed team members are valuable. Topics such as intercultural teamwork are helpful, and new members of virtual teams can especially benefit from teambuilding training.[73] Zoom happy hours are particularly despised by

team building An intervention designed to improve the effectiveness of a work group.

Companies like Tesla and American Express have used the Food Truck Challenge for team building.

remote workers, because they feel mandatory (even if they are not explicitly) and feel like forced fun. In addition, they're most often held after working hours on top of a stressful work day.[74]

18-6c Corporate Retreats

A corporate retreat (also known as company retreat) is an event lasting a day, a week, or longer in which employees engage in learning experiences away from the office and apart from their typical responsibilities. The objectives of a corporate retreat may be to allow employees to bond with each other, to reinforce company culture, to obtain new skills, or to allow employees to rest and relax. The retreat could involve the whole company, a subset of employees, or the executive team. In the era of remote work, retreats are becoming more popular as leaders seek to reinforce culture among employees who rarely interact face-to-face.

Corporate retreats range from simple and small-scaled to very extravagant. Scavenger hunts, axe throwing, golf getaways, and escape rooms are popular. One of the keys to success is having executives actively engaged during the retreat. In addition, planners should recognize that some employees do not see "forced fun" as enjoyable and some events should be non-mandatory.[75] Employees should be given substantial notice so they can plan to be away, and consideration of work piling up should be factored in. The goals of the retreat should be stated clearly, and the event should be evaluated at the end in terms of what was learned and what goals were achieved. A potential pitfall of corporate retreats is that people are tempted to let loose. Although no

one gets promoted on a retreat, people sometimes get demoted from their behavior on a retreat.

Some retreats are more lavish and include travel to destinations like Cancun, St. Tropez, Barcelona, and Cabo San Lucas. Uber employees' retreat in Las Vegas included a Beyonce concert. WeWork employees attended their retreat in the English countryside.[76] Although very expensive, some companies see corporate retreats as ways to give attractive perks to employees in a competitive labor market. During the pandemic, the online events via Zoom that were offered were much less expensive, but some employers felt that the events were too impersonal and did not have the desired impact. Offsite retreats may be welcome breaks for those remote workers experiencing Zoom fatigue.

18-6d Process Consultation

Pioneered by Edgar Schein, **process consultation** is an OD method that helps managers and employees improve the processes that are used in organizations.[77] The processes most often targeted are communication, conflict resolution, decision-making, group interaction, and leadership.

One of the distinguishing features of process consultation is that an outside consultant is used. The role of the consultant is to help employees help themselves. In this way, the ownership of a successful outcome rests with the employees.[78] The consultant guides the organization members in examining the processes in the organization and in refining them. The steps in process consultation are entering the organization, defining the relationship, choosing an approach, gathering data and diagnosing problems, intervening, and gradually leaving the organization.

Process consultation is an interactive technique between employees and an outside consultant, so it is seldom used as a sole OD method. Most often it is used in combination with other OD interventions.

All the preceding OD methods focus on changing the organization or the work group, whereas the following OD methods are aimed at individual change.

process consultation An OD method that helps managers and employees improve the processes that are used in organizations.

To build *learning teams*, members must be encouraged to seek feedback, discuss errors, reflect on successes and failures, and experiment with new ways of performing.

18-7 Individual-Focused Techniques for OD Intervention

OD efforts that are targeted at individuals include skills training, leadership training and development, executive coaching, role negotiation, job redesign, health promotion programs, and career planning.

18-7a Skills Training

The key question addressed by **skills training** is, "What knowledge, skills, and abilities are necessary to do this job effectively?" Skills training is accomplished either in formal classroom settings or on the job. The challenge is integrating skills training into OD in today's rapidly changing organizational environments. The job knowledge in most positions requires continual updates to keep pace with rapid change. As workplaces increasingly use robotics and artificial intelligence, they will require highly skilled employees for human work and judgment. Amazon, for example, is significantly upskilling its workforce by offering training like "Machine Learning University" and "Amazon Technical Academy." This action represents a significant investment in its people. Upskilling training for 100,000 employees will require more than $700 million to get the company ready for the next evolution in the digital age.[79]

Companies such as Google and Genentech are supplementing their traditional skills training with training in mindfulness skills. At Dow Chemical Company, researchers wondered whether mindfulness skills taught online would have as much impact as mindfulness skills taught in a classroom setting. A group of employees participated in an online

All of Genentech's employees have access to Headspace's app for mindfulness and meditation.

mindfulness course, and they were compared to a group of employees who were wait-listed for the training. The employees from the mindfulness online intervention reported decreased stress, better resilience and vigor, more work engagement, and higher overall well-being than those who had not yet completed the training.[80] Aetna, a U.S. health insurance company, continually trains employees at all levels in mindfulness, and reports a 28 percent reduction in stress levels and productivity improvements of $3,000 per employee per year.[81] Meetings at Aetna are often started with a brief mindfulness meditation session.

18-7b Leadership Training and Development

Companies invest millions of dollars in **leadership training and development**, a term that encompasses a variety of techniques that are designed to enhance individuals' leadership skills. One popular technique is to send future leaders to off-site training classes. Research shows that this type of education experience can have some impact, but participants' enthusiastic return to work may be short-lived due to the challenges and realities of work life. Classroom learning alone thus has a limited effect on leadership skills.

Some leadership training and development programs combine classroom learning with on-the-job experiences. One way of accomplishing development is with *action learning*, a technique that was pioneered in Europe. In action learning, leaders take on unfamiliar problems or familiar problems in unfamiliar settings. The leaders work on the problems

skills training Increasing the job knowledge, skills, and abilities that are necessary to do a job effectively.

leadership training and development A variety of techniques that are designed to enhance individuals' leadership skills.

and meet weekly in small groups made up of individuals from different organizations. The outcome of action learning is that leaders learn about themselves through the challenges of their comrades. Other techniques that provide action learning for participants are simulation, business games, role-playing, and case studies.[82]

The focus of leadership training is developing leadership skills, and for some companies, developing emotional intelligence (EI) skills. Google's Search Inside Yourself Leadership Institute focuses on training leaders in EI skills based in neuroscience. Topics include self-awareness, self-management, social awareness, and relationship management. The program was so successful that Google began offering it to other organizations, with the stated goal of making workplaces more compassionate and human.[83] Emotionally intelligent leadership helps leaders enact supportive behavior in stressful circumstances, such as the stress of mergers and acquisitions.[84] Compassionate leadership is a skill that allowed organizations to navigate the pandemic, and is also needed in the post-COVID era.[85]

Companies such as General Mills and Apple are integrating mindfulness training in their leadership development programs. Mindfulness training benefits the leaders themselves in terms of lower stress, more empathy, and improved well-being. Mindfulness training also has spillover effects for the leaders' employees. When leaders are more mindful, their employees have better job satisfaction and performance, along with improved well-being.[86]

The science of mindfulness shows three benefits of mindfulness that allow leaders to act more effectively in unpredictable, rapidly changing environments. The first of these benefits involves staying calm and remaining open-minded, which leads to mental agility. Another benefit is cognitive ability, the ability to think outside the box and navigate complex decisions. Finally, mindfulness provides focus and clear thinking. Regularly practicing mindfulness reduces distractibility by increasing awareness of the present moment.[87] All of these benefits are important to leader effectiveness.

Leadership training and development is an ongoing process that takes considerable time and effort. There are no quick fixes. At IBM, managers are held accountable for leadership development. In fact, IBM's managers will not be considered for promotion into senior executive positions unless they have a record of developing leaders. Top management must be committed to the process of leadership training and development if it wants to create a pipeline of high-potential employees to fill leadership positions.

18-7c Executive Coaching

Executive coaching is a technique in which managers or executives are paired with a coach in a partnership to help the executive perform more efficiently. Although coaching is usually done in a one-on-one manner, it is sometimes attempted in groups. The popularity of executive coaching has increased dramatically in recent years. The International Coach Federation, a group that trains and accredits executive coaches, doubled its membership in just two years of existence to 7,000 members in thirty-five countries.

Coaching is typically an investment in top-level managers. Coaches provide another set of eyes and ears and help executives see beyond their own blinders. They elicit solutions and ideas from the client rather than making suggestions. Thus they develop and enhance the talents and capabilities within the client. Many coaching arrangements focus on developing the emotional intelligence of the client executive and may use a 360-degree assessment in which the executive, her boss, peers, subordinates, and even family members rate the executive's emotional competencies.[88] The 360-degree feedback is critical, because many leaders are not self-aware. For example, 74 percent of executives think they are inspirational leaders, but only 27 percent of their employees agree.[89] This information is then fed back to the executive, and along with the coach, a development plan is put in place.

Good coaches form strong connections with clients, exhibit professionalism, and deliver forthright, candid feedback. The top reasons executives seek out coaches are to make personal behavior changes, enhance their effectiveness, and foster stronger relationships. Does executive coaching pay off? Research evidence indicates that coaching can yield positive results across a range

executive coaching A technique in which managers or executives are paired with a coach in a partnership to help them perform more efficiently.

of personal and leadership outcomes.[90] Successful coaching can result in sustained changes in executives' behavior, increased self-awareness and understanding, and more effective leadership competencies.[91] In addition, coaching allows leaders to better enact and manage change.[92] In one study, for example, executives who worked with executive coaches were more likely to set specific goals, ask for feedback from their supervisors, and were rated as better performers by their supervisors and subordinates when compared to executives who simply received feedback from surveys.[93] Effective coaching relationships depend on a professional, experienced coach, an executive who is motivated to learn and change, and a good fit between the two. The quality of the connection is particularly important.[94]

18-7d Role Negotiation

Individuals who work together sometimes have differing expectations of one another within the working relationship. **Role negotiation** is a technique whereby individuals meet and clarify their psychological contract, that is, their expectations of each other. The outcome of role negotiation is a better understanding between the two parties. When both parties have a mutual agreement on expectations, there is less ambiguity in the process of working together.

18-7e Wellness Programs

As organizations have become increasingly concerned with the costs of stress in the workplace, wellness programs have become a part of larger OD efforts. In Chapter 7, we examined stress and strain at work. To relieve stress and strain, companies such as Levi Strauss and Co., Motley Fool, Chesapeake Energy Co., and Johnson & Johnson have successfully integrated wellness programs into their organizations.

Wellness programs may include on-site fitness centers, smoking cessation and weight-loss programs, nutritional counseling, lunch and healthy snacks, yoga, and massage therapy, along with other options. One health risk that is of increasing concern is lack of sleep. Poor sleep quality and/or lack of sleep increases multiple health risks for employees and affects productivity at work. Companies that invest in employee well-being do so to preserve the

> As organizations have become increasingly concerned with the costs of stress in the workplace, health promotion programs have become a part of larger OD efforts.

health of their employees, and to reap the benefits of lower health care spending, higher productivity, and improved recruiting and retention of employees.[95]

Accenture, the business management consulting company, designed its wellness program with the goal of caring both about the minds and bodies of its employees. It offers services that provide support for stress, substance abuse, depression, and anxiety. Mental health for employees is a particular emphasis, and Accenture trained over 8,900 employees to become Mental Health Allies. These employees provide support to those who need it and connect them to professionals to get the help they need.[96] They also offer Teladoc services that provide access to a physician who can answer questions 24/7. The fitness program offers rewards to employees who set health goals and meet them. Special rates and discounts for fitness centers and an online fitness program encourage working out.

18-7f Career Planning

Matching an individual's career aspirations with the opportunities in the organization is career planning. This proactive approach to career management is often part of an organization's development efforts although it is a joint responsibility of organizations and individuals. Certainly career-planning activities benefit both the

Sam Whiteside, chief wellness officer at Motley Fool, says that wellness encompasses every facet that can make a person feel sound in mind, body, and spirit.

Bill O'Leary/The Washington Post/Getty Images

role negotiation A technique whereby individuals meet and clarify their psychological contract.

organization and its individuals. Through counseling sessions, employees identify their skills and skill deficiencies. The organization then can plan its training and development efforts based on this information. In addition, the process can be used to identify and nurture talented employees for potential promotion.

To sum up, managers can choose from a host of organization development techniques to facilitate organizational change. Large-scale changes in organizations require the use of multiple techniques. For example, implementing a new technology like robotics may require simultaneous changes in the structure of the organization, the configuration of work groups, and individual attitudes.

Since organization development is designed to help organizations manage change, it is important to evaluate the effectiveness of these efforts. The success of any OD intervention depends on a host of factors, including the technique used, the competence of the change agent, the organization's readiness for change, and top management commitment. No single method of OD is effective in every instance. Instead, multiple-method OD approaches are recommended because they allow organizations to capitalize on the benefits of several approaches.

Efforts to evaluate OD effects have focused on outcomes such as productivity. One review of more than 200 interventions indicated that worker productivity improved in 87 percent of the cases.[97] We can conclude that when properly applied and managed, organization development programs have positive effects on performance.[98]

The COVID-19 pandemic caused professionals to reevaluate the way OD is conducted, and to adapt. Learning events that once took place at a dedicated time and place are being supplemented with methods of learning while in the flow of work. Digital learning has emerged as a critical supplement to in-person learning. Self-paced learning provides flexibility and individualization. An emphasis on technical skills as supreme is being replaced with emphasis on capabilities for success in a post-COVID world, like inclusive leadership, curiosity, emotional intelligence and resilience.[99]

Experiential Exercise

Team Building for Team Effectiveness

This exercise will allow you and your team to engage in an organization development activity for team building. The two parts of the exercise are diagnosis and intervention.

Part 1. Diagnosis

Working as a team, complete the following four steps:

1. Describe how you have worked together this semester as a team.
2. What has your team done especially well? What has enabled this?
3. What problems or conflicts have you had as a team? (Be specific.) What was the cause of the problems your team experienced? Have the conflicts been over ideas, methods, or people?
4. Would you assess the overall effectiveness of your team as excellent, good, fair, poor, or a disaster? Explain your effectiveness rating.

Part 2. Intervention

A diagnosis provides the basis for intervention and action in organization development. Team building is a way to improve the relationships and effectiveness of teams at work. It is concerned with the results of work activities and the relationships among the members of the team. Complete the following three steps as a team.

Step 1. Answer the following questions with regard to the relationships within the team:

a. How could conflicts have been handled better?

b. How could specific relationships have been improved?

c. How could the interpersonal atmosphere of the team have been improved?

Step 2. Answer the following questions with regard to the results of the team's work:

a. How could the team have been more effective?

b. Are there any team process changes that would have improved the team's effectiveness?

c. Are there any team structure changes that would have improved the team's effectiveness?

Step 3. Answer the following questions with regard to the work environment in your place of employment:

a. What have you learned about team building that you can apply there?

b. What have you learned about team building that would not be applicable there?

Learning Objectives

18-1 **Identify the major external and internal forces for change in organizations.** When organizations are in a state of turmoil and transition, all members are affected. *External* forces that demand change are globalization, workforce diversity, technological change, and managing ethical behavior. *Internal* pressures for change are generally recognizable: declining effectiveness, crisis, changes in employee expectations, and a changed work climate. Adaptiveness, flexibility, and responsiveness are characteristics of the organizations that will succeed in meeting the challenges of change.

18-2 **Describe how different types of change vary in scope.** Change can be of a relatively small scope, such as a modification in a work procedure (an *incremental change*) or of a larger scale, such as the restructuring of an organization (a *strategic change*). The most massive scope of change is *transformational change*, in which the organization moves to a radically different, and sometimes unknown, future state. One of the toughest decisions faced by leaders is the "pace" of change. Researchers agree that pace is important; however, they can't agree on which pace of change is most beneficial.

18-3 **Discuss methods organizations can use to manage resistance to change.** The contemporary view holds that resistance is simply a form of feedback and that this feedback can be used very productively to manage the change process. Three key strategies for managing resistance to change are communication, participation, and empathy and support.

18-4 **Explain Lewin's organizational change model.** Lewin's model, the idea of force field analysis, contends that a person's behavior is the product of two opposing forces; one force pushes toward preserving the status quo and the other force pushes for change. Lewin's change model is a three-step process: *unfreezing*—encouraging individuals to discard old behaviors, *moving*—new attitudes, values, and behaviors are substituted for old ones, and *refreezing*—new attitudes, values, and behaviors are established as the new status quo.

18-5 **Explain how companies determine the need to conduct an organization development intervention.** *Organization development (OD)* is a systematic approach to organizational improvement. The first step, the diagnosis, should pinpoint specific problems and areas in need of improvement. Six areas to examine carefully are the organization's purpose, structure, reward system, support systems, relationships, and leadership. A needs analysis then determines the skills and competencies that employees must have to achieve the goals of the change.

18-6 **Discuss the major group-focused techniques for organization development intervention.** Some OD intervention methods emphasize changing the organization itself or changing the work groups within the organization. Intervention methods in this category include survey feedback, management by objectives, product and service quality programs, team building, and process consultation. All the preceding OD methods focus on changing the organization or the work group.

18-7 **Discuss the major individual-focused techniques for organization development intervention.** Managers have a host of organization development techniques to facilitate organizational change. Development efforts include skills training, leadership training and development, executive coaching, role negotiation, job redesign, health promotion programs, and career planning. Success depends on techniques used, competence of the change agent, the organization's readiness for change, and top management commitment. Programs do not drive change; business needs do.

Key Terms

change agent The individual or group that undertakes the task of introducing and managing a change in an organization. (p. 389)

executive coaching A technique in which managers or executives are paired with a coach in a partnership to help them perform more efficiently. (p. 399)

incremental change Change of a relatively small scope, such as making small improvements. (p. 388)

leadership training and development A variety of techniques that are designed to enhance individuals' leadership skills. (p. 398)

moving The second step in Lewin's change model, in which new attitudes, values, and behaviors are substituted for old ones. (p. 394)

organization development (OD) A systematic approach to organizational improvement that applies behavioral science theory and research in order to increase individual and organizational well-being and effectiveness. (p. 394)

planned change Change resulting from a deliberate decision to alter the organization. (p. 383)

process consultation An OD method that helps managers and employees improve the processes that are used in organizations. (p. 397)

refreezing The final step in Lewin's change model, in which new attitudes, values, and behaviors are established as the new status quo. (p. 394)

role negotiation A technique whereby individuals meet and clarify their psychological contract. (p. 400)

skills training Increasing the job knowledge, skills, and abilities that are necessary to do a job effectively. (p. 398)

strategic change Change of a larger scale, such as organizational restructuring. (p. 388)

survey feedback A widely used intervention method whereby employee attitudes are solicited using a questionnaire. (p. 395)

team building An intervention designed to improve the effectiveness of a work group. (p. 396)

transformational change Change in which the organization moves to a radically different, and sometimes unknown, future state. (p. 388)

unfreezing The first step in Lewin's change model, in which individuals are encouraged to discard old behaviors by shaking up the equilibrium state that maintains the status quo. (p. 393)

unplanned change Change that is imposed on the organization and is often unforeseen. (p. 383)

Ethical Dilemma

Alpha Consulting is a firm that offers a variety of consulting services for other businesses. There are three consulting divisions at Alpha: financial, strategic, and human resources. The financial division has always been smaller than the other two and lately has had very few clients.

Sofia is the manager for the financial division. She just learned from top management that the financial division will be closing at the end of the current quarter. She also gets a mandate that no consultants should be notified yet and that all work for all existing clients must be completed before the end of the quarter as well.

Sofia feels terrible that her divisional employees will be losing their jobs. She especially feels badly that she is going to have to ask a lot of her consultants in the next few weeks to complete their work and then she will have to let them go.

How can Sofia ask her employees to hurry up just to work themselves out of a job? She understands this is a necessary change. The division has been losing clients for a while and soon will be a cost center for Alpha if something isn't done. But how can she be asked to do this without allowing the consultants to know what is going on? It just does not feel right.

1. Using consequential, rule-based, and character theories, evaluate Sofia's options.

2. What should Sofia do? Why?

Endnotes

1

1. H. Schwartz, "The Clockwork or the Snakepit: An Essay on the Meaning of Teaching Organizational Behavior," *Organizational Behavior Teaching Review* 11, No. 2 (1987): 19–26.

2. P. Schilpzand, I. E. Depater, and A. Erez, "Workplace Incivility: A Review of the Literature and Agenda for Future Research," *Journal of Organizational Behavior*, early view published Online October 28, 2014.

3. Rath and Strong Management Consultants, "Creating an Energized Organization," http://www.rathstrong.com/whitepaper_creatingenergized.htm, accessed June 27, 2008.

4. H. G. Barkem, J. A. C. Baum, and E. A. Mannix, "Management Challenges in a New Time," *Academy of Management Journal* 45 (2002): 916–930.

5. K. Lewin, "Field Theory in Social Science: Selected Theoretical Papers" (edited by Dorin Cartwright) (New York: Harper, 1951).

6. N. Schmitt, ed., Industrial/Organizational Section in *Encyclopedia of Psychology* (Washington, D.C.: American Psychological Association, and New York: Oxford University Press, 2000).

7. R. E. Poyhart, N. Schmitt, and N. T. Tippins, "Solving the Supreme Problem: 100 years of selection and recruitment at the Journal of Applied Psychology," *Journal of Applied Psychology*, 102 (2017): 291–304.

8. R. Lopopolo, "Development of the Professional Role Behaviors Survey (PROBES)," *Physical Therapy* 81 (July 2001): 1317–1327.

9. F. W. Taylor, *The Principles of Scientific Management* (New York: Norton, 1911).

10. E. A. Locke and G. P. Latham, *A Theory of Goal Setting and Task Performance* (Englewood Cliffs, N.J.: Prentice-Hall, 1990).

11. A. L. Wilkins and W. G. Ouchi, "Efficient Cultures: Exploring the Relationship between Culture and Organizational Performance," *Administrative Science Quarterly* 28 (1983): 468–481.

12. M. F. R. Kets de Vries and D. Miller, "Personality, Culture, and Organization," *Academy of Management Review* 11 (1986): 266–279.

13. H. Schwartz, *Narcissistic Process and Corporate Decay: The Theory of the Organizational Ideal* (New York: NYU Press, 1990).

14. J. G. March and H. A. Simon, *Organizations* (New York: Wiley, 1958).

15. H. B. Elkind, *Preventive Management: Mental Hygiene in Industry* (New York: B. C. Forbes, 1931).

16. J. C. Quick, "Occupational Health Psychology: Historical Roots and Future Directions," *Health Psychology* 18 (1999): 82–88.

17. R. Eby and D. Mahone, "How to Use Ergonomics as a Loss Control Tool," *Risk Management* (March 1, 1991).

18. "Workplace Initiative Reduces Headaches, Neck and Shoulder Pain," *Occupational Health and Safety* (June 10, 2008), http://www.ohsonline.com/articles/64148.

19. B. M. Staw, L. E. Sandelands, and J. E. Dutton, "Threat-Rigidity Effects in Organizational Behavior: A Multilevel Analysis," *Administrative Science Quarterly* 26 (1981): 501–524.

20. D. Kirkpatrick, "The Net Makes It All Easier—Including Exporting U.S. Jobs," *Fortune* (May 26, 2003): 146.

21. C. Crosby, "Quest for Talent Is Driving Evolution in Outsourcing," *Banking Wire* (June 25, 2008): 59.

22. E. V. Brown, Vice President of Global Business Development, Alberto Culver, Inc., "Commencement Address—College of Business Administration, the University of Texas at Arlington" (December 2003).

23. T. Reay, K. Golden-Biddle, and K. Germann, "Legitimizing a New Role: Small Wins and Microprocesses of Change," *Academy of Management Journal* 49 (2006): 977–998.

24. H. A. Haveman, N. Jia, J. Shi, and Y. Wang, "The Dynamics of Political Embeddedness in China," *Administrative Science Quarterly* 62 (2017): 67–104.

25. R. L. A. Sterba, "The Organization and Management of the Temple Corporations in Ancient Mesopotamia," *Academy of Management Review* 1 (1976): 16–26; S. P. Dorsey, *Early English Churches in America* (New York: Oxford University Press, 1952).

26. Sir I. Moncreiffe of That Ilk, *The Highland Clans: The Dynastic Origins, Chiefs, and Background of the Clans and of Some Other Families Connected to Highland History*, rev. ed. (New York: C. N. Potter, 1982); D. Shambaugh, "The Soldier and the State in China: The Political Work System in the People's Liberation Army," *Chinese Quarterly* 127 (1991): 527–568.

27. L. L' Abate, ed., *Handbook of Developmental Family Psychology and Psychopathology* (New York: Wiley, 1993); J. A. Hostetler, *Communitarian Societies* (New York: Holt, Rinehart & Winston, 1974).

28. J. M. Lewis, "The Family System and Physical Illness," in *No Single Thread: Psychological Health in Family Systems* (New York: Brunner/Mazel, 1976).

29. D. Katz and R. L. Kahn, *The Social Psychology of Organizations*, 2nd ed. (New York: John Wiley, 1978); H. J. Leavitt, "Applied Organizational Change in Industry: Structural, Technological, and Humanistic Approaches," in J. G. March, ed., *Handbook of Organizations* (Chicago: Rand McNally, 1965): 1144–1170.

30. J. D. Thompson, *Organizations in Action* (New York: McGraw-Hill, 1967).

31. M. Malone, "The Twitter Revolution," *The Wall Street Journal* (April 18, 2009): A11.

32. P. E. Queen, "Enlightened Shareholder Maximization: Is This Strategy Achievable?" *Journal of Business Ethics* 127 (2015): 683–694.

33. A. K. Schnackenberg and E. C. Tomlinson, "Organizational Transparency: A New Perspective on Managing Trust in Organization—Stakeholder Relationships," *Journal of Management*, 42, No. 7 (November 2016): 1753–1783.

34. F. J. Roethlisberger and W. J. Dickson, *Management and the Worker* (Cambridge, Mass.: Harvard University Press, 1939).

35. W. L. French and C. H. Bell, *Organization Development*, 4th ed. (Englewood Cliffs, N.J.: Prentice-Hall, 1990).

36. S. G. Barsade and D. E. Gibson, "Why Does Affect Matter in Organizations?" *Academy of Management Perspectives*, 21 (2007): 36–59.

37. J. P. Kotter, "Managing External Dependence," *Academy of Management Review* 4 (1979): 87–92.

38. H. K. Steensma and D. G. Corley, "Organizational Context as a Moderator of Theories on Firm Boundaries for Technology Sourcing," *Academy of Management Journal* 44 (2001): 271–291.

39. M. Yunus, F. Dalsace, D. Menasce, and B. Faivre-Tavignot, "Reaching the World's Poorest Consumers," *Harvard Business Review* 93 (March 2015): 46–53.

40. T. B. Lawrence and V. Corwin, "Being There: The Acceptance and Marginalization of Part-Time Professional Employees," *Journal of Organizational Behavior* 24 (2003): 923–943.

41. M. K. Gowing, J. D. Kraft, and J. C. Quick, *The New Organizational Reality: Downsizing, Restructuring and Revitalization* (Washington, D.C.: American Psychological Association, 1998); T. Tang and R. M. Fuller, "Corporate Downsizing: What Managers Can Do to Lessen the Negative Effects of Layoffs," *SAM Advanced Management Journal* 60 (1995): 12–15, 31.

42. L. E. Thurow, *Head to Head: The Coming Economic Battle among Japan, Europe, and America* (New York: William Morrow, 1992).

43. S. Ovide, "Microsoft CEO Nadella Hints at Organizational Changes; Chief Asks Top Staff to Simplify Operations; Defends Xbox Business," *Wall Street Journal* (July 10, 2014).

44. B. Dattée and J. Barlow, "Multilevel Organizational Adaptation: Scale Invariance in the Scottish Healthcare System," *Organizational Science*, 28, No. 2 (March–April 2017): 301–319.

45. D. Ciampa, *Total Quality* (Reading, Mass.: Addison-Wesley, 1992).

46. T. J. Douglas and W. Q. Judge Jr., "Total Quality Management Implementation and Competitive Advantage: The Role of Structural Control and Exploration," *Academy of Management Journal* 44 (2001): 158–169.

47. American Management Association, *Blueprints for Service Quality: The Federal Express Approach* (New York: American Management Association, 1991); P. R. Thomas, L. J. Gallace, and K. R. Martin, *Quality Alone Is Not Enough* (New York: American Management Association, 1992).

48. J. de Mast, "A Methodological Comparison of Three Strategies for Quality Improvement," *International Journal of Quality & Reliability Management* 21 (2004): 198–213.

49. M. Barney, "Motorola's Second Generation," *Six Sigma Forum Magazine* 1, No. 3 (May 2002): 13.

50. S. Shahabudin, "Six Sigma: Issues and Problems," *International Journal of Productivity and Quality Management* 3 (2008): 145–160.

51. J. A. Edosomwan, "Six Commandments to Empower Employees for Quality Improvement," *Industrial Engineering* 24 (1992): 14–15.

52. N. T. Duarte, J. R. Goodson, and T. P. Dougherty, "Managing Innovation in Hospitals and Health Systems: Lessons from the Malcolm Baldrige National Quality Award Winners," *Journal of Healthcare Management* 7 (2014): 21–34.

53. See also the five articles in the Special Research Forum on Teaching Effectiveness in the Organizational Sciences, *The Academy of Management Journal* 40 (1997): 1265–1398.

54. L. Proserpio and D. A. Gioia, "Teaching the Virtual Generation," *Academy of Management Learning & Education* 6 (2007): 69–80.

55. L. W. Porter, G. A. Bigley, and R. M. Steers. *Motivation and Work Behavior*, 7th ed. (Burr Ridge, IL: Irwin/McGraw-Hill, 2003).

56. C. L. Cooper and J. C. Quick, *The Handbook of Stress and Health: A Guide to Research and Practice* (Chichester, UK: Wiley Blackwell, 2017).

57. D. L. Whetzel, "The Department of Labor Identifies Workplace Skills," *Industrial/Organizational Psychologist* 29 (1991): 89–90.

58. D. A. Whetton and K. S. Cameron, *Developing Management Skills*, 3rd ed. (New York: HarperCollins, 1995).

59. E. R. Kemery and L. T. Stickney, "A Multifaced Approach to Teamwork Assessment in an Undergraduate Business Program," *Journal of Management Education* 38 (2014): 462–479.

60. C. Argyris and D. A. Schon, *Organizational Learning: A Theory of Action Perspective* (Reading, Mass.: Addison-Wesley, 1978).

61. A. Y. Kolb and D. A. Kolb, "Learning Styles and Learning Spaces: Enhancing Experiential Learning in Higher Education," *Academy of Management Learning & Education* 4 (2005): 193–212.

2

1. M. A. Hitt, R. D. Ireland, and R. E. Hoskisson, *Strategic Management: Competitiveness & Globalization—Concepts and Cases, 13e* (Mason, OH: Cengage Learning, 2020).

2. H. G. Barkem, J. A. C. Baum, and E. A. Mannix, "Management Challenges in a New Time," *Academy of Management Journal* 45 (2002): 916–930.

3. J. Hilsenrath and A. Debarros, "Globalization Isn't Dead. But a Shake-Up Is Building," *The Wall Street Journal* (January 17, 2023): R1, R7; "Free Exchange: The Case for Optimism. Globalization Seems in Bad Shape," *The Economist* (February 18–24): 70.

4. A. Vonnegut, *Inside the Global Economy: A Practical Guide* (Lanham, MD: Rowman & Littlefield, 2018).

5. M. P. Bell and J. Leopold, *Diversity in Organizations, Fourth Edition* (Mason, OH: Cengage Learning, 2022).

6. J. C. Quick and J. L. Goolsby, "Integrity First: Ethics for Leaders and Followers," *Organizational Dynamics* 42 (2013): 1–7.

7. K. Sera, "Corporate Globalization: A New Trend," *Academy of Management Executive* 6 (1992): 89–96.

8. K. Ohmae, *Borderless World: Power and Strategies in the Interlinked Economy* (New York: Harper & Row, 1990).

9. C. A. Bartlett and S. Ghoshal, *Managing across Borders: The Transnational Solution* (Boston: Harvard Business School Press, 1989).

10. F. Warner, "Learning How to Speak to Gen Y," *Fast Company* 72 (July 2003): 36–37.

11. K. R. Xin and J. L. Pearce, "Guanxi: Connections as Substitutes for Formal Institutional Support," *Academy of Management Journal* 39 (1996): 1641–1658.

12. P. S. Chan, "Franchise Management in East Asia," *Academy of Management Executive* 4 (1990): 75–85.

13. H. Weihrich, "Europe 1992: What the Future May Hold," *Academy of Management Executive* 4 (1990): 7–18.

14. B. Schneider, V. Gonzalez-Roma, C. Ostroff, and M. A. West, "Organizational Climate and Culture: Reflection on the History of the Constructs in the *Journal of Applied Psychology*," *Journal of Applied Psychology* 102, No. 3 (2017): 468–482.

15. E. H. Schein, "Coming to a New Awareness of Organizational Culture," *MIT Sloan Management Review* 25 (1984): 3–16.

16. S. S. Sarwano and R. M. Armstrong, "Microcultural Differences and Perceived Ethical Problems: An International Business Perspective," *Journal of Business Ethics* 30 (2001): 41–56.

17. F. Warner, "Learning How to Speak to Gen Y," *Fast Company* 72 (July 2003): 36–37.

18. R. Sharpe, "Hi-Tech Taboos," *The Wall Street Journal* (October 31, 1995): A1.

19. G. Hofstede, *Culture's Consequences: International Differences in Work-Related Values* (Beverly Hills, Calif.: Sage Publications, 1980); G. Hofstede, "Motivation, Leadership, and Organization: Do American Theories Apply Abroad?" *Organizational Dynamics* (Summer 1980): 42–63.

20. G. M. Spreitzer, M. W. McCall, Jr., and J. D. Mahoney, "Early Identification of International Executive Potential," *Journal of Applied Psychology* 82 (1997): 6–29.

21. M. A. Hitt, L. Bierman, K. Uhlenbruck, and K. Shimizu, "The Importance of Resources in the Internationalization of Professional Service Firms: The Good, the Bad, and the Ugly," *Academy of Management Journal* 49 (2006): 1137–1157.

22. T. L. Quick, *The Global Nomad's Guide to University Transition, Second Edition* (London, UK: Summertime Publishing, 2022).

23. A. J. Michel, "Goodbyes Can Cost Plenty in Europe," *Fortune* (April 6, 1992): 16.

24. G. Hofstede, "Gender Stereotypes and Partner Preferences of Asian Women in Masculine and Feminine Countries," *Journal of Cross Cultural Psychology* 27 (1996): 533–546.

25. G. Hofstede, "Cultural Constraints in Management Theories," *Academy of Management Executive* 7 (1993): 81–94.

26. "IBM Offers Employees New 'Learning Accounts' and Global Training Programs," *InformationWeek* (July 26, 2007).

27. J. Sandberg, "Global-Market Woes Are More Personality Than Nationality," *The Wall Street Journal* (January 29, 2008).

28. M. P. Bell and J. Leopold, *Diversity in Organizations, 5ᵗʰ Edition* (Mason, OH: Cengage Learning, 2025).

29. American Psychological Association, *Publication Manual of the American Psychological Association, Seventh Edition* (Washington, DC: American Psychological Association, 2020).

30. APA, "Chapter 5: Bias-Free Language Guidelines," in *Publication Manual of the American Psychological Association, Seventh Edition*: (Washington, D.C.: American Psychological Association, 2020), pp. 131–149.

31. P. Gramm, R. Ekelund, and J. Early, *The Myth of American Inequality: How Government Biases Policy Debate* (Lanham, Boulder, New York, London: Rowman & Littlefield, 2022), p. 70.

32. S. Prasso, "Google Goes to India," *Fortune* (October 29, 2007).

33. "Women in the Labor Force: A Databook," http://www.bls.gov/opub/reports/cps/women-in-the-labor-force-a-databook-2014.pdf.

34. "Degrees Earned by Women," *Indicator* 27 (2008), http://nces.ed.gov/programs/coe/2008/section3/indicator27.asp.

35. Catalyst, *2007 Catalyst Census of Women Corporate Officers and Top Earners of the Fortune 500*, http://catalyst.org/publication/13/2007-catalyst-census-of-women-corporate-officers-and-top-earners-of-the-fortune-500.

36. National Association for Female Executives Names 2019, "Top 70 Companies for Executive Women" (Business Wire, A Berkshire Hathaway Company, March 5, 2019).

37. U.S. Department of Labor, BLS Report 1094 (September 2021), p. 1.

38. P. Gramm, R. Ekelund, and J. Early, *The Myth of American Inequality: How Government Biases Policy Debate* (Lanham, Boulder, New York, London: Rowman & Littlefield, 2022).

39. A. M. Morrison, R. P. White, E. Van Velsor, and the Center for Creative Leadership, *Breaking the Glass Ceiling: Can Women Reach the Top of America's Largest Corporations?* (Reading, Mass.: Addison-Wesley, 1987).

40. Catalyst, "Women on Corporate Boards" (New York: Catalyst, November 5, 2021).

41. R. Soares, H. Foust-Cummings, C. Francoeur, and R. Labelle, *Companies Behaving Responsibly: Gender Diversity on Boards* (New York: Catalyst, 2015).

42. D. L. Nelson and M. A Hitt, "Employed Women and Stress: Implications for Enhancing Women's Mental Health in the Workplace," in D. C. Quick, L. R. Murphy, and J. J. Hurrell, Jr., eds., *Stress and Well Being at Work* (Washington, D. C.: American Psychological Association, 1992), pp. 164–177.

43. M. Little, V. S. Major, A. S. Hinojosa, and D. L. Nelson, "Professional Image Maintenance: How Women Navigate Pregnancy in the Workplace," *Academy of Management Journal* 58 (2015): 8–37.

44. A Conversation with Indra Nooyi, The Maverick Speaker Series, The University of Texas at Arlington (March 21, 2023).

45. L. L. Martins and C. K. Parsons, "Effects of Gender Diversity Management on Perceptions of Organizational Attractiveness: The Role of Individual Differences in Attitudes and Beliefs," *Journal of Applied Psychology* 92 (2007): 865–875.

46. A. Eyring and B. A. Stead, "Shattering the Glass Ceiling: Some Successful Corporate Practices," *Journal of Business Ethics* 17 (1998): 245–251.

47. Catalyst, *Advancing Women in Business: The Catalyst Guide* (San Francisco: Jossey-Bass, 1998).

48. Department of Health and Human Services, "2021 Profile of Older Americans," https://acl.gov/sites/default/files/Profile%20of%20OA/2021%20Profile%20of%20OA/2021ProfileOlderAmericans_508.pdf.

49. W. B. Johnston, "Global Workforce 2000: The New World Labor Market," *Harvard Business Review* 69 (1991): 115–127.

50. S. Needleman, "The Last Office Perk: Getting Paid to Volunteer," *The Wall Street Journal* (April 29, 2008): D1, D5.

51. J. Li, C. W. L. Chu, K. C. K. Lam, and S. Liao, "Age Diversity and Firm Performance in an Emerging Economy," *Human Resource Management* 50, No. 2 (March–April 2011): 247–270.

52. M. Y. Byrd and C. L. Scott, *Diversity in the Workforce: Current Issues and Emerging Trends*, Second *Edition* (New York: Routledge, 2018).

53. "Managing Generational Diversity," *HR Magazine* 36 (1991): 91–92.

54. K. Tyler, "The Tethered Generation," *HR Magazine* (May 2007): 41–46.

55. S. R. Dobrow, Y. Ganzac, and Y. K. Liu, "Time and Job Satisfaction: A Longitudinal Study of the Differential Roles of Age and Tenure," *Journal of Management* 44 (2018): 2558–2579, https://doi.org/10.1177/0149206315624962.

56. K. Harris, S. Krygsman, J. Waschenko, and D. L. Rudman, "Ageism and the Older Worker: A Scoping Review," *The Gerontologist* 58 (2018): e1–e14, https://doi.org/10.1093/geront/gnw194.

57. U.S. Bureau of the Census, *Population Profile of the United States, 1997* (Washington, D.C.: U.S. Government Printing Office, 1997).

58. W. J. Rothwell, "HRD and the Americans with Disabilities Act," *Training and Development Journal* 45 (August 1991): 45–47.

59. J. J. Laabs, "The Golden Arches Provide Golden Opportunities," *Personnel Journal* (July 1991): 52–57.

60. APA, "Chapter 5: Bias-Free Language Guidelines," *Publication Manual of the American Psychological Association, Seventh Edition* (Washington, D.C.: American Psychological Association, 2020), pp. 131–149.

61. https://www.uwmedicine.org/practitioner-resource/lgbtq/lgbtq-inclusion-glossary.

62. *Bostock v. Clayton County*, 590 U.S. ___ (2020), decided by a 6-3 vote of the court.

63. A. N. Smith and S. V. Simms, "The Impact of Discrimination on Organizations," in A. J. Colella and E. B. King, eds., *Oxford Handbook of Workplace Discrimination* (New York: Oxford University Press, 2018).

64. L. Armstrong, "What Men Say behind Closed Doors," *Working Mother* (June–July 2008): 87–90.

65. J. E. Rigdon, "PepsiCo's KFC Scouts for Blacks and Women for Its Top Echelons," *The Wall Street Journal* (November 13, 1991): A1.

66. P. A. Galagan, "Tapping the Power of a Diverse Workforce," *Training and Development Journal* 26 (1991): 38–44.

67. C. L. Holladay, J. L. Knight, D. L. Paige, and M. A. Quinones, "The Influence of Framing on Attitudes toward Diversity Training," *Human Resource Development Quarterly* 14 (2003): 245–263.

68. R. Thomas, "From Affirmative Action to Affirming Diversity," *Harvard Business Review* 68 (1990): 107–117.

69. T. H. Cox, Jr., *Cultural Diversity in Organizations: Theory, Research and Practice* (San Francisco: Berrett-Koehler, 1994).

70. J. H. Gavin, J. C. Quick, C. L. Cooper, and J. D. Quick, "A Spirit of Personal Integrity: The Role of Character in Executive Health," *Organizational Dynamics* 32, No. 2: 165–179, https://doi.org/10.1016/S0090-2616(03)00016-0.

71. M. R. Fusilier, C. D. Aby, Jr., J. K. Worley, and S. Elliott, "Perceived Seriousness of Business Ethics Issues," *Business and Professional Ethics Journal* 15 (1996): 67–78.

72. L. Huang and T. A. Paterson, "Group Ethical Voice: Influence of Ethical Leadership and Impact on Ethical Performance," *Journal of Management* 43, No. 4 (April 2017): 1157–1184.

73. R. C. Solomon, "Corporate Roles, Personal Virtues: Aristotelean Approach to Business Ethics," *Business Ethics Quarterly* 2 (1992): 317–339; R. C. Solomon, *A Better Way to Think about Business: How Personal Integrity Leads to Corporate Success* (New York: Oxford University Press, 1999).

74. J. L. Goolsby, D. A. Mack, and J. C. Quick, "Winning by Staying in Bounds: Good Outcomes from Positive Ethics," *Organizational Dynamics* 39 (2010): 248–257.

75. M. Kouchaki and S. D. Desai, "Anxious, Threatened, and Also Unethical: How Anxiety Makes Individuals Feel Threatened and Commit Unethical Acts," *Journal of Applied Psychology* 100 (2015): 360–375.

76. C. Fried, *Right and Wrong* (Cambridge, Mass.: Harvard University Press, 1978).

77. I. Kant, *Groundwork of the Metaphysics of Morals*, trans. H. J. Paton (New York: Harper & Row, 1964).

78. J. S. Mill, Utilitarianism, Liberty, and Representative Government (London: Dent, 1910).

79. A. Smith, *An Inquiry into the Nature and Causes of the Wealth of Nations*: Vol. 10 Harvard Classics, ed. C. J. Bullock (New York: P. F. Collier & Son, 1909).

80. A. Smith, *The Theory of Moral Sentiments* (Scotland: Glasgow Edition, 1790).

81. C. Gregory, *Character Counts: Bringing the Rotary Four-Way Test to Life* (USA: Maestrowerks, 2017).

82. Rotary Club of Fort Worth, Rotary Minority-Owned Business Awards (RMBA): A Guide for Clubs. White Paper (2023).

83. J. W. Barfield, *Starting from Scratch: The Humble Beginnings of a Two Billion-Dollar Enterprise* (Bloomington, IN: WestBow Press, 2015).

84. W. Bulkeley, "Email Software Delves into Employees' Contacts," *The Wall Street Journal* (April 21, 2008): B9.

85. D. Kemp, "Employers and AIDS: Dealing with the Psychological and Emotional Issues of AIDS in the Workplace," *American Review of Public Administration* 25 (1995): 263–278.

86. J. J. Koch, "Wells Fargo's and IBM's HIV Policies Help Protect Employees' Rights," *Personnel Journal* (April 1990): 40–48.

87. J. C. Quick and M. A. McFadyen, "Sexual Harassment: Have We Made Any Progress?" *Journal of Occupational Health Psychology* 22, No. 3 (July 2017).

88. L. F. Fitzgerald, F. Drasgow, C. L. Hulin, M. J. Gelfand, and V. J. Magley, "Antecedents and Consequences of Sexual Harassment in Organizations: A Test of an Integrated Model," *Journal of Applied Psychology* 82 (1997): 578–589.

89. E. Felsenthal, "Rulings Open Way for Sex-Harass Cases," *The Wall Street Journal* (June 29, 1998): A10; S. J. Adler, "Lawyers Advise Concerns to Provide Precise Written Policy to Employees," *The Wall Street Journal* (October 9, 1991): B1.

90. K. T. Schneider, S. Swan, and L. F. Fitzgerald, "Job-Related and Psychological Effects of Sexual Harassment in the Workplace: Empirical Evidence from Two Organizations," *Journal of Applied Psychology* 82 (1997): 401–415.

91. A. M. O'Leary-Kelly, R. L. Paetzold, and R. W. Griffin, "Sexual Harassment as Aggressive Behavior: An Actor-Based Perspective," *Academy of Management Review* 25 (2000): 372–388.

92. L. M. Goldenhar, N. G. Swanson, J. J. Hurrell, Jr., A. Ruder, and J. Deddens, "Stressors and Adverse Outcomes for Female Construction Workers," *Journal of Occupational Health Psychology* 3 (1998): 19–32; C. S. Piotrkowski, "Gender Harassment, Job Satisfaction and Distress among Employed White and Minority Women," *Journal of Occupational Health Psychology* 3 (1998): 33–42.

93. K. Aquino, L. Sheppard, M. B. Watkins, J. O'Reilly, and A. Smith, "Social Sexual Behavior at Work," *Research in Organizational Behavior* 34 (2014): 217–236.

94. R. A. Posthuma, C. P. Maertz, Jr., and J. B. Dworkin, "Procedural Justice's Relationship with Turnover: Explaining Past Inconsistent Findings," *Journal of Organizational Behavior* 28 (2007): 381–398.

95. D. Fields, M. Pang, and C. Chio, "Distributive and Procedural Justice as Predictors of Employee Outcomes in Hong Kong," *Journal of Organizational Behavior* 21 (2000): 547–562.

96. H. L. Laframboise, "Vile Wretches and Public Heroes: The Ethics of Whistleblowing in Government," *Canadian Public Administration* (Spring 1991): 73–78.

97. E. J. Epstein, "Was Snowden's Heist a Foreign Espionage Operation," *Wall Street Journal* (May 10, 2014): A13.

98. L. J. Christensen, A. Mackey, and D. Whetton, "Taking Responsibility for Corporate Social Responsibility: The Role of Leaders in Creating, Implementing, Sustaining, or Avoiding Socially Responsible Firm Behaviors," *The Academy of Management Perspectives* 28 (2014): 164–178.

99. S. Covel, "Tours to Fair-Trade Farms Help Coffee Sellers Spread Word," *The Wall Street Journal* (March 11, 2008): B5.

100. D. B. Turban and D. W. Greening, "Corporate Social Performance and Organizational Attractiveness to Prospective Employees," *Academy of Management Journal* 40 (1996): 658–672.

101. R. Walker, "Sex vs. Ethics," *Fast Company* (June 2008): 74–78.

3

1. K. Lewin, "Formalization and Progress in Psychology," in D. Cartwright, ed., *Field Theory in Social Science* (New York: Harper, 1951).

2. N. S. Endler and D. Magnusson, "Toward an Interactional Psychology of Personality," *Psychological Bulletin* 83 (1976): 956–974.

3. R. Terborg, "Interactional Psychology and Research on Human Behavior in Organizations," *Academy of Management Review* 6 (1981): 561–576.

4. C. Spearman, "General Intelligence: Objectively Determined and Measured," *American Journal of Psychology* 15 (1904): 201–293.

5. F. L. Schmidt and J. Hunter, "General Mental Ability in the World of Work: Occupational Attainment and Job Performance," *Journal of Personality and Social Psychology* 86, No. 1 (2004): 162–173; C. Bertua, N. Anderson, and J. F Salgado, "The Predictive Validity of Cognitive Ability Tests: A UK Meta-Analysis," *Journal of Occupational and Organizational Psychology* 78 (2004): 387–409.

6. T. J. Bouchard, Jr., "Twins Reared Together and Apart: What They Tell Us about Human Diversity," in S. W. Fox, ed., *Individuality and Determinism* (New York: Plenum Press, 1984); R. D. Arvey, T. J. Bouchard, Jr., N. L. Segal, and L. M. Abraham, "Job Satisfaction: Environmental and Genetic Components," *Journal of Applied Psychology* 74 (1989): 235–248.

7. G. Allport, *Pattern and Growth in Personality* (New York: Holt, 1961).

8. R. B. Cattell, *Personality and Mood by Questionnaire* (San Francisco: Jossey-Bass, 1973).

9. J. M. Digman, "Personality Structure: Emergence of a Five-Factor Model," *Annual Review of Psychology* 41 (1990): 417–440.

10. T. A. Judge, J. J. Martocchio, and C. J. Thoresen, "Five-Factor Model of Personality and Employee Absence," *Journal of Applied Psychology* 82 (1997): 745–755.

11. H. J. Bernardin, D. K. Cooke, and P. Villanova, "Conscientiousness and Agreeableness as Predictors of Rating Leniency," *Journal of Applied Psychology* 85 (2000): 232–234.

12. K. A. Leger, S. T. Charles, N. A. Turiano, and D. M. Almeida, "Personality and Stressor-Related Affect," *Journal of Personality and Social Psychology* 111 (2016): 917–928.

13. T. A. Judge and R. Ilies, "Relationships of Personality to Performance Motivation: A Meta-Analytic Review," *Journal of Applied Psychology* 87 (2002): 797–807.

14. G. M. Hurtz and J. J. Donovan, "Personality and Job Performance: The Big Five Revisited," *Journal of Applied Psychology* 85 (2000): 869–879.

15. K. A. Byrne, C. D. Silasi-Mansat, and D. A. Worthy. "Who Chokes under Pressure? The Big Five Personality Traits and Decision-Making Pressure," *Personality and Individual Differences* 74 (2015): 22–28.

16. J. Sun, B. Neufeld, P. Snelgrove, and S. Vazire, "Personality Evaluated: What Do People Most Like and Dislike about Themselves and Their Friends?" *Journal of Personality and Social Psychology* 122 (2022): 731–748.

17. J. F. Salgado, S. Moscoso, and M. Lado, "Evidence of Cross-Cultural Invariance of the Big Five Personality Dimensions in Work Settings," *European Journal of Personality* 17 (2003): S67–S76; C. Rodriguez and T. H. Church, "The Structure and Personality Correlates of Affect in Mexico: Evidence of Cross-Cultural Comparability Using the Spanish Language," *Journal of Cross-Cultural Psychology* 34 (2003): 211–230.

18. J. Eck and J. E. Gebauer, "A Sociocultural Norm Perspective on Big Five Prediction," *Journal of Personality and Social Psychology* 122 (2022): 554–575.

19. M. Moody, "Adaptive Behavior in Intercultural Environments: The Relationship between Cultural Intelligence Factors and Big Five Personality Traits" (Ph.D. thesis, George Washington University, 2007).

20. T. F. Bainbridge, S. G. Ludeke, and L. D. Smillie, "Evaluating the Big Five as an Organizing Framework for Commonly Used Psychological Trait Scales," *Journal of Personality and Social Psychology* 122 (2022): 749–777

21. M. R. Barrick and M. K. Mount, "The Big Five Personality Dimensions and Job Performance: A Meta-Analysis," *Personnel Psychology* 44 (1991): 1–26.

22. D. D. Clark and R. Hoyle, "A Theoretical Solution to the Problem of Personality-Situational Difference Interaction," *Personality and Individual Differences* 9 (1988): 133–138.

23. D. Byrne and L. J. Schulte, "Personality Dimensions as Predictors of Sexual Behavior," in J. Bancroft, ed., *Annual Review of Sexual Research*, vol. 1 (Philadelphia: Society for the Scientific Study of Sex, 1990).

24. P. Harms, B. Roberts, and D. Wood, "Who Shall Lead? An Integrative Personality Approach to the Study of the Antecedents of Status in Informal Social Organizations," *Journal of Research in Personality* 41 (2007): 689–699.

25. T. A. Judge, E. A. Locke, and C. C. Durham, "The Dispositional Causes of Job Satisfaction: A Core Self-Evaluation Approach," *Research in Organizational Behavior* 19 (1997): 151–188.

26. M. Erez and T. A. Judge, "Relationship of Core Self-Evaluations to Goal Setting, Motivation and Performance," *Journal of Applied Psychology* 86 (2001): 1270–1279; R. F. Piccolo, T. A. Judge, K. Takahashi, N. Watanabe, and E. A Locke, "Core Self-Evaluations in Japan: Relative Effects on Job Satisfaction, Life Satisfaction, and Happiness," *Journal of Organizational Behavior* 26, No. 8 (2005): 965–984.

27. J. B. Rotter, "Generalized Expectancies for Internal vs. External Control of Reinforcement," *Psychological Monographs* 80, No. 609 (1966).

28. S. Aryee, F. O. Walumbwa, R. Mondejar, and C. W. L. Chu, "Core Self-Evaluations and Employee Voice Behavior: Test of a Dual-Motivational Pathway," *Journal of Management* 43 (2017): 946–966.

29. T. A. Judge and J. E. Bono, "Relationship of Core Self-Evaluations Traits—Self-Esteem, Generalized Self-Efficacy, Locus of Control, and Emotional Stability—With Job Satisfaction and Job Performance: A Meta-Analysis," *Journal of Applied Psychology* 86 (2001): 80–92.

30. Ibid.

31. S. S. K. Lam and J. Shaubroeck, "The Role of Locus of Control in Reactions to Being Promoted and to Being Passed Over: A Quasi Experiment," *Academy of Management Journal* 43 (2000): 66–78.

32. G. Chen, S. M. Gully, J. Whiteman, and R. N. Kilcullen, "Examination of Relationships among Trait-Like Individual Differences, State-Like Individual Differences, and Learning Performance," *Journal of Applied Psychology* 85 (2000): 835–847; G. Chen, S. M. Gully, and D. Eden, "Validation of a New General Self-Efficacy Scale," *Organizational Research Methods* 4 (2001): 62–83.

33. A. Bandura, *Self-Efficacy: The Exercise of Control* (San Francisco: Freeman, 1997).

34. D. R. Avery, "Personality as a Predictor of the Value of Voice," *Journal of Psychology* 137 (2003): 435–447.

35. T. A. Judge and J. E. Bono, "Relationship of Core Self-Evaluations Traits—Self-Esteem, Generalized Self-Efficacy, Locus of Control, and Emotional Stability—With Job Satisfaction and Job Performance: A Meta-Analysis," *Journal of Applied Psychology* 86 (2001): 80–92.

36. B. W. Pelham and W. B. Swann, Jr., "From Self-Conceptions to Self-Worth: On the Sources and Structure of Global Self-Esteem," *Journal of Personality and Social Psychology* 57 (1989): 672–680.

37. A. H. Baumgardner, C. M. Kaufman, and P. E. Levy, "Regulating Affect Interpersonally: When Low Esteem Leads to Greater Enhancement," *Journal of Personality and Social Psychology* 56 (1989): 907–921.

38. J. Schimel, T. Pyszczynski, J. Arndt, and J. Greenberg, "Being Accepted for Who We Are: Evidence That Social Validation of the Intrinsic Self Reduces General Defensiveness," *Journal of Personality and Social Psychology* 80 (2001): 35–52.

39. P. Tharenou and P. Harker, "Moderating Influences of Self-Esteem on Relationships between Job Complexity, Performance, and Satisfaction," *Journal of Applied Psychology* 69 (1984): 623–632.

40. R. A. Ellis and M. S. Taylor, "Role of Self-Esteem within the Job Search Process," *Journal of Applied Psychology* 68 (1983): 632–640.

41. J. Brockner and T. Hess, "Self-Esteem and Task Performance in Quality Circles," *Academy of Management Journal* 29 (1986): 617–623.

42. B. R. Schlenker, M. F. Weingold, and J. R. Hallam, "Self-Serving Attributions in Social Context: Effects of Self-Esteem and Social Pressure," *Journal of Personality and Social Psychology* 57 (1990): 855–863.

43. M. K. Duffy, J. D. Shaw, and E. M. Stark, "Performance and Satisfaction in Conflicted Interdependent Groups: When and How Does Self-Esteem Make a Difference?" *Academy of Management Journal* 43 (2000): 772–782.

44. T. Mussweiler, S. Gabriel, and G. V. Bodenhausen, "Shifting Social Identities as a Strategy for Deflecting Threatening Social Comparisons," *Journal of Personality and Social Psychology* 79 (2000): 398–409.

45. M. Snyder and S. Gangestad, "On the Nature of Self-Monitoring: Matters of Assessment, Matters of Validity," *Journal of Psychology and Social Psychology* 51 (1986): 125–139.

46. G. Toegel, N. Anand, and M. Kilduff, "Emotion Helpers: The Role of High Positive Affectivity and High Self-Monitoring Managers," *Personnel Psychology* 60, No. 2 (2007): 337–365.

47. A. Mehra, M. Kilduff, and D. J. Brass, "The Social Networks of High and Low Self-Monitors: Implications for Workplace Performance," *Administrative Science Quarterly* 46 (2001): 121–146.

48. W. H. Turnley and M. C. Bolino, "Achieving Desired Images while Avoiding Undesired Images: Exploring the Role of Self-Monitoring in Impression Management," *Journal of Applied Psychology* 86 (2001): 351–360.

49. M. Kilduff and D. V. Day, "Do Chameleons Get Ahead? The Effects of Self-Monitoring on Managerial Careers," *Academy of Management Journal* 37 (1994): 1047–1060.

50. A. H. Church, "Managerial Self-Awareness in High-Performing Individuals in Organizations," *Journal of Applied Psychology* 82 (1997): 281–292.

51. C. Douglas and W. L. Gardner, "Transition to Self-Directed Work Teams: Implications of Transition Time and Self-Monitoring for Managers' Use of Influence Tactics," *Journal of Organizational Behavior* 25 (2004): 45–67.

52. J. M. LeBreton, L. K. Shiverdecker, and E. M. Grimaldi, "The Dark Triad and Workplace Behavior," *Annual Review of Organizational Psychology and Organizational Behavior* 5 (2018): 387–414.

53. K. G. Melchers, N. Roulin, and A. Buehl, "A Review of Applicant Faking in Selection Interviews," *International Journal of Selection and Assessment* 28 (2021): 123–142.

54. K. Landay, D. J. Beal, and P. E. Tesluk, "Shall We Serve the Dark Lords? A Meta-Analytic Review of Psychopathy and Leadership," *Journal of Applied Psychology* 104 (2018): 183–196.

55. A. H. B. DeHoogh, D. N. Den Hartog, and F. D. Belschak, "Showing One's True Colors: Leader Machiavellianism, Rules and Instrumental Climate, and Abusive Supervision," *Journal of Organizational Behavior* 42 (2021): 851–866.

56. C. R. Boddy, "Organizational Psychopaths: A Ten Year Update," *Management Decision* 53 (2015), accessed at https://doi/org/10.1108/MD-04-2015-0114.

57. B. D. McLarty, D. S. Whitman, D. H. Kluemper, and S. Tao, "An Identity and Reputation Approach to Understanding the Dark Triad in the Workplace," *Journal of Organizational Behavior* 43 (2022): 524–545.

58. J. M. Twenge, and W. K. Campbell, *The Narcissism Epidemic: Living in the Age of Entitlement* (New York: Atria Books, 2009).

59. M. Kowalchyk, H. Palmieri, and E. Conte, "Narcissism through the Lens of Performative Self-Evaluation," *Personality and Individual Differences* 177 (2021), accessed at https://doi.org/10.1016/j.paid.2021.110780.

60. H. Rorschach, *Psychodiagnostics* (Bern: Hans Huber, 1921).

61. C. G. Jung, *Psychological Types* (New York: Harcourt & Brace, 1923).

62. Consulting Psychologists Press, http://www.cpp.com/products/mbti/index.asp, accessed June 30, 2008.

63. O. Kroeger and J. M. Thuesen, *Type Talk* (New York: Delacorte Press, 1988).

64. S. Hirsch and J. Kummerow, *Life Types* (New York: Warner Books, 1989).

65. I. B. Myers and M. H. McCaulley, *Manual: A Guide to the Development and Use of the Myers-Briggs Type Indicator* (Palo Alto, Calif.: Consulting Psychologists Press, 1990).

66. G. P. Macdaid, M. H. McCaulley, and R. I. Kainz, *Myers-Briggs Type Indicator: Atlas of Type Tables* (Gainesville, Fla.: Center for Application of Psychological Type, 1987).

67. J. B. Murray, "Review of Research on the Myers-Briggs Type Indicator," *Perceptual and Motor Skills* 70 (1990): 1187–1202; J. G. Carlson, "Recent Assessment of the Myers-Briggs Type Indicator," *Journal of Personality Assessment* 49 (1985): 356–365.

68. A. Thomas, M. Benne, M. Marr, E. Thomas, and R. Hume, "The Evidence Remains Stable: The MBTI Predicts Attraction and Attrition in an Engineering Program," *Journal of Psychological Type* 55 (2000): 35–42.

69. https://www.themyersbriggs.com.

70. D. P. Blevins, M. R. D. Stackhouse, and S. D. Dionne, "Righting the Balance: Understanding Introverts (and Extraverts) in the Workplace," *International Journal of Management Reviews* 24 (2021), accessed at https://onlinelibrary.wiley.com/doi/epdf/10.1111/ijmr.12268.

71. E. C. Webster, *The Employment Interview: A Social Judgment Process* (Schomberg, Canada: SIP, 1982).

72. L. M. Little, V. S. Major, A. S. Hinojosa, and D. L. Nelson, "Professional Image Maintenance: How Women Navigate Pregnancy in the Workplace," *Academy of Management Journal* 58 (2015): 8–37.

73. N. Adler, *International Dimensions of Organizational Behavior*, 2nd ed. (Boston: PWS-Kent, 1991).

74. L. R. Offerman and M. K. Gowing, "Personnel Selection in the Future: The Impact of Changing Demographics and the Nature of Work," in Schmitt, Borman & Associates, eds., *Personnel Selection in Organizations* (San Francisco: Jossey-Bass, 1993).

75. H. G. Halvorson, "Managing Yourself: A Second Chance to Make the Right Impression," *Harvard Business Review* 98 (2015, January–February): 108–111.

76. J. Park and M. R. Banaji, "Mood and Heuristics: The Influence of Happy and Sad States on Sensitivity and Bias in Stereotyping," *Journal of Personality and Social Psychology* 78 (2000): 1005–1023.

77. M. W. Levine and J. M. Shefner, *Fundamentals of Sensation and Perception* (Reading, Mass.: Addison-Wesley, 1981).

78. R. L. Dipboye, H. L. Fromkin, and K. Willback, "Relative Importance of Applicant Sex, Attractiveness, and Scholastic Standing in Evaluations of Job Applicant Resumes," *Journal of Applied Psychology* 60 (1975): 39–43; I. H. Frieze, J. E. Olson, and J. Russell, "Attractiveness and Income for Men and Women in Management," *Journal of Applied Social Psychology* 21 (1991): 1039–1057.

79. P. Ekman and W. Friesen, *Unmasking the Face* (Englewood Cliffs, N.J.: Prentice-Hall, 1975).

80. J. E. Rehfeld, "What Working for a Japanese Company Taught Me," *Harvard Business Review* 68 (November–December 1990): 167–176.

81. M. W. Morris and R. P. Larrick, "When One Cause Casts Doubt on Another: A Normative Analysis of Discounting in Causal Attribution," *Psychological Review* 102 (1995): 331–355.

82. G. B. Sechrist and C. Stangor, "Perceived Consensus Influences Intergroup Behavior and Stereotype Accessibility," *Journal of Personality and Psychology* 80 (2001): 645–654; A. Lyons and Y. Kashima, "How Are Stereotypes Maintained through Communication? The Influence of Stereotype Sharedness," *Journal of Personality and Social Psychology* 85 (2003): 989–1005.

83. S. P. King and F. B. Bryant, "The Workplace Intergenerational Climate Scale (WICS): A Self-Report Instrument Measuring Ageism in the Workplace," *Journal of Organizational Behavior* 38 (2017): 124–151.

84. A. Feingold, "Gender Differences in Effects of Physical Attractiveness on Romantic Attraction: A Comparison across Five Research Paradigms," *Journal of Personality and Social Psychology* 59 (1990): 981–993.

85. M. Snyder, "When Belief Creates Reality," *Advances in Experimental Social Psychology* 18 (1984): 247–305.

86. L. Praslova, "Neurodivergent People Make Great Leaders, Not Just Employees," *Fast Company*, December 15 (2021), accessed at https://www.fastcompany.com/90706149/neurodivergent-people-make-great-leaders-not-just-employees?utm_source=newsletters.

87. D. Motro and A. P. J. Ellis, "Boys, Don't Cry: Gender and Reactions to Negative Performance Feedback," *Journal of Applied Psychology* 102 (2017): 227–235.

88. L. Bian, S. Leslie, and A. Cimpian, "Gender Stereotypes about Intellectual Ability Emerge Early and Influence Children's Interests," *Science* 355 (2017): 389–391.

89. K. Tai, K. Lee, T. D. Johnson, W. Wang, M. K. Duffy, and S. Kim, "Gender, Bottom-Line Mentality, and Workplace Mistreatment: The Roles of Gender Norm Violation and Team Gender Composition," *Journal of Applied Psychology* 107 (2022): 854–865.

90. J. K. Kim, C. M. Harold, and B. C. Holtz, "Evaluations of Abusive Supervisors: The Moderating Role of the Abuser's Gender," *Journal of Organizational Behavior* 43 (2022): 465–482. accessed at https://doi.org/10.1002/job.2581.

91. K. Howansky, L. S. Wilton, D. M. Young, S. Abrams, and R. Clapham, "(Trans)Gender Stereotypes and the Self: Content and Consequences of Gender Identity Stereotypes," *Self and Identity* 20 (2021), accessed at https://www.tandfonline.com/doi/full/10.1080/15298868.2019.1617191.

92. C. H. Thoroughgood, K. B. Sawyer, and J. R. Webster, "Finding Calm in the Storm: A Daily Investigation of How Trait Mindfulness Buffers against Paranoid Cognition and Emotional Exhaustion Following Perceived Discrimination at Work," *Organizational Behavior and Human Decision Processes* 159 (2020): 49–63.

93. B. W. Swider, T. B. Harris, and Q. Gong, "First Impression Effects in Organizational Psychology," *Journal of Applied Psychology* 107 (2022): 346–369.

94. T. DeGroot and S. Motowidlo, "Why Visual and Vocal Cues Can Affect Interviewers' Judgments and Predict Job Performance," *Journal of Applied Psychology* 84 (1999): 986–993; M. C. L. Greene and L. Mathieson, *The Voice and Its Disorders* (London: Whurr, 1989).

95. R. L. Gross and S. E. Brodt, "How Assumptions of Consensus Undermine Decision Making," *MIT Sloan Management Review* 42 (Winter 2001): 86–94

96. R. Rosenthal and L. Jacobson, *Pygmalion in the Classroom: Teacher Expectations and Pupils' Intellectual Development* (New York: Holt, Rinehart & Winston, 1968).

97. D. Eden, "Pygmalion without Interpersonal Contrast Effects: Whole Groups Gain from Raising Manager Expectations," *Journal of Applied Psychology* 75 (1990): 394–398.

98. N. Chawla, A. S. Gabriel, C. C. Rosen, J. B. Evans, J. Koopman, W. A. Hochwarter, J. C. Palmer, and Jordan, S. L. "A Person-Centered View of Impression Management, Inauthenticity, and Employee Behavior. *Personnel Psychology* 74 (2021), 657–691.

99. A. Colella and A. Varma, "The Impact of Subordinate Disability on Leader–Member Exchange Relationships," *Academy of Management Journal* 44 (2001): 304–315.

100. D. H. M. Chng, M. S. Rodgers, E. Shih, and X. Song, "Leaders' Impression Management during Organizational Decline: The Roles of Publicity, Image Concerns, and Incentive Compensation," *The Leadership Quarterly*, published online January 2015.

101. S. Bozzolan, C. H. Cho, and G. Michelon, "Impression Management and Organizational Audiences: The Fiat Group Case," *Journal of Business Ethics* 126 (2015): 143–165.

102. R. A. Baron, "Impression Management by Applicants during Employment Interviews: The 'Too Much of a Good Thing' Effect," in R. W. Eder and G. R. Ferris, eds., *The Employment Interview: Theory, Research, and Practice* (Newbury Park, Calif.: Sage Publications, 1989).

103. F. Heider, *The Psychology of Interpersonal Relations* (New York: Wiley, 1958).

104. S. Graham and V. Folkes, *Attribution Theory: Applications to Achievement, Mental Health, and Interpersonal Conflict* (Hillsdale: L. Erlbaum and Associates, 1990).

105. P. D. Sweeney, K. Anderson, and S. Bailey, "Attributional Style in Depression: A Meta-Analytic Review," *Journal of Personality and Social Psychology* 51 (1986): 974–991.

106. P. Rosenthal, D. Guest, and R. Peccei, "Gender Differences in Managers' Causal Explanations for Their Work Performance," *Journal of Occupational and Organizational Psychology* 69 (1996): 145–151.

107. J. Silvester, "Spoken Attributions and Candidate Success in Graduate Recruitment Interviews," *Journal of Occupational and Organizational Psychology* 70 (1997): 61–71.

108. L. Ross, "The Intuitive Psychologist and His Shortcomings: Distortions in the Attribution Process," in L. Berkowitz, ed., *Advances in Experimental Social Psychology* (New York: Academic Press, 1977); M. O'Sullivan, "The Fundamental Attribution Error in Detecting Deception: The Boy-Who-Cried-Wolf Effect," *Personality & Social Psychology Bulletin* 29 (2003): 1316–1327.

109. D. T. Miller and M. Ross, "Self-Serving Biases in the Attribution of Causality: Fact or Fiction?" *Psychological Bulletin* 82 (1975): 313–325.

110. J. R. Schermerhorn, Jr., "Team Development for High-Performance Management," *Training and Development Journal* 40 (1986): 38–41.

111. D. Motro, J. B. Evans, A. P. Ellis, and L. Benson III, "Race and Reactions to Women's Expressions of Anger at Work: Examining the Effects of the 'Angry Black Woman' Stereotype," *Journal of Applied Psychology* 107 (2022), 142–152.

112. J. G. Miller, "Culture and the Development of Everyday Causal Explanation," *Journal of Personality and Social Psychology* 46 (1984): 961–978.

113. G. Si, S. Rethorst, and K. Willimczik, "Causal Attribution Perception in Sports Achievement: A Cross-Cultural Study on Attributional Concepts in Germany and China," *Journal of Cross-Cultural Psychology* 26 (1995): 537–553.

4

1. A. H. Eagly and S. Chaiken, *The Psychology of Attitudes* (Orlando, Fla.: Harcourt Brace Jovanovich, 1993).

2. M. Pounds, "Bring Positive Attitude to the Workplace Using Praise," in *South Florida Sun-Sentinel* (Fort Lauderdale, FL) (September 27, 2007), http://infotrac-college.thomsonlearning.com, accessed July 2, 2008.

3. M. J. Rosenberg, C. I. Hovland, W. J. McGuire, R. P. Abelson, and J. H. Brehm, *Attitude Organization and Change* (New Haven, Conn.: Yale University Press, 1960).

3a. H. M. Woznji, G. C. Banks, C. E. Whelpley, J. H. Batchelor, & F. A. Bosco, "Job attitudes: A meta-analytic review and an agenda for future research," *Journal of Organizational Behavior* 43 (2022): 946–964.

4. G. C. Banks, H. M. Woznji, & C. A. Mansfield, "Where is "behavior" in organizational behavior? A call for a revolution in leadership research and beyond. *The Leadership Quarterly* (2021).

5. L. Festinger, *A Theory of Cognitive Dissonance* (Evanston, Ill.: Row, Peterson, 1957).

6. B. E. Ashford, K. M. Rogers, M. G. Pratt, & C. Pradies, "Ambivalence in organizations: A multilevel approach," *Organization Science* 25 (2014): 1453–1478.

7. R. H. Fazio and M. P. Zanna, "On the Predictive Validity of Attitudes: The Roles of Direct Experience and Confidence," *Journal of Personality* 46 (1978): 228–243.

8. A. Tversky and D. Kahneman, "Judgment under Uncertainty: Heuristics and Biases," in D. Kahneman, P. Slovic, and A. Tversky, eds., *Judgment under Uncertainty* (New York: Cambridge University Press, 1982): 3–20.

9. A. Bandura, *Social Learning Theory* (Englewood Cliffs, N.J.: Prentice-Hall, 1977).

10. D. Vrontis, A. Makrides, M. Christofi, & A. Thrassou, "Social media influencer marketing: A systematic review, integrative framework and future research agenda," *International Journal of Consumer Studies*, 45 (2021): 617–644.

11. I. Ajzen and M. Fishbein, "Attitude–Behavior Relations: A Theoretical Analysis and Review of Empirical Research," *Psychological Bulletin* 84 (1977): 888–918.

12. B. T. Johnson and A. H. Eagly, "Effects of Involvement on Persuasion: A Meta-Analysis," *Psychological Bulletin* 106 (1989): 290–314.

13. K. G. DeBono and M. Snyder, "Acting on One's Attitudes: The Role of History of Choosing Situations," *Personality and Social Psychology Bulletin* 21 (1995): 629–636.

14. I. Ajzen and M. Fishbein, *Understanding Attitudes and Predicting Social Behavior* (Englewood Cliffs, N.J.: Prentice-Hall, 1980).

15. I. Ajzen, "From Intentions to Action: A Theory of Planned Behavior," in J. Kuhl and J. Beckmann, eds., *Action-Control: From Cognition to Behavior* (Heidelberg: Springer, 1985).

16. I. Ajzen, "The Theory of Planned Behavior," *Organizational Behavior and Human Decision Processes* 50 (1991): 1–33.

17. A. Sagie and M. Krausz, "What Aspects of the Job Have Most Effect on Nurses?" *Human Resource Management Journal* 13 (2003): 46–62.

18. J. Kettle, "Factors Affecting Job Satisfaction in the Registered Nurse," *Journal of Undergraduate Nursing Scholarship*, http://juns.nursing.arizona.edu/Default.htm, accessed July 1, 2008.

19. C. P. Parker, B. B. Baltes, S. A. Young, J. W. Huff, R. A. Altman, H. A. LaCost, and J. E. Roberts, "Relationships between Psychological Climate Perceptions and Work Outcomes: A Meta-Analytic Review," *Journal of Organizational Behavior* 24 (2003): 389–416.

20. E. A. Locke, "The Nature and Causes of Job Satisfaction," in M. Dunnette, ed., *Handbook of Industrial and Organizational Psychology* (Chicago: Rand McNally, 1976).

21. P. C. Smith, L. M. Kendall, and C. L. Hulin, *The Measurement of Satisfaction in Work and Retirement* (Skokie, Ill.: Rand McNally, 1969).

22. R. Ilies and T. A. Judge, "On the Heritability of Job Satisfaction: The Mediating Role of Personality," *Journal of Applied Psychology* 88 (2003): 750–759.

23. T. A. Judge, R. F. Piccolo, N. P. Podsakoff, J. C. Shaw, and B. Rich, "The Relationship between Pay and Job Satisfaction: A Meta-Analysis of the Literature," *Journal of Vocational Behavior* 77 (2010): 157–167.

24. D. J. Weiss, R. V. Davis, G. W. England, and L. H. Lofquist, *Manual for the Minnesota Satisfaction Questionnaire* (Minneapolis: Industrial Relations Center, University of Minnesota, 1967).

25. C. D. Fisher, "Why Do Lay People Believe that Satisfaction and Performance Are Correlated? Possible Sources of a Commonsense Theory," *Journal of Organizational Behavior* 24 (2003): 753–777.

26. Judge, T. A., Weiss, H. M., Kammeyer-Mueller, J. D., & Hulin, C. L. (2017). Job attitudes, job satisfaction, and job affect: A century of continuity and of change. *Journal of applied psychology*, 102(3), 356.

27. L. A. Bettencourt, K. P. Gwinner, and M. L. Meuter, "A Comparison of Attitude, Personality, and Knowledge Predictors of Service-Oriented Organizational Citizenship Behaviors," *Journal of Applied Psychology* 86 (2001): 29–41.

28. D. W. Organ, *Organizational Citizenship Behavior: The Good Soldier Syndrome* (Lexington, Mass.: Lexington Books, 1988).

29. P. M. Podsakoff, S. B. Mackenzie, and C. Hui, "Organizational Citizenship Behaviors and Managerial Evaluations of Employee Performance: A Review and Suggestions for Future Research," in G. Ferris, ed., *Research in Personnel and Human Resources Management* (Greenwich, Conn.: JAI Press, 1993): 1–40.

30. C. F. Lam, W. Wan, and C. J. Roussin, "Going the Extra Mile and Feeling Energized: An Enrichment Perspective of Organizational Citizenship Behaviors," *Journal of Applied Psychology* 101 (2016): 379–391.

31. W. H. Bommer, E. W. Miles, and S. L. Grover, "Does One Good Turn Deserve Another? Coworker Influences on Employee Citizenship," *Journal of Organizational Behavior* 24 (2003): 181–196.

32. J. P. Trougakos, D. J. Beal, B. H. Cheng, I. Hideg, and D. Zweig, "Too Drained to Help: A Resource Depletion Perspective on Daily Interpersonal Citizenship Behaviors," *Journal of Applied Psychology* 100 (2015): 227–236.

33. M. C. Bolino, H. Hsiung, J. Harvey, and J. A. LePine, "Well, I'm Tired of Tryin'! Organizational Citizenship Behavior and Citizen Fatigue," *Journal of Applied Psychology* 100 (2015): 56–74.

34. C. Ostroff, "The Relationship between Satisfaction, Attitudes and Performance: An Organizational Level Analysis," *Journal of Applied Psychology* 77 (1992): 963–974.

35. R. Griffin and T. Bateman, "Job Satisfaction and Organizational Commitment," in C. Cooper and I. Robertson, eds., *International Review of Industrial and Organizational Psychology* (New York: Wiley, 1986).

36. A. R. Wheeler, V. C. Gallagher, R. L. Brouer, and C. J. Sablynski, "When Person-Organization (Mis)Fit and (Dis)Satisfaction Lead to Turnover: The Moderating Role of Perceived Job Mobility," *Journal of Managerial Psychology* 22, No. 2 (2007): 203–219.

37. X. Huang and E. Van De Vliert, "Where Intrinsic Job Satisfaction Fails to Work: National Moderators of Intrinsic Motivation," *Journal of Organizational Behavior* 24 (2003): 133–250.

38. L. Sun, S. Aryee, and K. S. Law, "High-Performance Human Resource Practices, Citizenship Behavior, and Organizational Performance: A Relational Perspective," *Academy of Management Journal* 50 (2007): 558–577.

39. N. C. Carpenter and C. M. Berry, "Are Counterproductive Work Behavior and Withdrawal Empirically Distinct? A Meta-Analytic Investigation," *Journal of Management* 43 (2017): 834–863.

40. J. C. Palmer, M. Komarraju, M. Z. Carter, and S. J. Karau, "Angel on One Shoulder: Can Perceived Organizational Support Moderate the Relationship between the Dark Triad Traits and Counterproductive Work Behavior?" *Personality and Individual Differences* 110 (2017): 31–37.

41. N. C. Carpenter, D. S. Whitman, & R. Amrhein, "Unit-Level Counterproductive Work Behavior (CWB): A Conceptual Review and Quantitative Summary," *Journal of Management* Jul2021, Vol. 47 Issue 6: 1498–1527.

42. R. T. Mowday, L. W. Porter, and R. M. Steers, *Employee–Organization Linkages: The Psychology of Commitment* (New York: Academic Press, 1982).

43. N. Allen and J. Meyer, "Affective, Continuance, and Normative Commitment to the Organization: An Examination of Construct Validity," *Journal of Vocational Behavior* 49 (1996): 252–276.

44. J. P. Meyer, N. J. Allen, and C. A. Smith, "Commitment to Organizations and Occupations: Extension and Test of a Three-Component Model," *Journal of Applied Psychology* 78 (1993): 538–551.

45. J. P. Curry, D. S. Wakefield, J. L. Price, and C. W. Mueller, "On the Causal Ordering of Job Satisfaction and Organizational Commitment," *Academy of Management Journal* 29 (1986): 847–858; T. N. Bauer, T. Bodner, B. Erdogan, D. M. Truxillo, and J. S. Tucker, "Newcomer Adjustment during Organizational Socialization: A Meta-Analytic Review of Antecedents, Outcomes, and Methods," *Journal of Applied Psychology* 92 (2007): 707–721.

46. B. Benkhoff, "Ignoring Commitment Is Costly: New Approaches Establish the Missing Link between Commitment and Performance," *Human Relations* 50 (1997): 701–726; N. J. Allen and J. P. Meyer, "Affective, Continuance, and Normative Commitment to the Organization: An Examination of Construct Validity," *Journal of Vocational Behavior* 49 (1996): 252–276.

47. M. J. Somers, "Organizational Commitment, Turnover, and Absenteeism: An Examination of Direct and Interaction Effects," *Journal of Organizational Behavior* 16 (1995): 49–58; L. Lum, J. Kervin, K. Clark, F. Reid, and W. Sirola, "Explaining Nursing Turnover Intent: Job Satisfaction, Pay Satisfaction, or Organizational Commitment?" *Journal of Organizational Behavior* 19 (1998): 305–320.

48. F. Stinglhamber and C. Vandenberghe, "Organizations and Supervisors as Sources of Support and Targets of Commitment," *Journal of Organizational Behavior* 24 (2003): 251–270.

49. R. Eisenberger, S. Armeli, B. Rexwinkel, P. D. Lynch, and L. Rhoades, "Reciprocation of Perceived Organizational Support," *Journal of Applied Psychology* 86 (2001): 42–51; J. E. Finegan, "The Impact of Person and Organizational Values on Organizational Commitment," *Journal of Occupational and Organizational Psychology* 73 (2000): 149–169.

50. E. Snape and T. Redman, "Too Old or Too Young? The Impact of Perceived Age Discrimination," *Human Resource Management Journal* 13 (2003): 78–89.

51. A. McDonald, "Five Ways Managers can help Quiet Qutting," *Sloan Review*, https://sloanreview.mit.edu/article/five-ways-managers-can-help-prevent-quiet-quitting/, September 27th, 2022.

52. J. A. Conger, "The Necessary Art of Persuasion," *Harvard Business Review* 76 (1998): 84–96.

53. J. Cooper and R. T. Croyle, "Attitudes and Attitude Change," *Annual Review of Psychology* 35 (1984): 395–426.

54. B. Martin, D. Wentzel, and T. Tomczak, "Effects of Susceptibility to Normative Influence and Type of Testimonial on Attitudes toward Print Advertising," *Journal of Advertising* (Spring 2008), http://infotrac-college.thomsonlearning.com, accessed July 2, 2009.

55. D. M. Mackie and L. T. Worth, "Processing Deficits and the Mediation of Positive Affect in Persuasion," *Journal of Personality and Social Psychology* 57 (1989): 27–40.

56. J. W. Brehm, *Responses to Loss of Freedom: A Theory of Psychological Reactance* (New York: General Learning Press, 1972).

57. D. DeSteno, R. E. Petty, and D. D. Rucker, "Discrete Emotions and Persuasion: The Role of Emotion-Induced Expectancies," *Journal of Personality & Social Psychology* 86 (2004): 43–56.

58. R. Petty, D. T. Wegener, and L. R. Fabrigar, "Attitudes and Attitude Change," *Annual Review of Psychology* 48 (1997): 609–647.

59. P. Brinol and R. E. Petty, "Overt Head Movements and Persuasion: A Self-Validation Analysis," *Journal of Personality and Social Psychology* 84 (2003): 1123–1139.

60. W. Wood, "Attitude Change: Persuasion and Social Influence," *Annual Review of Psychology* 51 (2000): 539–570.

61. A. Ortony, G. L. Clore, and A. Collins, *The Cognitive Structure of Emotions* (Cambridge, England: Cambridge University Press, 1988).

62. R. S. Lazarus, *Emotion and Adaptation* (New York: Oxford University Press, 1991).

63. P. T. Van Katwyk, S. Fox, P. E. Spector, and E. K. Kelloway, "Using the Job-Related Affective Well-Being Scale to Investigate Affective Responses to Work Stressors," *Journal of Occupational Health Psychology* 52 (2000): 219–230.

64. E. Diener, S. Thapa, & L. Tay, "Positive Emotions at Work," *Annual Review of Organizational Psychology and Organizational Behavior*, 7 (2020): 451–477.

65. B. L. Fredrickson, "The Role of Positive Emotions in Positive Psychology: The Broaden-and-Build Theory of Positive Emotions," *American Psychologist* 56 (2001): 218–226.

66. S. S. Kaplan, J. C. Bradley, J. N. Luchman, and D. Haynes, "On the Role of Positive and Negative Affectivity in Job Performance: A Meta-Analytic Investigation," *Journal of Applied Psychology* 94 (2009): 162–178; B. Lawrence and S. L. Robinson, "Ain't Misbehavin: Workplace Deviance as Organizational Resistance," *Journal of Management* 33, No. 3 (2007): 378–394.

67. B. L. Fredrickson and C. Brannigan, "Positive Emotions," in G. Bonnano and T. Mayne, eds., *Emotions: Current Issues and Future Directions* (New York: Guilford Press, 2001): 123–152.

68. X. Hu and S. Kaplan, "Is 'Feeling Good' Good Enough? Differentiating Discrete Positive Emotions at Work," *Journal of Organizational Behavior* 36 (2015): 39–58.

69. D. Watson and L. A. Clark, "Affects Separable and Inseparable: On the Hierarchical Arrangement of Negative Affects," *Journal of Personality and Social Psychology* 62 (1992): 489–505.

70. A. M. Isen and R. A. Baron, "Positive Affect as a Factor in Organizational Behavior," *Research in Organizational Behavior* 13 (1991): 1–53; A. G. Miner and T. M. Glomb, "State Mood, Task Performance, and Behavior at Work: A Within-Persons Approach," *Organizational Behavior and Human Decision Processes* 112 (2010): 43–57.

71. S. G. Barsade, "The Ripple Effect: Emotional Contagion and Its Influence on Group Behavior," *Administrative Science Quarterly* 47 (2007): 644–675.

72. G. Kleef, & S. Côté, "The Social Effects of Emotions," *Annual Review of Psychology*, 73 (2021): 629–658.

73. J. E. Dutton, P. J. Frost, M. C. Worline, J. M. Lilius, and J. M. Kanov, "Leading in Times of Trauma," *Harvard Business Review* 80 (2002): 54–61.

74. T. A. Stewart, "The Highway of the Mind," *Harvard Business Review* 82 (2004): 116.

75. A. R. Ahmad, & H. R. Murad, "The Impact of Social Media on Panic During the COVID-19 Pandemic in Iraqi Kurdistan: Online Questionnaire Study," *J Med Internet Res*, 2020.

76. J. D. Mayer, P. Salovey, and D. R. Caruso, "Emotional Intelligence: Theory, Findings, and Implications," *Psychological Inquiry* 15 (2004): 197–215.

77. H. A. Elfenbein, S. G. Barsade, and N. Eisenkraft, "The Social Perception of Emotional Abilities: Expanding What We Know about Observer Ratings of Emotional Intelligence," *Emotion*, published online February 15, 2015.

78. A. R. Hochschild, *The Managed Heart: Commercialization of Human Feeling* (Berkeley: University of California Press, 1983).

79. A. A. Grandey, "When 'The Show Must Go On': Surface Acting and Deep Acting as Determinants of Emotional Exhaustion and Peer-Rated Service Delivery," *Academy of Management Journal* 46 (2003): 86–96; C. M. Brotherridge and A. A. Grandey, "Emotional Labor and Burnout: Comparing Two Perspectives of 'People Work'," *Journal of Vocational Behavior* 60 (2002): 17–39.

79a. D. Zapf, M. Kern, F. Tschan, D. Holman, & N. K. Semmer, "Emotion Work: A Work Psychology Perspective," *Annual Review of Organizational Psychology and Organizational Behavior*, 8 (2021): 139–172.

80. A. C. Troth, S. A. Lawrence, P. J. Jordan, & N. M. Ashkanasy, "Interpersonal Emotion Regulation in the Workplace: A Conceptual and Operational Review and Future Research Agenda." *International Journal of Management Reviews*, 20 (2017): 523–543.

81. L. M. Little, D.H. Kluemper, D.L. Nelson, & J. Gooty, "Development and validation of the interpersonal emotion management strategies (IEMS) scale," *Journal of Occupational and Organizational Psychology*, 85 (2012): 407–420.

81a. L. M. Little, J. Gooty, & M. Williams, "The role of leader emotion management strategies in leader member exchange and follower outcomes," *Leadership Quarterly*, 27 (2016): 85–97.

82. F. Navran, "Your Role in Shaping Ethics," *Executive Excellence* 9 (1992): 11–12.

83. K. Labich, "The New Crisis in Business Ethics," *Fortune* (April 20, 1992): 167–176.

84. L. S. Paine, *Value Shift: Why Companies Must Merge Social and Financial Imperatives to Achieve Superior Performance* (New York: McGraw-Hill, 2003).

85. D. B. Turban and D. M. Cable, "Firm Reputation and Applicant Pool Characteristics," *Journal of Organizational Behavior* 24 (2003): 733–751.

86. E. A. Lind, J. Greenberg, K. S. Scott, and T. D. Welchans, "The Winding Road from Employee to Complainant: Situational and Psychological Determinants of Wrongful-Termination Claims," *Administrative Science Quarterly* 45 (2000): 557–590.

87. "Stolen Birthrights; Australia's Aborigines," *The Economist* (US) (February 2, 2008), http://infotrac-college.thomsonlearning.com, accessed July 8, 2008; T. Johnston, "Australia Says 'Sorry' to Aborigines for Mistreatment," *The New York Times* (February 13, 2008), http://www.nytimes.com, accessed July 2, 2008.

88. Miriam Schulman, "Little Brother Is Watching You," Makkula Center for Applied Ethics, http://www.scu.edu/ethics/publications/iie/v9n2/brother.html, accessed July 1, 2008.

89. M. Oneal, P. Callahan, and E. Osnos, "Mattel Recalls 18 Million Toys," *Chicago Tribune* (August 15, 2007), http://www.chicagotribune.com/business/chi-toysaug15,0,7223810.story.

90. M. S. Baucus and D. A. Baucus, "Paying the Piper: An Empirical Examination of Longer-Term Financial Consequences of Illegal Corporate Behavior," *Academy of Management Journal* 40 (1997): 129–151.

91. J. O. Cherrington and D. J. Cherrington, "A Menu of Moral Issues: One Week in the Life of *The Wall Street Journal*," *Journal of Business Ethics* 11 (1992): 255–265.

92. B. L. Flannery and D. R. May, "Environmental Ethical Decision Making in the U.S. Metal-Finishing Industry," *Academy of Management Journal* 43 (2000): 642–662.

93. K. R. Andrews, "Ethics in Practice," *Harvard Business Review* (September–October 1989): 99–104.

94. M. T. Dasborough, S. T. Hannah, & W. Zhu, "The generation and function of moral emotions in teams: An integrative review," *Journal of Applied Psychology*, 105 (2020): 433–452.

94a. R. Greenbaum, J. Bonner, T. Gray, & M. Mawritz, "Moral emotions: A review and research agenda for management scholarship," *Journal of Organizational Behavior*, 41 (2019): 95–114.

95. M. Rokeach, *The Nature of Human Values* (New York: Free Press, 1973).

96. M. Rokeach and S. J. Ball-Rokeach, "Stability and Change in American Value Priorities, 1968–1981," *American Psychologist* 44 (1989): 775–784.

97. K. Parker & R. Igielnik, "On the Cusp of Adulthood and Facing an Uncertain Future: What We Know About Gen Z So Far," (2022).

98. S. P. Eisner, "Managing Generation Y," S.A.M. *Advanced Management Journal* 70, No. 4 (2005): 4–15.

99. M. Henderson and D. Thompson, *Values at Work: The Invisible Threads between People, Performance, and Profit* (Auckland, New Zealand: HarperBusiness, 2003).

100. E. C. Ravlin and B. M. Meglino, "Effects of Values on Perception and Decision Making: A Study of Alternative Work Values Measures," *Journal of Applied Psychology* 72 (1987): 666–673.

101. E. C. Ravlin and B. M. Meglino, "The Transitivity of Work Values: Hierarchical Preference Ordering of Socially Desirable Stimuli," *Organizational Behavior and Human Decision Processes* 44 (1989): 494–508.

102. B. M. Meglino, E. C. Ravlin, and C. L. Adkins, "A Work Values Approach to Corporate Culture: A Field Test of the Value Congruence Process and Its Relationship to Individual Outcomes," *Journal of Applied Psychology* 74 (1989): 424–432.

103. T. A. Judge and R. D. Bretz, Jr., "Effects of Work Values on Job Choice Decisions," *Journal of Applied Psychology* 77 (1992): 261–271.

104. R. H. Doktor, "Asian and American CEOs: A Comparative Study," *Organizational Dynamics* 18 (1990): 46–56.

105. R. L. Tung, "Handshakes across the Sea: Cross-Cultural Negotiating for Business Success," *Organizational Dynamics* (Winter 1991): 30–40.

106. C. Gomez, B. L. Kirkman, and D. L. Shapiro, "The Impact of Collectivism and In-Group/Out-Group Membership on the Evaluation Generosity of Team Members," *Academy of Management Journal* 43 (2000): 1097–1106; J. Zhou and J. J. Martocchio, "Chinese and American Managers' Compensation Award Decisions: A Comparative Policy-Capturing Study," *Personnel Psychology* 54 (2001): 115–145.

107. A. J. Ali and M. Amirshahi, "The Iranian Manager: Work Values and Orientations," *Journal of Business Ethics* 40 (2002): 133–143.

108. R. Neale and R. Mindel, "Rigging Up Multicultural Teamworking," *Personnel Management* (January 1992): 27–30.

109. J. B. Rotter, "Generalized Expectancies for Internal versus External Control of Reinforcement," *Psychological Monographs* 80 (1966): 1–28.

110. L. K. Trevino and S. A. Youngblood, "Bad Apples in Bad Barrels: A Causal Analysis of Ethical Decision-Making Behavior," *Journal of Applied Psychology* 75 (1990): 378–385.

111. H. M. Lefcourt, *Locus of Control: Current Trends in Theory and Research*, 2nd ed. (Hillsdale, N.J.: Erlbaum, 1982).

112. N. Machiavelli, *The Prince*, trans. George Bull (Middlesex, England: Penguin Books, 1961).

113. R. Christie and F. L. Geis, *Studies in Machiavellianism* (New York: Academic Press, 1970).

114. R. A. Giacalone and S. B. Knouse, "Justifying Wrongful Employee Behavior: The Role of Personality in Organizational Sabotage," *Journal of Business Ethics* 9 (1990): 55–61.

115. S. B. Knouse and R. A. Giacalone, "Ethical Decision Making in Business: Behavioral Issues and Concerns," *Journal of Business Ethics* 11 (1992): 369–377.

116. L. Kohlberg, "Stage and Sequence: The Cognitive Developmental Approach to Socialization," in D. A. Goslin, ed., *Handbook of Socialization Theory and Research* (Chicago: Rand McNally, 1969): 347–480.

117. C. I. Malinowski and C. P. Smith, "Moral Reasoning and Moral Conduct: An Investigation Prompted by Kohlberg's Theory," *Journal of Personality and Social Psychology* 49 (1985): 1016–1027; M. Brabeck, "Ethical Characteristics of Whistleblowers," *Journal of Research in Personality* 18 (1984): 41–53; W. Y. Penn and B. D. Collier, "Current Research in Moral Development as a Decision Support System," *Journal of Business Ethics* 4 (1985): 131–136; L. K. Trevino and S. A. Youngblood, "Bad Apples in Bad Barrels: A Causal Analysis of Ethical Decision-Making Behavior," *Journal of Applied Psychology* 75 (1990): 378–385.

118. C. Gilligan, *In a Different Voice: Psychological Theory and Women's Development* (Cambridge, Mass.: Harvard University Press, 1982).

119. S. Jaffee and J. S. Hyde, "Gender Differences in Moral Orientation: A Meta-Analysis," *Psychological Bulletin* 126 (2000): 703–726.

120. G. R. Franke, D. F. Crown, and D. F. Spake, "Gender Differences in Ethical Perceptions of Business Practices: A Social Role Theory Perspective," *Journal of Applied Psychology* 82 (1997): 920–934.

5

1. R. Kanfer, M. Frese, and R. E. Johnson, "Motivation Related to Work," *Journal of Applied Psychology* 102, No. 3 (March 2017): 338–355.

2. J. P. Campbell and R. D. Pritchard, "Motivation Theory in Industrial and Organizational Psychology," in M. D. Dunnette, ed., *Handbook of Industrial and Organizational Psychology* (Chicago: Rand McNally, 1976): 63–130.

3. M. Weber, *The Protestant Ethic and the Spirit of Capitalism* (London: Talcott Parson, tr., 1930).

4. S. Freud, *Civilization and Its Discontents*, trans. and ed. J. Strachey (New York: Norton, 1961).

5. J. C. Quick, A. McFadyen, and D. L. Nelson, 2014, "No Accident: Health, Well-Being, and Performance at Work." *Journal of Organizational Effectiveness: People & Performance* 1, No. 1 (2014): 98–119.

6. Y.-Q. Zhu, D. G. Gardner, and H.-G. Chen, "Relationships Between Work Team Climate, Individual Motivation, and Creativity," *Journal of Management*, 44 (2018): 2094–2115.

7. T. A. Judge, L. S. Simon, C. Hurst, and K. Kelley, "What I Experienced Yesterday Is Who I Am Today: Relationship of Work Motivations and Behaviors to Within-Individual Variation in the Five-Factor Model of Personality," *Journal of Applied Psychology* 99 (2014): 199–221.

8. A. Smith, *An Inquiry into the Nature and Causes of the Wealth of Nations*, Vol. 10 of *The Harvard Classics*, C. J. Bullock, ed. (New York: Collier, 1909).

9. J. Jennings, *Less Is More: How Great Companies Use Productivity as a Competitive Tool in Business* (New York: Portfolio, 2002).

10. F. W. Taylor, *The Principles of Scientific Management* (New York: Norton, 1911).

11. Hearings before Special Committee of the House of Representatives to Investigate the Taylor and Other Systems of Shop Management under Authority of House Resolution 90, Vol. 3, 1377–1508 contains Taylor's testimony before the committee from Thursday, January 25, through Tuesday, January 30, 1912.

12. J. Breal, "Secret Sauce," *Fast Company* 115 (May 2007): 61–63.

13. F. J. Roethlisberger, *Management and Morale* (Cambridge, Mass.: Harvard University Press, 1941).

14. L. Van Dyne and J. L. Pierce, "Psychological Ownership and Feelings of Possession: Three Field Studies Predicting Employee Attitudes and Organizational Citizenship Behavior," *Journal of Organizational Behavior* 25 (2004): 439–459.

15. A. H. Maslow, "A Theory of Human Motivation," *Psychological Review* 50 (1943): 370–396.

16. W. James, *The Principles of Psychology* (New York: H. Holt & Co., 1890; Cambridge, Mass.: Harvard University Press, 1983); J. Dewey, *Human Nature and Conduct: An Introduction to Social Psychology* (New York: Holt, 1922); S. Freud, *A General Introduction to Psychoanalysis: A Course of Twenty-Eight Lectures Delivered at the University of Vienna* (New York: Liveright, 1963); A. Adler, *Understanding Human Nature* (Greenwich, Conn.: Fawcett, 1927).

17. B. Litwiller, L. A. Snyder, W. D. Taylor, and L. M. Steele, "The Relationship Between Sleep and Work," *Journal of Applied Psychology*, 102, No. 4 (April 2017), 682–699.

18. N. K. Austin, "The Power of the Pyramid: The Foundation of Human Psychology and, Thereby, of Motivation, Maslow's Hierarchy Is One Powerful Pyramid," *Incentive* 176 (July 2002): 10.

19. D. M. McGregor, *The Human Side of Enterprise* (New York: McGraw-Hill, 1960).

20. D. M. McGregor, "The Human Side of Enterprise," *Management Review* (November 1957): 22–28, 88–92.

21. C. A. Fulmer and C. Ostroff, "Trust in Direct Leaders and Top Leaders: A Trickle-Up Model," *Journal of Applied Psychology*, 102, No. 4 (April 2017), 648–657.

22. Y. Berson, N. Halevy, B. Shamir, and M. Erez, "Leading from Different Psychological Distances: A Construal-Level Perspective on Vision Communication, Goal Setting, and Follower Motivation," *The Leadership Quarterly* 26 (2015): 143–155.

23. J. Boorstin, "No Preservatives. No Unions. Lots of Dough," *Fortune* 148 (September 15, 2003): 127–129.

24. C. P. Alderfer, *Human Needs in Organizational Settings* (New York: Free Press, 1972).

25. B. Schneider and C. P. Alderfer, "Three Studies of Need Satisfactions in Organizations," *Administrative Science Quarterly* 18 (1973): 489–505.

26. H. A. Murray, *Explorations in Personality: A Clinical and Experimental Study of Fifty Men of College Age* (New York: Oxford University Press, 1938).

27. D. C. McClelland, *Motivational Trends in Society* (Morristown, N.J.: General Learning Press, 1971).

28. D. C. McClelland, "Achievement Motivation Can Be Learned," *Harvard Business Review* 43 (1965): 6–24.

29. J. P. Chaplin and T. S. Krawiec, *Systems and Theories of Psychology* (New York: Holt, Rinehart & Winston, 1960); M. Stahl, *Managerial and Technical Motivation: Assessing Needs for Achievement, Power, and Affiliation* (Santa Barbara, CA: Praeger 1986).

30. J. S. Chun and J. N. Choi, "Members' Needs, Intragroup Conflict, and Group Performance," *Journal of Applied Psychology* 99 (2014): 437–450.

31. E. A. Ward, "Multidimensionality of Achievement Motivation among Employed Adults," *Journal of Social Psychology* 134 (1997): 542–544.

32. A. Sagie, D. Elizur, and H. Yamauchi, "The Structure and Strength of Achievement Motivation: A Cross-Cultural Comparison," *Journal of Organizational Behavior* 17 (1996): 431–444.

33. D. C. McClelland and D. Burnham, "Power Is the Great Motivator," *Harvard Business Review* 54 (1976): 100–111; J. Hall and J. Hawker, *Power Management Inventory* (The Woodlands, Tex.: Teleometrics International, 1988).

34. S. Schachter, *The Psychology of Affiliation* (Stanford, Calif.: Stanford University Press, 1959).

35. F. Herzberg, B. Mausner, and B. Snyderman, *The Motivation to Work* (New York: Wiley, 1959).

36. F. Herzberg, *Work and the Nature of Man* (Cleveland: World, 1966).

37. Y.-Q. Zhu, D. G. Gardner, and H.-G. Chen, "Relationships Between Work Team Climate, Individual Motivation, and Creativity," *Journal of Management*, 44 (2018): 2094–2115.

38. B. A. Scott, A. S. Garza, D. E. Conlon, and Y. J. Kim, "Why Do Managers Act Fairly in the First Place? A Daily Investigation of 'Hot' and 'Cold' Motives and Discretion," *Academy of Management Journal* 1015 (2015): 37–57.

39. G. van Houwelinger, M. van Dijke, and D. de Cremer, "Fairness Enactment as Response to Higher Level Unfairness," *Journal of Management*, 43, No. 2 (February 2017): 319–347.

40. J. I. Menges, D. V. Tussing, A. Wihler, and A. M. Grant, "When Job Performance Is All Relative: How Family Motivation Energizes Effort and Compensates for Intrinsic Motivation," *Academy of Management Journal*, 60 (April 2017): 695–719.

41. R. Griffin, "Organizational Behavior," *Oxford Annotated Bibliographies: Management* (2013): www.oxfordbibliographies.com.

42. D. L. Nelson and B. L. Simmons, "Health Psychology and Work Stress: A More Positive Approach," in J. C. Quick and L. E. Tetrick, eds., *Handbook of Occupational Health Psychology* (Washington, D.C.: American Psychological Association, 2003): 97–119.

43. K. S. Cameron, J. E. Dutton, and R. E. Quinn, eds., *Positive Organizational Scholarship: Foundations of a New Discipline* (San Francisco: Berrett-Koehler, 2003).

44. J. Loehr and T. Schwartz, "The Making of a Corporate Athlete," *Harvard Business Review* 79 (2001): 120–129.

45. J. Loehr and T. Schwartz, *The Power of Full Engagement: Managing Energy, Not Time, Is the Key to High Performance and Personal Renewal* (New York: Free Press, 2003).

46. G. Kholreiser, "Engaging Employees Crucial for Their Morale," *The Nation* (November 29, 2010), http://www.nationmultimedia.com/2010/11/29/business/Engaging-employees-crucial-for-their-morale-30143355.html, accessed May 12, 2011.

47. P. M. Blau, *Exchange and Power in Social Life* (New York: Wiley, 1964); N. Horster, *Principles of Exchange and Power: Integrating the Theory of Social Institutions and the Theory of Value* (New York: P. Lang, 1997).

48. A. Etzioni, "A Basis for Comparative Analysis of Complex Organizations," in A. Etzioni, ed., *A Sociological Reader on Complex Organizations*, 2nd ed. (New York: Holt, Rinehart & Winston, 1969): 59–76.

49. S. S. Masterson and C. L. Stamper, "Perceived Organizational Membership: An Aggregate Framework Representing the Employee–Organization Relationship," *Journal of Organizational Behavior* 24 (2003): 473–490.

50. L. J. Song, A. S. Tsui, and K. S. Long, "Unpacking Employee Responses to Organizational Exchange Mechanisms: The Role of Social and Economic Exchange Perceptions," *Journal of Management* 35 (2009): 56–93.

51. J. S. Adams, "Inequity in Social Exchange," in L. Berkowitz, ed., *Advances in Experimental Social Psychology*, Vol. 2 (New York: Academic Press, 1965): 267–299; J. S. Adams, "Toward an Understanding of Inequity," *Journal of Abnormal and Social Psychology* 67 (1963): 422–436.

52. J. Nelson-Horchler, "The Best Man for the Job Is a Man," *Industry Week* (January 7, 1991): 50–52.

53. P. E. Downes and D. Choi, "Employee Reactions to Pay Dispersion: A Typology of Existing Research," *Human Resource Management Review* 24 (2014): 53–66.

54. R. C. Huseman, J. D. Hatfield, and E. A. Miles, "A New Perspective on Equity Theory: The Equity Sensitivity Construct," *Academy of Management Review* 12 (1987): 222–234.

55. G. Lemmon and S. J. Wayne, "Underlying Motives of Organizational Citizenship Behavior: Comparing Egoistic and Altruistic Motivations," *Journal of Leadership & Organization Studies* 22 (2015): 129–148.

56. K. E. Weick, M. G. Bougon, and G. Maruyama, "The Equity Context," *Organizational Behavior and Human Performance* 15 (1976): 32–65.

57. R. C. Huseman, J. D. Hatfield, and E. W. Miles, "A New Perspective on Equity Theory: The Equity Sensitivity Construct," *The Academy of Management Review* 12 (1987): 222–234.

58. J. Greenberg, "Equity and Workplace Status: A Field Experiment," *Journal of Applied Psychology* 73 (1988): 606–613.

59. J. Greenberg, "Losing Sleep over Organizational Justice: Attenuating Insomniac Reactions to Underpayment Inequity with Supervisory Training in Interactional Justice," *Journal of Applied Psychology* 91 (2006): 58–69.

60. J. Greenberg and R. Alge, "Aggressive Reactions to Workplace Injustice," in R. W. Griffin, A. O'Leary-Kelly, and J. Collins, eds., *Dysfunctional Behavior in Organizations, Vol. 1: Violent Behaviors in Organizations* (Greenwich, CT: JAI, 1998): 119–145.

61. R. A. Cosier and D. R. Dalton, "Equity Theory and Time: A Reformulation," *Academy of Management Review* 8 (1983): 311–319.

62. J. E. Martin and M. W. Peterson, "Two-Tier Wage Structures: Implications for Equity Theory," *Academy of Management Journal* 30 (1987): 297–315.

63. R. J. Sanchez, D. M. Truxillo, and T. N. Bauer, "Development and Examination of an Expectancy-Based Measure of Test-Taking Motivation," *Journal of Applied Psychology* 85 (2000): 739–750.

64. V. H. Vroom, *Work and Motivation* (New York: Wiley, 1964/1970).

65. U. R. Larson, "Supervisor's Performance Feedback to Subordinates: The Effect of Performance Valence and Outcome Dependence," *Organizational Behavior and Human Decision Processes* 37 (1986): 391–409.

66. M. C. Kernan and R. G. Lord, "Effects of Valence, Expectancies, and Goal-Performance Discrepancies in Single and Multiple Goal Environments," *Journal of Applied Psychology* 75 (1990): 194–203.

67. R. J. Sanchez, D. M. Truxillo, and T. N. Bauer, "Development and Examination of an Expectancy-Based Measure of Test-Taking Motivation," *Journal of Applied Psychology* 85 (2000): 739–750.

68. W. VanEerde and H. Thierry, "Vroom's Expectancy Models and Work-Related Criteria: A Meta-Analysis," *Journal of Applied Psychology* 81 (1996): 575–586.

69. E. D. Pulakos and N. Schmitt, "A Longitudinal Study of a Valence Model Approach for the Prediction of Job Satisfaction of New Employees," *Journal of Applied Psychology* 68 (1983): 307–312; F. J. Landy and W. S. Becker, "Motivation Theory Reconsidered," in L. L. Cummings and B. M. Staw, eds., *Research in Organizational Behavior* 9 (Greenwich, Conn.: JAI Press, 1987): 1–38.

70. J. Gibbs, K. Basinger, and D. Fuller, *Moral Maturity: Measuring the Development of Sociomoral Reflection* (Hillsdale, NJ: L. Erlbaum, 1992).

71. N. J. Adler, *International Dimensions of Organizational Behavior*, 4th ed. (Mason, Ohio: South-Western, 2001).

72. D. E. Rupp, R. Shao, D. P. Skarlicki, E. L. Paddock, T. Kim, and T. Nadisic, "Corporate Social Responsibility and Employee Engagement: The Moderating Role of CSR-Specific Relative Autonomy and Individualism," *Journal of Organizational Behavior*, 39 (2018): 559–579.

73. G. Hofstede, "Motivation, Leadership, and Organization: Do American Theories Apply Abroad?" *Organizational Dynamics* 9 (1980): 42–63.

74. G. H. Hines, "Cross-Cultural Differences in Two-Factor Theory," *Journal of Applied Psychology* 58 (1981): 313–317.

75. M. C. Bolino and W. H. Turnley, "Old Faces, New Places: Equity Theory in Cross-Cultural Contexts," *Journal of Organizational Behavior* 29 (2008): 29–50; M. C. Bolino and W. H. Turnley, "Erratum: Old Faces, New Places: Equity Theory in Cross-Cultural Contexts," *Journal of Organizational Behavior* 29 (2008): i.

6

1. I. Goodfellow, Y. Bengio, and A. Courville, *Deep Learning* (Cambridge, MA: Massachusetts Institute of Technology, 2016).

2. B. Cannon, "Walter B. Cannon: Reflections on the Man and His Contributions," in *Centennial Session*, (Washington, D.C., American Psychological Association Centennial Convention, 1992).

3. B. F. Skinner, *The Behavior of Organisms: An Experimental Analysis* (New York: Appleton-Century-Crofts, 1938).

4. B. F. Skinner, *Science and Human Behavior* (New York: Free Press, 1953).

5. F. Luthans and R. Kreitner, *Organizational Behavior Modification and Beyond* (Glenview, Ill.: Scott, Foresman, 1985).

6. A. D. Stajkovic and F. Luthans, "A Meta-Analysis of the Effects of Organizational Behavior Modification on Task Performance, 1975–95," *Academy of Management Journal* 40 (1997): 1122–1149.

7. C. B. Cadsby, F. Song, and F. Tapon, "Sorting and Incentive Effects of Pay for Performance: An Experimental Investigation," *Academy of Management Journal* 50 (2007): 387–405.

8. K. K. Merriman, "Lost in Translation: Cultural Interpretations of Performance Pay," *Compensation and Benefits Review* 42 (2010): 403–410.

9. J. Hale, "Strategic Rewards: Keeping Your Best Talent from Walking Out the Door," *Compensation and Benefits Management* 14 (1998): 39–50.

10. B. F. Skinner, *Contingencies of Reinforcement: A Theoretical Analysis* (New York: Appleton-Century-Crofts, 1969).

11. J. P. Chaplin and T. S. Krawiec, *Systems and Theories of Psychology* (New York: Holt, Rinehart & Winston, 1960).

12. L. Bareket-Bojmel, G. Hochman, and D. Ariely, "It's (Not) All about the Jacksons: Testing Different Types of Short-Term Bonuses in the Field," *Journal of Management* (Advanced online publication May 27, 2014).

13. M. Maccoby, J. Hoffer Gittell, and M. Ledeen, "Leadership and the Fear Factor," *Sloan Management Review* 148 (Winter 2004): 14–18.

14. A. Bandura, *Social Learning Theory* (Englewood Cliffs, N.J.: Prentice-Hall, 1977); A. Bandura, "Self-Efficacy: Toward a Unifying Theory of Behavioral Change," *Psychological Review* 84 (1977): 191–215.

15. J. J. Martocchio and E. J. Hertenstein, "Learning Orientation and Goal Orientation Context: Relationships with Cognitive and Affective Learning Outcomes," *Human Resource Development Quarterly* 14 (2003): 413–434.

16. A. Bandura, "Regulation of Cognitive Processes through Perceived Self-Efficacy," *Developmental Psychology* (September 1989): 729–735.

17. J. M. Phillips and S. M. Gully, "Role of Goal Orientation, Ability, Need for Achievement, and Locus of Control in the Self-Efficacy and Goal-Setting Process," *Journal of Applied Psychology* 82 (1997): 792–802.

18. M. Tims, A. B. Bakker, and D. Derks, "Daily Job Crafting and the Self-Efficacy-Performance Relationship," *Journal of Managerial Psychology* 29 (2014): 490–507.

19. J. C. Weitlauf, R. E. Smith, and D. Cervone, "Generalization Effects of Coping-Skills Training: Influence of Self-Defense Training on Women's Efficacy Beliefs, Assertiveness, and Aggression," *Journal of Applied Psychology* 85 (2000): 625–633.

20. A. D. Stajkovic and F. Luthans, "Social Cognitive Theory and Self-Efficacy: Going beyond Traditional Motivational and Behavioral Approaches," *Organizational Dynamics* (Spring 1998): 62–74.

21. T. M. Amabile and S. J. Kramer, "The Power of Small Wins," *Harvard Business Review* 38, No. 5 (July 8, 2008): 70–80.

22. V. Gecas, "The Social Psychology of Self-Efficacy," *Annual Review of Sociology* 15 (1989): 291–316.

23. E. A. Locke and G. P. Latham, *A Theory of Goal Setting and Task Performance* (Englewood Cliffs, N.J.: Prentice-Hall, 1990).

24. A. D. Stajkovic, E. A. Locke, and E. S. Blair, "A First Examination of the Relationships between Primed Subconscious Goals, Assigned Conscious Goals, and Task Performance," *Journal of Applied Psychology* 91 (2006): 1172–1180.

25. T. O. Murray, *Management by Objectives: A Systems Approach to Management* (Fort Worth, Tex.: Western Company, n.d.).

26. W. T. Brooks and T. W. Mullins, *High Impact Time Management* (Englewood Cliffs, N.J.: Prentice-Hall, 1989).

27. E. A. Locke, "Toward a Theory of Task Motivation and Incentives," *Organizational Behavior and Human Performance* 3 (1968): 157–189.

28. J. C. Quick, "Dyadic Goal Setting within Organizations: Role Making and Motivational Considerations," *Academy of Management Review* 4 (1979): 369–380.

29. D. McGregor, "An Uneasy Look at Performance Appraisal," *Harvard Business Review* 35 (1957): 89–94.

30. J. R. Hollenbeck, C. R. Williams, and H. J. Klein, "An Empirical Examination of the Antecedents of Commitment to Difficult Goals," *Journal of Applied Psychology* 74 (1989): 18–23.

31. R. C. Rodgers and J. E. Hunter, "The Impact of Management by Objectives on Organizational Productivity," unpublished paper (Lexington: University of Kentucky, 1989).

32. E. A. Locke, K. N. Shaw, L. M. Saari, and G. P. Latham, "Goal Setting and Task Performance: 1969–1980," *Psychological Bulletin* 90 (1981): 125–152.

33. D. B. Fedora, W. D. Davis, J. M. Maslync, and K. Mathiesond, "Performance Improvement Efforts in Response to Negative Feedback: The Roles of Source Power and Recipient Self-Esteem," *Journal of Management* 27 (2001): 79–98.

34. J. C. Quick, "Dyadic Goal Setting and Role Stress," *Academy of Management Journal* 22 (1979): 241–252.

35. G. S. Odiorne, *Management by Objectives: A System of Managerial Leadership* (New York: Pitman, 1965).

36. American Management Association, *Blueprints for Service Quality: The Federal Express Approach* (New York: American Management Association, 1991).

37. P. F. Drucker, *The Practice of Management* (New York: Harper & Bros., 1954).

38. R. D. Prichard, P. L. Roth, S. D. Jones, P. J. Galgay, and M. D. Watson, "Designing a Goal-Setting System to Enhance Performance: A Practical Guide," *Organizational Dynamics* 17 (1988): 69–78.

39. C. L. Hughes, *Goal Setting: Key to Individual and Organizational Effectiveness* (New York: American Management Association, 1965).

40. M. E. Tubbs and S. E. Ekeberg, "The Role of Intentions in Work Motivation: Implications for Goal-Setting Theory and Research," *Academy of Management Review* 16 (1991): 180–199.

41. D. J. Schleicher, H. M. Baumann, D. W. Sullivan, and J. Yim, "Evaluating the Effectiveness of Performance Management: A 30-Year Integrative Conceptual Review," *Journal of Applied Psychology* 104 (2019): 851–887.

42. Y. Gong, M. Wang, J.-C. Huang, S. Y. Cheung, "Toward a Goal Orientation-Based Feedback Seeking Typology: Implications for Employee Performance Outcomes," *Journal of Management*, 43, No. 4 (April 2017), 1234–1260.

43. F. L. Oswald, T. S. Behrend, D. J. Putka, and E. Sinar, "Big Data in Industrial-Organizational Psychology and Human Resource Management: Forward Progress for Organizational Research and Practice," *Annual Review of Organizational Psychology and Organizational Behavior*, 7 (2020): 505–533.

44. J. R. Hollenbeck and A. P. Brief, "The Effects of Individual Differences and Goal Origin on Goal Setting and Performance," *Organizational Behavior and Human Decision Processes* 40 (1987): 392–414.

45. R. A. Katzell and D. E. Thompson, "Work Motivation: Theory and Practice," *American Psychologist* 45 (1990): 144–153; M. W. McPherson, "Is Psychology the Science of Behavior?" *American Psychologist* 47 (1992): 329–335.

46. A. S. DeNisi and K. R. Murphy, "Performance Appraisal and Performance Management: 100 Years of Progress?" *Journal of Applied Psychology*, 102, No. 3 (March 2017), 421–433.

47. F. L. Schmidt and J. Hunter, "General Mental Ability in the World of Work: Occupational Attainment and Job Performance," *Journal of Personality and Social Psychology* 86 (2004): 162–173.

48. D. L. Joseph, J. Jin, D. A. Newman, and E. H. O'Boyle, "Why Does Self-Reported Emotional Intelligence Predict Job Performance? A Meta-Analytic Investigation of Mixed EI," *Journal of Applied Psychology* 100 (2015): 298–342.

49. R. L. Cardy, *Performance Management: Concepts, Skills, and Exercises* (Armonk, New York, and London, England: M. E. Sharpe, 2004).

50. D. Hartley-Wilkins, "Getting the Best out of Your People: Managing Performance," *Human Resources* (April/May 2010): 26–27.

51. P. Cappelli and N. Rogovsky, "Employee Involvement and Organizational Citizenship: Implications for Labor Law Reform and 'Lean Production,'" *Industrial & Labor Relations Review* 51 (1998): 633–653.

52. L. D. Ordonez, M. E. Schweitzer, A. D. Galinskly, and M. H. Bazerman, "Goals Gone Wild: The Systematic Side Effects of Overprescribing Goal Setting," *Academy of Management Perspectives* 23 (2009): 6–16; E. A. Locke and G. P. Latham, "Has Goal Setting Gone Wild, or Have Its Attackers Abandoned Good Scholarship?" *Academy of Management Perspectives* 23 (2009): 17–23.

53. M. E. Tubbs and M. L. Trusty, "Direct Reports of Motivation for Task Performance Levels: Some Construct-Related Evidence," *Journal of Psychology* 135 (2001): 185–205.

54. S. Ellis, R. Mendel, and M. Aloni-Zohar, "The Effect of Accuracy of Performance Evaluation on Learning from Experience: The Moderating Role of After-Event Reviews," *Journal of Applied Social Psychology* 39, No. 3 (2009): 541–563.

55. D. J. Schleicher, H. M. Baumann, D. W. Sullivan, and J. Yim, "Evaluating the Effectiveness of Performance Management: A 30-Year Integrative Conceptual Review," *Journal of Applied Psychology* 104 (2019): 851–887.

56. R. R. Kilburg, *Executive Coaching: Developing Managerial Wisdom in a World of Chaos* (Washington, D.C.: American Psychological Association, 2000).

57. K. Y. Wilson, "An Analysis of Bias in Supervisor Narrative Comments in Performance Appraisal," *Human Relations* 63 (2010): 1903–1933.

58. H. H. Meyer, E. Kay, and J. R. P. French, "Split Roles in Performance Appraisal," *Harvard Business Review* 43 (1965): 123–129.

59. W. Lam, X. Huang, and E. Snape, "Feedback-Seeking Behavior and Leader-Member Exchange: Do Supervisor-Attributed Motives Matter?" *Academy of Management Journal* 50 (2007): 348–363.

60. D. Motro and P. J. Aleksander, "Boys, Don't Cry: Gender and Reactions to Negative Performance Feedback," *Journal of Applied Psychology* 102, No. 2 (February 2017): 227–235.

61. J. S. Goodman, R. E. Wood, and M. Hendrickx, "Feedback Specificity, Exploration, and Learning," *Journal of Applied Psychology* 89 (2004): 248–262.

62. M. B. DeGregorio and C. D. Fisher, "Providing Performance Feedback: Reactions to Alternative Methods," *Journal of Management* 14 (1988): 605–616.

63. G. C. Thornton, "The Relationship between Supervisory and Self-Appraisals of Executive Performance," *Personnel Psychology* 21 (1968): 441–455.

64. A. S. DeNisi and A. N. Kluger, "Feedback Effectiveness: Can 360-Degree Appraisals Be Improved?" *Academy of Management Executive* 14 (2000): 129–140.

65. F. Luthans and S. J. Peterson, "360-Degree Feedback with Systematic Coaching: Empirical Analysis Suggests a Winning Combination," *Human Resource Management* 42 (2003): 243–256.

66. G. Toegel and J. A. Conger, "360-Degree Assessment: Time for Reinvention," *Academy of Management Learning and Education 2* (2003): 297–311.

67. L. Hirschhorn, "Leaders and Followers in a Postindustrial Age: A Psychodynamic View," *Journal of Applied Behavioral Science* 26 (1990): 529–542.

68. T. C. Bednall, K. Sanders, and P. Runhaar, "Stimulating Informal Learning Activities through Perceptions of Performance Appraisal

Quality and Human Resource Management Strength: A Two-Wave Study," *Academy of Management Learning & Education* 13 (2014): 45–61.

69. D. J. Schleicher, H. M. Baumann, D. W. Sullivan, and J. Yim, "Evaluating the Effectiveness of Performance Management: A 30-Year Integrative Conceptual Review," *Journal of Applied Psychology* 104 (2019): 851–887.

70. E. D. Pulakos, R. Mueller-Hanson, and S. Arad, "The Evolution of Performance Management: Searching for Value," *Annual Review of Organizational Psychology and Organizational Behavior* 6 (2019): 249–271.

71. B. Buck, and J. Morrow, "AI, Performance Management and Engagement: Keeping Your Best Their Best, *Strategic HR Review* 17 (2018): 261–262.

72. J. Pfeffer, "Six Dangerous Myths about Pay," *Harvard Business Review* 76 (1998): 108–119.

73. L. M. Leslie, C. F. Manchester, and P. C. Dahm, "Why and When Does the Gender Gap Reverse? Diversity Goals and the Pay Premium for High Potential Women," *Academy of Management Journal* 60 (April 2017), 402–432.

74. "Six Employee Types Prefer Different Rewards," *HR Focus* 84, No. 4 (April 2007): 12.

75. M. Erez, "Work Motivation from a Cross-Cultural Perspective," in A. M. Bouvy, F. J. R. Van de Vijver, P. Boski, and P. G. Schmitz, eds., *Journeys into Cross-Cultural Psychology* (Amsterdam, Netherlands: Swets and Zeitlinger, 1994): 386–403.

76. G. T. Milkovich and J. M. Newman, *Compensation*, 4th ed. (Homewood, Ill.: Irwin, 1993).

77. T. Taylor, "The Challenge of Project Team Incentives," *Compensation and Benefits Review* 42 (2010): 411–419.

78. J. M. Bardwick, *Danger in the Comfort Zone* (New York: American Management Association, 1991).

79. D. F. Giannetto, "Get Your Money's Worth from Incentives," *Business Performance Management* 7 (2009): 12.

80. J. H. Han, K. M. Bartol, and S. Kim, "Tightening Up the Performance-Pay Linkage: Roles of Contingent Reward Leadership and Profit-Sharing in the Cross-Level Influence of Individual Pay-for-Performance," *Journal of Applied Psychology* 100 (2015): 417–430.

81. K. N. Wexley, R. A. Alexander, J. P. Greenawalt, and M. A. Couch, "Attitudinal Congruence and Similarity as Related to Interpersonal Evaluations in Manager-Subordinate Dyads," *Academy of Management Journal* 23 (1980): 320–330.

82. H. H. Kelley, *Attribution in Social Interaction* (New York: General Learning Press, 1971); H. H. Kelley, "The Processes of Causal Attribution," *American Psychologist* 28 (1973): 107–128.

83. B. Raabe and T. A. Beehr, "Formal Mentoring versus Supervisor and Coworker Relationships: Differences in Perceptions and Impact," *Journal of Organizational Behavior* 24 (2003): 271–293.

84. A. M. Young and P. L. Perrewe, "What Did You Expect? An Examination of Career-Related Support and Social Support among Mentors and Protégés," *Journal of Management* 26 (2000): 611–633.

85. K. Doherty, "The Good News about Depression," *Business and Health* 3 (1989): 1–4.

86. K. E. Kram, "Phases of the Mentor Relationship," *Academy of Management Journal* 26 (1983): 608–625.

87. T. D. Allen, L. T. Eby, M. L. Poteet, E. Lentz, and L. Lima, "Career Benefits Associated with Mentoring for Protégés: A Meta-Analysis," *Journal of Applied Psychology* 89 (2004): 127–136.

88. L. T. Eby, M. M. Butts, B. J. Hoffman, and J. B. Sauer, "Cross-Lagged Relations between Mentoring Received from Supervisors and Employee OCBs: Disentangling Causal Direction and Identifying Boundary Conditions," *Journal of Applied Psychology* (Advanced online publication January 19, 2015).

89. S. J. Wells, "Choices Flourish at IBM," *HR Magazine* (May 2009): 52–57.

90. K. E. Kram and L. A. Isabella, "Mentoring Alternatives: The Role of Peer Relationships in Career Development," *Academy of Management Journal* 28 (1985): 110–132.

91. J. Greco, "Hey, Coach!," *Journal of Business Strategy* 22 (2001): 28–32.

7

1. A. Kinder, R. Hughes, and C. L. Cooper, *Occupational Health and Wellbeing* (Oxon, UK, and New York, NY: Routledge, 2023).

2. American Psychological Association, *Stress in America Report* (Washington, DC, 2022).

3. M. Blake Hargrove, J. C. Quick, D. L. Nelson, and J. D. Quick, "The Theory of Preventive Stress Management: A 33-Year Review and Evaluation," *Stress and Health* 27 (2011): 182–193.

4. S. Benison, A. C. Barger, and E. L. Wolfe, *Walter B. Cannon: The Life and Times of a Young Scientist* (Cambridge, Mass.: Harvard University Press, 1987).

5. W. B. Cannon, *Bodily Changes in Pain, Hunger, Fear, and Rage: An Account of Recent Researchers into the Function of Emotional Excitement* (New York: Appleton-Century-Crofts, 1915).

6. W. B. Cannon, *The Wisdom of the Body* (New York: Norton, 1932).

7. J. B. Halbesleben, S. C. Paustian-Underdal, M. Westman, "Getting to the "COR": Understanding the Role of Resources in Conservation of Resources Theory," *Journal of Management* **40** (2014): 1334–1364.

8. R. S. Lazarus, *Psychological Stress and the Coping Process* (New York: McGraw-Hill, 1966).

9. M. R. Tuckey, B. J. Searle, C. M. Boyd, A. H. Winefield, and H. R. Winefield "Hindrances Are Not Threats: Advancing the Multimensionality of Work Stress," *Journal of Occupational Health Psychology* 20 (2015): 131–147.

10. R. Rau, K. Morling, and U. Rosler, "Is There a Relationship Between Major Depression and Both Objectively Assessed and Perceived Demands and Control?" *Work and Stress* 24 (2010): 88–106.

11. C. Liu, P. E. Spector, and L. Shi, "Cross-National Job Stress: A Quantitative and Qualitative Study," *Journal of Organizational Behavior* 28 (2007): 209–239.

12. J. Doron, Y. Stephan, C. Maiano, and C. LeScanff, "Motivational Predictors of Coping with Academic Examinations," *The Journal of Social Psychology* 151 (2011): 87–104.

13. J. D. Kammeyer-Mueller, T. A. Judge, and B. A. Scott, "The Role of Core Self-Evaluations in the Coping Process," *Journal of Applied Psychology* 94 (2009): 177–195.

14. D. Katz and R. L. Kahn, *The Social Psychology of Organizations*, 2nd ed. (New York: Wiley, 1978): 185–221.

15. H. Levinson, "A Psychoanalytic View of Occupational Stress," *Occupational Mental Health* 3 (1978): 2–13.

16. L. Yang, J. Bauer, R. E. Johnson, M. W. Groer, and K. Salomon, "Physiological Mechanisms That Underlie the Effects of Interactional Fairness on Deviant Behavior: The Role of Cortisol Activity," *Journal of Applied Psychology* 99 (2014): 310–321.

17. G-H. Huang, N. Wellman, S. J. Ashford, C. Lee, and L. Wang, "Deviance and Exit: The Organizational Costs of Job Insecurity and Moral Disengagement," *Journal of Applied Psychology* 102, No. 1 (January 2017): 26–42.

18. T. L. Friedman, *The Lexus and the Olive Tree* (New York: Vintage Anchor, 2000).

19. S. Zuboff, *In the Age of the Smart Machine: The Future of Work and Power* (New York: Basic Books, 1988).

20. C. L. Cooper, A. Pandey, and J. C. Quick (Eds), *Downsizing: Is More Less?* (Chichester, UK: Cambridge University Press, 2012).

21. N. P. Podsakoff, J. A. LePine, and M. A. LePine, "Differential Challenge Stressor-Hindrance Stressor Relationships with Job Attitudes, Turnover Intentions, Turnover, and Withdrawal Behavior: A Meta-Analysis," *Journal of Applied Psychology* 92 (2007): 438–454.

22. R. L. Kahn, D. M. Wolfe, R. P. Quinn, J. D. Snoek, and R. A. Rosenthal, *Organizational Stress: Studies in Role Conflict and Ambiguity* (New York: Wiley, 1964).

23. C. Vandenberge, A. Panaciio, K. Bentein, K. Mignonac, and P. Roussel, "Assessing Longitudinal Change of and Dynamic Relationships among Role Stressors, Job Attitudes, Turnover Intention, and Well-Being in Neophyte Newcomers," *Journal of Organizational Behavior* 34 (2011): 652–671.

24. L. B. Hammer and T. L. Cain, "The Work-Nonwork Interface: Policy and Practice," in L. E. Tetrick, G. Fisher, M. Ford, and J.C. Quick, eds., *Handbook of Occupational Health Psychology, Third Edition.* (Washington, DC: American Psychological Association, 2023).

25. W. J. Casper, J. H. Wayne, F. Rice, and H. Vaziri, "Work-Nonwork Balance and Employee Well-Being," in L. M. Lapierre and Sir C.L. Cooper, eds., *The Cambridge Companion to Organizational Stress and Well-Being* (Cambridge, UK: Cambridge University Press, 2023): 155–184.

26. S. Pal and P. O. Saksvik, "Work–Family Conflict and Psychosocial Work Environment Stressors as Predictors of Job Stress in a Cross-Cultural Study," *International Journal of Stress Management* 15, No. 1 (2008): 22–42.

27. A. Skogstad, S. Einarsen, T. Torsheim, M. S. Aasland, and H. Hetland, "The Destructiveness of Laissez-Faire Leadership Behavior," *Journal of Occupational Health Psychology* 12 (2007): 80–92.

28. A. A. Henderson, R. A., Matthews, and M. T. Ford. "The Temporal Dynamics Between Work Stressors and Health Behaviors," *Journal of Occupational Health Psychology* 28 (2023): 1–19.

29. P. J. Frost, *Toxic Emotions at Work: How Compassionate Managers Handle Pain and Conflict* (Boston: Harvard Business School Press, 2003).

30. T. Nicholson and B. Griffin, "Here Today but Not Gone Tomorrow: Incivility Affects After-Work and Next-Day Recovery," *Journal of Occupational Health Psychology* 20 (2015) 218–225.

31. S. Grebner, N. K. Semmer, L. L. Faso, S. Gut, W. Kalin, and A. Elfering, "Working Conditions, Well-Being, and Job-Related Attitudes among Call Centre Agents," *European Journal of Work and Organizational Psychology* 12 (2003): 341–365.

32. J. C. Quick and M. A. McFadyen. "Bad Behavior Is Preventable," *Harvard Business Review*, February 2 (2018).

33. L. T. Hosmer, "Trust: The Connecting Link between Organizational Theory and Philosophical Ethics," *Academy of Management Review* 20 (1995): 379–403; V. J. Doby and R. D. Caplan, "Organizational Stress as Threat to Reputation: Effects on Anxiety at Work and at Home," *Academy of Management Journal* 38 (1995): 1105–1123.

34. E. Lambert, H. Qureshi, and J. Frank. "Organization Trust and Job Stress: A Preliminary Study Among Police Officers," *Asian Journal of Criminology*, March 2022: 81–103.

35. M. F. Peterson and P. B. Smith, "Does National Culture or Ambient Temperature Explain Cross-National Differences in Role Stress? No Sweat!" *Academy of Management Journal* 40 (1997): 930–946.

36. R. S. DeFrank, "Executive Travel Stress: Perils of the Road Warrior," *Academy of Management Executive* 14 (2000): 58–72; M. Westman, "Strategies for Coping with Business Trips: A Qualitative Exploratory Study," *International Journal of Stress Management* 11 (2004): 167–176.

37. J. C. Quick, J. R. Joplin, D. A. Gray, and E. C. Cooley, "The Occupational Life Cycle and the Family," in L. L'Abate, ed., *Handbook of Developmental Family Psychology and Psychopathology* (New York: John Wiley, 1993).

38. S. Shellenbarger, "Work and Family," *The Wall Street Journal* (January 31, 1996): B1.

39. S. A. Lobel, "Allocation of Investment in Work and Family Roles: Alternative Theories and Implications for Research," *Academy of Management Review* 16 (1991): 507–521.

40. J. D. Quick, A. Henley, and J. C. Quick. "The Balancing Act—At Work and at Home," *Organizational Dynamics—Special Issue* 33 (2004): 426–438.

41. J. W. Pennebaker, C. F. Hughes, and R. C. O'Heeron, "The Psychophysiology of Confession: Linking Inhibitory and Psychosomatic Processes," *Journal of Personality and Social Psychology* 52 (1987): 781–793.

42. J. Loehr and T. Schwartz, "The Making of a Corporate Athlete," *Harvard Business Review* 79 (2001): 120–129.

43. J. D. Quick, R. S. Horn, and J. C. Quick, "Health Consequences of Stress," *Journal of Organizational Behavior Management* 8 (1986): 19–36.

44. R. M. Yerkes and J. D. Dodson, "The Relation of Strength of Stimulus to Rapidity of Habit-Formation," *Journal of Comparative Neurology and Psychology* 18 (1908): 459–482.

45. J. E. McGrath, "Stress and Behavior in Organizations," in M. D. Dunnette, ed., *Handbook of Industrial and Organizational Psychology* (Chicago: Rand McNally, 1976): 1351–1395.

46. S. T. Hannah, A. L. U. Perez, P.B. Lester, and J. C. Quick, "Bolstering Workplace Psychological Well-Being Through Transactional and Transformational Leadership," *Journal of Leadership & Organizational Studies* 27 (2020): 222–240.

47. W. B. Cannon, *Bodily Changes in Pain, Hunger, Fear, and Rage* (New York: Appleton, 1915).

48. P. A. Herbig and F. A. Palumbo, "Karoshi: Salaryman Sudden Death Syndrome," *Journal of Managerial Psychology* 9 (1994): 11–16.

49. S. Sauter, L. R. Murphy, and J. J. Hurrell, Jr., "Prevention of Work-Related Psychological Distress: A National Strategy Proposed by the National Institute for Occupational Safety and Health," *American Psychologist* 45 (1990): 1146–1158.

50. R. Cropanzano, D. E. Rupp, and Z. S. Byrne, "The Relationship of Emotional Exhaustion to Work Attitudes, Job Performance, and Organizational Citizenship Behaviors," *Journal of Applied Psychology* 88 (2003): 160–169.

51. A. A. Grandey, "When 'The Show Must Go On': Surface Acting and Deep Acting as Determinants of Emotional Exhaustion and Peer-Rated Service Delivery," *Academy of Management Journal* 46 (2003): 86–96.

52. G. B. Hall, M. F. Dollard, M. R. Tuckey, A. H. Winefield, and B. M. Thompson, "Job Demands, Work–Family Conflict, and Emotional Exhaustion in Police Officers: A Longitudinal Test of Competing Theories," *Journal of Occupational and Organizational Psychology* 83 (2010): 237–250.

53. C. Maslach and M. Leiter. *The Burnout Challenge: Managing People's Relationships with Their Jobs* (Cambridge, MA: Harvard University Press, 2022).

54. M. Valcour and C. Dierickx, "Beating Burnout," *Harvard Business Review*, January–February 2017, p. 19.

55. I. Wylie, "Routing Rust-Out," *Fast Company Magazine* (January 2004): 40 accessed at www.fastcompany.com/magazine/78/5things.html.

56. H. Selye, *Stress in Health and Disease* (Boston: Butterworth, 1976).

57. B. G. Ware and D. L. Block, "Cardiovascular Risk Intervention at a Work Site: The Ford Motor Company Program," *International Journal of Mental Health* 11 (1982): 68–75.

58. D. B. Kennedy, R. J. Homant, and M. R. Homant, "Perceptions of Injustice as a Predictor of Support for Workplace Aggression," *Journal of Business and Psychology* 18 (2004): 323–336.

59. C. M. Barnes, J. A. Miller, and S. Bostock, "Helping Employees Sleep Well: Effects of Cognitive Behavioral Therapy for Insomnia on Work Outcomes," *Journal of Applied Psychology* 102, No. 1 (January 2017): 104–113.

60. W. F. Cascio, *Managing Human Resources: Productivity, Quality of Life, Profits*, 9th ed. (New York: McGraw–Hill, 2013).

61. F. K. Cocchiara and J. C. Quick, "The Negative Effects of Positive Stereotypes: Ethnicity-Related Stressors and Implications on Organizational Health," *Journal of Organizational Behavior* 25 (2004): 781–785.

62. J. M. Ivancevich, M. T. Matteson, and E. Richards, "Who's Liable for Stress on the Job?" *Harvard Business Review* 64 (1985): 60–72.

63. Frank S. Deus v. Allstate Insurance Company, civil action no. 88-2099, U.S. District Court, Western District of Louisiana.

64. R. S. DeFrank and J. M. Ivancevich, "Stress on the Job: An Executive Update," *Academy of Management Executive* 12 (1998): 55–66.

65. P. Wilson and M. Bronstein, "Employers: Don't Panic about Workplace Stress," *Personnel Today* (November 4, 2003): 10.

66. J. E. Bono and M. A. Vey, "Personality and Emotional Performance: Extraversion, Neuroticism, and Self-Monitoring," *Journal of Occupational Health Psychology* 12 (2007): 177–192.

67. L. Verbrugge, "Recent, Present, and Future Health of American Adults," *Annual Review of Public Health* 10 (1989): 333–361.

68. D. L. Nelson and J. C. Quick, "Professional Women: Are Distress and Disease Inevitable?" *Academy of Management Review* 10 (1985): 206–218; T. D. Jick and L. F. Mitz, "Sex Differences in Work Stress," *Academy of Management Review* 10 (1985): 408–420.

69. J. H. Gavin, J. C. Quick, and D. J. Gavin, *Ending Sexual Violence on Campus: A Community-Based Approach* (Baltimore, MD: Johns Hopkins University Press, 2021).

70. M. P. Bell and J. Leopold, *Diversity in Organizations, 5th Edition* (Macon, OH: Cengage, 2025).

71. S. E. Taylor, L. C. Klein, G. P. Lewis, T. L. Gruenewald, R. A. R. Burung, and J. A. Updegraff, "Biobehavioral Responses to Stress in Females: Tend-and-Befriend, Not Fight-or-Flight," *Psychological Review* 107 (2000): 411–429.

72. M. D. Friedman and R. H. Rosenman, *Type A Behavior and Your Heart* (New York: Knopf, 1974).

73. L. Wright, "The Type A Behavior Pattern and Coronary Artery Disease," *American Psychologist* 43 (1988): 2–14.

74. S. O. C. Kobasa, "Conceptualization and Measurement of Personality in Job Stress Research," in J. J. Hurrell, Jr., L. R. Murphy, S. L. Sauter, and C. L. Cooper, eds., *Occupational Stress: Issues and Developments in Research* (New York: Taylor & Francis, 1988): 100–109.

75. J. K. Ito and C. M. Brotheridge, "Predictors and Consequences of Promotion Stress: A Bad Situation Made Worse by Employment Dependence," *International Journal of Stress Management* 16, No. 1 (2009): 65–85.

76. J. Borysenko, "Personality Hardiness," *Lectures in Behavioral Medicine* (Boston: Harvard Medical School, 1985).

77. R. Waldinger and M. Schulz, *The Good Life: Lessons from the World's Longest Scientific Study of Happiness* (New York: Simon & Schuster, 2023).

78. J. Bowlby, *A Secure Base* (New York: Basic Books, 1988).

79. C. Hazan and P. Shaver, "Love and Work: An Attachment-Theoretical Perspective," *Journal of Personality and Social Psychology* 59 (1990): 270–280.

80. J. C. Quick, D. L. Nelson, and J. D. Quick, *Stress and Challenge at the Top: The Paradox of the Successful Executive* (Chichester, England: Wiley, 1990).

81. M. G. Franco, "The Trait That 'Super Friends' Have in Common," *The Atlantic*, August 25 (2022).

82. J. C. Quick, J. R. Joplin, D. L. Nelson, and J. D. Quick, "Self-Reliance for Stress and Combat" (*Proceedings of the 8th Combat Stress Conference*, U.S. Army Health Services Command, Fort Sam Houston, Texas, September 23–27, 1991): 1–5.

83. R. Z. Goetzel, R. J. Ozminkowski, J. A. Bruno, K. R. Rutter, F. Issac, and S. Wang, "The Long-Term Impact of Johnson & Johnson's Health & Wellness Program on Employee Health Risks," *Journal of Occupational and Environmental Medicine* 44 (2002): 417–424

84. J. C. Dvorak, "Baffling," *PC Magazine* 3 (November 4, 2003): 61, accessed at http://www.pcmag.com/article2/0,4149,1369270,00.asp.

85. O. Janssen, "How Fairness Perceptions Make Innovative Behavior More or Less Stressful," *Journal of Organizational Behavior* 25 (2004): 201–215; T. A. Judge and J. A. Colquitt, "Organizational Justice and Stress: The Mediating Role of Work–Family Conflict," *Journal of Applied Psychology* 89 (2004): 395–404.

86. J. C. Quick, T. A. Wright, J. A. Adkins, and J. D. Quick, *Preventive Stress Management in Organizations, Second Edition* (Washington, DC: American Psychological Association, 2013).

87. A. Drach-Zahavy and A. Freund, "Team Effectiveness under Stress: A Structural Contingency Approach," *Journal of Organizational Behavior* 28 (2007): 423–450.

88. R. W. Griffin, A. O'Leary-Kelly, and J. M. Collins, eds., *Dysfunctional Behavior in Organizations: Violent and Deviant Behavior* (Stamford, Conn.: JAI Press, 1998).

89. M. Kouchaki and S. D. Desai, "Anxious, Threatened, and Also Unethical: How Anxiety Makes Individuals Feel Threatened and Commit Unethical Acts," *Journal of Applied Psychology* 100 (2015): 360–375.

90. W. L. French, C. H. Bell, Jr., and V. Vohra, *Organizational Development: Behavioral Science Interventions for Organization Improvement*, Revised 6th ed. (London, UK: Pearson, 2018).

91. C. Newton and S. Teo, "Identification and Occupational Stress: A Stress-Buffering Perspective," *Human Resource Management* 53 (2014): 89–113.

92. M. Macik-Frey, J. C. Quick, and J. D. Quick, "Interpersonal Communication: The Key to Unlocking Social Support for Preventive Stress Management," in C. L. Cooper, ed., *Handbook of Stress, Medicine, and Health*, rev. ed. (Boca Raton, FL: CRC Press).

93. J. C. Quick and C. L. Cooper, *FAST FACTS: Stress and Strain*, 2nd ed. (Oxford, England: Health Press, 2003).

94. M. E. P. Seligman, *Learned Optimism* (New York: Knopf, 1990).

95. F. Griva and F. Anagnostopoulos, "Positive Psychological States and Anxiety: The Mediating Effect of Proactive Coping," *Psychological Reports* 107 (2010): 795–804.

96. F. Luthans and C. M. Youssef-Morgan, "Psychological Capital: An Evidence-Based Positive Approach," *Annual Review of Organizational Psychology and Organizational Behavior* 4 (2017): 339–366.

97. W. T. Brooks and T. W. Mullins, *High-Impact Time Management* (Englewood Cliffs, N.J.: Prentice-Hall, 1989).

98. M. Westman and D. Eden, "Effects of a Respite from Work on Burnout: Vacation Relief and Fade-Out," *Journal of Applied Psychology* 82 (1997): 516–527.

99. K. H. Cooper, "The History of Aerobics (50 Years and Still Counting)," *Research Quarterly for Exercise and Sport* 89 (2018): 129–134. doi: 10.1080/02701367.2018.1452469.

100. R. Bachman, "Fitness: Five Secrets of Steady Exercisers," *Wall Street Journal*, May 22 (2017), p. A1534.

101. M. Davis, E. R. Eshelman, and M. McKay, *The Relaxation and Stress Reduction Workbook*, Seventh Edition (Oakland, Calif.: New Harbinger, 2019).

102. H. Benson, "Your Innate Asset for Combating Stress," *Harvard Business Review* 52 (1974): 49–60.

103. J. Gooty, "Just Breathe: Impact of Yoga on Work and Well-Being Outcomes from Two Longitudinal Quasi-Experiments," working paper.

104. D. Ornish, *Dr. Dean Ornish's Program for Reversing Cardiovascular Disease* (New York: Random House, 1995).

105. J. W. Pennebaker, *Opening Up: The Healing Power of Expressing Emotions* (New York: Guilford, 1997).

106. M. E. Francis and J. W. Pennebaker, "Putting Stress into Words: The Impact of Writing on Physiological, Absentee, and Self-Reported Emotional Well-Being Measures," *American Journal of Health Promotion* 6 (1992): 280–287.

107. Z. Solomon, B. Oppenheimer, and S. Noy, "Subsequent Military Adjustment of Combat Stress Reaction Casualties: A Nine-Year Follow-Up Study," in N. A. Milgram, ed., *Stress and Coping in Time of War: Generalizations from the Israeli Experience* (New York: Brunner/Mazel, 1986): 84–90.

108. C. L. Cooper and J. C. Quick, *The Handbook of Stress and Health: A Guide to Research and Practice* (Chichester, UK: Wiley-Blackwell, 2017).

109. D. Gebhardt and C. Crump, "Employee Fitness and Wellness Programs in the Workplace," *American Psychologist* 45 (1990): 262–272.

110. T. Wolf, H. Randall, and J. Faucett, "A Survey of Health Promotion Programs in U.S. and Canadian Medical Schools," *American Journal of Health Promotion* 3 (1988): 33–36.

111. S. Weiss, J. Fielding, and A. Baum, *Health at Work* (Hillsdale, N.J.: Erlbaum, 1990).

112. J. B. Bennett, C. Banks, and A. Chan, "An Integrated Framework for Organizational Well-Being: Updated Themes, Potential Competencies, and A Broader Horizon," in L. E. Tetrick, G. Fisher, M. Ford, and J. C. Quick, eds., *Handbook of Occupational Health Psychology, Third Edition* (Washington, D.C.: American Psychological Association, 2024).

8

1. E. James and L. P. Wooten, "In a Crisis, Great Leaders Prioritize Listening," *Harvard Business Review*, September 13 (2022).

2. M. Macik-Frey, J. C. Quick, and J. D. Quick, "Interpersonal Communication: The Key to Unlocking Social Support for Preventive Stress Management," in C. L. Cooper, ed., *Handbook of Stress, Medicine, and Health*, rev. ed. (Boca Raton, FL: CRC Press): 265–292.

3. *Richness* is a term originally coined by W. D. Bodensteiner, "Information Channel Utilization under Varying Research and Development Project Conditions" (Ph.D. diss., University of Texas at Austin, 1970).

4. T. J. Kiddie, "Text(ing) in Context: The Future of Workplace Communication in the United States," *Business and Professional Communication Quarterly* 77 (2014): 65–88.

5. B. Barry and I. S. Fulmer, "The Medium and the Message: The Adaptive Use of Communication Media in Dyadic Influence," *Academy of Management Review* 29 (2004): 272–292.

6. S. Aryee, F. O. Walumbwa, R. Mondejar, and C. W. L. Chu, "Core Self-Evaluations and Employee Voice Behavior: Test of a Dual-Motivational Pathway," *Journal of Management* 43, No. 3 (March 2017): 946–966.

7. F. M. Jablin, "Courage and Courageous Communication Among Leaders and Followers in Groups, Organizations, and Communities," *Management Communication Quarterly* 20 (2006): 94–110.

8. Y. J. Kim, C. F. Lam, J. Oh, and W. Sohn, "Employee Constructive Voice: An Integrative Review and a Dyadic Approach," *Journal of Management* 49 (2023): 430–473.

9. E. Rautalinko and H. O. Lisper, "Effects of Training Reflective Listening in a Corporate Setting," *Journal of Business and Psychology* 18 (2004): 281–299.

10. A. G. Athos and J. J. Gabarro, *Interpersonal Behavior: Communication and Understanding in Relationships* (Englewood Cliffs, N.J.: Prentice-Hall, 1978).

11. A. D. Mangelsdorff, "Lessons Learned from the Military: Implications for Management" (Distinguished Visiting Lecture, University of Texas at Arlington, January 29, 1993).

12. D. A. Morand, "Language and Power: An Empirical Analysis of Linguistic Strategies Used in Superior–Subordinate Communication," *Journal of Organizational Behavior* 21 (2000): 235–249.

13. S. Bates, "How Leaders Communicate Big Ideas to Drive Business Results," *Employment Relations Today* 33 (Fall 2006): 13–19.

14. F. Luthans, "Successful versus Effective Real Managers," *Academy of Management Executive* 2 (1988): 127–132.

15. L. E. Penley, E. R. Alexander, I. E. Jernigan, and C. I. Henwood, "Communication Abilities of Managers: The Relationship of Performance," *Journal of Management* 17 (1991): 57–76.

16. J. A. LePine and L. Van Dyne, "Voice and Cooperative Behavior as Contrasting Forms of Contextual Performance: Evidence of Differential Relationships with Big Five Personality Characteristics and Cognitive Ability," *Journal of Applied Psychology* 86 (2001): 326–336.

17. F. M. Jablin, "Superior-Subordinate Communication: The State of the Art," *Psychological Bulletin* 86 (1979): 1201–1222.

18. B. Barry and J. M. Crant, "Dyadic Communication Relationships in Organizations: An Attribution Expectancy Approach," *Organization Science* 11 (2000): 648–665.

19. J. Silvester, F. Patterson, A. Koczwara, and E. Ferguson, "'Trust Me . . .': Psychological and Behavioral Predictors of Perceived Physician Empathy," *Journal of Applied Psychology* 92 (2007): 519–527.

20. K. Mishra, L. Boynton, and A. Mishra, "Driving Employee Engagement: The Expanded Role of Internal Communications," *International Journal of Business Communications* 51 (2014): 183–202.

21. A. Furhham and P. Stringfield, "Congruence in Job-Performance Ratings: A Study of 360 Degree Feedback Examining Self, Manager, Peers, and Consultant Ratings," *Human Relations* 51 (1998): 517–530.

22. J. W. Gilsdorf, "Organizational Rules on Communicating: How Employees Are—and Are Not—Learning the Ropes," *Journal of Business Communication* 35 (1998): 173–201.

23. A. Malhotra and A. Majchrzak, "Enhancing Performance of Geographically Dispersed Teams through Targeted Use of Information and Communication Technologies," *Human Relations* 67 (2014): 389–411.

24. D. Tannen, *That's Not What I Mean! How Conversational Style Makes or Breaks Your Relations with Others* (New York, NY: Morrow, 1986); D. Tannen, *You Just Don't Understand* (New York, NY: Ballentine, 1990).

25. D. G. Allen and R. W. Griffeth, "A Vertical and Lateral Information Processing: The Effects of Gender, Employee Classification Level, and Media Richness on Communication and Work Outcomes," *Human Relations* 50 (1997): 1239–1260.

26. K. L. Ashcraft, "Empowering 'Professional' Relationships," *Management Communication Quarterly* 13 (2000): 347–393.

27. G. Hofstede, *Culture's Consequences: International Differences in Work-Related Values* (Beverly Hills, Calif.: Sage Publications, 1980).

28. G. Hofstede, "Motivation, Leadership, and Organization: Do American Theories Apply Abroad?" *Organizational Dynamics* 9 (1980): 42–63.

29. H. Levinson, *Executive* (Cambridge, Mass.: Harvard University Press, 1981).

30. B. M. Cole, "Lessons from a Martial Arts Dojo: A Prolonged Process Model of High-Context Communication," *Academy of Management Journal* 58 (2015): 567–591.

31. I. Setti, V. Sommovigo, and P. Argentero, "Enhancing Expatriates' Assignments Success: The Relationships between Cultural Intelligence, Cross-cultural Adaptation and Performance," *Current Psychology* 41 (2022): 4291–4311.

32. P. Schilpzand, I. E. de Pater, and A. Erez, "Workplace Incivility: A Review of the Literature and Agenda for Future Research," *Journal of Organizational Behavior* 37 (February 2016): S57–S88.

33. J. L. Welbourne, A. Gangadharan, and A. M. Sariol, "Ethnicity and Cultural Values as Predictors of the Occurrence and Impact of Experienced Workplace Incivility," *Journal of Occupational Health Psychology* 20 (2015): 205–217.

34. T. C. Reich and S. Hershcovis, "Observing Workplace Incivility," *Journal of Applied Psychology* 100 (2015): 203–215.

35. S. G. Taylor, A. G. Bedeian, M. S. Cole, and Z. Zhang, "Developing and Testing a Dynamic Model of Workplace Incivility Change," *Journal of Management* 43, No. 3 (March 2017): 645–670.

36. R. D. Enright and R. P. Fitzgibbons, *Forgiveness Therapy: An Empirical Guide for Resolving Anger and Restoring Hope*, 2nd ed. (Washington, D.C.: American Psychological Association, 2014).

37. R. D. Laing, *The Politics of the Family and Other Essays* (New York, NY: Pantheon, 1971).

38. H. S. Schwartz, *Narcissistic Process and Corporate Decay: The Theory of the Organizational Ideal* (New York, NY: New York University Press, 1990).

39. W. R. Forrester and M. F. Maute, "The Impact of Relationship Satisfaction on Attribution, Emotions, and Behaviors Following Service Failure," *Journal of Applied Business Research* 17 (2000): 1–45.

40. J. J. Lynch, *A Cry Unheard: New Insights into the Medical Consequences of Loneliness* (Baltimore, MD: Bancroft Press, 2000).

41. J. C. Quick, J. H. Gavin, C. L. Cooper, and J. D. Quick, "Working Together: Balancing Head and Heart," in N. G. Johnson, R. H. Rozensky, C. D. Goodheart, and R. Hammond, eds., *Psychology Builds a Healthy World* (Washington, D.C.: American Psychological Association, 2004): 219–232.

42. J. C. Quick, C. L. Cooper, J. H. Gavin and J. D. Quick. *Managing Executive Health: Building Strengths, Managing Risks* (Cambridge, UK: Cambridge University Press, 2008).

43. A. C. Edmondson and T. Besieux, "Reflections: Voice and Silence in Workplace Conversations," *Journal of Change Management* 21 (2021): 269–286

44. T. Foulk, A. Woolum, and A. Erez, "Catching Rudeness Is Like Catching a Cold: The Contagion Effect of Low-Intensity Negative Behaviors," *Journal of Applied Psychology* 101, No. 1 (January 2016): 50–67.

45. A. M. Katz and V. T. Katz, eds., *Foundations of Nonverbal Communication* (Carbondale, Ill.: Southern Illinois University Press, 1983).

46. M. D. Lieberman, "Intuition: A Social Cognitive Neuroscience Approach," *Psychological Bulletin* (2000): 109–138.

47. E. T. Hall, *The Hidden Dimension* (Garden City, N.Y.: Doubleday Anchor, 1966).

48. E. T. Hall, "Proxemics," in A. M. Katz and V. T. Katz, eds., *Foundations of Nonverbal Communication* (Carbondale, Ill.: Southern Illinois University Press, 1983).

49. R. T. Barker and C. G. Pearce, "The Importance of Proxemics at Work," *Supervisory Management* 35 (1990): 10–11.

50. R. L. Birdwhistell, *Kinesics and Context* (Philadelphia: University of Pennsylvania Press, 1970).

51. K. I. Ruys and D. A. Stapel, "Emotion Elicitor or Emotion Messenger?" *Psychological Science* 19 (2008): 593–600.

52. M. G. Frank and P. Ekman, "Appearing Truthful Generalizes across Different Deception Situations," *Journal of Personality and Social Psychology* 86 (2004): 486–495.

53. P. Ekman and W. V. Friesen, "Research on Facial Expressions of Emotion," in A. M. Katz and V. T. Katz, eds., *Foundations of Nonverbal Communication* (Carbondale, Ill.: Southern Illinois University Press, 1983).

54. H. H. Tan, M. D. Foo, C. L. Chong, and R. Ng, "Situational and Dispositional Predictors of Displays of Positive Emotions," *Journal of Organizational Behavior* 24 (2003): 961–978.

55. M. de Rond and J. Lok, "Some Things Can Never Be Unseen: The Role of Context in Psychological Injury at Ware," *Academy of Management Journal* 59 (December 2016): 1965–1993.

56. A. M. Katz and V. T. Katz, *Foundations of Nonverbal Communication* (Carbondale, IL: Southern Illinois University Press, 1983): 181.

57. K. Sanders, P. T. Nguyen, D. Bouckenooghe, A. Rafferty, and G. Schwarz, "Unraveling the What and How of Organizational Communication to Employees During COVID-19 Pandemic: Adopting an Attributional Lens," *Journal of Applied Behavioral Science* 56 (2020): 289–293.

58. E. DeFilippis, S. M. Impink, M., Singell, J. T. Polzer, and R. Sadun, "The Impact of COVID-19 on Digital Communication Patterns," *Humanities and Social Sciences Communications* 9 (2022). https://doi.org/10.1057/s41599-022-01190-9

59. D. Seetharaman, "Zuckerberg Lays Out Broad Vision for Facebook in 6,000-Word Mission Statement," *Wall Street Journal*, February 17 (2017).

60. C. Brod, *Technostress: The Human Cost of the Computer Revolution* (Reading, Mass.: Addison-Wesley, 1984).

61. S. Kiesler, "Technology and the Development of Creative Environments," in Y. Ijiri and R. L. Kuhn, eds., *New Directions in Creative and Innovative Management* (Cambridge, Mass.: Ballinger Press, 1988).

62. S. Adams, "Being There," *Forbes* 187 (2011): 94.

63. S. Kiesler, J. Siegel, and T. W. McGuire, "Social Psychological Aspects of Computer-Mediated Communication," *American Psychologist* 39 (1984): 1123–1134.

64. P. Shachaf, "Cultural Diversity and Information and Communication Technology Impacts on Global Virtual Teams: An Exploratory Study," *Information & Management* 45 (2008): 131–142.

9

1. R. Waldinger and M. Schulz, *The Good Life: Lessons from the World's Longest Scientific Study of Happiness* (New York, NY: Simon & Schuster, 2023).

2. S. S. Webber and R. J. Klimoski, "Crews: A Distinct Type of Work Team," *Journal of Business and Psychology* 18 (2004): 261–279.

3. J. L. Nemanich, S. Vélez-Castrillon, and S. Werner, "Knowledge-Based and Contextual Factors Associated with R&D Teams' Improvisation Capability," *Journal of Management* 42, No. 7 (November 2016): 1874–1903.

4. A. M. Towsend, S. M. DeMarie, and A. R. Hendrickson, "Virtual Teams: Technology and the Workplace of the Future," *Academy of Management Executive* 12 (1998): 17–29.

5. T. Neeley, "Global Teams That Work," *Harvard Business Review*, October (2015).

6. A. Taylor and H. R. Greve, "Superman or the Fantastic Four? Knowledge Combination and Experience in Innovative Teams," *Academy of Management Journal* 49 (2006): 723–740.

7. S. Faraj and A. Yan, "Boundary Work in Knowledge Teams," *Journal of Applied Psychology* 94 (2009): 604–617.

8. P. Shaver and D. Buhrmester, "Loneliness, Sex-Role Orientation, and Group Life: A Social Needs Perspective," in P. Paulus, ed., *Basic Group Processes* (New York: Springer-Verlag, 1985): 259–288.

9. K. L. Bettenhausen and J. K. Murnighan, "The Development and Stability of Norms in Groups Facing Interpersonal and Structural Challenge," *Administrative Science Quarterly* 36 (1991): 20–35.

10. N. Ellemers, S. Pagliaro, M. Barreto, and C. W. Leach, "Is It Better to Be Moral Than Smart? The Effects of Morality and Competence Norms on the Decision to Work at Group Status Improvement," *Journal of Personality and Social Psychology* 95 (2008): 1397–1410.

11. I. Adarves-Yorno, T. Postmes, and S. A. Haslam, "Creative Innovation or Crazy Irrelevance? The Contribution of Group Norms and Social Identity to Creative Behavior," *Journal of Experimental Social Psychology* 43 (2007): 410–416.

12. D. Tjosvold and Z. Yu, "Goal Interdependence and Applying Abilities for Team In-Role and Extra-Role Performance in China," *Group Dynamics: Theory, Research, and Practice* 8 (2004): 98–111.

13. M. S. Cole, F. Walter, and H. Bruch, "Affective Mechanisms Linking Dysfunctional Behavior to Performance in Work Teams: A Moderated Mediation Study," *Journal of Applied Psychology* 93 (2008): 945–958.

14. V. U. Druskat and S. B. Wolff, "Building the Emotional Intelligence of Groups," *Harvard Business Review* 79 (2001): 80–90.

15. I. Summers, T. Coffelt, and R. E. Horton, "Work-Group Cohesion," *Psychological Reports* 63 (1988): 627–636.

16. D. C. Man and S. S. K. Lam, "The Effects of Job Complexity and Autonomy on Cohesiveness in Collectivistic and Individualistic Work Groups: A Cross-Cultural Analysis," *Journal of Organizational Behavior* 24 (2003): 979–1001.

17. Y. Shin and J. N. Choi, "What Makes a Group of Good Citizens? The Role of Perceived Group-Level Fit and Critical Psychological States in Organizational Teams," *Journal of Occupational and Organizational Psychology* 83 (2010): 531–552.

18. K. H. Price, "Working Hard to Get People to Loaf," *Basic and Applied Social Psychology* 14 (1993): 329–344.

19. M. C. Schippers, "Social Loafing Tendencies and Team Performance: The Compensating Effect of Agreeableness and Conscientiousness," *Academy of Management Learning & Education* 13 (2014): 62–81.

20. R. Albanese and D. D. Van Fleet, "Rational Behavior in Groups: The Free-Riding Tendency," *Academy of Management Review* 10 (1985): 244–255.

21. E. Diener, "Deindividuation, Self-Awareness, and Disinhibition," *Journal of Personality and Social Psychology* 37 (1979): 1160–1171.

22. S. Prentice-Dunn and R. W. Rogers, "Deindividuation and the Self-Regulation of Behavior," in P. Paulus, ed., *Psychology of Group Influence* (Hillsdale, N.J.: Erlbaum, 1989): 87–109.

23. B. M. Bass and E. C. Ryterband, *Organizational Psychology*, 2nd ed. (Boston: Allyn & Bacon, 1979).

24. W. G. Bennis and H. A. Shepard, "A Theory of Group Development," *Human Relations* 9 (1956): 415–438.

25. A. Joshi and A. P. Knight, "Who Defers to Whom and Why? Dual Pathways Linking Demographic Differences and Dyadic Deference to Team Effectiveness," *Academy of Management Journal* 58 (2015): 59–84.

26. D. L. Fields and T. C. Bloom, "Employee Satisfaction in Work Groups with Different Gender Composition," *Journal of Organizational Behavior* 18 (1997): 181–196.

27. D. C. Lau and J. K. Murnighan, "Demographic Diversity and Faultlines: The Compositional Dynamics of Organizational Groups," *Academy of Management Review* 23 (1998): 325–340.

28. B. Tuckman, "Developmental Sequence in Small Groups," *Psychological Bulletin* 63 (1965): 384–399; B. Tuckman and M. Jensen, "Stages of Small-Group Development," *Group and Organizational Studies* 2 (1977): 419–427.

29. S. T. Bell and J. A. Belohlav, "The Power of 'We': The Effects of Psychological Collectivism on Team Performance over Time," *Journal of Applied Psychology* 96 (2011): 247–262.

30. D. Nichols, "Quality Program Sparked Company Turnaround," *Personnel* (October 1991): 24. For a commentary on Wallace's hard times and subsequent emergence from Chapter 11 bankruptcy, see R. C. Hill, "When the Going Gets Tough: A Baldrige Award Winner on the Line," *Academy of Management Executive* 7 (1993): 75–79.

31. M. Hardaker and B. K. Ward, "How to Make a Team Work," *Harvard Business Review* 65 (1987): 112–120.

32. C. R. Gowen, "Managing Work Group Performance by Individual Goals and Group Goals for an Interdependent Group Task," *Journal of Organizational Behavior Management* 7 (1986): 5–27.

33. K. L. Bettenhausen and J. K. Murnighan, "The Emergence of Norms in Competitive Decision-Making Groups," *Administrative Science Quarterly* 30 (1985): 350–372; K. L. Bettenhausen, "Five Years of Groups Research: What We Have Learned and What Needs to Be Addressed," *Journal of Management* 17 (1991): 345–381.

34. N. Li, B. L. Kirkman, and C. O. L. H. Porter, "Toward a Model of Work Team Altruism," *Academy of Management Review* 39 (2014): 541–565.

35. J. E. McGrath, *Groups: Interaction and Performance* (Englewood Cliffs, N.J.: Prentice-Hall, 1984).

36. K. L. Gammage, A. V. Carron, and P. A. Estabrooks, "Team Cohesion and Individual Productivity," *Small Group Research* 32 (2001): 3–18.

37. W. J. Becker and R. Cropanzano, "Good Acting Requires a Good Cast: A Meso-Level Model of Deep Acting in Work Teams," *Journal of Organizational Behavior* 36 (2015): 232–249.

38. N. Steckler and N. Fondas, "Building Team Leader Effectiveness: A Diagnostic Tool," *Organizational Dynamics* 23 (1995): 20–35.

39. D. Drews, *TEAMFLOW: The Science of Creating Positive Leadership Practices with IMPACT* (Austin, TX: Per Capita Publishing, 2022).

40. A. Carter and S. Holmes, "Curiously Strong Teamwork," *Business-Week* 4023 (February 26, 2007): 90–92.

41. W. R. Lassey, "Dimensions of Leadership," in W. R. Lassey and R. Fernandez, eds., *Leadership and Social Change* (La Jolla, Calif.: University Associates, 1976): 10–15.

42. B. Broysberg and L. Lee, "The Effect of Colleague Quality on Top Performance: The Case of Security Analysts," *Journal of Organizational Behavior* 29 (2008): 1123–1144.

43. J. D. Quick, G. Moorhead, J. C. Quick, E. A. Gerloff, K. L. Mattox, and C. Mullins, "Decision Making among Emergency Room Residents: Preliminary Observations and a Decision Model," *Journal of Medical Education* 58 (1983): 117–125.

44. J. Sieweke and B. Zhao, "The Impact of Team Familiarity and Team Leader Experience on Team Coordination Errors: A Panel Analysis of Professional Basketball Teams," *Journal of Organizational Behavior* 36 (2015): 382–402.

45. W. J. Duncan and J. P. Feisal, "No Laughing Matter: Patterns of Humor in the Workplace," *Organizational Dynamics* 17 (1989): 18–30.

46. L. Hirschhorn, *Managing in the New Team Environment* (Upper Saddle River, N.J.: Prentice-Hall): 521A.

47. G. Chen and R. J. Klimoski, "The Impact of Expectations on Newcomer Performance in Teams as Mediated by Work Characteristics, Social Exchanges, and Empowerment," *Academy of Management Journal* 46 (2003): 591–607.

48. B. Beersma, J. R. Hollenbeck, S. E. Humphrey, H. Moon, D. E. Conlon, and D. R. Ilgen, "Cooperation, Competition, and Team Performance: Toward a Contingency Approach," *Academy of Management Journal* 46 (2003): 572–590.

49. B. L. Bonner, A. T. Soderberg, N. L. Meikle and J. R. Overbeck, "Effects of Experience, Expertise, Reward Power, and Decision Power in Groups," *Group Dynamics: Theory, Research, and Practice* 26(2022): 309–321.

50. G. Parker, *Team Players and Teamwork* (San Francisco: Jossey-Bass, 1990).

51. N. R. F. Maier, "Assets and Liabilities in Group Problem Solving: The Need for an Integrative Function," *Psychological Review* 74 (1967): 239–249.

52. T. A. Stewart, "The Search for the Organization of Tomorrow," *Fortune* (May 18, 1992): 92–98

53. P. Chattopadhyay, M. Tluchowska, and E. George, "Identifying the Ingroup: A Closer Look at the Influence of Demographic Dissimilarity on Employee Social Identity," *Academy of Management Review* 29 (2004): 180–202.

54. M. M. Stewart and P. Garcia-Prieto, "A Relational Demography Model of Workgroup Identification: Testing the Effects of Race, Race Dissimilarity, Racial Identification, and Communication Behavior," *Journal of Organizational Behavior* 29 (2008): 657–680.

55. E. V. Hobman, P. Bordia, and C. Gallois, "Consequences of Feeling Dissimilar from Others in a Work Team," *Journal of Business and Psychology* 17 (2003): 301–325.

56. A. E. Randel and K. S. Jaussi, "Functional Background Identity, Diversity, and Individual Performance in Cross-Functional Teams," *Academy of Management Journal* 46 (2003): 763–774.

57. J. S. Bunderson, "Team Member Functional Background and Involvement in Management Teams: Direct Effects and the Moderating Role of Power Centralization," *Academy of Management Journal* 46 (2003): 458–474.

58. G. S. Van Der Vegt, E. Van De Vliert, and A. Oosterhof, "Informational Dissimilarity and Organizational Citizenship Behavior: The Role of Intrateam Interdependence and Team Identification," *Academy of Management Journal* 46 (2003): 715–727.

59. F. Balkundi, M. Kilduff, Z. I. Barsness, and J. H. Michael, "Demographic Antecedents and Performance Consequences of Structural Holes in Work Teams," *Journal of Organizational Behavior* 28 (2007): 241–260.

60. A. Pirola-Merlo and L. Mann, "The Relationship between Individual Creativity and Team Creativity: Aggregating across People and Time," *Journal of Organizational Behavior* 25 (2004): 235–257.

61. L. Thompson, "Improving the Creativity of Organizational Work Groups," *Academy of Management Executive* 17 (2003): 96–111.

62. J. Han and D. J. Brass, "Human Capital Diversity in the Creation of Social Capital for Team Creativity," *Journal of Organizational Behavior* 35 (2014): 54–71.

63. C. Ford and D. M. Sullivan, "A Time for Everything: How the Timing of Novel Contributions Influences Project Team Outcomes," *Journal of Organizational Behavior* 25 (2004): 279–292.

64. N. M. Llorinkova and S. J. Perry, "When Is Empowerment Effective? The Role of Leader-Leader Exchange in Empowering Leadership, Cynicism, and Time Theft," *Academy of Management* 43, No. 5 (May 2017): 1631–1654.

65. F. Shipper and C. C. Manz, "Employee Self-Management without Formally Designated Teams: An Alternative Road to Empowerment," *Organizational Dynamics* (Winter 1992): 48–62.

66. J. Hut and E. Molleman, "Empowerment and Team Development," *Team Performance Management* 4 (1998): 53–66.

67. J. E. Mathieu, L. L. Gilson, and T. M. Ruddy, "Empowerment and Team Effectiveness: An Empirical Test of an Integrated Model," *Journal of Applied Psychology* 91 (2006): 97–108.

68. H. Zhou and J. Chen, "How Does Psychological Empowerment Prevention Emotional Exhaustion? Psychological Safety and Organizational Embeddedness as Mediators," *Frontiers in Psychology* 12 (2021). https://doi.org/10.3389/fpsyg.2021.546687

69. T. Dennerlein and B. L. Kirkman, "The Hidden Dark Side of Empowering Leadership: The Moderating Role of Hindrance Stressors in Explaining When Empowering Employees can Promote Moral Disengagement and Unethical Pro-organizational Behavior," *Journal of Applied Psychology* 107 (2022): 2220–2242.

70. P. Block, *The Empowered Manager: Positive Political Skills at Work* (San Francisco: Jossey-Bass, 1987).

71. V. J. Derlega and J. Grzelak, eds., *Cooperation and Helping Behavior: Theories and Research* (New York: Academic Press, 1982).

72. C. Douglas and W. L. Gardner, "Transition to Self-Directed Work Teams: Implications of Transition Time and Self-Monitoring for Managers' Use of Influence Tactics," *Journal of Organizational Behavior* 25 (2004): 47–65.

73. A. G. Athos and J. J. Gabarro, *Interpersonal Behavior: Communication and Understanding in Relationships* (Englewood Cliffs, J.J.: Prentice-Hall, 1978).

74. C. Douglas, J. S. Martin, and R. H. Krapels, "Communication in the Transition to Self-Directed Work Teams," *Journal of Business Communication* 43 (2006): 295–321.

75. J. L. Cordery, W. S. Mueller, and L. M. Smith, "Attitudinal and Behavioral Effects of Autonomous Group Working: A Longitudinal Field Study," *Academy of Management Journal* 34 (1991): 464–476.

76. G. Moorhead, C. P. Neck, and M. S. West, "The Tendency toward Defective Decision Making within Self-Managing Teams: The Relevance of Groupthink for the 21st Century," *Organizational Behavior and Human Decision Processes* 73 (1998): 327–351.

77. S. O'Meara and C. Cooper, *Remote Workplace Culture: How to Bring Energy and Focus to Remote Teams* (London and New York: KoganPage, 2022).

78. B. M. Staw and L. D. Epstein, "What Bandwagons Bring: Effects of Popular Management Techniques on Corporate Performance, Reputation, and CEO Pay," *Administrative Science Quarterly* 45 (2000): 523–556.

79. R. M. Robinson, S. L. Oswald, K. S. Swinehart, and J. Thomas, "Southwest Industries: Creating High-Performance Teams for High-Technology Production," Planning Review 19: published by the Planning Forum (November-December 1991): 10–47.

80. D. C. Hambrick and P. Mason, "Upper Echelons: The Organization as a Reflection of Its Top Managers," *Academy of Management Review* 9 (1984): 193–206.

81. C. Heavey and Z. Simsek, "Distributed Cognition in Top Management Teams and Organizational Ambidexterity," *Academy of Management* 43, 3 (May 2017): 919–945.

82. D. C. Hambrick, "Upper Echelons Theory: An Update," *Academy of Management Review* 32 (2007): 334–343.

83. R. Krause, J. Rob, and K. A. Whitler, "The Top Management Team: Conceptualization, Operationalization, and a Roadmap for Scholarship," *Journal of Management* 48 (2022): 1548–1601.

84. A Conversation with Indra Nooyi, The Maverick Speaker Series, The University of Texas at Arlington, March 21, 2023.

85. D. C. Hambrick and G. D. S. Fukutomi, "The Seasons of a CEO's Tenure," *Academy of Management Review* 16 (1991): 719–742.

86. J. C. Quick, D. L. Nelson, and J. D. Quick, "Successful Executives: How Independent?" *Academy of Management Executive* 1 (1987): 139–145.

87. A. A. Cannella, Jr, J. Park, and H. Lee, "Top Management Team Functional Background Diversity and Firm Performance: Examining the Roles of Team Member Colocation and Environmental Uncertainty," *Academy of Management Journal* 51 (2008): 768–784. D. F. Larcker and B. Tayan, "Diversity in the C-Suite," Stanford Closer Look Series, Stanford Graduate School of Business, April 2020. https://www.gsb.stanford.edu/faculty-research/publications/diversity-c-suite

88. J. W. Ridge, A. D. Hill, and F. Aime, "Implication of Multiple Concurrent Pay Comparisons for Top-Team Turnover," *Academy of Management* 43, No. 3 (May 2017): 671–690.

89. N. J. Adler, *International Dimensions of Organizational Behavior* (Mason, Ohio: South-Western, 2001).

90. I. D. Steiner, *Group Process and Productivity* (New York: Academic Press, 1972).

91. Eaton Corporation plc, *The Power of Perspectives, 2021 Global Inclusion and Diversity Transparency Report*, Dublin, Ireland, 2022.

92. E. Kearney, D. Gebert, and S. C. Voelpel, "When and How Diversity Benefits Teams: The Importance of Team Members' Need for Cognition," *Academy of Management Journal* 52 (2009): 581–598.

93. T. Buyl, C. Boone, W. Hendriks, and P. Matthyssens, "Top Management Team Functional Diversity and Firm Performance: The Moderating Role of CEO Characteristics," *Journal of Management Studies* 48 (2011): 151–176.

10

1. H. A. Simon, *The New Science of Management Decision* (New York: Harper & Row, 1960).

2. T. Bove, "What's Behind Netflix's Culture Shift to Fear-Based Decision-Making?" *Fortune*, August 4 (2022), accessed at https://fortune.com/2022/08/04/netflix-culture-shifting-to-fear-based-decision-making/.

3. G. Huber, *Managerial Decision Making* (Glenview, Ill.: Scott, Foresman, 1980).

4. H. A. Simon, *Administrative Behavior* (New York: Macmillan, 1957).

5. L. Cabantous and J.-P. Gond, "Rational Decision Making as Performative Praxis: Explaining Rationality's *Eternel Retour*," *Organization Science* 22 (2011): 573–586.

6. R. L. Ackoff, "The Art and Science of Mess Management," *Interfaces* (February 1981): 20–26.

7. J. N. Marewski and G. Gigerenzer, "Heuristic Decision Making in Medicine," *Dialogues in Clinical Neuroscience* 14 (2012): 77–89.

8. J. S. Lerner, Y. Li, P. Valdesolo, and K. S. Kassam, "Emotion and Decision Making," *Annual Review of Psychology* 66 (2015): 799–823.

9. A. Saleh, "Brain Hemisphericity and Academic Majors: A Correlation Study," *College Student Journal* 35 (2001): 193–200.

10. D. Kahneman and A. Tversky, "Prospect Theory: An Analysis of Decision Under Risk," *Econometrica* 47 (1979): 263–291.

11. J. Kruger and D. Dunning, "Unskilled and Unaware of It: How Difficulties in Recognizing One's Own Incompetence Lead to Inflated Self-Assessments," *Journal of Personality and Social Psychology* 77 (1999):121–1134.

12. V. Berthet, "The Impact of Cognitive Biases on Professionals' Decision-Making: A Review of Four Occupational Areas," *Frontiers in Psychology* January 4 (2022), accessed at https://www.frontiersin.org/articles/10.3389/fpsyg.2021.802439/full.

13. N. Khatri, "The Role of Intuition in Strategic Decision Making," *Human Relations* 53 (2000): 57–86.

14. H. Mintzberg, "Planning on the Left Side and Managing on the Right," *Harvard Business Review* 54 (1976): 51–63.

15. D. J. Isenberg, "How Senior Managers Think," *Harvard Business Review* 62 (1984): 81–90.

16. R. N. Beck, "Visions, Values, and Strategies: Changing Attitudes and Culture," *Academy of Management Executive* 1 (1987): 33–41.

17. K. G. Ross, G. A. Klein, P. Thunholm, J. F. Schmitt, and H. C. Baxter, "The Recognition-Primed Decision Model," *Military Review*, Fort Leavenworth 84 (2004): 6–10.

18. C. I. Barnard, *The Functions of the Executive* (Cambridge, Mass.: Harvard University Press, 1938).

19. R. Rowan, *The Intuitive Manager* (New York: Little, Brown, 1986).

20. W. H. Agor, *Intuition in Organizations* (Newbury Park, Calif.: Sage, 1989).

21. D. J. Isenberg, *How Senior Managers Think* (Thousand Oaks, CA: Sage Publications, 1991).

22. H. A. Simon, "Making Management Decisions: The Role of Intuition and Emotion," *Academy of Management Executive* 1 (1987): 57–64.

23. J. L. Redford, R. H. McPhierson, R. G. Frankiewicz, and J. Gaa, "Intuition and Moral Development," *Journal of Psychology* 129 (1994): 91–101.

24. W. H. Agor, "How Top Executives Use Their Intuition to Make Important Decisions," *Business Horizons* 29 (1986): 49–53.

25. O. Behling and N. L. Eckel, "Making Sense out of Intuition," *Academy of Management Executive* 5 (1991): 46–54.

26. L. R. Beach, *Image Theory: Decision Making in Personal and Organizational Contexts* (Chichester, England: Wiley, 1990).

27. E. Bonabeau, "Don't Trust Your Gut," *Harvard Business Review* 81 (2003): 116–126.

28. L. Livingstone, "Person-Environment Fit on the Dimension of Creativity: Relationships with Strain, Job Satisfaction, and Performance" (Ph.D. diss., Oklahoma State University, 1992).

29. G. Wallas, *The Art of Thought* (New York: Harcourt Brace, 1926).

30. H. Benson and W. Proctor, *The Break-Out Principle* (Scribner: New York, 2003); G. L. Fricchione, B. T. Slingsby, and H. Benson, "The Placebo Effect and the Relaxation Response: Neural Processes and Their Coupling to Constitutive Nitric Oxide," *Brain Research Reviews* 35 (2001): 1–19.

31. M. D. Mumford and S. B. Gustafson, "Creativity Syndrome: Integration, Application, and Innovation," *Psychological Bulletin* 103 (1988): 27–43.

32. T. Poze, "Analogical Connections—The Essence of Creativity," *Journal of Creative Behavior* 17 (1983): 240–241.

33. I. Sladeczek and G. Domino, "Creativity, Sleep, and Primary Process Thinking in Dreams," *Journal of Creative Behavior* 19 (1985): 38–46.

34. F. Barron and D. M. Harrington, "Creativity, Intelligence, and Personality," *Annual Review of Psychology* 32 (1981): 439–476.

35. J. Zhou, G.R. Oldham, A. Chuang, and R.S. Hsu, "Enhancing Employee Creativity: Effects of Choice, Rewards, and Personality," *Journal of Applied Psychology* 107 (2022): 503–513.

36. A. M. Grant and J. W. Berry, "The Necessity of Others Is the Mother of Invention: Intrinsic and Prosocial Motivations, Perspective Taking, and Creativity," *Academy of Management Journal* 54, No. 1 (2011): 73–96.

37. A. M. Isen, "Positive Affect and Decision Making," in W. M. Goldstein and R. M. Hogarth, eds., *Research on Judgment and Decision Making* (Cambridge, England: Cambridge University Press, 1997).

38. G. L. Clore, N. Schwartz, and M. Conway, "Cognitive Causes and Consequences of Emotion," in R. S. Wyer and T. K. Srull, eds., *Handbook of Social Cognition* (Hillsdale, N.J.: Erlbaum, 1994): 323–417.

39. B. L. Frederickson, "What Good Are Positive Emotions?" *Review of General Psychology* 2 (1998): 300–319; B. L. Frederickson, "The Role of Positive Emotions in Positive Psychology," *American Psychologist* 56 (2001): 218–226.

40. L. Praslova, "Neurodiversity is Critical for Innovation in the Workplace," *Fast Company*, August 26 (2022), accessed at https://www.fastcompany.com/90782113/neurodiversity-is-critical-for-innovation-in-the-workplace.

41. A. Kasirer and N. Mashal, "Verbal Creativity in Autism," *Frontiers in Human Neuroscience* 8 (2014), accessed at https://www.frontiersin.org/articles/10.3389/fnhum.2014.00615/full.

42. H. A. White and P. Shah, "Uninhibited Imaginations: Creativity in Adults with Attention-Deficit/Hyperactivity Disorder," *Personality and Individual Differences* 40 (2006): 1121–1131.

43. J. Zhou, "When the Presence of Creative Coworkers Is Related to Creativity: Role of Supervisor Close Monitoring, Developmental Feedback, and Creative Personality," *Journal of Applied Psychology* 88 (2003): 413–422.

44. J. Peng, Y. Chen, Y. Xia, and Y. Ran, "Workplace Loneliness, Leader-Member Exchange and Creativity: The Cross-Level Moderating Role of Leader Compassion," *Personality and Individual Differences* 104 (2017): 510–515.

45. G. Koseoglu, C.E. Shalley, and G.J. Lemoine, "Every Sherlock Needs a Dr. Watson: A Theory of Creativity Catalysts in Organizations," *Journal of Organizational Behavior* 43 (2022): 840–857.

46. T. M. Amabile, R. Conti, H. Coon, J. Lazenby, and M. Herron, "Assessing the Work Environment for Creativity," *Academy of Management Journal* 39 (1996): 1154–1184.

47. T. Tetenbaum and H. Tetenbaum, "Office 2000: Tear Down the Wall," *Training* (February 2000): 58–64.

48. L. Livingstone, D. L. Nelson, and S.H. Barr, "Person-Environment Fit and Creativity: An Examination of Supply-Value and Demand-Ability Versions of Fit," *Journal of Management* 23 (1997): 119–146.

49. R. L. Firestein, "Effects of Creative Problem-Solving Training on Communication Behaviors in Small Groups," *Small Group Research* (November 1989): 507–521.

50. R. Von Oech, *A Whack on the Side of the Head* (New York: Warner, 1983).

51. A. G. Robinson and S. Stern, *How Innovation and Improvement Actually Happen* (San Francisco: Berrett Koehler, 1997).

52. M. D. Mumford, E. M. Todd, C. Higgs, and T. McIntosh, "Cognitive Skills and Leadership Performance: The Nine Critical Skills," *The Leadership Quarterly* 28 (2017): 24–39.

53. R. Y. J. Chua, Y. Roth, and J. Lemoine, "How Culture Impacts Creativity: Cultural Tightness, Cultural Distance, and Global Creative Work," *Administrative Science Quarterly* (in press), published online December 8, 2014.

54. G. Stasser, L. A. Taylor, and C. Hanna, "Information Sampling in Structured and Unstructured Discussion of Three- and Six-Person Groups," *Journal of Personality and Social Psychology* 57 (1989): 67–78.

55. E. Kirchler and J. H. Davis, "The Influence of Member Status Differences and Task Type on Group Consensus and Member Position Change," *Journal of Personality and Social Psychology* 51 (1986): 83–91.

56. R. F. Maier, "Assets and Liabilities in Group Problem Solving," *Psychological Review* 74 (1967): 239–249.

57. M. E. Shaw, *Group Dynamics: The Psychology of Small Group Behavior*, 3rd ed. (New York: McGraw-Hill, 1981).

58. P. W. Yetton and P. C. Bottger, "Individual versus Group Problem Solving: An Empirical Test of a Best Member Strategy," *Organizational Behavior and Human Performance* 29 (1982): 307–321.

59. W. Watson, L. Michaelson, and W. Sharp, "Member Competence, Group Interaction, and Group Decision Making: A Longitudinal Study," *Journal of Applied Psychology* 76 (1991): 803–809.

60. I. Janis, *Victims of Groupthink* (Boston: Houghton Mifflin, 1972); M. Kostera, M. Proppe, and M. Szatkowski, "Staging the New Romantic Hero in the Old Cynical Theatre: On Managers, Roles, and Change in Poland," *Journal of Organizational Behavior* 16 (1995): 631–646.

61. M. A. Hogg and S. C. Hains, "Friendship and Group Identification: A New Look at the Role of Cohesiveness in Groupthink," *European Journal of Social Psychology* 28 (1998): 323–341.

62. P. E. Jones and H. M. P. Roelofsma, "The Potential for Social Contextual and Group Biases in Team Decision Making: Biases, Conditions, and Psychological Mechanisms," *Ergonomics* 43 (2000): 1129–1152; J. M. Levine, E. T. Higgins, and H. Choi, "Development of Strategic Norms in Groups," *Organizational Behavior and Human Decision Processes* 82 (2000): 88–101.

63. A. L. Brownstein, "Biased Predecision Processing," *Psychological Bulletin* 129 (2003): 545–568.

64. C. P. Neck and G. Moorhead, "Groupthink Remodeled: The Importance of Leadership, Time Pressure, and Methodical Decision-Making Procedures," *Human Relations* 48 (1995): 537–557.

65. J. Schwartz and M. L. Ward, "Final Shuttle Report Cites 'Broken Safety Culture' at NASA," *The New York Times*, August 26 (2003), accessed at http://www.nytimes.com/2003/08/26/national/26CND-SHUT.html?ex=1077253200&en=882575f2c17ed8ff&ei=5070; C. Ferraris and R. Carveth, "NASA and the Columbia Disaster: Decision Making by Groupthink?" in Proceedings of the 2003 Convention of the Association for Business Communication Annual Convention, accessed at http://www.businesscommunication.org/conventions/Proceedings/2003/PDF/03ABC03.pdf.

66. W. P. Cheshire Jr., "Loopthink: A Limitation of Medical Artificial Intelligence," *Ethics & Medicine* 33 (2017): 7–12.

67. E. Dhawan, "How to Fight the Groupthink that Happens When We Work Virtually," *Fast Company*, November 11 (2020), accessed at https://www.fastcompany.com/90572111/how-to-fight-the-groupthink-that-happens-when-we-work-virtually.

68. A. C. Homan, D. van Knippenberg, G. A. Van Kleef, and K. W. C. De Dreu, "Bridging Faultlines by Valuing Diversity: Diversity Beliefs, Information Elaboration, and Performance in Diverse Work Groups," *Journal of Applied Psychology* 92, No. 5 (2007):1189–1199.

69. G. Moorhead, R. Ference, and C. P. Neck, "Group Decision Fiascoes Continue: Space Shuttle *Challenger* and a Revised Groupthink Framework," *Human Relations* 44 (1991): 539–550.

70. D. Streitfeld, "At eBay, Lurid Crimes and the Search for Punishment," *The New York Times*, September 16 (2022), accessed at https://www.nytimes.com/2022/09/16/technology/ebay-cyberstalking-crimes.html.

71. S. Moscovici and M. Zavalloni, "The Group as a Polarizer of Attitudes," *Journal of Personality and Social Psychology* 12 (1969): 125–135.

72. G. R. Goethals and M. P. Zanna, "The Role of Social Comparison in Choice of Shifts," *Journal of Personality and Social Psychology* 37 (1979): 1469–1476.

73. A. Vinokur and E. Burnstein, "Effects of Partially Shared Persuasive Arguments on Group-Induced Shifts: A Problem-Solving Approach," *Journal of Personality and Social Psychology* 29 (1974): 305–315; J. Pfeffer, "Seven Practices of Successful Organizations," *California Management Review* 40 (1998): 96–124.

74. J. K. Palmer and J. M. Loveland, "The Influence of Group Discussion on Performance Judgments: Rating Accuracy, Contrast Effects and Halo," *The Journal of Psychology: Interdisciplinary and Applied* 142 (2008): 117–130.

75. P. Paulus, N. W. Kohn, L. E. Arditti, and R. Korde, "Understanding the Group Size Effect in Electronic Brainstorming," *Small Group Research* 44 (2013): 332–352.

76. N. Michinov, E. Jamet, N. Metayer, and B. L. Henaff, "The Eyes of Creativity: Impact of Social Comparison and Individual Creativity on Performance and Attention to Others' Ideas During Electronic Brainstorming," *Computers in Human Behavior* 42 (2015): 57–67.

77. A. Van de Ven and A. Delbecq, "The Effectiveness of Nominal, Delphi and Interacting Group Decision-Making Processes," *Academy of Management Journal* 17 (1974): 605–621.

78. R. A. Cosier and C. R. Schwenk, "Agreement and Thinking Alike: Ingredients for Poor Decisions," *Academy of Management Executive* 4 (1990): 69–74.

79. D. M. Schweiger, W. R. Sandburg, and J. W. Ragan, "Group Approaches for Improving Strategic Decision Making: A Comparative Analysis of Dialectical Inquiry, Devil's Advocacy, and Consensus," *Academy of Management Journal* 29 (1986): 149–159.

80. G. Whyte, "Decision Failures: Why They Occur and How to Prevent Them," *Academy of Management Executive* 5 (1991): 23–31.

81. L. Scholten, D. van Knippenberg, B. A. Nijstad, and K. W. C. De Dreu, "Motivated Information Processing and Group Decision-Making: Effects of Process Accountability on Information Processing and Decision Quality," *Journal of Experimental Social Psychology* 43, No. 4 (2007): 539–552.

82. N. Adler, *International Dimensions of Organizational Behavior*, 3rd ed. (Mason, Ohio: South-Western, 1997).

83. K. W. Phillips and D. L. Lloyd, "When Surface- and Deep-Level Diversity Collide: The Effects on Dissenting Group Members," *Organizational Behavior and Human Decision Processes* 99, No. 2 (2006): 143–160.

84. T. Simons, L. H. Pelled, and K. A. Smith, "Making Use of Difference: Diversity, Debate, and Decision Comprehensiveness in Top Management Teams," *Academy of Management Journal* 42, No. 6 (1999): 662–673.

85. B. A. Livingston, P. Schilpzand, and A. Erez, "Not What You Expected to Hear: Accented Messages and Their Effect on Choice," *Journal of Management* 43 (2017): 804–833.

86. J. Pfeffer, "Seven Practices of Successful Organizations," *California Management Review* 40 (1998): 96–124.

87. L. A. Witt, M. C. Andrews, and K. M. Kacmar, "The Role of Participation in Decision Making in the Organizational Politics–Job Satisfaction Relationship," *Human Relations* 53 (2000): 341–358.

88. J. He and W. R. King, "The Role of User Participation in Information Systems Development: Implications from a Meta-Analysis," *Journal of Management Information Systems* 25 (2008): 301–331.

89. C. R. Leana, E. A. Locke, and D. M. Schweiger, "Fact and Fiction in Analyzing Research on Participative Decision Making: A Critique of Cotton, Vollrath, Froggatt, Lengnick-Hall, and Jennings," *Academy of Management Review* 15 (1990): 137–146; J. L. Cotton, D. A. Vollrath, M. L. Lengnick-Hall, and K. L. Froggatt, "Fact: The Form of Participation Does Matter—A Rebuttal to Leana, Locke, and Schweiger," *Academy of Management Review* 15 (1990): 147–153.

90. T. W. Malone, "Is Empowerment Just a Fad? Control, Decision Making, and Information Technology," *Sloan Management Review* 38 (1997): 23–35.

91. IBM Customer Success Stories, "City and County of San Francisco Lower Total Cost of Ownership and Build on Demand Foundation" (February 3, 2004), accessed at http://www-306.ibm.com/software/success/cssdb.nsf/cs/LWRT-5VTLM2?OpenDocument&Site=lotusmandc.

92. T. L. Brown, "Fearful of 'Empowerment': Should Managers Be Terrified?" *Industry Week* (June 18, 1990): 12.

93. P. G. Gyllenhammar, *People at Work* (Reading, Mass.: Addison-Wesley, 1977).

94. R. Tannenbaum and F. Massarik, "Participation by Subordinates in the Managerial Decision-Making Process," *Canadian Journal of Economics and Political Science* 16 (1950): 408–418.

95. H. Levinson, *Executive* (Cambridge, Mass.: Harvard University Press, 1981).

96. A. Kvamme, "The Self-Management Revolution is Here: How to Embrace It," *Forbes*, May 5 (2022), accessed at https://www.forbes.com/sites/forbestechcouncil/2022/05/05/the-self-management-revolution-is-here-how-to-embrace-it/?sh=4d7204fc635b.

97. "Riot's Agile Team Leadership Model: A Story of Challenging Convention (2017), https://www.riotgames.com/en/work-with-us/disciplines/dev-management/riots-agile-team-leadership-model-a-story-of-challenging-convention.

98. S. Khanagha, H.W. Volberda, A Alexiou, and M.C. Annosi, "Mitigating the Dark Side of Agile Teams: Peer Pressure, Leaders' Control, and the Innovative Output of Self-Managing Teams," *Journal of Product Innovation Management* 39 (2021), accessed at https://onlinelibrary.wiley.com/doi/full/10.1111/jpim.12589.

99. J. Auernhammer and B. Roth, "The Origin and Evolution of Stanford University's Design Thinking: From Product Design to Design Thinking in Innovation Management," *Journal of Product Innovation Management* 38 (2021): 623–644.

100. U. Johansson-Skoldberg, J. Woodilla and M. Cetinkaya, "Design Thinking: Past, Present, and Possible Futures," *Creativity and Innovation Management* 22 (2013): 121–146.

101. L. Thompson and D. Schonthal, "The Social Psychology of Design Thinking," *California Management Review*, January 7 (2020), accessed at https://journals.sagepub.com/doi/10.1177/0008125619897636.

102. R. F. Dam and T. Y. Siang, "What is Design Thinking and Why is it So Popular?" *Interaction Design Foundation*, accessed at https://www.interaction-design.org/literature/article/what-is-design-thinking-and-why-is-it-so-popular.

103. L. Vendraminelli, L. Macchion, A. Nosella, and A. Vinelli, "Design Thinking: Strategy for Digital Transformation," *Journal of Business Strategy*, March 21 (2022), accessed at https://www.emerald.com/insight/content/doi/10.1108/JBS-01-2022-0009/full/html?skipTracking=true.

104. J. Beshears and F. Gino, "Leaders as Decision Architects," *Harvard Business Review* 93 (2015): 52–62.

105. J. Davalos and D. Bennett, "The Nudge Conundrum," *Businessweek*, May 20 (2022), accessed at https://www.bloomberg.com/news/features/2022-05-27/how-uber-and-lyft-gamify-the-gig-economy.

11

1. G. C. Homans, "Social Behavior as Exchange," *American Journal of Sociology* 63 (1958): 597–606.

2. R. D. Middlemist and M. A. Hitt, *Organizational Behavior: Managerial Strategies for Performance* (St. Paul, Minn.: West Publishing, 1988).

3. C. Barnard, *The Functions of the Executive* (Cambridge, Mass.: Harvard University Press, 1938).

4. J. R. P. French and B. Raven, "The Bases of Social Power," in D. Cartwright, ed., *Group Dynamics: Research and Theory* (Evanston, Ill.: Row Peterson, 1962); T. R. Hinkin and C. A. Schriesheim, "Development and Application of New Scales to Measure the French and Raven (1959) Bases of Social Power," *Journal of Applied Psychology* 74 (1989): 561–567.

5. K. D. Elsbach and G. Elofson, "How the Packaging of Decision Explanations Affects Perceptions of Trustworthiness," *Academy of Management Journal* 43, No. 1 (2000): 80–89.

6. P. M. Podsakoff and C. A. Schriesheim, "Field Studies of French and Raven's Bases of Power: Critique, Reanalysis, and Suggestions for Future Research," *Psychological Bulletin* 97 (1985): 387–411.

7. M. A. Rahim, "Relationships of Leader Power to Compliance and Satisfaction with Supervision: Evidence from a National Sample of Managers," *Journal of Management* 15 (1989): 545–556.

8. C. Argyris, "Management Information Systems: The Challenge to Rationality and Emotionality," *Management Science* 17 (1971): 275–292; J. Naisbitt and P. Aburdene, *Megatrends 2000* (New York: Morrow, 1990).

9. P. P. Carson, K. D. Carson, E. L. Knight, and C. W. Roe, "Power in Organizations: A Look through the TQM Lens," *Quality Progress* (November 1995): 73–78.

10. K. Kruse, "Why Pepsi's CEO Writes to Her Employees' Parents," *Forbes*, February 6, 2014, accessed at http://www.forbes.com/sites/kevinkruse/2014/02/06/indra-nooyi-wholehearted-leader/.

11. J. Pfeffer and G. Salancik, *The External Control of Organizations* (New York: Harper & Row, 1978).

12. T. M. Welbourne and C. O. Trevor, "The Roles of Departmental and Position Power in Job Evaluation," *Academy of Management Journal* 43, No. 4 (2000): 761–771.

13. R. H. Miles, *Macro Organizational Behavior* (Glenview, Ill.: Scott, Foresman, 1980).

14. D. Hickson, C. Hinings, C. Lee, R. E. Schneck, and J. M. Pennings, "A Strategic Contingencies Theory of Intraorganizational Power," *Administrative Science Quarterly* 14 (1971): 219–220.

15. C. R. Hinings, D. J. Hickson, J. M. Pennings, and R. E. Schneck, "Structural Conditions of Intraorganizational Power," *Administrative Science Quarterly* 19 (1974): 22–44.

16. M. Velasquez, D. J. Moberg, and G. F. Cavanaugh, "Organizational Statesmanship and Dirty Politics: Ethical Guidelines for the Organizational Politician," *Organizational Dynamics* 11 (1982): 65–79.

17. D. E. McClelland, *Power: The Inner Experience* (New York: Irvington, 1975).

18. N. Shahinpoor and B. F. Matt, "The Power of One: Dissent and Organizational Life," *Journal of Business Ethics* 74, No. 1 (2007): 37–49.

19. N. Machiavelli, *The Prince*, trans. by G. Bull (Middlesex, England: Penguin Books, 1961).

20. S. Chen, A. Y. Lee-Chai, and J. A. Bargh, "Relationship Orientation as a Moderator of the Effects of Social Power," *Journal of Personality and Social Psychology* 80, No. 2 (2001): 173–187.

21. R. Kanter, "Power Failure in Management Circuits," *Harvard Business Review* (July–August 1979): 31–54.

22. F. Lee and L. Z. Tiedens, "Who's Being Served? 'Self-Serving' Attributions in Social Hierarchies," *Organizational Behavior and Human Decision Processes* 84, No. 2 (March 2001): 254–287.

23. M. Korda, *Power: How to Get It, How to Use It* (New York: Random House, 1975).

24. S. R. Thye, "A Status Value Theory of Power in Exchange Relations," *American Sociological Review* (2000): 407–432.

25. W. A. Hochwarter, C. C. Rosen, S. L. Jordan, G. R. Ferris, A. Ejaz, and L. P. Maher, "Perceptions of Organizational Politics Research: Past, Present, and Future," *Journal of Management*, 46 (2020): 879–907.

26. B. T. Mayes and R. T. Allen, "Toward a Definition of Organizational Politics," *Academy of Management Review* 2 (1977): 672–678.

27. M. Valle and P. L. Perrewe, "Do Politics Perceptions Relate to Political Behaviors? Tests of an Implicit Assumption and Expanded Model," *Human Relations* 53 (2000): 359–386.

28. W. A. Hochwarter, "The Interactive Effects of Pro-Political Behavior and Politics Perceptions on Job Satisfaction and Affective Commitment," *Journal of Applied Social Psychology* 33 (2003): 1360–1378.

29. W. A. Hochwarter, K. M. Kacmar, D. C. Treadway, and T. S. Watson, "It's All Relative: The Distinction and Prediction of Political Perceptions across Levels," *Journal of Applied Social Psychology* 33 (2003): 1955–2016.

30. D. A. Ralston, "Employee Ingratiation: The Role of Management," *Academy of Management Review* 10 (1985): 477–487; D. R. Beeman and T. W. Sharkey, "The Use and Abuse of Corporate Politics," *Business Horizons* (March–April 1987): 25–35.

31. C. O. Longnecker, H. P. Sims, and D. A. Gioia, "Behind the Mask: The Politics of Employee Appraisal," *Academy of Management Executive* 1 (1987): 183–193.

32. M. Valle and P. L. Perrewe, "Do Politics Perceptions Relate to Political Behaviors? Tests of an Implicit Assumption and Expanded Model," *Human Relations* 53, No. 3 (2000): 359–386.

33. D. Fedor, J. Maslyn, S. Farmer, and K. Bettenhausen, "The Contribution of Positive Politics to the Prediction of Employee Reactions," *Journal of Applied Social Psychology* 38, No. 1 (2008): 76–96.

34. D. Kipnis, S. M. Schmidt, and I. Wilkinson, "Intraorganizational Influence Tactics: Explorations in Getting One's Way," *Journal of Applied Psychology* 65 (1980): 440–452; D. Kipnis, S. Schmidt,

C. Swaffin-Smith, and I. Wilkinson, "Patterns of Managerial Influence: Shotgun Managers, Tacticians, and Bystanders," *Organizational Dynamics* (Winter 1984): 60–67; G. Yukl and C. M. Falbe, "Influence Tactics and Objectives in Upward, Downward, and Lateral Influence Attempts," *Journal of Applied Psychology* 75 (1990): 132–140.

35. A. Wilhelmy, M. Kleinmann, C. J. Konig, K. G. Melchers, and D. M. Truxillo, "How and Why Do Interviewers Try to Make Impressions on Applicants? A Qualitative Study," *Journal of Applied Psychology*, 10 (2016): 313–332.

36. G. Yukl, P. J. Guinan, and D. Sottolano, "Influence Tactics Used for Different Objectives with Subordinates, Peers, and Superiors," *Groups & Organization Management* 20 (1995): 272–296.

37. C. A. Higgins, T. A. Judge, and G. R. Ferris, "Influence Tactics and Work Outcomes: A Meta-Analysis," *Journal of Organizational Behavior* 24 (2003): 89–106.

38. K. K. Eastman, "In the Eyes of the Beholder: An Attributional Approach to Ingratiation and Organizational Citizenship Behavior," *Academy of Management Journal* 37 (1994): 1379–1391.

39. K. J. Harris, K. M. Kacmar, S. Zivnuska, and J. D Shaw, "The Impact of Political Skill on Impression Management Effectiveness," *Journal of Applied Psychology* 92, No. 1 (2007): 278–285.

40. J. D. Westphal and G. Shani, "Psyched-Up to Suck-Up: Self-Regulated Cognition, Interpersonal Influence, and Recommendations for Board Appointments in the Corporate Elite," *Academy of Management Journal*, 59 (2016): 479–509.

41. G. D. Keeves, J. D. Westphal, and M. L. McDonald, "Those Closest Wield the Sharpest Knife: How Ingratiation Leads to Resentment and Social Undermining of the CEO," *Administrative Science Quarterly*, published January 10 (2017) at http://journals.sagepub.com/action/doSearch?SeriesKey=asqa&AllField=westphal.

42. A. Drory and D. Beaty, "Gender Differences in the Perception of Organizational Influence Tactics," *Journal of Organizational Behavior* 12 (1991): 249–258.

43. S. Wellington, M. B. Kropf, and P. R. Gerkovich, "What's Holding Women Back?" *Harvard Business Review* (June 2003): 2–4.

44. P. Perrewe and D. Nelson, "Gender and Career Success: The Facilitative Role of Political Skill," *Organizational Dynamics* 33 (2004): 366–378.

45. R. Y. Hirokawa and A. Miyahara, "A Comparison of Influence Strategies Utilized by Managers in American and Japanese Organizations," *Communication Quarterly* 34 (1986): 250–265.

46. C. Anderson, S. E. Spataro, and F. J. Flynn, "Personality and Organizational Culture as Determinants of Influence," *Journal of Applied Psychology* 93 (May 2008): 702–710.

47. P. David, M. A. Hitt, and J. Gimeno, "The Influence of Activism by Institutional Investors on R&D," *Academy of Management Journal* 44, No. 1 (2001): 144–157.

48. G. R. Ferris, P. L. Perrewe, W. P. Anthony, and D. C. Gilmore, "Political Skill at Work," *Organizational Dynamics* 28 (2000): 25–37.

49. D. C. Treadway, W. A. Hochwarter, G. R. Ferris, C. J. Kacmar, C. Douglas, A. P. Ammeter, and M. R. Buckley, "Leader Political Skill and Employee Reactions," *Leadership Quarterly* 15 (2004): 493–513; K. K. Ahearn, G. R. Ferris, W. A. Hochwarter, C. Douglas, and A. P. Ammeter, "Leader Political Skill and Team Performance," *Journal of Management* 30, No. 3 (2004): 309–327.

50. P. L. Perrewé, K. L. Zellars, G. R. Ferris, A. M. Rossi, C. J. Kacmar, and D. A. Ralston, "Neutralizing Job Stressors: Political Skill as an Antidote to the Dysfunctional Consequences of Role Conflict Stressors," *Academy of Management Journal* 47 (2004): 141–152.

51. R. E. Frieder and K. J. Basik, "Political Skill, Behavioral Integrity, and Work Outcomes: Test of a Multistage Model," *Journal of Leadership and Organizational Studies*, 24 (2017): 65–82.

52. G. Meisler, "Exploring Emotional Intelligence, Political Skill, and Job Satisfaction," *Employee Relations* 36 (2014): 280–293.

53. D. C. Treadway, G. Adams, T. J. Hanes, P. L. Perrewe, M. J. Magnusen, and G. R. Ferris, "The Roles of Recruiter Political Skill and Performance Resource Leveraging in NCAA Football Recruitment Effectiveness," *Journal of Management* 40 (2014): 1607–1626.

54. S. Y. Todd, K. J. Harris, R. B. Harris, and A. R. Wheeler, "Career Success Implications of Political Skill," *The Journal of Social Psychology* 149, No. 3 (June 2009): 179–204; I. M. Jawahar, J. A. Meurs, G. R. Ferris, and W. A. Hochwarter, "Self-Efficacy and Political Skill as Comparative Predictors of Task and Contextual Performance: A Two-Study Constructive Replication," *Human Performance* 21 (2008): 138–157.

55. W. Ocasio, J. E. Pozner, and D. Milner, "Varieties of Political Capital and Power in Organizations: A Review and Integrative Framework," *The Academy of Management Annals*, 14 (2020): 303–338.

56. K. Kumar and M. S. Thibodeaux, "Organizational Politics and Planned Organizational Change," *Group and Organization Studies* 15 (1990): 354–365.

57. D. Buchanan, "You Stab My Back, I'll Stab Yours: Management Experience and Perceptions of Organization Political Behaviour," *British Journal of Management* 19 (March 2008): 49–64.

58. McClelland, *Power*.

59. D. R. Beeman and T. W. Sharkey, "Use and Abuse of Corporate Politics," *Business Horizons* 30 (1987): 26–30.

60. C. P. Parker, R. L. Dipboye, and S. L. Jackson, "Perceptions of Organizational Politics: An Investigation of Antecedents and Consequences," *Journal of Management* 21 (1995): 891–912.

61. S. J. Ashford, N. P. Rothbard, S. K. Piderit, and J. E. Dutton, "Out on a Limb: The Role of Context and Impression Management in Selling Gender-Equity Issues," *Administrative Science Quarterly* 43 (1998): 23–57.

62. J. Zhou and G. R. Ferris, "The Dimensions and Consequences of Organizational Politics Perceptions: A Confirmatory Analysis," *Journal of Applied Social Psychology* 25 (1995): 1747–1764.

63. M. L. Seidal, J. T. Polzer, and K. J. Stewart, "Friends in High Places: The Effects of Social Networks on Discrimination in Salary Negotiations," *Administrative Science Quarterly* 45 (2000): 1–24.

64. J. J. Gabarro and J. P. Kotter, "Managing Your Boss," *Harvard Business Review* (January–February 1980): 92–100.

65. P. Newman, "How to Manage Your Boss," *Peat, Marwick, Mitchell & Company's Management Focus* (May–June 1980): 36–37.

66. F. Bertolome, "When You Think the Boss Is Wrong," *Personnel Journal* 69 (1990): 66–73.

67. J. Conger and R. Kanungo, *Charismatic Leadership: The Elusive Factor in Organizational Effectiveness* (New York: Jossey-Bass, 1988).

68. G. M. Spreitzer, M. A. Kizilos, and S. W. Nason, "A Dimensional Analysis of the Relationship between Psychological Empowerment and Effectiveness, Satisfaction, and Strain," *Journal of Management* 23 (1997): 679–704.

69. L. D'Innocenzo, M. M. Luciano, J. E. Mathieu, M. T. Maynard, and G. Chen, "Empowered to Perform: A Multilevel Investigation of the Influence of Empowerment on Performance in Hospital Units," *Academy of Management Journal* 59 (2016): 1290–1307.

70. R. C. Ford and M. D. Fottler, "Empowerment: A Matter of Degree," *Academy of Management Executive* 9 (1995): 21–31.

71. M. R. Kukenberger, J. E. Mathieu, and T. Ruddy, "A Cross-Level Test of Empowerment and Process Influences on Members' Informal Learning and Team Commitment," *Journal of Management* 41 (2015): 987–1016.

72. X. Zhang and K. M. Bartol, "Linking Empowering Leadership and Employee Creativity: The Influence of Psychological Empowerment, Intrinsic Motivation, and Creative Process Engagement," *The Academy*

of Management Journal 53 (2010): 107–128; S. Seibert, G. Wang, and S. Courtright, "Antecedents and Consequences of Psychological and Team Empowerment in Organizations: A Meta-Analytic Review," *The Journal of Applied Psychology* 96, No. 5 (2011): 981–1003.

73. S. Patel, "10 Examples of Companies with Fantastic Cultures," *Enterpreneur* (August 6, 2015), accessed at https://www.entrepreneur.com/article/249174.

12

1. J. P. Kotter, "What Leaders Really Do," *Harvard Business Review* 68 (1990): 103–111.

2. D. A. Plowman, S. Solansky, T. E. Beck, L. Baker, M. Kulkarni, and D. V. Travis, "The Role of Leadership in Emergent, Self-Organization," *Leadership Quarterly* 18, No. 4 (2007): 341–356.

3. B. Stone, "Why Facebook Needs Sheryl Sandberg," *Bloomberg Businessweek* (May 12, 2011), accessed at http://www.businessweek.com/magazine/content/11_21/b4229050473695.htm.

4. A. Zaleznik, "HBR Classic—Managers and Leaders: Are They Different?" *Harvard Business Review* 70 (1992): 126–135.

5. "The World's 100 Most Powerful Women," *Forbes* (2016), accessed at https://www.forbes.com/profile/indra-nooyi/.

6. R. M. Stogdill, "Personal Factors Associated with Leadership: A Survey of the Literature," *Journal of Psychology* 25 (1948): 35–71.

7. K. L. Badura, B. M. Galvin, and M. Y. Lee, "Leadership Emergence: An Integrative Review," *Journal of Applied Psychology* 107 (2022): 2069–2100.

8. K. Lewin, R. Lippitt, and R. K. White, "Patterns of Aggressive Behavior in Experimentally Created 'Social Climates,'" *Journal of Social Psychology* 10 (1939): 271–299.

9. S. D. Sidle, "The Danger of Do Nothing Leaders," *The Academy of Management Perspectives* 21, No. 2 (2007): 75–77.

10. A. W. Halpin and J. Winer, "A Factorial Study of the Leader Behavior Description Questionnaire," in R. M. Stogdill and A. E. Coons, eds., *Leader Behavior: Its Description and Measurement*, research monograph No. 88 (Columbus, Ohio: Bureau of Business Research, The Ohio State University, 1957): 39–51.

11. E. A. Fleishman, "Leadership Climate, Human Relations Training, and Supervisory Behavior," *Personnel Psychology* 6 (1953): 205–222.

12. R. Kahn and D. Katz, "Leadership Practices in Relation to Productivity and Morale," in D. Cartwright and A. Zander, eds., *Group Dynamics, Research and Theory* (Elmsford, NY: Row, Paterson, 1960).

13. J. Stoker, H. Garretsen, and D. Soudis, "Tightening the Leash after a Threat: A Multi-Level Event Study on Leadership Behavior Following the Financial Crisis," *The Leadership Quarterly* 30, No. 2 (2019): 199–214.

14. F. E. Fiedler, *A Theory of Leader Effectiveness* (New York: McGraw-Hill, 1964).

15. F. E. Fiedler, *Personality, Motivational Systems, and Behavior of High and Low LPC Persons*, tech. rep. No. 70–12 (Seattle: University of Washington, 1970).

16. J. T. McMahon, "The Contingency Theory: Logic and Method Revisited," *Personnel Psychology* 25 (1972): 697–710; L. H. Peters, D. D. Hartke, and J. T. Pohlman, "Fiedler's Contingency Theory of Leadership: An Application of the Meta-Analysis Procedures of Schmidt and Hunter," *Psychological Bulletin* 97 (1985): 224–285.

17. F. E. Fiedler, "The Contingency Model and the Dynamics of the Leadership Process," in L. Berkowitz, ed., *Advances in Experimental and Social Psychology*, vol. 11 (New York: Academic Press, 1978).

18. S. Arin and C. McDermott, "The Effect of Team Leader Characteristics on Learning, Knowledge Application, and Performance of Cross-Functional New Product Development Teams," *Decision Sciences* 34 (2003): 707–739.

19. F. E. Fiedler, "Engineering the Job to Fit the Manager," *Harvard Business Review* 43 (1965): 115–122.

20. R. J. House, "A Path–Goal Theory of Leader Effectiveness," *Administrative Science Quarterly* 16 (1971): 321–338; R. J. House and T. R. Mitchell, "Path–Goal Theory of Leadership," *Journal of Contemporary Business* 3 (1974): 81–97.

21. C. A. Schriescheim and V. M. Von Glinow, "The Path–Goal Theory of Leadership: A Theoretical and Empirical Analysis," *Academy of Management Journal* 20 (1977): 398–405; E. Valenzi and G. Dessler, "Relationships of Leader Behavior, Subordinate Role Ambiguity, and Subordinate Job Satisfaction," *Academy of Management Journal* 21 (1978): 671–678; N. R. F. Maier, *Leadership Methods and Skills* (New York: McGraw-Hill, 1963).

22. J. P. Grinnell, "An Empirical Investigation of CEO Leadership in Two Types of Small Firms," *S.A.M. Advanced Management Journal* 68 (2003): 36–41.

23. P. Hersey and K. H. Blanchard, "Life Cycle Theory of Leadership," *Training and Development* 23 (1969): 26–34; P. Hersey, K. H. Blanchard, and D. E. Johnson, *Management of Organizational Behavior: Leading Human Resources*, 8th ed. (Upper Saddle River, N.J.: Prentice-Hall, 2001).

24. B. M. Bass, *Bass and Stogdill's Handbook of Leadership: Theory, Research, and Managerial Applications*, 3rd ed. (New York: Free Press, 1990).

25. D. Van Knippenberg and S. B. Sitkin, "A Critical Assessment of Charismatic—Transformational Leadership Research: Back to the Drawing Board?" *Academy of Management Annals* 7, No. 1 (2013): 1–60.

26. G. B. Graen, and M. Uhl-Bien, "Relationship-Based Approach to Leadership: Development of Leader Member Exchange (LMX) Theory of Leadership over 25 Years: Applying a Multi-Level Multi-Domain Perspective," *The Leadership Quarterly* 6, No. 2 (1995): 219–247.

27. G. B. Graen and M. Uhl-Bien, "Relationship-Based Approach to Leadership: Development of Leader–Member Exchange (LMX) Theory of Leadership over 25 Years," *Leadership Quarterly* 6 (1995): 219–247; C. R. Gerstner and D. V. Day, "Meta-Analytic Review of Leader–Member Exchange Theory: Correlates and Construct Issues," *Journal of Applied Psychology* 82 (1997): 827–844; R. C. Liden, S. J. Wayne, and R. T. Sparrowe, "An Examination of the Mediating Role of Psychological Empowerment on the Relations between the Job, Interpersonal Relationships, and Work Outcomes," *Journal of Applied Psychology* 85 (2001): 407–416.

28. J. H. Dulebohn, W. H. Bommer, R. C. Liden, R. L. Brouer, and G. R. Ferris, "A meta-Analysis of Antecedents and Consequences of Leader-Member Exchange: Integrating the Past with an Eye toward the Future," *Journal of Management* 38, No. 6 (2012): 1715–1759.

29. T. A. Scandura and J. D. Meuser, "Relational Dynamics of Leadership: Problems and Prospects," *Annual Review of Organizational Psychology and Organizational Behavior* 9 (2022): 309–337.

30. J. Gooty, A. Serban, J. S. Thomas, M. B. Gavin, and F. J. Yammarino, "Use and Misuse of Levels of Analysis in Leadership Research: An Illustrative Review of Leader-Member Exchange," *The Leadership Quarterly* 23, No. 6 (2012): 1080-1103.

31. J. Gooty and F. J. Yammarino, "Dyads in Organizational Research: Conceptual Issues and Multi-Level Analyses," *Organizational Research Methods* 14, No. 3 (2011): 456–483.

32. J. Gooty and F. J. Yammarino, "The Leader-Member Exchange Relationship: A Multi-Source, Cross-Level Investigation," *Journal of Management* 42, No. 4 (2016): 915–945.

33. M. Alvesson, Upbeat Leadership: A Recipe for–or against– "Successful" Leadership Studies. *The Leadership Quarterly* 31, No. 6 (2020): 101439.

34. J. M. Burns, *Leadership* (New York: Harper & Row, 1978); T. O. Jacobs, *Leadership and Exchange in Formal Organizations* (Alexandria, Va.: Human Resources Research Organization, 1971).

35. B. M. Bass, "From Transactional to Transformational Leadership: Learning to Share the Vision," *Organizational Dynamics* 19 (1990): 19–31; B. M. Bass, *Leadership and Performance beyond Expectations* (New York: Free Press, 1985).

36. P. M. Podsakoff, S. B. MacKenzie, and W. H. Bommer, "Transformational Leader Behaviors and Substitutes for Leadership as Determinants of Employee Satisfaction, Commitment, Trust, and Organizational Citizenship Behaviors," *Journal of Management* 22 (1996): 259–298.

37. W. Bennis, "Managing the Dream: Leadership in the 21st Century," *Training* 27 (1990): 43–48; P. M. Podsakoff, S. B. MacKenzie, R. H. Moorman, and R. Fetter, "Transformational Leader Behaviors and Their Effects on Followers' Trust in Leader, Satisfaction, and Organizational Citizenship Behaviors," *Leadership Quarterly* 1 (1990): 107–142.

38. "Starbucks Announces New Leadership Structure to Drive Global Growth," accessed at https://news.starbucks.com/news/starbucks-announces-new-leadership-structure.

39. X. H. F. Wang and J. M. Howell, "Exploring the Dual-Level Effects of Transformational Leadership on Followers," *Journal of Applied Psychology* 95 (2010): 1134–1144.

40. C. P. Egri and S. Herman, "Leadership in the North American Environmental Sector: Values, Leadership Styles, and Contexts of Environmental Leaders and Their Organizations," *Academy of Management Journal* 43 (2000): 571–604.

41. T. A. Judge and J. E. Bono, "Five-Factor Model of Personality and Transformational Leadership," *Journal of Applied Psychology* 85 (2001): 751–765.

42. H. J. Anderson, J. E. Baur, J. A. Griffith, and M. R. Buckley, "What Works for You May Not Work for (Gen)Me: Limitations of Present Leadership Theories for the New Generation," *The Leadership Quarterly* 28 (2017): 245–260.

43. The Jargon Dictionary, "The R Terms: Reality-Distortion Field," http://info.astrian.net/jargon/terms/r/reality-distortion_field.html.

44. R. J. House and M. L. Baetz, "Leadership: Some Empirical Generalizations and New Research Directions," in B. M. Staw, ed., *Research in Organizational Behavior*, vol. 1 (Greenwood, Conn.: JAI Press, 1979): 399–401.

45. J. Antonakis, N. Bastardoz, P. Jacquart, and B. Shamir, "Charisma: An Ill-Defined and Ill-Measured Gift," *Annual Review of Organizational Psychology and Organizational Behavior* 3 (2016): 293–319.

46. J. Antonakis, M. Fenley, and S. Liechti, Can charisma be taught? Tests of two interventions. *Academy of Management Learning & Education* 10, No. 3 (2011): 374–396.

47. J. Antonakis, M. Fenley, and S. Liechti, "Learning Charisma. Transform Yourself into the Person Others Want to Follow," *Harvard Business Review* 90, No. 6 (2012): 127–130.

48. G. C. Banks, K. N. Engemann, C. E. Williams, J. Gooty, K. D. McCauley, and M. R. Medaugh, "A Meta-Analytic Review and Future Research Agenda of Charismatic Leadership," *The Leadership Quarterly* (2017), accessed at http://www.sciencedirect.com/science/article/pii/S1048984316302971.

49. D. Van Knippenberg and S. B. Sitkin, "A Critical Assessment of Charismatic—Transformational Leadership Research: Back to the Drawing Board?" *Academy of Management Annals* 7, No. 1 (2013): 1–60.

50. J. Antonakis, S. Bendahan, P. Jacquart, and R. Lalive, "On Making Causal Claims: A Review and Recommendations," *The Leadership Quarterly* 21, No. 6 (2010): 1086–1120.

51. G. Stock, G. C. Banks, E. N. Voss, S. Tonidandel and H. Woznyj, "Putting Leader (Follower) Behavior Back into Transformational Leadership: A Theoretical and Empirical Course Correction," *The Leadership Quarterly* (2022): 101–632.

52. A. C. H. Schat, M. R. Frone, and E. K. Kelloway, "Prevalence of Workplace Aggression in the U.S. Workforce: Findings from a National Study," in E. K. Kelloway, J. Barling, and J. J. Hurrell, eds., *Handbook of Workplace Violence* (Thousand Oaks, CA: Sage, 2006): 47–89.

53. B. J. Tepper, C. A. Henle, L. S. Lambert, R. A. Giacalone, and M. K. Duffy, "Abusive Supervision and Subordinates' Organization Deviance," *Journal of Applied Psychology* 93 (2008): 721–732; P. A. Bamberger and S. B. Bacharach, "Abusive Supervision and Subordinate Problem Drinking: Taking Resistance, Stress and Subordinate Personality into Account," *Human Relations* 59 (2006): 1–30; B. J. Tepper, "Consequences of Abusive Supervision," *Academy of Management Journal* 43 (2000): 178–190; A. A. Grandey, J. Kern, and M. Frone, "Verbal Abuse from Outsiders versus Insiders: Comparing Frequency, Impact on Emotional Exhaustion, and the Role of Emotional Labor," *Journal of Occupation Health Psychology* 12 (2007): 63–79.

54. B. J. Tepper, M. K. Duffy, C. A. Henle, and L. S. Lambert, "Procedural Injustice, Victim Precipitation and Abusive Supervision," *Personnel Psychology* 59 (2006): 101–123.

55. S. Thau and M. S. Mitchell, "Self-Gain or Self-Regulation Impairment? Tests of Competing Explanations of the Supervisor Abuse and Employee Deviance Relationship through Perceptions of Distributive Justice," *Journal of Applied Psychology* (in press).

56. S. H. Courtright, R. G. Gardner, T. A. Smith, B. W. McCormick, and A. E. Colbert, "My Family Made Me Do It: A Cross-Domain, Self-Regulator Perspective on Antecedents to Abusive Supervision," *Academy of Management Journal* 59 (2016): 1630–1652.

57. J. Hu and R. C. Liden, "Antecedents of Team Potency and Team Effectiveness: An Examination of Goal and Process Clarity and Servant Leadership," *Journal of Applied Psychology* 96, No. 4 (2011): 851–862.

58. R. K. Greenleaf, L. C. Spears, and D. T. Frick, eds., *On Becoming a Servant-Leader* (San Francisco: Jossey-Bass, 1996).

59. W. L. Gardner, C. C Cogliser, K. M. Davis, and M. P. Dickens, "*Authentic Leadership: A Review of the Literature and Research Agenda,*" *The Leadership Quarterly* 22, No. 6 (2011): 1120–1145.

60. F. Luthans and B. J. Avolio, "Authentic Leadership: A Positive Development Approach," in K. S. Cameron, J. E. Dutton, and R. E. Quinn, eds., *Positive Organizational Scholarship: Foundations of a New Discipline* (San Francisco: Berrett-Koehler, 2004): 241–261.

61. O. Epitropaki, R. Kark, C. Mainemelis, and R. G. Lord, "Leadership and Followership Identity Processes: A Multilevel Review," *The Leadership Quarterly* 28 (2017): 104–129.

62. M. Alvesson, and K. Einola, "Warning for Excessive Positivity: Authentic Leadership and Other Traps in Leadership Studies," *The Leadership Quarterly* 30, No. 4 (2019): 383–395.

63. W. L. Gardner, E. P. Karam, M. Alvesson, and K. Einola, "Authentic Leadership Theory: The Case for and against," *The Leadership Quarterly* 32, No. 6 (2021): 101495.

64. M. E. Brown, L. K. Treviño, and D. A. Harrison, "Ethical Leadership: A Social Learning Perspective for Construct Development and Testing," *Organizational Behavior and Human Decision Processes* 97, No. 2 (2005): 117–134.

65. G. J. Lemoine, C. A. Hartnell, and H. Leroy, "Taking Stock of Moral Approaches to Leadership: An Integrative Review of Ethical, Authentic, and Servant Leadership," *Academy of Management Annals* 13, No. 1 (2019): 148–187.

66. B. J. Avolio, W. L. Gardner, F. O. Walumbwa, F. Luthans, and D. R. May, "Unlocking the Mask: A Look at the Process by Which Authentic Leaders Impact Follower Attitudes and Behaviors," *The Leadership Quarterly* 15 (2004): 801–823.

67. M. E. Heilman, C. J. Block, R. F. Martell, and M. C. Simon, "Has Anything Changed? Current Characteristics of Men, Women, and Managers," *Journal of Applied Psychology* 74 (1989): 935–942.

68. A. H. Eagly, S. J. Darau, and M. Makhijani, "Gender and the Effectiveness of Leaders: A Meta-Analysis," *Psychological Bulletin* 117 (1995): 125–145.

69. J. Gooty, E. N. Ruggs, H. Aguinis, D. L. Bergeron, L. Eby, D. van Knippenberg, C. Post, D. Rupp, S. M. B. Thatcher, S. Tonidandel, and F. J. Yammarino, "Gender Inclusive Leadership in Business Schools: Current Challenges and Actionable Solutions," *Journal of Management* (in press).

70. K. Sergent, and A. D. Stajkovic, "Women's Leadership Is Associated with Fewer Deaths during the COVID-19 Crisis: Quantitative and Qualitative Analyses of United States Governors," *Journal of Applied Psychology* 105, No. 8 (2020): 771.

71. B. T. Hyacinth, *The Future of Leadership: Rise of Automation, Robotics and Artificial Intelligence* (2017).

72. C. Y. Tsai, J. D. Marshall, A. Choudhury, A. Serban, Y. T. Y. Hou, M. F. Jung, and F. J. Yammarino, "Human-Robot Collaboration: A Multilevel and Integrated Leadership Framework," *The Leadership Quarterly* 33, No. 1 (2022): 101594.

73. M. J. Matthews, S. H. Matthews, D. D. Wang, and T. K. Kelemen, "Tweet, Like, Subscribe! Understanding Leadership through Social Media Use," *The Leadership Quarterly* 33, No. 1 (2022): 101580.

74. M. K. Ryan, S. A. Haslam, and T. Postmes, "Reactions to the Glass Cliff: Gender Differences in the Explanations for the Precariousness of Women's Leadership Positions," *Journal of Organizational Change Management* 20, No. 2 (2007): 182–197.

75. E. P. Hollander and L. R. Offerman, "Power and Leadership in Organizations: Relationships in Transition," *American Psychologist* 45 (1990): 179–189.

76. H. P. Sims, Jr, and C. C. Manz, *Company of Heros: Unleashing the Power of Self-Leadership* (New York: John Wiley & Sons, 1996).

77. C. C. Manz and H. P. Sims, "Leading Workers to Lead Themselves: The External Leadership of Self-Managing Work Teams," *Administrative Science Quarterly* 32 (1987): 106–128.

78. L. Hirschhorn, "Leaders and Followers in a Postindustrial Age: A Psychodynamic View," *Journal of Applied Behavioral Science* 26 (1990): 529–542.

79. R. E. Kelley, "In Praise of Followers," *Harvard Business Review* 66 (1988): 142–148.

80. S. A. Eisenbeiss and D. van Knippenberg, "On Ethical Leadership Impact: The Role of Follower Mindfulness and Moral Emotions," *Journal of Organizational Behavior* 36 (2014): 182–195.

81. G. A. Yukl, *Leadership in Organizations*, 2nd ed. (Upper Saddle River, N.J.: Prentice-Hall, 1989).

82. D. A. Garvin and J. D. Margolis, "The Art of Giving and Receiving Advice," *Harvard Business Review* (January–February 2015): 61–71.

13

1. Definition adapted from D. Hellriegel, J. W. Slocum, Jr., and R. W. Woodman, *Organizational Behavior* (St. Paul: West, 1992); and from R. D. Middlemist and M. A. Hitt, *Organizational Behavior* (St. Paul, Minn.: West, 1988).

2. D. Tjosvold, *The Conflict-Positive Organization* (Reading, Mass.: Addison-Wesley, 1991).

3. K. Thomas and W. Schmidt, "A Survey of Managerial Interests with Respect to Conflict," *Academy of Management Journal* 19 (1976): 315–318; G. L. Lippitt, "Managing Conflict in Today's Organizations," *Training and Development Journal* 36 (1982): 66–74.

4. M. Rajim, "A Measure of Styles of Handling Interpersonal Conflict," *Academy of Management Journal* 26 (1983): 368–376.

5. M. M. Hopkins and R. D. Yonker, "Managing Conflict with Emotional Intelligence: Abilities That Make a Difference," *Journal of Management Development* 34 (2015): 226–244.

6. "The Seven Costs of Conflict Incompetence," Center for Creative Leadership, accessed at https://www.ccl.org/articles/leading-effectively-articles/the-cost-of-conflict-incompetence/.

7. R. Saundry and P. Urwin, "Estimating the Costs of Workplace Conflict," Advisory, Conciliation, and Arbitration Service (ACAS) (2021), accessed at https://www.acas.org.uk/estimating-the-costs-of-workplace-conflict-report.

8. Tjosvold, *The Conflict-Positive Organization* (Reading, MA: Addison-Wesley, 1991).

9. R. A. Cosier and D. R. Dalton, "Positive Effects of Conflict: A Field Experiment," *International Journal of Conflict Management* 1 (1990): 81–92.

10. D. Tjosvold, "Making Conflict Productive," *Personnel Administrator* 29 (1984): 121–130.

11. I. Janis, *Groupthink*, 2nd ed. (Boston: Houghton Mifflin, 1982).

12. A. C. Amason, W. A. Hochwarter, K. R. Thompson, and A. W. Harrison, "Conflict: An Important Dimension in Successful Management Teams," *Organizational Dynamics* 24 (1995): 25–35.

13. J. C. Quick, A. McFadyen, and D. L. Nelson, "No Accident: Health, Well-Being, Performance … and Danger," *Journal of Organizational Effectiveness: People and Performance* 1 (2014): 98–119.

14. R. Nibler and K. L. Harris, "The Effects of Culture and Cohesiveness on Intragroup Conflict and Effectiveness," *The Journal of Social Psychology* 143 (2003): 613–631.

15. R. Shaukat, A. Yousaf, and K. Sanders, "Examining the Linkages Between Relationship Conflict, Performance and Turnover Intentions: Role of Job Burnout as a Mediator," *International Journal of Conflict Management* 28 (2017): 4–23.

16. G. Walker and L. Poppo, "Profit Centers, Single-Source Suppliers, and Transaction Costs," *Administrative Science Quarterly* 36 (1991): 66–87.

17. R. Miles, *Macro Organizational Behavior* (Glenview, Ill.: Scott, Foresman, 1980).

18. H. Levinson, "The Abrasive Personality," *Harvard Business Review* 56 (1978): 86–94.

19. J. C. Quick and J. D. Quick, *Organizational Stress and Preventive Management* (New York, NY: McGraw-Hill, 1984).

20. F. N. Brady, "Aesthetic Components of Management Ethics," *Academy of Management Review* 11 (1986): 337–344.

21. J. R. Ogilvie and M. L. Carsky, "Building Emotional Intelligence in Negotiations," *The International Journal of Conflict Management* 13 (2002): 381–400.

22. A. M. Bodtker and R. L. Oliver, "Emotion in Conflict Formation and Its Transformation: Application to Organizational Conflict Management," *International Journal of Conflict Management* 12 (2001): 259–275.

23. D. E. Conlon and S. H. Hunt, "Dealing with Feeling: The Influence of Outcome Representations on Negotiation," *International Journal of Conflict Management* 13 (2002): 35–58.

24. J. Schopler, C. A. Insko, J. Wieselquist, M. Pemberton, B. Witcher, R. Kozar, C. Roddenberry, and T. Wildschut, "When Groups Are More Competitive Than Individuals: The Domain of the Discontinuity Effect," *Journal of Personality and Social Psychology* 80 (2001): 632–644.

25. M. Sherif and C. W. Sherif, *Social Psychology* (New York: Harper & Row, 1969).

26. M. A. Zarate, B. Garcia, A. A. Garza, and R. T. Hitlan, "Cultural Threat and Perceived Realistic Group Conflict as Dual Predictors of Prejudice," *Journal of Experimental Social Psychology* 40 (2004): 99–105; J. C. Dencker, A. Joshi, and J. J. Martocchio, "Employee Benefits as Context for Intergenerational Conflict," *Human Resource Management Review* 17, No. 2 (2007): 208–220.

27. J. Wombacher and J. Felfe, "The Interplay of Team and Organizational Commitment in Motivating Employees' Interteam Conflict Handling," *Academy of Management Journal*, June 2016.

28. W. Tsai and S. Ghoshal, "Social Capital and Value Creation: The Role of Intrafirm Networks," *Academy of Management Journal* 41 (1998): 464–476.

29. K. J. Hurt and M. A. Abebe, "The Effect of Conflict Type and Organizational Crisis on Perceived Strategic Decision Effectiveness," *Journal of Leadership and Organizational Studies*, published online February 4, 2015.

30. D. L. Nelson and J. C. Quick, "Professional Women: Are Distress and Disease Inevitable?" *Academy of Management Review* 10 (1985): 206–218; D. L. Nelson and M. A. Hitt, "Employed Women and Stress: Implications for Enhancing Women's Mental Health in the Workplace," in J. C. Quick, J. Hurrell, and L. A. Murphy, eds., *Stress and Well-Being at Work: Assessments and Interventions for Occupational Mental Health* (Washington, D.C.: American Psychological Association, 1992).

31. E. C. Dierdorff and J. K. Ellington, "It's the Nature of Work: Examining Behavior-Based Sources of Work–Family Conflict across Occupations," *Journal of Applied Psychology* 93 (2008): 883–892.

32. M. G. Pratt and J. A. Rosa, "Transforming Work–Family Conflict into Commitment in Network Marketing Organizations," *Academy of Management Journal* 46 (2003): 395–418.

33. W. R. Boswell and J. B. Olson-Buchanan, "The Use of Communication Technologies after Hours: The Role of Work Attitudes and Work–Life Conflict," *Journal of Management* 33, No. 4 (2007): 592–610.

34. R. L. Kahn, D. M. Wolfe, R. P. Quinn, J. D. Noek, and R. A. Rosenthal, *Organizational Stress: Studies in Role Conflict and Ambiguity* (New York, NY: Wiley, 1964).

35. J. R. B. Halbeslaben, "A Meta-Analysis of Work Engagement: Relationships with Burnout, Demands, Resources, and Consequences," in A. Bakker and M. Leiter, eds., *Work Engagement: A Handbook of Essential Theory and Research* (New York, NY: Psychology Press, 2010); M. Wang, S. Liu, Y. Zhan, and J. Shi, "Daily Work–Family Conflict and Alcohol Use: Testing the Cross-Level Moderation Effects of Peer Drinking Norms and Social Support," *Journal of Applied Psychology* 95 (2010): 377–386.

36. C. Nohe, A. Michel, and K. Sonntag, "Family-Work Conflict and Job Performance: A Diary Study of Boundary Conditions and Mechanisms," *Journal of Organizational Behavior* 35 (2014): 339–357.

37. J. L. Badaracco, Jr., "The Discipline of Building Character," *Harvard Business Review* (March–April 1998): 115–124.

38. B. Schneider, "The People Make the Place," *Personnel Psychology* 40 (1987): 437–453.

39. C. A. O'Reilly, J. Chatman, and D. F. Caldwell, "People and Organizational Culture: A Profile Comparison Approach to Assessing Person-Organization Fit," *Academy of Management Journal* 34 (1991): 487–516.

40. I. Dayal and J. M. Thomas, "Operation KPE: Developing a New Organization," *Journal of Applied Behavioral Science* 4 (1968): 473–506.

41. R. H. Miles, "Role Requirements as Sources of Organizational Stress," *Journal of Applied Psychology* 61 (1976): 172–179.

42. W. F. G. Mastenbroek, *Conflict Management and Organization Development* (Chichester, England: Wiley, 1987).

43. C. Porath, "Frontline Work When Everyone Is Angry," *Harvard Business Review*, November 8 (2022), accessed at https://hbr.org/2022/11/frontline-work-when-everyone-is-angry?utm_medium=email&utm_source=bigidea_incivility&utm_campaign=promo_20221110&utm_content=actsubs&deliveryName=DM227874.

44. L. M. Cortina, M. S. Hershcovis, and K. B. H. Clancy, "The Embodiment of Insult: A Theory of Biobehavioral Response to Workplace Incivility," *Journal of Management* 48 (2022): 738–763.

45. U. R. Hulsheger, S. van Gills, and A. Walkowiak, "The Regulating Role of Mindfulness in Enacted Workplace Incivility: An Experience Sampling Study," *Journal of Applied Psychology* 106 (2021): 1250–1265.

46. N. I. Eisenberger, "The Neural Bases of Social Pain: Evidence for Shared Representations with Physical Pain," *Psychosomatic Medicine* 74 (2012): 126–135.

47. A. Gallo, "How to Respond to a Rude Comment at Work," Harvard Business Review, November 8 (2022), accessed at https://hbr.org/2022/11/how-to-respond-to-a-rude-comment-at-work.

48. I. A. Smith and A. Griffiths, "Microaggressions, Everyday Discrimination, Workplace Incivilities, and Other Subtle Slights at Work: A Meta-Synthesis," *Human Resource Development Review* 21 (2022): 275–299.

49. Deloitte, "Women @ Work 2022: A Global Outlook," accessed at https://www2.deloitte.com/content/dam/Deloitte/global/Documents/deloitte-women-at-work-2022-a-global-outlook.pdf.

50. X. T. Wang, "Microaggressions at Work: Here's How to Push Back, *Inc.*, October 26 (2022), accessed at https://www.inc.com/xintian-tina-wang/microaggression-integrating-women-leaders-workplace-equity.html.

51. D. D. King, E. S. M Fattoriacci, D. W. Hollingsworth, E. Stahr, and M. Nelson, "When Thriving Requires Effortful Surviving: Delineating Manifestations and Resource Expenditure Outcomes of Microaggressions for Black Employees," *Journal of Applied Psychology* (2022), accessed at https://psycnet.apa.org/record/2022-56902-001.

52. E. F. Washington, "Recognizing and Responding to Microaggressions at Work," *Harvard Business Review*, May 10 (2022), accessed at https://hbr.org/2022/05/recognizing-and-responding-to-microaggressions-at-work.

53. H. H. Meyer, E. Kay, and J. R. P. French, "Split Roles in Performance Appraisal," *Harvard Business Review* 43 (1965): 123–129.

54. T. W. Costello and S. S. Zalkind, *Psychology in Administration: A Research Orientation* (Englewood Cliffs, N.J.: Prentice-Hall, 1963).

55. Snapshot Spy, "Employee Computer & Internet Abuse Statistics," http://www.snapshotspy.com/employee-computer-abuse-statistics.htm; data sources include U.S. Department of Commerce—Economics and Statistics Administration and the National Telecommunications and Information Administration—Greenfield and Rivet, "Employee Computer Abuse Statistics."

56. P. F. Hewlin, "And the Award for Best Actor Goes to . . . : Facades of Conformity in Organizational Settings," A*cademy of Management Review* 28 (2003): 633–642.

57. C. A. Insko, J. Scholper, L. Gaertner, T. Wildschut, R. Kozar, B. Pinter, E. J. Finkel, D. M. Brazil, C. L. Cecil, and M. R. Montoya, "Interindividual–Intergroup Discontinuity Reduction through the Anticipation of Future Interaction," *Journal of Personality and Social Psychology* 80 (2001): 95–111.

58. D. Tjosvold and M. Poon, "Dealing with Scarce Resources: Open-Minded Interaction for Resolving Budget Conflicts," *Group and Organization Management* 23 (1998): 237–255.

59. R. Miles, *Macro Organizational Behavior* (Glenview, IL: Scott, Foresman, 1980); R. Steers, *Introduction to Organizational Behavior*, 4th ed. (Glenview, Ill.: Harper-Collins, 1991).

60. A. Tyerman and C. Spencer, "A Critical Text of the Sherrif's Robber's Cave Experiments: Intergroup Competition and Cooperation between Groups of Well-Acquainted Individuals," *Small Group Behavior* 14 (1983): 515–531; R. M. Kramer, "Intergroup Relations and Organizational Dilemmas: The Role of Categorization Processes," in B. Staw and L. Cummings, eds., *Research in Organizational Behavior* 13 (1991): 191–228.

61. E. B. Shiraev, J. Keohane, M. Icks, and S. A. Samoilenko, *Character Assassination and Reputation Management: Theory and Applications* (Oxfordshire, UK: Routledge).

62. S. Mukherjee, "Why Fauci's Role as the Face of Science Made Him a Hero –and a Villian," *Fast Company*, August 24 (2022), accessed at https://www.fastcompany.com/90781634/why-faucis-role-as-the-face-of-science-made-him-a-hero-and-a-villain.

63. J. Cohen, "Fauci Looks Back—and Ahead," *Science* 377 (2022): 1137–1138.

64. A photo of Dr. Fauci would be a nice addition here, with a caption referring to character assassination.

65. A. Carmeli, "The Relationship between Emotional Intelligence and Work Attitudes, Behavior and Outcomes: An Examination among Senior Managers," *Journal of Managerial Psychology* 18 (2003): 788–813.

66. R. Blake and J. Mouton, "Overcoming Group Warfare," *Harvard Business Review* 64 (1984): 98–108.

67. D. G. Ancona and D. Caldwell, "Improving the Performance of New Product Teams," *Research Technology Management* 33 (1990): 25–29.

68. M. A. Cronin and L. R. Weingart, "Representational Gaps, Information Processing and Conflict in Functionally Diverse Teams," *Academy of Management Review* 32, No. 3 (2007): 761–773.

69. C. K. W. DeDreu and L. R. Weingart, "Task versus Relationship Conflict, Team Performance, and Team Member Satisfaction: A Meta-Analysis," *Journal of Applied Psychology* 88 (2003): 741–749.

70. R. J. Lewicki, J. A. Litterer, J. W. Minton, and D. M. Saunders, *Negotiation*, 2nd ed. (Burr Ridge, Ill.: Irwin, 1994).

71. J. Brett and L. Thompson, "Negotiation," *Organizational Behavior and Human Decision Processes* 136 (2016): 68–79.

72. G. Ku, C. S. Wang, and A. D. Galinsky, "Promise and Perversity: Towards a Comprehensive Model of Perspective Taking," *Research in Organizational Behavior* (in press).

73. J. R. Curhan, J. R. Overbeck, Y. Cho, T. Zhang, and Y. Yang, "Silence Is Golden: Extended Silence, Deliberative Mindset, and Value Creation in Negotiation," *Journal of Applied Psychology* 107 (2022): 78–94.

74. S. Aslani, J. Ramirez-Marin, J. Brett, J. Yao, Z. Semnani-Azad, Z. Zhang, C. Tinsley, L. Weingart, and W. Adair, "Dignity, Face, and Honor Cultures: A Study of Negotiation Strategy and Outcomes in Three Cultures," *Journal of Organizational Behavior* 37 (2016): 1178–1201.

75. J. Mazei, J. Huffmeier, P. A. Freund, A. F. Stuhlmacher, L. Bilke, and G. Hertel, "A Meta-Analysis on Gender Differences in Negotiation Outcomes and Their Moderators," *Psychological Bulletin* 141 (2015): 85–104.

76. C. K. W. De Dreu and A. E. M. Van Vianen, "Managing Relationship Conflict and the Effectiveness of Organizational Teams," *Journal of Organizational Behavior* 22 (2001): 309–328.

77. R. A. Baron, S. P. Fortin, R. L. Frei, L. A. Hauver, and M. L. Shack, "Reducing Organizational Conflict: The Role of Socially Induced Positive Affect," *International Journal of Conflict Management* 1 (1990): 133–152.

78. S. L. Phillips and R. L. Elledge, *The Team Building Source Book* (San Diego: University Associates, 1989).

79. R. Fehr and M. J. Gelfand, "When Apologies Work: How Matching Apology Components to Victims' Self-Construals Facilitates Forgiveness," *Organizational Behavior and Human Decision Processes* 113 (2010): 35–70.

80. J. Corliss, "The Art of a Heartfelt Apology," *Harvard Medical School Health Blog*, April 13 (2021), accessed at https://www.health.harvard.edu/blog/the-art-of-a-heartfelt-apology-2021041322366.

81. J. R. Curhan, M. A. Neale, L. Ross, and J. Rosencranz-Engelmann, "Relational Accommodation in Negotiation: Effects of Egalitarianism and Gender on Economic Efficiency and Relational Capital," *Organizational Behavior and Human Decision Processes* 107 (2008): 192–205.

82. T. N. Gladwin and I. Walter, "How Multinationals Can Manage Social and Political Forces," *Journal of Business Strategy* 1 (1980): 54–68.

83. A. Solomon, "Howard Schultz Once Spoke of the Reservoir of Trust He had With Starbucks Employees—But His War On Unions Risks Destroying That Bond," *Fortune*, August 15 (2022), accessed at https://fortune.com/2022/08/15/howard-schultz-union-trust-workers-starbucks-employment-leadership-aron-solomon/.

84. K. W. Thomas, "Toward Multidimensional Values in Teaching: The Example of Conflict Behaviors," *Academy of Management Review* 2 (1977): 484–490.

85. S. Alper, D. Tjosvold, and K. S. Law, "Conflict Management, Efficacy, and Performance in Organizational Teams," *Personnel Psychology* 53 (2000): 625–642.

86. A. Burton and P. Confino, "Remote Work has Created a Power Struggle between CEOs and CHROs," *Fortune*, August 29 (2022), accessed at https://fortune.com/2022/08/29/remote-work-created-power-struggle-between-ceo-and-chro/.

87. A. Somech, H. S. Desvililya, and H. Lidogoster, "Team Conflict Management and Team Effectiveness: The Effects of Task Interdependence and Team Identification," *Journal of Organizational Behavior* 30 (2009): 359–378.

88. W. King and E. Miles, "What We Know and Don't Know about Measuring Conflict," *Management Communication Quarterly* 4 (1990): 222–243.

89. D. Ni, X. Zheng, and L. H. Liang, "Rethinking the Role of Team Mindfulness in Team Relationship Conflict: A Conflict Management Perspective," *Journal of Organizational Behavior* 43 (2022): 878–891.

90. J. Barker, D. Tjosvold, and I. R. Andrews, "Conflict Approaches of Effective and Ineffective Project Managers: A Field Study in a Matrix Organization," *Journal of Management Studies* 25 (1988): 167–178.

91. K. A. Way, N. L. Jimmieson, and P. Bordia, "Shared Perceptions of Supervisor Conflict Management Style," *International Journal of Conflict Management* 27 (2016): 25–49.

14

1. S. O'Meara and C. Cooper, "It's Not Just Where We Work, It's How We Work," in *Remote Workplace Culture* (London, UK and New York, NY: Kogan Page Limited, 2022): 21–43.

2. B. L. Berkelaar and P. M. Buzzanell, "Bait and Switch or Double-Edged Sword? The (Sometimes) Failed Promises of Calling," *Human Relations* 68 (2014): 157–178.

3. G. W. England and I. Harpaz, "How Working Is Defined: National Contexts and Demographic and Organizational Role Influences," *Journal of Organizational Behavior* 11 (1990): 253–266.

4. L. R. Gomez-Mejia, "The Cross-Cultural Structure of Task-Related and Contextual Constructs," *Journal of Psychology* 120 (1986): 5–19.

5. A. Wrzesniewski and J. E. Dutton, "Crafting a Job: Revisioning Employees as Active Crafters of Their Work," *Academy of Management Review* 26 (2001): 179–201.

6. D. T. Hall and M. Las Heras, "Reintegrating Job Design and Career Theory: Creating Not Just Good Jobs but Smart Jobs," *Journal of Organizational Behavior* 31 (2010): 448–462.

7. F. W. Taylor, *The Principles of Scientific Management* (New York, NY: Norton, 1911).

8. T. Bell, *Out of This Furnace* (Pittsburgh: University of Pittsburgh Press, 1941); J. H. Gittell, D. B. Weinberg, A. L. Bennett, and J. A. Miller, "Is the Doctor in? A Relational Approach to Job Design and the Coordination of Work," *Human Resource Management* 47 (Winter 2008): 729–755.

9. N. D. Warren, "Job Simplification versus Job Enlargement," *Journal of Industrial Engineering* 9 (1958): 435–439.

10. T. Moller, S. E. Mathiassen, H. Franzon, and S. Kihlberg, "Job Enlargement and Mechanical Exposure Variability in Cyclic Assembly Work," *Ergonomics* 47 (2004): 19–40.

11. C. R. Walker and R. H. Guest, *The Man on the Assembly Line* (Cambridge, Mass.: Harvard University Press, 1952).

12. M. A. Campion, L. Cheraskin, and M. J. Stevens, "Career-Related Antecedents and Outcomes of Job Rotation," *Academy of Management Journal* 37 (1994): 1518–1542.

13. H. R. Nalbantian and R. A. Guzzo, "Making Mobility Matter," *Harvard Business Review* (March 2009): 76–84

14. E. Santora, "Keep Up Production through Cross-Training," *Personnel Journal* (June 1992): 162–166.

15. S. Leroy, "Why Is It So Hard to Do My Work? The Challenge of Attention Residue When Switching between Work Tasks," *Organizational Behavior and Human Decision Processes* 109 (2009): 168–181.

16. R. P. Steel and J. R. Rentsch, "The Dispositional Model of Job Attitudes Revisited: Findings of a 10-Year Study," *Journal of Applied Psychology* 82 (1997): 873–879; C. S. Wong, C. Hui, and K. S. Law, "A Longitudinal Study of the Job Perception–Job Satisfaction Relationship: A Text of the Three Alternative Specifications," *Journal of Occupational & Organizational Psychology* 71 (Part 2, 1998): 127–146.

17. F. Herzberg, "One More Time: How Do You Motivate Employees?" *Harvard Business Review* 46 (1968): 53–62.

18. R. N. Ford, "Job Enrichment Lessons from AT&T," *Harvard Business Review* 51 (1973): 96–106.

19. K. A. Whitler and N. Morgan, "Why CMOs Never Last," *Harvard Business Review*, July–Aug. 2017.

20. A. N. Turner and P. R. Lawrence, *Industrial Jobs and the Worker* (Cambridge, Mass.: Harvard University Press, 1965).

21. D. H. McKnight, B. Phillips, and B. C. Hardgrave, "Which Reduces IT Turnover Intention the Worst: Workplace Characteristics or Job Characteristics?" *Information & Management* 46 (2009): 167–174.

22. J. R. Hackman and G. R. Oldham, "The Relationship among Core Job Dimensions, the Critical Psychological States, and On-the-Job Outcomes," in *The Job Diagnostic Survey: An Instrument for the Diagnosis of Jobs and the Evaluation of Job Redesign Projects* (New Haven, Conn.: Department of Administrative Sciences, Yale University, 1974).

23. J. L. Pierce, I. Jussila, and A. Cummings, "Psychological Ownership within the Job Design Context: Revision of the Job Characteristics Model," *Journal of Organizational Behavior* 30 (2009): 477–496.

24. J. R. Hackman and G. R. Oldham, "Development of the Job Diagnostic Survey," *Journal of Applied Psychology* 60 (1975): 159–170.

25. E. Sadler-Smith, G. El-Kot, and M. Leat, "Differentiating Work Autonomy Facets in a Non-Western Context," *Journal of Organizational Behavior* 24 (2003): 709–731.

26. H. P. Sims, A. D. Szilagyi, and R. T. Keller, "The Measurement of Job Characteristics," *Academy of Management Journal* 19 (1976): 195–212.

27. H. P. Sims and A. D. Szilagyi, "Job Characteristic Relationships: Individual and Structural Moderators," *Organizational Behavior and Human Performance* 17 (1976): 211–230.

28. Y. Fried, "Meta-Analytic Comparison of the Job Diagnostic Survey and Job Characteristic Inventory as Correlates of Work Satisfaction and Performance," *Journal of Applied Psychology* 76 (1991): 690–698.

29. D. R. May, R. L. Gilson, and L. M. Harter, "The Psychological Conditions of Meaningfulness, Safety, and Availability and the Engagement of the Human Spirit at Work," *Journal of Occupational and Organizational Psychology* 77 (2004): 11–37.

30. D. DClercq, D. Bouckenooghe, U. Raja, and G. Matsyborska, "Unpacking the Goal Congruence-Organizational Deviance Relationship: The Roles of Work Engagement and Emotional Intelligence," *Journal of Business Ethics* 124 (2014): 695–711.

31. R. Wagner, "Nourishing Employee Engagement," *Gallup Management Journal* (February 12, 2004): 1–7, accessed at http://gmj.gallup.com/content/default.asp?ci=10504.

32. M. Soyars and J. Brusino, "Essentials of Engagement," *T&D* (March 2009): 62–65.

33. J. Loehr and T. Schwartz, *The Power of Full Engagement: Managing Energy, Not Time, Is the Key to High Performance and Personal Renewal* (New York, NY: Free Press, 2003).

34. M. F. R. Kets de Vries, "Creating Authentizotic Organizations: Well-Functioning Individuals in Vibrant Companies," *Human Relations* 54 (2001): 101–111.

35. G. R. Salancik and J. Pfeffer, "A Social Information Processing Approach to Job Attitudes and Task Design," *Administrative Science Quarterly* 23 (1978): 224–253.

36. J. Pfeffer, "Management as Symbolic Action: The Creation and Maintenance of Organizational Paradigms," in L. L. Cummings and B. M. Staw, eds., *Research in Organizational Behavior*, vol. 3 (Greenwich, Conn.: JAI Press, 1981): 1–52.

37. C. Clegg and C. Spencer, "A Circular and Dynamic Model of the Process of Job Design," *Journal of Occupational & Organizational Psychology* 80 (2007): 321–339.

38. J. K. Jo, D. A. Harrison, S. M. Gray, "The Ties That Cope? Reshaping Social Connections in Response to Pandemic Distress," *Journal of Applied Psychology* 106 (2021): 1267–1282.

39. H. H. Zhao, N. H. Li, T. B. Harris, C. C. Rosen, and X. Zhang, "Information Advantages in Social Networks: The Core-Periphery Divide in Peer Performance Ratings," *Journal of Applied Psychology* 106 (2021): 1093–1102.

40. Y. S. Scharp, K. Breevaart, and A. B. Bakker, "Using Playful Work Design to Deal with Hindrance Job Demands: A Quantitative Diary Study," *Journal of Occupational Health Psychology* 26 (2021): 175–188.

41. D. R. May, K. Reed, C. E. Schwoerer, and P. Potter, "Ergonomic Office Design and Aging: A Quasi-Experimental Field Study of Employee Reactions to an Ergonomics Intervention Program," *Journal of Occupational Health Psychology* 9 (2004): 123–135.

42. M. A. Campion and P. W. Thayer, "Job Design: Approaches, Outcomes, and Trade-Offs," *Organizational Dynamics* 16 (1987): 66–79.

43. J. Teresko, "Emerging Technologies," *Industry Week* (February 27, 1995): 1–2.

44. M. A. Campion and C. L. McClelland, "Interdisciplinary Examination of the Costs and Benefits of Enlarged Jobs: A Job Design Quasi-Experiment," *Journal of Applied Psychology* 76 (1991): 186–199.

45. B. Kohut, *Country Competitiveness: Organizing of Work* (New York: Oxford University Press, 1993).

46. D. Holman, S. Frenkel, O. Sorensen, and S. Wood, "Work Design Variation and Outcomes in Call Centers: Strategic Choice and Institutional Explanations," *Industrial and Labor Relations Review* 62 (July 2009): 510–532.

47. L. E. Tetrick, G. G. Fisher, M. T. Ford, and J. C. Quick, eds., *Handbook of Occupational Health Psychology, Third Edition* (Washington, D.C.: American Psychological Association, 2024).

48. W. E. Deming, *Out of the Crisis* (Cambridge, Mass.: MIT Press, 1986).

49. L. Thurow, *Head to Head: The Coming Economic Battle among Japan, Europe, and America* (New York: Morrow, 1992).

50. M. A. Fruin, *The Japanese Enterprise System—Competitive Strategies and Cooperative Structures* (New York: Oxford University Press, 1992).

51. W. Niepce and E. Molleman, "Work Design Issue in Lean Production from a Sociotechnical System Perspective: Neo-Taylorism or the Next Step in Sociotechnical Design?" *Human Relations* 51 (1998): 259–287.

52. S. K. Parker, "Longitudinal Effects of Lean Production on Employee Outcomes and the Mediating Role of Work Characteristics," *Journal of Applied Psychology* 88 (2003): 620–634.

53. E. Furubotn, "Codetermination and the Modern Theory of the Firm: A Property-Rights Analysis," *Journal of Business* 61 (1988): 165–181.

54. H. Levinson, *Executive: The Guide to Responsive Management* (Cambridge, Mass.: Harvard University Press, 1981).

55. B. Gardell, "Scandinavian Research on Stress in Working Life" (Paper presented at the IRRA Symposium on Stress in Working Life, Denver, September 1980).

56. L. Levi, "Psychosocial, Occupational, Environmental, and Health Concepts; Research Results and Applications," in G. P. Keita and S. L. Sauter, eds., *Work and Well-Being: An Agenda for the 1990s* (Washington, D.C.: American Psychological Association, 1992): 199–211.

57. L. E. Tetrick, G. Fisher, M. Ford, and J. C. Quick, *Handbook of Occupational Health Psychology, Third Edition* (Washington, DC: American Psychological Association, 2023).

58. J. Seigrist, "The Effort-Reward Imbalance Model," in C. L. Cooper and J. C. Quick, eds., *The Handbook of Stress and Health: A Guide to Research and Practice* (Chichester, UK: Wiley Blackwell, 2017): 24–35.

59. A. B. Bakker and E. Demerouti, "Job Demands-Resources Theory: Taking Stock and Looking Forward," *Journal of Occupational Health Psychology* 22, No. 3 (July 2017): 273–285.

60. Y. Shin and W.-M. Hur, "Having Control or Lacking Control? Roles of Job Crafting and Service Scripts in Coping with Customer Incivility," *Journal of Occupational Health Psychology* 27 (2022): 104–118.

61. E. Carleton and J. Barling, "Sleep, Work, and Well-Being," in C. L. Cooper and J. C. Quick, eds., *The Handbook of Stress and Health: A Guide to Research and Practice* (Chichester, UK: Wiley Blackwell, 2017): 485–500; C. M. Barnes, J. A. Miller, and S. Bostock, "Helping Employees Sleep Well: Effects of Cognitive Behavioral Therapy for Insomnia on Work Outcomes," *Journal of Applied Psychology* 102, No. 1 (2017): 104–113.

62. M. Shoss, "Occupational Health Psychology Research and the COVID-19 Pandemic," *Journal of Occupational Health Psychology* 26 (2021): 259–260.

63. A. Idris, "Flexible Working as an Employee Retention Strategy in Developing Countries," *Journal of Management Research* 14 (2014): 71–86.

64. M. Aleem, M. Sulyan, I. Ameer, and M. Mustak, "Remote Work and the COVID-19 Pandemic: An Artificial Intelligence-Based Topic Modeling and Future Agenda," *Journal of Business Research* 154 (2023). doi: 10.1016/j.jbusres.2022.113303

65. A. Wontorczyk and B. Rożnows, "Remote, Hybrid, and On-Site Work during the SARS-CoV-2 Pandemic and the Consequences for Stress and Work Engagement," *International Journal of Environmental Research and Public Health* 19 (2022). https://doi.org/10.3390/ijerph19042400

66. S. Leroy, A. M. Schmidt, and N. Madjar, "Working from Home during COVID-19: A Study of the Interruption Landscape," *Journal of Applied Psychology* 106 (2021): 1448–1465.

67. H. Vaziri, W. J. Casper, J. H. Wayne, and R. A. Matthews, "Changes to the Work–Family Interface During the COVID-19 Pandemic: Examining Predictors and Implications Using Latent Transition Analysis," *Journal of Applied Psychology* 105 (2020): 1073–1087.

68. M. Shirmohammadi, W. C. Au, and M. Beigi, "Remote Work and Work-Life Balance: Lessons Learned from the COVID-19 Pandemic and Suggestions for HRD Practitioners," *Human Resource Development International* 25 (2022): 163–181.

69. B. Robinson, "Is Working Remote A Blessing or Burden? Weighing the Pros and Cons," *Forbes*, June 19 (2020).

70. L. Gratton, "Four Principles to Ensure Hybrid Work is Productive Work," *MIT Sloan Management Review*, November 09 (2020).

71. https://www.forbes.com/sites/bryanrobinson/2022/10/27/4-day-workweek-catching-on-in-the-united-states/?sh=38f2b4c65a93.

72. C. Hilberath, J. Kilmann, D. Lovich, T. Tzanetti, A. Bailey, S. Beck, E. Kaufman, B. Khandelwal, F. Schuler, and K. Wooley, *Hybrid Work Is the New Remote Work* (Boston: Boston Consulting Group, 2020).

73. L. Gratton, "How to do Hybrid Right," *Harvard Business Review*, May–June (2021).

74. J. Trevor and M. Holweg, "Managing the New Tensions of Hybrid Work," *MIT Sloan Management Review*, Winter (2023).

75. B. Ziegler, "Your Company May be Watching You," *Wall Street Journal*, August 22 (2022), R1, R6.

76. C. E. Thiel, J. Bonner, J. T. Bush, D. T. Welsh, and N. Garud, "Stripped of Agency: The Paradoxical Effect of Employee Monitoring on Deviance," *Journal of Management* 49 (2023): 709–740.

77. A. Tangel, "When Will You Hail a Taxi that Flies?" *Wall Street Journal*, November 10 (2022), R3.

78. P. Budden and F. Murray, "Strategically Engaging with Innovation Ecosystems," *MIT Sloan Management Review*, Fall 2022.

79. B. Marr, *Future Skills* (Hoboken, NJ and Chichester, UK: Wiley, 2022).

80. D. A. Whetten and K. S. Cameron, *Developing Management Skills*, 10th ed. (Upper Saddle River, N.J.: Pearson, 2019).

15

1. M. A. Hitt, R. D. Ireland, and R. E. Hoskisson, *Strategic Management: Competitiveness & Globalization—Concepts and Cases*, 13th ed. (Mason, OH: Cengage Learning, 2020).

2. J. Child, *Organization* (New York, NY: Harper & Row, 1984).

3. P. Lawrence and J. Lorsch, *Organization and Environment: Managing Differentiation and Integration*, rev. ed. (Cambridge, Mass.: Harvard University Press, 1986).

4. J. Hage, "An Axiomatic Theory of Organizations," *Administrative Science Quarterly* 10 (1965): 289–320.

5. "The Army Reserve at 100: An Emerging Operational Force," *Army Logistician* (November–December, 2008): 15–16.

6. W. Ouchi and J. Dowling, "Defining the Span of Control," *Administrative Science Quarterly* 19 (1974): 357–365.

7. L. Porter and E. Lawler, III, "Properties of Organization Structure in Relation to Job Attitudes and Job Behavior," *Psychological Bulletin* 65 (1965): 23–51.

8. A. Ollier-Malaterre and A. Foucreault, "Cross-National Work-Life Research: Cultural and Structural Impacts for Individuals and Organizations," *Journal of Management* 43, No. 1 (January, 2017): 111–136.

9. R. Dewar and J. Hage, "Size, Technology, Complexity, and Structural Differentiation: Toward a Theoretical Synthesis," *Administrative Science Quarterly* 23 (1978): 111–136.

10. F. C. Vasoncelos and R. Ramirez, "Complexity in Business Environments," *Journal of Business Research* 64 (2011): 236–241.

11. Paul R. Lawrence and Jay W. Lorsch, "Differentiation and Integration in Complex Organizations," *Administrative Science Quarterly* 12, No. 1 (1967): 1–47.

12. J. R. R. Galbraith, *Designing Complex Organizations* (Reading, Mass.: Addison-Wesley-Longman, 1973).

13. W. Altier, "Task Forces: An Effective Management Tool," *Management Review* 76 (1987): 26–32.

14. P. Lawrence and J. Lorsch, "New Managerial Job: The Integrator," *Harvard Business Review* 45 (1967): 142–151.

15. J. Lorsch and P. Lawrence, "Organizing for Product Innovation," *Harvard Business Review* 43 (1965): 110–111.

16. D. Pugh, D. Hickson, C. Hinnings, and C. Turner, "Dimensions of Organization Structure," *Administrative Science Quarterly* 13 (1968): 65–91; B. Reimann, "Dimensions of Structure in Effective Organizations: Some Empirical Evidence," *Academy of Management Journal* 17 (1974): 693–708; S. Robbins, *Organization Theory: The Structure and Design of Organizations*, 3rd ed. (Englewood Cliffs, N.J.: Prentice-Hall, 1990).

17. M. C. Andrews, T. L. Baker, and T. G. Hunt, "The Interactive Effects of Centralization on the Relationship between Justice and Satisfaction," *Journal of Leadership & Organizational Studies* 15 (2008): 135–144.

18. A. Arora, S. Belenzon, and L. A. Rios, "Make, Buy, Organize: The Interplay Between Research, External Knowledge, and Firm Knowledge," *Strategic Management Journal* 35 (2014): 317–337.

19. N. J. Foss and T. Saebi, "Fifteen Years of Research on Business Model Innovation: How Far Have We Come, and Where Should We Go?" *Journal of Management* 43 (2017): 200–227.

20. H. Mintzberg, *The Structuring of Organizations* (Englewood Cliffs, N.J.: Prentice-Hall, 1979).

21. J. A. Kuprenas, "Implementation and Performance of a Matrix Organization Structure," *International Journal of Project Management* 21 (2003): 51–62.

22. Mintzberg, *Structuring of Organizations*.

23. K. Weick, "Educational Institutions as Loosely Coupled Systems," *Administrative Science Quarterly* (1976): 1–19.

24. D. Miller and C. Droge, "Psychological and Traditional Determinants of Structure," *Administrative Science Quarterly* 31 (1986): 540; H. Tosi, Jr. and J. Slocum, Jr., "Contingency Theory: Some Suggested Directions," *Journal of Management* 10 (1984): 9–26.

25. K. Singh, I. P. Mahmood, and S. Natarajan, "Capital Market Development and Firm Restructuring During an Economic Shock," *Organizational Science* 28, No. 3 (May–June, 2017): 552–573.

26. M. Meyer, "Size and the Structure of Organizations: A Causal Analysis," *American Sociological Review* 37 (1972): 434–441; J. Beyer and H. Trice, "A Reexamination of the Relations between Size and Various Components of Organizational Complexity," *Administrative Science Quarterly* 24 (1979): 48–64; B. Mayhew, R. Levinger, J. McPherson, and T. James, "Systems Size and Structural Differentiation in Formal Organizations: A Baseline Generator for Two Major Theoretical Propositions," *American Sociological Review* 37 (1972): 26–43.

27. M. Gowing, J. Kraft, and J. C. Quick, *The New Organizational Reality: Downsizing, Restructuring, and Revitalization* (Washington, D.C.: American Psychological Association, 1998).

28. M. Brauer and L. Laamanen, "Workforce Downsizing and Firm Performance: An Organizational Routine Perspective," *Journal of Management Studies* 51 (2014): 1311–1333.

29. L. Donaldson and G. Joffe, "Fit—The Key to Organizational Design," *Journal of Organization Design* 3 (2014): 38–45.

30. J. Werth and D. Fleming, "Creating a 'Super' Agency in San Diego County," *The Public Manager* (Fall 2008): 21–26.

31. J. Woodward, *Industrial Organization: Theory and Practices* (London: Oxford University Press, 1965).

32. C. Perrow, "A Framework for the Comparative Analysis of Organizations," *American Sociological Review* 32 (1967): 194–208; D. Rosseau, "Assessment of Technology in Organizations: Closed versus Open Systems Approaches," *Academy of Management Review* 4 (1979): 531–542.

33. C. Perrow, "A Framework for the Comparative Analysis of Organizations," *American Sociological Review* 32, No. 2 (1967): 194–208.

34. J. D. Thompson, *Organizations in Action* (New York: McGraw-Hill, 1967).

35. J. R. Baum and S. Wally, "Strategic Decision Speed and Firm Performance," *Strategic Management Journal* 24 (2003): 1107–1129.

36. X. R. Luo, D. Wang, and J. Zhang, "Whose Call to Answer: Institutional Complexity and Firms' CSR Reporting," *Academy of Management Journal* 60 (2017): 321–344.

37. Thompson, *Organizations in Action*.

38. H. Downey, D. Hellriegel, and J. Slocum, Jr., "Environmental Uncertainty: The Construct and Its Application," *Administrative Science Quarterly* 20 (1975): 613–629.

39. G. Dess and D. Beard, "Dimensions of Organizational Task Environments," *Administrative Science Quarterly* 29 (1984): 52–73.

40. J. A. Cogin and I. O. Williamson, "Standardize or Customize: The Interactive Effects of HRM and Environment Uncertainty on MNC Subsidiary Performance," *Human Resource Management* 53 (2014): 701–721.

41. G. G. Dess and D. W. Beard, "Dimensions of Organizational Task Environments," *Administrative Science Quarterly* 29, No. 1 (1984): 52–73.

42. T. Burns and G. Stalker, *The Management of Innovation* (London: Tavistock, 1961); Mintzberg, *Structuring of Organizations*.

43. M. Chandler and L. Sayles, *Managing Large Systems* (New York: Harper & Row, 1971).

44. M. Sanchez-Manzanares, R. Rico, and F. Gil, "Designing Organizations: Does Expertise Matter?" *Journal of Business Psychology* 23 (2008): 87–101.

45. R. E. Hoskisson, F. Chirico, J. (D.) Zyung, and E. Gambeta, "Managerial Risk Taking: A Multitheoretical Review and Future Research Agenda," *Journal of Management* 43, No. 1 (January 2017): 137–169.

46. R. Daft, *Organization Theory and Design*, 10th ed. (Mason, Ohio: South-Western, 2010).

47. R. S. Kaplan and D. P. Norton, "How to Implement a New Strategy without Disrupting Your Organization," *Harvard Business Review* (March 2006): 100–109.

48. L-H Lin, "Organizational Structure and Acculturation in Acquisitions: Perspectives of Congruence Theory and Task Interdependence," *Journal of Management* 40 (2014): 1831–1856.

49. N. J. Foss, J. Lyngsie, and S. A. Zahra, "Organizational Design Correlates of Entrepreneurship: The Roles of Decentralization and Formalization for Opportunity Discovery and Realization," *Strategic Organization* 13 (2015): 32–60.

50. W. R. Scott, *Organizations: Rational, Natural, and Open Systems*, 6th ed. (Upper Saddle River, N.J.: Prentice-Hall, 2006).

51. D. Miller and P. Friesen, "A Longitudinal Study of the Corporate Life Cycle," *Management Science* 30 (1984): 1161–1183.

52. S. Raisch, "Balanced Structures: Designing Organizations for Profitable Growth," *Long Range Planning* 41 (2008): 483–508.

53. M. H. Overholt, "Flexible Organizations: Using Organizational Design as a Competitive Advantage," *Human Resource Planning* 20 (1997): 22–32; P. W. Roberts and R. Greenwood, "Integrating Transaction Cost and Institutional Theories: Toward a Constrained-Efficiency Framework for Understanding Organizational Design Adoption," *Academy of Management Review* 22 (1997): 346–373.

54. G. Davidson, "Organisation Structure: The Life Cycle of an Organization," *New Zealand Management* 56 (2008): 58–60.

55. C. W. L. Hill and G. R. Jones, *Strategic Management: An Integrated Approach*, 12th ed. (Boston: Cengage Learning, 2017).

56. T. Fountaine, B. McCarthy, and T. Saleh, "Building the AI-Powered Organization," *Harvard Business Review*, July-August 2019.

57. S. Chaudhary, V. Gkigoulos, and S. Katsikas, "Developing Metrics to Assess the Effectiveness of Cybersecurity Awareness Program," *Journal of Cybersecurity* 8 (2022).

58. H. R. Gregg, S. L. Restubog, M. Dasborough, C.(M.) Xu, C. M. Deen, and Y. He, "When Disaster Strikes! An Interdisciplinary Review of Disasters and Their Organizational Consequences," *Journal of Management* 48 (2022): 1382–1429.

59. K. E. Weick and K. M. Sutcliff, *Managing the Unexpected: Sustained Performance in a Complex World* (Hoboken, NJ: John Wiley & Sons, 2015).

60. A. Kinder, R. Hughes, and Sir C. L. Cooper, *Occupational Health and Wellbeing* (London and New York: Routledge, Taylor & Francis Group).

61. B. Brown and S. D. Anthony, "How P&G Tripled Its Innovation Success Rate," *Harvard Business Review* 89 (June 2011): 64–72.

62. P. J. Brews and C. L. Tucci, "Exploring the Structural Effects of Internetworking," *Strategic Management Journal* 25 (2004): 429–451.

63. J. Kroezen, D. Ravasi, I. Sasakik, M. Zebrowska, and R. Suddaby, "Configurations of Craft: Alternative Model for Organizing Work," *Academy of Management Annals* 15 (2021): 502–536.

64. J. Fulk, "Global Network Organizations: Emergence and Future Prospects," *Human Relations* 54 (2001): 91–100.

65. K. Kelley, A. Toma, F. Roghé, and S. Baxter, *The Power of Distributed Organization Design* (Boston: Boston Consulting Group, 2020).

66. S. O'Meara and Sir C. Cooper, *Remote Workplace Culture* (London and New York: Kogan Page Limited, 2022).

67. R. Teerlink and L. Ozley, *More Than a Motorcycle: The Leadership Journey at Harley-Davidson* (Boston: Harvard Business School Press, 2000).

68. W. A. Cohen and N. Cohen, *The Paranoid Organization and 8 Other Ways Your Company Can Be Crazy: Advice from an Organizational Shrink* (New York: American Management Association, 1993).

69. P. E. Tetlock, "Cognitive Biases and Organizational Correctives: Do Both Disease and Cure Depend on the Politics of the Beholder?" *Administrative Science Quarterly* 45 (2000): 293–326.

70. J. C. Quick, J. H. Gavin, and D. J. Gavin, "Mental Health: A Twenty-First Century Imperative for Workplace Wellbeing," in A. Kinder, R. Hughes, and C. L. Cooper, eds., *Occupational Health and Wellbeing* (London and New York: Routledge, Taylor and Francis, 2022): 95–105.

16

1. T. E. Deal and A. A. Kennedy, *Corporate Cultures* (Reading, Mass.: Addison-Wesley, 1982).

2. W. Ouchi, *Theory Z* (Reading, Mass.: Addison-Wesley, 1981).

3. T. J. Peters and R. H. Waterman, *In Search of Excellence* (New York, NY: Harper & Row, 1982).

4. M. Gardner, "Creating a Corporate Culture for the Eighties," *Business Horizons* (January–February 1985): 59–63.

5. S. J. Hogan and L. V. Coote, "Organizational Culture, Innovation, and Performance: A Test of Schein's Model," *Journal of Business Research* 67 (2014): 1609–1621.

6. Definition adapted from E. H. Schein, *Organizational Culture and Leadership* (San Francisco: Jossey-Bass, 1985): 9.

7. C. D. Sutton and D. L. Nelson, "Elements of the Cultural Network: The Communicators of Corporate Values," *Leadership and Organization Development* 11 (1990): 3–10.

8. A. Gara, "Visa's CEO Charlie Scharf Steps Down After Four Years, Sick of San Francisco Travel," *Forbes* October 17 (2016), accessed at https://www.forbes.com/sites/antoinegara/2016/10/17/visas-ceo-charlie-scharf-steps-down-after-four-years-sick-of-san-francisco-travel/#666533b199e0.

9. "Walgreeens CEO Roz Brewer to Leaders: Put Your Phones Away and Listen to Employees," *Harvard Business Review*, December 9 (2021), accessed at https://hbr.org/2021/12/walgreens-ceo-roz-brewer-to-leaders-put-your-phones-away-and-listen-to-employees.

10. "Hershey CEO Michele Buck on Empowering Internal Change Agents," *Harvard Business Review*, April 29 (2022), accessed at https://hbr.org/2022/04/hershey-ceo-michele-buck-on-empowering-internal-change-agents.

11. A. Bandura, *Social Learning Theory* (Englewood Cliffs, N.J.: Prentice-Hall, 1977).

12. J. A. Chatman, "Leading by Leveraging Culture," *California Management Review* 45 (2003): 20–34.

13. J. M. Beyer and H. M. Trice, "How an Organization's Rites Reveal Its Culture," *Organizational Dynamics* 16 (1987): 5–24.

14. H. M. Trice and J. M. Beyer, "Studying Organizational Cultures through Rites and Ceremonials," *Academy of Management Review* 9 (1984): 653–669.

15. "Recap: The 2014 Berkshire Hathaway Annual Meeting," *The Wall Street Journal* May 3 (2014), accessed at http://blogs.wsj.com/moneybeat/2014/05/03/live-blog-the-2014-berkshire-hathaway-annual-meeting/.

16. H. Levinson and S. Rosenthal, *CEO: Corporate Leadership in Action* (New York, NY: Basic Books, 1984).

17. V. Sathe, "Implications of Corporate Culture: A Manager's Guide to Action," *Organizational Dynamics* 12 (1987): 5–23.

18. J. Schlecker, "Using Stories and Symbols to Build a Powerful Culture," *Inc.*, January 24 (2015), accessed at https://www.inc.com/jim-schleckser/use-stories-and-symbols-to-build-a-powerful-culture.html.

19. J. Martin, M. S. Feldman, M. J. Hatch, and S. B. Sitkin, "The Uniqueness Paradox in Organizational Stories," *Administrative Science Quarterly* 28 (1983): 438–453.

20. J. Lofstock, "Applauding the QuikTrip Culture," http://www.quiktrip.com/aboutqt/news.asp.

21. https://www.uschamber.com/co/good-company/growth-studio/successful-companies-that-reinvented-their-business.

22. S. K. Johnson, "How CEOs Can Lead Selflessly Through a Crisis," *Harvard Business Review*, May 14 (2020), accessed at https://hbr.org/2020/05/how-ceos-can-lead-selflessly-through-a-crisis.

23. S. R. Martin, "Stories About Values and Valuable Stories: A Field Experiment of Narratives to Shape Newcomers' Actions," *Academy of Management Journal* 59 (2016): 1707–1724.

24. T. Kim, O. Sezer, J. Schroeder, J. Risen, F. Gino, and M. I. Norton, "Work Group Rituals Enhance the Meaning of Work," *Organizational Behavior and Human Decision Processes* 165 (2021): 197–212.

25. K. Senz, "Rituals at Work: Teams That Play Together Stay Together," *Harvard Business Review*, March 24 (2022), accessed at https://hbswk.hbs.edu/item/rituals-at-work-teams-that-play-together-stay-together.

26. R. Goffee and G. Jones, "What Holds the Modern Company Together?" *Harvard Business Review* (November–December 1996): 133–143.

27. https://www.clifbar.com/who-we-are/our-aspirations.

28. D. Sull, S. Turconi, and C. Full, "When It Comes to Culture, Does Your Company Walk the Talk?" *MIT Sloan Management Review*, July 21 (2020), accessed at https://sloanreview.mit.edu/article/when-it-comes-to-culture-does-your-company- walk-the-talk/.

29. K.M. Kroeper, H.E. Williams, and M.C. Murphy, "Counterfeit Diversity: How Strategically Misrepresenting Gender Diversity Dampens Organizations' Perceived Sincerity and Elevates Women's Identity Threat Concerns," *Journal of Personality and Social Psychology* 122 (2022): 399–326.

30. http://www.capspire.com/careers/life-at-capspire/.

31. L. Smircich, "Concepts of Culture and Organizational Analysis," *Administrative Science Quarterly* 28 (1983): 339–358.

32. Y. Weiner and Y. Vardi, "Relationships between Organizational Culture and Individual Motivation: A Conceptual Integration," *Psychological Reports* 67 (1990): 295–306.

33. M. R. Louis, "Surprise and Sense Making: What Newcomers Experience in Entering Unfamiliar Organizational Settings," *Administrative Science Quarterly* 25 (1980): 209–264.

34. T. L. Doolen, M. E. Hacker, and E. M. van Aken, "The Impact of Organizational Context on Work Team Effectiveness: A Study of Production Teams," *IEEE Transactions on Engineering Management* 50 (2003): 285–296.

35. O. A. O'Neill and N. P. Rothbard, "Is Love All You Need? The Effects of Emotional Culture, Suppression, and Work-Family Conflict on Firefighter Risk-Taking and Health," *Academy of Management Journal* 60 (2017): 78–108.

36. J. P. Kotter and J. L. Heskett, *Corporate Culture and Performance* (New York: Free Press, 1992); A. S. Boyce, L. R. G. Nieminen, M. A. Gillespie, A. M. Ryan, and D. R. Denison, "Which Comes First, Organizational Culture or Performance? A Longitudinal Study of Causal Priority with Automobile Dealerships," *Journal of Organizational Behavior*, published online January 15, 2015.

37. Deal and Kennedy, *Corporate Cultures.*

38. D. R. Katz, *The Big Store* (New York, NY: Viking, 1987).

39. G. G. Gordon, "Industry Determinants of Organizational Culture," *Academy of Management Review* 16 (1991): 396–415.

40. G. Donaldson and J. Lorsch, *Decision Making at the Top* (New York, NY: Basic Books, 1983).

41. R. H. Kilman, M. J. Saxton, and R. Serpa, eds., *Gaining Control of the Corporate Culture* (San Francisco: Jossey-Bass, 1986).

42. J. P. Kotter, *A Force for Change: How Leadership Differs from Management* (New York, NY: Free Press, 1990); R. M. Kanter, *The Change Masters* (New York, NY: Simon & Schuster, 1983).

43. J. A. Chatman, D. F. Caldwell, C. A. O'Reilly, and B. Doerr, "Parsing Organizational Culture: How the Norm for Adaptability Influences the Relationship Between Culture Consensus and Financial Performance in High-Technology Firms," *Journal of Organizational Behavior* 35 (2015): 785–808.

44. J. Kantor and A. Sundaram, "The Rise of the Worker Productivity Score," *The New York Times*, August 14 (2022), accessed at https://www.nytimes.com/interactive/2022/08/14/business/worker-productivity-tracking.html.

45. Schein, *Organizational Culture and Leadership.*

46. F. Ekelman and J.P. Kantor, *Thrive With a Hybrid Workplace* (London: Rowman & Littlefield, 2023).

47. A. Burgess, "Remote Work Might Damage Your Career Advancement," Remote Work Study by Alliance Virtual Offices, accessed at https://www.alliancevirtualoffices.com/virtual-office-blog/remote-work-study-career-advancement/.

48. J. A. Pearce II, T. R. Kramer, and D. K. Robbins, "Effects of Managers' Entrepreneurial Behavior on Subordinates," *Journal of Business Venturing* 12 (1997): 147–160.

49. A. Bryant, "Barbara Corcoran on the Power of a Positive Attitude," *The New York Times*, June 2 (2017), accessed at https://www.nytimes.com/2017/06/02/business/barbara-corcoran-shark-tank-html?_r=o;

50. P. W. Braddy, A. W. Meade, and C. M. Kroustalis, "Organizational Recruitment Website Effects on Viewers' Perceptions of Organizational Culture," *Journal of Business and Psychology* 20, No. 4 (2006): 525–543.

51. A. Xenikou and M. Simosi, "Organizational Culture and Transformational Leadership as Predictors of Business Unit Performance," *Journal of Managerial Psychology* 21, No. 6 (2006): 566–579.

52. D. C. Feldman, "The Multiple Socialization of Organization Members," *Academy of Management Review* 6 (1981): 309–318.

53. A. M. Ellis, T. N. Bauer, L. R. Mansfield, B. Erdogan, D. M. Truxillo, and L. S. Simon, "Navigating Uncharted Waters: Newcomer Socialization through the Lens of Stress Theory," *Journal of Management* 41 (2015): 203–235.

54. D. L. Nelson, "Organizational Socialization: A Stress Perspective," *Journal of Occupational Behavior* 8 (1987): 311–324.

55. E. Van Vulpen, "The Realistic Job Preview Explained," *Academy to Innovate HR*, (2022), accessed at https://www.aihr.com/blog/realistic-job-preview/.

56. J. Fan and J. P. Wanous, "Organizational and Cultural Entry: A New Type of Orientation Program for Multiple Boundary Crossings," *Journal of Applied Psychology* 93 (2008): 1390–1400.

57. D. M. Cable, L. Aiman-Smith, P. W. Mulvey, and J. R. Edwards, "The Sources and Accuracy of Job Applicants' Beliefs about Organizational Culture," *Academy of Management Journal* 43 (2000): 1076–1085.

58. J. D. DeBode, K. W. Mossholder, and A. G. Walker. "Fulfilling Employees' Psychological Contracts: Organizational Socialization's Role," *Leadership and Organization Development Journal* 38 (2017): 42–55.

59. D. L. Nelson, J. C. Quick, and M. E. Eakin, "A Longitudinal Study of Newcomer Role Adjustment in U.S. Organizations," *Work and Stress* 2 (1988): 239–253.

60. N. J. Allen and J. P. Meyer, "Organizational Socialization Tactics: A Longitudinal Analysis of Links to Newcomers' Commitment and Role Orientation," *Academy of Management Journal* 33 (1990): 847–858.

61. T. N. Bauer, E. W. Morrison, and R. R. Callister, "Organizational Socialization: A Review and Directions for Future Research," *Research in Personnel and Human Resources Management* 16 (1998): 149–214.

62. D. M. Cable and C. K. Parsons, "Socialization Tactics and Person–Organization Fit," *Personnel Psychology* 54 (2001): 1–23.

63. S. H. Harrison, D. M. Sluss, and B. E. Ashforth, "Curiosity Adapted the Cat: The Role of Trait Curiosity in Newcomer Adaption," *Journal of Applied Psychology* 96 (2011): 211–220; M. Wang, Y. Zhan, E. McCune, and D. Truxillo, "Understanding Newcomers' Adaptability and Work-Related Outcomes: Testing the Mediating Roles of Perceived P-E Fit Variables," *Personnel Psychology* 64 (2011): 163–189.

64. A. M. Saks, J. A. Gruman, and H. Cooper-Thomas, "The Neglected Role of Proactive Behavior and Outcomes in Newcomer Socialization," *Journal of Vocational Behavior* 79 (2011): 36–46.

65. D. M. Rousseau, "Assessing Organizational Culture: The Case for Multiple Methods," in B. Schneider, ed., *Organizational Climate and Culture* (San Francisco: Jossey-Bass, 1990).

66. R. A. Cooke and D. M. Rousseau, "Behavioral Norms and Expectations: A Quantitative Approach to the Assessment of Organizational Culture," *Group and Organizational Studies* 12 (1988): 245–273.

67. R. H. Kilmann and M. J. Saxton, *Kilmann-Saxton Culture-Gap Survey* (Pittsburgh: Organizational Design Consultants, 1983).

68. W. J. Duncan, "Organizational Culture: 'Getting a Fix' on an Elusive Concept," *Academy of Management Executive* 3 (1989): 229–236.

69. P. Bate, "Using the Culture Concept in an Organization Development Setting," *Journal of Applied Behavior Science* 26 (1990): 83–106.

70. K. R. Thompson and F. Luthans, "Organizational Culture: A Behavioral Perspective," in B. Schneider, ed., *Organizational Climate and Culture* (San Francisco: Jossey-Bass, 1990).

71. S. Seren and U. Baykal, "Relationships between Change and Organizational Culture in Hospitals," *Journal of Nursing Scholarship* 39, No. 2 (2007): 191–197.

72. M. Blanding, "Amazon vs. Whole Foods: When Cultures Collide," *Harvard Business Review*, May 14 (2018), accessed at https://hbswk.hbs.edu/item/amazon-vs-whole-foods-when-cultures-collide.

73. M. Gelfand, S. Gordon, C. Li, V. Choi, and P. Prokopowicz, "One Reason Mergers Fail: The Two Cultures Aren't Compatible," *Harvard Business Review*, October 2 (2018), accessed at https://hbr.org/2018/10/one-reason-mergers-fail-the-two-cultures-arent-compatible.

74. D. Full, C. Full, W. Cipolli, and C. Brighenti, "Why Every Leader Needs to Worry About Toxic Culture," *MIT Sloan Management Review*, March 16 (2022), accessed at https://sloanreview.mit.edu/article/why-every-leader-needs-to-worry-about-toxic-culture/.

75. M. Arena, S. Hines, and J. Golden III, "The Three Cs for Cultivating Organizational Culture in a Hybrid World," *Organizational Dynamics*, January 23 (2023), accessed at https://www.sciencedirect.com/science/article/abs/pii/S0090261623000025.

76. C. Reilly, "Chief Well-Being Officer Takes a Collective Approach to Solve Burnout," *Forbes*, October 6 (2020), accessed at https://www.forbes.com/sites/colleenreilly/2020/10/06/chief-well-being-officer-takes-a-collective-approach-to-solve-burnout/?sh=f438fb92f983.

77. "Workers Appreciate and Seek Mental Health Support in the Workplace," *APA's 2022 Work and Well-Being Survey*, accessed at https://www.apa.org/pubs/reports/work-well-being/2022-mental-health-support.

78. S. Gupta, "Many Veterans Struggle to Hold Down a Job Due to Struggles with Mental Health," *Fast Company*, November 11 (2022), accessed at https://www.fastcompany.com/90808498/veterans-mental-health-employment-substance-abuse?utm_medium=Notification&utm_source=Pushly&utm_campaign=2483547&cid=pushly.

79. V. Sathe, "How to Decipher and Change Corporate Culture," in R. H. Kilman et al., eds., *Managing Corporate Cultures* (San Francisco: Jossey-Bass, 1985).

80. M. E. Johnson-Cramer, S. Parise, and R. L. Cross, "Managing Change through Networks and Values," *California Management Review* 49, No. 3 (2007): 85–109.

81. L. K. Trevino and K. A. Nelson, *Managing Business Ethics: Straight Talk about How to Do It Right* (New York, NY: John Wiley & Sons, 1995).

82. "The State of Ethics & Compliance in the Workplace: A Look at Global Trends," *Ethics Research Center*, (2021), accessed at https://www.ethics.org/wp-content/uploads/2021-ECI-GBES-State-Ethics-Compliance-in-Workplace.pdf.

83. B. Murphy, Jr., "The CEO of McDonald's Is Making a Big Change. It's the Hardest Thing Any Leader Can Ever Do," *Inc.*, January 11 (2020), accessed at https://www.inc.com/bill-murphy-jr/the-ceo-of-mcdonalds-is-making-a-big-change-its-hardest-thing-any-leader-can-ever-do.html.

84. M. Jin, J. Lee, and M. Lee, "Does Leadership Matter in Diversity Management? Assessing the Relative Impact of Diversity Policy and Inclusive Leadership in the Public Sector," *Leadership and Organization Development Journal* 38 (2017), accessed at http://www.emeraldinsight.com/doi/abs/10.1108/LODJ-07-2015-0151.

85. L. Quast, "6 Tips for an Inclusive Organizational Culture," *Forbes*, April 17 (2017), accessed at https://www.forbes.com/sites/lisaquast/2017/04/17/combating-gender-discrimination-6-tips-for-an-inclusive-organizational-culture/#12deecabf5da.

86. "Corporate Equality Index 2022," *Human Rights Campaign*, (2022), accessed at https://reports.hrc.org/corporate-equality-index-2022?_ga=2.20449855.688856217.1676934111-494136316.1676934111.

87. https://www.mondelezinternational.com/Snacking-Made-Right/Diversity-Equity-and-Inclusion.

88. J. Beer, "Oreo Continues its LGBTQ+ Allyship Despite the Culture War Against 'Woke' Companies," *Fast Company*, April 4 (2022), accessed at https://www.fastcompany.com/90737822/oreo-continues-its-lgtbq-allyship-despite-the-culture-war-against-woke-companies?partner=rss&utm_source=rss&utm_medium=feed&utm_campaign=rss+fastcompany&utm_content=rss&cid=search.

89. http://about.att.com/pages/diversity/employee_groups.

17

1. J. H. Greenhaus, *Career Management* (Hinsdale, Ill.: CBS College Press, 1987).

2. D. T. Hall, *Careers in Organizations* (Pacific Palisades, Calif.: Goodyear, 1976).

3. Greenhaus, *Career Management;* T. G. Gutteridge and F. L. Otte, "Organizational Career Development: What's Going on Out There?" *Training and Development Journal* 37 (1983): 22–26.

4. M. B. Arthur, P. H. Claman, and R. J. DeFillippi, "Intelligent Enterprise, Intelligent Careers," *Academy of Management Executive* (November 1995): 7–22.

5. M. Lips-Wiersma and D. T. Hall, "Organizational Career Development Is Not Dead: A Case Study on Managing the New Career during Organizational Change," *Journal of Organizational Behavior* 28, No. 6 (2007): 771–792.

6. D. Jemielniak, "Managers as Lazy, Stupid Careerists?" *Journal of Organizational Change Management* 20, No. 4 (2007): 491–508.

7. R. Cropanzano, K. Keplinger, B. K. Lambert, B. Caza, and S.J. Ashford, "The Organizational Psychology of Gig Work: An Integrative Conceptual Review," *Journal of Applied Psychology* (2022), accessed at https://psycnet.apa.org/doiLanding?doi=10.1037%2Fapl0001029.

8. J. Fuller, M. Raman, A. Bailey, and N. Vaduganathan, "Rethinking the On-Demand Workforce," *Harvard Business Review* 98 (2020): 96–103.

9. D. E. Super, *The Psychology of Careers* (New York, NY: Harper & Row, 1957); D. E. Super and M. J. Bohn, Jr., *Occupational Psychology* (Belmont, Calif.: Wadsworth, 1970).

10. J. L. Holland, *The Psychology of Vocational Choice* (Waltham, Mass.: Blaisdell, 1966); J. L. Holland, *Making Vocational Choices: A Theory of Careers* (Englewood Cliffs, NJ: Prentice-Hall, 1973).

11. F. T. L. Leong and J. T. Austin, "An Evaluation of the Cross-Cultural Validity of Holland's Theory: Career Choices by Workers in India," *Journal of Vocational Behavior* 52 (1998): 441–455.

12. C. Morgan, J. D. Isaac, and C. Sansone, "The Role of Interest in Understanding the Career Choices of Female and Male College Students," *Sex Roles* 44 (2001): 295–320.

13. J. K. Hellerstein and M. S. Morrill, "Dads and Daughters: The Changing Impact of Fathers on Women's Occupational Choices," *Journal of Human Resources* 46, No. 2 (2011): 333–372; S. H. Osipow, *Theories of Career Development* (Englewood Cliffs, NJ: Prentice-Hall, 1973).

14. J. P. Wanous, T. L. Keon, and J. C. Latack, "Expectancy Theory and Occupational/Organizational Choices: A Review and Test," *Organizational Behavior and Human Performance* 32 (1983): 66–86.

15. P. O. Soelberg, "Unprogrammed Decision Making," *Industrial Management Review* 8 (1967): 19–29.

16. J. P. Wanous, *Organizational Entry: Recruitment, Selection, and Socialization of Newcomers* (Reading, Mass.: Addison-Wesley, 1980).

17. S. L. Premack and J. P. Wanous, "A Meta-Analysis of Realistic Job Preview Experiments," *Journal of Applied Psychology* 70 (1985): 706–719.

18. https://jobs.spectrum.com/call-center

19. https://jobs.netflix.com/podcast

20. P. W. Hom, R. W. Griffeth, L. E. Palich, and J. S. Bracker, "An Exploratory Investigation into Theoretical Mechanisms Underlying Realistic Job Previews," *Personnel Psychology* 41 (1998): 421–451.

21. J. A. Breaugh, "Realistic Job Previews: A Critical Appraisal and Future Research Directions," *Academy of Management Review* 8 (1983): 612–619.

22. G. R. Jones, "Socialization Tactics, Self-Efficacy, and Newcomers' Adjustment to Organizations," *Academy of Management Journal* 29 (1986): 262–279.

23. M. R. Buckley, D. B. Fedor, J. G. Veres, D. S. Wiese, and S. M. Carraher, "Investigating Newcomer Expectations and Job-Related Outcomes," *Journal of Applied Psychology* 83 (1998): 452–461.

24. J. Oliver, R. T. Erk, A. Koch, T. L. Russell, N. E. Babin, S. A. Ardison, and M. C. Young, "Identification and Accessioning of Individuals for Officer Candidate School: Developing Realistic Job Previews," technical report, United States Army Research Institute for Behavioral and Social Sciences (2014), accessed online.

25. A. De Vos and C. Freese, "Sensemaking During Organizational Entry: Changes in Newcomer Information Seeking and the Relationship with Psychological Contract Fulfillment," *Journal of Occupational and Organizational Psychology* 84 (2011): 288–314.

26. P. Buhler, "Managing in the '90s," *Supervision* (July 1995): 24–26.

27. D. T. Hall and J. E. Moss, "The New Protean Career Contract: Helping Organizations and Employees Adapt," *Organizational Dynamics* (Winter 1998): 22–37.

28. S. A. Zahra, R. L. Priem, and A. A. Rasheed, "Understanding the Causes and Effects of Top Management Fraud," *Organizational Dynamics* 36, No. 2 (2007): 122–139.

29. A. Fisher, "Don't Blow Your New Job," *Fortune*, June 22 (1998), 159–162.

30. D. Goleman, *Working with Emotional Intelligence* (New York, NY: Bantam, 1998); A. Fisher, "Success Secret: A High Emotional IQ," *Fortune*, October 26 (1998), 293–298.

31. N. Libbrecht, F. Lievens, B. Carette, and S. Cote, "Emotional Intelligence Predicts Success in Medical School," *Emotion* 14 (2014): 64–73.

32. K. V. Petrides, A. Furnham, and G. N. Martin, "Estimates of Emotional and Psychometric Intelligence," *Journal of Social Psychology* 144 (April 2004): 149–162.

33. C. Chermiss, "The Business Case for Emotional Intelligence," *The Consortium for Research on Emotional Intelligence in Organizations* (2003), accessed at http://www.eiconsortium.org/research/business _case_for_ei.htm; L. M. Spencer, Jr., and S. Spencer, *Competence at Work: Models for Superior Performance* (New York, NY: John Wiley & Sons, 1993); L. M. Spencer, Jr., D. C. McClelland, and S. Kelner, *Competency Assessment Methods: History and State of the Art* (Boston: Hay/McBer, 1997).

34. J. O. Crites, "A Comprehensive Model of Career Adjustment in Early Adulthood," *Journal of Vocational Behavior* 9 (1976): 105–118; S. Cytrynbaum and J. O. Crites, "The Utility of Adult Development in Understanding Career Adjustment Process," in M. B. Arthur, D. T.

Hall, and B. S. Lawrence, eds., *Handbook of Career Theory* (Cambridge: Cambridge University Press, 1989): 66–88.

35. D. E. Super, "A Life-Span, Life-Space Approach to Career Development," *Journal of Vocational Behavior* 16 (1980): 282–298; L. Baird and K. Kram, "Career Dynamics: Managing the Superior/Subordinate Relationship," *Organizational Dynamics* 11 (1983): 46–64.

36. D. J. Levinson, *The Seasons of a Man's Life* (New York, NY: Knopf, 1978); D. J. Levinson, *The Seasons of a Woman's Life* (New York, NY: Knopf, 1996).

37. D. J. Levinson, "A Conception of Adult Development," *American Psychologist* 41 (1986): 3–13.

38. D. L. Nelson, "Adjusting to a New Organization: Easing the Transition from Outsider to Insider," in J. C. Quick, R. E. Hess, J. Hermalin, and J. D. Quick, eds., *Career Stress in Changing Times* (New York, NY: Haworth Press, 1990): 61–86.

39. J. P. Kotter, "The Psychological Contract: Managing the Joining Up Process," *California Management Review* 15 (1973): 91–99.

40. D. M. Rousseau, "New Hire Perceptions of Their Own and Their Employers' Obligations: A Study of Psychological Contracts," *Journal of Organizational Behavior* 11 (1990): 389–400; D. L. Nelson, J. C. Quick, and J. R. Joplin, "Psychological Contracting and Newcomer Socialization: An Attachment Theory Foundation," *Journal of Social Behavior and Personality* 6 (1991): 55–72.

41. H. Zhao, S. Wayne, B. Glibkowski, and J. Bravo "The Impact of Psychological Breach on Work-Related Outcomes," *Personnel Psychology* (2007): 647–680.

42. L. Zhou, J. Park, J. D. Kammeyer-Mueller, P. P. Shah, and E. M. Campbell, "Rookies Connected: Interpersonal Relationships Among Newcomers, Newcomer Adjustment Processes, and Socialization Outcomes, *Journal of Applied Psychology* 107 (2022): 370–388.

43. D. J. Levinson, "A Conception of Adult Development," *American Psychologist* 41, No. 1 (January 1986): 3–13.

44. S. Shaffakat, L. Otaye-Ebede, J. Reb, R. Chandwanai, and P. Vongswasdi, "Mindfulness Attenuates Both Emotional and Behavioral Reactions Following Psychological Contract Breach: A Two-Stage Moderated Mediation Model," *Journal of Applied Psychology* 107 (2022): 425–443.

45. J. W. Walker, "Let's Get Realistic about Career Paths," *Human Resource Management* 15 (1976): 2–7.

46. E. H. Buttner and D. P. Moore, "Women's Organizational Exodus to Entrepreneurship: Self-Reported Motivations and Correlates," *Journal of Small Business Management* 35 (1997): 34–46; Center for Women's Business Research Press Release, "Privately Held, 50% or More Women-Owned Businesses in the United States," 2004, accessed at http://www.nfwbo.org/pressreleases/nationalstatetrends/total.htm.

47. D. G. Collings, H. Scullion, and M. J. Morley, "Changing Patterns of Global Staffing in the Multinational Enterprise: Challenges to the Conventional Expatriate Assignment and Emerging Alternatives," *Journal of World Business* 42, No. 2 (2007): 198–213.

48. B. Filipczak, "You're on Your Own," *Training* (January 1995): 29–36.

49. K. E. Kram, *Mentoring at Work: Developmental Relationships in Organizational Life* (Glenview, Ill.: Scott, Foresman, 1985).

50. T. D. Allen, L. T. Eby, G. T. Chao, and T. N. Bauer, "Taking Stock of Two Relational Aspects of Organizational Life: Tracing the History and Shaping the Future of Socialization and Mentoring Research," *Journal of Applied Psychology*, 102 (2017): 324–337.

51. J. Arnold and K. Johnson, "Mentoring in Early Career," *Human Resource Management Journal* 7 (1997): 61–70.

52. B. P. Madia and C. J. Lutz, "Perceived Similarity, Expectation–Reality Discrepancies, and Mentors' Expressed Intention to Remain in the Big Brothers/Big Sisters Programs," *Journal of Applied Social Psychology* 34 (March 2004): 598–622.

53. "A Guide to the Mentor Program Listings," *Mentors Peer Resources*, accessed at http://www.mentors.ca/mentorprograms.html.

54. http://www.diversityinc.com/mentoring/why-mentoring-is-not-an-option-at-ibm/

55. S. E. Seibert, M. L. Kraimer, and R. C. Liden, "A Social Capital Theory of Career Success," *Academy of Management Journal* 44 (2001): 219–237.

56. https://about.nike.com/en/impact/initiatives/building-and-investing-in-our-teams

57. M. A. Covaleski, M. W. Dirsmuth, J. B. Heian, and S. Samuel, "The Calculated and the Avowed: Techniques of Discipline and Struggles over Identity in Big Six Public Accounting Firms," *Administrative Science Quarterly* 43 (1998): 293–327.

58. E.A. Ensher, W. B. Johnson, and D.G. Smith, "How to Mentor in a Remote Workplace," *Harvard Business Review*, March 22 (2022), accessed at https://hbr.org/2022/03/how-to-mentor-in-a-remote-workplace.

59. Ibid.

60. A. Ramaswami, G. F. Dreher, R. Bretz, and C. Wiethoff, "Gender, Mentoring and Career Success: The Importance of Organizational Context," *Personnel Psychology* 63, No. 2 (2010): 385–405.

61. W. Whiteley, T. W. Dougherty, and G. F. Dreher, "Relationship of Career Mentoring and Socioeconomic Origin to Managers' and Professionals' Early Career Progress," *Academy of Management Journal* 34 (1991): 331–351; G. F. Dreher and R. A. Ash, "A Comparative Study of Mentoring among Men and Women in Managerial, Professional, and Technical Positions," *Journal of Applied Psychology* 75 (1990): 539–546; T. A. Scandura, "Mentorship and Career Mobility: An Empirical Investigation," *Journal of Organizational Behavior* 13 (1992): 169–174.

62. G. F. Dreher and T. H. Cox, Jr., "Race, Gender and Opportunity: A Study of Compensation Attainment and Establishment of Mentoring Relationships," *Journal of Applied Psychology* 81 (1996): 297–309.

63. B. R. Ragins, J. L. Cotton, and J. S. Miller, "Marginal Mentoring: The Effects of Type of Mentor, Quality of Relationship, and Program Design on Work and Career Attitudes," *Academy of Management Journal* 43 (2000): 1177–1194.

64. C. Buengeler, A. C. Homan, and S. C. Voelpel, "The Challenge of Being a Young Manager: The Effect of Contingent Reward and Participative Leadership on Team-Level Turnover Depend on Leader Age," *Journal of Organizational Behavior* 37 (2016): 1224–1245.

65. C. R. Masterson and J. M. Hoobler, "Care and Career: A Family Identity-Based Typology of Dual-Earner Couples," *Journal of Organizational Behavior* 36 (2015), accessed online, doi:10.1002/job.1945.

66. A. Croft, T. Schmader, K. Block, and A. S. Baron, "The Second Shift Reflected in the Second Generation," *Psychological Science* (2015), accessed online, doi:10.1177/0956797614533968.

67. B. Morris, "Is Your Family Wrecking Your Career? (And Vice Versa)," *Fortune*, March 17 (1997), 70–80.

68. Ibid.

69. L. K. Barber, S. G. Taylor, J. P. Burton, and S. F. Bailey, "A Self-Regulatory Perspective of Work-to-Home Undermining Spillover/Crossover: Examining the Roles of Sleep and Exercise," *Journal of Applied Psychology* 102 (2017): 753–763.

70. E. McGrath, H. D. Cooper-Thomas, E. Garrosa, A. I. Sanz-Vergel, and G. W. Cheung, "Rested, Friendly, and Engaged: The Role of Daily Positive Collegial Interactions at Work," *Journal of Organizational Behavior* (2017), accessed at http://onlinelibrary.wiley.com/doi/10.1002/job.2197/full.

71. R. G. Netemeyer, J. S. Boles, and R. McMurrian, "Development and Validation of Work–Family Conflict and Family–Work Conflict Scales," *Journal of Applied Psychology* 81 (1996): 400–410.

72. B. Livingston and T. A. Judge, "Emotional Responses to Work-Family Conflict: An Examination of Gender Role Orientation among Working Men and Women," *Journal of Applied Psychology* 93 (2008): 207–216.

73. N. Yang, C. C. Chen, J. Choi, and Y. Zou, "Sources of Work–Family Conflict: A Sino–U.S. Comparison of the Effects of Work and Family Demands," *Academy of Management Journal* 43 (2000): 113–123.

74. McKinsey & Company, "Americans Are Embracing Flexible Work—And They Want More of It," (2023), accessed at https://www.mckinsey.com/industries/real-estate/our-insights/americans-are-embracing-flexible-work-and-they-want-more-of-it#/.

75. Mitchell Gold Co., "Day Care," accessed at http://www.mitchellgold.com/daycare.asp.

76. R. Stephens, "Turning the 4-day Week Dream Into a Reality," *Fortune*, September 22 (2022), accessed at https://fortune.com/2022/09/22/battle-for-talent-job-recruitment-4-day-week/.

77. C. Lockhart, "4-Day Week Pioneering Pilot Program a Huge Success, New Research Reveals," (2022), accessed at https://www.4dayweek.com/news-posts/4-day-week-pioneering-pilot-program-a-huge-success-new-research-reveals.

78. McKinsey & Co., "The Childcare Conundrum." May 9 (2022), accessed at https://www.mckinsey.com/featured-insights/sustainable-inclusive-growth/future-of-america/the-childcare-conundrum-how-can-companies-ease-working-parents-return-to-the-office.

79. H. Zacher and H. Schultz, "Employees' Eldercare Demands, Strain, and Perceived Support," *Journal of Managerial Psychology* 30 (2015): 183–198.

80. Cincinnati Area Senior Services, "Corporate Elder Care Program," accessed at http://www.senserv.org/elder.htm.

81. E. E. Kossek, J. A. Colquitt, and R. A. Noe, "Caregiving Decisions, Well-Being, and Performance: The Effects of Place and Provider as a Function of Dependent Type and Work–Family Climates," *Academy of Management Journal* 44 (2001): 29–44.

82. http://www.parentsinapinch.com/sitters-and-nannies/

83. B. Schulte, "Aging Population Prompts More Employers to Offer Elder-Care Benefits to Workers," *The Washington Post*, November 16 (2014), accessed at http://www.washingtonpost.com/local/aging-population-prompts-more-employers-to-offer-elder-care-benefits-to-workers/2014/11/16/25f9c8e6-6847-11e4-a31c-77759fc1eacc_story.html.

84. J. B. Fuller and M. Raman, "The Caring Company," *Harvard Business School*, (2019), accessed at https://www.hbs.edu/managing-the-future-of-work/research/Pages/the-caring-company.aspx.

85. N. P. Rothbard, K. W. Phillips, and T. L. Dumas, "Managing Multiple Roles: Work-Family Policies and Individuals' Desires for Segmentation," *Organization Science* 16 (2005): 243–258.

86. N. P. Rothbard, "Building Work-Life Boundaries in the WFH Era," *Harvard Business Review*, July 15 (2020), accessed at https://hbr.org/2020/07/building-work-life-boundaries-in-the-wfh-era.

87. https://www.zillow.com/careers/benefits/.

88. D. Burkus, "Research Shows that Organizations Benefit When Employees Take Sabbaticals," *Harvard Business Review*, August 10 (2017), accessed at https://hbr.org/2017/08/research-shows-that-organizations-benefit-when-employees-take-sabbaticals.

89. J. W. Gilsdorf, "The New Generation: Older Workers," *Training and Development Journal* (March 1992): 77–79.

90. H. Weisman, U. K. Bindl, C. B. Gibson, and K. L. Unsworth, "It's About Time: Understanding Job Crafting Through the Lens of Individuals' Temporal Characteristics," *Group & Organization Management* 47 (2022), accessed at https://journals.sagepub.com/doi/10.1177/10596011221081586.

91. S. Dust, "Job Hopping Shouldn't Be Your First Instinct. Try Job Crafting Instead," *Fast Company*, April 5 (2022), accessed at https://www.fastcompany.com/90737833/does-the-perfect-fit-job-exist-this-strategy-may-bring-workers-closer-to-finding-one.

92. M. Gerhardt, J. Nachemson-Ekwall, and P. Fogel, *Gentelligence: The Revolutionary Approach to Leading an Intergenerational Workforce* (Washington, D.C.: Rowman & Littlefield, 2021).

93. L. Alton, "How Reverse Mentoring Can Help Promote Generational Diversity Awareness," (2022), accessed at https://www.adp.com/spark/articles/2022/01/how-reverse-mentoring-can-help-promote-generational-diversity-awareness.aspx.

94. J. F. Quick, "Time to Move On?" in J. C. Quick, R. E. Hess, J. Hermalin, and J. D. Quick, eds., *Career Stress in Changing Times* (New York, NY: Haworth Press, 1990): 239–250.

95. D. Machan, "Rent-an-Exec," *Forbes*, January 22 (1990), 132–133.

96. S. Kim and D. C. Feldman, "Working in Retirement: The Antecedents of Bridge Employment and Its Consequences for Quality of Life in Retirement," *Academy of Management Journal* 43 (2000): 1195–1210.

97. https://news.gallup.com/poll/394943/retiring-planning-retire-later.aspx

98. H. Van Solinge, A. Vanajan, and K. Henkens, "Does Phased Retirement Increase Vitality in Older Workers? Findings From a 3-Year Follow-Up Panel Study," *Journal of Aging and Social Policy* (2022), accessed at https://www.tandfonline.com/doi/full/10.1080/08959420.2022.2029270.

99. T. A. Beehr, "To Retire or Not to Retire: That Is Not the Question," *Journal of Organizational Behavior* 35 (2014): 1093–1108.

100. S. E. Sullivan and A.A. Ariss, "Employment After Retirement: A Review and Framework for Future Research," *Journal of Management* 45 (2019): 262–284.

101. G. W. Dalton, "Developmental Views of Careers in Organizations," in M. B. Arthur, D. T. Hall, and B. S. Lawrence, eds., *Handbook of Career Theory* (Cambridge: Cambridge University Press, 1989): 89–109.

102. D. C. Feldman, "Careers in Organizations: Recent Trends and Future Directions," *Journal of Management* 15 (1989): 135–156.

18

1. M. A. Verespej, "When Change Becomes the Norm," *Industry Week*, March 16 (1992): 35–38.

2. World Health Organization, "COVID-19 Pandemic Triggers 25% Increase in Prevalence of Anxiety and Depression Worldwide," March 2 (2022), accessed at https://www.who.int/news/item/02-03-2022-covid-19-pandemic-triggers-25-increase-in-prevalence-of-anxiety-and-depression-worldwide.

3. V. H. Murthy, "Confronting Health Worker Burnout and Well-Being," *New England Journal of Medicine*, August 18 (2022), accessed at https://www.nejm.org/doi/full/10.1056/NEJMp2207252.

4. K. Bach, "New Data Shows Long COVID Is Keeping As Many As 4 Million People Out of Work," *The Brookings Institution Report*, accessed at https://www.brookings.edu/research/new-data-shows-long-covid-is-keeping-as-many-as-4-million-people-out-of-work/.

5. A. Basiouny, "Why Hybrid Work Will Reign in 2023," *Knowledge at Wharton*, January 17 (2023), accessed at https://knowledge.wharton.upenn.edu/podcast/wharton-business-daily-podcast/why-hybrid-work-will-reign-in-2023/.

6. "Number of Freelancers in the United States from 2017 to 2028," *Statista*, September 30 (2022), accessed at https://www.statista.com/statistics/921593/gig-economy-number-of-freelancers-us/.

7. "The World in 2050," Price Waterhouse Coopers, accessed at https://www.pwc.com/gx/en/research-insights/economy/the-world-in-2050.html.

8. "World's Largest Companies in 2022," *Global Finance*, March 9 (2023), accessed at https://www.gfmag.com/global-data/economic-data/largest-companies.

9. C. Cote, "Five Common Challenges of International Business You Should Consider," *Harvard Business School Online*, November 24 (2020), accessed at https://online.hbs.edu/blog/post/challenges-of-international-business.

10. "Women in the Workforce: United States," *Catalyst*, August 29 (2022), accessed at https://www.catalyst.org/research/women-in-the-workforce-united-states/.

11. C. Suddath, "It's Getting Harder to Be a Woman in America," *Bloomberg Businessweek*, August 9 (2022), accessed at https://www.bloomberg.com/news/features/2022-08-03/roe-decision-epitomizes-increasing-burnout-among-women.

12. A. M. Valerio, "Supporting Women Leaders: Research-Based Directions for Gender Inclusion in Organizations," *Consulting Psychology Journal* 74 (2022): 178–193.

13. "Barilla: An Italian Family-Owned Company's Journey to Global Inclusion," *Catalyst*, January 26 (2021), accessed at https://www.catalyst.org/research/barilla-journey-to-global-inclusion/.

14. G. Tsipursky, "This Simple Shift in Perspective Can Increase Your Talent Pool by 15%," *Fast Company*, November 20 (2022), accessed at https://www.fastcompany.com/90813887/increase-talent-pool-diverse-candidates?utm_medium=Notification&utm_source=Pushly&utm_campaign=2500499&cid=pushly.

15. K. Roose, "How ChatGPT Kicked Off an AI Arms Race," *The New York Times*, February 3 (2023), accessed at https://www.nytimes.com/2023/02/03/technology/chatgpt-openai-artificial-intelligence.html.

16. J. Korn, "Vanderbilt University Apologies for Using ChatGPT to Write Mass-Shooting Email," *CNN Business*, February 22 (2023), accessed at https://www.cnn.com/2023/02/22/tech/vanderbilt-chatgpt-shooting-email/index.html.

17. R. M. Kanter, "Improving the Development, Acceptance, and Use of New Technology: Organizational and Interorganizational Challenges," in *People and Technology in the Workplace* (Washington, D.C.: National Academy Press, 1991): 15–56.

18. https://www.patagonia.com/ownership/.

19. https://apparelcoalition.org/.

20. S. A. Mohrman and A. M. Mohrman, Jr., "The Environment as an Agent of Change," in A. M. Mohrman, Jr., et al., eds., *Large-Scale Organizational Change* (San Francisco: Jossey-Bass, 1989): 35–47.

21. T. D'Aunno, M. Succi, and J. A. Alexander, "The Role of Institutional and Market Forces in Divergent Organizational Change," *Administrative Science Quarterly* 45 (2000): 679–703.

22. https://www.4dayweek.com/.

23. M. Jarman, "Intel Opens 'Leading-Edge Fab: Plant to Build Most Powerful Chips'," *The Arizona Republic*, October 21 (2007), accessed at http://www.azcentral.com/arizonarepublic/business/articles/1021biz-intel1021.html.

24. Q. N. Huy, "Emotional Balancing of Organizational Continuity and Radical Change: The Contribution of Middle Managers," *Administrative Science Quarterly* 47 (March 1, 2002): 31–69.

25. D. Nadler, "Organizational Frame-Bending: Types of Change in the Complex Organization," in R. Kilmann and T. Covin, eds., *Corporate Transformation* (San Francisco: Jossey-Bass, 1988): 66–83.

26. R. Winkler, "YouTube: 1 Billion Viewers, No Profit," *The Wall Street Journal*, February 15 (2015), accessed at http://www.wsj.com/articles/viewers-dont-add-up-to-profit-for-youtube-1424897967.

27. L. Ackerman, "Development, Transition, or Transformation: The Question of Change in Organizations," *OD Practitioner* (December 1986): 1–8.

28. T. D. Jick, *Managing Change* (Homewood, Ill.: Irwin, 1993): 3.

29. J. M. Bloodgood and J. L. Morrow, "Strategic Organizational Change: Exploring the Roles of Environmental Structure, Internal Conscious Awareness, and Knowledge," *Journal of Management Studies* 40 (2003): 1761–1782.

30. D. Miller and M. J. Chen, "Sources and Consequences of Competitive Inertia. A Study of the U.S. Airline Industry," *Administrative Science Quarterly* 39 (1994): 1–23.

31. S. L. Brown and K. M. Eisenhardt, "The Art of Continuous Change: Linking Complexity Theory and Time-Paced Evolution in Relentlessly Shifting Organizations," *Administrative Science Quarterly* 42 (1997): 1–34.

32. J. Child and C. Smith, "The Context and Process of Organizational Transformation: Cadbury Ltd. in Its Sector," *Journal of Management Studies* 12 (1987): 12–27.

33. M. Uhl-Bien and M. Arena, "Complexity Leadership: Enabling People and Organizations for Adaptability," *Organizational Dynamics* 46 (2017): 9–20.

34. R. M. Kanter, *The Change Masters* (New York: Simon & Schuster, 1983).

35. J. R. Katzenbach, *Real Change Leaders* (New York: Times Business, 1995).

36. J. L. Denis, L. Lamothe, and A. Langley, "The Dynamics of Collective Leadership and Strategic Change in Pluralistic Organizations," *Academy of Management Journal* 44 (2001): 809–837.

37. M. Beer, *Organization Change and Development: A Systems View* (Santa Monica, Calif.: Goodyear, 1980): 78.

38. K. Whalen-Berry and C. R. Hinings, "The Relative Effect of Change Drivers in Large-Scale Organizational Change: An Empirical Study," in W. Passmore and R. Goodman, eds., *Research in Organizational Change and Development*, vol. 14 (New York: JAI Press, 2003): 99–146.

39. J. L. Denis, L. Lamothe, and A. Langley, "The Dynamics of Collective Leadership and Strategic Change in Pluralistic Organizations," *Academy of Management Journal* 44 (2001): 809–837.

40. J. W. Brehm, *A Theory of Psychological Reactance* (New York: Academic Press, 1966).

41. J. A. Klein, "Why Supervisors Resist Employee Involvement," *Harvard Business Review* 62 (1984): 87–95.

42. B. L. Kirkman, R. G. Jones, and D. L. Shapiro, "Why Do Employees Resist Teams? Examining the 'Resistance Barrier' to Work Team Effectiveness," *International Journal of Conflict Management* 11 (2000): 74–92.

43. D. L. Nelson and M. A. White, "Management of Technological Innovation: Individual Attitudes, Stress, and Work Group Attributes," *Journal of High Technology Management Research* 1 (1990): 137–148.

44. S. Elias, "Employee Commitment in Times of Change: Assessing the Importance of Attitudes toward Organizational Change," *Journal of Management* 35 (2009): 37–55; J. B. Avey, T. S. Wernsing, and F. Luthans, "Can Positive Employees Help Positive Organizational Change? Impact of Psychological Capital and Emotions on Relevant Attitudes and Behaviors," *Journal of Applied Behavioral Science* 44 (2008): 48–70.

45. T. Diefenbach, "The Managerialistic Ideology of Organisational Change Management," *Journal of Organizational Change Management* 20, No. 1 (2007): 126–144.

46. N. Sverdlik and S. Oreg, "Beyond the Individual-Level Conceptualization of Dispositional Resistance to Change: Multilevel Effects on the Response to Organizational Change," *Journal of Organizational Behavior* (2022), accessed at https://onlinelibrary.wiley.com/doi/epdf/10.1002/job.2678.

47. A. E. Rafferty, N. L. Jimmieson, and A. A. Armenakis, "Change Readiness: A Multilevel Review," *Journal of Management* 39 (2013): 110–135.

48. T. G. Cummings and E. F. Huse, *Organizational Development and Change* (St. Paul, Minn.: West, 1989).

49. N. L. Jimmieson, D. J. Terry, and V. J. Callan, "A Longitudinal Study of Employee Adaptation to Organizational Change: The Role of Change-Related Information and Change-Related Self Efficacy," *Journal of Occupational Health Psychology* 9 (2004): 11–27.

50. N. DiFonzo and P. Bordia, "A Tale of Two Corporations: Managing Uncertainty during Organizational Change," *Human Resource Management* 37 (1998): 295–303.

51. J. de Vries, C. Webb, and J. Eveline, "Mentoring for Gender Equality and Organisational Change," *Employee Relations* 28, No. 6 (2006): 573–587.

52. A. H. Hon, M. Bloom, and J. M. Crant, "Overcoming Resistance to Change and Enhancing Creative Performance," *Journal of Management* 40 (2014): 919–941.

53. A. Shatte, A. Perlman, B. Smith, and W. D. Lynch, "The Positive Effect of Resilience on Stress and Business Outcomes in Difficult Work Environments," *Journal of Occupational and Environmental Medicine* 59 (2017): 135–140.

54. C. S. Dweck, *Mindset: The New Psychology of Success* (New York: Random House, 2006).

55. J. M. Berg, A. Wrzesniewski, A Grant, J. Kurkoski, and B. Welle, "Getting Unstuck: The Effects of Growth Mindsets about the Self and Job on Happiness at Work," *Journal of Applied Psychology* 108 (2023): 152–166.

56. K. Lewin, "Frontiers in Group Dynamics," *Human Relations* 1 (1947): 5–41.

57. C. Bareil, A. Savoie, and S. Meunier, "Patterns of Discomfort with Organizational Change," *Journal of Change Management* 7, No. 1 (2007): 13–24.

58. W. Mc Whinney, "Meta-Praxis: A Framework for Making Complex Changes," in A. M. Mohrman, Jr., et al., eds., *Large-Scale Organizational Change* (San Francisco: Jossey-Bass, 1989): 154–199.

59. M. Beer and E. Walton, "Developing the Competitive Organization: Interventions and Strategies," *American Psychologist* 45 (1990): 154–161.

60. B. Bertsch and R. Williams, "How Multinational CEOs Make Change Programs Stick," *Long Range Planning* 27 (1994): 12–24.

61. J. Amis, T. Slack, and C. R. Hinings, "Values and Organizational Change," *Journal of Applied Behavioral Science* 38 (2002): 356–385.

62. W. L. French and C. H. Bell, *Organization Development: Behavioral Science Interventions for Organization Improvement*, 4th ed. (Englewood Cliffs, N.J.: Prentice-Hall, 1990); W. W. Burke, *Organization Development: A Normative View* (Reading, Mass.: Addison-Wesley, 1987).

63. A. O. Manzini, *Organizational Diagnosis* (New York: AMACOM, 1988).

64. M. R. Weisbord, "Organizational Diagnosis: Six Places to Look for Trouble with or without a Theory," *Group and Organization Studies* 1 (December 1976): 430–444.

65. H. Levinson, *Organizational Diagnosis* (Cambridge, Mass.: Harvard University Press, 1972).

66. J. Nicholas, "The Comparative Impact of Organization Development Interventions," *Academy of Management Review* 7 (1982): 531–542.

67. W. G. Dyer, *Team Building: Issues and Alternatives*, 2nd ed. (Reading, Mass.: Addison-Wesley, 1987).

68. E. Stephan, G. Mills, R. W. Pace, and L. Ralphs, "HRD in the Fortune 500: A Survey," *Training and Development Journal* 42 (January 1988): 26–32.

69. A. Edmondson, "Psychological Safety and Learning Behavior in Work Teams," *Administrative Science Quarterly* 44 (1999): 350–383.

70. https://www.teambonding.com/programs/team-food-truck -challenge/.

71. F. Campbell, A. Gast, K. Morton, and F. Tonies, "(Extremely) Out of Office: Let Nature Boost Your Team's Creativity and Performance," *McKinsey & Co.* (2023), accessed at https://www .mckinsey.com/capabilities/people-and-organizational-performance/ our-insights/extremely-out-of-office-let-nature-boost-your-teams -creativity-and-performance#/.

72. C. G. Myers and M. Doyle, "Get Adventurous with Your Leader-ship Training," *Harvard Business Review*, February 13 (2020), accessed at https://hbr.org/2020/02/get-adventurous-with-your-leadership -training.

73. L. L. Gilson, M. T. Maynard, N. C. J. Young, M. Vartiainen, and M. Hakonen, "Virtual Teams Research: 10 Years, 10 Themes, and 10 Opportunities," *Journal of Management*, published online before print on November 24, 2014, accessed at http://jom .sagepub.com.argo.library.okstate.edu/content/early /2014/11/21/0149206314559946.full.

74. A. Cohen, "Stop with the Zoom Happy Hours. Workers Really Hate Them, Says This Study," *Fast Company*, March 1 (2021), accessed at https://www.fastcompany.com/90609140/stop-with-the -zoom-happy-hours-workers-really-hate-them-says-this-study.

75. D. Wilkie, "Executive View: A New Approach to Executive and Company Retreats," *SHRM Executive Network*, accessed at https:// www.shrm.org/executive/resources/articles/pages/new-approach -to-company-retreats.aspx.

76. L. Kelley, "For Workers Who Are Never On Site, the "Off-Site" Still Beckons," *The New York Times*, February 22 (2022), accessed at https://www.nytimes.com/2022/02/25/business/offsite-corporate -retreats.html.

77. E. Schein, *Its Role in Organization Development, Process Consultation*, vol. 1 (Reading, Mass.: Addison-Wesley, 1988).

78. H. Hornstein, "Organizational Development and Change Man-agement: Don't Throw the Baby Out with the Bath Water," *Journal of Applied Behavioral Science* 37 (2001): 223–226.

79. "Amazon to Spend $700 Million to Train 100,000 Workers for Digital Age," *CBS News*, July 11 (2019), accessed at https://www .cbsnews.com/news/amazon-to-spend-700-million-training-100000 -employees-digital-age/.

80. K. A. Aikens, J. Astin, K. R. Pelletier, K. Levanovich, C. M. Baase, Y. Y. Park, and C. M. Bodnar, "Mindfulness Goes to Work: Impact of an Online Workplace Intervention," *Journal of Occupational and Environmental Medicine* 56 (2014): 721–731.

81. C. Greiser and P. Martini, "How Companies Can Instill Mind-fulness," *Knowledge at Wharton*, April 19 (2018), accessed at https:// knowledge.wharton.upenn.edu/article/how-companies-can-instill -mindfulness/.

82. I. L. Goldstein, *Training in Organizations*, 3rd ed. (Pacific Grove, Calif.: Brooks/Cole, 1993).

83. https://www.siyglobal.com/announcement-siy-global-launch/.

84. S. R. Giessner, J. F. Dawson, K. E. Horton, and M. West, "The Impact of Supportive Leadership on Employee Outcomes during Organizational Mergers: An Organizational-Level Field Study," *Journal of Applied Psychology* (2022), accessed at https://psycnet.apa .org/doiLanding?doi=10.1037%2Fapl0001042.

85. T. Maak, N. M. Pless, and F. Wohlgezogen, "The Fault Lines of Leadership: Lessons from the Global Covid-19 Crisis," *Journal of Change Management* (2021), accessed at https://www.tandfonline .com/doi/full/10.1080/14697017.2021.1861724?src=.

86. J. Reb, J. Narayanan, and S. Chaturvedi, "Leading Mindfully: Two Studies on the Influence of Supervisor Trait Mindfulness on Employee Well-Being and Performance," *Mindfulness* 5 (2014): 36–45.

87. D. Goleman and R. Davidson, *Altered Traits: Science Reveals How Meditation Changes Your Mind, Brain and Body* (New York: Avery, 2017).

88. M. Jay, "Understanding How to Leverage Executive Coaching," *Organization Development Journal* 21 (2003): 6–13; D. Goleman, R. Boyaysis, and A. McKee, *Primal Leadership: Learning to Lead with Emotional Intelligence* (Boston: Harvard Business School Press, 2004).

89. S. Gupta, "Leaders, Your Employees Think You Lack Self-Awareness. Consider Soft-Skills Coaching for Everyone," *Fast Company*, July 20 (2022), accessed at https://www.fastcompany.com/90770313/ leaders-your-employees-think-you-lack-self-awareness-consider -soft-skills-coaching-for-everyone?partner=rss&utm_source=rss& utm_medium=feed&utm_campaign=rss+fastcompany& utm_content=rss.

90. E. de Hand and V. O Nillson, "What Can We Know about the Effectiveness of Coaching? A Meta-Analysis Based Only on Randomized Controlled Trials," *Academy of Management Learning and Education*, February 13 (2023), accessed at https://journals.aom.org/ doi/abs/10.5465/amle.2022.0107.

91. K. M. Wasylyshyn, "Executive Coaching: An Outcome Study," *Consulting Psychology Journal* 55 (2003): 94–106.

92. A. M. Passarelli, S. Moore, and E. B. Van Oosten, "How Leaders and Their Coaches Describe Outcomes of Coaching for Intentional Change," *Consulting Psychology Journal* 74 (2022): 239–346.

93. J. W. Smither, M. London, R. Flautt, Y. Vargas, and I. Kucine, "Can Working with an Executive Coach Improve Multisource Feedback Ratings over Time? A Quasi-Experimental Field Study," *Personnel Psychology* 56 (2003): 23–44.

94. K. M. Wasylyshyn, "The Art of Executive Coaching at the Top: Using Clients' Self-Imagery as a Tool for High Impact," *Consulting Psychology Journal* 72 (2022): 1–18.

95. W. N. Burton, C. Chen, A. Schultz, and X. Li, "Association between Employee Sleep with Workplace Health and Economic Outcomes," *Journal of Occupational and Environmental Medicine* 59 (2017): 177–183.

96. https://www.accenture.com/us-en/blogs/blogs-careers/from-the -top-down-were-prioritizing-mental-health-and-well-being.

97. R. A. Katzell and R. A. Guzzo, "Psychological Approaches to Worker Productivity," *American Psychologist* 38 (1983): 468–472.

98. P. F. Sorenson, T. Yaeger, and R. Narel, "The New Golden Age of Organization Development Research and Knowledge," *Organization Development Journal* 35 (2017): 47–55.

99. M. Parmelee, "5 Ways the Pandemic Has Changed Professional and Staff Development Forever," *Fast Company*, November 6 (2020), accessed at https://www.fastcompany.com/90571147/ 4-ways-the-pandemic-has-changed-professional-and-staff -development-forever?partner=rss&utm_source=rss&utm _medium=feed&utm_campaign=rss+fastcompany&utm _content=rss.

Index

Test Your Knowledge

Chapter 1 Organizational Behavior and Opportunity

1. Define *organizational behavior*. What is its focus?
2. Identify the four action steps for responding positively to change.
3. What is an organization? What are its four system components? Give an example of each.
4. Briefly describe the elements of the formal and the informal organization. Give examples of each.
5. Describe how competition and total quality are affecting organizational behavior.

Chapter 2 Challenges for Managers

1. What are Hofstede's five dimensions of cultural differences that affect work attitudes?
2. What are the primary sources of diversity in the U.S. workforce?
3. What are the potential benefits and problems of diversity?
4. What are some of the ethical challenges encountered in organizations?
5. Describe the difference between distributive and procedural justice.

Chapter 3 Personality, Perception, and Attribution

1. What are individual differences, and why should managers understand them?
2. Define *personality* and describe its origins.
3. Describe two theories of personality and explain what each contributes to our knowledge of personality.
4. What factors influence social perception? What are the barriers to social perception?
5. Describe the errors that affect the attribution process.

Chapter 4 Attitudes, Emotions, and Ethics

1. Discuss cultural differences in job satisfaction and organizational commitment.
2. Define *values*. Distinguish between instrumental values and terminal values.
3. What is the relationship between values and ethics?
4. How does locus of control affect ethical behavior?
5. What is Machiavellianism, and how does it relate to ethical behavior?

Chapter 5 Motivation at Work

1. What are the five categories of motivational needs described by Maslow? Give an example of how each can be satisfied.
2. What are the Theory X and Theory Y assumptions about people at work? How do they relate to the hierarchy of needs?
3. What three manifest needs does McClelland identify?
4. How do hygiene and motivational factors differ?
5. What are two new ideas in motivation that managers are using?

Chapter 6 Learning and Performance Management

1. Define the terms *learning, reinforcement, punishment*, and *extinction*.
2. What are the differences in the way introverted and extraverted and intuitive and sensing people learn?
3. What are the five characteristics of well-developed goals?
4. What are the benefits of 360-degree feedback?
5. What are the two possible attributions of poor performance? What are the implications of each?

Chapter 7 Stress and Well-Being at Work

1. Define *stress, distress*, and *strain*.
2. Describe four approaches to understanding stress.
3. What are the four changes associated with the stress response?
4. What is a nonwork demand? How does it affect an individual?
5. What are primary prevention, secondary prevention, and tertiary prevention?

Chapter 8 Communication

1. Why is reflective listening important in interpersonal communication?
2. What are the five communication skills of effective supervisors and managers?
3. What are the costs of incivility and blessings of civility?
4. How does nonverbal communication affect interpersonal relationships?
5. What is communicative disease?

Chapter 9 Work Teams and Groups

1. What is the difference between a group and a team?
2. What are the components of Tuckman's Five-Stage Model?
3. Describe the four characteristics of mature groups.
4. Describe five task and five maintenance functions that effective work teams must perform.
5. What are the benefits and potential drawbacks of selfmanaged teams?

Chapter 10 Decision Making by Individuals and Groups

1. List and describe Jung's four cognitive styles.
2. What are the individual and organizational influences on creativity?
3. What are the individual and organizational foundations of empowerment and teamwork?
4. Describe the advantages and disadvantages of group decision making.
5. Describe the symptoms of groupthink, and identify actions that can be taken to prevent it.

Chapter 11 Power and Political Behavior

1. What are the five types of power according to French and Raven? What are their effects?
2. What is information power?
3. What are the intergroup sources of power?
4. What are the four power-oriented characteristics of the best managers?
5. What are the symbols of power according to Kanter?

Chapter 12 Leadership and Followership

1. Define leadership and followership.
2. Distinguish between formal leadership and informal leadership.
3. Define transformational, charismatic, and authentic leadership.
4. Describe the differences between autocratic and democratic work environments. How do they differ from a laissez-faire workplace?
5. Define initiating structure and consideration as leader behaviors.

Chapter 13 Conflict and Negotiation

1. Discuss the differences between functional and dysfunctional conflict.
2. Identify the structural and personal factors that contribute to conflict.
3. Discuss the four major forms of conflict in organizations.
4. What defense mechanisms do people use in interpersonal conflict?
5. Identify five styles of conflict management.

Chapter 14 Jobs and the Design of Work

1. Describe six patterns of working that have been studied in different countries.
2. Describe four traditional approaches to the design of work in America.
3. What are the salient features of the social information-processing (SIP) model of job design?
4. How do the Japanese, German, and Scandinavian approaches to work differ from one another and from the American approach?
5. What are five emerging issues in jobs and the design of work?

Chapter 15 Organizational Design and Structure

1. Define differentiation and integration.
2. Describe the six basic dimensions of organizational design.
3. Identify four forces that are reshaping organizations today.
4. Discuss the nature of emerging organizational structures.
5. List four symptoms of structural weakness.

Chapter 16 Organizational Culture

1. Explain the three levels of organizational culture.
2. Describe five artifacts of culture and give an example of each.
3. Explain three theories about the relationship between organizational culture and performance.
4. Contrast adaptive and nonadaptive cultures.
5. Describe the three stages of organizational socialization. How is culture communicated in each stage?

Chapter 17 Career Management

1. What is a realistic job preview, and why is it important?
2. What are psychological contracts?
3. What stressors are associated with socialization?
4. What are the career functions provided by a mentor?
5. What are the two key issues to deal with during the maintenance career stage?

Chapter 18 Managing Change

1. What are the major external and internal forces for change in organizations?
2. Contrast incremental, strategic, and transformational change.
3. Name the four behavioral reactions to change.
4. Describe force field analysis and its relationship to Lewin's change model.
5. What is organization development? Why is it undertaken by organizations?